EGERTON RYERSON

THE MAKERS OF CANADA

EGERTON RYERSON

BY

NATHANAEL BURWASH

TORONTO
MORANG & CO., LIMITED
1910

PREFACE

THIS book does not profess to be either a
minute biography or a detailed history. It is
the presentation to our countrymen of the various
aspects of the work of a great man who has left his
impress upon several of the important institutions
of our province, and in each case for good. In these
sketches we have made no attempt, except in the
first brief chapter, to trace the record, either of his
personal or public life, or the development of his
character, or the lessons which might be gathered
from the example of his life. We have rather considered his work as one of the makers of Canada,
and necessarily with that, something of the great
movements of the days in which he lived. The subject is a noble one, and we must acknowledge that
we have done it but scant justice.

The volume is the product of joint labour with
my life-long friend and colleague, Dr. A. H.
Reynar. He has specially prepared the first chapter

PREFACE

dealing with the early life and ministry of Dr. Ryerson, and the eleventh, dealing with the literary work of Dr. Ryerson.

We must both acknowledge our constant indebtedness to the indefatigable labours of Dr. J. George Hodgins, LL.D. The rich storehouse of historic material which he is accumulating in his many works will place all future labourers in this field under lasting obligations.

With the hope that our work may prove useful to the thousands who in our schools are now reaping the advantages of Dr. Ryerson's labours, we commit it to our fellow-citizens of Ontario.

N. BURWASH.

VICTORIA COLLEGE, *Feb. 28th, 1901.*

CONTENTS

CONTENTS

CHAPTER I

EARLY LIFE AND MINISTRY

IN his book entitled "The Story of My Life," Dr. Ryerson speaks thus of his birth and parentage: "I was born on March 24th, 1803, in the township of Charlotteville, near the village of Vittoria, in the then London district, now the county of Norfolk. My father had been an officer in the British army during the American Revolution, being a volunteer in the Prince of Wales' Regiment of New Jersey, of which place he was a native. His forefathers were from Holland, and his more remote ancestors were from Denmark. At the close of the American revolutionary war, he, with many others of the same class, went to New Brunswick, where he married my mother, whose maiden name was Stickney, a descendant of one of the early Massachusetts Puritan settlers. Near the close of the last century, my father with his family followed an elder brother to Canada, where he drew some 2,500 acres of land from the government for his services in the army, besides his pension."

Believers in the strong influence of heredity will say that the child of such parents should inherit a nature, sturdy, militant, and loyal on the one hand,

1

and on the other hand, earnest, inward and devout. Those again who magnify the influence of nurture in the making of the man will find support for their view in the following statement of this man, so distinguished as one of the makers of Canada: "That to which I am principally indebted for any studious habits, mental energy, or even capacity or decision of character, is religious instruction, poured into my mind in my childhood by a mother's counsels, and infused into my heart by a mother's prayers and tears. When very small, under six years of age, having done something naughty, my mother took me into her bed-room, told me how bad and wicked what I had done was and what pain it caused her, kneeled down, clasped me to her bosom and prayed for me. Her tears, falling upon my head, seemed to penetrate to my very heart. This was my first religious impression, and was never effaced. Though thoughtless and full of playful mischief, I never afterwards knowingly grieved my mother, or gave her other than respectful and kind words." Such is the beautiful tribute that the old man, full of years and honours, pays to the mother that looked on his childhood.

> "Happy he
> With such a mother! Faith in womankind
> Beats in his blood, and trust in all things high
> Comes easy to him, and though he trip and fall,
> He shall not blind his soul with clay."

Whatever heredity alone may do or fail to do, and

however the influences of early training alone may make or mar the man, it is impossible to think that the nature and the nurture that combined to bless the early life of Egerton Ryerson could fail to lead him to a place amongst the great and good.

The life of the first settler is sometimes described as a life of many hardships and few privileges. But except in a few cases and for a short time, the hardships were not more than enough to make the people hardy, and their privations were less dangerous and hurtful than the ease and plenty that so often leave the body and the mind without struggle, and therefore without strength. And as for the comparative dearth of instruction in the early times, it may be doubted whether the present generation, beschooled and bechurched as it often is, and oppressed with the surfeit and disgust of learning, has after all so great an advantage over the people of the earlier time. Then, the schools and the churches may have been few and far between, but there was a better relish and digestion of the simpler moral and intellectual fare. It was in those times of hard work and few privileges that the boyhood of Egerton Ryerson was passed. He tells us that he learned to do all kinds of farm work. And before he had reached his majority he "ploughed every acre of ground for the season, cradled every stalk of wheat, rye, and oats, and mowed every spear of grass, pitched the whole first on a wagon, and then from the wagon to the hay-mow or stack." Well might he look back without regret to the hardships of his youth, if they built up the well-knit frame and much-enduring strength that marked his manhood and his age.

The story of Egerton Ryerson's school days is not long. He had such advantages from the district grammar school as might be had in those days by a boy who was at the same time learning "to do all kinds of farm work," and when he was fourteen years of age he was sent to attend a course of lectures "given by two professors, the one an Englishman and the other an American, who taught nothing but English grammar." Into this study he threw himself with great enthusiasm, and he made such progress that his instructors were glad to secure his help as a teacher when one of them was incapacitated by illness. In this way the chief maker of the Ontario school system tried his prentice hand as a teacher when a lad of only fifteen summers. Further instruction from teachers was not given him in his boyhood, but as soon as he reached his majority and had the direction of his own life, he sought for himself the best help available in the pursuit of learning. In the story of his life he writes: "I felt a strong desire to pursue further my classical studies, and determined, with the kind counsel and aid of my eldest brother, to proceed to Hamilton and place myself for a year under the tuition of a man of high reputation both as a scholar and a teacher, the late John Law, Esq., then headmaster of the

Gore district grammar school. I applied myself with such ardour, and prepared such an amount of work, both in Latin and Greek, that Mr. Law said it was impossible for him to give the time and hear me read all that I had prepared, and that he would therefore examine me on the translation and construction of the more difficult passages, remarking more than once that it was impossible for any human mind to sustain long the strain that I was imposing upon mine. In the course of some six months his apprehensions were realized, as I was seized with a brain fever, and on partially recovering took cold, which resulted in inflammation of the lungs, by which I was so reduced that my physician pronounced my case hopeless, and death was hourly expected." From this illness he slowly recovered, thanks to his good constitution and to his mother's care. He took up his classical studies again, but almost immediately afterwards began his work as a Methodist preacher. This is all the story of the schooling received by one who for so many years, and with so great distinction at home and abroad, directed, and indeed created, the school system of Ontario.

The story of the moral development of a young life is always interesting, but it is peculiarly so in the case of a man who may be regarded as a type. Such a man was the subject of this memoir. He furnishes an example of the development of the religious life in one who has grown up under the influences of Christian nurture, and at the same time an example of the way in which that life is unfolded under the conditions found in the great religious body to which he belonged, and to which his talents and energies were given as an honoured leader for nearly three score years. We have already seen what he tells us of the religious influences and impressions of his childhood. At the age of twelve, when the passive and receptive stage is rising into the stage of more serious reflection and more active self-determination, he passed into a higher form of religious life, a life in which he not merely accepted the traditional teachings as to sin and salvation, but realized in his own soul the profound interests of the moral life, and bravely took up its struggle, trusting all the issues of this life and of the great hereafter to the High God and to Jesus Christ, who had made His mercy known. He tells of the change that took place in these words: "My consciousness of guilt and sinfulness was humbling, oppressive and distressing; and my experience of relief, after lengthened fastings, watchings, and prayers, was clear, refreshing, and joyous. In the end I simply trusted in Christ and looked to Him for a present salvation; and as I looked up in my bed the light appeared to my mind, and, as I thought, to my bodily eye also, in the form of one, white-robed, and with more of the expression of the countenance of Titian's Christ than of any person I have ever seen. I turned, rose to my knees, bowed my head

6

and covered my face, rejoiced with trembling, saying to a brother who was lying beside me that the Saviour was now near us. The change within was more marked than anything without, and perhaps the inward change may have suggested what appeared an outward manifestation."

It may be interesting to compare this experience with that of Thomas Carlyle, who at about the same time was passing through the pangs of a belated and abnormal spiritual birth. He tells the story in the *Sartor Resartus*, and he says it actually took place in his own experience. "The heart within me, unvisited by any heavenly dewdrop, was smouldering in sulphurous, slow-consuming fire. . . . I lived in a continual, indefinite, pining fear. . . . It seemed as if all things in the heavens above and in the earth beneath would hurt me. . . . When all at once there rose a thought in me, and I asked myself: 'What art thou afraid of? Wherefore, like a coward, dost thou forever pip and whimper, and go cowering and trembling? Despicable biped! What is the sum total of the worst that lies before thee? Death? Well, death, and say the pangs of Tophet too, and all that the devil and man may, will, or can do against thee! Hast thou not a heart; canst thou not suffer whatever it be; and, as a child of freedom, though outcast, trample Tophet itself under thy feet, while it consumes thee?'... And as I so thought, there rushed like a stream of fire over my whole soul; and I shook base fear away

7

from me forever. . . . The everlasting No had said: 'Behold thou art fatherless, outcast, and the universe is mine (the devil's);' to which my whole Me now made answer: 'I am not thine, but free, and forever hate thee!'" Elsewhere Carlyle writes: "Foreshadows—call them rather fore-splendours— of that truth, that beginning of truths, fell mysteriously over my soul. . . . The universe is not dead and demoniacal, a charnel-house with spectres, but God-like, and my Father's!"

It is of this experience that Carlyle says, " I found it to be essentially what Methodist people call their conversion—the deliverance of their souls from the devil and the pit. Precisely that in a new form. And there burned accordingly a sacred flame of joy in me, silent in my inmost being, as of one henceforth superior to fate. This *holy joy* lasted sensibly in me for several years. . . . . . nor has it proved what I can call fallacious at any time since." Carlyle was wont to assure his pious mother that his opinions, although clothed in a different garb, remained essentially the same as her own, and we may well believe him for he would lie to no man and he could not lie to his mother. But in comparing the experience of what he calls his new birth with that of Egerton Ryerson, we must remember that the one was a rugged man, hardheaded and metaphysical, and a worshipper of will and force, whilst the other was a bright but unsophisticated boy who followed without doubting

8

his moral intuitions and affections and recognized the eternal goodness in the Son of Man. The one was like an oak tree that grew alone, through the scorching heat of summer and the winter's cold and tempests, the other was like a pine tree that grew tall and shapely in the forest.

This story of the moral and spiritual development of Egerton Ryerson has a historical as well as a psychological interest. It is an example of the change that usually attended the ministrations of the pioneer preachers, and its presence or absence is still looked upon amongst Methodists as the sign of a standing or falling church. In telling the story some of the converts, especially in later times, use language less intense and striking than that of Egerton Ryerson, and others use language almost as mystical and imaginative as that of Carlyle, but the essential things are always the same and in harmony with the inwardness of the Great Apostle's preaching, "repentance towards God and faith toward our Lord Jesus Christ."

The circumstances of the early settlers and their habits of life and thought were in some respects most favourable to the work of the first preachers. The lives of the people were simple, laborious and comparatively free from the distractions and dissipations of later times. They had no relish for the fine-spun and mystifying speculations that so often befog and enervate the mind. They had not learned to question the truthfulness of the intuitive reason, and they no more called for logical demonstrations of the Good than for logical demonstrations of the Beautiful. Their intellectual palate had not been vitiated and their digestion spoiled by daily doses of newspaper omniscience or by a supping of the devil's broth in low comedy and fiction. Whatsoever things commended themselves to their simple minds as lovely and of good report, those things were beautiful and good to them beyond all dispute. And they must either revere and obey or feel that they were in opposition to the Eternal order. When, therefore, the pioneer preacher came to those people, he found the way open to their hearts and minds. And the preachers were, as a rule, men of the people, and they knew their hearers though they did not always know Greek. They preached the facts of the inner life and of the gospel of the grace of God, rather than theories about the facts and the gospel; and above all things, they sought to help the people to the supreme moral choice which brought inward peace and supplied a fixed principle of life.

A passing notice may here be given to the scenes of the early religious experiences and labours of the first makers of this country. Except in the cities and towns a regular religious service seldom occurred more than once a week. In many places it would take two or three or even six weeks before the pioneer preacher could complete his round of hundreds of miles. But when the work of the year was slack and the weather favourable, special religious services were held as if to compensate for the usual dearth of religious privileges. In the larger places what were called "protracted services" were held, when evening after evening for two or three weeks the preacher and his helpers brought all their powers of instruction and persuasion to bear on their hearers. These services were commonly held in the winter season; but in the pleasant summer weather, between the spring work and the harvest there were held in the sparsely settled districts camp meetings, when for a week or ten days the people would dwell in tents and give themselves to religious exercises. They would then return to their homes, some of them to have few opportunities for public worship for the rest of the year. As the places for regular religious services multiplied, these protracted meetings and camp meetings gradually fell into disuse, but in the old time they often served a good purpose.

Returning from these observations on the religious life of Canada in the early days, observations intended to show something of the environment in which Egerton Ryerson grew up, we resume the story of his own life on the religious side. From his thirteenth to his eighteenth year, no events of much note are put on record. When, however, at the age of eighteen he formally joined the Methodist Church, he was met by his father with these words: "Egerton, I understand you have joined the

11

Methodists. You must either leave them or leave my house." The military spirit of his early habits seems to have followed the father into his domestic life, and the young man knew him too well to expect that there would be any change in the word of command. But the son too was a good soldier when called upon to endure hardness for what he considered a sacred cause. His decision was soon made, and the next day he left his father's roof to begin the struggle of life on his own account. "In this trying time," he says, "I had the aid of a mother's prayers and a mother's tenderness, and a conscious divine strength according to my need." It is a further mark of his noble character that he utters no word of reproach or bitterness on account of treatment he had received, but to the end of his life speaks words of tenderness and reverence for his father.

For the next two years he was employed as an assistant in the London district grammar school and at the same time he diligently pursued his own studies. The bent of his mind even at this early period is seen in the character of the works that he read with greatest interest:—"Locke, 'On the Human Understanding'; Paley's 'Moral and Political Philosophy,' and Blackstone's 'Commentaries,' especially the sections of the latter on the Prerogatives of the Crown, the Rights of the Subject and the Province of Parliament."

His return for a year to his father's home and his

12

selection of a course of life for himself may best be told in his own words :

" As my father had complained that the Methodists had robbed him of his son, and of the fruits of that son's labours, I wished to remove that ground of complaint as far as possible by hiring an English farm-labourer, then just arrived in Canada, in my place, and paid him out of the proceeds of my own labour for two years. But although the farmer was the best hired man my father had ever had, the result of his farm productions during these two years did not equal those of the two years that I had been the chief labourer on the farm, and my father came to me one day uttering the single sentence: 'Egerton, you must come home,' and then walked away. . . . I had left home for the honour of religion, and I thought the honour of religion would be promoted by my returning home and showing still that the religion so much spoken against would enable me to leave the school for the plough and the harvest field, as it had enabled me to leave home without knowing at the moment whether I should be a teacher or a farm-labourer. I relinquished my engagement as a teacher within a few days, engaging again on the farm. . . . My father then became changed in regard both to myself and the religion I professed, desiring me to remain at home; but having been enabled to maintain a good conscience in the sight of God, and a good report before men in regard to my filial duty during my minority, I felt that my life's work lay in another direction." What that other direction was he does not tell us in the story of his life, but his love for the study of political philosophy and constitutional law, and the quality of mind exhibited throughout his life, incline us to think that the legal profession was the one to which he was attracted. However that may be, his first care was to qualify himself for his life's work by a better intellectual equipment and discipline. In those good old times the study of the classics was the approved method of preparation for all professional life. The young man accordingly placed himself under the tuition of the best scholar and teacher within his reach, and applied himself to his classical studies with great zeal and success. But as we have already seen, his zeal was not according to knowledge, for the close hard work induced brain fever and led to further illness from which it was thought he would not recover.

During his illness, and in the prospect of death— a prospect not dreaded at the time,—he looked again over his plans of life and asked himself what might have been, and again what ought to be if his life should be prolonged. Then he resolved that he would not follow his own counsels, but "would yield to the openings and calls which might be made in the church by its chief ministers." With this resolve, peace and joy came to his mind and healing to his body, so that his mother, entering his

14

room soon after, exclaimed: "Egerton, your countenance is changed: you are getting better." He recovered, to the surprise of his friends, and in due time resumed his classical studies at Hamilton. A few days later he went to attend a religious service where his brother William was expected to preach. His brother, however, did not appear at the appointed time, being prevented by serious illness, and the young student was suddenly called upon by the authorities of the church to take his brother's place in the ministry for the rest of the year. He was astonished, and for a time speechless from emotion, but, as St. Paul was "not disobedient unto the heavenly vision" which appeared unto him to make him "a minister and a witness," so did this young Canadian student at the call of the church give up his early plans and take upon himself the care of souls. His first sermon was preached on Easter Sunday, April 3rd, 1825, and his text was: "They that sow in tears shall reap in joy."—Psa. 126: 5.

The brief records of his early ministry contained in the young preacher's diary throw much light on the condition of the country and the habits of the people in the first half of the last century. At the same time they reveal the spirit of the men who, in the heroic days gone by, attempted and achieved great things for God and for their country. Our respect for those men is none the less but rather greater because they did not think that they were great men or imagine that they were attempting extraordinary things. They thought humbly of themselves, they felt the weaknesses and limitations of mortal men, but through all the changes of feeling and through good report and ill, they persisted in the brave endeavour to do their duty. They were without the smug content that sometimes marks the clever men of an inferior grade. They rather felt—and felt most painfully at times—the depression of the truly great who realize how little they know as compared with what they have yet to learn, and how imperfect are their best works as compared with the ideals towards which they struggle and aspire. The following brief extracts from his diary will tell of the young itinerant's character and labours with simple eloquence:

"*April 3rd, 1825 (Easter Sunday).*—I this day commenced my ministerial labours. . . . Oh, my soul, hang all thy hopes upon the Lord! Forbid that I should seek the praise of men, but may I seek their good and God's glory. . . ."

"*April 8th.*—The Lord being my helper, my little knowledge and feeble talents shall be unreservedly devoted to His service. I do not yet regret giving up my worldly pursuits for the welfare of souls. . . ."

"*April 10th (Sabbath).*—. . . . I felt much of the presence of the Lord, and I do bless the Lord he has converted one soul in this place to-day. I feel encouraged to go on."

"*April 15th.*—So bowed down with temptation

16

to-day I almost resolved to return to my native place. But, in God's strength, I will try to do my best during the time I have engaged to supply my brother William's place."

"*April 25th and 26th.*—And thus I go on, depressed and refreshed; almost discouraged because of the way, and then cheered by the kind and fatherly conversation of the Rev. Thomas Madden."

"*May 12th.*—I have this day ridden nearly thirty miles, preached three times and met two classes. I felt very much fatigued, yet the Lord has given me strength equal to my day."

"*May 19th.*—. . . . Since I commenced labouring for my Master I have found fathers and mothers, brothers and sisters, all ready to supply my every want."

"*May 29th.*—For many days I have been cast down by a weight of care. My father is exceedingly anxious that I should return home and remain with him during his lifetime. A position in the Church of England has presented itself, and other advantageous attractions with regard to this world offer themselves. It makes my heart bleed to see the anxiety of my parents. But is it my duty? If they were in want I would return to them without hesitation, but when I consider they have everything necessary, can it be my duty to gratify them at the expense of the cause of God? Surely if a man may leave father and mother to join himself to a wife, how much more reasonable to leave all to join himself to the Christian ministry! My parents are dear to me, but my duty to God is dearer still. One thing I do desire, that I may live in the house of the Lord forever.[1] And shall I leave a church through whose faithful instructions I have been brought to know God for any advantages that the entrance of another might afford me? No, far be it from me. As I received the Lord Jesus, so I will walk in Him. . . ."

"*August 10th.*—My soul rejoices at the news I have heard from home, that my eldest brother (George) has resolved to join the Methodists and become a missionary to the Indians. . . . My father has become reconciled, and my mother is willing to part with her sons for the sake of the church of Christ."

In September, 1825, Mr. Ryerson was appointed an assistant preacher on the York and Yonge street circuit. This circuit comprised the town of York (now Toronto) and the surrounding country, "over which," he says, "we travelled, and preached from twenty-five to thirty-five sermons in four weeks, preaching generally three times on Sabbath, and attending three class meetings, besides preaching and attending class meetings on week days."

[1] It is worthy of note just here that Colonel Ryerson lived to an advanced age, and died in 1854. If, therefore, his son had at this time (1825) considered his filial emotions only and not also the work to which he was called, he would have waited for twenty-nine years to bury his father, and his duty to his church and country would have been left undone.

In the early part of the following year (April and May 1826) these labours of the intinerant preacher, excessive and exhausting as they must appear, were greatly increased by the controversy that arose on the question of the Clergy Reserves and by his defence of his co-labourers and co-religionists from the ungenerous and unjust charges brought against them by their privileged ecclesiastical opponents. In the next chapter the origin of this controversy will be explained and the story told of Egerton Ryerson's valiant championship of the cause of religious liberty and equal rights. It was not of choice that he engaged in controversy, but he was constrained by the urgent appeals of those who felt themselves wronged to undertake their defence. Again and again he tells of his preference for the care of souls and the preaching of the gospel. At the same time we may be allowed to think that his soldierly ancestral instincts found a certain satisfaction in the fray when he was once committed to it, and when he knew that he was fighting for a good cause. His controversial life seems to have been guided throughout by the precept of the old councillor in *Hamlet,*—

> "Beware
> Of entrance to a quarrel, but, being in,
> Bear't that the opposed may beware of thee."

There was another conflict, however, into which he threw himself with all the generous enthusiasm of a good soldier. His arduous pastoral duties and his exciting theological and semi-political controversies did not so engross him as to prevent the outgoing of his heart and mind in sympathy with those who were in greatest need of light and help, viz., the heathen aborigines of the country who were then very numerous. So strongly did he feel on this matter that he resolved to give his life to these poor people; to turn aside and share their affliction and poverty rather than go out to meet the comfort and distinction that appeared before him on another path. The following quotation from his diary will reveal his mind on this matter:

"August 17th.—Scarcely a day passes without beholding new openings to extend my ministerial labours. To-day, in an affecting manner, I witnessed the hands of suffering humanity stretched forth to receive the word of life. More than five hundred aborigines of the country were assembled in one place. In a moral point of view they may be said to be 'sitting in the valley of the shadow of death.' 'The day star from on high' has not yet dawned upon them. Alas! are they to perish for lack of knowledge? . . . Oh, Lord, if Thou wilt qualify me and send me to dispense to them the Bread of Life, I will throw myself upon Thy mercy and submit to Thy will!"

In accordance with this desire, Mr. Ryerson received an appointment as missionary to the Indians at the Credit, but at the same time he was required to preach on two Sundays out of four in the town of York. He commenced his work among the Indians in the middle of September, 1826. That he endured some hardness may be gathered from his account of his place of abode. " In one of these bark-covered and brush-enclosed wigwams, I ate and slept for some weeks, my bed consisting of a plank, a mat, and a blanket, and a blanket also for my covering ; yet I was never more comfortable and happy." The spirit of chivalry in which he entered upon this work is clearly seen in his diary when he says, "I feel an inexpressible joy in taking up my abode with them. I must acquire a new language to teach a new people."

The practical nature of his work is seen in his immediate effort to lift the people out of their heathenish degradation into a higher state where the comfortable environment of a Christian civilization might foster the moral and intellectual life of a people just emerging from paganism. And the energy and perseverance of this young missionary and maker of his country is seen in the fact that in less that ten days after his arrival amongst the Indians, they resolved to build a house "to answer the double purpose of a school house and a place for divine worship." The Indians under his charge were about two hundred in number, and very poor, but they entered with enthusiasm into the new enterprise. They subscribed one hundred dollars towards the building in less than an hour. The missionary mounted his horse and visited his old friends in Hamilton, and in the York and Yonge street and Niagara circuits, and begged the rest of the money required. At the end of six weeks the house was built and paid for. All this was done, as he says, with a touch of humour, "while our 'swell' friends of the government and of the Church of England were consulting and talking about the matter. It was thus that the church-standing of these Indian converts was maintained, and they were enabled to walk in the Lord Jesus as they had found Him."

The methods of missionary work followed by Mr. Ryerson some five and seventy years ago, were of the most modern and approved kind and worthy of imitation by the missionaries of the present day. He did not take his stand on a height of privilege and attainment and call to the people, bidding them to come up to him, but he came down to them and helped them to ascend. He shared their humble dwellings, lived on their homely fare, and, like the Divine Teacher, he too became poor that through his poverty his heathen brethren might become rich. Writing to one of his brothers he says: "I am very unpleasantly situated at the Credit during the cold weather, as there are nearly a dozen in the family, and only one fire-place. I have lived at different houses among the Indians, and thereby learned some of their wants, and the proper remedies for these. Having no place for retirement, and living in the midst of bustle and noise, I have forgotten a good deal of my Greek and Latin and made but little progress in other things. My desire and aim is to live solely to the glory of God and the good of men." Again he writes in his diary, "I have been often quite unwell, owing to change of living and being out at night; my fare, as to food, *is very plain* but wholesome, and I generally lie on boards with one or two blankets intervening." He could not but feel the hardship of the situation and suffer from it, yet even as he speaks of these things, he gives expression to his admiration of the noble character of his humble hosts.

In his endeavours to enlighten and uplift the heathen he proclaimed "the grace of God that bringeth salvation to all men," but he preached also a gospel of cleanliness, and decency, and industry, and intelligence. He brought help to them, and, better still, he taught them to help themselves. He stirred them up to build the House of the Lord. And whilst that House was primarily a place for preaching the Word and administering the sacraments in the congregation, it was also a Sunday school and a day school, whence light as well as sweetness might come into the lives of the children of the forest. Nor did the missionary despise the work of an instructor in mechanics and agriculture. In "The Story of My Life," Ryerson says: "After collecting the means necessary to build the house of worship and school-house, I showed the Indians how to enclose and make gates for their gardens, having some knowledge and skill in mechanics.

"Between daylight and sunrise, I called out four of the Indians in succession, and showed them how and worked with them, to clear and fence in, and plow and plant their first wheat and corn fields. In the afternoon I called out the school-boys to go with me, and cut and pile, and burn the brushwood in and around the village. The little fellows worked with great glee as long as I worked with them, but soon began to play when I left them."

His brother William, writing to the Rev. George Ryerson tells of his observations made on the mission : "I am very certain I never saw the same order and attention in any school before. Their progress in spelling, reading and writing is astonishing, but especially in writing, which certainly exceeds anything I ever saw. They were getting forward with their work. When I was there they were fencing the lots in the village in a very neat substantial manner. On my arrival at the mission, I found Egerton about half a mile from the village, stripped to the shirt and pantaloons, clearing land with between twelve and twenty little Indian boys who were all engaged in chopping and picking up the brush. It was an interesting sight. Indeed he told me that he spent an hour or more every morning and evening in this way, for the benefit of his own health and the improvement of the Indian children. He is almost worshipped by his people,

24

and, I believe, under God, will be a great blessing to them."

Here we come again in sight of that first and last great qualification of the noblest helpers of mankind. Something of their work may be done from the sense of duty, and there may be times when nothing but the sense of duty, that "stern daughter of the voice of God," can hold them to their work; but their noblest inspiration is drawn from the heart of God rather than from His will, and their greatest success is achieved through the labour of love. This generous affection transpires in many passages in the diary of Egerton Ryerson. On coming to his charge among the Indians he writes, "I feel an inexpressible joy in taking up my abode with them," and again "my heart feels one with them." And when he had had experience of the privations of Indian life and suffered frequent and depressing illness from the hardship endured, he exclaims on returning to his work after a short absence, "I am now among the dear objects of my care. My heart leaped for joy as I came in sight of the village and received such a hearty welcome."

At the conference of 1827, Mr. Ryerson was appointed to the Cobourg circuit which at that time extended from Bowmanville to Brighton. The Indian work at the Rice Lake and Mud Lake missions was still an object of his care, but his work was on the whole of a more pastoral and evangelistic character than that of his Credit and York

25

appointment. He speaks of the kindness received from his people and of the greater comfort of his circumstances and the corresponding advancement in his studies. But the work of controversy continued with increasing pressure and anxiety. It was about two years before this time that he was forced, much against his own inclination, into controversial writing. He speaks of it as of an affliction, but adds, "I feel it to be the cause of God, and I am resolved to follow truth and the holy scripture in whatever channel they will lead me." A few months later he writes: "My engagement in controversial writing savours too much of dry historical criticism to be spiritual, and often causes leanness of soul; but it seems to be necessary in the present state of matters in this colony, and it is the opinion of my most judicious friends that I should continue it till it comes to a successful termination." Again he writes, "During the past year (1826-7) my principal attention has been called to controversial labours. If the Lord will, may this cup pass by in my future life."

It was not the Lord's will, however, to answer this prayer. On the contrary, controversy was more and more required of the man who would have chosen for himself the work of a missionary and of an itinerant preacher. Mr. Ryerson tells us how he had to compose on horseback sermons and replies to his ecclesiastical adversaries as he passed from end to end of his extensive and laborious circuit.

CONTROVERSY

Indeed, in Cobourg, stories are still told to the third generation of the way in which those replies were written. The young preacher would come in at nightfall from his long ride and sit up till morning looked in upon him and saw the pile of firewood consumed on the one side of him and a pile of manuscript grown up on the other. In this work thus thrust upon him, he so fulfilled the Apostolic precept, " Quit you like men, be strong," that when the conference in 1829 established the *Christian Guardian* newspaper, Mr. Ryerson was placed in the editorial chair and charged with the duty of vindicating the character and contending for the civil and religious rights of his people.

CHAPTER II

RELIGION AND POLITICS IN UPPER CANADA
IN 1826

MR. RYERSON had not completed his first year of ministration to the religious wants of the settlers in Upper Canada when a new work was thrust upon him. This was no other than the consideration of the relation of the Christian church which he was serving and of sister churches to the political movements of the time. Such consideration was a necessary part of the work of a Methodist minister of that day. It was, indeed, forced upon him, if, as a citizen and a freeman, he would secure for himself and his posterity the rights and liberties which are now acknowledged without dispute to be the glory of our province, viz., perfect liberty of conscience and the absolute equality of all the churches in relation to the state. To understand this question it will be necessary to study somewhat carefully the constitution of Upper Canada as a British colony at this date, and also the peculiar working of this constitution under successive administrations for the preceding thirty-five years.

The Constitutional Act of 1791 separated Upper Canada from the old province of Quebec, and created it what was known as a free crown colony. The government was vested in:

1. A governor appointed by the British crown, with constitutional powers to be exercised either at his discretion, or on the advice of an executive council appointed by and responsible to himself alone, or under instructions which accompanied his appointment, or were received from the colonial office in England from time to time. To this office he was directly responsible.

2. A legislative council composed of life-members holding their appointment from the crown, and with legislative powers similar to those exercised by the House of Lords in England.

3. A legislative assembly elected by the people and with legislative powers defined by the act.

The prerogatives of the governor as defined in the act were: *(a)* the summoning or appointment of members of the legislative council; *(b)* the division of the province into electoral districts for the election of members of the assembly, and the making of all other provisions for the first election; *(c)* the giving or withholding of the royal assent to the legislative acts of the council and assembly; and *(d)* the calling and proroguing of the legislature and the dissolution of the assembly, and the calling for a new election, provision being made that not more than twelve months shall elapse without a session of the legislature. The appointment of the executive council is also alluded to in the act, but rather as a prerogative already existing than as constituted by this act. But this appointment of the executive council was not the only power vested in the governor apart from the provisions of the Constitutional Act. As the council held control of the great departments of executive government, and was responsible to the governor only, the governor, by virtue of this authority, became *de facto* the prime minister of the colony. He stood not simply as the representative of the sovereign, maintaining the constitution and seeing that it was obeyed by all subordinate branches of the government, but he became the political leader of the government, making appointments and controlling policy in the great executive departments, though without control of the legislation necessary for the execution of that policy except in the upper chamber. On the other hand it lay in his power to prevent any legislation intended to obstruct the successful event of his executive policy. Of this government Sir Erskine May, in his "Constitutional History of England," chapter seventeen, says: "Self-government was then the theory; but in practice, the governors, aided by dominant interests in the several colonies, contrived to govern according to the policy dictated from Downing Street. Just as at home, the crown, the nobles, and an ascendant party were supreme in the national councils, so in the colonies the governors and their official aristocracy were generally able to command the adhesion of the local legislatures." This, however, was far from being the case in Upper Canada, for reasons which our author proceeds to point out: "A more direct interference, however, was often exercised. Ministers had no hesitation in disallowing any colonial acts of which they disapproved.[1] They dealt freely with the public lands as the property of the crown, often making grants obnoxious to the colonists, and peremptorily insisting on the conditions under which they should be sold and settled. Their interference was also frequent regarding church establishments and endowments, official salaries and the colonial civil lists. Misunderstandings and disputes were constant, but the policy and will of the home government usually prevailed. Another incident of colonial administration was that of patronage. The colonies offered a wide field of employment for the friends, connections, and political partisans of the home government." In Upper Canada this exercise of patronage by the colonial office never reached the extremity of abuse described by May as prevailing in the American colonies during the preceding century. But there was scarcely less objection to the irresponsible exercise of patronage by the governor and his council on behalf of their adherents in the colony itself.

[1] The Constitutional Act provided that all acts of the colonial legislature might be disallowed within two years after being officially laid before the secretary of state. The colonial office thus held a two-fold veto on colonial legislation, first indirectly through the governor, and later directly in the royal name.

IMPERIAL INTEREST SUPREME

A constitution with such inherent liability to abuse could scarcely be expected to work to the satisfaction of an intelligent people who had continually before them the example of the operation of a more thoroughly responsible system of government immediately to the south, and who were many of them but lately immigrants from the parent land, where already the principles of responsible government were being far more effectively carried into practice. There was, of course, a bare possibility that such a constitution might afford a tolerably satisfactory government. If the colonial office on the one hand and the governor on the other used their large powers with wise consideration and discretion, anticipating the needs and wishes of the people as expressed through their legislative assembly, it might have been possible to avoid what otherwise must lead to inevitable conflict. But the spirit which framed this colonial constitution was evidently still jealously tenacious of imperial prerogatives, and determined to govern the colonies for the good of the colonists, as they viewed it, but at the same time in subordination to what they considered the paramount interests of the mother land. The constitution framed in this spirit gave to the colonists the name, the idea of, and the desire for self-government, while it withheld the reality, and thus of itself planted the seeds of dissatisfaction in the minds of a progressive people.

But this was not its only weakness. Its very

33

efforts after good became in themselves the greatest of evils. The colonial office itself was by no means either regardless or forgetful of what it considered the best interests of the colonists; and a large part of the Constitutional Act is devoted to making provision for what it considered the highest interests of these loyal children of the empire. To say nothing of mistakes in the province of Lower Canada, in Upper Canada two most serious errors were the provisions for the endowment of an established church and for the creation of a titled hereditary aristocracy with places in the upper legislative chamber. These provisions, both embodied in the new colonial constitution, both destined to utter practical failure, but both acting as irritants provoking unfortunate conflicts, were the beginning of misfortunes from which we have not perfectly escaped even to-day, though we have passed a century of effort to counteract their far-reaching influence. These provisions, with others which followed, were the result of the spirit of an age when the supreme care of the state was for what was regarded as the superior class of people, and when the great body of the population, whose labour and virtue constitute its wealth and strength, were passed over with but little consideration. To such an age a governing class, of which the clergy of the established church were regarded as a part, seemed a prime necessity; and to create and educate such a class and provide for their maintenance seemed an imperative duty. The rest of the people were expected "to labour truly to get their own living, and to do their duty in that state of life unto which it pleased God to call them." It can now scarcely be doubted that some such conception was in the minds of the framers of the Constitutional Act; and it is even more certain that such was the policy inaugurated by the first governor of Upper Canada, Lieut.-General John Graves Simcoe. His educational policy alone is proof of this. It was more concerned with the erection of schools after the model of the English classical schools, and with the founding of a university, than with the elementary education of all the people; and while for the one class it provided an endowment, which, if not sufficient, has at least supplied our wants for an entire century in high schools and university, it left the other to care for itself.

But the population which laid the foundations of Upper Canada was not of the material to be treated after this fashion. The men whose intelligence and whose moral and political principles were so matured as to lead them to sacrifice almost their entire worldly fortune for the sake of those principles, were not easily to be divided into upper and lower classes, or relegated to any inferior position while their neighbours were constituted a governing class. Moreover, they were men of various forms of religious faith. There were Puritan Independents from New England, Quakers from Pennsylvania and Rhode Island, Lutherans and Dutch Reformed from New York and Pennsylvania, Presbyterians from New Jersey, and from various parts a large body of the followers of John Wesley, and not a few Baptists. Probably from the beginning the adherents of the Church of England were a decided minority of the population, while Presbyterians, Methodists, Roman Catholics and Baptists together constituted the majority. The founding of an endowed and established church under such circumstances was as serious a mistake and as difficult an enterprise as the creation of a titled governing class. The body whom it was proposed to make the established church was from the beginning behind in the race, while energy, zeal, self-denying labour and sympathy with the progressive spirit of the age were largely if not exclusively on the side of the so-called sects.

The policy then inaugurated might thus have expired with its founder's term as governor, and was liable at any time to have been abandoned by the coming to the colony of an intelligent and liberal-minded governor, had not two or three notable circumstances combined to give it a living continuity and fictitious support. The first of these was the coming to the country in 1799, to inaugurate the educational side of the policy, of John Strachan, afterwards first Anglican bishop of Toronto. The post was first offered to the famous

Thomas Chalmers, then also a young man fresh
from college, and by him declined. What might
have been the result of his acceptance no one can
now venture to conjecture. The event proved that
the man to whom it fell was preëminently fitted
for the work, and would have succeeded in its
accomplishment had it been possible to mortal man.
This young man, then a mere youthful school
teacher, was employed solely for that purpose, and
because of his success in that profession. But he
was endowed with all the qualities of a great political leader, a pleasing personality, intense energy,
tireless pertinacity of purpose, a mind fruitful of
resources for the practical accomplishment of his
purposes, and a judgment of men and of circumstances which enabled him to take their measure
with accuracy and to make both serve his purposes.
He was not long in the country before he had
fully grasped the dominant policy and had shaped
himself and his life work for its accomplishment.
Though a divinity student of the Church of Scotland his association with the rector of the Church
of England in Kingston, and with Mr. Cartwright
a leading layman of that body, led to his taking
orders in that church ; and from that day, May,
1803, his future course was determined. His great
talents were soon recognized and in a few years his
appointment as rector of York, and a little later
as member of the executive council, made him
virtual leader of the Church of England party

in the province, and gave at once continuity, guidance and energy to its policy. Henceforth his ambition was to make the Church of England dominant as the established church in the country with full control of the vast clergy reserve endowments and of the superior education as well as the government of the province.

A circumstance which afforded some fictitious strength to this ambitious politico-religious policy was the relation of several of the other religious bodies and particularly of the Methodists to the sister or rather parent churches in the United States. These churches had sprung from the American colonies at the era of the Revolution, through the United Empire Loyalist emigration which founded Upper Canada. Methodist preachers, themselves also, almost to a man, of Loyalist sympathies, had followed their people to their new homes in the northern wilderness and had shared all their early privations and trials. But under the Methodist itinerant economy they did not establish a separate church, judging that the work of preaching the gospel was not limited by political boundaries. As the Methodists were the most effectual obstacle in the way of the success of the church policy, their opponents were not slow to attach to them the opprobrium of being republicans, annexationists, and not loyal to the British throne and institutions. The reproach was most unjust, for Canadian Methodism was born out of the great United Empire Loyalist movement, and this was quite as true of her first preachers as of her people, except that they had little or no property to lose and were precluded by their clerical profession from taking up arms.

A second circumstance tending in the same direction was the prestige afforded to the English church by its relations to the established church in England. If the relation of Methodism to the parent church in the United States was a disadvantage to Canadian Methodism, the relation of the Anglican church in Canada to the parent Church of England operated to the advantage of the colonial church. It thus secured not only prestige, but also, by the transfer of British law and usage to the new colony, a legal status denied to other bodies of Christians. Under that advantage it even laid claim to be the established church of all the colonies as well as of the parent country. This claim was not made good, as the example of the older American colonies was against it, and as the established Church of Scotland at once put forth a similar claim on the same ground. But both bodies secured in this way rights of property and of the legal performance of ministerial or clerical functions. On the other hand the other denominations could hold no property, and baptisms or marriages performed by their ministers were not recognized in law; and only after a struggle of thirty years were these disabilities removed. The facts thus recited are the key to a large part of the first fifty

years of the history of Upper Canada, and to a
good deal which has happened since that time. At
first indeed the people were so occupied with their
individual struggle in the wilderness for a bare
subsistence, that they scarcely noticed the lack
of these political rights and privileges. They built
their humble places of worship on a site cheerfully
offered by one of themselves and accepted and used
in simple christian confidence. The question of the
legal bearings of baptism was scarcely raised, and
as for marriage, while its importance could not be
overlooked, they accepted the legal provisions existing, though often at great inconvenience and
sacrifice.

During this first period also, the ecclesiastical
policy, while it had laid some foundations, had not
developed any considerable strength. Neither the
clergy reserves nor the educational endowment had
as yet become productive of appreciable revenue,
and the superior advantages of the Anglican church
were as yet imported from the old country rather
than acquired here. If the English church was
supported by government grants, they were made
in England and not in Canada.

But even in these times when the Methodists
and others were quietly making the best of their
disadvantages, the existence of a spirit of arrogant
enmity towards them was manifest not only in
social life, but also in the exercise of civil authority
in forms which exhibited the persecuting spirit

of barbarous ages. The death of Charles Justin McCarthy through the action of the civil authorities at Kingston, was the extreme instance of this. He was the martyr of early Canadian Methodism.

But this preliminary period was brought to an end by a convulsion thrust into our history from without. This was the war of 1812-14. With the causes or the events of this war we have nothing to do, except to say that in it the Canadian Methodists abundantly vindicated their loyalty to the British throne and institutions. In the noble rally to drive the invader from our soil they bore a manly part; and while all Canadian hearts were united by the common danger and in the common struggle, no one was found base enough even to whisper a slander against either their loyalty or their courage.

With the close of the war came a new era of political and industrial life to Upper Canada. The wave of imperialism which through the South African war has stirred our own time, is largely sentimental. But it has made us feel that we are not only Canadians but a part of Greater Britain. The wave which followed the war of 1812 was intensely sentimental. It made us feel that we were Canada, a country, able to defend its rights and soil; not a mere outlying territory which our neighbours might covet and take possession of. But that wave was one of great material uplift as well. The expenditure of British money during the war introduced an era of prosperity. The desperate struggle with want and sometimes with starvation was over, and the whole population began to feel that our country was a home worth fighting for, dying for, and living for, that it might become still more worthy of our affection. A new public interest was created in all that belonged to the country, and the country began to feel the pulsations of political life. It was such an awakening as in all ages has led nations into larger life and liberty. Nor was Canada alone in feeling the power of this movement. It stirred all western Europe, and it led in England itself to the perfecting of her system of responsible government. In fact, our Canadian movement might in comparison seem to be but an insignificant side current of the great movement of the time. But little as it might appear in the great world's history, it had a distinctive unity and character of its own; and to us it is all-important—it is the foundation history of our own country. It was not entirely an isolated history. It had very definite relations to the greater movement in the older lands, especially in England, as we shall see presently. But the forces by which it was propelled were not extraneous; they arose from within, and out of the facts and conditions which we have already described. It therefore assumed a character distinctively Canadian. It was neither American republicanism nor English chartism, but Canadian reform. It was the movement of the great body of the people of

CANADIAN REFORM

Upper Canada toward perfect civil and religious equality and political manhood and freedom.

This movement was along three distinct yet closely related and parallel lines. One was political, and its goal was responsible government. A second was religious, and its goal was equal civil rights of free churches in a free state. The third was educational, and its goal was common provision for all the people, without distinction of class or creed. It would be a mistake to suppose that the actors in this movement always clearly grasped the results for which they were struggling, or against which they were striving in vain. Each felt the force and direction of the current in his own immediate vicinity, and was making as best he could for some objective point within his own range of vision; but the far-off goal of the unexplored river in the still distant sea, none as yet fully knew. In dealing, therefore, with any one of these men of that time as makers of Canada, we must judge of them not only by final results, but also by the human motives and limitations of their time. They sometimes laboured more wisely and sometimes more vainly than they knew. Their apparent defeats were sometimes real successes, and at others their seeming success was a real disaster. To impute to them moral inconsistency because to us now, or even to their neighbours then in another part of the current, they seemed to be moving in a wrong direction, would be a great injustice. Such movements growing out of and impelled by the needs of a whole nation are too great to be controlled or even fully grasped by the mind of any one man. But yet they call for and make great men, and find the materials out of which they may be made.

It was to the second and third of these movements that Mr. Ryerson gave his life, and he was led into the third from the second. Both movements, of necessity, touched politics, and were often closely related to, if not identified with, the political movement. But from the beginning he was a Methodist preacher and not a politician. Had he been a politician his connection with these movements would have thrown him into the ranks of political reform, if not revolution. But for such an alliance he had no sympathy. His political predilections were thoroughly conservative. Through his studies of Blackstone and Paley, at an age when very few have formed clearly defined political opinions, he had settled his conceptions of the rights of the crown, the parliament, and the people; and from the constitutional principles thus defined he would have considered it a sin in morals as well as a crime in law to depart. It is scarcely necessary to say that these conceptions were not republican; and it could scarcely be said that they included all that is understood by constitutional liberty and responsible government in our time. What he was seeking was not a change of constitution, but the righting of wrongs. He wished that what he believed to be justice should be done under the existing constitution. The constitutional reformers on the other hand were firmly of opinion that justice to the masses of the people would never be done until the constitution itself was so reformed as to give the voice of the people power to determine the policy of the government. Forming their judgment from the standpoint of men of the world, and not from that of a devout and enthusiastic young clergyman, they were quite convinced that so long as the constitution placed the power of shaping public policy and controlling legislation in the hands of a ruling class, they would be shaped and controlled for the advantage of that class. And in this opinion they were quite right, and the whole course of subsequent history has justified their struggle for constitutional reform. But Mr. Ryerson's ideal objects were not of this radical character. He sought equal rights for all the churches, and equal and efficient provision of education for all the people. He perhaps at first did not even see the necessity of complete separation of church from state, although he fully recognized the injustice of the establishment of one church as a state, and so a dominant, church. The state might assist religion,[1] but there must be no favouritism. In the same way he did not begin with a theory of secular education separated from all religious bodies. His earnest religious nature was in full sympathy

---

[1] Even W. L. Mackenzie in 1824 held this view. See the first number of the *Colonial Advocate*.

with the idea that true education must be moral and religious as well as intellectual. He would not have divorced education from the influence of the churches. But he could not brook the injustice of having the educational endowments of the country controlled for their own advantage by one religious body.

Simple, practical, and conservative as these ideas appear to us to-day, they brought him into direct conflict with the policy of Dr. Strachan. In 1813, Dr. Strachan had been appointed a member of the executive council of Upper Canada; in 1820 he was made a member of the legislative council, and in 1827 was made Archdeacon of York. These appointments gave him a position of commanding influence in both church and state for the successful development of his politico-ecclesiastical policy. In fact, by 1820 it is clear that the policy and patronage of Upper Canada were controlled not so much by the lieutenant-governor for the time being as by the rector of York and the chief justice of the province. It is not necessary for our purpose to enlarge upon all the aspects of their exercise of this irresponsible power; we are concerned with the facts only along the ecclesiastical and educational lines.

The Constitutional Act of 1791 had authorized the setting apart for the support of a Protestant clergy of a quantity of land equal in value to one seventh of all the lands granted by the crown for

46

settlement. This was in lieu of the tithes granted to the Roman Catholic church in Lower Canada. The lands so reserved in Upper Canada finally amounted to nearly 2,400,000 acres. Although the intention of some of the framers of the act was probably to make these lands the foundation of an established church—and this was certainly the policy of Simcoe, both for political and religious reasons—yet the act did not specifically assign either the lands or their revenue to the Anglican church. In fact, by giving the governors power to assign a portion or the whole of them in each township for the support of a rectory, it excluded any legal claim to them on the ground of the original grant. Until after the war the lands were not productive of any appreciable revenue, and the support of the Anglican clergy was derived from grants made by the home government and by the Society for the Propagation of the Gospel in Foreign Parts. Up to 1819 the annual product of the reserves did not exceed £700. But before this date the clergy reserve question was forced upon the attention of the people and the legislature in another form. These blocks of unoccupied land obstructed settlement by separating the settlers by intervening tracts of forest without roads, as well as by increasing by one-sixth the burden of taxation for any local purpose. A resolution was introduced in 1817 on this subject, and in 1819 the House asked for a return of the lands leased and of the revenue derived therefrom. The governor referred the matter to England for instructions. At the same time a congregation of the Church of Scotland in the town of Niagara petitioned the governor for an allowance of £100 a year for the support of a minister. The governor transmitted the petition to England, and with it he raised the question as to whether the Church of Scotland was entitled to participate in the reserves. These circumstances stirred up the Anglicans to immediate action, and in the next year, through the application of their bishop, Dr. Mountain, they were created a corporation in each province and invested with the management of the clergy reserves. But under the advice of the law officers of the crown, who recognized the claims of the Church of Scotland, and as a matter of policy, this power of management was not made to include any right of ownership. This was to be reached, if reached at all, by the establishment and endowment of rectories by the governor under the existing act. On this, under the existing temper of the people, they did not venture, resting satisfied for the present with the prestige of being guardians of the property.

But the question, once raised, could not be postponed. The claim of the Church of Scotland, now supported by eminent legal authority at home, as well as by the advice of the Earl of Bathurst to give them a share in the reserves, was at once pressed. In 1823 they secured from the legislature

48

a presentation to the King in their favour which was rejected by the legislative council, and also pressed their claims upon the lieutenant-governor for aid from any source. In the meantime Dr. Strachan prepared a petition to the King asserting the full pretensions of the Anglican church, and supporting them by statements concerning the religious state of the province as unfounded as were those which a few years later in his sermon were destined to bring an entirely new force into the contest. These statements, the same in substance whether embodied in petition, chart, or sermon, were, however, not yet made public in the province. They were only for the sympathetic ears of councillors of state.

The question has been asked, why did not the Anglican party call into effect the power of the governor to establish rectories in every township, and endow them with the lands, and so secure legal possession? The reason would seem to be that they could not be satisfied with anything less than the exclusive possession of the whole; and this they could not expect to secure in the face of the political advice of the Earl of Bathurst that they should divide with the Church of Scotland. Without his assent they could not take action; and that assent they were not likely to secure in the face of the storm of opposition which such a course would have aroused in the province. The next year, Dr. Strachan, now the leader of the Anglican cause, was sent to England with the proposal "that the

clergy corporation should be empowered to sell
one-half of the lands thus appropriated, to fund
the money derived from their sale, and to apply the
interest towards the support of the clergy." Such is
the statement of the proposition as given by Dr.
Bethune in his "Memoirs of Bishop Strachan."
This proposal again failed through Dr. Strachan's
desire to secure the largest possible advantage to
the church. The Canada Company offered to become the purchasers, but he objected to their price
as too low; the project was delayed for the appointment of commissioners to value the lands, and
finally fell through. This termination was not
reached until after Dr. Strachan's return, and until
events made it perfectly clear that his plan for the
establishment and endowment of some hundreds of
Anglican clergy in the province could not be carried
into effect. This was doubtless in large part due to
the influence upon the home government of the
action of the legislative assembly from 1824 to
1826, and of a petition from the province of Upper
Canada praying that the proceeds of the clergy
reserve lands be divided among the Protestant
denominations, or applied to the purpose of general
education. This petition was called out by Dr.
Strachan's famous chart, and was, with other Canadian questions, referred to a select committee of
the British House of Commons in 1827. It was
during this juncture that Dr. Strachan preached
his famous sermon on the death of the Bishop of

Quebec, which called Mr. Ryerson into the conflict in April, 1826.

We may now turn to the other question of the time, the effort to control for denominational purposes the education of the country. The circumstances that meet us here are very different from those which we have just been considering. The early settlers in Upper Canada were generally religious people. By the end of thirty years they had largely supplied themselves with the means of grace. At that date the population of Upper Canada is estimated at 120,000, and a trustworthy contemporary document gives the following statement of the Protestant ministry in the province:

Church of England	16
Presbyterian and Congregational	15
Baptist	18
Methodist	33
Mennonites	7
Friends	10
Total	99

Besides these the Methodists employed 112 lay preachers. These statistics are of themselves the clearest evidence of the conditions which precluded the monopoly of religious functions or even rights and privileges by any one denomination. On the other hand there was no such preëmption of the field of education. Here was a sphere of influence at first entirely unoccupied, and one in which by the aid of public endowments the policy inaugurated by Governor Simcoe, and followed up with such marked ability by Dr. Strachan, could find free and ample scope. The fundamental mistake in their policy and one that doomed it from the beginning to ultimate failure was its neglect of the common people.

The education of a nation naturally falls into three grand divisions: first, the primary, which should reach all the people; then, the secondary, which at best will not touch more than ten per cent., generally not more than five; and last, the university, reached by less than one-half of one per cent. It was to these two last fields of education that the policy we are considering was directed. And its method from the beginning was the building of a system of class education reserved for the rightful rulers of the people, and with no broad basis of universal instruction as its foundation. The grammar schools and university which they projected were not the higher departments of a comprehensive system of education which knows no distinction of class or rank, but opens the door of learning wide for the humblest child to whom God has given the ability to reach its very summit. They were shaped rather as an exclusive system for a caste; if they admitted the gifted child of poverty, it was an accorded privilege. They were never expected to draw their patronage from the whole body of the people. For these they did not attempt any provision. Fortunately they did not attempt to interfere with their making provision for themselves.

FIRST SCHOOL LEGISLATION

The original plan of Governor Simcoe, as carried into effect by President Russell, set apart 550,000 acres of public lands for the establishment of a university and four royal grammar schools. These were a little later proposed to be located—the university at York, and the grammar schools at Cornwall, Kingston, Newark, and Sandwich. It is evident that from the outset the character of the schools thus proposed was not to the mind of the legislative assembly, for nothing further was done till 1804, and then a motion for the establishment of these schools was negatived by a vote of seven to five. The reason for this defeat seems to have been not so much opposition to public provision for education, though there may have been both indifference and opposition, as a feeling that the scheme was not sufficiently comprehensive. A motion following, to establish a school in each of the districts was lost by the casting vote of the speaker. An act to this effect was finally passed in 1807, placing the appointment of trustees for these district schools in the hands of the lieutenant-governor, and such trustees were appointed for eight districts, viz., Eastern, Johnstown, Midland, Newcastle, Home, Niagara, London, and Western.

The legislation thus carried through both branches of the legislature and acted upon by the lieutenant-governor, finally became effective in the establishment of district grammar schools in the eight districts, and, after repeated amendments, its operation was extended to the establishment of twenty-five schools, twenty of which reported an attendance of 627 pupils, or an average of $31\frac{1}{2}$ for each school. Allowing the same for the five which made no returns, the whole number of children being educated under this system in 1845 was less than 800. The feeling of the great mass of the people towards the system may perhaps be judged from two petitions presented to the legislature shortly after its inauguration. One of these, from the Newcastle district, set forth, "That your petitioners find the said appropriation (£100 for the district grammar school) to be entirely useless to the inhabitants of this district in general." They therefore pray that the said acts "may be repealed, and that such other provision may be made to encourage common schools throughout this district as to you in your wisdom may seem meet." The other, from the Midland district, where one of the oldest and one of the best of these schools was established at Kingston, speaks in these terms: "Its object, it is presumed, was to promote the education of our youth in general, but a little acquaintance with the facts must convince every unbiased mind that it has contributed little or nothing to the promotion of so laudable a design. By reason of the place of instruction being established at one end of the district, and the sum demanded for tuition, in addition to the annual compensation received from the public, most of the people are unable to avail themselves of the advantages contemplated by the institution. A few wealthy inhabitants and those of the town of Kingston reap exclusively the benefit of it in this district. The institution, instead of aiding the middle and poorer classes of His Majesty's subjects, casts money into the lap of the rich, who are sufficiently able, without public assistance, to support a school in every respect equal to the one established by law."

This want of the people also voiced itself in another and more practical form. It led to the large establishment of private and subscription schools, some of them of the more elementary character afterwards known as common schools, and others more pretentious and known as academies—a term borrowed from the United States. It is not possible for us now to obtain exact statistics of the number of the common schools in existence throughout the province prior to the triumph of popular education in the act of 1816. But in the next year, 1817, Mr. Gourlay collected statistics of no less than 259 common schools already in operation, and these were by no means the whole number in the province. From this we may safely infer that the voluntary efforts of the people to provide for the education of their own children had, even before the act of 1816, far outstripped in extent of influence the class system inaugurated in 1807.

The extension of the public schools to each of the eight districts, while seemingly in the interests of the mass of the people, did not prove so from several causes. They were secondary rather than primary schools; there was but one in each district —a district covering the area of three or more counties; the trustees were appointed by the governor and the executive council, *i.e.*, the irresponsible ruling class; and finally the teachers selected by them were men fitted to support their views, and frequently clergymen of the English church. The schools were, besides this, beyond the reach of the people, on account of the expense of residence at a distance from home, and of the high fees charged. Their unpopularity appears from the fact that in almost every session a repeal bill was introduced, though failing either in the assembly, which at this time was Conservative through the influence of the war, or in the legislative council. The influence of popular feeling finally resulted in the passage of the Common School Bill of 1816. The main provisions of this act were the following:—(1) It authorized the inhabitants of any locality to convene a meeting at which provision might be made for building or providing a school-house, securing the necessary number of scholars (twenty or more), providing for the salary of a teacher, and electing three trustees for the management of a school. (2) It conferred upon the trustees power to examine teachers as to qualification, to appoint such to the school, to dismiss them if unsatisfactory, to make rules for the governing of the school, including books to be used, and to grant the teacher a certificate on presentation of which he would be entitled to his proportion of the legislative grant to the district. (3) It made provision for grants in aid to the several districts, amounting in all to £6,000 per annum. (4) It authorized the lieutenant-governor to appoint for each district a board of education with the following powers:—to receive quarterly reports from the trustees of each school; to exercise superintendence over the schools; to disallow at their discretion the regulations made by the trustees, or the books used in the schools; to make further rules and regulations for the schools, and to distribute or apportion the legislative grant. These district boards were required to report to the lieutenant-governor. Their power to "proportion" the legislative grant was unrestricted, and they could use a part of it—up to £100—in purchasing books for use in the schools.

It will be seen that the first part of these provisions relating to school meetings, trustees and their powers, was simply a continuation of the existing institutions which the people had already created for themselves. The loyalist immigrants, from the time of their first arrival in the country, had organized voluntary municipal institutions for themselves on popular principles, and before the passing of this act a considerable number of schools had been thus created and supported in the older settlements. The new provisions of the act were the legislative grant and the district boards, and the chief purpose of the latter would seem to have been, besides the apportionment of the money, the exclusion of disloyal teachers and text books.

The educational development of the province from the passing of this act (1816) to 1825 may be summarized as follows: (1) The reduction of the grant to common schools in 1820 from £6,000 to £2,500; (2) the introduction into a central school in York of the Bell system (the Church of England national system); (3) the constitution and appointment in 1823 of a general board of education for the province, consisting of the following gentlemen: the Honourable and Reverend John Strachan, D.D., Chairman; the Honourable Joseph Wells, M.L.C.; the Honourable George H. Markland, M.L.C.; the Reverend Robert Addison; John Beverley Robinson, Esquire, Attorney-General; Thomas Ridout, Esquire, Surveyor-General; (4) the passage of the extension and amendment act of 1824, which continued the grant and other provisions of 1820, made a further grant of £150 to be expended by the general board in the purchase of books for Sunday schools, to be equally distributed among the districts of the province, made provision for the extension of the benefits of the common school acts to Indian schools, and required that all teachers participating in legislative aid should pass an examination before the district board of education.

In this act the provincial board of education was

recognized as in existence or about to be appointed by the lieutenant-governor for the superintendence of education, but it is not specifically constituted by the act, nor are its powers defined other than in the matter of the purchase of the books for Sunday schools. It seems, therefore, that the appointment of this board and the definition of its powers was a matter of executive and not legislative authority. Its initiation by communication with the colonial office points in the same direction.[1]

On the incoming of the new legislative assembly elected in 1824, we thus find an educational system in existence, directed or supervised by district and provincial boards appointed by the lieutenant-governor, and at the head of the system the Reverend John Strachan, D.D., as chairman of the provincial board. The next steps in the development of this system were the university charter of 1827, and the founding of Upper Canada College in 1829; but as these enter into the struggle for equal rights, which began in deadly earnest the next year, and in which Mr. Ryerson was henceforth to take part as a prominent actor, we need not consider them in this preliminary review of the initial situation.

[1] An incidental circumstance, showing the trend or intent of movements at this time, is the petition of Dr. Strachan in 1818 for legislative aid for theological students.

CHAPTER III

THE BEGINNING OF THE STRUGGLE FOR
EQUAL RIGHTS

DR. STRACHAN, in one of his published papers, refers to the year 1820 as a memorable one in the history of Upper Canada. The reason for this was the erection of the clergy of the Church of England into a body corporate, and their control of the clergy reserves. This, with his own personal accession to power and the hold which he was gradually securing on the educational work of the country, evidently made him sanguine of success in the prosecution of his far-reaching policy of making the Church of England the established and endowed, and so the dominant church of the young province, controlling the religious life and education of the whole people. The era is indeed memorable in the history of Upper Canada, but for just the opposite reason. It is the period from which dates the awakening of the people to a full sense of their political and religious danger, and the beginning of that struggle which finally resulted in the overthrow of the Strachan policy and the complete civil and religious emancipation of the province. For this result two things were necessary: the people must be aroused, and competent leaders must be found. The first of these needed elements was furnished by the ruling party, even the wise and far-seeing Strachan himself contributing an essential part of the stimulus which goaded the people into strenuous self-defence. From this period we may date the beginning of distinct party life and spirit in the politics of the province, and this life was created, not by academic theory, nor by the assembly of a convention, or the formation of a platform, or the election of political leaders. It was the spontaneous revolt of manly independence both in church and state against unjust and arrogant assumptions and cruel wrongs.

As we are not attempting the political history of the province we cannot enter into the detailed statement of these wrongs, or of the political evils which culminated at this period. It will be sufficient to mention a few events which combined to awaken the mind of the whole province to a true sense of the situation. It took not a little to do this. The Upper Canadians were a loyal people. The older—and on the whole, more influential—families were United Empire Loyalists. No stronger appeal could be made than to their loyalty. The war of 1812 had continued and strengthened this feeling. Since the war, here and there a bolder spirit had called in question wrong-doing in high places, or had claimed recognition for the just rights of the people. The school bill of 1816 was one concession to such rights. But the voice of this party was constantly hushed by the cry of disloyalty set up against all who dared to call in question the policy or acts of the ruling power; and without leadership and cohesion the voice of the people was as "one crying in the wilderness." Besides all this the people were too busy with the hard necessities of life to give the needed time and energy to these things. The first event which contributed to the awakening of the people was the prosecution and imprisonment of Gourlay, and his banishment from the country after his harsh treatment in prison had reduced him to shattered senility. The story has been told with thrilling effect by Dent, and the feelings stirred by its recital to-day are but a reflection of those aroused in the country at the time.

The election contests of Barnabas Bidwell followed, and, extending over two years or more, served to perpetuate the feelings aroused and to give them a more decidedly political direction. The Appleton case following awakened interest in the educational aspects of the question. Finally the sermon preached by Dr. Strachan on the occasion of the death of Bishop Mountain aroused the religious feeling of the entire body of the people who were not attached to the Church of England. This sermon, the immediate occasion of calling Mr. Ryerson into the field, will require fuller attention presently.

In the meantime we must deal with the more immediate effects of the general political awakening caused by these events. These effects were clearly manifest in the general election of 1824 and in the first session of the newly-elected legislative assembly. Probably for the first time in the history of the colony an election contest was carried on in which not so much the individual candidates as the principles which they represented were prominently before the minds of the people. Nothing but the influence of a new political life could have produced this. This consciousness of a distinct issue before the electors was not the result of any of the political agencies of our time. A party or provincial press scarcely existed—Mackenzie's *Colonial Advocate* was only a few weeks old. No great conventions had been held. There were no clearly recognized leaders of public opinion, and there was no party organization. This movement seemed to be the spontaneous uprising of political manhood against assumptions and injustice which could no longer be endured. The result was the return to the assembly of a majority of members opposed to the ruling party and their policy, and the election of one of their number, John Wilson, as speaker, by a majority of two. This narrow majority by no means represented their influence in the House. Feebler men whose convictions were with them were not yet prepared to cut loose from the old party still in power.

But this return of a majority to the assembly did not introduce an era of political reform. It was only the beginning of an era of political conflict culminating in the new constitution of 1840. The ruling party represented by the governor and the executive council owed no responsibility to the assembly, and through the legislative council and the governor they held a negative control over all legislation. The direct advantage gained by the triumph of reform at the polls was the power to prevent any legislation which would further sacrifice the interests of the people. The assembly alone could make no positive progress towards even legislative improvement. But outside of this they gained another important advantage; they could express the sentiment and wants of the people to the people themselves. The popular branch of parliament became at least an organ for the clear and definite expression of political ideas and ideals. In it the people found set forth in speech what they had felt, but scarcely understood, and perhaps, as isolated individuals, would not have dared to utter. It even went further. It soon became the organ for the expression of the same ideas at the foot of the throne and before the parliament of England. It was especially in this latter way that it was able to forward largely and effectively the cause of constitutional reform in the colony.

Another and scarcely less important result of this new political life was the creation of leadership. Four men of conspicuous ability at once came to the front in the assembly,—John Wilson, the new speaker of the House, John Rolph, member for

Middlesex, and Peter Perry and M. S. Bidwell, members for Lennox and Addington. Three others, the Baldwins and W. L. Mackenzie, were as yet co-workers outside of the House. Mackenzie worked especially through his paper *The Colonial Advocate*, and the creation of a press through which the people could be kept in touch with the new political life was another most important event of the period.

The new movement from the political side had thus in the course of a very few years risen to commanding influence among the people, had acquired for itself a standing ground and organ of influential work in parliament itself, had called to its front able and energetic leaders, and had created a press through which it could disseminate necessary information among the people.

But important and far-reaching in its results as was this political side of the movement it by no means exhausted its force. From the political point of view, many of the religious questions raised were quite excluded, and others occupied a subordinate place. But the religious interests of a people are too important and lie too near to their hearts to be relegated to any secondary place; and the party in power were at this juncture fated to awaken against themselves the full force of the religious as well as the political sentiments of the people. This was brought about by three or four acts of Dr. Strachan following close on the political events just sketched.

AN AWAKENING SERMON

The first of these was the sermon preached at York on July 3rd, 1825, on the death of the late Lord Bishop of Quebec. In this sermon, preached before a sympathetic audience of his own people, he expounded somewhat freely, not only his own ecclesiastical views and policy, but also his sentiments towards the other religious bodies of the country. The main points were the following: (1) The maintenance of the Divine authority and exclusive validity of the Episcopal Church polity; (2) the necessity of a state church and the moral obligation of the government to provide for its establishment and support; (3) the claim of the Church of England to be the established church of this colony and to the exclusive enjoyment of the clergy reserves; (4) disparaging references to other religious bodies, in which he represents them as disloyal, as imbued with republican and levelling opinions, as ignorant, incapable, and idle, and pictures the country which was largely supplied with the means of grace through their services as in a state of utter moral and religious destitution.

The persecution of Gourlay and the expulsion of Bidwell from the House of Assembly were scarcely more effective in arousing the political feelings of the country than was this unfortunate utterance in arousing the indignation of the religious community. This indignation immediately found a voice and a capable leader in the person of Egerton Ryerson, a young Methodist preacher then in the

67

first year of his ministry. He had been received on trial at the conference of 1825 and was stationed with the Rev. James Richardson on the Yonge Street and York circuit. His entrance upon the present controversy is thus described in "The Story of My Life": "The Methodists in York at that time numbered about fifty persons, young and old. The two preachers arranged to meet once in four weeks on their return from their country tours, when a social meeting of the leading members of the society was held for consultation, conversation, and prayer. One of the members of this company obtained and brought to the meeting a copy of the Archdeacon's sermon, and read the parts of it which related to the attacks on the Methodists, and the proposed method of exterminating them. The reading of these extracts produced a thrilling sensation of indignation and alarm, and all agreed that something must be written and done to defend the character and rights of Methodists and others assailed, against such attacks and such a policy. The voice of the meeting pointed to me to undertake the work. I was then designated as 'The Boy Preacher,' from my youthful appearance and as the youngest minister in the church (he was then just twenty-three years of age). I objected on account of my youth and incompetence, but my objections were overruled, when I proposed as a compromise, that during our next country tour the Superintendent of the circuit (the Rev. James Richardson) and myself should each write on the subject, and from what we should both write, something might be compiled to meet the case. This was agreed to, and at our next social monthly meeting in the town, inquiry was made as to what had been written in defence of the Methodists and others against the attacks and policy of the Archdeacon of York. It was found that the Superintendent of the circuit had written nothing; and on being questioned, I said I had endeavoured to obey the instructions of my senior brethren. It was then insisted that I must read what I had written. I at length yielded and read my answer to the attacks made on us. The reading of my paper was attended with alternate laughter and tears on the part of the social party, all of whom insisted that it should be printed. I objected that I had never written anything for the press, and was not competent to do so, and advanced to throw my manuscript into the fire, when one of the elder members caught me by the arms and another wrenched the manuscript out of my hands, saying he would take it to the printer. Finding my efforts vain to recover it, I said if it were restored I would not destroy but re-write it and return it to the brethren to do what they pleased with it. I did so. Two of the senior brethren took the manuscript to the printer, and its publication produced a sensation scarcely less violent and general than a Fenian invasion. It is said that before every house in Toronto (then the town

of York) might be seen groups reading and discussing the paper on the evening of its publication
in June; and the excitement spread throughout the
country. It was the first defiant defence of the
Methodists, and of the equal and civil rights of all
religious persuasions, the first protest and argument
on legal and British constitutional grounds, against
the erection of a dominant church establishment
supported by the state in Upper Canada. It was
the Loyalists of America and their descendants
who first lifted up the voice of remonstrance against
ecclesiastical despotism in the province, and un-
furled the flag of equal religious rights and liberty
for all religious persuasions. The sermon of the
Archdeacon of York was the third formal attack
made by the Church of England clergy upon the
character of their unoffending Methodist brethren
and those of other religious persuasions, but no
defense of the assailed parties had as yet been
written. At that time the Methodists had no law to
secure a foot of land on which to build parsonages
or chapels and in which to bury their dead; their
ministers were not allowed to solemnize matrimony, and some of them had been the objects
of cruel and illegal persecution on the part of
magistrates and others in authority. And now they
were the butt of unprovoked and unfounded asper-
sions from two heads of Episcopal clergy, while
pursuing the 'noiseless tenor of their way' through
trackless forests and bridgeless rivers and streams,

to preach among the scattered inhabitants the unsearchable riches of Christ."

These words from Dr. Ryerson's own pen indicate most clearly the circumstances under which and the motives by which he was led into this controversy. It was no itching for political notoriety, but rather manly indignation against wrong which forced the young Methodist preacher into the strife. But the extract gives us no conception of the ability and thoroughness with which he performed his task. Replies from the Church of England side quickly appeared, and again and again he returned to the conflict. In a short time a volume of the letters of two hundred and fifty pages was written which forms to-day a most valuable historical document. In these letters he shows himself a master of the scriptural and even of the patristic argument on the fundamental question of church polity, taking a position which is now conceded by the very best Anglican divines. He discusses the question of a church establishment with wonderful practical insight as well as wide historical learning. With keen satire he contrasts the self-denying life and labours, and the consecrated purity and zeal of the Methodist preachers with the lives, work and emoluments of their detractors. While not claiming for them scholastic learning, he shows that they were at least men of good sound fundamental education, practically fitted and able for their work; and finally he vindicates their loyalty as citizens in words of burning eloquence.

Before the review of his sermon appeared in print Dr. Strachan had left the province on a visit to England where he spent some eighteen months improving the opportunity for the furtherance of his ecclesiastical and educational policy. The character of his efforts to this end appeared in three public documents which bear date in 1827. The first of these was a bill introduced into the Imperial parliament in February, 1827. Of it, Dr. Strachan himself writes: "I should now be on my way to Canada, but I got a bill introduced, in February, into parliament, to enable the crown to sell a portion of the clergy reserves, as they are at present totally unproductive, and a cause of clamour as being a barrier to improvement. I was anxious to avoid the great question that has been agitated in the colony about the meaning of the words 'Protestant Clergy,' and confined myself simply to the power of sale. But Mr. Stanley came forward with a motion to investigate the whole matter, and of consequence, the second reading of my bill is put off to the first of May. In the meantime the old ministry has fallen to pieces, and whether the new ministry will attend to my business or not remains to be seen." The second was the charter of King's College, dated March 15th, 1827. Of this he speaks in the same letter: "I am happy to tell you that I had the good fortune to accomplish the most material part of my mission before the crash amongst the ministry took place. *My* university charter was issued on March 22nd, and I have had a few copies printed."

This charter, which was to be the subject of acrimonious dispute for more than twenty years to come, and the end of which we have not yet reached, deserves attention as one of the most important parts of Dr. Strachan's educational policy. We have already seen his relation, first to the district or secondary schools, and later to the common or primary. Over each he had secured some measure of control, but as yet by no means complete in the case of the latter. *His* charter was now about to leave no room for question as to the ecclesiastical control of the university, as will appear from the following provisions of the charter:

1. The bishop of the diocese was made the visitor of the university. This placed the supreme power of investigating and vetoing all questions as to its management and work in ecclesiastical hands.

2. The president must be a clergyman in holy orders of the united Church of England and Ireland, and the Rev. John Strachan, D.D., was appointed the first president.

3. The college was to be governed by a council consisting of the chancellor, the president, and seven professors who should be members of the united Church of England and Ireland and subscribe to the thirty-nine articles. In the lack of

seven such professors the council was to be filled by graduates who should be members of the Church of England and subscribe as above.

4. Degrees in divinity were conditioned on the same declarations, subscriptions and oaths as were required at that date in the University of Oxford. They were thus confined to the clergy of the established church.

The third document was a letter to Mr. Horton, Under-Secretary of State for the Colonies, setting forth the needs and claims of the church in Upper Canada to an establishment of two or three hundred clergymen deriving the greater portion of their income from *funds deposited in England.* This letter was seemingly connected with the bill already referred to, and contained statements very similar to those made in the sermon of 1825, and was accompanied by an ecclesiastical chart or table setting forth Dr. Strachan's estimate of the different religious bodies in Upper Canada. In this chart the names of thirty-one Anglican clergymen were given and the whole number was put at thirty-nine. The Presbyterians were placed as eight, the Methodists were said to be very uncertain, "perhaps twenty or thirty," and all others "very few" and "very ignorant."

These documents once more awakened the political and religious sentiment of the province. Petitions extensively signed by the inhabitants of the province were forwarded to England, and representations by resolution of the House of Assembly were laid before the British House of Commons, and the whole subject of the civil government of both Upper and Lower Canada, which also had its important grievances, was referred to a select committee of the House, which, after taking voluminous evidence on all the questions raised, reported to the House in July 1828. Before this committee Mr. George Ryerson appeared on behalf of the Upper Canadian petitioners touching the university charter and the clergy reserves and the ecclesiastical chart. The petitioners presented a counter chart, compiled by the Rev. Dr. Lee of the Presbyterian Church. These facts are evidence of the earnestness of the people in the assertion of their civil and religious liberties at this juncture.

In the meantime, Dr. Strachan, having returned to Canada on March 7th, 1828, delivered a speech before the legislative council "to repel the charges against his conduct in relation to a certain letter and ecclesiastical chart, said to have been addressed by him to the Under-Secretary of State for the Colonies, and in his agency in procuring the charter for the University of King's College for many months past circulated in the public journals." This speech, which once more called forth the pen of Mr. Ryerson, is largely occupied with the defence of personal rectitude and consistency. Apart from this, its most important elements were the history of the bill in the English parliament in the summer of 1827, and of Dr. Strachan's relations to it ; his appeal to the self-interest of the Church of Scotland; his defence of the Church of England's claim to be the established church of Canada and to exclusive right as such to the clergy reserves; and his defence of his university charter as "the most liberal that has ever been granted." As a minor point it may be noted that it contains an indirect appeal to the "Wesleyan Methodists," by which at this time he means the British missionaries as distinguished from " those Methodists who get their teachers and preachers from the United States." These last he holds to be " the enemies of the established church," because they are " at this moment labouring to separate religion from the State, with which it ought ever to be firmly united, since one of its great objects is to give stability to good government; nor can it be separated with impunity in any Christian country."

It was scarcely to be expected that the Methodists would sit down quietly under such a challenge. The address was published by request of the legislative council in March or April, and by the beginning of May Mr. Ryerson had commenced his reply, which was completed by June 14th, in a series of eight letters addressed to Dr. Strachan. In these letters he cheerfully admits Dr. Strachan's sincerity, but makes a very strong case against his consistency, and exposes the artful character of his appeals to self-interest. Once more he vindicates the rights and the loyalty of the Christian body to which he belongs, and points out the fictitious character of the Doctor's sneering references to their ecclesiastical movement toward independence of the American Church as due to his advice. But by far the weightiest part of his reply is his masterly attack upon Dr. Strachan's fundamental principles and policy. He discusses the great questions raised as follows:

1. Is an established church a benefit to the state?

2. Is such the necessary or best means for promoting the interests of religion?

3. Is the Church of England already the established church of Canada?

4. Ought it to be so established with peculiar privileges and endowments?

To each of these questions the reply is a most emphatic negative, enforced by such considerations as these:—The great work of the church is not political, but purely moral and spiritual. When it enters the political sphere its presence there is productive of evil and a menace to the liberty of the citizen and the unity of the state. History proves that the establishment and endowment of a church has a tendency to destroy its spiritual vitality and power, the Church of England herself, according to the testimony of her own divines, being an example. The answer to the question, Is the Church of England by law established in Upper Canada, is a clear and comprehensive piece of legal argument founded on the Constitutional Act of 1791, which is interpreted by its own internal use of the terms employed, and by the fact that to secure certain special privileges to the Church of England, specific enactments are made, such specifications excluding a general comprehensive interpretation by a recognized principle of law. The claim that the Church of England is by law established in all the British colonies under acts of parliament from Elizabeth onward, by the language of the Coronation Oath and by acts of royal prerogative is clearly disposed of by the example of numerous British colonies since that time, in which such claim was neither recognized nor enforced, and by the fact that when it was so established it was done by express Royal Charter, and further by the recognition of the Roman Catholic Church in Lower Canada. Finally he concludes the fourth question in the negative by showing that every ground upon which such establishment might be based is lacking in the case of Upper Canada. It is not the church of the majority, nor does its moral and religious influence justify any such claim ; and to so establish and force it upon the people would be to its own fatal disadvantage.

Turning from the church to the university charter, he points out its sectarian character, its lack of adaptation to the wants of our country, its injustice to all religious bodies except the Anglican, the misrepresentations by which it had been secured, and he concludes by contrasting Dr. Strachan's educational system forced upon the people against their will and under the complete domination of the Anglican Church with the Scottish system founded by act of their own parliament, fitted to their national circumstances, commanding the general assent and confidence of the people, and subject to no undue interference or control from their clergy. By this second effort Mr. Ryerson became the recognized leader of the religious side of this great movement for religious liberty and equal civil rights. The other side, involving the fundamental question of a government completely responsible to the people, was, as we have seen, led by other men of acknowledged political ability; but while they were contending for closely related and no less important rights, there is nothing to show that he stepped aside from his important religious responsibilities to interfere in these political questions. It is not even evident that he sympathized with the political side of the reform movement, but rather probable that he held to the old conservative political faith of not intermeddling with those who are given to change.

Especially was the Methodist Church (numbering at this time about ten thousand members and fifty thousand adherents, with fifty-six ministers), fully awakened to the dangers which now threatened its liberties and progress, and under a leadership seemingly raised up for the time by Divine Providence, it moved forward to meet the needs of the situation with an energy and self-sacrificing enterprise which must command our highest admiration.

CHAPTER IV

A METHODIST PRESS AND A METHODIST COLLEGE

DURING these years in which he was engaged in this first controversy, Mr. Ryerson was still a young preacher, not yet admitted to the full responsibilities of the Christian ministry. At the conference of 1829 he was ordained an elder, being then twenty-six years of age. From this time forward he takes a prominent place in the councils of the church. But even on this occasion the powerful impulse which his writings had given to the thoughts and energies of Methodism was seen in two important actions of the conference. At the conference of 1824 the Canadian Methodists had felt and expressed the desire for an independent organization which would free them from the reproach of being subject to the jurisdiction of a church belonging to a foreign country. At that date they were constituted a distinct conference but still connected with and under the jurisdiction of the General Conference of the Methodist Episcopal Church in the United States. In 1828 they had been erected into an independent Canadian Church with the full consent of their American brethren. This action was creditable to the Christian spirit and patriotism of both parties. The American Church recognized the obligations which rested on the Canadians as citizens of another country; the Canadians recognized their obligations to the parent church, through whose missionary zeal their churches had been planted, and both recognized that the work of God should not be hindered or prejudiced by any political complications. The separation was with mutual good-will and affection, a voluntary sacrifice of personal feelings and historic sentiment to the higher interests of religion and citizenship. No refutation of the slander that Canadian Methodism was disloyal could be more complete than that which was afforded by this action. Nor was it without important results for the political future of Upper Canada. An independent Canadian Methodism has been no small factor in the creation of a united Canadian national spirit as a part of the British Empire.

The new Canadian Methodist Church was now free to develop a thoroughly Canadian policy in founding church enterprises adapted to its distinctive Canadian needs. The first of these was a Methodist press. At the conference of 1829 steps were taken for the establishment of a weekly paper, to be called *The Christian Guardian* and Mr. Ryerson was elected editor and stationed at York. Henceforth this journal was to be the exponent of the views of Methodism on the great questions which agitated both the religious and the political sentiment of the country, and in the hands of Mr. Ryerson was shortly to be acknowledged by the lieutenant-governor himself as the leading paper of the province, whose influence was of the highest importance in the critical times which even then were so close at hand. The editorial chair was the official recognition by the Canadian Methodist Church of Mr. Ryerson's leadership in the great issues which were agitating the country and the churches. The financial side of *The Guardian* was characteristic of the self-denying spirit and enterprise of this heroic age. Stock to the amount of $2,000 in 100 shares of $20 each was subscribed, the greater part of it by the fifty-four ministers and preachers who composed the conference of that year. The first number was issued on November 21st, 1829. The spirit and attitude of the paper may be judged from the following extract, quoted from an editorial in the first volume in Dr. Webster's excellent history of the Methodist Episcopal Church in Canada: "The constitution of a Church and State establishment is not suited to the atmosphere of Canada. Such a monster, whether with one, two or three heads, must very soon share the fate in this country which he has lately met with in France; for the unobstructed air of free discussion is his mortal poison, and never can he long maintain a successful contest against the deathly piercings of that triple sword of *truth, justice and Puritan independence*, which is turning every way, guarding the intellectual citadels of the good people of Canada against his blasphemous approach. 'Many are running to and fro, and knowledge is increasing,' and it is too late in the day to attempt to introduce into British North America the policy of Portugal and Spain, or that of Charles the Tenth."

The second important interest to which the attention of the Methodist conference was directed at this early period was that of education. The entire question, not only of religious instruction in the fundamental doctrines of religion, but also the broader question of higher education for ministers and people occupied the attention of the conference. At that date the other churches differed as widely from Methodism in theology as they did in their quality and methods of work. The conference of 1829 organized a Sunday School Union, the first in Upper Canada, and the foundation of a Sunday School organization which is to-day by far the largest and most influential in our country. In 1830 the first formal steps were taken for the establishment of a Seminary of Learning. Mr. Ryerson's name does not appear on the first committee as he was still a junior member of the conference, but before the project was carried into successful operation, he was to become a foremost worker in the labours by which its almost insuperable difficulties were overcome. But a Methodist college, truly Christian in its educational influence, yet broadly liberal in its constitution and work, as became the doctrines and spirit of Methodism, was an essential part of the far-seeing and aggressive policy which he had marked out for Methodism. This policy had not been propounded in any conventional platform. It had scarcely been expressed in words, perhaps not formulated to his own mind in very definite propositions. It was a spirit which found expression in deeds as well as words. This spirit fired his own youthful impetuosity, and it was thoroughly contagious, and the whole Methodist Church felt its influence. Its voice was, we will submit to no ecclesiastical domination, we will acknowledge ourselves inferior to no other body of people, we will assert our rightful place and influence as citizens on an equality with every other citizen of this free new country. But it was a spirit of wisdom as well as of manly independence, and that wisdom clearly indicated that to hold their own in this struggle for their rights, the young Methodists must be as well educated and as thoroughly intelligent as their neighbours. In the pursuit of this noble policy Mr. Ryerson had already led the way by the example of his own young life. Since his conversion no opportunity of gaining knowledge had been allowed to pass unimproved. He had devoured both the English and the ancient classics with a greedy appetite. He had become thoroughly at home in the history of ancient and modern times, he had studied the jurisprudence of

Blackstone and the philosophy of Paley as well as the best English divines, and at twenty-six he was perhaps the "best informed" man of his years in the country. His example, his ambitions, as well as his words thus aroused the whole Methodist ministry and people to the importance of the most ample learning in ministers and laity if they were to assert their rights against supercilious arrogance. Victoria College was thus born out of the struggle for religious liberty and equal civil rights. But before entering upon the consideration of Mr. Ryerson's active part in this new enterprise, we must give our attention to another development of the great struggle in which he was now so thoroughly engaged.

We have seen that in his address before the legislative council, in March, 1828, Dr. Strachan made a bid not only for the aid of the Old Kirk Presbyterians, but also for that of the English Wesleyan missionaries, a few of whom were already in Upper Canada. The action of the General Conference of the Methodist Episcopal church in the United States providing for the independence of the Canadian Methodists was taken a very few weeks after the delivery of this address, and the fact that this was in contemplation was already well known and is referred to by Dr. Strachan. But another important circumstance was not so well known, though possibly known to Dr. Strachan even at this date. What that circumstance was appears from the evidence of Dr. Alder before the select committee of the English House of Commons in July, 1828, a few months after Dr. Strachan's address, and three months before the independence of the Canadian Methodist church was formally completed, but two months after the action of the American conference which provided for it. In that evidence Dr. Alder reveals these important facts :

1. That the English Methodist authorities were already looking forward to the annexation of Upper Canadian Methodism as a part of their work.

2. That for this purpose they were looking to securing a share in the clergy reserves.

3. That this policy, if not based upon and originated by, was at least associated with communications which they had received from the Governor-General, and communications to the colonial office from Sir Peregrine Maitland, with which Dr. Alder had evidently become acquainted. The references in the evidence to these documents is as follows:—"This is the opinion of the Governor-General, from whose letter to me (which I received a few days before I left the province) I beg permission to read an extract. 'We all know,' His Lordship observes, 'that the Established Church cannot provide clergymen at all places where they are required and desired; in that difficulty the Wesleyan ministers have rendered most valuable services, and I think they are qualified and capable to render much

greater services under the protection and encouragement which they desire from His Majesty's government.' Do you conceive that the colonial government has manifested any desire for the extension of the British Wesleyan Methodists in that province? I believe there are documents in the colonial office addressed to Earl Bathurst and to Mr. Huskisson from Sir Peregrine Maitland which will show that His Excellency is very anxious that the number of British Methodist ministers should be increased as far as possible in Upper Canada; and I understand that he wrote home a short time ago recommending that pecuniary aid might be allowed us for that purpose." One further extract in answer to the claim of Methodists on the clergy reserves will serve to make clear the whole situation. "There is a difference of opinion among us on this subject; but the general opinion of our ministers in Lower Canada, I believe, is this, that if the reserves be appropriated to the sole use of the Church of England, we shall offer no objection to it; but if the Presbyterians are to have any part of these reserves, then we conceive that we have at least an equally good claim with them; and we should be very much dissatisfied if our claims were disallowed."

This new factor, which speedily developed into more definite form, introduced an entirely new problem into the struggles in which the Methodists and Mr. Ryerson were engaged. They were now called to meet not only the ecclesiastical and political influences which opposed them from without, but also the possibility of weakness and division from within. There appear to be good grounds for the belief that this difficulty was itself brought about by the insidious plans of the dominant party. They expected, and with good reason, that the English Wesleyans, who up to this time in the mother land had always been politically subservient to the established church, would here also be willing to yield to their claims. In looking back now this should not be ascribed as a reproach to these English Wesleyans. As yet they, with the great body of the people of England, had not been awakened to a sense of political responsibilities and rights. It seemed to them quite right and natural that the institutions of the old land should without change be transplanted to Canada.

Notwithstanding the anticipations of Dr. Alder in 1828 that "the Methodists of Upper Canada will soon be brought to act under the direction of the British conference," they held on their way with increasing influence and prosperity for four years. In May, 1832, a communication was received from Dr. Alder that the Wesleyan Missionary Committee in London had again resolved to send missionaries to Upper Canada, and that Dr. Alder and twelve missionaries would sail shortly. "This announcement," says Mr. John Ryerson, then president of the Canada Conference Missionary Society, "was to us like a thunderclap. For eight or nine years our church had been wading through deep waters of affliction, and enduring fightings without and fears within, while contending for the right to hold property on which to erect places of worship and in which to bury our dead, for right to solemnize matrimony, against the clergy reserve monopoly, and for equal rights and privileges before the law with the Church of England, in effecting by mutual consent our separation from the Methodist Episcopal Church in the United States, and our organization into an independent church, preceded and followed as it was by the tumults and schisms of Ryanism. And now when peace and quiet had apparently returned, and when expectations of increased prosperity were beginning to cheer us, to receive such an announcement was disheartening and crushing beyond what can be expressed. It was easy to predict what would be the result of rival Methodist congregations in every town and principal neighbourhood, and the rival congregations served by able ministers from England."

This resolution of the London Wesleyan Missionary Committee was not, however, altogether sudden. As we have seen, it was foreshadowed as a plan of absorption by Dr. Alder four years before; and during a visit of Mr. Case and Peter Jones to England in 1831, it had been intimated to them that the London committee purposed undertaking

missions to the Indians and new settlers in Upper
Canada. On his return home Mr. Case laid the
matter before his own missionary committee; and
an earnest appeal was made to the London Wesleyan Missionary Committee against such unfortunate rivalry of work, as contrary to the agreement
of 1820, in which the English Wesleyans agreed to
confine their labours to Lower Canada, and the
American missionaries to limit theirs to Upper
Canada, the town of Kingston, as a military station, being made an exception. The reply to this
remonstrance was that this agreement was made
with the Methodist Episcopal Church of the United
States, and not with the now independent Methodist Episcopal Church of Canada, a reply which
was valid neither in law, equity, nor Christian
charity.

It is not surprising that United Empire Loyalists, who, for loyalty's sake, had just severed themselves from their parent church, and who had just
entered upon the onerous task of building up a
loyal Canadian Methodism in the face of great
difficulties, should feel deeply wounded and discouraged by such treatment from their English
brethren, who refused to them as Canadians the
consideration accorded to the Methodist Church of
the United States. The difficulty of their position
was enhanced by another circumstance. Their Indian missions providently placed in their hands by
the remarkable conversion of over a thousand pagan

Indians since 1824, were a heavy financial burden.
Up to the time of their independence, and for two
or three years after, they had received aid from the
United States. In 1831 they were induced to make
an appeal to England, with the result that they
received the intimation already referred to and a
gift of £300. It is difficult to resist the conclusion
that the London Wesleyan Missionary Committee
was at this time under other influence than that
which Dr. Carroll so charitably assigns, the belief
"that the provincial conference had more missionary ground than it had men and means to
occupy." But setting this question aside, the Canadian Methodists, after serious deliberation over the
situation, first in their missionary committee and
subsequently in their conference, resolved to seek a
union with the English Wesleyans. By the terms
of this union the identity of their conference and
church was to be preserved, and to be related to
the British conference after the model of the Irish
Wesleyan conference. But their missions, including
both the Indian missions and missions to the new
settlements, were handed over to the London Wesleyan Missionary Committee to be controlled by
a superintendent appointed from England. This
arrangement seemingly retained for the Canadian
conference the control of its own work, and granted
to the English Methodism what it sought, the new
mission field. It also relieved the Canadian conference of the heavy financial responsibility of the

missionary work, which was entirely undertaken by the London Wesleyan Missionary Committee, to which the Canadian conference contributed its missionary funds.

Up to this point the basis of union seems reasonable and just from the standpoint of both bodies, and most likely to result in the best interests of Methodism and religion. But there were two ominous facts behind the entire arrangement which were portentous of future trouble. One was the fact that the London Wesleyan Missionary Committee were already committed to a subsidy from the colonial office of the British government. The other was the fact that the Canadian Methodist conference was most decidedly, by public conference action, committed to opposition to the government policy on the questions of an established state church and the clergy reserves. These questions were not referred to in the articles of union. Both parties were aware of the facts, for the previous correspondence indicates such knowledge on the part of the English committee, and that correspondence was afterwards pleaded as if it were a stipulation of the union. There is nothing to shew that it was so intended or understood. On the other hand there is nothing to shew that the Canadian conference protested against the position of the London Wesleyan Missionary Committee. If these difficulties were at all referred to in the negotiations, the reference was verbal, and would seem to have amounted to a tacit understanding that the unpleasant facts would be ignored, each body being responsible for its own action. If such was the case the hope was illusory, the unpleasant facts would not disappear, and to no one did they cause more trouble than to Mr. Ryerson himself.

Further difficulties arose from two provisions of the basis of union adopting the English form of church government and an English presidency. These soon became the occasion of serious trouble. Of Mr. Ryerson's personal relations to the preliminary negotiations we have no record. Probably as a younger man he deferred to his seniors. But his attitude seems clear from the subsequent history. At the close of the negotiations with Dr. Alder at the conference of 1832, he at first refused to allow his name to be put in nomination for editor. Later he assented, but James Richardson was elected editor. Mr. Ryerson was elected representative to England for the purpose of the negotiations with the British conference. In those negotiations he was entirely bound by the articles of union to which his conference had agreed. Six years later, when the difficulties arising from the union were approaching a crisis, it was claimed that he was bound by other matters of verbal agreement between Mr. Alder and the leading representatives of the Canadian conference. That there had been conversation on the two points of the political relations of *The Christian Guardian*,

and on the grant from the British government
to the London Wesleyan Missionary Committee of
a subsidy from the casual and territorial revenue,
there seems to be no room for doubt. That the
Canadians assented to the general principle that
The Guardian should not intermeddle in politics
is probably also correct; as also that they agreed
to leave the responsibility of accepting aid from
the government entirely to the British conference
without interference on their part. But the evidence seems clear that they reserved their right to
independent action on the questions of a state
church and the clergy reserves, as these were not
merely political but also religious questions. That
this was the exact position of affairs appears, first
of all, from the fact that before the British conference, when presenting the Canadian case, Mr.
Ryerson made a full historic statement vindicating
the action of the Canadian conference and Methodist people, as well as the course of *The Guardian*
on these points. It is further confirmed by the fact
that when in England Mr. Ryerson presented to
the secretary of state for the colonies the complete
case for the Canadian opponents of an established
and endowed church in Canada. In this presentation he sets forth that the English Church is not
the established church in Canada; replies to the
petition of the English Church in Canada; defends
the Methodists as to their loyalty, work and numbers, and concludes by pressing that the reserves

be not invested in the home government; that they be not given to the English Church; that they be not divided among the Canadian Protestant churches, but that they be sold and the proceeds applied for education. Before this presentation was sent to the colonial secretary, it was endorsed by at least one of the English missionary secretaries.

Again, after his return to Canada, Mr. Ryerson was elected once more to the editorial chair. Almost his first work was the publication of this presentation in *The Guardian.* At the same time he claims that his views on these great questions are unchanged, and that he will maintain them as consistently as ever. These facts seem to prove that the clergy reserve question and the state church question in Canada were reserved in the general understanding that the Canadian conference and *The Guardian* were to refrain from interference in politics. Mr. Ryerson's subsequent course, resulting finally in the disruption of the union, is further confirmation of this. Possibly these facts as they became generally known to the friends of reform, and especially to the Methodist people, would have quieted the fears that their political freedom had been betrayed by union, but for another product of Mr. Ryerson's facile pen which appeared at the same time. And yet this was perhaps no less conducive to the best interests of the country than his previous battle for equal civil rights.

"IMPRESSIONS"

While in England, from March to August, he had abundant opportunities of becoming acquainted with English institutions and people. The results he gave to the readers of *The Guardian* in a series of articles entitled "Impressions." The first of these dealt with political parties and leaders in England. These he divided into ultra-Tories, whom he described as tyrants and bigots; moderate Tories, whom he praises as men distinguished for justice, conscientiousness and religion; Whigs, who act from expediency, whom he describes as including the infidels and socinians, and as being republicans with a king instead of a president, and as an obstacle to true reforms. There can be no doubt that in this article Mr. Ryerson's true political sympathies appear. As a United Empire Loyalist he was himself a moderate Conservative, and already Canadian reform was developing a radical wing with which he could have no affinity. It is not at all impossible that he already discerned that the goal of this radical tendency was rebellion or annexation, and that the articles were written to awaken the loyal fears of Methodists that they might not be led into a compromising political position. If so they served their purpose, and it was his boast in later times that not a member of the Wesleyan Methodist Church in Canada was implicated in the rebellion.

But the "Impressions" fell like a spark in a tinder box among the Canadian radicals, and the next issue of Mr. Mackenzie's *Colonial Advocate* contained the following: "*The Christian Guardian*, under the management of our reverend neighbour Egerton Ryerson, has gone over to the enemy, press, types and all, and hoisted the colours of a cruel and vindictive Tory priesthood. His brother George, when sent to London, became an easy convert to the same cause, and it appears that the parent stock were of those who fought to uphold unjust taxation, stamp acts and Toryism in the United States. The contents of *The Guardian* to-night tell us in language too plain, too intelligible to be misunderstood that a deadly blow has been struck in England at the liberties of the people of Upper Canada by as subtle and ungrateful an adversary in the guise of an old and familiar friend as ever crossed the Atlantic. The Americans had their Arnold, and the Canadians have their Egerton Ryerson." It is quite unnecessary to follow the political storm, of which this is a first gust, through all its tempestuous course during the next three years. It resulted as Mr. Ryerson had partially foreseen and predicted, in a check to the reform movement in 1836, in the rebellion in 1837, and in the final triumph of constitutional reform in 1840.

But before we turn our attention to these final results, we must take note of an ecclesiastical tempest scarcely less violent, and much more extended in its results. In fact, say what men would, and do what they could to prevent it, at this period religion and politics were inevitably intermingled. The party in power was an ecclesiastical as well as a political party, and its policy was an ecclesiastical as well as a political policy, and men could not contend for their political rights without religious feeling, nor could they defend their religious liberties without political weapons. But at this time the most violent animosities were to be found in the political arena, and to a large number their political rights were quite as dear as any other. But there were purely ecclesiastical questions which were to co-operate with the political suspicions already aroused in creating the new struggle. It not infrequently happens that a progressive spirit in politics is associated with the conservative spirit in religious or ecclesiastical matters. Mr. Gladstone affords a good example. The Methodist union involved a large change in the polity of the church. Into its particulars it is by no means necessary that we should now enter. It is sufficient to say that the change raised a number of questions as to the constitution of Methodism, the rights of the laity, the orders of the ministry and so forth, which the subsequent progress of the church to a higher ground has completely left behind. They are many of them now ecclesiastical antiquities. Others involved fundamental principles of religious liberty which are now fully recognized under the new constitution of the reunited church. Before the union of Canadian and British Methodism had been in existence two years, these forces brought about a schism, which left the main body in 1835 just about where it stood in 1832.

But this was not to be the end of ecclesiastical disaster to Methodism. Immediately after the rebellion, Mr. Ryerson, after an interval of three years, one-half of which had been spent in England on college matters, was again called in 1838 to the editorial chair of *The Guardian*. It was the juncture at which the great constitutional and religious questions which had been pending for years in Upper Canada were about to be settled, and it was admitted by all that at this time his influence should once more be felt through the official journal of the church. With all his former earnestness of purpose and vigour of argument he applied himself to the question of the clergy reserves, which was now the centre of the religious or ecclesiastical side of the matter. *The Guardian* was used with great power as of old, and a new volume of letters, addressed to the Hon. W. H. Draper, discussed the entire question in its legal and historical aspects, supported distinctly the voluntary system as the only religious system suitable to a country like Canada, and advocated the application of the clergy reserves to the purposes of education. In the progress of affairs towards what seemed to promise a settlement, but which was finally found to be a delusive hope, it was proposed to divide the reserves between the several Protestant bodies, allowing all to use their share for such purposes as they might judge right. Under this proposal the representatives of the London Wesleyan Missionary Committee insisted that as this settlement was to terminate all religious grants from other sources, and they had been the recipients of a grant from the casual and territorial revenue of the British crown, they should be the recipients of the apportionment of the clergy reserves. Mr. Ryerson, on the other hand, insisted that as this was a Canadian question, and the apportionment to Canadian churches of a fund derived from the sale of Canadian lands, the Canadian conference should receive and control the apportionment, which he proposed to devote to the work of education. In a few months the dispute led to another schism in Canadian Methodism, and at the census of 1842 Methodism stood divided between three major bodies and a minor group, as follows:—

Canadian Wesleyan Methodists................... 32,313
British Wesleyan Methodists................... 23,342
Episcopal Methodists 20,125
Other Methodist Bodies 7,141

Such an outcome of the policy and convulsions of ten years can scarcely be regarded in any other light than as a disaster. It was the very outcome which in 1832 all parties were seeking by right methods or wrong to prevent, viz., a divided and weakened Methodism. The question is natural—what were the causes of such a result? A further question is almost unavoidable—where lay the mistake, and who was to blame?

The causes of this misfortune lay in no single circumstance, nor yet in the action of any single individual. They lay in the meeting at various points of institutions and ideas which had grown up on opposite sides of the Atlantic and embodied in the life of this young country thoroughly antagonistic elements. Between these elements, whether in the political or the religious field, a conflict was inevitable. Well meant efforts at compromise might postpone it for a little, but they scarcely secured even a truce. Peace could be secured only by victory, and that victory was certain to be on the side of the young free life of the new world, before which the effete and already corrupting ideas and forms of the old world must certainly go down. Crown colony absolutism must inevitably disappear before the sturdy Anglo-Saxon capacity for self-government. Aristocratic officialism must certainly give way before the rising spirit of independence and the asserted rights of the people. And in the religious field the voluntary principle full of spiritual zeal and life and appealing to the religious conscience and intelligence for its support, could not fail to displace all forms dependent on state aid and endowment for support. The English Church was only saved from utter failure by being forced back upon the powers of its own spiritual life. The conflict of fifty years, through which our young

country passed, was inevitable, and its unfortunate results were a part of the price of our political and religious liberties.

If we ask where was the mistake, the answer is: the first mistake was in the attempt to transplant to this new world the decadent institutions of the old world. Whether that mistake was made on the larger scale in the Constitutional Act of 1791; or on a minor scale in the policy and ambitions of English Methodism, it was only a mistake. English Methodism has long since rectified that mistake at home, and now almost unanimously casts in her lot with the free churches of England. The subserviency to and dependence upon the established church which prevailed there seventy years ago have given place to an independent church life, independent politically as well as financially and spiritually. This result was not reached without sore conflict, and before the demon was exorcised, English Methodism was well-nigh as sorely riven as Canadian Methodism.

The second mistake lay in either a partial compromise or an unconscious compromise of the young life of progress with the opposing forces. That compromise was probably disguised even from those who made it. They were seeking not loaves and fishes, as they were sometimes slanderously said to be doing, but, as they supposed, the unity and peace of the church and the furtherance of the gospel. They thought that their responsibility was

103

discharged by asserting the voluntary principle for themselves; and permitting others to act according to their own convictions of right. In seven short years the development of circumstances made such a working arrangement impossible, and the union became a rope of sand. In the meantime all those whose convictions were such that no compromise was possible had also separated and formed a third Methodist Church.

Who was to blame? In one sense no one was altogether blameworthy. It must be borne in mind that the fundamental principles which appear so clear to us through the development of subsequent history were two generations ago but very imperfectly apprehended even by the clearest minds. Men were convinced of them rather by an instinctive feeling than by reason. They felt injustice, revolted against submission to arrogance, were spurred on to action by manly independence and generous ambition, before they understood the great ethical principles towards which they were making progress. And they moved towards these results, as the world of humanity has ever moved, in two grand divisions, the one restless, impatient, eager, impetuous, dissatisfied with the past, impatient for the lifting of the veil of the future; the other cautious, and timid, clinging to the seen and tried, and even asserting that it alone is eternal, immutable and divine. It is not given to mortals in such historic movements to be infallible; and in

awarding praise or blame we must credit their good intentions.

But, on the other hand, all were more or less to blame, inasmuch as the individual passions and frailties of humanity added fuel to the fire, and so aggravated the evils which are inseparable from such a conflict of moral forces. But after we have said this, as we see such men as William Case, James Richardson and Egerton Ryerson stand at the parting of the ways, those of us who knew them all will most heartily acknowledge that few men of any age could have acquitted themselves better under the circumstances. As this later mistake was the mistake of Methodism, so Methodism alone was the sufferer. The healing of her schisms was to take nearly half a century, and was not to be accomplished till all the actors in the original struggle had passed away. But her misfortunes tended on the whole to the political redemption of the country. Methodism has, in fact, been closely identified with every forward step in the history of Upper Canada. She was present at its foundations as the chief agency for the maintenance of moral and religious life among the first settlers. Her people formed the first influential body to protest against the incubus which threatened her civil and religious liberty. Her self-sacrifice of early religious attachments rendered permanent the attachment of the colony to the British empire. And now her very divisions were to be made subservient in the

order of an over-ruling Providence to the more
perfect establishment of civil and religious liberty
in the country. The introduction of British Methodism was a conservative influence at a point where
a conservative influence was essentially necessary.
The later growth to extensive influence of the
Methodist Episcopal Church and the severance of
the Canadian Wesleyans from the British once
more reinforced the ranks of reform and progress
at a point when powerful forces in this direction
were needed; and thus a divided Methodism, while
the least political of all our Canadian churches,
has been most potential in the political advancement of the province. But this will appear more
fully as we turn back for a few years to follow up
another chapter in the life work of Mr. Ryerson as
one of the makers of Canada.

CHAPTER V

MR. RYERSON IN THE POLITICAL ARENA

DOWN to 1833 Mr. Ryerson's work in its interest and motive was purely religious. He was a Methodist preacher standing for the rights and liberties, the interests and prosperity of the church and people which he represented. The circumstance that these rights and interests must be maintained on the side of their political relations was entirely beyond his control. The circumstance that they coincided with the principles of one political party, and that they were invaded and threatened by the policy of the other, was also a matter beyond his control. The party with which he acted was not the party of his hereditary sympathies or of his settled political convictions, so far as he had formed any; but he was working not for political party or policy, but for religious freedom and equal civil rights. So far as one may judge he was as sensible as any other clergyman of that time of the gravity of unnecessary intermeddling with politics; and the concessions made to Dr. Alder in 1832 were doubtless due in part to the influence of this principle on his own mind and those of his associates. So far was he from having formed any new or progressive political theories that it may be questioned whether he had fully comprehended the importance and far-reaching influence of the voluntary principle, notwithstanding the fact that it was a principle as important to religion as to political life. He was rather seeking justice under the existing constitution of government than such a change of political constitution as would conform the government to the will of the people. His method, too, had been appeal to argument and free discussion by the use of the press. We have no intimation that he took any part in political meetings or conventions, or in the elections, or in the petitions which moved the legislative assembly to action. For the first time, so far as we can learn, in 1833 he stepped aside from this guarded course by becoming the bearer to England of a petition, signed by 20,000 people, setting forth the grievances of the Canadian people, and praying that the clergy reserves be devoted to education. The passage of the Reform Bill in 1832 and the accession to power of the Whigs under Earl Grey had doubtless raised hopes in the minds of the advocates of Canadian reform that their cause might be undertaken by the home government. In the fulfillment of this mission he not only presented the petition of which he was the bearer, but also, as we have seen, supported it by an able presentation of the entire Canadian case to the secretary of state for the colonies. At this time, also, he gave close attention to the debates in the British House of Commons and studied the English political parties and party leaders with careful scrutiny. We have already referred to the results of this new experience, as embodied in the series of papers known as the "Impressions," published in *The Guardian* in November, 1833. These studies, without doubt, shaped more definitely Ryerson's future political opinions and conduct. Of the English parties, the moderate Tories represented by Mr. Gladstone secured his most complete approval as guided by justice and religion. The ultra Tories and even the Duke of Wellington seemed too near akin to the Canadian Tories—arrogant, despotic and bigoted; while the Whigs seemed to be too much governed by "expediency." But of all the English political parties the most abhorrent to him seemed to be the Radicals, and these, unfortunately, were the friends and almost representatives in the English parliament of the Canadian party of constitutional reform. We have already seen how the "Impressions" affected Mr. Mackenzie's attitude towards Mr. Ryerson. The effect of these first studies of English politics was scarcely less pronounced on the mind of Mr. Ryerson himself. Seeing danger both to British monarchical government and to religion and morality in the principles of the English Radicals, he began to be suspicious of their Canadian friends. The treatment which he received from the reform press on his return home certainly did not tend to allay this feeling; and the extreme language which they used and the covert threats they uttered led him to a full conviction that they were secretly meditating the erection of a republic in Canada, or the annexation of the province to the United States. This conviction he did not hesitate to express thirty years later. It cannot be said, in view of subsequent events, to have been an altogether groundless suspicion, and yet it did injustice to the great body of honest reformers, including many who were still Methodists, though now separated from the Wesleyan body.

For two years Mr. Ryerson contended, as editor of *The Guardian*, against this new and now rapidly increasing danger, at the same time endeavouring to maintain, as best he could, his old-time position of contention against a state church and for equal civil rights in religious matters. Speaking three years later of his efforts at this time, he says: "It will be seen that the object I have had in view at all times and under all circumstances was a just, liberal, and popular, as well as constitutional government, in this province. The majority of the late House of Assembly (*i.e.*, the House prior to the election of 1836) put it out of my power to act with them because they made the clergy reserve question subservient to other objects which I had never embraced and with which I could not identify myself individually nor the Methodists as a body, whatever might be the free opinions of the individual members."

110

THE AFFAIRS OF THE CANADAS

In the year 1835 the Rev. E. Evans was elected to the editorial chair, and Mr. Ryerson, though still a member of the "Committee for Guarding our Religious Privileges," was relieved of the responsibility which had devolved upon him for the past two years. During the course of the year he proceeded to England to seek funds and a charter for the new academy, now nearing completion. On arriving in England he soon found that his suspicions—or rather convictions—as to the tendencies of Mr. Mackenzie's policy were confirmed by rumours, which appear to have originated with Mr. Hume, that Canada was quite prepared to declare her independence and to set up a republican government. This called out one of his strongest and most famous pamphlets, a series of letters to *The Times* on "The Affairs of the Canadas." The object of these letters was the vindication of the loyalty of Canada against the "machinations and misstatements of Messrs. Hume and Roebuck, shewing from their own letters to Messrs. Papineau and Mackenzie that they were the first promoters of the project." But while thus maintaining and vindicating Canadian loyalty to the British crown and British institutions, he was by no means unmindful of the questions which disturbed the colony so long as they remained unsettled, and in an interview with Lord Glenelg and Mr. Stephen, he discussed the clergy reserve question, the legislative council, and the executive council. What his proposals were on these three important questions does not now appear. They were certainly more conservative than those which finally prevailed under the constitution of 1840, and probably more of the nature of administrative than of constitutional reform. As his letters to *The Times* were conservative in their tendency and intended to prove that the people would be satisfied by a righteous administration of the existing constitution, this was probably also the purport of his recommendations to Lord Glenelg. If so, his views had already been anticipated.

It is very certain that English statesmen were now more perfectly informed on Canadian affairs, and quite prepared to inaugurate a new policy, though not so radical as that proposed by Mr. Mackenzie in his "Seventh Report on Grievances." Sir Francis Bond Head had been sent to the province in the preceding January with instructions which, if carried out in a liberal, conciliatory spirit, might still have prevented the outbreak of the now ominous storm. The people were certainly expecting great things from him, and when, in 1834— shortly after his entrance on office,—he appealed to them on the ground of loyalty and the constitution, he was sustained by a large majority. But "it was not," as Mr. Ryerson says in reviewing this period a little later, "on the ground of the constitution in utter opposition to every kind of reform. It was by his taking his stand upon the constitution in connection with the elaborate conciliatory despatch of Your Lordship to him, dated December 15th, 1835, and the elaborate conciliatory despatch of the Earl of Ripon, dated November 8th, 1832, to which Your Lordship referred him as his guide; it was by his assuring the people of Upper Canada in every possible form of address that if they would support him, he would 'correct every grievance' according to the letter and spirit of those conciliatory instructions, while he maintained the happy constitution inviolate." This conciliatory policy of just, and impartial, and liberal administration of the existing form of government had doubtless been Mr. Ryerson's own ideal of reform in Upper Canada. And it would appear that even early in 1836 he was not without faith in this as a political remedy. This faith, however, was to be rudely shaken by subsequent events. Sir Francis Bond Head did not fulfill "the expectations which his promises and pledges had created. His administration in financial as well as in ecclesiastical and general affairs fell so far short of [these] expectations that he was aware that he would have been left in the minority in his own House of Assembly during the late (1838) session, had it not been for the insurrection."

Such was the political course of Mr. Ryerson up to the rebellion of 1837-8—an earnest pressure for such administration of the government as would secure equal civil rights, and just and faithful administration, and religious liberty to all His Majesty's subjects, while at the same time he was not in sympathy with any radical constitutional changes.

Sir Francis Bond Head's administration terminated in March, 1838. A month later Mr. Ryerson wrote to a leading member of the government in England in the terms which we have just quoted, and once more took his stand maintaining the cause of the people of Upper Canada against the dominant oligarchy. At the following conference he was again elected to the editorial chair under circumstances and influences which clearly appear from the following letter written by Dr. Stinson to the Rev. John Ryerson:—"I am quite of your opinion that Bro. Egerton [Ryerson] ought to take *The Guardian* next year. There is a crisis approaching in our affairs which will require a vigorous hand to wield the defensive weapon of the conference. There can be no two opinions as to whom to give that weapon. We now stand on fair grounds to maintain our own against the encroachments of the oligarchy, and we must do it or sink into a comparatively uninfluential body. This must not be." Such was the opinion even of the representative of the London Wesleyan Missionary Committee, who, after five years' residence in Canada, now understood and at least in part sympathized with the situation.

Mr. Ryerson was now once more fairly in the field of battle for religious liberty and equal civil rights and against a state church and a political oligarchy. In accepting this official position, to which was added the further responsibility of being secretary and convener of the Committee for the Protection of Civil and Religious Privileges, he at once fully and clearly defined his platform both before the conference and in his editorial inaugural. He says:—"In respect to the ecclesiastical affairs of this province I still adhere to the principles and views upon which I set out in 1826. I believe the endowment of the priesthood of any church in this province will be an evil to that church, as well as impolitic in the government. In accordance with the declaration put forth by several principal ministers in the Methodist Church in January last, I believe that the appropriation of the proceeds of the clergy reserves to general educational purposes will be the most satisfactory disposal of them that can be made. If in the way of such a disposal of the clergy reserves insuperable obstacles should be thrown or found to exist, although I believe nothing is impossible with the Earl of Durham in these provinces, I think the next best settlement of that question will be to divide the proceeds of the clergy reserves among different religious denominations in proportion to what is raised by each, leaving to the discretionary disposal of each religious body its own apportionment." . . . . "To the very natural and important inquiry, in relation to civil affairs 'Do you intend to be neutral?' I

answer 'No, I do not,' and for this simple reason:—
I am a man, am a British subject, am a professing
Christian, and represent a British community. The
present is a period in the affairs of this province in
which no man of intelligence or consideration can
be safely or justifiably neutral. The foundation of
our government is being laid anew, the future
character and relations and destinies of the country
are involved in pending deliberations, the last whisper of rebellion is to be silenced in the land. My
decision, however, is to be not one of party but of
principle; not one of passion but of conviction; not
one of partial proscription but of equitable comprehensiveness. To be explicit as well as brief, I am
opposed to the introduction of any new and un-
tried theories of government. I assume that this
country is to remain a portion of the British empire, and view every measure, not in reference to
every or any abstract political theory, however
plausible that theory may be, but in reference to
the well-being of the country in connection with
Great Britain. I take my stand upon the established
constitution of the country as expounded by royal
despatches, and as illustrated by the usages of the
British parliament, British courts of justice, and
the common law of England. Nothing more is
wanted to render the province happy and prosperous, than the practical and efficient application
to every department of our government and to our
whole system of legislation of the principles and

instructions laid down in the despatch of the Earl
of Ripon addressed to Sir John Colborne, dated
November 8th, 1832, and the despatch of Lord
Glenelg, addressed to Sir Francis Bond Head,
dated December 15th, 1835."

To the platform thus candidly set before the
church and the country, we think it must be
admitted Mr. Ryerson held fast during the two
stormy years which followed. It was a time of
intense excitement both in church and state. Political parties became more distinct than ever before;
the Wesleyan Methodist Church was rent in twain
on an issue in part ecclesiastical and yet growing
out of the political situation; recriminations and
imputations abounded; in the heat of passion parliamentary proprieties were often transgressed; but
throughout this strenuous period the powerful influence of Mr. Ryerson's pen and personality was
courageously and continuously exerted.

To the policy proposed by the Earl of Durham
and elaborated in his able report on the affairs of
British North America, Mr. Ryerson gives in his
editorials repeated and cordial assent. To Sir George
Arthur's efforts to repel the attacks upon the province from the American frontier he gave hearty
support, which appears to have been attended with
the best results in leading the people to respond
to the governor's call for volunteers. But while
thus loyal in support of the government, he was
equally faithful in pressing upon their attention the

demands of the people, and pointing out to them the still existing causes of dissatisfaction, which he regards as more dangerous than the incursion of foreign foes. These he sums up as follows:—

1. Lack of just consideration in the treatment of the volunteers in the late campaign.

2. Appointments of adventurers and youths to office over the heads of old and influential residents of the country.

3. Slanderous imputation of the insurrection to reformers generally, when four-fifths or nine-tenths of them had proved their loyalty by their acts.

4. Unnecessary severity towards the rebel prisoners.

5. Abuse of Her Majesty's government in England by the high church party.

6. The non-settlement of the clergy reserve question, and the establishment and endowment of the fifty-seven rectories.

It is noteworthy that every one of these was a question of administration or public conduct, and not of constitutional change, shewing how practical and conservative his ideas of needed reform still continued to be. But of even these moderated hopes he was as much disappointed in Sir George Arthur as he had previously been in Sir Francis Bond Head. This disappointment especially culminated in his replies to various Methodist addresses at the close of 1838 and the beginning of 1839, in which he expresses his gratification that

the Methodists were loyal, but his disappointment
that they had not rallied to the support of the
English Church. The significance of this complaint
will appear from the fact that in the October
preceding, the church party had memorialized the
home government asking for a judicial decision as
to their exclusive right to the reserves, or, if this
was refused, that the provincial assembly might
pass a bill re-investing them in the British crown,
subject once more to their disposal. Both requests
were refused. The opinion of the law officers of
the crown had been given as far back as 1819. The
management of the reserves was a subject for the
Canadian House and not for the British parliament,
and the imperial government expressed their un-
willingness to interfere in the matter. This led to a
proposition from Sir George in his speech from the
throne, February 27th, 1839, for division of the
fund if the bill for reinvestment failed. To the
reinvestment scheme Mr. Ryerson was thoroughly
opposed. He was willing to assent to division provided each denomination were free to determine
the disposition to be made of its apportionment.
His clearly expressed judgment favoured the appropriation of the whole proceeds to education. He
accepted division only as a *dernier ressort* for the
sake of settlement, and with an expressed expectation that the Methodist apportionment would in
that case be devoted to education and the building
of churches, and not to clerical endowment. These

119

views he presented not only in his weekly editorials
but also in a series of ten letters to the Hon. W.
H. Draper, Her Majesty's Solicitor-General. The
scheme of division was thus clearly a compromise,
and we have already seen how speedily it became a
ground of contention in the Methodist Church
itself; and how fatal were its results to the peace
and unity of that body. The outcome was another
division of Methodism. But that division, by re-
uniting the forces of reform, probably saved the
country from what would have been an unfortunate
mode of settlement, giving us several endowed
churches instead of one. The division bill was indeed passed under Lord Sydenham in 1840, but the
forces arrayed against it by the division of Methodism, and a little later, by the disruption of the
Presbyterian Church, made the apparent settlement
a temporary affair. It served one important purpose in bringing the whole fund once more under
the control of the Canadian government, where
it remained until its settlement in 1854.

While the clergy reserve battle was thus being
fought out in church and state, Mr. Ryerson's voice
was also uplifted on behalf of wider reform, and his
letters to Lord Normanby once more brought
important aspects of the Canadian cause before the
government at a time when Lord Durham's report
was opening the way for the most successful remedy.
Lord Durham's report reached this country early
in the summer, and was the subject of universal

discussion both in the press and by the provincial legislatures. Mr. Ryerson supported Lord Durham's proposals, not only in his letters to the Marquis of Normanby, but also in reply to the attacks which identified it with the system of "responsible government proposed by the Canadian Alliance society in 1834." He dwells with special emphasis on the conservative and moderate character of Lord Durham's proposals. He says:—"Does Lord Durham propose a government purely democratic, under the name of responsible government? No. Does he propose to abolish one branch of the present government? No. Does he propose that our relations with foreign countries, or our military affairs, or the crown lands or crown resources be placed under the control of the provincial legislature? No, he proposes to place them exclusively in the control of the imperial parliament. What does His Lordship propose then? Lord Durham, except in the single case of the union of the Canadas, proposes not the alteration of a single letter of the established constitution; he proposes nothing more or less than that the people of Upper Canada within the defined and secured limits of local legislation and government, should be governed, as in England, by the men, as well as institutions of their choice." He thus vindicates his own consistency and that of thousands of the staunchest constitutionalists who had opposed Mackenzie, but were now prepared to support Lord Durham's responsible government.

A later editorial brings out the fact that the form of responsible government to which Mr. Ryerson so strenuously objected was that of purely elective institutions, such as are so largely adopted in the United States; and yet that he saw clearly that no system of responsibility was a guarantee for satisfactory administration, save responsibility to the people, directly or indirectly.

After the departure of the Earl of Durham, Mr. Poulett Thomson (afterwards Lord Sydenham) came to Canada as governor-general. He, as well as his successor, Sir Charles Bagot, received from Mr. Ryerson cordial and able support in the delicate task of introducing the new constitution, and the principles of responsible government. Lord Sydenham in the introduction of the system determined to ignore party, and in this step was supported by the wisest and best men of both the old parties. As was said by contemporary writers, such a step brought to the province "peace." Lord Sydenham's first ministry was composed of moderate men of both parties in about equal numbers, but did not include a French Canadian. At the opening of the House, Mr. Baldwin resigned because his advice for a reconstruction of the ministry was not followed, and with Mr. Hincks, LaFontaine and others, formed an opposition party, who pressed for a more explicit declaration of the principles upon which responsible government was to be conducted. For this purpose Mr. Baldwin moved a series of resolutions to which Mr. Harrison moved in amendment three resolutions, said to have been drawn up by the hand of Lord Sydenham himself, and which are sometimes referred to as the Magna Charta of Canadian responsible government. These resolutions in amendment were as follows:—

1. That the head of the executive government of the province, being within the limits of his government the representative of the sovereign, is responsible to the imperial authority alone.

2. That, nevertheless, the management of our local affairs can only be conducted by him by and with the assistance, counsel and information of subordinate officers in the province.

3. That in order to preserve between the different branches of the provincial parliament that harmony which is essential to the peace, welfare and good government of the province, the chief advisers of the representative of the sovereign, constituting a provincial administration, ought to be men possessed of the confidence of the representatives of the people, thus affording a guarantee that the well understood wishes and interests of the people, which our gracious sovereign has declared shall be the rule of the provincial government, will on all occasions be faithfully represented and advocated.

By these resolutions the general principles of responsible government as involved in the relations between the crown and the representative branch of parliament were declared. The concurrence of the two was required for all legislation and all executive acts. That concurrence is to be mediated by the executive council or ministry, who shall always command the confidence of and hence represent the representatives of the people. The prerogative of the crown is limited by the requirement that it shall be exercised by and with the assistance, counsel and information of the executive council. These principles, so fundamental in the British constitution, admit of considerable latitude of interpretation and application. They require, indeed, the concurrence of two powers before aught can be executed in government or enacted in law. But they do not define the source from which such acts or laws shall originate. Does the initiation of all legislation and executive action belong to parliament or to the ministry, and is the prerogative of the crown merely judicial, revisory and negative? It is upon this question that the character of British institutions as affording a perfectly free government must ultimately depend. The answer gives the advantage of positive power to one side or other of the two estates. This answer has not been given by positive constitutional declaration, but by procedure established by usage. From the date of the constitutional or limited monarchy in 1688, that usage has passed through a process of evolution. It is true that all our parliamentary language and the terms of all commissions to office and warrants for executive acts imply the supreme authority of the crown. But to-day in practice, if we reckon the executive council as an expression of the power of the people, the initiative has largely passed to that side. The calling to his councils of a new body of advisers is now the most important act of initiative on the part of the crown, and even then he calls a leader, giving him wide discretion in the selection of his associates.

But we have not to go very far back in the history of British constitutional monarchy to find a time when the crown exercised a far more positive and initial influence in the work of government. Even in 1841 when responsible government was being introduced in Canada, the change which took place between the days of George III. and Victoria was not yet complete. It is thus by no means surprising that during the first ten years of responsible government in Canada, there should be conflict between advanced Liberal and Conservative ideas on this point. This arose the more easily inasmuch as up to this time the executive council, representing not the people, but the crown and the governor, had been in a position to control the whole policy of the country, the representative assembly possessing a power which could do little but object and set forth grievances. It is possible that with the incoming of the new system the reformers expected too much. It may be that the colonial governors, acting under a sense of responsibility to the home government, and with express reserve of all questions affecting imperial interests, were disposed to assert too positive an influence over the policy of the Canadian government. It is certain that not till the coming of Lord Elgin was there a clear understanding established on these delicate points. Certain it is that almost from the beginning, notwithstanding the wisdom of the measures proposed both by Lord Sydenham and his successor, Sir Charles Bagot, there was dissatisfaction on the part of the reformers. An attempt to allay this by a reconstruction of the ministry, in which the reformers had a majority and the French Canadians were represented, served only to bring the matter to a crisis. Some minor appointments and the reserve of the Secret Societies' Bill, aimed at the Orange Societies, served to precipitate a conflict between the governor-general and his ministers, and led finally to an appeal to the country. It was at this crisis that Dr. Ryerson, now president of Victoria College, once more took a prominent place in the political arena in defence of Sir Charles Metcalfe. On the opposite side of the conflict new names came into prominence, especially George Brown and Adam Ferguson. The leaders in parliament were W. H. Draper and Robert Baldwin.

The facts from which the crisis was precipitated were two—the appointment of a clerk of the peace in Dalhousie district and the reservation of the Secret Societies' Bill for Her Majesty's pleasure. Other appointments were referred to, but all were admitted to be of minor importance. But from the outset the leaders of the reform party made a mistake both in parliamentary procedure and in political tactics. On the question of the reservation of the bill against the secret societies the governor was so clearly within his rights that even they could not object. They could only point to the act as a proof of his sympathy with the Tory party. As to the question of appointments it appears that the appointments were actually made, and as they could be made only by the commission being signed by the responsible minister who held the provincial seal in his keeping, they had thus become formally consenting parties. To complain of an act to which they had formally assented by seal and signature was technically a violation of the faith required of Her Majesty's privy councillors. The appointments should have been prevented by the refusal of the seal and signature, and if the persons recommended by the ministry for appointment were objected to and refused by the governor, they should have resigned. The governor could make no appointment without the assistance of a responsible minister, and if he dismissed his ministry or accepted their resignation, then upon him devolved the task of finding a ministry willing to be responsible for the measure which he proposed, and able to secure the confidence of parliament. This method of procedure secures at once the prerogative and influence of

the crown and the power of parliament, and is the
very essence of British responsible government.
Mr. Baldwin's ministry on the other hand allowed
the appointments to be made, and then sought
from the governor "an understanding" that in
future no appointments should be made without
previously taking the advice of the council; that
the lists of the candidates should in every instance
be laid before the council; that the council should
recommend any others at discretion; and that the
governor-general, in deciding after taking their advice, "should not make any appointment prejudicial
to their influence." To these stipulations or understandings the governor-general refused to commit
himself, and in his refusal was sustained by the
imperial government and probably by all British
precedent. On this refusal the ministry, with one
exception, tendered their resignations. Upon this
resignation the whole matter was thrown back
upon parliament, and a few months later—by the
dissolution of the House—upon the country. The
contest was one of the most bitter in Canadian
political history, accompanied by scenes of violence and bloodshed. The reformers made not only
the mistake in procedure referred to, but also
what seems now a mistake in political tactics by
introducing two or three extraneous elements into
the arena. One was the race and provincial difficulty. They allied themselves with the French
Canadians, and as a result were beaten in the

election by an Upper Canadian majority sufficient to give their opponents a majority of the whole House. This interprovincial jealousy was tided over for a time by the "double majority," and finally led to a deadlock, out of which confederation arose. Possibly the ghost is not yet laid. Another source of trouble was the prominence given to *party* in the working of responsible government. There can, we think, be no doubt that even in their communications with the governor they introduced this matter to some extent. In their discussions before the House and the country it was not concealed. They even called upon the country to define more distinctly party lines. The governor, on the other hand, took his stand on the principle that in the making of appointments he should not be asked to do so on party lines. This doubtless secured him the support of many moderate men of both parties, who desired the cessation of extreme party conflict.

Dr. Ryerson's defence of Sir Charles Metcalfe is, we think, his ablest piece of political writing. His positions are taken with the clearest judgment, and defended with consummate logical skill, and with a mastery of constitutional principles and a wealth of historical learning which is amazing when we consider his times and his opportunities. Examples and illustrations are taken from all periods of English history and made to tell on the argument and case in hand with wonderful force, and one can scarcely study the case as a grand debate without awarding

129

him the victory. And yet within half a dozen years the fundamental principle which no one had as yet clearly defined, but towards which the country was unconsciously tending, was admitted by all as henceforth an element of our responsible government. The whole responsibility of public policy now rests with the ministry, and there is scarcely even a practical reservation of imperial interests except of the most vital character. The royal prerogative guards the constitution and the whole people against wrong and injustice, and graciously modifies by the power of moral influence the policies of all parties, bringing them into more perfect harmony with truth, and justice, and liberty, and mercy, and at times it curbs the violence of party impetuosity and passion. But for this higher task it must stand above party and policies. Yet this result has been attained not by the destruction of the royal prerogative, which might have resulted had the reformers of 1844 secured their "stipulations," but by a mode of exercise which, perhaps, was beyond the wisest and best of men at that date.

In one respect both parties erred through fear, and each did injustice to the other. The reformers looked upon Sir Charles Metcalfe and Dr. Ryerson as the foes of responsible government, and predicted the return of the absolutism of the "family compact." We can see now no ground for such a fear. Dr. Ryerson certainly never was disposed to make a truce with the "family compact," or to submit to

the injustice of absolutism, and Sir Charles's only
desire seemed to be to avoid such a one-sided distribution of government patronage as would renew
the old evil in another form. On the other hand
even a Liberal imperial government and Sir Charles
as their representative seemed afraid to trust the
young Canadian baby to walk alone, and wished to
keep a good hand on its legislation and policy.
They seemed to be still afraid of republican tendencies, and possibly another insurrection. We do
not forget that though Canada had passed under
the administration of three governors her constitution was then but four years old; and that the
guiding hand of Lord Sydenham in legislation,
as well as his comprehensive administration of
affairs with equal favour to all parties tended to
strengthen the better political life of the province
and to heal the sores of the past. These things fully
explain the course of Sir Charles Metcalfe, and of
the Whig government at home, as well as the attitude of Dr. Ryerson in their defence. But they too
were not yet fully conscious of the power of the new
political life which was now becoming national, nor
did they foresee either the exact form or the magnitude to which it must shortly grow.

After this contest Dr. Ryerson never again returned to the arena of general politics. His position
in the educational work of the country brought him
into contact with both parties, as one or the other
held the reins of power. In the early fifties he

contributed some letters on the clergy reserve question, otherwise his future work was exclusively in the field of education. In 1867, as united Canada entered upon her larger life as a young dominion, he addressed to his fellow-countrymen a letter replete with wise counsels and patriotic sentiment. But in this there was but the loving advice of a father, and no more the strenuous contest of the man who is fighting the battle of national life. Reviewing his work in the political field we think we may safely say that from first to last in the three great conflicts in which it was exercised it was conservative, timely, and, in the result, for the good of the country.

CHAPTER VI

THE UNIVERSITY QUESTION

A THIRD important question involved in the early struggle of the province was that of education. The policy inaugurated as we have seen in Governor Simcoe's day was too comprehensive and far-seeing to omit this. To control the executive government, the religion and the education of the country was to mould its future at will; and while the dominant party doubtless believed they were discharging their duty by their trust, and acting for the highest interest of the country, they quite forgot the fact that the men to whom they thus extended a paternal government were men of equal capacities as men and of equal rights as citizens with themselves.

In the matter of education, the early policy projected a university and four royal grammar schools, two in the east at Cornwall and Kingston, and two in the west at Newark (Niagara) and a place undetermined. The university was reserved for York, the new capital of Upper Canada. Had this policy been carried into effect, though some of the locations might have proved unfortunate, it might have resulted, with subsequent change of location to suit the needs of the population, in a most compre-

133

hensive and efficient scheme of higher education.
Even now, a central university with strong affiliated collegiate institutes at centres of population
solves the problem of the wider diffusion of at least
a portion of university education.

We have already seen that the secondary part of
this scheme shaped itself into the district schools as
early as 1807 and 1816. The lack of funds delayed
the university part until the royal charter of 1827,
and even then the only practical result was Upper
Canada College, an institution answering to the
royal grammar schools as originally projected.

But the entire system thus created was dominated throughout by the idea of a state church, with
exclusive privileges in religion, education, and even
civil power. When, therefore, in 1826, and again in
1828, Mr. Ryerson took up his pen in defence of
the rights of the great majority of the people
against this unjust policy, the subject of education,
and, in 1828, the subject of the proposed constitution of the new university occupied a prominent
place. On taking his position as editor of *The
Christian Guardian* in 1829, he made full use of
the columns of the new journal to awaken the
country to a proper estimate of the importance of
this subject, and practical results almost immediately followed. In the conference of the Methodist
Church of 1829, the subject of an institution of
learning was discussed, and while it was postponed
for that year in order to establish *The Guardian*,

in the following year the subject was again taken up and practical measures adopted, resulting in the opening of Upper Canada Academy in June, 1836.

The Presbyterians were actuated by the same spirit, and two movements appear among them, one to establish a literary and theological institution at Pleasant Bay, in the township of Hillier, Prince Edward County, and the other to secure from the government the appointment of a theological professor on a status of equality with the professor of divinity of the English Church in the staff and council of King's College. These Presbyterian movements reached their final results in the opening of Queen's College in March, 1842. A third movement, quite independent of these two and antedating both, appears in the Upper Canadian legislative assembly. As soon as the nature of Dr. Strachan's charter and ecclesiastical chart was known in the province, the assembly prepared an address to the King on the political affairs of the country, based on a report of a select committee of the House, in which this passage closes the reference to the new university charter following an expression of strong condemnation of its exclusive sectarian provisions: "It should not be a school of political or sectarian views. It should have about it no appearance of a spirit of partiality or exclusion. Its portals should be thrown open to all, and upon none who enter should any influence be exerted to attach them to any particular creed or church. It should be a source of intellectual and moral light and animation, from which the glorious irradiations of literature and science may descend upon all with equal lustre and power. Such an institution would be a blessing to the country, its pride and glory. Most deeply, therefore, is it to be lamented that the principles of the charter are calculated to defeat its usefulness, and to confine to a favoured few all its advantages." (*Report* of March 17th, 1828.) The address of the colonial assembly to the King brought the matter before the British House of Commons in 1828, where it was further pressed by petitions signed by thousands of Upper Canadian subjects. Mr. George Ryerson, an elder brother of Mr. Egerton Ryerson, was the bearer of these petitions. A select committee of the British House of Commons took up the matter in connection with other Canadian affairs, and in regard to the university reported in the following terms: "It cannot be doubted as the guidance and government of the college is to be vested in the hands of members of the Church of England, that in the election of professors, a preference would inevitably be shown to persons of that persuasion; and in a country where only a small proportion of the inhabitants adhere to that church a suspicion and jealousy of religious interference would necessarily be created." This declaration is followed by the recommendation of essential changes in the charter, both as to its theological faculty and the appointment of professors generally. One of these provisions was adopted in the first amendment of the charter by the provincial legislature in 1837.

It was with the movement in the Methodist Church that Mr. Ryerson was most directly connected. During the first two or three years his official influence as editor of *The Guardian* and his personal influence as a member of the conference and church were very helpful to the committee who were struggling with the difficult task of bringing into operation a large literary institution without any aid from public sources. The following extract from an editorial in April, 1831, will indicate the character of his support, as well as the principles upon which the new institution was being founded:—"It is the first literary institution which has been commenced by any body of ministers in accordance with the frequently expressed wishes of the people of Upper Canada. The Methodist conference have not sought endowments of public lands for the establishment of an institution contrary to the voice of the people as expressed by their representatives; much less have they sought to acquire such endowments to erect 'essentially a missionary college' for the purpose of carrying on an extensive proselytizing warfare upon the territories of their religious neighbours. But the Methodist conference, in the manner in which they have commenced and are proceeding in the establishment of this institution, say, in effect, to the people of Upper Canada, 'We have not laboured among you for the promotion of selfish and party purposes, but for the diffusion of pure and undefiled religion; nor have we sought or received any other subsistence than the voluntary offerings of your liberality. Desirous of promoting more extensively the interests of the rising generation and of the country generally, we have resolved upon the establishment of a seminary of learning. We have done so upon liberal principles; we have not reserved any peculiar privileges to ourselves for the education of our own children; we have published the constitution for your examination; and now we appeal to your liberality for assistance, we feel confident that you will not withhold it; we believe your good wishes are with us in this undertaking, and we submit to your decision for the success or failure of it.'"

The undertaking proved much more arduous and costly than its promoters had anticipated. When completed the building was by far the most classic in architecture and imposing in appearance of any up to that time erected in Upper Canada for educational purposes, not excepting Upper Canada College; and instead of costing £6,000 as estimated, the cost, with furnishings, reached £9,000. The perfection of the workmanship may be estimated from the fact that after seventy years the government of Ontario find it still a substantial, valuable building. The amount collected by the trustees from the Canadian

Methodist people and their friends, who by 1834 had been thoroughly canvassed, was £4,000. By that date the building was enclosed and well advanced towards completion; but the trustees, who were not a body corporate, and had hitherto proceeded entirely upon their personal responsibility, were under obligations to the banks and for private loans to the extent of £2,000. It was at this difficult juncture that Mr. Ryerson became officially connected with the college, being appointed by the trustees as their agent to England to solicit aid for the institution, and to petition the imperial government for a royal charter. The first part of this commission was to him exceedingly uncongenial, as literally it was true of him "To beg I am ashamed." But this is the letter which followed him from Mr. Lord, the English president of the Canadian conference:—"You must stay in England until the money is got. Use every effort, harden your face to flint, and give eloquence to your tongue. This is your calling. Excel in it. Be not discouraged with a dozen refusals in succession. The money must be had, and it must be begged. My dear brother, work for your life, and I pray God to give you success. Do not borrow if possible. Beg, *beg, beg* it all. It must be done."

But the more difficult, as well as more important part of Mr. Ryerson's commission was the securing of the royal charter. It must be borne in mind that up to this time no such legal recognition had been afforded to a body of non-conformist ministers, either in England or in any of the colonies. A bill for the purpose of incorporating the trustees had already failed to pass the Canadian legislature. There was thus no precedent to which he could appeal, and no model which he could copy, and his sole hope was in the justice of his cause, and in the spirit, now rapidly growing in England, of equal civil and religious rights and privileges.

To grant the Methodists equal legislative, if not equal governmental support for their college, with that which had already been conceded to Dr. Strachan on behalf of the Church of England, was only a fair practical outcome of this spirit. But a technical difficulty was at once proposed by the law officers of the crown. How could a body unknown to the law be officially recognized as the recipients of a royal charter? Mr. Ryerson's legal acumen here stood him in good stead, and found a way out of the difficulty. Although the Methodist conference, as such, was as yet unknown to English law, the Methodist preacher as such had already been given a recognized legal status by the grant of legal authority for the solemnization of matrimony. Mr. Ryerson accordingly constituted his fundamental chartered body of all men so recognized by law in Upper Canada, and the charter granted to these authorized them to elect trustees and visitors who should be a body corporate for all the purposes of the college. The first legal name of the college was Upper Canada Academy, its name at once designating its comprehensive character, offering its services to all the people of the province, and yet distinguishing it from Upper Canada College, already in operation. Both were designed to prepare the way for higher institutions of learning in the immediate future, when the number of students prepared for a university course should warrant the advance. In the race toward this goal the Methodist institution won by two years, commencing university work in 1841 and reaching its first graduating class in 1845.

Mr. Ryerson's return from his English mission was a veritable triumph of patient industry and remarkable ability devoted unsparingly to a high purpose. It was but five years since a governor-general had superciliously replied to a loyal address of the Methodist conferenee, in which they ventured to refer to their projected college, of which a stone had not yet been laid, "That the system of education which has produced the best and ablest men in the United Kingdom, will not be abandoned here to suit the limited views of the leaders of societies who perhaps have neither experience nor judgment to appreciate the value or advantages of a liberal education." Within three years Mr. Ryerson, one of the leaders referred to in this disparaging paragraph, was on his way to England with recommendatory letters from this same governor-general, who had already learned to form a truer estimate of the

141

Methodist people and their leaders; and now after nearly two years of arduous toil and able work for his church and his country, he returned home with the first royal charter ever granted by the imperial government for an educational institution outside of an established church, and with a fair prospect of its release from financial embarrassment. Already as the result of his labours he found, on his arrival home, the buildings completed and occupied by a promising body of teachers and pupils, under the principalship of Rev. Matthew Richey, M.A., who had opened the academy on June 18th, 1836. This step had been secured through the financial assistance which he had obtained from friends in England.

But financial difficulties were as yet by no means ended. He had received in England from Lord Glenelg instructions to the new governor-general, Sir Francis Bond Head, to recommend to the Canadian legislature a grant in assistance of the institution. Mr. Ryerson, who knew well the state of affairs in the two branches of the legislature at that date, was fully aware that this last recommendation would be of no practical service. He therefore persisted in his efforts, until in April, 1837, a few days before sailing for home, he secured further instructions from the imperial government to Sir Francis Bond Head to advance the amount, £4,100, out of the unappropriated revenues of the crown. One-half of this amount was paid in November following, in the midst of the excitement which immediately preceded the insurrection. The balance was withheld by the governor until the whole matter was brought before parliament by petition from Mr. Ryerson. The question was carried back to Lord Glenelg, but upon report and address of the House of Assembly to the governor it was settled.

The establishment of responsible government in Canada in 1840 led to important consequences in regard to university work. During the first session of the provincial legislature a bill prepared by Mr. Ryerson was introduced, and passed both Houses, extending the charter of Upper Canada Academy under the new name of "Victoria College," so as to confer university powers. This bill received the royal assent at the hand of Lord Sydenham, August 27th, 1841. In October of that year Mr. Ryerson was appointed the first president under the enlarged charter, and opened the session on the 21st of that month. His formal inaugural took place on June 21st, 1842, and on August 3rd following he was honoured by the Wesleyan University, Middletown, Connecticut, with the degree of doctor of divinity.

The official relation to Victoria College thus begun he held for four years, during which time students flocked to the college from all parts. Among those who became eminent in after years in various walks of life were the late Judge Springer; S. S. Nelles, afterwards his successor in office; the Hon. J. C. Aikins; the Hon. Wm.

Macdougall, C.B.; J. George Hodgins, his life-long friend and associate in work; the Rev. Wm. Ormiston, D.D., one of the brightest ornaments of the Presbyterian Church; Col. Walker Powell, Adjutant-General; Stoughton Dennis, Surveyor-General; the Hon. W. H. Brouse, and James L. Biggar, M.P. Out of such materials as these were organized in four years four undergraduate classes, under a curriculum equal in extent of science, literature and philosophy to that of the best American colleges of the time. Its matriculation embraced both Latin and Greek—in the former Nepos, Cæsar, Sallust, and Virgil,—arithmetic and algebra in mathematics, with English grammar, history, geography, and elementary science. The subsequent course included four years' work in the Latin and Greek languages, four in mathematics, three in science, two years each in English constitution and history, philosophy, evidences of natural and revealed religion, Hebrew and French. Rhetoric, composition and elocution received attention throughout the course, and the study of the Greek testament and Biblical literature was also provided for.

The following words from the pen of the late gifted Dr. Ormiston give a most vivid portraiture of the impression made upon his students by Dr. Ryerson as college president: " Dr. Ryerson was at that time in the prime of a magnificent manhood. His well-developed, finely-proportioned, firmly-knit frame, his broad, lofty brow, his keen, penetrating eye, and his genial, benignant face, all proclaimed him every inch a man. His mental powers, vigorous and well disciplined; his attainments in literature, varied and extensive; his experience, extended and diversified; his fame as a preacher of great pathos and power, widely spread; his claims as a doughty, dauntless champion of the rights of the people to civil and religious liberty, generally acknowledged; his powers of expression, marvellous in readiness, richness and beauty; his manners affable and winning; his presence magnetic and impressive,—he stood in the eye of the youthful, ardent, aspiring student, a tower of strength, a centre of healthy, helpful influences, a man to be admired and honoured, loved and feared, imitated and followed. And I may add, that frequent intercourse for nearly forty years, and close official relations for more than ten, only deepened and confirmed the impression first made. A more familiar acquaintance with his domestic, social and religious life, a more thorough knowledge of his mind and heart constantly increased my appreciation of his worth, my esteem for his character, and my affection for his person.

"Not a few misunderstood, undervalued or misrepresented his public conduct, but it will be found that those who knew him best, loved him most, and that many who were constrained to differ from him in his management of public affairs, did full justice to the purity and generosity of his motives, to the nobility, loftiness and ultimate success of his aims, and to the disinterestedness of his manifold labours for the country and the church of Christ.

"As a teacher he was earnest and efficient, eloquent and inspiring, but he expected and exacted too much work from the average student. His own ready and affluent mind sympathized keenly with the apt, bright scholar, to whom his praise was warmly given, but he scarcely made sufficient allowance for the dullness or lack of previous preparation which failed to keep pace with him in his long and rapid strides; hence his censures were occasionally severe. His methods of examination furnished the very best kind of mental discipline, fitted alike to cultivate the memory and to strengthen the judgment. All the students revered him, but the best of the class appreciated him most. His counsels were faithful and judicious, his admonitions paternal and discriminating, his rebukes seldom administered, but scathingly severe. No student ever left his presence without resolving to do better, to aim higher and to win his approval."

While Mr. Ryerson was thus engaged in laying the foundations of Victoria College, two other colleges were being brought into operation. The Presbyterian Church had in 1839 petitioned the legislature of Upper Canada for an act of incorporation for a university at Kingston. The act was passed in 1840, but as they desired a royal charter, it was found necessary to ask for its disallowance, and the charter was issued October 14th, 1841. The institution was accordingly opened for the reception of students on March 7th, 1842, and as the curriculum for the degree of B.A. extended over three years, the first graduates had completed their course in 1845. Finally King's College after long delay was brought into operation, and on June 8th, 1843, the inauguration took place, the college being located in the Parliament Buildings. The practical work of instruction appears to have commenced in October following, and the warrants of the first professors in arts bear date September, 1843. On March 4th, 1837, the royal assent had been given by His Excellency, the Governor-General, to a bill incorporating Regiopolis College, Kingston, under the direction of the Roman Catholic Church.

These various steps growing out of the exclusive character of the university charter obtained in 1827, and which Dr. Strachan so innocently called his charter, presented Upper Canada as early as 1843 with her university problem. There were then in operation in the province four colleges, the best equipped of which had not more than four full professors in arts. One of these, King's College, was in possession of the provincial endowment, consisting of nearly £39,000 in provincial debentures and other stock, besides a large quantity of lands. Although no building had been erected or instruction given, there was already a considerable debt against this endowment. The other colleges were without endowments or property other than the buildings which had been erected for Victoria as already related, and real estate and buildings which had been secured by the Roman Catholic Church for Regiopolis. Queen's was as yet without buildings, and was seriously considering the problem before her. Victoria and Queen's had each been voted a legislative grant of £500, but apart from that were dependent on fees and church funds. The total number of undergraduate students in arts in the province was less than fifty, and these were divided among three colleges.

It was at this juncture that in 1843 the first effort to secure a truly provincial university was made by the Honourable Robert Baldwin. His scheme embraced a large number of the distinctive features of the Federation Act of 1887. It proposed to include all the existing colleges by removing them to Toronto; also any that might hereafter be founded. It deprived all the colleges of their degree conferring powers. It proposed to erect a central university, with teaching faculty, in which the students of all the colleges should receive instruction on equal terms. The only subjects excluded from the university course were the divinity subjects. Each college was left free to teach whatever it chose. The colleges were placed somewhat largely under the control of the central university authority or council, in which they were all equally represented; and while the university endowment was to remain intact and for the university, for a period of four years each college was to receive a grant in aid of £500. A minimum amount invested in buildings, outfit, and endowment was required to entitle a college to claim its place and status in the university. It is said that this scheme was the work of Mr. Baldwin's own mind, having been prepared after a single interview with each of the parties concerned.

From the Anglican party, who were now in possession of the endowment, this bill met with the most uncompromising opposition. They claimed that the endowment belonged by gift of the crown to King's College exclusively; that King's College had been constituted by royal charter a Church of England institution; and that the provincial parliament had no power to interfere with either the property or the charter. They petitioned parliament for leave to present their case by counsel at the bar of the House, and the Hon. W. H. Draper was deputed for that purpose, and in an able address of over two hours laid the constitutional argument before the members.

The Presbyterians, whose college had been in operation for a year and a half, but who had not yet erected buildings, and had thus no financial complication, supported the proposed plan most heartily, and were prepared to surrender their university powers and remove to Toronto at once. In fact the whole movement originated with the expressed desire of Queen's to take part in the provincial university. Dr. Liddell, the principal of Queen's, was a very hearty advocate of the scheme, and pressed it upon the Methodists in a series of letters to Dr. Ryerson. The Methodists, on the other hand, were in a most embarrassing position. They were now divided into three bodies, the largest numbering 32,000 and the smallest 20,000 adherents. They had only some three or four years previously completed a most exhausting effort to secure the last of the nine thousand pounds needed for the building of their college, and they were as yet entirely without endowment. The most toilsome labour of this work had, as we have already seen, fallen on Dr. Ryerson. He was now asked to leave the institution thus founded to fall back upon its previous work of an academy or minor college, and begin anew the task of founding a Methodist college in the provincial university. His reply— penned by his own hand, though presented as that of his church through resolution of the college board —is such as Methodism need never be ashamed of. The essential parts of this document are contained in the fourth and fifth resolutions, as follows:—

"4. That viewing the general objects and opinions of the University Bill in this light we cordially concur in them, and give that bill our warm approbation and support; although its present application to the Wesleyan Methodist Church as a body, from circumstances peculiar to ourselves, deprives us of important rights and privileges which we now enjoy, without conferring upon us any corresponding advantages, since all the resources which we have been able to obtain both in this country and in England for the erection of college buildings have been expended in the completion of a commodious and expensive edifice at too great a distance from the seat of the University of Toronto to render any of its advantages available to the scholars and students of Victoria College.

"5. That in view of the peculiar inconveniences and disadvantages to which the operation of the bill must necessarily subject us, without its being in our power to enjoy the advantages of the university, we appeal to the just and enlightened consideration of the government to grant us such assistance as our peculiar circumstances suggest, and to aid us to the utmost of its power in making any arrangements which may hereafter be deemed expedient and advisable to secure to the persons under our institution the advantages of the university."

But this expression of approval and of desire as soon as possible to take part in the project did not end Dr. Ryerson's efforts on its behalf. The bill was meeting with powerful opposition on plausible constitutional grounds. Into its defence he threw himself with all his ability, energy, and learning, and in a most complete reply to Mr. Draper's address to the parliament, he proved that the

province had a right to a truly provincial university;
that the original endowment was not a gift to the
English Church or to a particular college, but was
granted by the crown for the education of the
people of Canada in response to a request from the
legislative assembly of the province, and that over
both the charter and the endowment, parliament—
which includes the crown itself—possessed complete power, and that over both of these the present
tenants had no personal rights or control, being but
trustees for the people.

The political complication to which we have
already referred, ending in the resignation of Mr.
Baldwin and the majority of his colleagues, brought
this first promising effort for the establishment of a
provincial university to an end, but the fundamental principles of the whole question were developed in this first attempt at solution, and were
clearly grasped and maintained both by Mr. Baldwin and Dr. Ryerson. Their effort was to build the
new university into the past history of the people;
to make it include rather than antagonize or destroy
existing institutions; to make it comprehensive,
meeting the wants, conciliating the sympathies,
and enlisting the support of all the people; and
finally to make it impartial, offering perfectly equal
rights and privileges to all. The province was destined to wait for fifty years before another measure
equally comprehensive would be proposed, and in
those fifty years the university question was to

pass through six successive phases of attempted legislation and party conflict. Before this history was completed, if completed it be even yet, Robert Baldwin, Bishop Strachan, Dr. Ryerson, W. H. Draper, J. B. Robinson, R. B. Sullivan, and all the other actors in the beginning of things had passed from the scene.

The second attempt at the solution of the university question was made by Mr. Draper in 1846. The general principles of Mr. Draper's bill were the same as those presented by the Baldwin Bill, and it was supported and opposed by the same parties, and on the same grounds. Dr. Ryerson at this time defined his position in the following propositions:—

1. That there should be a provincial university furnishing the highest academical and professional education, at least in respect to law and medicine.

2. That there should be a provincial system of common school education, commensurate with the wants of the entire population.

3. That both the university and the common school system should be established and conducted upon Christian principles, yet free from sectarian bias or ascendency.

4. That there should be an intermediate class of seminaries in connection with the different religious persuasions who have ability and enterprise to establish them, providing, on the one hand, a theological education for their clergy, and, on the other

hand, a thorough English and scientific education and elementary classical instruction for those of the youth of their congregations who might seek for more than a common school education, or who might wish to prepare for the university, and who, not having the experience of university students, required a parental and religious oversight in their absence from their parents.

5. That it would be economic as well as patriotic on the part of the government to grant a liberal aid to such seminaries, as well as to provide for the endowment of a university or a common school system.

It is evident from the contemporary press that already a new principle was making its way into the university question, viz., the entire separation of the higher education from religion, leaving that entirely to the voluntary efforts of the churches. "I cannot, for the life of me, see," says a prominent editor of that time, "what religion has to do with the department of the university devoted to arts and sciences." Dr. Ryerson's view was the very opposite of this, religion with him forming an essential element in all education.

Another element in the educational problem of that time was the appearance of residential secondary schools either owned by or patronized by the principal religious denominations. Upper Canada College was really such under the control of the Church of England. Upper Canada Academy, still

continued as a preparatory adjunct of Victoria
College, was another. Knox College filled for some
years a similar place for the Free Church Presbyterians, and the Society of Friends were establishing another in Bloomfield. Those institutions,
the outcome of the religious and intellectual spirit
of the age, were destined for a time to be eclipsed
by the rise of the high schools as a part of the
system which Dr. Ryerson was now inaugurating;
but their persistence to the present and their large
extension in secondary colleges, both for young
men and young women, is the best proof of their
value in an educational system.

Mr. Draper's bill was lost by the carrying of an
amendment to the second reading, and so ended
the second attempt at the formation of a provincial
university. Its failure was due to two causes. The
voluntary party in the House and outside were
now taking the ground that even for education no
state grants should be made to churches. The
church party, on the other hand, were making a
most determined effort to retain control of the
university and its endowment. Mr. Draper's bill
suited neither, and was killed by their combined
vote.

A similar fate befell the effort in 1847 made by
the solicitor-general, Mr. John A. Macdonald, to
solve the university problem. His bill offered the
largest concessions yet tendered to the church
party. He proposed to hand over to them King's

College, with the building now completed, together with an annual income of $12,000, and to give to Queen's and Victoria and Regiopolis $6,000 each. The balance of the annual income arising from the university endowment was to be expended on the district grammar schools and in promoting the teaching of scientific agriculture. This bill, known as the partition scheme, called forth the most strenuous opposition of the Liberals, who had now planted themselves firmly on the principle that the university endowment should not be divided, and that the provincial university should be completely secularized. On the other hand, it was rejected by the church party, who still claimed the whole endowment, as well as the college. The combined opposition of these two parties caused its withdrawal.

This partition bill of Mr. Macdonald was the introduction of an entirely new phase of the university question. Hitherto all were agreed on the idea of a single provincial university. The question at issue was its control in the interests of a single religious body, as opposed to the equal rights and privileges of all. Nor was there any question as to the relation of the churches and religious teaching to university education. All university reforms proposed to retain this by the incorporation of the existing colleges. The principle of historic continuity was thus maintained. There was no proposal to destroy existing institutions for the erection of the new. Mr. Macdonald's proposition was thoroughly conservative. It proposed to do full justice to all existing institutions, but at the expense of the central university, which had now become the ideal of liberal thought. The ground of conflict was thus shifted, and henceforth the battle was to be between one secular state university and the four church colleges. Mr. Macdonald's partition bill received Dr. Ryerson's strong support, and determined his position on the university question to the end of his life, for the following reasons:

1. It appeared to him to meet the full extent of the needs of university education as at that time existing in the leading colleges of the English-speaking world. The vast modern extension of the sphere of the university was then unknown.

2. It coincided with his conservative instincts, which always led him to work with spontaneous historic growth rather than upon theory.

3. It satisfied his convictions of the need of religion as an essential part of all education.

4. He judged that the four colleges already established would afford the advantages of higher education to a larger number than would receive them in one central university.

The defeat of the Conservative government at the next election and the return of the Liberals to power, placed the university question once more in the hands of Mr. Baldwin, and his now largely advanced positions were embodied in the bill of

1849. The central idea of this bill was the complete separation of the provincial university from all ecclesiastical influence and control. The subject of divinity was excluded from the university; all religious tests, subscriptions and exercises were done away with; it was forbidden to the government to appoint an ecclesiastic on the senate, and such could not fill the office of chancellor. The only privilege offered to the outlying colleges established by the churches was the right to appoint one member of the senate, and this privilege was offered only on condition of their being deprived at once and forever of the power to confer degrees except in divinity. The central idea was the extinction of all other colleges as educational institutions and their conversion into theological schools, and this to be accomplished either by their voluntary surrender, or by the force of state-endowed competition.

It is not surprising that this bill satisfied neither the high church party, who found themselves stripped by it of the college and endowments to which they had held so tenaciously, nor the other religious bodies, who at so much sacrifice, had founded colleges of their own. It met the wishes of the thorough "voluntaries" alone, who as yet had not founded colleges of their own. It certainly was at variance with Dr. Ryerson's fundamental principles of education, which sought to combine morals and religion with intellectual culture and to unite

158

voluntary effort with the aid of the state. The fundamental principle of the new bill was that the state alone should control and maintain education, and that all alliance of the churches with the state was to be avoided. It cut loose from all past history of education in the province, ignored all church institutions, and built upon a purely secular foundation.

In four years' time the exclusive rigidity of this bill was broken, and a bill apparently more liberal in its attitude to outlying colleges was introduced by Mr. Hincks in 1853. Dr. Ryerson, who had strongly opposed the Baldwin Bill in 1849, in 1850 had secured legislative authority for the removal of Victoria College to Toronto; and in 1852 he addressed a series of open letters to the Hon. Sir Francis Hincks, now the head of the Canadian government, outlining a most comprehensive and patriotic plan for the establishment of the provincial university upon a basis which might secure the coöperation of all the sections of the community.

The Hincks Bill of 1853 did not follow Dr. Ryerson's outline, which anticipated some of the most important features of the Federation Act of 1887, but was modelled on the example of the London University, and possibly implied, though it did not specifically enact, the partition features of Mr. Macdonald's bill of 1847. It made more liberal provision for the affiliation of the outlying colleges, separated the teaching faculty of arts from the university, making provision for its support as a state college from the university endowments, and provided that the balance of income from the university endowment after meeting the wants of the university and college should be at the disposal of the legislature for the aid of higher education. These provisions were accepted by the outlying colleges as a promise of more harmonious relations, and they all accepted affiliation with the reconstructed university, and for a time their representatives took their places on the university senate.

Parliamentary acts, however, can change names and constitution, but not spirit, policy or nature; they can constitute an institution the provincial university in form and theory without making it such in the affections and support of the people or in its spirit and attitude toward the other educational institutions of the country. The new university and state college consisted still very largely of the same men; its policy was still the policy of the old state church college, to use the provincial endowments as the rival of the outlying colleges. The Baldwin Act had, as we have seen, converted this policy into one of extinction; and although the new act pointed towards a better way, there was under it not the slightest effort toward a combination of resources and colleges for the building up of a truly provincial university. If such a result was ever to come it could under this policy come only when the outlying colleges had been destroyed by the force of an unfair financial competition. These colleges had from the very first maintained the attitude of willingness or even desire for friendly coöperation in some form to build up a truly provincial university. They were now doomed to see all hope in this direction extinguished.

Dr. Ryerson had from the first been a leader in this movement. He had throughout opposed all sectional and exclusive policies, whether ecclesiastical or political. When, therefore, the sectional character of the university policy—for the policy rather than the constitution was at fault—culminated in the conflict of 1860, he threw himself with all his force and ability into it and in favour of a comprehensive policy. The particular form of that policy was not the best. It still clung to the old partition scheme of John A. Macdonald, which would have been a fatal mistake. The conflict resulted for a little time in increased legislative aid to the denominational colleges, in itself a very doubtful advantage. But it embittered the state university party, and at the first opportunity all state aid was taken from the denominational colleges, their affiliation with the provincial university was cancelled, and they were left, as was supposed, to die, but in reality to renew their youth when once they were left to live by the merit of their work and the truth of the principles upon which they were founded. Dr. Ryerson was their consistent friend and supporter by pen and tongue and purse to the end. He believed in religion and morals in all education.

He believed in a comprehensive unity of all forces in a truly provincial system. His chief mistake was, perhaps, that he did not unflinchingly apply the voluntary principle to the religious side of the work. It, perhaps, was financially impossible in his time. If so, then even this was not an error on his part, for in maintaining the religious principle even at the compromise of the other he has preserved for us a goal which is most abundantly vindicated by the strength and influence of the religious colleges to-day, and the reflex influence of which has been of the greatest benefit to the state college itself.

CHAPTER VII

FOUNDING THE COMMON SCHOOL SYSTEM

IN Mr. Ryerson's last interview with Lord Sydenham, shortly before the accident which resulted
in His Excellency's death, the governor discussed
with him his contemplated measures for the improvement of popular education, and proposed that
Mr. Ryerson should take charge of that important
work. The matter was again considered under Sir
Charles Bagot's administration in 1842, but the
Rev. Mr. Murray was appointed. Near the close
of 1843 Sir Charles Metcalfe conferred with Dr.
Ryerson on educational matters and again suggested that he should undertake the necessary
work, which had made no progress under Mr.
Murray's tenure of office. A few weeks later the
rupture took place between the governor and his
cabinet. At first Mr. Ryerson was disposed to take
a view unfavourable to the position assumed by the
governor. But after a careful study of the question
involved, as it was set forth by the newly organized
Reform Association, he took up his pen in defence
of Sir Charles, at the same time avowing his intention to accept no office until this question had been
settled by the voice of the people at the polls.
At the election in the autumn of 1844, the new

advisers of Sir Charles, led by Mr. Draper, were sustained, and in September Dr. Ryerson was appointed superintendent of schools under the act of 1843, with permission to visit the United States and Europe for the purpose of studying the best systems then in operation before preparing a new bill for the improvement of common schools in Upper Canada. On this tour of investigation and study, Dr. Ryerson started in November, 1844, returning early in 1846. We cannot follow him through the various interesting episodes of this visit, but before taking up his work on his return, as it appears in the Common School Act of 1846 and the reports which preceded and followed immediately on that measure, it will be necessary to review briefly the state of the common schools of Canada West when he accepted office.

The elementary schools of Upper Canada had been organized into something approaching system by the acts of 1841 and 1843. Parliamentary aid to the extent of £20,000 annually supplemented the local effort. Schools were generally established in all the older settled parts of the country, and were to some extent under the oversight of a provincial superintendent and local superintendents. But there were several fatal defects in the so-called system. The central authority was weak. It was authorized by the law to apportion the grant, to receive reports, and to make regulations for the schools. But it lacked authority to enforce its regulations or to secure proper reports, and its principal function was the distribution of the parliamentary grant. The local authorities, consisting of the district or township superintendent, the district, town or city municipal council, and the trustees, were possessed of large powers, but were generally incompetent for their exercise. The powers and duties of the local superintendents were the examination and licensing of teachers, the inspection of the schools, the making of reports to the provincial superintendent and the distribution of the provincial and county grant. But as these duties were associated most frequently with other employment, they were often performed in the most superficial manner, and there was absolutely no uniformity of standard in the qualification of teachers; and it is perhaps not too much to say that the majority of them were quite inefficient. The municipal councils possessed absolute authority in the selection and appointment of these superintendents, there being no standard of qualification; and the same body fixed their remuneration, and hence the grade of service which they were able to render. The other powers of the municipal council consisted in levying a county assessment to equal the parliamentary grant, and the formation of school sections. To the local trustees were assigned some of the most important functions. They selected and *hired* the teacher, they determined the character and appointments of the schoolroom and the text books to be used, and to their regulations the teacher was responsible, as the regulations of the provincial authorities were recommendatory and not imperative. One power they lacked: they could establish a school only for those who desired it and were willing to pay, they could not make it a school for all the children. Finally, while model schools were encouraged and established in the older districts at which teachers might learn by example, there was no efficient high class provision for the thorough professional training of teachers.

Such a system among a people the most of whom had grown up without enjoyment of proper school advantages and whose circumstances made the keeping down of expenses one of the most influential considerations of their lives, was certain to produce miserable school houses, haphazard school books and poor teachers, and even these inefficient provisions reached only a part of the population. In the state of New York from which they had been originally borrowed they were already largely modified so as to obviate the chief objections.

For the work of reconstructing this inefficient system and of remedying its great defects, no man was better qualified than Dr. Ryerson. He had himself grown up and had been educated under its influence. He had seen it in its best and in its worst results. He had lived in touch with it all his life, now over forty years. A large part of his life work had been in the field of education, and he knew the people of the country, their wants and their possibilities as few men knew them. Moreover his careful conservative habit of mind made him a safe as well as a practical and successful reformer of defects. In addressing himself to his task, the comprehensive grasp of his mind, his clear judgment, and keen observation revealed to him at once both the important defects in the existing system and their real causes. He has set these before us very fully in his first and fundamental reports, and with the defects he sets forth the remedies. First of all, properly qualified teachers must be provided, proper school house accommodation and equipment, proper and uniform text books and proper inspection of schools. To secure these with fair uniformity and efficiency they must be more largely controlled or directed from the central provincial department. These important elements were now entirely in the hands of the local authorities, and the result was a body of starved and inefficient schools with here and there a notable exception. To secure the necessary central control and direction without creating fatal antagonism was a task calling for the very highest qualities of the wise statesman, clearly defined ends, good judgment as to ways and means, courage and firmness in administration, and yet sympathy with the difficulties and forbearance with even the prejudices of the people. The success of Dr. Ryerson's effort is the

best proof of the high order of ability which he
brought to his work.

As we have seen, before entering upon his work
he had devoted a year to the study of the school
systems of many lands, but it is evident from the
results that he was most deeply impressed by three,
those of Prussia, Ireland and Massachusetts. In
Prussia he had seen the advantages of strong and
wise central direction and authority. In Ireland he
had found a promising solution of the religious
question in education to which we must presently
devote specific attention, and in Massachusetts he
had found examples and methods of dealing with
many of the problems which arise in the application
of a central administrative system to a free people
in this western world. But while learning from all
these, his mind was too independent and original to
borrow any one of them or use it as a model.
His strong conservative instinct led him to build
upon historic foundations and to use the materials
which had grown up ready to his hand. His work
was not to sweep these away but to mould them to
his great ends. He found a central superintendency
and a board of education; he increased the power
and extended the functions of these until they were
sufficient for his purposes. He found a local superintendency; he brought it under proper control
and responsibility, made it a profession in the work
of education, occupying the entire time and gifts of
qualified men who should make this their only and

lifelong calling. He found the municipal councils
taking part in the work, and he skilfully encouraged as well as directed their co-operation in the
task without depriving them of a single function
which they had previously exercised, and, as in a
few years the municipal system was perfected in
form, he adapted its educational functions to the
more perfect municipal institutions. He found as
the fundamental element of the whole system
boards of school trustees elected according to immemorial Saxon custom by the assembly of the
people. These too he adopted, and without seeming
to deprive them of any of their accustomed functions, he first of all gave them experience and
continuity of life as a body corporate by making
each member hold office for three years, while the
continuous interest was maintained by the annual
election of one new member of the board, and
by the annual discussion of all school matters at
the school meeting of all the ratepayers. While
skilfully stimulating their ambition to have a good
school through the inspectors' reports and free publication of results and honourable mention whenever possible or deserved, and by insisting on at
least a minimum of efficiency, he secured them
from personal liability by making them a corporate
body of trustees, so that the whole people whom
they represented, and not the mere patrons of the
school were liable for their lawful action; and at the
same time he gave them such power to levy school

rates as well as fees as should secure adequate support. As an offset to the limited financial views of local authorities, he made the parliamentary grant a stimulus to larger liberality, helping those who helped themselves, and making the minimum of efficiency an indispensable condition to sharing in the public grants.

The Common School Act of 1846 seemed then to be but an amendment here and there, somewhat thorough it is true, but still no more than an amendment of that of 1843. But in reality it was inspired by a new principle of life. The old system dealt out a legislative grant and left the individual schools very much to care for themselves, scarcely securing even a complete return of the number and attendance at the schools. The new system directed the whole educational force of the country into a combined, wise, scientific effort for the proper education of every child of the land, and held every officer of the system to proper responsibility both to the people and to the central government. On no point was Dr. Ryerson more careful than to make it appear that his system was in thorough harmony with the principles of responsible government. At the one end of the system he maintained the most thorough responsibility to parliament through report of the entire work of the department as a branch of the civil service. At the other end he brought the local trustees of each school section under responsibility to the local meeting of ratepayers, as well as the local superintendents to the municipal authorities. The new political principle was that, under this universal responsibility, there was instituted all along the line a strong executive. Every officer from the chief superintendent to the local trustee was invested with power, and held responsible for its exercise, both to the people and their representatives, and also to the higher executive authorities. But on the other hand the enforcement of responsibility or of penalty for neglect was in no case matter of individual judgment. The delinquent could be displaced only by the authority by which he was appointed, or punished by regular process of law. There was no room for individual caprice.

It is thus evident that Dr. Ryerson very fairly claimed that his system was based throughout on the principles of responsible government; at the same time it is equally certain that it was animated by the idea of a thoroughly effective government. To this efficiency his own strong convictions, clear judgment and masterful character were largely contributory. Separated as he was by at least one remove from the changing forces of popular political life, he felt himself, like the men who have with so remarkable a record presided in our courts of justice, shielded from those transient and changeful currents of popular influence which must be felt by the ordinary minister of the crown. The latter can assert his manhood and his convictions only by

171

holding office loosely, as a thing which he will at any time resign rather than compromise his principles. Dr. Ryerson held that the dignity and importance of the work in which he was engaged demanded, as in the administration of justice, absolute independence of action and position. He felt that this work was a sacred calling to be directed by fundamental principles, and not by considerations of temporary expediency, as expressed by the changes of popular opinion, and that it demanded, by its very nature, stability and permanency of method as well as of ideal.

Two principles which he adopted from the outset as the very basis of his system were destined to give rise to no little difficulty in the future. One was that religion and morality are essential elements in all education. We have already seen how steadily he held by this principle in the discussion of the university question, and we shall presently see how large and difficult were the problems to which it gave rise in the field of elementary schools.

The other was that the state provision of education should be comprehensive, bringing its advantages as a matter of equal rights to every child irrespective of creed, wealth, or class. We have seen that these two principles were to him matters of sacred conviction and essential justice at every period of his career. They appear in every controversy in which he took part, and always ranked with him as higher and more imperative than even the very important political maxim of the complete independence of church and state.

Before entering on the special study of the free school question and the separate school question as they appear in the work of Dr. Ryerson, we must devote a little space to another important aspect of his system as he introduced it from the beginning, viz., the normal school as a provision for the training of teachers. Up to the time of Dr. Ryerson's taking office the only provision in this direction was the model school in each district. These were merely better schools, they made no provision for either practical or theoretical training in the art of teaching. As usual, in this work he started from a sound fundamental principle, to create a fountain-head of good teaching and well-trained teachers and wait till its streams flowed forth to enrich the whole land. His report on a normal school followed close upon his report on a system of common schools, and a year later he succeeded in his task of founding the Toronto Normal school.

His wisdom in this foundation was in no way more conspicuous than in the choice of the principal and first masters of the school. Thomas Jaffray Robertson, M.A., was a man whose power over students has seldom been equalled. In remote parts of the country long years after they had left the "Normal," we have met with students still under the spell of his power. His original methods of teaching reappeared in every county in Ontario and passed down to the second and third generations of teachers. Henry Youle Hind, M.A., the distinguished scientist, was afterward to win fame in a wider field. The Rev. William Ormiston, M.A., was another of the mighty men of his choice in that early day, followed by J. H. Sangster, M.A., M.D., another strong man. Dr. Ryerson was preëminently a believer that the power to educate lay in the mental and moral power of the teacher and not in his mere technical learning, and in the choice of such men he laid one of the very strongest foundations of his new system.

No large part of the instruction of the normal school in those days was devoted to theories of education, or to what is known as "scientific pedagogics." Lectures were given on the management and organization of a school, and perhaps on the history of education, but the strength of the school lay in thorough mastery of the subjects to be subsequently taught, in the example and influence of master teachers, and the criticism of the practical efforts of the normal students by experienced teachers in the model school. But though the method might to-day be considered empirical, the results in a very few years raised the standard of teaching in every part of the province, and provided able teachers for all the centres of population, as well as many of the better rural schools, and also furnished an experienced and efficient class of men to act as local inspectors.

174

SUMMARY OF THE SYSTEM

The system thus introduced by Dr. Ryerson in 1846, and much more completely by the act of 1850 which has really been the foundation of all subsequent school legislation, was by no means completed at one stroke. Apart from the great questions of free schools, separate schools, and grammar or high schools which have in some sense a distinct history of their own, experience suggested many minor improvements and adaptations to the growing development of the country and the rising standard of intellectual life which was the result of the successful work of the school systems. But the fundamental principles and even machinery were adopted from the very outset, and were so wisely chosen that each subsequent change seemed only natural historic growth. The following summary may represent the main elements of the system as introduced between 1846 and 1850, the principles of which we have already discussed:

1. It was brought into operation in every school section in the province by an annual meeting of the freeholders and householders of the section. At this meeting school matters were reported and discussed, a trustee board formed or filled for the ensuing year, and the manner of raising school monies for the next year determined, whether by fees, by taxation, or both.

2. The trustee board thus formed was made a body corporate, responsible for and holding all school property for the section, and with full

175

powers to provide school room, teachers and equipment, and to appoint a secretary-treasurer and a collector, or to apply to the township or municipality for the collection of all such school rates as were raised by general taxation of all taxable property in the section. They were required to see that the school was conducted according to law, that uniform and authorized text books were used, and to make a full annual report according to legal form to the local superintendent, which report was also read at the annual school meeting, the report to shew the time the school was kept open, the money expended and how raised, the number of children in the section and the number attending school, the branches of education taught and the visits of inspection, examinations and other special exercises connected with the school during the year, thus bringing the whole work of the school for the year under review.

3. It made full provision for the proper qualification of teachers, and made them accountable for their duties in the school to the trustees and to the local superintendent of schools. The qualification of teachers was secured through a county board of education consisting of the grammar school trustees and the local superintendent or superintendents of schools for the county.

4. It made it the duty of municipal councils in the townships and in cities, towns and incorporated villages, to levy assessments as desired by the

trustees, or to authorize loans for the purchase or erection of school buildings, to form proper school sections, and to report all acts of the council affecting the schools to the local superintendent.

5. It made it the duty of the county municipal council to appoint the local superintendents and the grammar school trustees, who formed the county board of education, and to levy, by a county school rate, a sum at least equal to the share of the parliamentary school grant allotted to the county. The provision of public libraries was also placed in the hands of the municipal council of the county and the county board of education.

6. It made full provision for the appointment, support and duties of the local superintendents of schools. It not only provided for thorough inspection of schools, but it placed in the hands of the inspectors power to enforce the observance of the law by giving them authority to distribute the school grant under conditions of the fulfilment of all legal requirements, and also power to act as arbitrators in case of dispute on school matters, subject to appeal to the chief superintendent. It gave also the power to cancel or suspend teachers' certificates for neglect of duty, or inefficiency in its discharge or breach of law. The local superintendents thus became the executive officers through whom the most important provisions of the law were enforced. A local visitorial power was also placed in the hands of clergymen, judges, members

of parliament, magistrates, and municipal council-lors, by which a local interest and confidence in the schools might be created in the minds of the people.

7. At the centre of this system, with adequate powers to secure energy and efficiency in its entire working, was placed the chief superintendent of schools, and the council of public instruction. The chief superintendent was invested with duties and powers for the province corresponding to those of the local superintendents in their district. They were required to report to him, and the final executive administration of the whole system was under his supervision, with power to direct and enforce its efficient operation, and with judicial powers either on reference or appeal. His direct power of enforcement lay in the administration of the legislative grant. The law must be observed, or the warrant for the money was not issued. His power of direction lay in, the preparation of the forms and regulations through which the provisions of the law were to be observed.

Matters of more obvious legislation, such as the authorization of text books, rules for the govern-ment and discipline of schools, and the entire responsibility and direction of the normal school were wisely placed in the hands of the council of public instruction, who also prescribed the classi-fication, qualification, and subjects of examination of teachers.

PERSONAL INFLUENCE

The simplicity, unity, and efficiency of this system are its highest praise. It was built upon no theory of education. It involved no complicated machinery. It was not unduly centralized. It involved the intelligent coöperation of the people of the whole country, and of all the bodies responsible for executive government and legislation. It thus made the schools at once the schools of the people, of the counties and of the province, almost compelling an interest in them at every point. But beyond all this, its grand success—for its success every one must acknowledge — depended in no small measure upon the energy, the wisdom, the administrative ability and the tireless industry of the grand personality who stood at its head as chief superintendent. Devoting his magnificent abilities to this one work, turned aside from it by no complications of the political, the ecclesiastical, or the commercial world, he put the energy of his life into it, and that energy was felt throughout the entire system. But even his work could not have been so complete apart from the coöperation of a younger man who mastered all details, compiled all reports, and generalized all particulars, and kept before the eye of his chief the entire working of the system. J. George Hodgins was the indispensable complement of Dr. Ryerson, and no one knew or appreciated this more than the doctor himself.

A system introducing forces and principles so decidedly new in Canadian educational life was not

to be launched without strong opposition. Perhaps
its most disturbing characteristic was the fact that
in almost all its features it touched the pockets of
the people who had never before regarded education as a matter in which they had any special
concern, and also of the people who desired education, but at as cheap a rate as possible. It demanded qualified and efficient teachers, and this
called for better salaries; the Gore district council
proclaimed throughout the country that old men
and cripples, who could do nothing else, and poor
immigrants, glad of work at any wage, were quite
competent for this work. It demanded uniform
text books of better quality, and loyal and British
in their teachings; many people thought that the
school books were a matter of indifference. It called
for school houses properly built, warmed and ven-
tilated, and provided with proper furniture, maps,
and other means of teaching; the whole community
who were taxed for these purposes rebelled against
the expense. It required a moderate outlay for
administration and inspection, both general and
local; several district councils united in proclaiming
this a useless waste of money. All the essential
features of the system which contributed directly
to improve the character of the schools were thus
assailed, nominally as unnecessary, but really on
the ground of expense. A people who had grown
up themselves under the school bill of 1816 were
seemingly utterly without power to appreciate the

need of better things. A few places were noble exceptions to this outburst of ignorant opposition. The municipal council of the Colborne district (Peterborough) was conspicuous in its enlightened support of the new measures, while in the far east municipal authorities refused to recognize or to act under the new law.

The opposition was first encountered in the parliament itself. As the bill was prepared by Dr. Ryerson and introduced by the government, it aimed at bringing education within reach of all the people, poor as well as rich. For this purpose it proposed not at first to make the schools entirely free, but it looked in this direction, and many clauses of the bill making provision for this were eliminated or so modified as to be ineffective. In 1848 a new administration came into power, personally opposed or unfavourable to Dr. Ryerson, and, without consulting him, a new bill was introduced in 1849 making still further changes, crippling the power of administration and inspection. One of the objections of those who were unwilling to appear illiberal in the matter of education was that the system placed too much power in the hands of the central authority; that in fact it was the introduction of a Prussian despotism, with the chief superintendent as absolute monarch. While the new bill copied verbatim all the local provisions of the act of 1846, and thus seemed to maintain the system in the main intact, yet by restoring the old

181

township superintendents, by making the district board of education an appointment not of the municipal council but of the governor-in-council (and so political), and by limiting the powers of the chief superintendent and council of public instruction, and throwing the text book question back upon local authorities, it took the strength, the unity and the efficiency out of the system, and gave scope once more for that ignorant prejudice and selfish penuriousness which had nullified all previous attempts at educational advancement. The animus of the whole measure was manifest in one of its first clauses, which reduced the moderate salary of £500 assigned to the chief superintendent to £420, a magnificent saving to the country of $320! Mr. Baldwin, fortunately, was too enlightened and high-minded a statesman to descend to pettiness or to be deceived as to the results of such a measure, and although the bill—introduced by an individual member, who lived to see his mistake and make generous amends—was passed through the House, it was, on Mr. Baldwin's advice, disallowed by the governor, and in 1850 Dr. Ryerson was given opportunity in a new school act to advance the system towards his ideal conception.

The act of 1850 was the complete foundation of that school system which Ontario maintains to-day, and which has commanded the admiration of the whole civilized world. The battle for the fundamentals of the system was by no means ended when the act of 1850 was passed. Other grave questions arose, the history of which is still before us. But with the passage of the act of 1850 the victory was won for the system, and in contending for that victory Dr. Ryerson had exhibited all the characteristics of the true British statesman. He was courageous in the face of opposition, patient and wise in his measures in the midst of difficulty, strong and clearly defined in his convictions and policy, and not afraid to resign at once when by the passage of the bill of 1849 he seemed to be defeated, thus maintaining his manly independence and the strength and truth of his principles. The results have more than justified his course.

Our review of Dr. Ryerson's system of common schools would be incomplete without some reference to two or three important adjuncts of that system, which furnished excellent service at this time, but which are now remembered only by the older people. The first of these was the educational depository. The supply of the new uniform text books to the 200,000 school children of the country offered so obvious a field for commercial enterprise that it might safely be left to the trade, only taking care to protect the public as to price and quality. This was from the beginning the policy both of the council of public instruction and of the chief superintendent. Having obtained permission for the free use of the Irish national series of text books, which they resolved to adopt, these rights were transferred to responsible dealers who agreed to furnish books of approved workmanship and reasonable price. But other matters requisite for efficient or high-class schools did not as yet offer the same encouragement to commercial enterprise. They were not the things universally necessary and soon worn out by use, and hence in continuous demand in large quantities. Such were philosophical apparatus, illustrative specimens, and advanced books required by teachers, or for school libraries or prizes. All these were at first the luxuries of education, the demand for them was limited, and their use needed encouragement, as leading to the highest perfection in the work of education Such encouragement Dr. Ryerson secured in the form of government assistance to all schools making an effort to secure these higher and more perfect aids in their work. The requisite voucher being presented that the articles required were *bona fide* for the use of the teacher or of the school, they were furnished from the educational depository at half the cost price. The teachers of forty and fifty years ago will remember very distinctly the large assistance afforded in their work and especially in the improvement of their schools or of their own scholarship by those simple, liberal, but thus necessary provisions. A holiday visit to Toronto nearly always resulted in bringing home something which added to the interest and intellectual life of the school. Even the country log

184

school house often had its case in which were preserved the means of illustrating the zones and the changes of the seasons, and the mysteries of square and cube root; and a few well-selected prize books were indeed light-bearers in the darkness in the days when books were still not abundant.

Associated with this depository was the educational museum, which still survives in its enlarged and modern form. The art critics of to-day will perhaps smile at the copies of the old masters imported from France, Germany and Italy. But in those days they served their purpose, and sowed the seeds of that æsthetic life which to-day is developing a true Canadian art.

Closely associated with the depository was the scheme for the establishment of public school libraries throughout the country. These were not libraries for use in the school, but libraries for the people and attached to the school. The object was to improve the taste and intelligence of the adult population, as well as of the senior scholars. This had been a favourite idea with Dr. Ryerson for many years. When the first suggestion was made to him by Lord Sydenham of undertaking the superintendence and improvement of the public school system, he connected with it in his own mind and in his private letters this wider object. In his opinion no people could exercise the exalted responsibilities of self-government apart from morality and intelligence, and at a time when the intelligence of the people was far less widely affected by the public press than now, he looked very largely to the public library planted in the public school to give the whole people that higher knowledge which would make them wise, patriotic, broad-minded citizens. Science, too, was then beginning the wonderful and brilliant career of discovery which has been the most remarkable characteristic of the nineteenth century, and her work had not yet grown so technical as to be beyond the power of ordinary intelligence to follow with both profit and interest. The refinement of the public taste by means of poetry and literature was also before his mind. In all these respects he had been deeply interested and impressed by the ideas of Horace Mann, as expressed in his reports and addresses on the school system of Massachusetts. His earlier conceptions on this subject may be illustrated by the following paragraph from the close of his report of 1846:—"The advantages of the school can be but very partially enjoyed unless they are continued and extended by means of books. As the school is the pupil's first teacher, so books are his second; in the former he acquires the elements of knowledge, in the latter he acquires knowledge itself; in the former he converses with the schoolmaster, in the latter he holds intercourse with the greatest and wisest men in all ages, and countries and professions, on all subjects and in every variety of style. But in any community few persons can be expected to possess the means necessary to procure anything like a general assortment of books—in a new and rural community perhaps none. One library for the whole community is the best substitute. Each one acquires the fruits of the united contributions of all, and the teacher and the poor man with his family participate in the common advantage."

The outcome of these ideas was the provision made in the early school acts for the establishment of township or district circulating libraries. Through the depository a supply of appropriate and judiciously selected books was brought within easy reach. By means of a supplementary legislative grant the effort to secure this boon was substantially aided. By a simple system of sections circulating from school to school, a very considerable library was brought within reach of every school section in the township or county. The care of the books was provided for through the municipal officers, the trustees and the teachers; and many older persons will remember with hearty appreciation the advantages accruing to many municipalities forty years ago from these provisions.

CHAPTER VIII

THE DEVELOPMENT OF THE SCHOOL SYSTEM

THE school system established on a firm foundation by the act of 1850, contemplated two main objects, comprehensiveness or universality and efficiency. While there were many obstacles which interfered with the attainment of the latter object, such as the lack of qualified teachers, the lack of proper school buildings and furniture, and the lack of proper text books, the great obstacle to the accomplishment of the first purpose was the matter of expense. Under the act of 1843 the expense of the school fell largely upon the parents of the children attending school, who paid by subscription or rate bill, seldom less than 7s., 6d. a quarter. The result of the system was that in 1845, when Dr. Ryerson began his work, the number of children in the province of school age was estimated by Mr. Hodgins at 198,434, of whom 110,002, or 55 per cent., attended school. This included all who were in attendance during any part of the year, and as the average time during which the school was kept open was $9\frac{2}{3}$ months, when the usual allowance is made for absence it will be seen that the schools, such as they were, were not reaching at any time one half of the children of the country. Dr.

Ryerson's first object was to give the advantages of a good school to every child in the land from five to sixteen years of age. This object attained would certainly mean a high average of intelligence for the whole country. Even eight years of effective schooling out of the eleven years of school age would be a vast advance on the state of things with which he commenced.

His practical knowledge of the country and of the people convinced him at the outset that the remedy lay in free schools and compulsory education. But these two means involved an exercise of executive authority for which the country was by no means prepared. The first school bill introduced by Dr. Ryerson contained provision for the option of free schools by a majority of the ratepayers of the school section. The provision was eliminated by the legislature. The act of 1850 restored this provision, and so opened the question in every school section of the province. Many can still remember the contention which arose through the country over this measure and the profound discussions by political philosophers over the rights of property and the responsibilities of parents. Dr. Ryerson was too wise to propose any arbitrary measure. He secured provision of law by which the people could all in their own time ordain that their own school should be free, and left that provision to work its own way through the influence of enlightened convictions and higher interests. But in each annual report, as well as in his public addresses, he kept before the minds of the people such principles as these : a free country requires an intelligent people ; a common school education is the right of every child in the land ; the property which is accumulated by the help of the common industry and intelligence of the people, and protected as well as increased in value by the institutions of the land, is justly chargeable with that which is absolutely necessary for the general welfare of the country, and to enable every man born in the country to discharge the common duties of citizenship for the common good. Slowly, it is true, but still surely these principles made their way, assisted by the fact that the majority of ratepayers, especially in the newer parts of the country, had children of their own to be educated. In 1858, 45 per cent. of the schools were wholly free, and 38 per cent. more partially so, *i.e.*, they charged less than the legal maximum of school fees, while 74 per cent. of the children of school age were now found in the schools. In 1865, no less than 83 per cent. of the schools of the province were entirely free, and nearly 85 per cent. of the school population were in attendance at the schools. It easily and naturally followed that in 1871 all the schools were made free by law. No better illustration could be given of the patient wisdom by which Dr. Ryerson pursued and attained his great ends.

The other aspect of the development of the

school system in the quality and efficiency of the schools involved much more complicated problems and a much more varied history.

The first point in the efficiency of a school is the qualification of the teacher. We have no means of ascertaining the average or even the maximum qualification of the teachers of Upper Canada in 1845. The average salary paid, £29, or $116 a year, indicates a low standard. For the first few years the certificates were issued by the local superintendents, and while the total number of teachers possessing such certificates was nearly equal to that of the schools, no certain opinion can be formed as to the extent of qualification. There was no definite standard of attainments; and the examination of the teacher was entirely personal.

In 1847 the normal school was opened and a standard was prescribed for first and second class provincial certificates of qualification. This was shortly afterwards followed up by the act of 1850 establishing county boards of education with authority to issue first, second and third class certificates of qualification according to a specific programme of examination. In 1857 the results of these measures were apparent in the fact that of nearly 4,000 teachers, 640 possessed first class certificates, over 2,000 second class, and less than 1,000 were teaching on certificates of the lowest class. By this date 734 teachers had already graduated from the normal school in the first or the second class, constituting a considerable percentage of the teachers of that class throughout the province and extending the influence of their professional training throughout the schools of the entire system. County teachers' associations were now very generally established under the advice and influence of the county superintendents, and through the aid of these the influence of the normal school graduates was extended to all grades of teachers, as their methods of teaching were used as examples and illustrations. In the schools conducted by the normal graduates many of the county teachers received their training under what might be termed a Lancasterian system. By this date, through this improvement in the qualification of teachers, there might be found in almost every county in Ontario schools of a grade of efficiency of which any country might be proud. The people who ten years before had rebelled against the expensiveness of the new system and were willing to place the education of their children in the hands of cripples, worn out old men and stranded immigrants, were now becoming jealous of the reputation of their school and quite ambitious to have the very best in the county.

The furnishing of the schools was also rapidly improved. Brick and stone buildings of handsome architectural appearance replaced the old log and frame structures; proper means of heating and ventilation were supplied; maps, blackboards and other apparatus were secured; and above all, the old benches and high wall desks were superseded by comfortable seats and desks in which the pupils were ranged two and two, facing the teacher and the long platform from which his blackboards and maps were displayed. With these improvements new methods of order and systematic work were introduced, class instruction superseded the individualism of the early days, and an orderly programme, in itself an important element of education, became possible in every school.

At the very outset of his work Dr. Ryerson recognized the possibility of a still higher standard of school work in the towns, cities and even incorporated villages. In 1847, his first bill, making special provision for these centres of population, was introduced. The object from the beginning of these special provisions was the construction of the schools of the city or town into an educational system. The first step in this direction was the appointment of a larger board of trustees who had charge of all the public schools of the municipality, maintained them from a common school fund, and appointed a local superintendent of the whole. From this the steps were easy to a graded school system for the city or town. Primary schools were established for the several sections or wards in which the junior pupils were taught by themselves in schools convenient to their homes, while the elder pupils were massed in a graded central school of more advanced forms, and this at a later period was sometimes combined with the grammar school, under the designation of a union school. Perhaps the most widely known example of the successful working of this system was to be found in the city of Hamilton under the direction of Mr. A. Macallum, one of the first graduates of the normal school. It was no slight tribute to Dr. Ryerson that in the very district which was the centre of rebellion against his new system in 1847, there should be found the most successful illustration and the most enthusiastic working out of his most advanced ideas of high class public schools.

In the larger city of Toronto the graded school system was worked out on another model. The ward schools were each one a graded school covering the whole field of public school work from the most elementary to the highest form. Here the grammar school work was always kept distinct. In smaller towns and villages, the graded system was introduced as a single central school with several rooms and teachers covering the whole work as in the ward schools of Toronto.

Such were some of the steps by which the school system through the fifties and the sixties was gradually developed to higher perfection. In this process much was left to local enterprise and co-operation. From time to time legislation was introduced which opened the way for improvement. Especially after the perfection of our municipal system, by the act of 1856, the whole school system was harmonized with the improved forms of municipal government. But the object of these new provisions of the school law was not to force a cast-iron form of schools upon the people, but to provide facilities by which they could themselves work out in their own way and according to local needs and ability the higher models which were thus placed before them. The municipal relations of education were thus very fully developed under Dr. Ryerson's direction. As the school law finally passed from his hands, all common or public schools, whether in townships, incorporated villages, towns or cities, were placed under the control of trustees elected directly by the people and forming a distinct body corporate for the purpose of the school alone. Education was in this way separated, not only from general politics, but also from municipal interests of other kinds. Constituting in itself an interest of the most permanent character, requiring continuity of policy and an income not subject to fluctuations, the independence of the educational work and of the board to which it is committed is a most important principle in the system.

It was a bold policy which ventured to place so much power in the hands of trustees, enabling them to apply to the municipal council for the levying of all monies required for the proper maintenance of the schools. Had such a provision been suggested in 1846, or even in 1850, it would in all probability have been at once rejected. But after the schools had advanced step by step both in efficiency and popularity, until by the voluntary act of an intelligent people they were made free to all, it was an easy matter to secure assent to a law, which required the municipal councils to collect with the other local taxes, the ways and means for the support of the schools. To transfer the management of the schools even now to the municipal bodies would doubtless result in their rapid deterioration. To give these bodies power to limit the expenditure of the school trustees would tend in the same direction. It is a peculiar feature under any government, that one body should be responsible for raising the funds and another for their expenditure. But the peculiar circumstances and the unusual importance of the interest involved we think fully justify the anomaly, and have commended it to the common sense of the people. The school under Dr. Ryerson's system is not a local but rather a national interest. The child is educated not merely as an inhabitant of a particular locality, but also as a future citizen. The whole country on that basis contributes to the support of every local school. The county school rate is an intermediate link in the same direction. The school trustees are thus not merely the representatives of the local interest. Theirs is like that of members of parliament, a wider responsibility. Their duty is not merely to furnish public services, sidewalks, street lights and so forth, to a locality for the

197

coming year, but to furnish the country with an intelligent citizenship for a whole generation. Such wider and higher responsibility demands a centralization of power and an independence of action, passing beyond the ordinary limits of municipal government, and justifies the apparent anomaly. Occasionally attempts are made from the municipal side to create dissatisfaction by representing the school trustees as an irresponsible body who load the people with taxes. But the patriotic instinct of the people has protected them against such unworthy suggestions. They are well satisfied, provided they have really good schools, to provide the means for their support, and they do not forget that school trustees as well as municipal councils are directly and finally responsible to the people, and they have manifested no desire to make them, in addition to this, responsible to the municipal council. The collection of the school funds by the officers of the municipality is after all only a matter of economy and convenience. In the nature of the case it cannot imply that the municipal body is responsible either for the amount or for its proper expenditure. To attempt because of this common sense economical provision to bring the educational system completely under municipal control would prove fatal. Education, like the administration of justice to which Dr. Ryerson often compared it, is an interest of the nation, as well as of the locality and the individual. It is one of the glories of the Ontario system that it has so well preserved the balance of controlling forces, keeping both these important interests so largely out of the field both of local and general politics, and combining both local and central supervision and support.

A second municipal duty in relation to public school education is provision for supervision by the appointment of public school inspectors. These officers constitute one of the most important elements in the system. When Dr. Ryerson began his work, inspection was provided for by township superintendents, but, as we have seen, these officers, except as clerks for the distribution of the school fund, were either in large part incompetent or perfunctory in the discharge of their duty. The superintendency of the schools was not their chief work. The first step was the appointment of county inspectors, whose whole time should be given to this work. A second step was provision for thorough qualification. Professional training, experience in practical teaching, and a high-grade teacher's certificate were successively demanded for this important work. The rapid improvement of the schools was doubtless largely due to this feature of the system. At an early day the best graduates of the normal school were rapidly passed into this commanding office, and through them the influence of the normal school reached every part of their district. In the cities and towns the inspector was appointed by the public school board directly, and became their executive officer and professional counsel. In no part of the system was the influence of the inspector as an efficient officer more evident than here. With the development of graded schools along the two lines which we have already described, under efficient and able inspectors the organization and perfection of the schools made very rapid and gratifying progress in all the cities, and the larger towns, where the system but slightly differed, by no means fell behind. We have before referred to the cities of Toronto and Hamilton as conspicuous examples of the two methods of grading schools, and as forming city systems, one adapted to a city covering a more extended area, the other to a city where all the older children were within reach of a central school. This latter system, slightly modified, became the type for the larger towns, and in a short time beautiful and commodious central schools, as well as neat, comfortable and conveniently located primary schools, became a prominent feature of our then rising towns, which are now numbered among our cities.

The material and visible improvement in school buildings and architecture was, perhaps, the readiest measure of the improvement in the educational status of the schools. Dr. Ryerson served his province as chief superintendent thirty-three years, the life of a single generation. At the beginning of that time the public school buildings even of Toronto were an eyesore; at the end they were in almost every town of ambition or consequence the pride of the people and the chief ornament of the place, fitly representing the high character of the intellectual life within. It may be said that all this was the natural result of the growth of the people in wealth and intelligence. True, but it was the result of that growth under a system which called out their enterprise, enlisted their interest, wisely composed their differences and united their energies, and which directed their efforts by placing before them patiently and continuously the best models and methods.

It is not easy to form a true estimate of the personal influence of Dr. Ryerson in this remarkable process of the development of our public school system. We have already noted that at its very foundation he wisely utilized the common forces which move human society in such a way as to make the work grow by its own inner vitality. His work was not so much to force a system upon an unwilling people, as to construct a system so accommodated to the needs, the interests, the habits, and even the selfish motives of the people, that they would readily and naturally adopt it as their own. In a few years its success became to them a matter of honest pride. The intelligence and enterprise of trustees, the ambition of teachers to excel, the patriotic liberality of municipal bodies, the fidelity and ability of inspectors, even the emulation of the school children and the sympathetic

coöperation of the whole people became powerfully
enlisted in this work. The schools seemed to grow
of themselves. But behind all this there was a wise,
sympathetic, unostentatious, but powerful mind at
the helm. One secret of his success, as we have
already seen, lay in the choice of the ablest young
men as his helpers in various departments of the
work. Another lay in his unusual skill in avoiding
or overcoming difficulties. His interpretation and
administration of school law was remarkable in its
success, and in this Dr. Hodgins was his right-hand
man. But these were a part of the progressive
movement of the system; his most important work
was always in advance of that movement, the
discovery and the devising of new and more perfect
things as the country was prepared for them. For
this purpose he kept in constant touch with the
school work and the men most intelligently interested in it throughout the entire province. He
made a special study of the county superintendents' reports. He made periodical tours through
the province, calling conventions of trustees, superintendents, municipal officers, teachers, and all persons interested in education, and discussing at
length with them the questions which seemed to
require advanced legislation. He was at the same
time a diligent student of the progress of education
in other countries, and for this purpose made
extended and repeated visits abroad, to become
personally acquainted with the working of new

methods and educational theories. And yet he was least of all things a theorist. His mind was peculiarly practical and conservative, and adopted nothing except under conviction of its utility, and with most intimate knowledge of the conditions of his own people, he moulded all new things to their needs and capacity.

The results of this constant mental activity appear in his annual reports which are admirable digests not only of the progress of the work but also of suggested improvements, which were frequently the precursors of new legislation. As we have already seen, the School Act of 1850 was the broad and fairly complete basis of the whole educational system. Dr. Ryerson was too wise a legislator to render his work nugatory by too frequent or too radical changes. When the act of 1850 was followed up by the supplementary act of 1855 it was merely a step forward. The powers of trustees were more clearly defined and extended, so that the efficiency of the school could not be prevented by legal quibbles or individual obstinacy. The danger that separate schools might be made to destroy the unity and comprehensiveness of the system was guarded against, and provision was made for the extended usefulness of the Journal of Education, for the establishment of the Museum of Art, and for larger legislative aid to the schools. In like manner the amendment act of 1860 secured more perfectly the discharge of the duties of trustees by enforcing reports, providing for proper audit, insisting that trustees should be properly qualified in the section for which they were elected, and by demanding proper notice of all legal meetings of school trustees. It prohibited trustees from any interest in contracts for school supplies or buildings, gave them power to sell school property, called for definite written agreement between trustees and teacher. It provided a more definite programme for the examination and classification of teachers by the county boards. From these examples it will be seen that the successive acts of legislation proposed by Dr. Ryerson for twenty years after the full establishment of the new system in 1850, involved no important change of the system. They aimed rather at growth and perfection, and at remedy of practical defects, which the working out of the system had revealed.

The second most important period in the history of our common school legislation was ushered in by the act of 1870-71. The subject of education had at confederation been placed in the hands of the provincial legislature, and in this act it for the first time grappled with the problems presented by the common schools, which were now named public schools. The act of 1870-71 was supplemented by that of 1874, and the two together represent Dr. Ryerson's last legislative work on behalf of the schools of Ontario.

Preceding this legislation Dr. Ryerson made his

fourth and final educational tour in Europe and America, and also held his fifth and last series of conventions through the province, discussing the most important features of the new legislation. The legislation itself was also shaped on the basis of our new federal and provincial constitution, and thus may be considered as the beginning of what may be regarded as a reconstruction of the school system. It is a fact noted by Dr. Hodgins that a principal objection to this proposed legislation was the fear of the people that the system of 1850 would be materially changed. The system which in 1848-9 had excited such violent opposition as an introduction of Prussian despotism was in 1870 so prized and had so completely commended itself to the judgment and affections of the people, that they looked with jealousy upon any proposal for change. Commended abroad as one of the best, if not the best in the world, and the ground of honest pride at home, it was now being carefully shielded by the very people who once regarded it as a foreign intrusion.

But when we come to examine in detail the changes of 1870-71 we find that they were not radical. They did not in any way disturb the established method of working with which the people had now become familiar and which had been productive of such excellent results. They perfected the free school system, and introduced a carefully guarded and most moderate form of compulsion.

To the schools under this new extension of public interest was given the designation, not of "common" schools, as open to all, but of "public" schools, as belonging to and used by all the people. The principle of compulsory attendance at school for at least four months in each year was the most radical change introduced. This Ryerson had made the subject of most careful study both in Europe and America, and it was only when fully convinced of its necessity by such study, and with the example before him of its success in several states of the Union, as well as in several countries of Europe, that he ventured upon its introduction. Even then he guarded scrupulously against any undue pressure upon the poor. The trustees and magistrates by whom the law was to be enforced were given wide power of discretion, and the term made compulsory was but four months in the year, as against six months required in Massachusetts.

A very important part of the legislation of 1870-71 was the effort to render uniform and to improve the standard of qualification of teachers. For this purpose the examination for teachers seeking first class certificates was placed in the hands of the council of public instruction, and such certificates became provincial. The county boards were also improved, being composed with the inspector of two persons who themselves held certificates of qualification for that purpose from the council of public instruction. Provision was also made that certificates should be given to inspectors, the condition being a university degree or the highest grade of provincial certificate, experience in teaching, and proof by written thesis of mastery of the fundamental principles of the science of education.

In this effort to elevate the standard of qualification in the interest of the schools, the interests of the teachers were never forgotten. It is true their ranks were thinned by the elimination of incompetent or unqualified persons, but at the same time every effort was made to render their position and work such as might be desired as a permanent calling or profession in life. The period of service of even one third of the early normal school graduates was three and a half years on the average. Every year scores of the best teachers after a short term of service entered the Christian ministry, or law or medicine, often attaining the highest eminence in these professions. But others left the teaching profession, not for a wider or more ambitious sphere of usefulness, but from pecuniary and family considerations alone. As teachers they were not secure of a permanent position, and a home and status in the community. Teachers were still frequently changed at the end of a year, and the average length of service was scarcely three years. Few schools made provision for a residence for the teacher, and in a large number of the country schools the teacher must of necessity be an unmarried man or woman. Many of these final provisions devised by Dr.

Ryerson aimed at the remedy or at least alleviation of these evils, by making the work of the teacher a profession, by providing him a home in connection with the school, by improving the scale of remuneration, and by making provision for a retiring allowance for teachers who had given their life to the service. The evil of frequent change of teachers and of the employment of young and inexperienced teachers was easily seen; but the causes lay deeper perhaps than the reach of any legislative enactment. In any case they could be removed only by a long and patient policy in which the government and the people would unite in continuous effort to make the position and work of the teacher as desirable as those of any other profession. Dr. Ryerson's work was now too near its close to permit of his accomplishing so desirable a result.

The introduction of compulsory education brought to the front the problem of the neglected and unfortunate classes of our population. The recognition of the principle that the education of all the children was the duty of the state, made more prominent the condition of the street arabs of our cities, of the children of criminal and inebriate parents, and of those who come into the world deprived of sight, or speech, or ordinary mental powers. These problems were also the subject of Dr. Ryerson's latest studies and reports and were matters left, as he retired from his life work in the seventy-fourth year of his age, to be wrought out by his successors. But before he passed from his office at least legislative provision was made for the better care of all these classes of the population.

The later years of Dr. Ryerson's work were not without their prophecy of several minor though still important changes in his school system. The date was the time of the high tide of the *laisser faire* system both in England and Canada. The doctrine that the needs of the country should be supplied by private enterprise as far as possible without legislative interference was just then popular. The government ownership and control of all public franchises, or the communistic supply of common needs was then looked upon as a dream of wild theorists. And yet the very idea of an educational system is paternal; and the system built up by Dr. Ryerson was certainly such. It was in its very nature the undertaking by the government, whether provincial, municipal or local, of the supply of one of the most universal needs of the people. To-day we think it quite reasonable to consider and even vote upon the public supply of light, of transportation, and of telegraphic as well as postal communication. The justification of all these projects is the well-being of the whole people. This certainly was the justification of the paternalism involved in Dr. Ryerson's system. It had worked well for the people. The children were being educated as never before. Illiteracy was disappearing from the land, and the standard of intelligence was being advanced beyond all precedent in all classes of society. No one could venture to criticize a system marked by such success as a whole.

The cry of Prussian despotism had quite disappeared, but against some of its features the cry was raised of interference with the interests of trade. The educational depository was the ground of objection. It had in its day accomplished a most important and excellent work. It had placed nearly two hundred thousand volumes, not of inferior fiction, but of high class science, history, travel and literature in public libraries throughout the country, and it had furnished the schools of the country with an equipment of school apparatus which would have been beyond their reach otherwise for years to come. It had accomplished this work without other expense to the country than the legislative grants in aid which were wholly employed in supplementing the money raised by the schools and in thus furnishing them with apparatus at one half the cost price. The depository had thus served the three-fold purpose of bringing into the country the best school apparatus, of furnishing it at cost price, and of distributing the grant in aid of the purchase of such outfit on the basis of local contribution. The attack on this section of the education department, and the personal form which it assumed, was a matter upon which one can now look back only with pain and shame. It was poor requital to the man who had done so much for his country, and the so-called principles upon which it was grounded will scarcely bear critical examination in the light of history. But at the time it carried with it a large section of the public, and under its influence the depository came to an end. It can be said now, with no little confidence, that the depository was in its day at least, one of the most important contributory means to the success of Dr. Ryerson's work. Fortunately for the country it was not destroyed until the need which it supplied was so manifest that other means could be used to do its work. Private enterprise would have failed completely in that work at an earlier date, and even now it succeeds in some measure only by the help of legislative enactment. What Dr. Ryerson tempted the schools to do as a benefit to their children, we now command them to do under pain of loss of the legislative grant.

Another and much more important change in the central education department Dr. Ryerson himself anticipated, and proposed almost immediately after the introduction of the federal system of government into Canada. This was the creation for the province of a minister of education as a member of the executive council of the province, placing the department on the same footing as then were the public works, the crown lands, and the executive administration of law. There was no little hesitation on this point on the part of leading statesmen. Dr. Ryerson urged the supreme importance of the work involved, the need of direct and authoritative representation of that work on the floor of the legislature, and in the executive council. He proposed that the educational system should be unified from the provincial university to the elementary school under the control of a minister of the crown, as a most important department of the provincial government. For this purpose he voluntarily placed his resignation in the hands of the lieutenant-governor.

The hesitancy of the government and of the public mind to accede to this change arose from a consideration of the danger of the intervention of party politics in so important and national an interest. Here, if anywhere, the interests of the public service should not be subordinated to, or even for a moment endangered by the unfortunate tendency to reward political adherents by appointments in the public service. Dr. Ryerson himself acknowledged the difficulty and continued in office for several years after making this proposition. Immediately on his retirement in 1876, the proposal was carried into effect, and has powerfully influenced the history of education in Ontario for the last twenty-five years. During that time the political danger has not appeared to be so important. The appointing power is so diffused among municipal and local bodies that there has scarcely been room for criticism even by the most suspicious; and the few appointments at the central office have been very judiciously made. Dr. Ryerson's idea of greater facility and effectiveness in the presentation of educational interests to the legislature has been fully sustained by the results in the hands of able ministers of education. Perhaps the one weakness of the new system was scarcely anticipated at the time. The minister of education, under the pressure of the general work of government, and of the demands made upon a political leader, must depend to no small degree upon subordinates, and he himself is liable at any time to step out of office. There can scarcely be thus the same conservative unity and continuity of policy and the same careful development of great principles which were such conspicuous features of Dr. Ryerson's administration. Perhaps we could not have secured them under any other man as chief superintendent.

CHAPTER IX

THE SEPARATE SCHOOL QUESTION

AT the date of the founding of our Upper Canadian school system all parties were agreed
that religion and morality should form an essential
part of the education of the young. Puritans and
Presbyterians, Anglicans and Roman Catholics,
stood firmly by this principle as a matter of conviction as well as of traditional usage, and Methodists
were no exception to the consensus. They had shewn
their faith by their works in the building of their
college. When, therefore, Dr. Ryerson addressed
himself to his important task, he did so upon the
basis of this principle, believing that he had behind
him the support of almost unanimous conviction
on the subject; and he took especial pains to make
provision for the recognition of religion in the
schools, and for the instruction of the children in
the fundamental principles of religion and morality.
This provision was made in three ways—first the
trustees were given power for the regulation of
religious teaching and exercises in the schools in
harmony with the desires of the parents; again all
clergymen were made visitors of the schools with
the right to instruct the children of their com-
munion by themselves for an hour each week; and

215

in addition the text books selected for the schools were made to embody a very considerable amount of religious and scriptural knowledge, without involving any dogmas called in question among the religious bodies. As a result of these provisions it is a well-remembered fact that at least in the rural schools religious influence and instruction were fairly well maintained. In the year 1859, with 3,665 schools, 4,360 visits were made by clergymen; in 2,510 schools the scriptures were read daily, and 1,708 schools were opened and closed with prayer. In all the schools the text books used contained the moral and religious lessons referred to. In the last report issued by Dr. Ryerson, of 4,758 schools reported, 4,033 were opened and closed with prayer, and the ten commandments were taught in 3,167. On these facts Dr. Ryerson in his report makes the following remarks:—"The religious instruction, reading, and exercises, are, like religion itself, a voluntary matter with trustees, teachers, parents, and guardians. The council of public instruction provides facilities, even forms of prayer, and makes recommendations on the subject, but does not assume authority to enforce or compel compliance with those provisions or recommendations. As Christian principles and morals are the foundation of all that is most noble in man, and the great fulcrum and lever of public freedom and prosperity in a country, it is gratifying to see general and avowed recognition of them in public schools."

While Dr. Ryerson with his strong personal influence continued at the head of the school system, these general provisions exerted a distinct moral and religious influence on the schools, but they were by no means a complete solution of the educational and political questions involved. To one class of the people the religious instruction thus given appeared altogether inadequate. They would be satisfied with nothing short of full instruction in the doctrines and usages of their own church; and they were not satisfied to confine this extended religious instruction to the Sunday school or catechumen class, or to a weekly hour in the public school under the direction of the clergyman. Another tendency due to the growth of the modern spirit which would completely separate the work of the church from the political sphere is thus referred to by Dr. Ryerson in his last report:—"There are many religious persons who think the day school, like the farm fields, the place for secular work, the religious exercises of the workers being performed in the one case as in the other in the household and not in the field of labour." This class of the people would, of course, find the solution of the problem in a strictly secular government school for all classes of the population.

The first of these two classes had, as early as 1841 (*i.e.*, when the first attempt at a general system of public schools was made, three years before Dr. Ryerson's appointment, and five years before the introduction of his first Common School Act,) already secured for themselves the concession of separate schools. They were thus in possession of a vested right; and of this the act of 1846 did not attempt to deprive them. The act of 1849, which failed to come into effect, dropped the provision and would apparently have resulted in purely secular schools, and this formed one of Mr. Ryerson's most serious objections to it. From the very outset of Mr. Ryerson's carefully conceived plan of schools on a moral and religious basis which might be accepted by all the members of a Christian community, it was thus exposed to two antagonistic influences which were at the same time directly and irreconcilably in conflict with each other. The separate school party were anxious to strengthen and extend their position, and the other party were anxious to extinguish the separate schools by the general enforcement of a purely secular system. Dr. Ryerson desired to secure the maintenance of the general moral and Christian aspect of the common schools, making them free from any valid objection on the ground of sectarian teaching, with at the same time such supervision of the separate schools as would secure their efficiency, and prevent their being forced upon any person without his free consent or desire. The common schools were to be maintained in their true position as the schools of all the people.

The active conflict of these opposing parties may

be said to date from 1852. Up to that date the number of separate schools established had been fifty, of which thirty-two had been discontinued in the last three years. Of the remaining eighteen, three were Protestant, two being in sections where the majority of the population was French, and two were schools for coloured children in Kent and Essex, leaving only thirteen Roman Catholic separate schools in operation at the close of 1852. No better proof could be afforded of the success of the fair and conciliatory policy of Dr. Ryerson. Up to the time of his death, Bishop Power acted as chairman of the council of public instruction and was a most valued member of the board, and by his presence, counsel, and general attitude, contributed not a little to make the common school system acceptable to the Roman Catholic population. During the first three years of his administration the attitude of Bishop Charbonnel was at least not antagonistic, and the aggressive position assumed in 1852 was, to the friends of a common school system, a surprise.

But on looking back, a circumstance connected with the passing of the School Act of 1850 seems to indicate that the new bishop, while seemingly acquiescent, was at heart anxious for thoroughly Roman Catholic schools. The bill of 1849 had disturbed the confidence created under the policy of Dr. Ryerson, and gave occasion for a movement on the part of those desirous of denominational schools. In this the high church party of the Anglicans and the Roman Catholics united their forces. Dr. Ryerson's bill as introduced proposed to place the power of establishing separate schools in the hands of the board of trustees, instead of making it possible for ten householders to demand a separate school. To this the separate school party proposed an amendment, making it possible for any ten householders, either Catholic or Anglican, to demand a denominational school without restriction. The acts of 1843 and 1846 had restricted this power to cases when the teacher was a Protestant in a Protestant community, or a Catholic in a district mainly Catholic, and so made no provision for the subdivision of Protestantism and the establishment of Protestant denominational schools. By means of strong influence brought to bear on the members, this amendment was on the verge of passing when Dr. Ryerson fell back on a slight modification of the provisions of 1843 and 1846, which satisfied the Roman Catholics and broke up the combination, and so prevented a most serious inroad upon the principle of common schools. But shortly after this difficulty had passed another circumstance brought the question again to the front. The city of Toronto was under the new act but a single school section divided for municipal and other purposes into wards, in each of which there was a graded common school. The trustees, who were decidedly opposed to the separate schools, refused to grant more than a single separate school under the provisions of the act, and the courts sustained them in the refusal. Dr. Ryerson used his influence to secure more favourable consideration for the Roman Catholics, but without avail. It was certainly within the power of the trustees to grant such consideration, as the law specified "one or more," but equally within their right, as interpreted by the court, to grant but the one, and upon that right they took their stand. This led to the demand for an amendment to the act, giving room for a more aggressive separate school policy. This Dr. Ryerson refused, but provided an amendment in 1851 which conferred the right of a separate school on each ward or union of wards for that purpose. During this period also, and for several years following, the advocates of the bill of 1849 kept the question alive by a constant effort to eliminate from the common school act all provision for or concession of the right of separate schools. Dr. Ryerson consistently opposed this policy, believing that such a concession constituted a means of rendering the great body of the Roman Catholic inhabitants satisfied with the provisions of the law, and thus secured a more general acceptance of the common school system than would be otherwise possible. While Dr. Ryerson's policy, as we have seen, was, down to 1852, largely successful, the agitation against separate schools and the other circumstances referred to kept alive an opposing

221

force which suddenly became active in 1852. By his fair consideration of the claims of the Roman Catholics in the Toronto separate school case in 1850-1, as well as by his consistent opposition to all attempts to deprive them of the rights already conceded by law, Dr. Ryerson had gained the ill-will of the radical party who wished to abolish all separate schools at once. He was now doomed to encounter almost equal difficulty from the ultra separate school party.

The initial point of the agitation was furnished by the growing establishment of free schools. These schools were supported entirely by their apportionment of the school fund, made up of legislative grant and county school tax, in which the separate school shared *pro rata*, and supplemented by a municipal tax upon all the property of the school section. In this last tax the Roman Catholics now demanded that the separate schools should also share *pro rata* of their average attendance. The case was brought up on appeal from the towns of Belleville and Chatham, in which Dr. Ryerson sustained the trustees in refusing to the separate schools a share in the second part of their school revenue. This led to the preparation by the Roman Catholic authorities of a bill which they were determined to press through parliament, and which, in the opinion of Sir Francis Hincks, would be a serious blow to the common school system and to free schools. To meet this emergency the Supplemental Act of 1853 was prepared by Dr. Ryerson and passed through parliament. The opportunity afforded by the passage of this act was embraced to define and improve many of the general provisions of the act of 1850, but in regard to separate schools its essential feature was the exemption from the local or municipal school tax of all who were contributing supporters of a separate school. In making this equitable concession to the supporters of the separate school, care was taken to guard the rights of the common schools by provisions which Dr. Ryerson summarizes as follows:—

1. No separate school can be established or continued otherwise than on the conditions and under the circumstances specified in the nineteenth section of the School Act of 1850.

2. No part of the municipal assessment can be applied, and no municipal authority or officer can be employed to collect rates for the support of any separate school.

3. If any persons, whether Roman Catholic or Protestant, demand a separate school in the circumstances in which it may be allowed, they must tax themselves for its support, and they must make returns of the sums they raise and of the children they teach.

4. Separate schools are subject to the same inspection and visits as common schools.

5. All ground and semblance of complaint of injustice is taken away from the supporters of a

separate school, while they no longer employ municipal authority and municipal assessments for sustaining their school.

6. The supporters of separate schools cannot interfere in the affairs of the public schools.

The new act was thus a fresh proof of Dr. Ryerson's consistent support of the fundamental principle of a common school system, and of the separation of the state from entanglement with any church.

By this date the separate school question had aroused an intensely violent discussion and political contention on the part of two extreme parties. We have already seen that a party, led in the House of Parliament by Messrs. W. L. Mackenzie, George Brown and Malcolm Cameron, and joined by a very few of the extreme opposite political faith, maintained a most active crusade against separate schools, whether maintained as a matter of principle or as a compromise. With these Dr. Ryerson agreed in principle but not in policy. Of both his principle and policy he made the most open avowal, saying in an official letter to Bishop Charbonnel (afterwards published):—"I always thought the introduction of any provision for separate schools in a popular system of common education like that of Upper Canada was to be regretted and inexpedient; but finding such a provision in existence, and that parties concerned attached great importance to it, I have advocated its continuance, leaving separate schools to die out not by force of legislative enact-

ment, but under the influence of increasingly enlightened and enlarged views of Christian relations,
rights, and duties between different classes of the
community. I have at all times endeavoured to
secure to parties desiring separate schools, all the
facilities which the law provides, though I believe
the legal provision for separate schools has been
and is seriously injurious rather than beneficial to
the Roman Catholic portion of the community, as
I know very many intelligent members of that
church believe as well as myself." As this calm
statement was written in reply to a letter from the
Bishop inveighing in very forcible language against
the whole system of common schools, there can be
no question that it candidly and clearly expresses
Dr. Ryerson's position and policy.

The leader in the opposition to this policy was
Mr. Brown, then influential in parliament and
throughout the province as the editor and proprietor of *The Globe*. Mr. Brown's policy, in which
he was supported not only by a large section of
Liberals but also by a section of the Orange body,
was the radical one of no separate schools. His
contention is fully expressed by the following quotation given by Dr. Hodgins from *The Globe*.
Addressing Dr. Ryerson, he says: "And did this
third concession to the claimants of separate schools
satisfy them? Was your oft-repeated assurance realized that 'the existence of the provision for separate schools' in the national system prevented

'oppositions and combinations which would otherwise be formed against it?' On the contrary the separatists only advanced in the extent of their demands, and became more resolute in enforcing them. The very next year the matter was again brought to a crisis, a general election came on, Bishop Charbonnel pressed his demands, and Mr. Hincks consented to bring in yet another sectarian school act." The position of the Bishop will fully appear from another extract from a letter written by him to Dr. Ryerson in March, 1852:—"Therefore, since your school system is the ruin of religion, and persecution of the church; since we know, at least as well as anybody else, how to encourage, diffuse, promote education, and better than you how to teach respect toward authority, God, and His church, parents and government; since we are under the blessed principles of religious liberty and equal civil rights, we must have and we will have, the full management of our schools, as well as Protestants in Lower Canada; or the world of the nineteenth century will know that here as elsewhere, Catholics, against the constitution of the country, against its best and most sacred interests, are persecuted by the most cruel, hypocritical persecution."

No analysis or description of the case could more clearly present the situation than do these three extracts. Each of the extremists stands on his ideal principle and is ready to carry it in practice to its logical conclusion regardless of the convictions of his opponent and of all collateral interests; Dr. Ryerson stands in a *via media*, striving to reconcile their conflicting ideas of right and truth and to harmonize both with other equally important interests of religion and patriotism, only to find himself the object of bitter invective from both. Dr. Ryerson's letters at this period rank again amongst the best work of his life as an exposition of the principles ethical, political and religious, which should govern in a mixed community of varying religious convictions, in matters in which, as citizens, they are called upon to coöperate with each other. We cannot, of course, claim that in the enunciation of these principles there does not appear at times some evidence of a strong and fiery spirit. It is scarcely given to a great soul pursuing with single purpose a great object of life, not at times to be roused to ire when needless difficulties are thrown across his pathway by men of alien ideas and spirit. Hence we must not be surprised if at times his words are almost as strong as those of Mr. Brown or Bishop Charbonnel. But the *via media* for which he contended throughout was respect to conscientious convictions on both sides and patient waiting for that unity of thought which truth is sure to bring in the long run. But for many years the conflict of parties made the *via media* a very thorny path to the chief superintendent of education.

Returning from the field of controversy to that of legislative and political action, we scarcely find the supplemental act of 1853 in operation before the occasion arises for further agitation and new demands. There can be no doubt that the underlying cause of the new agitation was a clearly defined and persistent policy on the part of the Bishop to separate the entire body of Catholic children from the common schools and place the management of their education under the control of the church. To this policy Dr. Ryerson was, as we have seen, strenuously and inflexibly opposed. But as the Bishop was careful to wait for a reasonable occasion or favourable opportunity for each forward step in his policy, Dr. Ryerson was equally careful in his opposition not to contravene any principle of equity or fairness.

The occasion for the new agitation again arose in Toronto, where the extreme party opposed to separate schools was strong and quite ready for heroic measures. In St. David's ward one Roman Catholic teacher was employed in a school of six teachers, and on this ground the application of the Roman Catholics for a separate school was refused. This refusal Dr. Ryerson pronounced contrary to law. In the next year, by error, some supporters of the separate schools were included in the common school taxation and a refund of the amount so paid was refused on the ground that the proper returns of names had not been made by the separate school trustees. These circumstances were made the foundation of the following complaints by Bishop Charbonnel:—

1. That the supporters of separate schools were unjustly required to pay amounts equal to those required for common schools in order to secure exemption from the common school taxation, and that for the same purpose the trustees were required to make returns not required of common school trustees.

2. That the trustees of the several wards of a city or town could not act together as one board as could the trustees of the common schools.

3. That the government grant was distributed by the city or town board, or in the townships by the local superintendent, a provision which did not secure impartiality. It does not appear that any instance of partiality was cited.

To remedy these complaints Dr. Ryerson added to a short grammar and common school bill of 1854 three clauses touching separate schools proposing: (1) To relieve the supporters of separate schools of the defined rate at which they must be taxed and also the trustees of the obnoxious returns; (2) To enable the trustees to unite as one board in towns and cities; (3) To place the distribution of the legislative grant in the hands of the chief superintendent of education. These provisions Dr. Ryerson calls his ultimatum of legislation on separate schools, but as they were not accepted they appear to have been withdrawn from the bill.

Early in the following year the Roman Catholic Bishops of Toronto, Bytown and Kingston prepared a comparative table of the Upper and Lower Canada school laws and a draft of a separate school bill setting forth their terms. This bill proposed to repeal all previous provisions for separate schools; to empower any number of dissidents of any profession to form a separate school board; to give such board all the rights and powers of common school boards; to erect a single board in a town or city; gave the trustees power to fix their own limits to their separate school sections, and their own standard of qualification for separate school teachers, and to claim their share not only of all legislative grants but also of all provincial or municipal school funds and of all taxes for school and library purposes in proportion to the population which they claimed to represent. This bill was immediately answered by Dr. Ryerson in a thorough and able exposure of its objectionable features involving, as he truly and emphatically asserted, "the complete destruction of our public school system." Notwithstanding this opposition of Dr. Ryerson, six weeks later and without his knowledge or consent, a bill very similar in many of its provisions was introduced into the legislative council by Sir E. P. Taché. Mr. Gamble at once telegraphed Dr. Ryerson and mailed him a copy of the bill.

THE TACHÉ BILL

Dr. Ryerson telegraphed the Hon. J. A. Macdonald asking that the bill should be restricted to Roman Catholics, and should not admit the separate schools to the municipal council assessment. To these amendments Mr. Macdonald assented and the bill, as so largely amended, became the Roman Catholic separate school law.

Dr. Ryerson always denied all responsibility for this act, though as amended he considered it harmless in its effect upon the common school system. In his view, the bulwark of that system lay in the principle that the machinery of the government could be used to raise funds only for the support of common schools and not for the purposes of sectarian education, and that no individual should be compelled to contribute to such education without his consent. The most objectionable feature of the law was its utterly inefficient provision for the qualification of teachers, but this was a defect which concerned only those who voluntarily placed themselves under it. The large majority by which the bill was passed even in amended form was secured from Lower Canadian votes which stood forty-five to two, those from the upper province, which alone was affected, being sixteen to fifteen. Dr. Ryerson gives great credit to Church of England members on both sides of the House for their aid in amending the bill and supporting the common school system, naming Gamble, Stevenson, Robinson, Langton and Crawford.

It will be seen that in this second stage the separate school question had now passed into the purely political arena. It was no longer a question of what was in the best interests of the country, or of what was wise, and just, and practicable in the furtherance of those interests, but rather this: what are the demands of the contending parties? and what votes and influence can they bring to bear to enforce those demands? This political relation gave to the separate school question not only a new though extrinsic interest and importance, but also the fierce intensity of conflict which marked its history for the next few years. It became part of a new constitutional question in Canadian politics, should Upper Canadian interests be determined by Lower Canadian votes?—a question the solution of which was tentatively sought in the principle of the double majority, but which finally forced all parties to turn to the broader principle of federal government now embodied in the constitution of our Dominion and its provinces.

Thus, once again, Dr. Ryerson found himself at the very centre of an intensely active and highly important political movement in our Canadian history. But in this movement he was now not so much the active participator as the passive occasion. On the school question the position of the extreme parties was now clearly defined. The Liberal party demanded the abolition of separate schools, and whatever measure of secularization was necessary for that purpose. The Roman Catholic authorities sought the complete control of the education of the children of their church, holding that education must be moral and religious as well as secular or else be defective and even injurious. Dr. Ryerson stood between the two parties, by turns fighting the battles of each, and yet hated and assailed by both. He recognized that the Roman Catholics had conscientious convictions, and also vested rights which he felt bound to respect and protect. But while he maintained this position, he recognized the vested rights, the conscientious convictions, and the political equity which required that the rights of the Roman Catholic population should not infringe upon the equally important and much more extensive rights of the great body of citizens who desired an effective system of common schools.

With this position of Dr. Ryerson, the Hon. John A. Macdonald, now coming into the foremost rank in the Conservative party, was in full sympathy, although through the exigency of party interests he was forced to compromise, as in the Taché Bill. The Liberal party, on the other hand, identified Dr. Ryerson, Mr. Macdonald, and the Roman Catholic hierarchy as the common foes of a common school system, and thus the conflict between Dr. Ryerson and Mr. Brown was for some years of a most intensely bitter and even personal character.

In the meantime the separate school party were

very far from confining their efforts to the legislative and political arena. Every effort was put forth to bring the provisions of the separate school law into operation. Even under the act of 1853 the Roman Catholic separate schools were increased from thirteen in 1852 to forty-four in 1855. Under the Taché Act the number was raised to one hundred in 1857-8, attended by nearly 10,000 pupils, an increase due, perhaps, not so much to any change in the law as to the active efforts of the ecclesiastical authorities, of which the lenten pastoral of Bishop Charbonnel in 1856 may be cited as an example. In this pastoral he says:— "Catholic electors who do not use their electoral power on behalf of separate schools are guilty of mortal sin. Likewise parents who do not make the sacrifices necessary to secure such schools, or send their children to mixed schools."

During this period the agitation of the public mind over this question was such that the governor-general, Sir Edmund Head, requested from Dr. Ryerson a special report. In this report, of which Dr. Hodgins has published extracts in his comprehensive history of separate schools in Upper Canada, he exposes very clearly the attitude of the Roman Catholic hierarchy at this period toward the common school system, summing it up in these words:—"It is this double aggression by Roman Catholic bishops and their supporters, in assailing on the one hand our public schools and school

system, and invading what has been acknowledged
as sacred constitutional rights of individuals and
municipalities; and, on the other hand, in demanding the erection and support at the public expense
of a Roman Catholic hierarchal school system,
which has aroused to so great an extent the people
of Upper Canada against permitting the continuance any longer of the provisions of the law for
separate schools." At the same time he deprecates
the interference of bishops and priests in Lower
Canada, or of their representatives, with the school
system of Upper Canada, pointing out that "there
has been no interference in Upper Canada with the
school system of Lower Canada." Many of the
most essential parts of this report, re-written and
enlarged, were laid before parliament in the same
year.

The next important attempt at separate school
legislation began in 1860 with the introduction of
a separate school bill by Mr. R. W. Scott, then
member for Ottawa. Mr. Scott's first attempt failed,
and was repeated in 1861 and 1862 with the same
result. Finally, in 1863, a modified bill to which
Dr. Ryerson consented was passed. Mr. Scott was
a Liberal in politics, as well as a Roman Catholic
in religion. His introduction of the question thus
marks a new phase of the movement.

Early in 1860 Bishop Charbonnel had resigned
the charge of the diocese of Toronto, and Bishop
Lynch became his successor. His policy does not

appear to have been as aggressive as that of his predecessor. There was now no attempt to break up the public school system by provisions for a general introduction of denominational schools. Several provisions aimed at the removal of disabilities which Roman Catholics had imposed upon themselves by the Taché Act, which, in 1855, repealed indiscriminately the provisions of 1853. Other clauses attempted once more to introduce provisions to which Dr. Ryerson had from the outset been inflexibly opposed, especially two, the distribution of all school funds according to population, and the employment in any form of the municipal authorities to collect funds for the purposes of denominational schools.

In 1862, Dr. Ryerson, willing to concede the more equitable parts of Mr. Scott's bill, and if possible to reconcile the authorities of the Roman Catholic church to the public system of common schools, at least through the country generally, proposed the name of Bishop Lynch as a member of the council of public instruction for Upper Canada, finding, as he says, that his views on the subject "were moderate and constitutional, appreciating the rights of citizens and the institutions of our country, as well as the interests and institutions of their own church." He accordingly prepared a draft of a bill repealing the objectionable requirement of an oath to returns, providing for separate schools in incorporated villages as in towns and cities, enabling separate school trustees to form union school sections for their purposes, and exempting the ratepayer who has once formally given notice that he is a supporter of a separate school from the necessity of annual renewal of such notice, substituting therefor a return by the trustees of the names of all supporters of their school.

This draft seems never to have come before the House, as Mr. Scott again introduced his bill with the two objectionable demands. These were, however, removed in committee, and to the bill as thus amended, Dr. Ryerson assented on condition that the bill should be accepted as a settlement of the question by the authorities of the Roman Catholic Church and should receive the assent of the government. For this purpose the bill was thoroughly revised by Dr. Ryerson in consultation with the representatives of the Roman Catholic Church, accepted by them, two copies prepared, and the assent of the government asked to Mr. Scott's proceeding with the bill in this form. Of it Dr. Ryerson says:—"Everyone who examines the bill will see that it brings back the school system in respect to separate schools as near as possible to what it was before the passing of the Roman Catholic Separate School Bill of 1855 . . . . an object I have been most anxious to accomplish."

The parliament was now, however, approaching that period of perplexity which finally forced confederation to the front, and the defeat of the government laid the school bill over for another year. Early in the following session, under the Sandfield Macdonald administration, Mr. Scott once more introduced the bill, and it was accepted as a government measure and passed shortly before another change of administration. In the final vote the double majority principle announced by Mr. Sandfield Macdonald failed, as there was an Upper Canadian majority of ten against it. The act was, notwithstanding, assented to on May 5th, and so became law a week before the defeat of the ministry.

The passage of this Separate School Act of 1863 may be regarded as the final settlement of the principle of Roman Catholic separate schools as a part of the public school system of Canada. In that part of his school policy in which Dr. Ryerson hoped through careful and impartial administration of the common schools to make them so acceptable to the Roman Catholic population that separate schools would disappear as undesirable, he had not been able to succeed. In spite of his liberal measures and strenuous efforts, the vigorous policy of the Roman Catholic authorities from 1852 onward gave strong and rapid growth to the separate schools. This growth was stimulated, as is always the case, by the efforts of the opposite party to wipe out separate schools by adverse legislation. The number of separate schools then in existence was 120, attended by 15,859 pupils, nearly one fourth of the Roman Catholic school population of the province.

A PERMANENT INSTITUTION

Yet this fact afforded no ground for discouragement as to the success of the public schools, which commanded a voluntary attendance of more than four-fifths of the whole school population of the province, and employed the services of 333 Roman Catholic teachers, or nearly twice as many as were employed in the separate schools.

But while these figures prove that the strength and comprehensive character of the common school system had been maintained without serious break, they also show that the separate schools had grown too strong to be overthrown by any form of policy, and that Dr. Ryerson was now wisely accepting the logic of facts, in making every provision for their equitable treatment and their highest efficiency. On the defensive side of his policy, he had certainly succeeded, and had foiled every attempt either to make the municipal authorities an agency for the maintenance of denominational schools, or to make the property of any but their declared supporters contribute thereto. They were thus left to work their own way on the voluntary principle, a right to which certainly every citizen is entitled in matters affecting his religious convictions, and for this purpose they were freed from all contributions to the public system of common schools, an exemption which, if not imperative on rigid political principles, is certainly fair as between Christian neighbours.

But notwithstanding the importance of the position thus reached, the story of Dr. Ryerson's struggle with this problem is not yet quite complete. In 1865 a new agitation of the separate school question was begun in Kingston and Toronto the principal importance of which was the occasion which it furnished for one of Dr. Ryerson's ablest deliverances on the subject. After meeting the main objections of his opponents and reviewing the whole history of the question from 1840 onward, showing that no privilege was granted to common school trustees which was not accorded to separate schools, with the single exception that they were not permitted to employ the municipal machinery for sectarian purposes, and pointing out the injustice of using general taxation for denominational purposes against the will of the majority, he states the fundamental political principle involved in the question as follows:—"Separate schools cannot be claimed on any ground of right, as I have often shown in discussing the subject in former years. All that any citizen can claim as a right on this subject is equal and impartial protection with every other citizen. All that can be claimed or granted beyond this must be on the ground of compact or of expediency or indulgence. I have ever regarded the existence of the separate school provisions of the law in the light of a compact commencing with the union of the Canadas; and, as such, in behalf of the public, I have endeavoured to maintain it faithfully and liberally. But if the supporters of separate schools continue to violate that compact, as they have done repeatedly, by denouncing it, and demanding its modification and extension, then they forfeit all right to the original terms and conditions of it, and reduce the whole question to one of expediency, in which light I will briefly consider it.

"I think no one will maintain that separate schools are expedient for the interests of the state. Nay, those interests are more or less injured by every act of class legislation, and the strength of the state is weakened by every sectional division which its citizens have created by law. If it was a source of individual pride and of the strength of the state, in ancient days, for every man to say '*Romanus sum*'—'I am a Roman'—so would it be now, under a legislation of equal rights and privileges, without the shadow of distinction in regard to sect or party, for a man to say 'I am a Canadian.' For every man to feel that he stands in all respects upon equal ground of right and privilege with every other man in relation to the state and law, must best contribute to the true interests and real strength of the state, and best respond to the spirit and principles of free government. Upon public grounds, therefore, the law for separate schools cannot be maintained."

After pointing out at a considerable length that separate schools are equally inexpedient for the educational, social and political interests of Roman Catholics themselves, he concludes thus:—"The fact is that the tendency of the public mind and of the institutions of Upper Canada is to confederation and not to isolation, to united effort, and not to divisions and hostile effort in those things in which all have a common interest. The efforts to establish and extend separate schools, though often energetic and made at great sacrifice, are a struggle against the instincts of Canadian society, against the necessities of a sparsely populated country, against the social and political, present and future interests of the parents and youth separated from their fellow-citizens. It is not the separate school law which renders such efforts so fitful, feeble, and little successful; their paralysis is caused by a higher than human law—the law of circumstances, the law of nature, the law of interest, if not the law of duty from parent to child.

"If, therefore, the present separate school law is not to be maintained as a final settlement of the question, and if the legislature finds it necessary to legislate on the separate school question again, I pray that it will abolish the separate school law altogether; and to this recommendation I am forced, after having long used my best efforts to maintain and give the fullest and most liberal application to successive separate school acts; and after twenty years experience and superintendence of our common school system."

This discussion was followed by a single abortive effort to secure further separate school legislation in 1866. In 1867 the question was finally settled by the following provisions of the British North America Act:—"In and for each province, the legislature may exclusively make laws in relation to education, subject and according to the following provisions:—

"1. Nothing in any such law shall prejudicially affect any right or privilege with respect to denominational schools which any class of persons have by law in the province at the union.

"2. All the powers, privileges and duties at the union conferred and imposed in Upper Canada on the separate schools and school trustees of the Queen's Roman Catholic subjects shall be and the same are hereby extended to the dissentient schools of the Queen's Protestant and Roman Catholic subjects in Quebec."

These two fundamental provisions are followed by right of appeal to the governor-general-in-council, and the right of remedial legislation by the parliament of Canada.

Before dismissing this important subject we may give a brief notice to the efforts of the Anglican Church in Upper Canada to secure separate church schools. The first of these efforts preceded Dr. Ryerson's appointment, and was made by Bishop Strachan in 1841 and 1843. The effort was renewed in 1850. Of this effort Dr. Ryerson says:—"An amendment to the nineteenth section was concocted and agreed upon by the clerical Roman Catholic and high Episcopalian parties, by which any twelve members of either church could demand a separate school in any school section of Upper Canada. The leaders on both sides of this new combination were very active, and in the course of a few days boasted that they would have a majority of fourteen or twenty votes against the government on the nineteenth section of the bill. I saw at once that the proposed amendment, if carried, would destroy the school system, and in order to break up the combination and save the school system, I proposed to amend the nineteenth section of the bill so as to secure the right of establishing separate schools to the applicants (Roman Catholics) as provided in the school acts of 1843 and 1846."

The Taché Bill, as introduced, embodied a similar provision, opening the door to a general system of denominational schools, and very strenuous efforts, as we have seen, were required to secure the elimination of its objectionable features. Even during the legislation of 1860-63 the attempt was renewed, but in all these cases the effort was defeated by the liberal and intelligent stand taken by lay members of the Church of England.

In closing this review of the separate school agitation it would be very wrong to attribute other than honourable motives to the supporters of the movement. Denominational ambitions may, of course, have had an influence; but behind all else there was, without doubt, a deep conviction of the importance, or rather necessity of religion and morals in the education of the young. In that conviction Dr. Ryerson shared, and his whole lifework was proof of its deep hold upon his own mind. As a result, from the beginning he sought to make the common schools Christian in a broad, comprehensive, unsectarian sense of the term. Beyond that he provided facilities for more specific religious teaching after school hours by the pastors of the several churches, and took great pains to interest them in this work. It cannot be said that this last provision has been a success. The children generally cannot be held after four o'clock for another hour of school, even by the minister. But side by side with the school system was growing up in all the churches an independent and purely voluntary system of moral and religious education, in the Sunday school, the Bible class, the Sunday school teachers' normal class, the catechumen class, and in the efforts after higher religious intelligence of the young people's societies. In these lies the true solution of the moral and religious side of education, a solution in which the conscientious and pious zeal of our churches should keep pace with the intelligent and harmonious work of the state.

CHAPTER X

THE GRAMMAR OR HIGH SCHOOLS

THE foundation of the present high school system of Ontario was laid in 1798 when half a million acres of public lands were set apart for education, to include both a university and four secondary schools. This wise provision was vitiated by the class-spirit in which it was proposed to be carried into effect; but before it was made available by the Act of 1807, the growth of the country expanded it into a provision for a system of district grammar schools, at first eight in number. Each of these district schools was placed under the complete control of a board of trustees for the district, appointed by the lieutenant-governor-in-council. These trustees appointed the teacher, made regulations for the school and issued the certificates under which the teacher received from the government the legislative appropriation for his salary which was £100 for each school. No provision was made for uniformity in curriculum or text books, nor was any standard of qualification prescribed for the teacher, and the governor-in-council was the only central authority supervising the appointments made by the trustees. In 1819 this act was amended so as to require the trustees to hold an annual

247

examination of the school in which they were required to take part and also to make an annual report to the governor of the state of the school, the number of pupils, the branches taught and any other matters pertaining to the prosperity of the school. Provision was also made for ten *free* scholars in each school. In 1831 a proposal was made in the legislature to make these schools free with a grant of £400 a year to each school, and in 1832, a bill was introduced to place them under the direction of a general board of education for the province, but neither of these measures was carried through.

In 1839 a new Grammar School Act was passed under which the schools were conducted until 1853. By this act the district schools were henceforth legally known as grammar schools, and were thus brought under the provisions of the royal grant of 1797. For each school the board of trustees was appointed as before to have the superintendence of the school and to receive the monies authorized to be paid for its support. The rules and regulations for the conduct and good government of all the schools were placed in the hands of the council of King's College, thus bringing them for the first time under a uniform system. A not less important provision of the act was a more definite and liberal financial policy and provision, under which a permanent grammar school fund was created from the investment of the proceeds of the sale of the old school lands and from a new appropriation of

250,000 acres for this purpose; and the proceeds of this investment were placed in the hands of King's College council for distribution according to the needs of the schools. In addition to the £100 heretofore paid to each district school, a further grant of an additional £100 each was authorized for the establishment under certain conditions of two additional schools in each district, and a sum of £200 to aid in the erection of a suitable schoolhouse in each district. A full financial as well as educational report was also required from each district board of trustees. The council of King's College was further authorized to apply a portion of the monies from invested endowment in aid of the grammar schools, and to extend aid from this and the grammar school revenue at their disposal to four additional grammar schools in any district where they deemed it necessary. Under the impulse of this act the grammar schools, then twelve in number, rose by 1842 to twenty-five, and by 1845 to thirty in number; and when to the more liberal provisions of the law there was added the stimulus and even competition of the new common school system, the number of grammar schools was rapidly multiplied, rising in 1853 to sixty-four. Many of these new schools were of a respectable character and in some places the old schools were doing good work. But the influence of the university council in their direction was exceedingly feeble, the majority of well-prepared university matriculants were furnished by Upper Canada College, and the majority of the old schools continued to be schools of a class, doing, with the addition of Latin, elementary work in English, mathematics and science below the standard of the best common schools, and taking their pupils from private schools in which they were taught the first rudiments. There was still no legal standard of qualification for the teacher, and the teacher was not seldom the local curate. There was no provision for inspection, and although the number of schools was multiplied, there was no guarantee that the large amount of public monies expended on their maintenance was profitably employed. They were now teaching 3,221 pupils, of whom 102 were returned as unable to read and 285 unable to write. About one-sixth (556) studied Latin, and one-ninth algebra and Euclid. The expenditure on these schools was £10,743. 11s. 1d., or nearly $43,000—$13.35 for each pupil.

The situation was thus one which demanded the attention of the legislature, and the Grammar School Act accompanying the new University Act of 1853 was the result. By this act the grammar schools were separated from the university in administration and made for the first time a part of the public system of which Dr. Ryerson was the superintendent, and it is with the preparation and administration of this act that his work on a grammar or secondary school system begins.

He began by placing the whole system on a more

popular basis by vesting the appointment of trustees in the hands of the municipal councils and providing a separate board for each school. This was effected gradually, the change of system being completed in three years. At the same time the responsibility for the support of the schools was placed upon the municipalities acting through their trustees, the legislative grant and the income from the invested proceeds of the grammar school lands forming a grammar school fund to aid the municipalities in their work. These two radical changes brought the grammar schools under the same fundamental principles as the common schools. They henceforth belonged not to the government but to the people. They were immediately controlled by their representatives and supported by their money contributed either as fees or by direct municipal taxation. The whole body of the people were thus brought to feel a direct and financial as well as educational interest in their secondary schools.

The third principle of the new act was equally important and also on a line with the constitution of the common school system. This was an efficient system, not only for the distribution of grants in aid, but also for making proper regulations for the government of the schools, and for their inspection. This system was administered as in the common schools through the council of public instruction, of which the president of University College and of the other colleges affiliated to the provincial university were now made members for this purpose, and through the chief superintendent of education. These provisions included a standard of qualification for all teachers in the grammar schools, and the appointment of a provincial board of examination for that purpose; a curriculum which covered all subjects required for matriculation in the provincial university as well as the elements of science, needed for industrial and commercial education; provision of proper text books for use in the schools; directions as to organization of the schools, and provision of suitable apparatus and equipment, including provision for a system of meteorological observations throughout the province, and the appointment of provincial inspectors of grammar schools. The chief superintendent was authorized to require complete reports of the grammar schools as of the public schools according to forms provided, and again as in the common schools satisfactory compliance with these regulations was made the condition of receiving the annual government grant. The trustee boards were also clothed with all the necessary powers for the efficient discharge of their duties placing them on a footing in this respect approaching to that of the common school trustees, to whom such large powers had been safely entrusted under the common school acts.

It is not too much to say that here again these fundamental principles, few and simple as they are, brought order out of chaos. To call into exercise the local interest, authority and responsibility of the people, to aid it by judicious grants, to direct it by wise regulation and inspection, these were the simple principles from which the practical genius of this man of the people constructed one of the most efficient systems of education that the world has known. These principles once established were never disturbed, and all subsequent amendments were minor provisions for their more perfect development.

The first of these provisions to become effective were the appointment of inspectors and the proper qualification of masters. At the end of three years thirty-eight out of sixty-one headmasters were graduates in arts—twenty-three of Canadian and thirteen of British universities, while two held American degrees. Of the rest, ten had qualified by examination, the others holding their position in virtue of appointment before the passing of the act.

The first inspectors, the Rev. Wm. Ormiston, M.A., and T. J. Robertson, M.A., were men of great ability, thorough scholarship, experience in educational work, and masters in the organization and management of schools, and under their influence the schools rapidly improved in system and method of work. Pupils fit only for primary schools were excluded by means of entrance examinations, the pupils were properly classified, and something like an orderly curriculum of school work was intro-

duced. Still the work of the first few years served
rather to bring to light the defects of the schools
than to bring them up to a satisfactory degree of
perfection. The masters were under-paid, the school
houses defective and unsuitable, the schools without needed equipment, many of them without even
suitable maps and blackboards, and the county
councils unwilling to furnish trustees with funds,
since they looked on the schools as belonging to the
towns and villages, while these complained that the
control of the schools through appointment of
trustees was not in their hands. Notwithstanding
these complaints it did not seem desirable to change
the law, as the schools were intended not for the
benefit of the immediate locality but of the entire
county or section of the county in which and for
which they were established.

To obviate these financial difficulties in villages,
and even in some towns and cities, the trustees
took advantage of the provision for the union of
the grammar with the common school, giving for
the united school the powers of local taxation
enjoyed by the common school board. In 1858 no
less than thirty-nine of the seventy-five grammar
schools were so united. The report of the inspector
shows that while such union resulted in financial
advantages, it was detrimental to the higher work
of the school. In fact Dr. Ormiston soon reported
that it furnished satisfactory work neither in the
common school nor in the grammar school depart-

ment. The motive—a cheap school—reduced it too
often to an attempt to carry on the union school
with a staff sufficient for a good common school.
Under these circumstances the high school work
was reduced to a minimum, and that minimum
became an incubus on the common school. Notwithstanding these difficulties a steady and gratifying progress was made in the character of the
grammar school work and also in the buildings and
equipment used for grammar school purposes. This
was especially the case in the western and central
parts of the province. The attendance of county as
against town pupils was gradually increased. The
influence of the universities as directing the curriculum of the grammar schools was making itself
felt. And while the intense local interest attached
to the common schools was not yet awakened for
the secondary schools, a deeper and more intelligent
interest was being created.

After ten years experience of the new law, in
which the schools had increased in number from
64 to 95 and the attendance from 3,221 to 5,589,
while the classical pupils had risen from 556 to
2,825, we meet the next important movement in
advance. In the year 1863, the Rev. George Paxton
Young was appointed inspector of grammar schools.
This was another example of Dr. Ryerson's peculiar
wisdom in the choice of able co-workers. In his
reports for 1864 and 1865, Mr. Young presents an
exhaustive statement of the still existing defects in

the grammar school system, and of the remedies which in his judgment should be applied.

The first point to which Mr. Young calls attention is the abuse of the power of county councils to establish new schools whenever their proportion of the grammar school fund enabled them to do so without lowering the grant to each school beneath the prescribed minimum of $200. This results, as he finds, in the establishment of weak grammar schools. In fact Mr. Checkley, his predecessor, had already reported some of these as positively inferior to good common schools. This undue multiplication of schools he found, further, to affect the attendance, finances, and consequently the efficiency of the existing schools. It was, besides, bringing the whole system of grammar schools into contempt, and depressing the average work of the common schools by substituting poor grammar schools for good common schools. The remedy for this abuse Mr. Young leaves to the chief superintendent, though he quietly suggests the application of Dr. Ryerson's old device of a solid financial requirement.

Next to this undue multiplication of schools, Mr. Young places the evils growing out of the union of the common with the grammar schools. He reports that now three out of every five grammar schools in the province have common schools united with them. He points out the cause of this in the financial provisions of the law, giving the united board of trustees a power of direct taxation not possessed by the grammar school trustees alone. He also shows the advantage which it possesses of bringing the whole body of common school pupils into touch with the higher work and exciting their ambition to continue their studies beyond the limits of the common school programme. But he finds that these advantages are far more than counterbalanced by the resulting evils which Dr. Ormiston had already pointed out. It put upon the grammar school master the burden of instructing the common school pupils in their higher work, to the detriment of his own curriculum. It filled up the common school department with inferior teachers, and led to cheaper and poorer schools in both departments.

While Mr. Young, in common with his predecessors, deplored the still existing defects of buildings and equipment, and urged strong pressure for reform in this direction, he does not consider it advisable to extend the power of direct taxation to a second board of trustees. He considers rather that pressure should be brought to bear upon the municipal councils to secure the needed improvements. The last item of Mr. Young's exceedingly able report deals with improvements in the method of teaching such subjects as algebra, geometry, and the Latin and Greek languages, and strikes at an evil which has persisted to our own time, the lack of thorough elementary instruction, and the use of methods suitable only for advanced pupils.

On this report was founded Dr. Ryerson's Act of 1865 "for the further improvement of grammar schools in Upper Canada." The main features of this act were:—

1. A change in the method of distributing the grammar school fund. The old distinction between senior and other schools was abolished. The county lines were also virtually abolished as a basis of distribution according to population; and the fund was distributed directly to the several schools of the whole province according to their works, *i.e.*, the average attendance of *bona fide* grammar school pupils. To prevent abuse here the entrance examination to the grammar school was placed entirely in the hands of the inspector, also in this way securing uniformity throughout the province. This provision at once put a premium upon really strong schools.

2. To maintain these schools efficiently it was required that in every case a local contribution, outside of fees, equal to the grant from the grammar school fund should be raised by the municipality or by the trustees.

3. To create a more directly local interest in the school, in towns and incorporated villages one half the trustee board was appointed by the council of the town or village and one half by the county, while the cities were separated from the county for grammar school purposes, except in the rare instances where the city was the location of the

only grammar school in the county, in which case the county council appointed one half. These enactments were of themselves a strong influence against the undue multiplication of schools; but in the same direction was the further proviso that no new school should be established until it could secure a grant of $300 from the grammar school funds without diminishing the grants to existing schools. Provision was also made for the dissolution of the union between grammar and common school boards by the vote of a majority of the united board. One of the last but not least important of the new provisions made a university degree necessary for the head master of a grammar school.

The new law was immediately followed up by a revised and thoroughly graded programme of studies for the pupils of the grammar schools, accompanied by a completely revised code of regulations. These regulations were scarcely less important than the act, as conformity with these was a condition of participation in the grammar school fund. By these regulations elementary English was excluded from the grammar school programme, and the schools were made strictly secondary schools. A programme of modern languages was provided for students who did not wish to take classics, and to this course girls were, at the option of the trustees, admitted on the same terms as boys. This step, taken apparently with a good deal of hesitation and conditioned upon the assent of the trustees, was one of the most important of all the new features now introduced.

These new departures were still considered somewhat tentative, and in his succeeding report Mr. Young examines with care their results. The expected diminution of the number of grammar schools did not follow. Two fell off the first year, but from that time there was a steady though more moderate rate of increase. The non-classical course for grammar school pupils was another feature which did not meet with large response in the public demand. The inspector himself, while not approving of this course, was decidedly in favour of it for the girls; but although the girls were not encouraged in this direction, their avidity for Latin seemed almost increased by the fact that it had been so long to them forbidden ground. In five years the attendance on the grammar schools had risen to 7,280, an increase of 36 per cent., while the number studying Latin had risen to 6,658, an increase of 81 per cent. Greek had in the same period experienced a relative decline, falling from $12\frac{3}{4}$ to $10\frac{1}{2}$ per cent., a decline which has continued steadily to the present time.

The transfer of the entrance examination to the inspector revealed the fact that the preparation of the pupils was still largely defective, pointing to the need of a more definite course in the public school before coming up for the entrance examination. In fact, the lack of a solid foundation in the elementary English branches was now clearly apparent as the most serious drawback to the success of the secondary schools. The new law was also still found defective as a means of making adequate financial provision for first class schools. The trustees were, as a rule, anxious to improve the schools, but being entirely dependent upon the municipal bodies and upon fees for financial support, they were quite unable to give effect to their wishes. In the meantime the completion of confederation and the formation of the new Dominion had given to the country the impulse of a new national life. With that life Dr. Ryerson, a Canadian of the Canadians, was himself in the warmest sympathy. The provincial legislature, to whom the whole field of education was now entrusted, was likely to be a far more progressive body in the matter of educational legislation than the united parliament of the past, and Dr. Ryerson, under its auspices, once more addressed himself to the work of advancing and perfecting both the public and high school systems.

The legislation of 1874 and its immediate results in the new regulations issued by the council of public instruction, was without doubt the most important in the history of education from 1850 onward. Its chief features were the following:—

1. It introduced the representative principle into the composition of the council of public instruction, thereby bringing it into distinct touch with

261

the universities, the high schools and the public schools and inspectors. This feature, which might have been productive of most important practical results, was discontinued at the reorganization of the education department under a minister of education.

2. It reorganized the grammar schools as high schools and collegiate institutes, providing in the latter for a far more complete programme of secondary education than had ever been attempted in the country before.

3. To maintain this advanced programme efficiently, the trustees of the high schools and collegiate institutes were now for the first time authorized to make requisition upon the municipal council or councils of their district, for such sums in addition to the government grant and its equivalent, as were necessary for the maintenance of the school, thus placing them in this respect on an equality with the public school trustees. It will be seen that this provision was carried into effect only after twenty years of effort in this direction. The provision for new buildings or grounds was still left to the voluntary action of the municipal bodies.

4. The union of public with high school boards was discontinued, and the provision for dissolving existing unions was re-enacted.

5. In the distribution of the high school grant the principle of payment according to results was now first introduced. The regulations under which

these results were to be ascertained were placed in the hands of the council of public instruction.

6. The conditions of the establishment of collegiate institutes were definitely fixed by law ; four qualified masters must be fully employed in teaching the subjects of the prescribed curriculum, and a daily average of not less than sixty male pupils must be pursuing the study of Latin or Greek. On fulfilment of these conditions the lieutenant-governor-in-council was authorized to confer on any high school the name of collegiate institute, with an additional grant from the grammar school fund of $750.

Under these provisions of the law the council of public instruction, with Dr. Ryerson at its head, proceeded with great energy in their important work. The programme of studies was once more completely revised, and especially for the work of the collegiate institutes, extended in the lines of modern literature and science. Three able men were appointed as inspectors, devoting their entire time to this work, and representing by their eminent attainments as specialists, the three great branches of the curriculum, classics, mathematics and science, and modern literature, especially English. But perhaps the most influential step of all taken by the council was the establishment of the intermediate examination at the end of the work of the second form as a means of testing the results of the work of the school as a basis for the distribution of the grant. This was the first introduction in a truly influential form of the examination system into our school work below the university. In twenty-five years it has extended its influence, until now it dominates our whole educational work.

The devising of these last measures for the perfecting of the high school system, we may call Dr. Ryerson's last great contribution to the educational work of Upper Canada. For twenty years he had devoted his energies to the perfecting of the high schools, as for thirty he had laboured on the public school system. In both cases he had found it necessary to overcome the obstacles arising from popular ignorance, apathy, or penuriousness, by wise enactments and patient effort. He was especially patient of delay. With remarkable accuracy of judgment he was able to discern the true ends to be ultimately attained, and to gauge the ability and willingness of the majority of the people to furnish the means for their attainment; and we have found him waiting patiently and working steadfastly for the accomplishment of such ends as the establishment of free common schools, or properly sustained high schools. And this labour he continued for ten or even twenty years, never losing sight of his ultimate object, employing gentle pressure whenever necessary, but always avoiding a friction which would render the whole system unpopular. It was doubtless of great advantage to him during his life-long labour that his work, like the administration of justice, stood just outside the field of politics, and was thus not subject to the ordinary contingencies of political changes. If it made his difficulties a little greater, and his progress somewhat more tardy, as he overcame difficulties with the people, difficulties with municipal bodies, difficulties with the legislature and the government of the day, this very slowness of growth and absence of startling change made his work in the end more strong and gave it a deeper foundation in the habits as well as the confidence of the people. Retiring from this work in the seventyfourth year of his age, after devoting thirty years of his matured manhood and great endowments to this service of his country, with an old man's pardonable pride, he thus, in his last report, sums up the results of his work:—

"In concluding this report for 1874, I may be permitted to note the progress which has been effected in the development of the public school system, of which I took charge in 1844. At that time there were 2,706 public school teachers, in 1874 there were 5,736, increase 3,030. In 1844 the amount paid for salaries of teachers was $206,856; in 1874 the amount paid for salaries of teachers was $1,440,894. In 1844 the total amount raised and expended for public school purposes was $275,000; in 1874 it was $2,865,332, increase $2,590,332. In 1844 the number of pupils in the public schools was 96,756; in 1874 the number of pupils was 464,047, increase 367,291. In 1844 the number of school-houses was 2,495, in 1874, 4,827, increase 2,332. The number of log school-houses in 1844 was 1,334; in 1874, 115, decrease 1,229. The number of frame school-houses in 1844 was 1,028; in 1874, 2,080, increase 1,052. The number of stone school-houses in 1844 was 84; in 1874, 463, increase 379. The number of brick school-houses in 1844 was 49; in 1874, 1,169, increase 1,120. These are mere naked figures, which convey no idea of the improved character, furniture and fittings of the school-houses, the improved character, uniformity and greater cheapness of the text books, the introduction of maps, globes, blackboards, etc., in the schools, the improved character, qualifications and position of teachers and their teaching. In 1844 maps and globes were unknown in the public schools; up to 1874, 2,785 globes and 47,413 maps and charts have been furnished to the schools, nearly all of which are now manufactured in the country. In 1844 there were no public libraries or library books; in 1874 there were 1,334 public school libraries, containing 266,046 volumes, provided and sent out by the department. In 1844 there were no prize books distributed as rewards for good conduct, diligence and success in the schools; up to 1874, 766,645 prize books had been sent out by the department and distributed in the schools. In this summary statement no mention has been made of the normal schools and their work, the standard of qualification and examination of teachers, and the improved organization and inspection of the schools.

"In regard to the grammar or high schools the duty was imposed upon me in 1852 of framing and administering the law respecting this important class of our public institutions. The number of these schools then in existence was 84; the number in 1874 was 108, increase 24. The number of pupils in 1852 was 2,643; in 1874 it was 7,871, increase 5,228. In 1852 the amount of legislative grant or grammar school fund was $20,567; in 1874 it was $75,553; besides a sum equal to half that amount, raised by county and city councils, and corporate powers in boards of trustees to provide additional means for the payment of teachers and the building and repair of school houses, many of which are now amongst the finest school buildings in the province. In 1852 the amount paid for the salaries of teachers was $38,533; in 1874 it was $179,946, increase $141,413. In 1852 the grammar schools received pupils from their 'a-b-c's' upwards; now pupils are only admitted on an entrance examination from the fourth form of the public schools, and the high schools have uniform programmes and text books, and are under the semi-annual inspection of three able inspectors. It is by the coöperation of successive administrations of government and parliaments, and the noble exertions of the country at large that this great work has been developed and advanced to its present state."

Such was the kindly and honourable farewell of a great man to the country for which he had wrought out his noble work. That work was built upon such secure foundations that not only its permanency but also its perpetual expansion was insured. It was sustained by the common sense and best feelings of all the people. It is now more than a quarter of a century since this report was issued, and the statistics of the first year of the new century are in our hands, showing 5,663 public schools, 379 separate schools, 414,619 pupils in the public schools and 43,978 in the separate schools, and a total expenditure for schools of $4,328,682. In the high schools there is an attendance of 22,523 pupils, with a total expenditure of $728,132. While these figures indicate the growth among us of a population who are neglecting the education of their children, the vast increase in the expenditure for education shows the continuous growth of interest in and appreciation of this work.

CHAPTER XI

LATER LITERARY WORK

TOWARDS the close of his long and honoured life, Dr. Ryerson was for a long time one of a very few surviving actors in the stirring and important events of the early years of the nineteenth century. His intimate knowledge of the past was frequently of great use in the conduct of affairs ecclesiastical and civil, and it was frequently sought and highly prized. Those who had the benefit of his experience and counsel could not but think themselves happy, and they could not but think that the time would soon come when his genial presence could no more be found amongst them, and the rich treasure-house of his memory would be forever darkened and sealed up by death. Hence it came that he was again and again importuned to commit to writing the story of his life, and to leave some record of the observations and experiences of his long and eventful career. It was felt that such a record would not only be interesting as a story of the beginnings of our Canadian life, but it would be helpful as a guide to a true policy for the present and the future—a policy well grounded on the foundations of the past. And it was but natural that such a man would love to tell the

269

story of his life, and that all who knew him would love to hear the story told.

It was not till about six years before his death that Dr. Ryerson found time to enter seriously upon the work in question. The makers of history are not often at the same time the writers of history, and Dr. Ryerson was engaged in making the history of his country till he had passed three years beyond the three score years and ten. This was in 1876, when he retired from the office of chief superintendent of education. Between that date and his death in 1882 he prepared his three works of chief literary and historical interest. They are "The Story of My Life," "Canadian Methodism, Its Epochs and Characteristics," and "The Loyalists of America and Their Times."

The writings of Dr. Ryerson are all marked by the complete subordination of the style to the matter. Indeed there is no pretence at style. Sometimes, it is true, a certain stateliness and formality of expression appears, such as was often found in the old-time writers and speakers, and was thought becoming in treating serious things, just as the powdered wig or swallow-tailed coat was thought becoming on occasions of ceremony. As a general thing, however, the style is familiar and idiomatic, and such as marks a ready speaker rather than a writer.

"The Story of My Life," an octavo of more than six hundred pages, is in part only an autobiography.

"THE STORY OF MY LIFE"

It may have been the original intention of Dr. Ryerson to tell the story of his life as an ordinary autobiography, and some part of the work is actually written in that way. On the seventieth anniversary of his birthday he wrote a short sketch of his life. This sketch ends with an account of his first sermon, preached on Whit Sunday, 1825. The story is continued to 1832 chiefly by extracts from a diary kept from 1829 to 1832. Beyond that time the title, "The Story of My Life," if taken too literally, would not be correct, for Dr. Ryerson's work becomes less and less and the book becomes more and more the story of Dr. Ryerson's life, prepared with admirable skill and loving care by Dr. J. George Hodgins, the faithful friend and fellow-labourer of Dr. Ryerson for many years. The grand old man never found time to tell more than the beginning of the story and some later fragments, and the work as completed was prepared by Dr. Hodgins as a monument to his revered friend. It is at the same time a noble monument to the friend who made it for his friend, and for long years to come it will associate in the story of the making of Canada the names of Ryerson and Hodgins.

The second of the three works to be mentioned here is that entitled "Canadian Methodism, its Epochs and Characteristics." It is a collection of articles or essays, as they are called, prepared at the request of the Methodist conferences of London,

Toronto and Montreal, and first published in the Canadian Methodist Magazine. The essays were collected into a volume of 440 pages by the Rev. Dr. Withrow, the editor of the magazine.

When we remember the militant character of the Methodist church for many years after Dr. Ryerson had entered the ministry, and especially when we remember the heroic part taken by him in the religious conflicts forced upon his people, we cease to wonder at the warmth that sometimes is displayed in the narrative. We rather wonder that there is so little warmth and we admire the evident and heartfelt charity that forgave the offences of the past and would even forget all that the fidelity of a historian would permit him to forget. Can we wonder, for example, that in the essay on the *Loyal Origin of Methodism*, some warmth of feeling should be kindled when the men who fought, bled, and suffered exile for the flag of England, flung back the charge of disloyalty brought against them by sectarian prejudice and animosity? In like manner we may look for some indignation when the writer sees the eccentricities and vagaries of excited and uncultivated people held up as the standard of doctrine and practice of a whole church, in spite of the clear statements of their acknowledged teachers. The marvel rather was, and that marvel still remains in this new century, that men of intelligence and conscience in ordinary affairs should lose all conscience and intelligence under

the blinding influence of religious antipathy. Even
to-day the caricatures and slanders of the early part
of the last century are repeated, and if Dr. Ryerson
were living still, he might find a respectable authority
amongst his old antagonists, gravely charging him
with the absurd doctrine that genuine conversions
and convulsions go regularly and properly together.
Such being the case, some men might say that it is
vain to contend against religious prejudice for it
can not be eradicated, but others would reply
as would Dr. Ryerson, that we must not cease
to contend against noxious weeds and venomous
creatures, though we may scarcely hope to see them
utterly eradicated and destroyed.

In the same volume of essays the whole story of
the clergy reserves controversy is told from Dr.
Ryerson's point of view. There are also five essays
on the divisions amongst the Methodists in Canada.
These essays are written by the Rev. John Ryerson,
a brother of Dr. Ryerson and a highly respected
authority on the history and usages of Canadian
Methodists. There are also several essays on the
relations of the Canadian Methodists to the British
conference. Happily all the misunderstandings and
divisions recorded in these essays have given way to
union at home and the most cordial relations
with the mother churches in England and the
United States, and the essays may ere long be
of interest to none but historians and antiquarians
and book collectors.

EGERTON RYERSON

The most considerable of Dr. Ryerson's literary works and the only one remaining for consideration in this volume is his "Loyalists of America and their Times." It is in two octavo volumes and contains over a thousand pages. For some twenty years the author had this work in mind, and as he could find time from his official duties he prepared for its publication. But long before he had any thought of authorship, and indeed from his earliest youth, he was himself in course of preparation for the task. Remote as the subject may seem to this generation, it was the great subject of family history and table talk in the home of young Egerton Ryerson. His father, Col. Joseph Ryerson, when only fifteen years of age, joined the royal army on the breaking out of the American Revolution in 1775. About eighteen months later he received an ensign's commission as a reward for distinguished service. And soon after that his skill and energy and daring secured the further promotion to a lieutenancy in the Prince of Wales Regiment. Throughout the war he fought under the royal standard and at the close of the war in 1783, when Great Britain acknowledged the independence of the United States, Joseph Ryerson and his brother Samuel left the young republic to seek new homes under the old flag in that true North that had remained loyal to the empire. The brothers went first to New Brunswick, and afterwards removed to Ontario, or Upper Canada,

as it was then called, where they settled on lands
awarded to them by the government in consideration of their services and sacrifices in the cause
of a united empire. Then came the experiences
of pioneer settlers in the Canadian wilderness, the
journeyings and toils and privations, the enterprise
and success, the simple life, the neighbourly help-
fulness and generous hospitality of the good old
times. These all were familiar to Egerton Ryerson,
as they came to him fresh from the fountains of
household talk, or as they were matters of personal
experience.

The manner in which Dr. Ryerson tells the story
of the United Empire Loyalists and their times, is
strongly suggestive of the manner in which he
became familiar with the facts. His work is not
history, such as we think of it from the examples
of our great historians. The scenes and events are
seen at short distance, and the reader is left to
supply proportion and perspective to the narrative.
But if the enchantment that distance lends is wanting, we find ourselves carried away by a new
enchantment back into the closest contact with the
persons and events described. We seem to listen to
the story as it falls in the twilight from the lips of
the sturdy old United Empire Loyalists and their
brave wives and children. We catch the tones of
strife, and pain, and pathos, and humour, and we
lend ourselves to this new enchantment with no
less pleasure than we do to that of the grand

panorama of Gibbon and the brilliant pictures of
Macaulay.

There is, however, a distinct historic value in
this work of Dr. Ryerson's in that it has helped to
qualify and correct an opinion that has obtained
too widely even amongst Canadians and Englishmen—the opinion that the English people were all
wrong in the unhappy struggle of the American
revolution, and the colonists all right. In his attempt to change what was to many of his readers
a fixed opinion, Dr. Ryerson thought it necessary
to produce copious documentary evidence to prove
that the prevailing impressions were seriously at
fault. The following is his apology for this method—
a method that is to some readers tedious enough:—
"The United Empire Loyalists were the losing
party; their history has been written by their adversaries and strangely misrepresented. In the vindication of their character I have not offered
assertion against assertion; but in correction of
unjust and untrue assertions I have offered the
records and documents of the actors themselves,
and in their own words. To do this has rendered
my history to a large extent *documentary*, instead
of being a mere popular narrative. The many fic-
tions of American writers will be found corrected
and exposed in the following volumes, by authorities and facts which cannot be successfully denied.
In thus availing myself so largely of the proclama-
tions, messages, addresses, letters and records of

the times when they occurred, I have only followed the example of some of the best historians and biographers."

It is pleasing to note that the latest and best of the American historians themselves have come round to views substantially the same as those of Dr. Ryerson on some of the important issues in the history of the American revolution. And especially do they, in just and generous spirit, maintain that the men who staked all and lost all for the integrity of the empire were in numbers far more considerable than had long been supposed, and that they were in standing and character of the very best in the colonies. Dr. Ryerson does not undertake any defence of the conduct of the English government. On the contrary he condemns it in strong terms. He maintains, however, that the bad policy of compulsion was not that of the English people but of the king and of a court party whose overthrow was desired by the mass of the English people and whose success would have been as great a disaster to England as it would have been to the colonies. The true thought of England found expression in the words of Chatham and Burke and not in the message of the king and his ministers. Neither does Dr. Ryerson blame the colonists for resisting the attempt to subvert their liberties. He rather commends them for it, even to the length of taking up arms as a last resort. But he does blame them for their secession from the empire when further patience and forbearance would inevitably have secured all their rightful demands—and their demands were in the main rightful. Moreover this would have been secured with the good will and assistance of their kin beyond the sea from whom the colonists derived their English love of liberty, and without the help of their French allies, who were actuated by the hate of England rather than by the love of America.

The part of Dr. Ryerson's book which treats of the American revolution seems to be wholly in favour of those who maintain that war is always a blunder and a crime. But we are left in some uncertainty in this case as to which party is entitled to the bad preëminence as blunderers and criminals.

We still ask ourselves sometimes what might have been if the counsels of Edmund Burke in England and Joseph Galloway in America had prevailed, and the whole British people had presented a united front against all falsehood and oppression. But the God of battles, the God of all the earth, ruled otherwise. His thoughts were not our thoughts, neither were our ways His ways. We submit to His ruling, and yet we trust that He was in those troublous times leading His people by ways they knew not to the larger and more steadfast achievement of both law and liberty for all the nations.

That portion of Dr. Ryerson's work which treats of the United Empire Loyalists in their pioneer Canadian life has always been interesting, but in

our times there is a new awakening of interest in
the subject. We are now far enough away from the
times of the first settlers to find a certain quaint-
ness in all that was theirs, and we are also in
danger of losing many of the traditions of those
times if we do not speedily secure in some way the
collections and recollections of those who stood in
closest connections with the past. Dr. Ryerson's
book is of special value to Canadians from this
point of view. It is written by a maker and the son
of a maker of Canada. And if it has something of
the irregularity of all such early things, it is full of
the spirit of liberty and law and truth, and buoyant
with the breezy strength that makes "this Canada
of ours" so dear to all Canadians.

CHAPTER XII

LATER CHURCH WORK AND CLOSING DAYS

AFTER his appointment to the office of chief superintendent of education, Dr. Ryerson still maintained both his connection with and his active influence and leadership in the Methodist conference. In that influence he was closely associated with his two elder brothers, the Revs. John and William Ryerson. The former down to his death in 1878, was respected by the whole conference for his eminent gifts as a legislator and administrator of Methodist polity. All three were active and able promoters of the reunion of the British with the Canadian Wesleyans which took place in 1847, and in the union of the Lower Canada District which took place in 1854. These various unions as well as the growth of the church introduced new elements and new leadership into the church in which three parties might now be distinctly traced. The British members of the conference with such men as Dr. Wood, Dr. Rice and Dr. Evans as prominent representatives constituted an able class of preachers, strongly conservative of all the views and usages of English Methodism. A thoroughly Canadian and progressive section of the conference was led and represented by such men as the Hurlburts, James Elliott, Jeffers and Spenser; while a more conservative Canadian section was represented by the Ryersons, Green, Jones, and Rose, with such younger men as Sanderson and Nelles. It would not be right to call these sections of the conference parties in the modern sense of the term, for there was no organization or pledged following; and in all the sections there were many men of such strong individuality that they followed no man. But history had given to each of these sections its peculiar tendency and character so definitely that the attitude of each on any great question might be safely predicted. The Ryersons, with the more conservative Canadians, were in general a mediating influence between the British and the more radical Canadians, and in that way did not a little to bring about and cement the unity of the body.

But in 1854 an incident occurred which for a time made Dr. Ryerson appear as the most extreme of radicals in Methodist polity, and even threatened to sever his connection with the conference. An intimate friend, a man whose Methodist lineage reached back to John Wesley's day, a man of spotless Christian character and life, and one active and useful in many fields of Christian work was "dropped" from church membership for non-attendance at class. The circumstance was at once so painful, and, though according to the letter of the law as well as the practice of the time, so anomalous from the broader point of view, that Dr. Ryerson took up the question with great earnestness, published a pamphlet on the subject, and when his views were not sustained by the majority of the conference, emphasized his protest by tendering his resignation as a minister of the church. In his pamphlet he claimed that membership in the Christian church was a sacred right as inviolable as the rights of citizenship and only forfeited by positive wrong doing. He held that now that Methodism had assumed the status and responsibilities of a church, a condition of membership which was established for a society in the church was no longer the proper test of true church membership, which should be based only upon the requirements of the New Testament. Beyond this he also pressed the right of all baptised children to more definite recognition and admission to the full privileges of church membership.

Dr. Ryerson's presentation of the case made at the time a deep impression upon the younger members of the conference. It certainly contained large elements of truth which were obviously neglected by the Methodism of that day. These truths were emphasized by the constant exercise of a somewhat arbitrary power to drop members from the church roll by simply omitting their names in the copying of the list to a new page at the end of the quarter. Wesley's regulations required that this should be done only after the cases had been examined in the leaders' meeting and admonition had been duly given. But even this safeguard was now very largely omitted. In the majority of cases where the member had grown careless and no longer valued his position and privilege as a member of the church, it might be that no substantial injustice was done. It was but the lopping off of dead branches which would in time fall off themselves if they had not already done so. But in seasons of ecclesiastical convulsion both in Canada and in England this had without doubt been used as an easy way of getting rid of troublesome persons. On the other hand, up to this time both in Canada and in the old country Methodism laid the emphasis in all her work upon the revival as the important means of filling the ranks of her membership, and upon the class meeting as the manifestation of a living Christian experience. To admit as co-ordinate or even superior to these two fundamentals, the use of catechumen classes and a permanent roll of membership conditioned upon the maintenance of a consistent Christian life, appeared to the old country Methodists and to the more conservative Canadians, and even to many who ranked as progressives, but were intensely earnest in their religious spirit, a most serious forsaking of the old ways. Strong pamphlets were written in reply to Dr. Ryerson's tract, and one important truth was brought into prominence, viz., that Christian fellowship was in the Apostolic

church a co-ordinate means of grace with the Word
or teaching of the apostles, the stated seasons of
prayer, and the sacraments of baptism and the
Lord's Supper. It was recognized as a scriptural
ordinance and not simply as a human and pru-
dential institution. On the other hand, from that
date onward the legislation of Canadian Methodism
moved steadily in the direction of more ample
provision and more careful effort to gather the
children into the church, and also in the direction
of more careful guarding of the sacred right of
church membership until finally the class meeting
has been placed on a par with the other scriptural
means of grace as a condition of membership in
the church.

In 1866-7, while making an educational tour
of Great Britain and Europe, Dr. Ryerson was
once more brought into close touch with English
Methodism, and especially with the late honoured
William Morley Punshon, then at the height of
his fame as a pulpit orator. The acquaintance
ripened into fast friendship and resulted in Mr.
Punshon's devoting his services for the benefit
of Canadian Methodism for the five years following
the summer of 1868, perhaps the most effective
period of his pulpit and platform work. The impulse
given to Canadian Methodism by this term of
service can never be fully estimated. He began by
attracting crowds of all classes of the population to
the old, and hitherto often despised Methodist

chapels. Easily outranking in oratorical powers the men of all other churches, he gave to Methodism an acknowledged status, corresponding to her superior numbers and rapidly increasing wealth and social position. With such a man in their pulpits even men of the world were no longer ashamed to be called Methodists. He made the Methodists respect themselves, and inspired them in all parts of the country with the ambition to erect places of worship commensurate with the work which they were called in the providence of God to perform. He met a crisis in the affairs of Victoria College by helping to establish that institution on the firm foundation of purely voluntary support. He attracted the attention of all branches of Methodism to the larger body, and by his relations to England smoothed the way to those needed adjustments which removed all obstacles to union and finally resulted in the consolidation of Canadian Methodism, first in part in 1874 and in full in 1883.

Into all this work of his chosen friend, Dr. Ryerson entered with the fire and enthusiasm of youth, mingled with the sagacity and wise experience of age. It became a favourite saying of his that one of his most important works for his church and country was the bringing of Mr. Punshon to Canada. With this new inspiration of church life throughout Canadian Methodism, the fifty years' services of Dr. Ryerson for his native land began to be estimated at their true value; while his wisdom and experience as a legislator placed him in the forefront of the negotiations for the first union. To him no more congenial task could be assigned than the healing of these breaches, which had all occurred in his own lifetime and as the result of struggles in which he himself had borne a prominent part; and when in 1874 the first stage of success was reached, he was by the united voice of all parties to the union, placed in the chair of the first general conference of united Canadian Wesleyan Methodism.

In the constitution of the united church, over which Dr. Ryerson was thus called to preside, two great principles were incorporated which had not previously obtained in the larger bodies composing the union. These were lay representation in the supreme assembly of the church, and a representative general conference for legislation, and the administration of the common connexional work of missions, education and religious literature. It was into this body alone that lay representation was introduced, the executive pastoral functions continuing in the annual conferences whose rights were very carefully guarded. In the hands of these annual courts, and their subordinate courts, district and circuit or station, the administration of the general work of the church was vested. Four departments, missions, education, book and publishing interests, and the support of worn-out ministers and widows were placed under separate bodies corporate, and administered by boards constituted by the

287

general conference in accordance with their several corporate charters. The president of the general conference presided in these boards, but exercised no general pastoral function in the church at large.

This form of organization continued for nine years, or until the completion of the second union in 1883, and was presided over by Dr. Ryerson from 1874 to 1878. From the beginning it was clearly seen that the solidarity and connexional spirit of the whole church were seriously imperilled by such a constitution. Even uniformity in the administration of the law and discipline of the church could scarcely be secured where the annual presidency changed yearly, and where, as in the east and west, historic traditions and usages had been somewhat different. The compactness, and, within the law of the discipline, the complete autonomy of the annual conferences, gave them, on the other hand, great efficiency in the building up of all local interests, and under strong leadership could easily make them a unit in their vote and influence in the general conference. The one influence to counterbalance these strong tendencies was the strength of the men at the head of the general conference administration, and their ability to reach the whole church at least every year.

The following extract from a letter to Dr. Ryerson from the late Dr. Punshon will illustrate this point:—"I am looking with some solicitude to the result of the appeal to the quarterly meetings on the union question. I hope it will be carried, though your modifications of the scheme do not quite meet my approval, as one who would like to see a statesman's view taken of things. I do not see the bond of cohesion twenty years hence when those who are now personally known to and therefore interested in each other, have passed off the stage. Then the general conference will meet as perfect strangers, having hardly a common interest but that of a common name, and as there are no general superintendents who know all the conferences there will not be, as in the States, any link to bind them together."

The history of the first and even of the second quadrennium was on these accounts very much of the nature of an experiment, and did not afford to Dr. Ryerson such an opportunity as would have made his large experience and great administrative ability most widely useful to the church. But as opportunity offered he gave most freely of his ability to the services of the church, and was found once more not only presiding over the great church boards and attending their great anniversary meetings, but also occupying the prominent pulpits of the church to lend assistance both in connexional and local work. His work in this way and still more that of his successor, the eloquent Dr. Douglas, did much to prepare the way for conferring larger powers on the chief executive officer at the second union.

One of the most interesting and important duties

imposed upon Dr. Ryerson by the general conference was a visit to England as representative of the Methodist Church of Canada to the British Wesleyan Methodist Conference. This mission he accomplished in the summer of 1876. Forty-three years earlier he had occupied a similar position for the first time, and thrice since he had been deputed to the same honourable duty. On this last visit his dignified and venerable appearance, his courteous manners, his eloquent and impressive address, and above all, the rich fulness of matter furnished by the experience of fifty years in the Christian ministry all combined to make his appearance before the conference an unusually marked event.

Apart from his duties as representative, his time in England was largely occupied in the collection of material for the completion of his last great work, the history of the United Empire Loyalists, to which we have already referred. Visiting the London annual conference assembled in Guelph there was laid upon him another literary labour, in response to which he prepared a most valuable volume entitled the "Epochs of Canadian Methodism," also already referred to in these pages.

There was now wanting but one year before the next assembly of the general conference, and already its important interests were engaging his earnest attention. His experience had deepened the conviction of the necessity of some form of general superintendency by which the community of interest and unity of action of the whole church might be more fully maintained. At the same time in the several conferences there were forming strong democratic tendencies and most pronounced opposition to any policy of greater centralization. The final conflict on this point did not take place until after Dr. Ryerson's death. But even as early as 1878 the opposing forces were cohering into defined parties and policies under able and active leadership. The general conference held in Montreal in 1878 was thus one of significant importance, starting as it did some of the movements which almost suddenly culminated in action, and in the union of the several annual and two general conferences of 1882 and 1883. Before these years with their strenuous conflict and victory for union and greater solidarity arrived, Dr. Ryerson had passed to his rest. It is therefore a matter of greater interest to trace his active part in the legislation of the preceding conference of 1878 which proved to be his last general conference.

As retiring president he opened the conference with an address in which, after sketching the history and growth of Methodism during his fifty years of ministerial life, he thus refers to the changes which he regards as necessary for its effective constitution:—" I doubt not you will deem it necessary to revise and improve the system of the transfer of the preachers from one part of the conferential work to another when judged necessary, as the

experiment of a transfer committee introduced four
years ago has proved cumbrous, expensive and inefficient. Equally, if not more important will it be
for you to supply some principle or authority of
connexional unity, as at present our connection
consists of a mere *congeries* of co-ordinate annual
conferences, and your president is the mere chairman of the general conference and is not even
a member of any annual conference except that
from which he happens to have been elected. The
oneness and unity of the body of the church obviously requires not merely a figurehead, but a real
head, like that of the natural body, as illustrated
by the example of the Methodist church both in
England and in the United States."

The two points thus referred to were intimately
related. The men who are called from one part of
the work to another are generally the men of mark.
They become known in all parts of the church. By
their personal knowledge of the different sections
and great centres of the work, they acquire a
broader interest and a wider outlook than if they
spent their whole life in a single conference and
were always identified with its interests. Nothing is
more conducive to the unity of interest and to
broad sympathy in all parts of the church than this
free circulation of the strongest men throughout
the work. If they breathe the free air of the west,
if they feel the full life of the great cities with their
manifold moral need, if they come into contact

292

with the great problems of different races and faiths, if from the seaports of the east they learn to look out upon the whole world, they cannot but carry with them throughout the church the influence of this varied life, and so bring its various sections into sympathy with each other. A general superintendency brings the power of one man to bear upon this problem of unification; a free transfer brings the power of scores of such to bear in the same direction. At best, the general superintendent can be but a passing visitor. The transferred pastor, on the other hand, remains long enough both to take in and to transmit the spirit of his successive environments.

But, accustomed as Dr. Ryerson had been all his life to strong leadership and central government, the superintendency appeared to him at present the most important need of the church. Two facts since demonstrated by history were not then so fully manifest. Individual leadership was weakening. The great leaders of the past, men who had entered the ministry in the twenties and the thirties were on the eve of passing. Ryerson himself, Green, Carroll, Douse, Evans, Rose, James Elliott, George Young, J. H. Robinson, Borland, were members of a general conference for the last time, Lachlin Taylor was present only as a visitor, and Asahel Hurlburt, elected a member, died before the session. The younger men, even if equal in ability, could not wield the same influence in the larger sphere and over men who were more nearly their equals in intellectual power. On the other hand, constitutional forces were increasing in influence and becoming far more powerful and important than individual men. The transfer system and the status and attitude of the annual conference were thus more important questions than the general superintendency, and as the result has proved much more difficult to solve.

Early in the conference Dr. Ryerson gave notice of motion on the subject of a virtual superintendency as follows:—"That the president of the general conference shall devote his time, as far as possible, in visiting every part of the work ; that he shall be considered a member of each of the several annual conferences, and when present at their sessions shall preside over their proceedings ; and that the president of each annual conference shall preside over its proceedings in the absence of the president of the general conference."

A discussion of this resolution resulted only in provision for such assistance to the president of the general conference as would enable him to give more time to travel throughout the church, but gave him no status in the annual conference. The subject of transfers was taken up by younger legislators but no very substantial progress was made towards its solution. Both of these important questions thus stood over for the second union.

The close of the general conference was virtually

the close of Dr. Ryerson's active ministerial life. In 1879 after fifty-four years' active work, the longest period on record in Canadian Methodism, he took his place on the list of superannuates, being now in the seventy-sixth year of his age. His remaining days were spent in the quiet of his home near the scene of his life work, and in visits to the home of his boyhood and to his aged brother. As strength permitted he continued his literary work almost to the last, often assisted by younger friends who counted it a privilege to be associated with a great and good man in the closing labours of his life. Into the beautiful scenes of affectionate tenderness and Christian hope of these last days it would not become this work to enter. They belong rather to the field of personal and religious biography. But we cannot forbear to copy the words in which his lifelong friend and co-labourer, Dr. Hodgins, depicts the final scene:—

"To such a man death had no terrors, the heart had no fear. It was cheering and comforting to listen to him (as I often did alone) and to hear him speak of his near departure as of one preparing for a journey, ceasing from duty in order to be ready to be conveyed away and then resuming it when the journey was over. Thus he spoke of the time of his departure as at hand, and he was ready for the messenger when he should call for him. He spoke of it trustfully, hopefully, cheerfully, neither anxious nor fearful, and yet, on the other hand, neither elated nor full of joy. But he knew in whom he had trusted, and was persuaded, and was not afraid of evil tidings either of the dark valley or of the river of death. He knew whom he believed, and was persuaded that He was able to keep that which he had committed unto Him against that day.

"Thus the end drew near, and with it, as the outward man began to fail, the feeling of unwavering trust and confidence was deepened and strengthened. At length hearing failed, and the senses one by one partially ceased to perform their functions. Then to him were fully realized the inspired words of Solomon: 'Desire failed, and the silver cord was loosed, the golden bowl was broken, the pitcher broken at the fountain, and the wheel broken at the cistern.' Gradually the weary wheels of life stood still, and at seven o'clock on Sunday morning February 19th, 1882, in the presence of his loved ones and dear friends, gently and peacefully the spirit of Egerton Ryerson took its flight."

After such a life the pageant of a funeral and the pomp of monumental grandeur are empty trifles. But to honour him in his death, as he had served them in his life the whole country seemed assembled in its representatives. Government house, legislative halls, the bench of judges, university and academic authorities, ecclesiastical dignitaries of all names, thousands from the schools which he had founded, and above all, the common people

HONOURED IN DEATH

for whose cause he never failed to stand, followed
to the grave the remains of the great Canadian
who had lived so faithfully and well for his country.

> " Hush, the dead march wails in the people's ears;
> The dark crowd moves, and there are sobs and tears;
> The black earth yawns, the mortal disappears;
> Ashes to ashes, dust to dust;
> He is gone who seemed so great,—
> Gone; but nothing can bereave him
> Of the force he made his own
> Being here, and we believe him
> Something far advanced in state,
> And that he wears a truer crown
> Than any wreath that man can weave him."

INDEX

INDEX

INDEX

BALDWIN LAFONTAINE HINCKS

BALDWIN LAFONTAINE HINCKS

RESPONSIBLE GOVERNMENT

BY

STEPHEN LEACOCK

TORONTO
MORANG & CO., LIMITED
1910

PREFACE

IN the present volume the narrative of personal biography is subordinated to the record of political achievement. The name of Robert Baldwin and that of his distinguished colleague Louis La-Fontaine will always be associated with the words responsible government. Baldwin was frequently de-rided by his contemporaries as a "man of one idea." Time has shown that this "one idea" of Robert Baldwin,—the conception of responsible govern-ment,—has proved the corner-stone of the British imperial system. It is fitting, therefore, that this brief account of the political career of Robert Baldwin and his associates should centre round the evolution of responsible government in the province of Can-ada. In other works of the present series the periods of Canadian history preceding and following the LaFontaine-Baldwin administrations have already been treated. The biography of Papineau, already published, and the forthcoming biography of William Lyon Mackenzie offer an ample ac-count of the stirring events of the rebellion. Sir John Bourinot in his *Lord Elgin* and Mr. Lewis in his *George Brown* have told the story of the ad-ministration of Hincks and Morin after the retire-ment of their former chiefs. The present narrative is therefore especially concerned with the two LaFon-

PREFACE

taine-Baldwin ministries and with the great political controversy during the administration of Sir Charles Metcalfe.

The author desires to express his sincere thanks for the very valuable assistance and useful suggestions received from Dr. James Bain, Librarian of the Toronto Public Library, and from Mr. Charles Gould, Librarian of McGill University. The author owes much also to the kindness of Dr. A. G. Doughty, C.M.G., Archivist of the Dominion Government.

STEPHEN LEACOCK.

McGill University,
July 31st, 1906.

x

CONTENTS

CONTENTS

CHAPTER I

INTRODUCTORY

FROM the time of the surrender of Canada by the capitulation of Vaudreuil at Montreal in 1760, the government of the province presented an unsolved problem, whose difficulties finally culminated in the outbreak of 1837. In the beginning the country was entirely French, an appanage of the British Crown by right of conquest. Its population, some seventy thousand in number, thinly spread along the valley of the St. Lawrence, was almost entirely an agricultural peasantry. Ignorant and illiterate as they were, they cherished towards their Church an unfailing devotion, while a stubborn pride of nationality remained with them as a heritage from the great country from which they had sprung. Of initial loyalty to the British Crown there could be no question. Still less could there be any question of self-government. Military rule was established as a necessity of the situation. Even when, in 1764, a year after the final treaty of cession, the purely military rule was superseded by the institution of an executive council, this body consisted merely of a group of officials appointed by the governor of the province. Nor is it to be said that this form of government was of itself an injustice. The

1

inhabitants of French Canada had known nothing of political rights[1] or representative institutions. Only in rare cases had offices, favour, or promotion been bestowed upon native Canadians. Even the Church itself, in spite of its democratic tradition in favour of capacity and zeal, had withheld all superior offices from the children of the humble peasantry of the St. Lawrence. To have instituted among such a people a system of democratic self-government on the morrow of the conquest, could only have ended in chaos and disaster.

The government thus established by royal proclamation was systematized and consolidated by the British parliament through the Quebec Act of 1774.[2] This statute established in Canada a province of magnificent extent. Northward it extended to the Hudson Bay Territory; on the south it bordered New England, New York, Pennsylvania and the Ohio; westward it reached to where all trace of civilization ended with the Mississippi River. The Ohio valley was already dotted here and there in its forests and open meadow lands with the cabins of adventurous settlers. Of the rest of Canada the valley of the St. Lawrence was the only occupied part. Thither had come already, since the conquest, a few British immigrants, for the most part small traders[3]

[1] Kingsford, *History of Canada*, Vol. IX., pp. 190 *et seq.*

[2] 14 Geo. III., c. 83.

[3] See V. Coffin, *The Province of Quebec and the Early American Revolution* (1896), Ch. II. pp. 303 *et seq.*

and needy adventurers. The upper portion of the province was still a wilderness. The Quebec Act restored to the country the old French civil law, the "*Coutume de Paris*," under which it had lived before the conquest. It retained the English criminal law. It repeated the guarantee of freedom of worship already extended to the adherents of the Roman Catholic Church, and, in permitting to the clergy of that Church the enjoyment of their "accustomed dues and rights," it legalized the collection of the tithe.[1] The government was committed to a governor with a legislative council to be nominated by the Crown, to which was added by Major-General Carleton (1776), in accordance with instructions from England, an executive (or privy) council of five members. The Act declared it "inexpedient to call an assembly." Fox, indeed, pleaded in the House of Commons in favour of representative institutions, but was met with the argument that a Protestant government could not safely entrust power to a Roman Catholic legislature.[2]

It is a disputed point how far the concessions thus granted to the French were adopted as a means of preserving the country from the infection of the revolutionary discontent, widespread in the colonies of the Atlantic sea-board, and of preventing the French *habitant* from making common cause with

[1] The tithe was, however, only to be collected from persons professing the Roman Catholic religion.

[2] Sir H. Cavendish, *Debates on the Quebec Act*, (1839), pp. 246-8.

the malcontents of New England and Virginia. Such, if not the purpose, was at any rate the effect of the Act. The pulpits of Massachusetts were loud with denunciation of the toleration of popery embodied in the statute. The American congress (September 5th, 1774) expressed its alarm in documentary form, and the small British minority already settled in Lower Canada forwarded to England a petition of energetic protest. The fact that the British government, in the face of bigoted opposition, passed and maintained the statute which stands as the charter of religious liberty for Roman Catholic Canada, may be said to have laid the foundation of that firm attachment of the Canadian French to the Crown, which, after the lapse of four generations, has become one of the fundamental factors of the political life of Canada. The effect of the Act in preventing the adherence of the *habitants* to the cause of the American revolution is undoubted. The clergy of the province threw the whole weight of their influence in favour of the British side. The agitators sent into the country found but few sympathizers of influence, and the attempt at military conquest ended in failure.

The issue of the Revolutionary War and the separation of the revolted colonies from Great Britain had a momentous effect upon the destinies of British North America. That province now became a haven of refuge for the distressed Loyalists, who abandoned the United States in thousands rather than sever their allegiance from their mother country. Of these nearly thirty thousand found their way into the Maritime Provinces. Others, ascending the St. Lawrence or coming by Lake Champlain, settled in the Eastern Townships of Quebec or near to Montreal itself. Still others, pushing their way up the river or passing over the rough wagon-trails of the forest country of New York, embarked on Lake Ontario to find new homes upon its northern shores. Liberal grants of land were made. Settlements sprang up along the Bay of Quinté, on the Niagara frontier, on the Grand River, on the Thames and as far west as the Detroit River. By the year 1791 there were some thirty thousand settlers in the districts thus thrown open. The newcomers, impoverished as most of them were, made excellent pioneers. Their conviction of the righteousness of their cause lent vigour to their arduous struggle with the wilderness. The sound of the axe resounded amid the stillness of the pine forest; farmsteads and hamlets arose on the shores of the lake and beside its tributary streams. But with the coming of the Loyalists Canada became a divided country. The population of the upper country was British, that of the lower, French. French law and custom seemed to the new settlers anomalous and unjust. British Protestantism was abhorrent to the devout Catholics of French Canada. The new settlers, too, accustomed to the political freedom which they had enjoyed in the colonies of their origin, chafed under autocratic control, and in repeated petitions demanded of the home government the privilege of a representative assembly.[1]

To meet this situation the British parliament adopted the Constitutional Act of 1791,[2] by which the province was separated into two distinct governments under the names of Upper and Lower Canada. It was presumed that a natural solution of the vexed question of British and French rivalry had thus been found. " I hope," said Pitt, "that this settlement will put an end to the competition between the old French inhabitants and the new settlers from Britain and the British colonies." Burke at the same time expressed the opinion that "to attempt to amalgamate two populations composed of races of men diverse in language, laws, and customs, was a complete absurdity."[3] To each province was given a legislature consisting of two Houses, the Lower House, or assembly, being elected by the people, the Upper, called the legislative council, being nominated for life by the Crown. By the Crown also were to be appointed all public officers of each district, including the governor-general of the two provinces, the lieutenant-governor who conducted the administration of Upper Canada, and the members of the executive councils which aided in

[1] *Canadian Archives*, Q. 24. 1. pp., 76, 232.

[2] 31 Geo. III. c. 31.

[3] See *Parliamentary History*. Vol. xxvii, p. 1271, Vol. xxxix, pp. 359-459.

the administration of each province. The British parliament reserved to itself the right of imposing duties for the regulation of navigation and commerce. The free exercise of the Roman Catholic religion was again guaranteed. It was further enacted that the Crown should set apart one-eighth of all the unallotted Crown land in the province for the maintenance of a Protestant clergy, a provision which subseqently entailed the most serious consequences.

The measure was undoubtedly liberal, and at the time of its passage furnished an instrument of goverment well suited to the requirements of the situation. It was intended to extend to Canada something of the degree of political liberty enjoyed by the people of Great Britain. Its object was declared by Lord Grenville,[1] to be to "assimilate the constitution of Canada to that of Great Britain as nearly as the difference arising from the manners of the people and from the present situation of the province will admit." Lieutenant-Governor Simcoe, speaking to his "parliament" of twenty-three members in the rough frame-house at Niagara where first they met, spoke of the new government as "an image and transcript of the British constitution."[2] For some years, indeed, after the adoption of the new constitution, the government of the provinces was carried on with reasonable success

[1] Letter to Lord Dorchester, Oct. 20th, 1789.

[2] Consult D. B. Read, *Life and Times of Governor Simcoe*, Ch. XI. and D. C. Scott, *John Graves Simcoe* (Makers of Canada Series) (1905), Ch. VI.

and a fair amount of harmony. Had the constitution been of a more flexible character and had the conduct of the administration been adapted to the progressive settlement of the country, its success might have continued indefinitely. The incoming century found a contented country;[1] wealth and population were on the increase. A tide of immigration from Scotland and Ireland turned steadily towards Upper Canada. Pennsylvania farmers crossed the lakes to find new homes in the fertile land of the province. The little hamlet of York, on the site of the old Indian post of Toronto, became the seat of government. To the north of it a wide, straight road, called Yonge Street in honour of the secretary of war, carried the tide of settlement towards Lake Simcoe. At the head of Lake Ontario, Dundas Street ran from the settlement at Hamilton to the Thames, and presently was opened eastward as far as York. The inhabitants of the province in the year 1811 were estimated at seventy-seven thousand.[2] Into Lower Canada also British immigrants had come in considerable numbers. Ere long it began to appear that the racial conflict, which it was the intention of the Act of 1791 to obviate, had but shifted its ground and was renewed with increasing bitterness in the province of Lower Canada. The War of 1812, in which the energies of both French and British settlers were absorbed in repelling American invasion,

[1] McMullen, *History of Canada* (1868), pp. 222 *et seq.*

[2] J. Bouchette, *British Dominions in North America* (1832), Vol. 1. p. 108.

stilled for the time the internal conflict of races. But with the renewal of peace the political difficulties of both Upper and Lower Canada assumed an increasingly serious aspect.

The political situation in the two provinces in the twenty years succeeding the peace of 1815 presented analogous, though not identical, features. In each of them the fact that the executive was not under the control of the representatives of the people constituted the main cause of complaint. But in the Lower Province the situation was aggravated by the fact that the executive heads of the administration were identified with the interests of the British minority and opposed to the dominance of the French-Canadians. Even in Upper Canada, however, the position of affairs was bad enough. The actual administration of the province was in the hands of the lieutenant-governor and his executive council of five, later of seven, members, a wholly irresponsible body of placemen appointed by the Crown from among the judges, public officers and members of the legislative council. Of the legislature itself the Upper House, or legislative council, was, as already said, a nominated body. Under such circumstances the political control of the colony had passed into the hands of a privileged class who engrossed the patronage of the Crown, received liberal grants of land and were able to bid defiance to the efforts of the assembly to free itself from oligarchical control.

9

Had the constitution been in any real sense a "transcript" of the constitution of Great Britain, the assembly might have fallen back upon the power of the purse as an effective method of political control. But this remedy, under the system in vogue, was inadequate, owing to the fact that the assembly possessed only a limited power over the finances of the colony. The Crown was in enjoyment of a permanent civil list. Exclusive of the revenue from the clergy reserve, it had at its disposal a patronage of fifty thousand pounds a year. Local expenditure within the province was under the direction of magistrates appointed by the Crown meeting in Quarter Session.[1] The legislative council itself claimed the right to reject, and even to amend, the money bills passed by the representatives of the people. Under such circumstances the House of Assembly found itself deprived of any effective means of forcing its wishes upon the administration.[2] Quite early in the history of the period, it had vigorously protested against the impotence to which it was reduced. In an address presented to the acting governor in 1818, the assembly drew attention to the " evil that must result from the legislative and executive functions being materially vested in the same persons, as is unfortunately the case in this province, where His Majesty's executive council is almost wholly com-

---

[1] See in this connection C. Lindsey, *Life and Times of William Lyon Mackenzie* (1862), Vol. I., pp. 330-2.

[2] Kingsford, Vol. IX., pp. 216 *et seq.*

posed of the legislative body, and consisting only of
the deputy superintendent-general of the Indian
department, the receiver-general and the inspector-
general, the chief-justice, the speaker of the legislative council, and the honourable and reverend chap-
lain of that House." The essence of the financial situation appears in the famous Seventh Report of the
Committee on Grievances[1] drawn up in 1835. "Such
is the patronage of the colonial office," it declares,
"that the granting or withholding of supplies is of
no political importance, unless as an indication of
the opinion of the country concerning the character
of the government."

It has become customary to apply to the privileged class who thus engrossed political power and
office in the colony of Upper Canada, the term
Family Compact. The designation itself appears to
be, in strictness, a misnomer, for there existed among
the ruling class no further family relationship than
what might naturally be expected in a community
whose seat of government contained, even in 1830,
only two thousand eight hundred and sixty persons.
But it is undoubted that, from 1815 onwards, the
members of the administration with their friends and
adherents formed a distinct political party united
by ties of mutual interest and social cohesion, de-

[1] The report was published in detail by M. Reynolds, King's Printer,
Toronto (1835), and contains an index and much valuable material. It
must, of course, be remembered that the report is a document of a partisan character, but the quotation in the text above may be accepted as
representing the situation.

11

termined to retain the influence they had acquired, and regarding the protests of the plainer people of the province with a certain supercilious contempt. Nor is it to be supposed that the adherents of the Family Compact embodied in themselves the very essence of tyranny. They represented merely, within their restricted sphere, those principles of class government and vested interests which were still the dominant political factor in every country of Europe. Of the high moral quality and sterling patriotism of such men as Robinson, the attorney-general, there can be no doubt. The exaggerated diatribes of the indignant Radicals in which the ruling class figure as the "tools of servile power,"[1] are as wide of the mark as the later denunciations launched against the party of Reform.

The growing agitation in Upper Canada presently found an energetic leader in William Lyon Mackenzie, a Scotchman of humble parentage. Born at Springfield in Forfarshire in 1795, he came in 1820 to try his fortunes in Canada. He set up in business in a small way at the village of York, removing presently to Dundas. It is typical of the restricted commercial life of the time that Mackenzie and his partner dealt in drugs, hardware, jewelry, toys, confections, dye stuffs

[1] Mackenzie's *Colonial Advocate*, No. I. Compare the petition prepared for presentation to the home government by Robert Fleming Gourlay, whose agitation in the second decade of the century was one of the first expressions of the gathering discontent : " Corruption, indeed, has reached such a height in this province that it is thought no part of the British empire witnesses the like."

12

and paints, and maintained in addition a circulating library. From Dundas, Mackenzie moved to Queenston. Interested from the first in the political affairs of the colony, he started in 1824 the publication of the *Colonial Advocate*, the first number of which, distributed gratuitously through the countryside, commenced an unsparing attack upon the governing class. Its editor, the "westernmost journalist in the British dominions on the continent of America," assumed, as he himself subsequently expressed it, "the office of a public censor." He denounced the Family Compact and all its works. He denounced the jobbery of the public land. He denounced the land monopoly of the Church of England, the lack of schools, the perversion of justice and the greed of the official class. The appearance of the *Colonial Advocate* aided in consolidating the party of Reform. In the elections of 1824 they carried a majority of the seats in the House of Assembly, a victory which only served to reveal the impotence of the opposition in the face of the established system. Dr. Rolph, elected for Middlesex, the stalwart Peter Perry, member for Lennox and Addington, and other leaders of the Reform party, found they could do little beyond selecting a farmer speaker of their own liking and passing resolutions condemning the existing conduct of affairs. None the less their presence as a majority of the House remained as a standing protest and threw into a clearer light the irresponsible position of the executive.[1] The better to aid their opposition Mackenzie moved his printing presses to York. The virulence of his pen awoke embittered opposition in return. His printing office was sacked in broad daylight by a gang of young men whom his biographer has called an "official mob." A lawsuit ensued with mutual recriminations, followed presently by prosecutions for libel. Mackenzie, in historic phrase, denounced the minority party in the assembly as an "ominous nest of unclean birds," and invited the people of Upper Canada to sweep them from the "halls that have been so long and shamefully defiled with their abominations."

The provincial quarrel went from bad to worse. The election of 1828 again returned a majority of Reformers, this time including Mackenzie himself. Resolutions of grievances were presented to the House. A select committee on grievances, of which Mackenzie was chairman, was called upon to report. A new lieutenant-governor in the person of Sir John Colborne, a tried soldier and a veteran of Waterloo, appeared on the scene (1828). Him the assembly hastened to warn against the "unhappy policy they [the executive council] had pursued in the late administration." The assembly asserted its right to the full control of the revenue and demanded (1830) the dismissal of the executive councillors. "Gentlemen," was the curt reply of Sir

[1] A list of the members of the assembly is given by Lindsey, *op. cit.* p. 59.

PETITIONS AND COUNTER-PETITIONS

John, "I thank you for your address." In the election of 1830, following on the death of George III, the party of the Compact, aided by an influx of British immigrants, regained a majority of the assembly. Mackenzie, elected for the county of York, was expelled from the House for libel and branded as a "reptile unworthy of the notice of any gentleman."[1] Reëlected by his constituents, he was again expelled and declared disqualified to sit in the existing parliament, a proceeding which occasioned wild tumult in the village capital, with sympathetic meetings in the other settlements of the colony. The Tory party retaliated, perpetrated a second attack on the printing office of the *Advocate*, and burned Mackenzie in effigy in the streets of York. Mackenzie, seizing the moment of martyrdom, sailed for England laden with indignant petitions from his constituents and their sympathizers, (April, 1832). The signatures on the documents numbered twenty-five thousand, but the counter-petitions forwarded by the party of the Compact were subscribed with twenty-six thousand names. Mackenzie received at the colonial office a not unfavourable hearing. Lord Goderich, the colonial secretary, forwarded to the colony a censorious despatch, characterized by the indignant Tories as an "elegant piece of fiddle faddle." Hagerman, the solicitor-general, was removed

[1] A phrase used by Solicitor-General Hagerman. See *Colonial Advocate*, Dec. 15th, 1831.

from office, only to be restored when Lord Goderich gave place to Mr. Stanley. Boulton, the
attorney-general, was permanently removed. Beyond this nothing of account was done by the
home government to remedy the situation in the
colony. Mackenzie on his return again presented
himself to his constituents for election, (December
16th, 1833), only to be again expelled from the
House. The general election of the ensuing year,
(October, 1834), resulted in the return of a majority of the Reform party to the House, Mackenzie
being among those then elected. Opposition to the
oligarchical system now became more and more
pronounced. A "Canadian Alliance Society" was
founded at York, (henceforth incorporated as a city
and known as Toronto), whose political programme
opened with the demand for responsible government and the abolition of the nominated legislative
council. A select committee on grievances, appointed
by the assembly, drew up a voluminous report, in
which the misgovernment of Upper Canada was
scathingly reviewed. Such was the position of affairs
in the province at the time when Sir Francis
Bond Head entered upon his momentous administration.

During the same period a still more aggravated
situation had been developed in Lower Canada.
Here the conflict represented something more
than a struggle between an office-holding minority
and the excluded masses. It was a conflict inten-

sified by the full bitterness of racial and religious antagonism. It was not merely as in Upper Canada, (to use the historic phrases of Lord Durham), " a contest between a government and a people; " the spectacle presented was that of " two nations warring in the bosom of a single state," a " struggle, not of principles, but of races."[1] The British minority in the province, insignificant in the early years of the new régime, had grown constantly in numbers and influence. The incoming of the United Empire Loyalists and of immigrants from the mother country had swelled the ranks of a party which, though small in proportion, was determined to assert its claims against the preponderating race. British merchants controlled the bulk of the sea-going trade of the colony.[2] An Anglican bishop of Quebec had been appointed (1793), and an Anglican cathedral erected (1804) on the site of an ancient convent of the Récollets. The governors of the province looked to the British party for support, and selected from its ranks the majority of their legislative and executive councillors. In the minds of the latter the French-Canadians still figured as a conquered people whose claims to political ascendency were equivalent to disloyalty. The blundering patriotism of such a governor as Craig (1807-11), widened the cleavage between the rival races and intensified in the

[1] *Report of the Earl of Durham*, (Ed. 1902) p. 8.
[2] D. B. Read, *Rebellion of 1837*, p. 49.

minds of the French inhabitants the sentiment of their national solidarity. Excluded from the control of the executive government, the French fell back upon the assembly in which they commanded an easy and permanent majority. Nor were they, although in opposition, altogether powerless against the government. The public revenue of Lower Canada during the period under review was raised, in part by virtue of imperial statutes,[1] in part by the provincial legislature itself. To these sources of income were added the "casual and territorial" revenue of the Crown arising from the Jesuits' Estates, the postal service, the land and timber sales and other minor items. The duties raised by the imperial government,[2] together with the casual and territorial revenue, were inadequate to meet the public expenditure, and it was necessary, therefore, to have recourse to the votes of supply passed by the House of Assembly. The House of Assembly, dominated by the French-Canadian party, made full use of the power thus placed in its hands. It insisted (1818) that the detailed items of expenditure should be submitted to its consideration. It asserted its claim to appropriate not merely the revenue raised by its own act, but the whole expenditure of the province. It insisted on voting the civil list from year to year, refusing to vote a permanent provision for the salaried servants of the

[1] 14 Geo. III. c. 88, and later 3 Geo. IV. c. 119.

[2] The appropriation of this revenue was surrendered in 1831.

Crown. On each point it met with a determined opposition, not only from the governor-general but from the legislative council, whose existence thus began to appear as the main obstacle to that full control of the province which had become the avowed aim of the popular party.

With the advent of Lord Dalhousie as governor-general (1820) the quarrel between the two branches of the legislature and the conflict of races from which it had sprung, reached an acute stage. Dalhousie, one of Wellington's veterans, was more fitted for the camp than the council chamber, a disciplinarian devoid of diplomacy who naturally upheld the side of the British party and discountenanced the financial claims of the assembly.[1] Meantime the occasion had found the man, and a leader had appeared well-fitted to head the agitation in the province. Louis-Joseph Papineau, born in Montreal in 1789, had been elected to the assembly in 1812 and early distinguished himself by the brilliance of his oratory. In 1815 he was elected speaker of the House, a position which he filled with decorum until the trend of affairs under the Dalhousie administration aroused him to virulent and sustained opposition to the governing class. From now on, petitions and addresses for redress of grievances in Lower Canada poured in upon the imperial government. The French-Canadian press roused the simple farm-

[1] See A. D. DeCelles, *Papineau*, (Makers of Canada Series) 1904. Ch. VI.

ers of the countryside with the cry of national rights;
even a certain minority of the English residents, led
by such men as Cuthbert of Berthier and Neilson of
Quebec, in close alliance with Papineau, made common cause with the French for a reform of the
government of the province. On the other hand, the
adherents of the ruling powers openly expressed
their desire to rid the country of every vestige of
French control. "This province" the Quebec *Mer-
cury* had said as long ago as 1810, "is far too French
for a British colony. After forty-seven years' possession it is now fitting that the province become truly
British." Such indeed had become the avowed policy
of the dominant faction. Papineau, supported alike
by the people, the clergy[1] and the majority of the
assembly, became emphatically the man of the hour
and figured as the open adversary of the governor-
general. A petition signed with eighty-seven thousand names was forwarded (1827) to the home government. Dalhousie, departing in 1828 to take command of the forces in India, was succeeded by Sir
James Kempt whose efforts at conciliation proved
unavailing. In vain the imperial government surrendered its control over the proceeds of its customs
duties (1831). The assembly refused to grant a
permanent civil list and the leaders of the popular
party clamoured for the abolition of the nominated
Upper House. Against such a measure of reform,
which appeared out of harmony with monarchical

[1] DeCelles, *op. cit.* p. 61.

institutions, the British ministry resolutely set its face. Stanley, the colonial secretary, hinted that the government might be forced to curtail even the existing privileges of its colonial subjects. Aroused to furious opposition the assembly adopted the famous "Ninety-two resolutions," indicating a long catalogue of grievances and denouncing the existence of the Upper House (February 21st, 1834). The elections of 1834 were attended with riots and tumultuous gatherings. Revolutionary committees sprang into being. Votes of supplies since 1832 had come to a full stop and the governor, Lord Aylmer, (1831-5), had been driven to pay salaries by loans taken from the war chest. The malcontents of French Canada corresponded busily with the "patriot" party of the Upper Province. The current of the two movements ran side by side with increasing swiftness, approaching rapidly the vortex of insurrection.

CHAPTER II

THE MODERATE REFORMERS AND THE CANADIAN REBELLION

SUCH was the environment in which Robert Baldwin and his future colleagues in the Reform ministry of Canada, entered upon political life. The Baldwins were sprung from an Irish family resident on a little property called Summer Hill, near Carragoline, in the county of Cork. The father of Robert Baldwin had come out to Canada with his father (himself a Robert Baldwin) in 1798. The family settled on a tract of land on the north shore of Lake Ontario, in the present county of Durham, where Robert Baldwin (senior) set himself manfully to work to clear and cultivate a farm to which he gave the name of Annarva.[1] His eldest son, William Warren Baldwin, did not, however, remain upon the homestead. He had already received at the University of Edinburgh a degree in medicine and, anxious to turn his professional training to account, he went to the little village of York. Here he took up his abode with a Mr. Wilcocks of Duke Street, an Irish friend of his family, who had indeed been instrumental in inducing the Baldwins to come to Canada. In a pioneer

---

[1] The details which follow are taken from the *Memorial of the Baldwin Family*, (*Archives of Canada*, M. 393) and from the *Canadian Portrait Gallery*, published at Toronto, 1881.

colony like the Upper Canada of that day, the health of the community is notoriously sound, and Dr. Baldwin soon saw that the profession of medicine at York could offer but a precarious livelihood. He determined, therefore, to supplement it with school-teaching and inserted in the *Gazette* an announcement of his intention to open a classical school:—
"Dr. Baldwin, understanding that some gentlemen of this town have expressed an anxiety for the establishment of a classical school, begs leave to inform them and the public that he intends on Monday, the first of January next [1803], to open a school in which he will instruct twelve boys in writing, reading, classics and arithmetic. The terms are, for each boy, eight guineas per annum, to be paid quarterly or half yearly; one guinea entrance and one cord of wood to be supplied by each of the boys on opening the school." It is interesting to note that among the earliest of Dr. Baldwin's pupils was John Robinson, distinguished later as a leading spirit in the Family Compact and chief-justice of the province.

School-teaching with the ambitious Irishman was, however, only a means to an end. The legal profession, then in its infancy in the colony, offered a more lucrative and a more honourable field, and for this in his leisure hours Baldwin hastened to prepare himself. Indeed no very arduous preparation or profound knowledge was needed in those days for admission to the legal fraternity of "Muddy York." A

24

summary examination, conducted in person by the chief-justice of the province, was all that was required of Baldwin as a candidate for the bar, and on April 6th, 1803, he was admitted as a duly qualified practitioner. His entry upon his new profession was signalized by his marriage in the same year with Miss Phœbe Wilcocks, a daughter of the family friend with whom he had lived. The newly married couple took up their quarters in a new house on the corner of Frederick and Palace Streets,[1] the latter a street running parallel with the shore of the bay and receiving its grandiloquent name from the expectation that it would presently become the site of a gubernatorial "palace." In this house Robert Baldwin, eldest son of William Warren Baldwin was born on May 12th, 1804.

Little need be said of Robert Baldwin's youth and school days. By no means a precocious child, he was distinguished at school rather for a painstaking diligence than for exceptional natural aptitude. He received his education at the Home District Grammar School, at the head of which was Dr. John Strachan, then rector of York and subsequently distinguished as Bishop of Toronto and champion of the Anglican interest. Baldwin's conscientious industry presently made him "head boy" of the Grammar School, from whose walls he passed with credit to enter upon the study of the law (1819). After spending some years in his father's office, he was called

[1] Palace Street is the present Front Street.

to the bar in Trinity Term, 1825, and became a partner in his father's business under the firm name of "W. W. Baldwin and Son." The fortunes of the elder Baldwin had in the meantime rapidly improved. Not only had he met with success in his dual profession, but he had the good fortune to fall heir to the property of a Miss Elizabeth Russell, a distant connection of the Baldwins, and sister to a certain Peter Russell, a bygone magnate of the little colony whose extensive estates she had herself inherited and now bequeathed to William Baldwin. Desirous to use his new found wealth for the foundation of a family estate,[1] Dr. Baldwin purchased a considerable tract of land to the north of the little town on the summit of the hill overlooking the present city of Toronto. To this property the name " Spadina " was given, and the wide road opened by Dr. Baldwin southward through a part of the Russell estate was christened Spadina Avenue.

Both father and son were keenly interested in the political affairs of the province. The elder Baldwin was a Liberal and prominent among the Reformers who, even before the advent of William Lyon Mackenzie, denounced the oligarchical control of the

[1] "His purpose was to establish in Canada a family whose head was to be maintained in opulence by the proceeds of an entailed estate. There was to be forever a Baldwin of Spadina." H. Scadding, *Toronto of Old*, p. 66. The same work contains many interesting details in reference to the Baldwin residences and some account of the "closing exercises" of Dr. Strachan's school (Aug. 11-12, 1819) at which Robert Baldwin delivered a "prologue." *Op. cit.* Index. Art. Baldwin.

Family Compact. But he was at the same time profoundly attached to the British connection and averse by temperament to measures of violence. While making common cause with the Mackenzie faction in the furtherance of better government, Dr. Baldwin and his associates were nevertheless separated from the extreme wing of the Reformers by all the difference that lies between the Whig and the Radical. The political aims were limited to converting the constitution of the colony into a real, and not merely a nominal, transcript of the British constitution. To effect this, it seemed only necessary to render the executive officers of the government responsible to the popular House of the legislature in the same way as the British cabinet stands responsible to the House of Commons. This one reform accomplished, the other grievances of the colonists would find a natural and immediate redress. Robert Baldwin sympathized entirely with the political views of his father. Moderate by nature, he had no sympathy with the desire of the Radical section of the party to abolish the legislative council, or to assimilate the institutions of the country to those of the United States. The Alpha and Omega of his programme of political reform lay in the demand for the introduction of responsible government. His opponents, even some of his fellow Reformers, taunted him with being a "man of one idea." Viewed in the clearer light of retrospect it is no reproach to his political insight

27

that his "one idea" proved to be that which ultimately saved the situation and which has since become the corner stone of the British colonial system.

The year 1829 may be said to mark the commencement of Robert Baldwin's public life. He had already taken part in election committees and was known as one of the rising young men among the moderate Reformers. He had, moreover, in the election of 1828, unsuccessfully offered himself as a candidate for the county of York. But in 1829 we find him figuring as the draftsman of the petition addressed to George IV in connection with the Willis affair. Willis, an English barrister of some prominence, had been appointed in 1827 to be one of the judges of the court of king's bench in Upper Canada. While holding that office he had held aloof from the faction of the Family Compact and had thereby incurred the displeasure of the authorities, who had become accustomed to view the judges as among their necessary adherents. A technical pretext being found,[1] Sir Peregrine Maitland dismissed Willis from office. The cause of the latter was at once espoused by the Reform party. A public meeting of protest was called at York under the chairmanship of Dr. Baldwin, and a petition drawn up addressed "to the king's most excellent Majesty, and to the several other branches of the imperial

[1] Willis had refused to sit in term at Toronto on the ground that the court was not properly constituted.

and provincial legislatures." The petition is said to
have been drafted, at least in part, by Robert Baldwin. The occasion was considered a proper one, not
only for protesting against the injustice done to
Judge Willis, but for drawing the attention of the
Crown to the numerous evils from which the colony
was suffering. The list of grievances, arranged under
eleven heads, included the already familiar protests
against the obstructive action of the legislative
council, the precarious tenure of the judicial offices,
and the financial extravagance and favouritism of
the executive government. Of especial importance is the eighth item of the list, which called
attention to "the want of carrying into effect that
rational and constitutional control over public functionaries, especially the advisers of your Majesty's
representative, which our fellow-subjects in England enjoy in that happy country." Following the
catalogue of grievances is a list of "humble suggestions" of adequate measures of reform. The
essential contrast between the moderate Reformers of Upper Canada on the one hand, and the
Radical wing of their party and the Papineau
faction of the Lower Province on the other, is
seen in the fact that no request is made for an
elective legislative council. It is merely asked that
only a "small proportion" of the council shall be
allowed to hold other offices under the government, and that neither the legislative councillors
nor the judges shall be permitted to hold places

in the executive council.[1] The sum and substance of the wishes of the petitioners appears in the sixth of their recommendations, in which they pray "that a legislative Act be made in the provincial parliament to facilitate the mode in which the present constitutional responsibility of the advisers of the local government may be carried practically into effect; not only by the removal of these advisers from office when they lose the confidence of the people, but also by impeachment for the heavier offenses chargeable against them." The petition was forwarded for presentation to Viscount Goderich and the Hon. E. G. Stanley, from each of whom Dr. Baldwin duly received replies. A quotation from the letter sent by Stanley, who became shortly afterwards colonial secretary, may serve to show to how great an extent the British statesmen of the period failed to grasp the position of affairs in Upper Canada. "On the last and one of the most important topics," wrote Stanley, "namely, the appointment of a local ministry subject to removal or impeachment when they lose the confidence of the people, I conceive there would be great difficulty in arranging such a plan, for in point of fact the remedy is not one of enactment but of practice—and a constitutional mode is open to the people, of addressing for a removal of advisers of the Crown and refusing supplies, if

[1] The full text of the petition and of the letters from Stanley and Goderich to Dr. Baldwin is given in the *Seventh Report of the Committee on Grievances* already mentioned.

30

necessary to enforce their wishes." From what has been said above it is clear that this was the very mode of redress which was not open to the people of the province.

In this same year (1829) Robert Baldwin first entered the legislature of the province. John Beverley Robinson, the member for York and attorney-general, had been promoted to the office of chief-justice of the court of king's bench, his seat in the assembly being thereby vacated. Baldwin contested the seat and was successful in his canvass, being strongly aided by the influence of William Lyon Mackenzie. A petition against his election, on the ground of an irregularity in the writ, caused him to be temporarily unseated, but in the second election Baldwin was again successful and entered the legislature on January 8th, 1830. In the ensuing session he appears to have played no very conspicuous part, his membership being brought to a premature termination by the death of George IV. The demise of the Crown necessitating a dissolution of the House. Baldwin again presented himself to the electors of York. In this election the adherents of the Family Compact contrived to carry the day, and Baldwin was among the number of Reformers who lost their seats in consequence. During the year that ensued he had no active share in the government of the country but continued to be prominent among the ranks of the moderate Reformers of York with whom his influence was constantly on the increase. To his professional career also he devoted an assiduous attention. He had, in 1827, married Augusta Elizabeth Sullivan, whose mother was a sister of Dr. William Baldwin. He now (1829) entered into partnership with his wife's brother, Robert Baldwin Sullivan, who had been his fellow-student in his father's law office, a young man whose showy intellectual brilliance and lack of conviction contrasted with the conscientious application of his painstaking cousin. Of Baldwin's public life there is, however, during this period, nothing to record until the advent of Sir Francis Bond Head brought him for the first time into public office.

Among the intimate associates of the Baldwins in the year preceding the rebellion, there was no one who sympathized more entirely with their political views than Francis Hincks. Hincks came to Canada in the year 1830. He was born at Cork on December 14th, 1807, and descended from an old Cheshire family which for two generations had been resident in Ireland, in which country he spent his youth. He received at the Royal Belfast Institution a sound classical training. He had early conceived a wish to embark in commercial life, which his father, the Rev. T. D. Hincks, a minister of the Irish Presbyterian Church, did not see fit to combat. He entered as an articled clerk in the business house of John Martin & Co., Belfast, where he spent five years.[1] On the termination of his period of ap-

[1] See Sir F. Hincks, *Reminiscences of his Public Life*, (Montreal, 1884) Chap. i.

prenticeship Hincks resolved to see something of the world and sailed for the West Indies (1830), visiting Barbadoes, Demerara and Trinidad. At Barbadoes, he accidentally fell in with a Mr. George Ross of Quebec, by whom he was persuaded to sail for Canada. After spending some time in Montreal he determined to visit Upper Canada and set out for the town of York, travelling after the arduous fashion of those days "by stage and schooner," a journey which occupied ten days. Hincks spent the winter of 1830-1 at York, conceived a most favourable idea of the commercial possibilities of the little capital, and interested himself at once in the threatening political crisis. He was a frequent visitor at the Parliament House, a brick structure at the foot of Berkeley Street, intended presently "to be adorned with a portico and an entablature,"[1] whose gallery was open to the public. Here, and in the hall of the legislative council, which, in the words of an enthusiastic writer, "corresponded to the House of Lords" (being "richly carpeted, while the floor of the House is bare,"[2]) Hincks listened to the exciting debates of the session in which Mackenzie was denounced as a "reptile" and a "spaniel dog," and expelled by the indignant majority of the Tory faction. Early in 1831 he left Canada for Belfast to "fulfil a matrimonial engagement" which he had already

[1] J. S. Buckingham, *Canada*, (1843) p. 14. See also H. Scadding, *Toronto of Old*, pp. 27, 28.

[2] Buckingham, *Op. cit., loc. cit.*

contracted. The matrimonial engagement being duly fulfilled (July, 1832), Hincks returned to Canada to settle in York. Here he became one of the promoters and a director of the Farmers' Joint Stock Banking Company; from this institution Hincks very shortly seceded, on account of its connection with the Family Compact. In company with two or three other seceding directors he joined the Bank of the People, which was established in the interests of the Reform party. Of this bank Hincks was manager during the troubled period of the rebellion. With Robert Baldwin and his father the young banker had already formed an intimate connection. Hincks's house at No. 21 Yonge Street was next door to the house occupied at this time by the Baldwins, to whom both houses belonged.[1] The acquaintance thus formed between the families ripened into a close friendship from the time of his arrival at York. Hincks's practical good sense had led him to sympathize with the moderate party of Reform, and he now found in Robert Baldwin an associate whose political views harmonized entirely with his own. In addition to his management of the Bank of the People, Hincks was active in other commercial enterprises. He became the secretary of the Mutual Assurance Company,

[1] According to Walton's *York Directory* (1833-4), No. 23 Yonge Street was occupied by "Baldwin, Dr. W. Warren; Baldwin, Robert, Esq., Attorney, etc., Baldwin and Sullivan's office and Dr. Baldwin's surrogate office round the corner in King Street, 195½." Dr. Baldwin lived at Spadina only a part of each year.

founded at Toronto shortly after his coming, and appears also to have carried on a general warehouse business at his premises on Yonge Street. That his eminent financial abilities met with ready recognition, is seen from the fact that he was appointed, in 1833, one of the examiners to inspect the accounts of the Welland Canal, at that time the subject of a parliamentary investigation. The practical experience and insight into the commercial life of the colony which Hincks thus early acquired, enabled him presently to bring to the financial affairs of Canada the trained capacity of an expert.

At the time when Baldwin, Hincks, and their friends among the constitutional Reformers of Upper Canada were viewing with alarm the increasing bitterness which separated the rival parties, a new lieutenant-governor arrived in the province whose coming was destined to bring matters rapidly to a crisis. Francis Bond Head was one of those men whose misfortune it was to have greatness thrust upon them unsought. He was awakened one night at his country home in Kent by a king's messenger, who brought a letter from the colonial-secretary offering to him the lieutenant-governorship of Upper Canada. Head was a military man, a retired half-pay major who received his sudden elevation to the governorship with what he himself has described as "utter astonishment." On the field of Waterloo and during his experience as an engineer in the

Argentine Republic,[1] he had given proof that he was not wanting in personal courage. Of civil government, beyond the fact that he had been an assistant poor law commissioner, he had no experience. Of politics in general he knew practically nothing; of Canada even less. Nor had he a range of intellect such as to enable him to rise to the difficulties of his position. With a natural incapacity he combined a natural conceit, to be presently enhanced still further by his elevation to a baronetcy. Convinced of his own ability from the very oddness of his appointment, he betook himself to Canada puffed up with the pride of a professional pacificator. How Lord Glenelg, the colonial secretary, could have been induced to make such an appointment, remains one of the mysteries of Canadian history. Rumour indeed has not scrupled to say that the whole affair was an error, that the name of Francis Head had been confused with that of Sir Edmund Head, also a poor law commissioner and a young man of rising promise and attainments. Hincks in his *Reminiscences*[2] asserts that he was informed of this fact in later years by Mr. Roebuck and that a "distinguished imperial statesman had also spoken of it."

In so far as he had had any political affiliations in England, Head had been a Whig. The news of this simple fact had gone before him, and the Reform

[1] D. B. Read, *Lieutenant-Governors of Upper Canada and Ontario* (Toronto, 1900), pp. 153 *et seq.*

[2] *Reminiscences*, pp. 14, 15.

party were prepared to find in him a champion of
their interests; Sir Francis in consequence found
the rôle of saviour of the country already prepared
for his acceptance. "It was with no little surprise,"
he writes in his *Narrative*, in speaking of his first
entry into Toronto (January, 1836), "I observed
the walls placarded with large letters which designated me as Sir Francis Head, a tried Reformer."[1] The administration on which the new
governor now entered was from first to last a
series of blunders. It had been impressed upon
him by the British cabinet that he must seek to
conciliate the Reform party and to compose the
factious differences by which the province was torn.
The *Seventh Report on Grievances* had become,
since his appointment, the object of his constant
perusal, and the Reformers of the province crowded
about him in the fond hope of political redress. It
was impossible, therefore, that Sir Francis should
fail to make some advances to the Reform party.
This indeed he was most anxious to do, although
the tone of his opening address to his parliament, in
which he asked for a loyal support of himself, already began to alienate the sympathy of those
whose support he was most anxious to secure. As a
pledge, however, of his good intentions, he determined to add three members to his executive council and to fill their places from among the Reform
party. The men upon whom his choice fell were

[1] Sir Francis B. Head, Bart., *A Narrative* (London, 1839),
pp. 32, 33.

Robert Baldwin, Dr. John Rolph, a leader of the Mackenzie faction, and John Henry Dunn who had filled the office of receiver-general but had not been identified with either of the rival parties. In a despatch addressed to the colonial secretary,[1] the lieutenant-governor speaks thus of Baldwin:—" After making every enquiry in my power, I became of opinion that Mr. Robert Baldwin, advocate, a gentleman already recommended to your Lordship by Sir John Colborne for a seat in the legislative council, was the first individual I should select, being highly respected for his moral character, being moderate in his politics and possessing the esteem and confidence of all parties."

Now came a critical moment in the history of the time. With a majority in the assembly and with a proper control over the executive offices, the Reform party would find themselves arrived at that goal of responsible government which had been the object of their every effort. They conceived, nevertheless, that the acceptance of office was of no import or significance unless it were conjoined with an actual control of the policy of the administration. Such, however, was by no means the idea of Sir Francis Head. The "smooth-faced insidious doctrine"[2] of responsible government, as he afterwards called it, and the self-effacement of the governor which it implied, could commend itself but little to one who had con-

[1] Head to Glenelg, February 22nd, 1836

[2] Sir Francis Bond Head, *A Narrative*, p. 71.

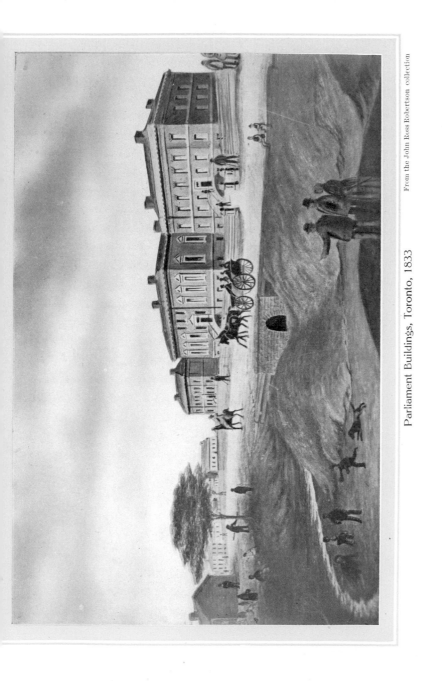

Parliament Buildings, Toronto, 1833

fessedly come to Canada as a "political physician" proposing to rectify the troubled situation by his own administrative skill. Interviews followed between Baldwin and Sir Francis Head, at which the former refused to hold office unless the remaining Tory members of the executive, who were also legislative councillors,[1] should be dismissed. Baldwin indeed, suffering from the domestic affliction he had just sustained in the loss of his wife, appears to have been reluctant to assume the cares of office. On reconsideration, however, the Reformers decided to accept the positions offered and were duly appointed (February 20th, 1836). It was, nevertheless, made quite clear to the governor that Baldwin and his friends accepted office only on the understanding that they must have his entire confidence. A letter, written at this time by Baldwin to Peter Perry, his father's friend and fellow Reformer, accurately explains the situation and elucidates also the full force of the "one idea" by which the writer was animated. "His Excellency having done me the honour to send for me . . . . expressed himself most desirous that I should afford him my assistance by joining his executive council, assuring me that in the event of my acceding to his proposals I should enjoy his full and entire confidence . . . . I proceeded to state that . . . . I would not be performing my duty to my sovereign or the country, if I did not with His Excellency's permission, explain fully to His Ex-

[1] See Lord Durham's *Report* (Ed. 1902), p. 111.

cellency my views of the constitution of the province and the change necessary in the practical administration of it, particularly as I considered the delay in adopting this change as the *great and all absorbing grievance* before which all others in my mind sank into insignificance, and the remedy for which would most effectually lead, and that in a constitutional way, to the redress of every other grievance . . . . and that these desirable objects would be accomplished without the least entrenching upon the just and necessary prerogative of the Crown, which I consider, when administered by a lieutenant-governor through the medium of a provincial ministry responsible to the provincial parliament, to be an essential part of the constitution of the province." Baldwin adds that the "call for an elective legislative council which had been formally made from Lower Canada, and which had been taken up and appeared likely to be responded to in this province, was as distasteful to me as it could be to any one."

The new ministry were no sooner appointed than they found themselves in a quite impossible position. Head had no intention of governing according to their advice. On the contrary he proceeded at once to make official appointments from among the ranks of their opponents, calling down thereby the censure of the assembly. The new council now found themselves called to account by the country for executive acts in which they had had no share. The formal remonstrances which they addressed to the lieutenant-governor drew from him a direct denial of their cardinal principle of government. "The lieutenant-governor maintains," they were informed, "that responsibility to the people who are already represented in the House of Assembly, is unconstitutional; that it is the duty of the council to serve him, not them." To say this was, of course, to throw down the gauntlet. The new ministers resigned at once (March 4th, 1836), and henceforth there was war to the knife between the governor and the party of Reform. The majority of the assembly, espousing the cause of the outgoing ministers, refused to vote the appropriation of the moneys over which it had control. Sir Francis had recourse to a dissolution (May 28th, 1836). In the general election which followed, he exerted himself strenuously on the side of the Tories.[1] To Lord Glenelg he denounced the "low-bred antagonist democracy" which he felt it his duty to combat. In an address issued to the electors of the Newcastle district,[2] the voters were told, "if you choose to dispute with me and live on bad terms with the mother country, you will, to use a homely phrase, only quarrel with your bread and butter." The Tories made desperate efforts. Large sums of money were subscribed. The Anglican interest was enlisted on behalf of the clergy reserves,

[1] Durham's *Report* (Ed. 1902), pp. 115 *et seq*. C. Lindsey, *Life and Times of William Lyon Mackenzie*, pp. 371 *et seq*.

[2] See D. B. Read, *Rebellion of 1837*, p. 241.

the special landed provision for the Anglican Church (under the Constitutional Act of 1791) out of which Sir John Colborne, the preceding governor, had endowed forty-four rectories, a policy to which the Reformers were bitterly opposed. The Methodists, fearing to be carried to extremes, veered away from the party of Reform.[1] The latter, meanwhile, were not idle. Baldwin himself, indeed, had no share in the campaign, having sailed for England shortly after his resignation, pursued by a letter from the irate governor to Lord Glenelg in which he was denounced as an agent of the revolutionary party.

Meantime the Reform party had organized a Constitutional Reform Society of Upper Canada (July 16th, 1836) of which Dr. William Baldwin was president and Francis Hincks secretary. The programme of the society called for "responsible advisers to the governor" and the "abolition of the rectories established by Sir John Colborne." In the tumultuous election which ensued, the governor and his party, with the aid of intimidation, violence and fraud, carried the day. Sir Francis found himself supported by a "bread and butter parliament," as the new assembly was christened in memory of the Newcastle address. Henceforth the extreme party of the Reformers lost hope of constitutional redress.

It is no part of the present narrative to relate the story of the armed rebellion which followed and in

---

[1] See Egerton Ryerson, *Story of my Life*, Chapters xviii-xxx, and see also Hincks, *Reminiscences*, pp. 18, 19.

which the subjects of the present biography had no share. Mackenzie and his adherents now gathered the farmers of the colony into revolutionary clubs. Messengers went back and forth to the malcontents of Lower Canada. Vigilance committees were formed, and in secret hollows of the upland and in the openings of the forest the yeomanry of the countryside gathered at their nightly drill. Mackenzie passed to and fro among the farmers as a harbinger of the coming storm. He composed and printed a new and purified constitution for Upper Canada, blameless save for its unconscionable length.[1] An attack on Toronto, unprotected by royal troops and offering a fair mark for capture, was planned for December 7th, 1837. A veteran soldier, one Van Egmond who had been a colonel under Napoleon, was made generalissimo of the rebel forces. The whole affair ended in a fiasco. Rolph, joint organizer of the revolt with Mackenzie, fearing detection, hurriedly changed the date of the rising to December 4th. The rebels gathering from the outlying country moved in irregular bands to Montgomery's tavern, some three miles north of the town, and waited in vain for the advent of sufficient members to hazard an attack. In Toronto, for some days intense apprehension reigned. The alarm bells rang, the citizens were hurriedly enrolled and the onslaught of the rebels was hourly expected. With the arrival of support from the outside in the shape of a steamer from

[1] The text is given in D. B. Read's *Rebellion of 1837*, pp. 282 *et seq.*

the town of Hamilton with sixty men led by Colonel Allan MacNab, confidence was renewed. More reinforcements arriving, the volunteer militia on a bright December afternoon (December 7th, 1837) marched northward with drums beating, colours flying, two small pieces of artillery following their advance guard, and scattered the rebel forces in headlong flight. The armed insurrection, save for random attempts at invasion of the country from the American frontier in the year following, had collapsed.

In the insurrectionary movement, neither Baldwin nor Hincks, as already said, had any share. The former who had now returned from England, did, however, play a certain part in the exciting days of December, a part which in later days his political opponents wilfully misconstrued. Sir Francis Bond Head in the disorder of the first alarm, whether from a sudden collapse of nerves or with a shrewd idea of gaining time, was anxious to hold parley with the rebels. Robert Baldwin was hurriedly summoned to the governor and despatched, along with Dr. John Rolph, under a flag of truce, to ask of the rebels the reason of their appearance in arms. Baldwin and Rolph rode out on horseback to Montgomery's tavern, where Mackenzie informed them that the rebels wanted independence and that if Sir Francis Head wished to communicate with them it must be done in writing. Rolph meanwhile, who was himself one of the organizers of the revolt, entered into private conversation with Samuel Lount (hanged

44

later in Toronto for his share in the rebellion), telling Lount in an undertone to pay no attention to the message. Baldwin returned to Toronto, but, finding that the governor would put no message in writing, he again rode out to the rebel camp and apprised Mackenzie of this fact. The peculiar nature of this embassy and the known complicity of Rolph in the revolt, gave a false colour in the minds of the malicious to Baldwin's conduct. By the partisan press he was denounced as a rebel and a traitor. Even on the floor of the Canadian parliament (October 13th, 1842) Sir Allan MacNab did not scruple to taunt him with his share in the events of the revolt. But it is beyond a doubt that Baldwin had no complicity in the rebellion, nor was his embassy anything more than a reluctant task undertaken from a sense of public duty.

While these affairs were happening in Upper Canada, the insurrectionary movement in the Lower Province had run a like disastrous course. The home government, alarmed at the continued legislative deadlock, had ordered an investigation at the hands of a special commission with a new governor-general, Lord Gosford, (who arrived on August 23rd, 1835) at its head. Gosford tried in vain the paths of peace, spoke the malcontents fair and invited the leaders of the party to his table. But the assembly would nothing of Lord Gosford's overtures. Papineau denied the powers of the imperial commissioners and boasted on the floor of the assembly that an "epoch is approaching when America will give republics to Europe." The report of the commissioners (March, 1837) dissipated the last hopes of constitutional redress. It condemned the principle of an elective Upper House, declared that ministerial responsibility was inadmissible, suggested that means should be found to elect a British majority by altering the franchise, and recommended coercion in the last resort. Following on the report came a series of resolutions moved in the House of Commons by Lord John Russell, who declared in terms that "an elective council for legislation and a responsible executive council combined with a representative assembly would be quite incompatible with the rightful inter-relationship of any colony with the mother country." A bill was brought forward to dispose of the revenue of Lower Canada without the consent of the assembly. After this the leader of the movement saw no recourse but open rebellion. The peasanty of the Montreal district, obedient to the call, took up arms. There was a short, sharp struggle along the Richelieu, at the little villages of St. Denis and St. Charles, and southward on the American frontier. Sir John Colborne, hurriedly recalled to Canada to take command, crushed out the revolt. Papineau fled to the United States, leaving to his followers nothing but the memory of a lost cause.

Among those who had warmly espoused the side of Reform in Lower Canada, but who, like Baldwin and Hincks in the Upper Province, had had no sympathy with armed insurrection, was Louis-Hippolyte LaFontaine. LaFontaine, the son of a farmer of Boucherville,[1] in the county of Chambly, was born in October, 1807. His grandfather had been a member of the assembly of Lower Canada from 1796 until 1804. LaFontaine was educated at the College of Montreal, where he distinguished himself as well by the natural alertness of his mind as by a stubborn self-assertion which rendered somewhat irksome to him the narrow, clerical discipline of the institution. After studying law in the office of a Mr. Roy, LaFontaine entered upon legal practice in the town of Montreal. Here in 1831 he married Mlle. Adèle Berthelot, daughter of a Lower Canadian advocate, who died, however, a few years later leaving no children. Into the political struggle of the time Lafontaine threw himself with great activity. He was elected a member of the assembly for Terrebonne in 1830 and became a supporter, though not entirely a follower, of the turbulent Papineau. Between the two French-Canadian leaders, there were from the start marked differences both of opinion and of purpose. Papineau, aware of the great influence of the clergy,[2] was anxious to conciliate their interests and enlist their support. LaFontaine, bold if not heterodox in his views, stood out as the champion of *Le Jeune Can-*

[1] L. O. David, *Biographies et Portraits*, (Montreal, 1876), pp. 96 *et seq.*

[2] Kingsford, Vol. IX, p. 453.

ada, against the traditional dominance of the priesthood. Although LaFontaine had no sympathy whatever with violent measures, he distinguished himself during the constitutional agitation as one of the boldest of the agitators. His first action in the legislature was to second a motion for the refusal of supplies, and throughout the years preceding the rebellion, both from his place in parliament and in the press, he exerted himself unceasingly in the cause of the popular party. When the storm broke in 1837, he endeavoured in vain to dissuade his fellow-countrymen from taking up arms. A few days after the skirmishes on the Richelieu (December, 1837) he went from Montreal to Quebec to beg Lord Gosford to call a meeting of the legislature with a view to prevent further violence. On the refusal of the governor to do so, LaFontaine took ship for England. Fearing, however, that his complicity in the agitation preceding the Canadian revolt might lead to his arrest, he fled from England and spent some little time in France. Thence he returned to Canada in May, 1838. This was the moment when Sir John Colborne was busily employed in extinguishing the still smouldering ashes of revolt. Wholesale arrests of supposed sympathizers were made. An ordinance passed by Sir John Colborne and his special council, appointed under the Act suspending the constitution of Lower Canada,[1] declared the Habeas Corpus Act

[1] 1 and 2 Vict. c. g. For the Habeas Corpus Act question see R. Christie, *History of the Late Province of Lower Canada,* Vol. VI., pp. 263 *et seq.*

to be without force in the province. The prisons were soon filled to overflowing. Among those arrested was Hippolyte LaFontaine, an arrest for which legal grounds were altogether lacking. La-Fontaine, since his return to Canada, had written a letter to Girouard, one of his associates in the constitutional agitation, in regard to the frontier disturbances of 1838, recommending, in what was clearly and evidently an ironical vein, a continuance of the insurrection. On the strength of this and on the ground of his having been notorious as a leader of the French-Canadian faction, he was arrested on November 7th, 1838, and imprisoned at Montreal. The evident insufficiency of the charges against him, led shortly to his release without trial.[1] The collapse of the rebellion, the flight of Papineau and O'Callaghan, and the arrest of Wolfred Nelson and many other leaders, naturally induced the despairing people of Lower Canada to look for guidance to the moderate members of the party who had realized from the first the folly of armed revolt. In the period

[1] The following extract from a letter written by Sir Charles Bagot to Lord Stanley under date of November 25th, 1842, is of interest in this connection :—"With regard to Mr. LaFontaine, I have always understood that he was arrested upon mere suspicion. He protested strongly at the time, and subsequently, against the unjustifiableness of the proceeding, and demanded, but in vain, to see the warrant or affidavit on which he was arrested. The public offices furnish no record of the transaction, but Mr. Daly has supplied me with a copy of a letter which Mr. LaFontaine addressed to him from New York, and which was shown by him to Lord Durham. This document bears satisfactory evidence of his readiness to court inquiry." (*Archives of Canada. MS. Letters of Sir C. Bagot.*)

49

of reconstruction which now followed under the rule of Lord Durham and Lord Sydenham, LaFontaine was recognized as the leader of the national Reform party of Lower Canada, energetic in its protest against the proposed system of union and British preponderance but determined by constitutional means, when the union was forced upon them, to turn it to account in the interest of French Canada.

CHAPTER III

THE UNION OF THE CANADAS

THE collapse of the rebellion of 1837 opens a new era, not merely in the history of Canada itself, but in the history of colonial government. The revolt, unsuccessful though it was, had brought into clear light the fact that the previous system of colonial management could not permanently endure, that its continuance must inevitably mean discontent and discord which could only terminate in forcible separation. The lesson that the mother country had failed to learn from the loss of its Atlantic colonies in 1776 had now been repeated. This time, fortunately for the mother country and the colonies, there were statesmen ready to give heed to the lessons of the past. The years of reconstruction that ensued may be considered to constitute the truly critical period of our colonial history. The position was indeed a difficult one. England found itself in possession of a colony still bleeding from the strife of civil war, and torn with racial and religious antagonism. The majority of its inhabitants cherished, indeed, a conscientious loyalty to the British connection, but smarted from a sense of unredressed wrongs and long-continued misgovernment, while those who had been forced into submission at the point of the bayonet, harboured an

51

embittered hatred against their conquerors. That a means was found to establish, in such a situation, a form of government fitted to restore peace, prosperity and loyalty, ranks among the finest triumphs of British administrative skill; and it stands as the great political achievement of the colonial statesmen whose work forms the subject of the present volume, that they both planned the adoption and sustained the execution of the sole policy that could preserve to an illustrious future the colonial system of Great Britain. Responsible government was the chief, indeed the only, demand of Robert Baldwin and his associates; it had been a leading demand of the Radicals in Upper Canada who had been drawn into revolt, and it had been one of the demands of the French-Canadian party of discontent. The history of British administration, like the structure of British government, is filled with inconsistencies and contradictions. Nor is there any inconsistency more striking than this: that the imperial government, after strenuously denying the possibility of colonial self-government and suppressing the rebellion of its subjects who had taken up arms largely to obtain it, proceeded to grant to the conquered colony the privilege which peaceful agitation had constantly failed to obtain.

The British government, stirred from the lethargy and ignorance which had so long characterized its colonial administration, was now anxious to redeem the past. "The Downing Street conscience," as a

LORD DURHAM

Canadian historian[1] has called it, was quickened
into a belated activity. With a view to ascertaining
the grievances of the Canadians and enabling the
government of Lord Melbourne to adopt remedial
measures, a special high commissioner and governor-
general was sent out to British North America in
the person of Lord Durham. John George Lambton, created Baron Durham in 1828, and Earl of
Durham in 1832, is one of the notable characters of
Canadian history, and one whose name will ever be
associated with the grant of responsible government
to Canada. The scion of a Whig family whose members had represented the city of Durham in the
House of Commons continuously from 1727 until
1797,[2] Durham came honestly by Liberal principles,
which his ardent temperament and domineering
intellect carried to the verge of radicalism. He had
already enjoyed a career of distinction, had served
in the army, sat in the House of Commons and
had held the post of Lord Privy Seal in the ministry of Earl Grey (1830). Over Lord Grey, whose
eldest daughter he had married, Durham possessed
an unusual ascendency, *"une funeste influence"* the
aged Talleyrand had called it.[3] Prominent as
one of the leading supporters of the British Reform
Bill and identified in ideas, if not in practice, with

[1] Dr. George Bryce, *Short History of the Canadian People*, Ch. xi.
Section iii.

[2] Justin McCarthy, *History of Our Own Times*, Vol. I. Ch. iii.

[3] *Greville Memoirs*, Ch. xvi.

the Liberal creed of equal rights, Lord Durham appeared preëminently suited to typify to the people of Canada the earnest desire of the mother country to redress their wrongs. From the moment of his arrival at Quebec (May 29th, 1838), he threw himself with characteristic energy into the task before him. The powers conferred upon him as high commissioner, Lord Durham interpreted with the utmost latitude. He regarded himself in the light of a benevolent dictator, and supported the extraordinary powers which he thus assumed with an ostentatious magnificence. He reconstructed Sir John Colborne's council in Lower Canada, issued an amnesty to the generality of political prisoners still in confinement and to the participants in the late rebellion, and, on his own authority, banished to Bermuda certain leaders in the insurrection.[1] He set up at the same time special commissions to enquire into education, immigration, municipal government and Crown lands; paid a brief visit to Upper Canada, where he was received with enthusiasm,[2] and in his short stay of five months gathered together the voluminous materials which formed the basis of the celebrated report. Meanwhile, however, the governor-general's enemies in England were working busily against him. The illegal powers which he had seen fit to assume were made the basis of an

[1] F. Bradshaw, *Self-government in Canada* (London, 1902), p. 142.

[2] R. Christie, *History of the Late Province of Lower Canada,* Vol. V., Ch. xliii.

unsparing attack. Durham's actions were denounced in the House of Lords and but feebly defended by the government. The ordinance by which he had granted political amnesty was disallowed by the Crown. On the news of this, Durham, conscious of the real utility of his work in Canada, and stung to the quick at the pettifogging legality of the government, issued (October 9th, 1838) an ill-considered proclamation, in which he recited the aims of his mission and declared that "if the peace of Lower Canada is to be again menaced, it is necessary that its government should be able to reckon on a more cordial and vigorous support at home than has been accorded to me." This was too much. The high commissioner had become, in the words of the London *Times*, a "High Seditioner," and the government reluctantly ordered Lord Durham's recall. For this, however, the governor-general had not waited. He had already reëmbarked for England, and completed during the voyage the preparation of his report.

Among all the state papers on British colonial administration, the report of Lord Durham, both in point of form and of substance, stands easily first. It is needless here to discuss how much of its preparation was owed to the ability of the governor-general's secretaries; it is certain that a part of it at any rate was the personal work of Lord Durham himself. In its bearing upon the topic which is the main subject of the present volume, it stands as a

Magna Charta of colonial liberty. The report contains a masterly analysis of the origin and progress of those grievances which had driven the provinces to revolt, together with a survey of the existing situation with recommendations for its amelioration. The distracted condition of the Canadian provinces was attributed by Lord Durham to two causes. The first of these was the intense racial animosity existing between the English and the French, an animosity still further inflamed by the arrogant pretensions of the English minority in Lower Canada, which the report pitilessly exposed. The second cause of disturbance was found in the absence of that system of responsible government which could alone confer upon the people of Canada the political liberty to which they were entitled. As a remedy Durham proposed the reunion of the two Canadas into a single province, with a legislature representative of both the races. Such a union he anticipated would necessarily mean, sooner or later, the dominance of British interests and British nationality.

"I have little doubt," wrote Lord Durham,[1] "that the French when once placed, by the legitimate course of events and the working of natural causes, in a minority, would *abandon their vain hope of nationality* . . . . I certainly shall not like to subject the French-Canadians to the rule of the identical English minority with whom they

[1] *Report of the Earl of Durham*, (Methuen & Co., new edition, 1902,) pp. 227, 228.

have so long been contending; but from a majority
emanating from so much more extended a source, I
do not think that they would have any oppression
or injustice to fear." Had Lord Durham's report
rested for its reputation upon his view of the probable future of French Canada it would never have
achieved its historic distinction. Indeed Durham's
political foresight failed him in that he did not see,
as LaFontaine, Morin and the leaders of the moderate party presently demonstrated, that the system
of government which he went on to recommend for
the united provinces would prove the very means
of sustaining the nationality and influence of the
French-Canadians. It is in its recommendation of a
change in the system of government that the chief
merit of the report is to be found. "Without a
change in our system of government the discontent
which now prevails will spread and advance . . . .
It is difficult to understand how any English statesman could have imagined that representative and
irresponsible government could be successfully combined . . . . It needs no change in the principles
of government, no invention of a new constitutional
theory, to supply the remedy which would, in my
opinion, completely remove the existing political
disorders. It needs but to follow out consistently
the principles of the British constitution, and introduce into the government of these great colonies
those wise provisions by which alone the working of
the representative system can in any country be

rendered harmonious and efficient . . . . The responsibility to the united legislature of all officers of the government, except the governor and his secretary, should be secured by every means known to the British constitution."

The administration of Lord Durham and the policy which he was about to recommend to the imperial government, commanded among the Reformers of Upper Canada a cordial support. Hincks established at Toronto, July 3rd, 1838, a weekly paper called the *Examiner*, (there was as yet no daily published in the little town) which bore as its motto the words, " Responsible Government." On the first page of it Hincks printed each week for some months "three extracts which were intended to explain the principles it was intended to advocate."[1] The first of these was the well-worn saying of Lieutenant-governor Simcoe, that the constitution of the colony was nothing less than "the very image and transcript of that of Great Britain." In a leading article of the first number of the *Examiner*, Hincks wrote in support of Lord Durham: "We trust his advice will be followed by all parties in this province, and we would urge those Reformers, who, guiltless of any violation of the laws, have been wantonly oppressed and insulted for the last six months, to forget their injuries, and repose confidence in the illustrious individual to whom the government of these provinces has been entrusted."

[1] *Reminiscences*, p. 22.

LORD SYDENHAM

Meantime the imperial government had decided to act upon the advice presented in Lord Durham's report and to effect a union of the Canadas. A bill to that effect was brought into parliament, but on reconsideration was withdrawn, in order that still further information might be obtained about the state of opinion in the colony, and in order that, as far as might be, the terms of the union should be proposed by the colonists themselves. To effect this purpose a new governor-general was dispatched to the Canadian provinces, in the person of Mr. Charles Poulett Thomson. Thomson came of a mercantile family, had been in the Russian trade at St. Petersburg, had sat in the Commons, had served as vice-president of the Board of Trade in the ministry of Lord Grey, and had no little reputation as a Liberal economist and tariff expert. His business career enabled him at his coming to make a pleasing show of democratic equality with the colonial community. "Bred a British merchant myself," he told the Committee of Trade at Quebec, "the good opinion of those who follow the same honourable career is to me naturally and justly dear." The "British merchant" was, however, very shortly removed to a higher plane by his elevation to the peerage as Baron Sydenham and Toronto. At Quebec the governor-general took over the administration of Lower Canada from the hands of Sir John Colborne. Thence he went to Montreal, where he arrived on October 22nd, 1839, and proceeded to lay the imperial plan of union before the special council, a body of nominated members appointed by Colborne, the representative institutions of the colony being still in suspense. This plan, as conceived in outline by the imperial government, involved the establishment of a legislature in which the two provinces should be equally represented, the creation of a permanent civil list, and the assumption by the united provinces of the debt already incurred in public works in Upper Canada.

Sydenham had come to Canada in the now familiar role of pacificator general, and in especial as the apostle of union. Being endowed, moreover, in a high degree with that firm belief in his own abilities and in the efficacy of his own programme, which was the especial prerogative of so many colonial governors, he was fatuous enough to suppose that the plan of union was highly acceptable to the people of Canada. To Lord John Russell, now colonial secretary, he wrote in the following terms: "The large majority of those whose opinions I have had the opportunity of learning, both of British and French origin, and of those, too, whose character and station entitle them to the greatest authority, advocate warmly the establishment of the union."[1] It was indeed easy enough for His Excellency to obtain a vote of approval from the special council convoked at Montreal, (November 13th,

[1] *Parliamentary Papers*, Canada, 1840.

1839). But as a matter of fact the mass of the people of French Canada were bitterly opposed both to the union in general and to the special terms on which it was offered. Nor was there a more outspoken opponent of the union than La-Fontaine, now recognized as the leader of French-Canadian opinion. Under his auspices a public meeting was held at Montreal, at which he delivered a powerful address of protest against the proposed amalgamation of the two Canadas. Lord Sydenham, aware of the influence of LaFontaine and anxious to conciliate all parties, offered to him the post of solicitor-general of Lower Canada. This position, in view of the existing suspension of constitutional government, LaFontaine did not see fit to accept.

Before, however, these advances were made to LaFontaine, Sydenham had already visited Upper Canada (November 21st, 1839 and February 18th, 1840), in the interests of the project of Canadian union. Here his task was decidedly easier. The Reformers who were led, as will presently be seen, to identify the Union Bill with the adoption of responsible government, were strongly in its favour. The party of the Family Compact were indeed opposed to the scheme, fearing that it might put an end to the system of privileged control which they had so long enjoyed. Chief-justice Robinson, then, as ever, the protagonist of the party, hastened to draw up a pamphlet of protest, which voiced the sentiments of his immediate adherents but had little effect upon the public at large.[1] The Tories found themselves, moreover, in a perplexing position. Attachment to the imperial tie, obedience to the imperial wish,— this, if anything, had been their claim to virtue. To oppose now the project offered them by the mother country, seemed to do violence to their loyal past. A formidable secession took place from their ranks, and very few of their number in the legislature were prepared to offer to the union an uncompromising opposition. It was owing to this that the assembly elected in 1836 as the Tory parliament of Sir Francis Head, was now prepared to vote resolutions in favour of the union. The utmost that the extreme Tories would do was to endeavour to make the terms of union as onerous as possible to the French-Canadians. For this purpose they attempted to pass in the assembly a resolution[2] demanding a representation for Upper Canada, not merely equal but superior to that of the Lower Province. In view of the fact that the populations of the two provinces of Upper and Lower Canada stood at this time respectively at four hundred and seventy thousand and six hundred and thirty thousand, the proposal for a representation inversely proportionate to population only evinced the obstinate determination of the Upper Canadian Tories to ex-

[1] Sir John B. Robinson, *Canada and the Canada Bill.* London, 1840.

[2] *Journals of the Assembly,* 1825-40, p. 338. The resolution in question appears as an amendment by Mr. Sherwood to the resolution finally passed.

tinguish the influence of French Canada. The result of their attempts was merely to hasten on that alliance between the Reformers of the two provinces which offered presently the key to the situation. Francis Hincks had, during a visit paid to Montreal and Quebec in 1835, made the acquaintance of LaFontaine, Morin and other leaders of the moderate party in French Canada. He now, in common with Robert Baldwin, entered into a correspondence with them in which the principles of responsible government and the part it might play in the interests of both races in Canada, were fully discussed.

It is to be observed that to the Reform party, the essence of the union question lay in the adoption of responsible government. Without this their projected alliance with the French-Canadian leaders could have no significance save to establish a factious opposition of continued hopelessness. With responsible government a fair prospect was opened for reconciling the divergent interests of the Canadian races and carrying on a united government resting upon common consent. It is important to appreciate this point, since the conduct of Robert Baldwin in what followed has been freely censured. Baldwin had been appointed by Sydenham, in pursuance of his policy of conciliation, to be solicitor-general of Upper Canada (February, 1840) without, however, being offered a seat in the executive council. Baldwin accepted the office, and, after the proclamation of the union (February 5th, 1841), was made in addition an executive councillor. On the day of the opening of parliament (June 14th, 1841), however, Baldwin resigned his office, thus laying himself open to the charge at the hands of Lord Sydenham's biographer[1] of being guilty of conduct "impossible to reconcile with the principles of political honour by which British statesmen are governed." To understand the motives by which Robert Baldwin was animated in his acceptance of the office which he subsequently so suddenly resigned, it is necessary to review the position in which the question of responsible government stood while the union was in course of making (1839-40).

Lord Sydenham himself in reality had no more idea of applying colonial self-government in the sense in which it is now known and in which it was understood by Robert Baldwin, than had Sir Francis Head. Indeed a system of administration which would have reduced his own part to a benevolent nullity was foreign to his temperament, and the thought of it occasioned him serious apprehension for the welfare of the colony. This has since been fully disclosed by his published correspondence. "I am not a bit afraid," he wrote (December 12th, 1839), "of the responsible government cry; I have already done much to put it down *in its inadmis-*

[1] G. Poulett Scrope, *Life of Lord Sydenham*, (1844), p. 219. See also Major Richardson, *Eight Years in Canada*, (1847), pp. 190, 191.

sible sense, namely, the demand that the council shall be responsible to the assembly, and that the governor shall take their advice and be bound by it . . . . And I have not met with any one who has not at once admitted the absurdity of claiming to put the council over the head of the governor . . . . I have told the people plainly, that, as I cannot get rid of my responsibility to the home government, I will place no responsibility on the council; that they are a council for the governor to consult, but no more." Sydenham might claim to have told the people plainly this old-time doctrine of gubernatorial autocracy, but the people had certainly not so understood his views. Indeed they had good reason for believing the contrary. The governor-general had received from Lord John Russell, under date of October 16th, 1839, a despatch in which the position to be held by colonial executive officers was explained. "You will understand, and will cause it to be generally made known, that hereafter the tenure of colonial offices held during Her Majesty's pleasure, will not be regarded as equivalent to a tenure during good behaviour: but that not only such officers will be called upon to retire from the public service as often as any sufficient motives of public policy may suggest the expediency of that measure, but that a change in the person of the governor will be considered as a sufficient reason for any alterations which his successor may deem it expedient to make in the list of public functionaries, subject, of course, to the future confirmation of the sovereign."[1]

The publication of this despatch had been put by Lord Sydenham (who laid it before the legislature of Upper Canada), to a special purpose. It served as a notice to the office-holding Tories of the legislative council that they must either conform to the wishes of the imperial government in proposing the union or forfeit the positions which they held. But the Reform party, not without justice, read in it a still further significance. Interpreted in the light of Lord Durham's recommendations, it distinctly implied that the executive council, of which in a later paragraph it made particular mention, should be expected by the governor to resign when no longer commanding the confidence of the country. This view had been, moreover, distinctly emphasized by the presentation (December 13th, 1839) of an address to the governor-general, in which it was requested that he would be pleased to inform the House whether any communications had been received from Her Majesty's principal secretary of state for the colonies on the subject of responsible government. To this Lord Sydenham replied that "it was not in his power to communicate to the House of Assembly any despatches upon the subject referred to," but added, that "the governor-general has received Her Majesty's commands to

[1] For the full despatch see *Journal of the Legislative Assembly of Upper Canada*, 1839-40, p. 51.

administer the government of the provinces *in accordance with the well understood wishes and interests of the people*, and to pay to their feelings, as expressed through their representatives, the deference that is justly due to them." The matter had thus been left, purposely perhaps, in a half light. But in order that there might be no doubt as to the views of the Reform party whose wishes he represented, Baldwin, on accepting office, had addressed to Lord Sydenham and had caused to be published the following statement of his position: "I distinctly avow that in accepting office I consider myself to have given a public pledge that I have a reasonably well grounded confidence that the government of my country is to be carried on in accordance with the principles of responsible government which I have ever held." In this position, then, the matter rested until the resignation of Baldwin after the union, under circumstances described in the following chapter.

Meantime the union project was carried forward. The special council of Lower Canada, the assembly and the legislative council of Upper Canada, had all adopted resolutions accepting the basis of union proposed by Lord Sydenham on the part of the imperial government. The assembly of Upper Canada accompanied its resolutions with an address requesting that "the use of the English language in all judicial and legislative records be forthwith introduced, and that at the end of a space of a

given number of years after the union, all debates
in the legislature shall be in English." It was asked
also, that the seat of government should be in Upper Canada.

The intelligence of the proceedings having been
forwarded to England, the Act of Union was duly
enacted by the imperial parliament. Its terms, in
summary, were as follows.[1] In the place of the two
former colonies of Upper and Lower Canada, there
was to be a single province of Canada. A legislature
was instituted consisting of two Houses, the Upper
House, or legislative council, consisting of not fewer
than twenty persons appointed for life by the
Crown, and the Lower House, or assembly, being
elected by the people. Of the eighty-four members
of the Lower House, forty-two were to be elected
from each of the former divisions of the province.
English was made the sole official language of
legislative records. Out of the consolidated revenue
of the province the sum of seventy-five thousand
pounds was to be handed over yearly to the Crown
for the payment of the civil list, namely, certain
salaries, pensions and other fixed charges of the
government. The executive authority was vested
in a governor-general, to whom was adjoined an
executive council appointed by the Crown.[2] The
extent of the responsibility of this council to the

[1] 3 and 4 Vict. c. 35. See Houston, *Constitutional Documents of Canada,* for the text of the Act with comments.

[2] 3 and 4 Vict. c. 35, sec. xlv.

parliament is not defined in the Act. Inasmuch, however, as the entire system of responsible, or cabinet government, in Great Britain itself is only a matter of convention and not of positive law, a definite statement of responsibility was in the present case not to be expected. The debt previously contracted in the separate provinces now became a joint burden.

The union thus prepared went into operation (by virtue of a proclamation of the governor-general) on February 10th, 1841.[1] On the thirteenth of the same month the writs were issued for the election of members of the legislature, returnable on April 8th. Robert Baldwin was elected in two constituencies, the south riding of York and the county of Hastings. Francis Hincks offered himself as a candidate to the electors of Oxford, a county which he had been invited to visit shortly before on the strength of his writings in the *Examiner*,[2] and in which he secured his election. To the electors he published an address in which he took his stand on the principle of responsible government, a system, "which by giving satisfaction to the colonists, would secure a permanent connection between the British empire and its numerous dependencies." The elections in Lower Canada were marked by scenes of unusual fraud and corruption. No pains were spared by the administration to carry the

---

[1] The proclamation itself was issued under date of February 5th.

[2] *Reminiscences*, p. 44.

day in favour of union candidates. The governor-general, by virtue of a power conferred under the Act of Union, reconstructed the boundaries of the constituencies of Quebec and Montreal. Elsewhere intimidation and actual violence were used to stifle the hostile vote of the anti-union party.[1] To this was due the defeat of the French-Canadian leader, LaFontaine, in the county of Terrebonne. The latter, in his electoral address, had again denounced the union in embittered terms. "It is," he said, "an act of injustice and of despotism, in that it is forced upon us without our consent; in that it robs Lower Canada of the legitimate number of its representatives; in that it deprives us of the use of our language in the proceedings of the legislature against the faith of treaties and the word of the governor-general; in that it forces us to pay, without our consent, a debt which we did not incur." But LaFontaine realized the futility of blind opposition to an accomplished fact. The attempt to repeal the union, he argued, would merely lead to a continuation of despotic government by an appointed council. To him the key to the situation was to be found in the principle of ministerial responsibility. "I do not hesitate to say," he said, "that I am in favour of this English principle of responsible government. I see in it the only guarantee that we can have for good, consti-

[1] L. P. Turcotte, *Canada sous l'Union*, (1891), pp. 62, 63. See also C. H. Dent, *The Last Forty Years*, (1881), Vol. I., pp. 50, 51

tutional and effective government. . . . The Reformers in the two provinces form an immense majority. . . . Our cause is common. It is in the interest of the Reformers of the two provinces to meet in the legislature in a spirit of peace, union, friendship and fraternity. Unity of action is necessary now more than ever."

In despite, however, of the defeat of LaFontaine and several other Reform candidates in Lower Canada, the result of the election of 1841 was not unfavourable to the cause of Reform. Of the eighty-four members of the Lower House only twenty-four were pledged supporters of the governor-general,[1] while the Reform party, together with the French Nationalists, included well over forty members of the House.

[1] Poulett Scrope, *Life of Lord Sydenham* (1844), p. 217.

CHAPTER IV

LORD SYDENHAM AND RESPONSIBLE GOVERNMENT

UNDER the Act of 1840 (sec. xxx), the choice of a seat of government for the united provinces was left to the governor-general. In the troubled state of racial feeling, such a selection was naturally a matter of difficulty. While it was clear that the capital city of the country must be chosen in Upper Canada, Sydenham was, nevertheless, anxious to conciliate the French-Canadians as far as might be by appointing a capital neither too remote from their part of the province, nor too little associated with their history. Kingston, situated on the north shore of Lake Ontario, at the point where the lake narrows to the river St. Lawrence, seemed best to fulfil these requirements. The foundation of the settlement antedated by nearly a century the English occupation of Canada, and the fort and trading station then established had been one of the western outposts of the French régime, while its erstwhile name of Frontenac associated the place with the bygone glory of New France. British loyalty, with a characteristic lack of inventiveness, had altered the name of the little town to Kingston. A strong fort built upon the limestone hills that commanded the sheltered harbour, and garrisoned by imperial troops, testified to the military importance of the place. Its central position rendered it at once the key to the navigation of the lake and river, while the construction of the Rideau Canal had placed it in control of an inland waterway whose possession minimized the dangers of an American frontier attack. In this favoured situation there had now sprung up a town, of some seven thousand inhabitants, built largely of the limestone on which it stands and patterned upon the now inevitable rectangular plan. At the time of the union Kingston was a town of about a mile and a half in length, with a breadth of three-quarters of a mile. [1] It contained six churches, was able to boast of three newspapers, and was, moreover, the seat of a very considerable milling industry, large quantities of grain being brought across the lake to be ground at Kingston and exported thence to Great Britain, thereby enjoying the special tariff preference accorded to colonial products. The one hundred and sixty miles which separated it from Toronto represented in those days a steamboat voyage of about eighteen hours, or in winter time a sleigh-drive, under favourable conditions, of about a day and a night's duration. From Montreal to Kingston, a distance of about one hundred and seventy miles, the journey was accomplished while navigation was open, partly by steamer, partly by stage. A letter of Lord Sydenham's under date of

---

[1] J. S. Buckingham, *Canada* (London, 1843), Chap. v., pp. 62 *et seq.*

December 3rd, 1839, illustrates the arduousness of travel to and from the new provincial capital. "The journey," he writes, "was bad enough. A portage (from Montreal) to Lachine; then the steamboat to the cascades, twenty-four miles further; then road again (if road it can be called) for sixteen miles; then steam to Cornwall, forty miles; then road, twelve miles; then by a change of steamers, into Lake Ontario to Kingston." The all-water route by the Rideau Canal, passing through Bytown (now Ottawa) occupied some forty-eight hours. It was in Kingston, then, that Lord Sydenham had summoned the new Canadian legislature to meet on June 14th, 1841, and in the early summer of that year the little town was already astir with sanguine hopes of becoming the metropolis of Canada.

Before, however, the legislature had as yet come together, the governmental problem, which was to be the central feature of the political life of Canada from now until the administration of Lord Elgin, the problem of ministerial responsibility, had already developed itself. Under the new régime it fell to the task of Lord Sydenham to appoint not only the members of the legislative council, which was to form the Upper House of the parliament, but also those of the executive council. These appointments were made a few days after the inauguration of the union (February 13th, 1841). The list of executive councillors was as follows: from Upper Canada,

W. H. Draper as attorney-general of Upper Canada; Robert Baldwin Sullivan, president of the council; J. H. Dunn, receiver-general; S. B. Harrison, provincial secretary for Upper Canada; and Robert Baldwin, solicitor-general for that province. The Lower Province was represented in the executive government by C. R. Ogden, attorney-general for Lower Canada; Dominick Daly, provincial secretary; and C. D. Day as solicitor-general. Mr. H. H. Killaly was presently added to the ministry (March 17th, 1841), as commissioner of public works. We have already seen that in accepting a seat in the executive council Robert Baldwin had made it abundantly clear that he did so on the presumption that the operation of the incoming government would be based upon the principle of executive responsibility. Beyond this preliminary declaration, however, Baldwin did not think it desirable to take any further action until the election of the assembly and the relative representation of political parties should have given some indication of the standing of the ministry with the country at large.

The executive council, as thus constituted, was a body of multicoloured complexion and varying views. Ability it undoubtedly possessed, but it represented at the same time so little agreement in political sentiment or conviction, that it might well be doubted whether joint and harmonious action would be possible. Baldwin, as we have seen, was an uncompromising Reformer, devoted to the principles of popular sovereignty and executive responsibility. Sullivan, his cousin, was a man of different temper. Keen in intellect, ready in debate, he brought to the practical business of politics the point of view of the lawyer, the tactician, the man of the world. For abstract principles of government he cared not a brass farthing. It was his wont to say to his colleagues, "Fix on your policy. Take what course you like, and I will find you good reason for doing so."[1]

William Henry Draper, the attorney-general, differed still more radically in his political outlook from Robert Baldwin. Draper, after an adventurous and wandering youth, had come to Canada some twenty years before, had drifted from school-teaching into law and politics, and at this time belonged, like Baldwin and Sullivan, to the legal fraternity of York. He had sat in the Upper Canadian assembly, been one of the council of Sir Francis Bond Head and had succeeded Christopher Hagerman in 1840 as attorney-general of Upper Canada. This office he still held in the ministry of the united provinces. Draper was a man of great ability, eloquent and persuasive of speech, skilled as a parliamentary manager and dexterous in the game of politics. He was by principle and temperament a Conservative, and although of undoubted patriotism and devoted to the cause of good government, he viewed with alarm the increasing tendency of his time towards the extension of democratic rule.

[1] N. F. Davin, *The Irishman in Canada* (London, 1887), p. 545.

Harrison and Killaly were Liberals of a moderate cast. John Henry Dunn has already been noticed as one of Baldwin's colleagues of the short-lived ministry of Sir Francis Head, and may be considered as sharing the opinions of the moderate Reform party. The councillors for Lower Canada could lay but little claim to be representative of the sentiments of that province. Dominick Daly, the provincial secretary, and presently member for Megantic, an Irishman now nearly twenty years in Canada, of an easy and affable personality, was not displeasing to the French-Canadians whose religion he shared. Ogden, a lawyer and a former office-holder in the government of Lower Canada, was identified with the British interests and was unpopular with the French. Day represented the same class. It will be observed that the refusal of LaFontaine to accept office left the French-Canadians wholly without representation in the executive government.

Baldwin appears to have been convinced from the outset that such a ministry would be quite incompatible with any system of government save one under which the governor-general would be the sole motive force of the administration. To his published communication, already cited, he shortly added a letter to Lord Sydenham (February 19th, 1841) in which he wrote : " With respect to those gentlemen [his fellow-members of the council], Mr. Baldwin has himself an entire want of political confidence in all of them except Mr. Dunn, Mr. Harrison and

78

Mr. Daly. He deems it a duty which he owes to the governor-general, at once to communicate his opinion that such an arrangement will not command the support of parliament." This opinion had been confirmed by the result of the elections and by the correspondence [1] which had ensued between the leaders of the Reform party in the two provinces. In despite of the defeat of LaFontaine, it was plain that the Upper Canadian section of that party would find in Morin, the member for Nicolet, Aylwin of Portneuf, Viger of Richelieu, and others of LaFontaine's party, a group of sympathizers with whom they might enter into a natural and profitable alliance. On the strength of this expectation, Baldwin called together at Kingston, a few days before the opening of the session, a meeting of the Reform party. The attending members, while not agreeing on a decisive line of public policy, expressed themselves as unanimous in their want of confidence in the administration as existing.[2] Shortly after this meeting, Baldwin addressed to the governor-general (June 12th, 1841) a letter in which he recommended that a reconstruction of the ministry should be made in such a way that the Reform party of French Canada, now prepared to coöperate with their Upper Canadian allies, should be represented in the executive. The Reformers, said

[1] See in this connection a letter from Morin to Hincks, May 8th, 1841, fully reviewing the situation. Sir F. Hincks, *Reminiscences*, pp. 50-6.

[2] *Ibid*, p. 58.

Baldwin, could not extend their support to a ministry which included Messrs. Draper, Sullivan, Ogden and Day, whose views differed so entirely from their own. Lord Sydenham, in answer, drew attention to the fact that such a request, at the very moment of the assembly of parliament, was inopportune, and that the French-Canadians whom he proposed to substitute for the ministers to be dismissed, had been radical opponents of the very union of which the new government was the embodiment. The governor-general's communication, followed by further correspondence of the same tenor, left Baldwin no choice but to resign his office. His resignation, offered on June 12th (1841), was still awaiting its formal acceptance when the House met on the fourteenth.

The action of Robert Baldwin in this connection has been, as already indicated, roundly censured by Lord Sydenham's biographer. " This transaction," writes the latter, " looking to the character of the gentleman who was the principal actor in it, and to the manner in which he conducted his negotiation with the representative of the Crown, illustrates more clearly than anything else, the ignorance at that time prevailing, even among the leaders of the political parties in Canada, as to the principles on which a system of responsible government can alone be carried on."[1] The true explanation of the matter is to be found in reality in the uncompromising

[1] Poulett Scrope, *Life of Lord Sydenham* (1844), p. 223.

stand which Robert Baldwin was prepared to take in defence of his "one idea." To have formed part of a ministry which would inevitably find itself voted down in the popular assembly (as Baldwin expected would now be the case), and which would have to rely on the expedients of political management for the conduct of public affairs, would have seemed to him nothing short of trafficking with the fundamental right of the people whom he represented. The error that Baldwin made, speaking from the standpoint of practical politics, lay in his overestimating the union and power of the Reform party. He did not fully realize that the party had as yet but an imperfect basis of organization, that its programme was not one of positive agreement but merely of negative opposition, and that this alone was not calculated to give it the cohesion requisite for its ends. The expectation that the government could be voted out of office and that the system of ministerial responsibility could thereby be forced upon Lord Sydenham, was not borne out by the sequel.

The difficulties, moreover, of establishing at once an operative system of cabinet government is realized when one views the complex character of the party divisions among the newly-elected members of the assembly. One may distinguish among them at least five different groups. There was, first of all, the party pledged to the support of the administration, drawn chiefly from Upper Canada and led by Attorney-General Draper, as member for the county of Russell. To these were closely affiliated the members elected, largely by coercion, in the British interest in Lower Canada, among whom was Dr. McCulloch who had defeated LaFontaine in Terrebonne. These two groups numbered together about twenty-four. As an extreme Conservative wing, were the Upper Canadian Tories, the remnant of the days of the Compact, some seven in number. These were under the redoubtable leadership of Sir Allan MacNab, the hero of the "men of Gore" of 1837, by whose direction the *Caroline* had been sent over Niagara Falls, a feat which had earned him the honour of knighthood, a man of the old school, the sterling qualities of whose character redeemed the rigidity of his intellect. Of quite opposed complexion were the Reformers, a large and somewhat uncertain group including the moderates of both provinces, and shading off into the ultra-Reformers and into the group of French Nationalists who as yet stood in no affiliation to the English party of Reform. The classification thus adopted would indicate in the assembly the following numerical divisions: 1st, the party supporting Lord Sydenham, twenty-four; 2nd, the party of Sir Allan MacNab, seven; 3rd, the moderate Reformers, twenty; 4th, ultra-Reformers, five; 5th, French Nationalists, twenty. There were, in addition to these, eight doubtful members that cannot be classified with any of the groups, making up in all eighty-four members of the assembly. Such classification is, however, too precise to indicate the true state of affairs. Party lines were not as yet drawn with precision. The system of the union being still in its experimental stage, party tradition and parliamentary precedent were absent, and individual members were naturally led to follow the dictates of their own judgment, and voted sometimes with and sometimes against the particular group with which their names were chiefly associated.

Meantime a legislative council of twenty-four members had been appointed (June 9th, 1841) by Lord Sydenham. The French-Canadians were represented by René Caron, mayor of Quebec, (a man of liberal views and subsequently a member of LaFontaine's ministry), Barthélémy, Joliette and six others. Of the sixteen British members of the council, Robert Baldwin Sullivan, Peter McGill of Montreal, William Morris, formerly of the legislative council of Upper Canada and notable as the champion of the Presbyterian Church in the matter of the Clergy Reserves,[1] were of especial prominence.

The constitutional history of the first session of the union parliament which now ensued, and in which the first test was made of the operation of the united government, has the appearance of an indecisive battle. The Reform party, anxious to force the issue, endeavoured to obtain an expres-

---

[1] H. J. Morgan, *Sketches of Celebrated Canadians* (1862), pp. 429 *et seq.*

sion of want of confidence sufficiently emphatic to
compel the government to resign office. The government, on the other hand, strove to put the question of parliamentary theory in the background
by bringing forward a programme of great public
utility and inviting for its accomplishment a united
support. The members of the Reform party found
themselves thus placed in a dilemma. Should they
persist in an uncompromising attitude of opposition, they might delay the carrying out of public
works of whose urgency they were themselves
convinced. Should they break their ranks and
vote with the party of the government in favour
of measures of undoubted utility, they thereby
seemed to justify the existence of an administration of which they had at the outset expressed their disapproval. It was, in a word, the oft-
recurring dilemma occasioned by the conflicting
claims of party policy and public welfare. In a long-
established legislature where rival parties of balanced powers alternate in office, such a dilemma
presents less difficulty, since, with the defeat of the
government, the incoming party is enabled to carry
on such part of the programme of its opponents as
may enlist its support. But in the case of the newly
inaugurated government of Canada, both the urgency of the time and the doubtful complexion of
the parties themselves seemed to favour individual
action as against the claims of party cohesion. It
followed as a consequence that the question of re-

sponsible government, albeit the real issue of the
moment, remained for the time in suspense. Lord
Sydenham with his able lieutenant, Attorney-general Draper, was enabled to obtain sufficient support to carry on his government, while the Reformers contrived, nevertheless, to force from the administration a somewhat reluctant assent to the proposition that only this fortuitous support gave them a
valid claim to office. It has been necessary to undertake this preliminary explanation in order to make
it clear how men, so like-minded in their political
views as Hincks and Baldwin, should presently be
found voting on opposite sides of the House. But if
the state of public affairs at the time is properly
understood, it appears but natural that Hincks, as
a man of affairs, should have preferred a policy of
immediate effectiveness, while Baldwin, of a more
theoretical temperament, clung fast to his uncompromising principle.

As already mentioned, the first united parliament met at Kingston on Monday, June 14th,
1841. The place of its meeting was a stone building about a mile to the west of the town, that
had been intended to serve as a general hospital,
but for the time being was given over for the use of
the legislature. The comfort of the members appears to have been well cared for. The halls, both of
the council and the assembly, were spacious and
well furnished, " with handsome, stuffed arm-chairs
of black walnut, covered with green moreen, with

a small projection on the side to write upon." Sydenham himself seems to have been somewhat impressed with the luxurious surroundings of his colonial legislators. "The accommodation," he wrote home to England, "would be thought splendid by our members of the English House of Commons. But these fellows in their colonies have been spoilt by all sorts of luxuries,—large arm-chairs, desks with stationery before each man, and Heaven knows what,—so I suppose they will complain."

The governor-general was not present in person at the first meeting of the Houses. In his absence the members were sworn in, and the proclamation convening the parliament read by the clerk of the assembly. After this the assembly addressed itself to the task of electing one of their number as Speaker. Here occurred, in accordance with a plan prearranged[1] by the Reformers, the first passage-at-arms between the government and its opponents. The Reformers had decided to nominate for the speakership a Mr. Cuvillier, member for Huntingdon, a man fluent in both English and French, identified formerly with the popular party in Lower Canada, but moderate[2] in his views and acceptable on all sides. It had been hoped by the Reformers that the government might oppose Mr. Cuvillier's nomination,

[1] Hincks, *Reminiscences*, p. 58.

[2] Cuvillier had been one of those deputed, in 1828, to carry the petition of the eighty-seven thousand to the imperial government, but he had voted against Papineau's "Ninety-two Resolutions."

and thus be led to make a trial of strength by which means the election of Mr. Cuvillier would appear as an initial defeat of the administration. It seemed, however, as if the administration, either because they considered Mr. Cuvillier well suited to the office or in order to avoid a hostile vote, would allow that gentleman to be elected without opposition. This the Reformers were minded to prevent. " I was determined," wrote Hincks in a letter to the *Examiner* in which he described this preliminary onslaught on the government, "that the advisers of His Excellency should swallow the bitter pill by publicly voting for a gentleman who had declared his entire want of confidence in them." In order, therefore, to force the government into a corner, Hincks rose and stated that he considered it his duty to his constituents of North Oxford to explain publicly why he supported the nomination of Mr. Cuvillier. His reason was, he said, that that gentleman had opposed certain provisions of the Union Bill of which he himself disapproved, notably the provision for a permanent civil list. He was furthermore led to support Mr. Cuvillier because of "his [Mr. Cuvillier's] entire want of confidence in the present administration."

This, of course, was a direct challenge, and left the government and the Tories no choice but to come out and fight. Sir Allan MacNab was proposed as a rival candidate. Aylwin of Portneuf, Morin and others, followed the lead of Hincks. A heated debate followed, in which Mr. Cuvillier's "want of confidence" did service as an opportune bone of contention. Peace-loving members begged Mr. Cuvillier to state, in the interests of harmony, whether he had, or had not, a "want of confidence." Mr. Cuvillier did not see fit to do so. The situation became somewhat confused. Smith of Frontenac, an over-belligerent friend of the government, attacked the bad taste of the member for North Oxford in trying to force an adverse vote at such a time, and spoke of a dissolution of parliament as the possible outcome of the day's proceedings. The dangerous word "dissolution" brought Attorney-general Draper to his feet with soothing words in the interests of peace. MacNab having meanwhile caused his name to be withdrawn, the discussion subsided, and Mr. Cuvillier was declared unanimously elected. Baldwin, being still technically a member of the government (his resignation awaiting its formal acceptance), took no part in this preliminary discussion.

There was some debate over the question whether, as the governor-general had not come down to parliament on the day for which it was summoned, it could be said, legally, to have met at all. A motion for adjournment was, however, carried, which practically affirmed the proposition that the House had legally meet.

Next day Lord Sydenham appeared in person, and with no little pomp, in the chamber of the legislative council, and read to the assembled members of the two Houses the speech from the throne. The measures outlined therein showed that the governor and his advisers were prepared to adopt a vigorous forward policy in the administration of the country.[1] They declared their intention to adopt legislation for " developing the resources of the province by well considered and extensive public works," to obtain a reduction of the rate of postage and a speedier conveyance of letters, and to effect the improvement of the navigation from the shores of Lake Erie and Lake Huron to the ocean. The governor had, moreover, the satisfaction of informing the members of the two Houses that he had received authority from Her Majesty's government to state that they were prepared to call upon the imperial parliament to afford assistance towards these important undertakings. It was announced that the imperial parliament would be asked to guarantee a loan of one and a half million pounds sterling, to be raised for the expenditure on public works in the province. The intention of the government to complete the establishment of representative institutions in Canada by a law providing for municipal self-government was also indicated, and a promise was given of a law for the establishment of a system of common schools.

No practical programme could have been better devised at this juncture for enlisting public support, especially among the people of Upper Canada, in

[1] *Journal of the Legislative Assembly* (Canada, 1841),Vol. I., pp. 7, 8.

whose division of the country the rapid progress of immigration and settlement called urgently for generous public expenditure. It was part of the shrewdness of the concerted policy of Sydenham and Draper that they sought thus to remove attention from questions of theory to questions of practical utility, while the promise of the imperial government to assist the province by a guaranteed loan and by public aid to immigration into Canada, seemed to hold out a strong inducement towards reconciliation and harmonious action. The Reformers, however, were determined that the question of principle, the question of the constitution itself, should not be forced altogether into the background. Before coming to a vote upon the resolutions on which the address in answer to the speech from the throne was to be framed, they pressed the administration for a definite statement in regard to the all-important subject of responsible government. The House being then in committee of the whole upon the speech from the throne, Malcolm Cameron opened the discussion by declaring that "the dry and parched soil is not more eager for the coming shower than all the people of this country for the establishment of the administration of the government of this province upon such a basis as will ensure its tranquillity."[1] Mr. Cameron, followed by Buchanan, Hincks

---

[1] The debates of the parliament were not officially reported. What follows is based on the report published in *The Church* (Toronto), June 26th, 1841.

and others, urged upon the government the desirability of a definite explanation of principle. The attorney-general, fortified with a budget of manuscript notes whereby he might speak the more accurately, then undertook a formal statement of the principle of colonial government as he conceived it. In the first place, he would declare, he said, for the information both of those who act with him and those who act against him, that so long only as he could give a conscientious support to those measures which the head of the government might deem it his duty to submit to that House, so long only would he continue to hold office under the government. . . . . He would next, he continued, state the views which he entertained respecting the duties of His Excellency : he looked upon the governor as having a mixed character, firstly, as being the representative of royalty ; secondly, as being one of the ministers of Her Majesty's government, and responsible to the mother country for the faithful discharge of the duties of his station—a responsibility that he could not avoid by saying that he took the advice of this man or that man. He looked upon it as a necessary consequence of this doctrine, that where there is responsibility there shall be power also. For he could not admit the idea that one man should possess the power, and another be liable for the responsibility. . . . The attorney-general went on to explain that this same doctrine of responsibility corresponding to power, applied not only to the governor but to the ministers below him. " Whenever," he said, " I find the head of the government and the minister of the Crown desirous of propounding measures which I cannot conscientiously support, honour and duty point out but one path, and that is resignation. There are few men who have long acted in a public capacity, who have escaped animadversion and censure, but a man must indeed be hardened in sentiment and feeling who does not acknowledge *a degree of responsibility to public opinion.* . . . It is to be desired above all things that between the government and the people there should exist the greatest possible harmony and mutual good understanding. . . . It is the duty of the head of the government to preserve that harmony by all the means in his power. . . . If he find that he has been led astray by incapable or dishonest advisers, he may relieve himself of them by their dismissal."

The attorney-general, with his usual persuasiveness of speech, had succeeded in talking all round the question of responsible government without really touching upon it. The blunt question, do the ministers resign when they have no majority behind them, was still left unanswered. Not without cause, indeed, had Draper's oratorical powers earned him the nickname of "Sweet William." In this instance, the Reformers were quick to see the weak side of the attorney-general's presentation. Baldwin, rising to reply, brushed aside the subtleties of the leader of the government and forced the question to a direct issue. He agreed, he said, that the head of the government is of a mixed character, and that he is responsible to the home government for the proper administration of the government of the colony. He would admit that, in the administration of the government, questions may arise in which he may not be prepared to adopt the advice which may be tendered to him. But if he (Mr. Baldwin) understood the honourable and learned gentleman aright, that the council of His Excellency are to offer their advice only when it is demanded of them, and on all occasions remain mere passive observers of the measures adopted by the government, he would beg leave from such a system as this entirely to dissent. . . . Such a council would be no council at all. The honourable and learned gentleman, Mr. Baldwin continued, admits that in the event of the administration not retaining the confidence of parliament, they should resign ; if he had understood the honourable gentleman aright as intending to go to this extent, then it would seem that the difference between the views of that honourable gentleman and his own amounted only to a difference in terms and not a difference in fact. But should those gentlemen be prepared, notwithstanding a vote of want of confidence should be passed by that House, to retain their seats in the council, then he must say that he entirely dissented from them. . . . If the honourable gentleman had intended to be understood as going to this length, then he would perfectly concur with him.

Baldwin expressed his regret that this important matter had not been made the subject of a distinct communication in the speech from the throne. "It was," he said "a great and important principle, on the faithful carrying out of which *the continuation of the connection with the mother country in great measure depends.*" The comprehensive refutation of Mr. Draper's position thus made by Mr. Baldwin was followed up by a series of "teasing questions"[1] from other Reformers determined to force the attorney-general to a direct answer to the question whether or not he would resign. Brought to bay finally by these attacks and having in the series of seven speeches which he made during the debate involved the issue in as much intricacy as possible, Mr. Draper admitted that he would resign.

So prolonged, however, had been the debate, and so confused had become the theoretical arguments pro and con, that at the end of it the members seem to have been but little the wiser. Some supposed that responsible government was now a fact, others that it had been merely the subject of a meaningless wrangle. The Montreal *Herald*[2] announced that Mr. Draper's final and reluctant "Yes," had been "*succeeded by a burst of applause*

[1] New York *Albion*, July 3rd, 1841.

[2] Cited by the *Albion*, July 3rd, 1841.

*from the House. The cry is, responsible govern-
ment is come at last.*" The Kingston *Chronicle*[1] informed its readers that "the great monster, responsible government, was actually ground into
nothing," but added in a tone of complacent patronage that this "seeming waste of powder ought
not to be considered as altogether unprofitable."
The same journal, in its discussion of the great
debate, informed its readers that "the perpetual
foaming and puffing of the honourable gentlemen
reminded us of a set of small steam engines whose
safety valves kept them from actually bursting
their boilers on the floor of the House." Then, as if
apprehensive of the consequences of its own wit,
the journal hastened to add : "By this passing remark we do not mean any disrespect to the honourable House, far from it, for we think it altogether
the most talented and respectable House of Assembly that ever met in this section of the province.

In despite of the seeming harmony of opinion
thus established, the fact remained that the attorney-general had to a large extent come off victori-
ous. His opponents had wished to make the question one of men; Draper had succeeded in making
it one of measures. His declaration was in reality
an invitation to the members to judge the programme of the government upon its merits, and to
accord it their support irrespective of any previous

[1] Wednesday, June 22nd, 1841.

confidence, or want of it, in the originators of the programme. Mr. Draper's difficulties were not, however, at an end. The Upper Canada Reform party being for the moment placated, he had yet to deal with the French-Canadian section, whose opposition to the terms of the union itself now sought expression. Neilson of Quebec moved an amendment to the address, to the effect that " there are features in the Act now constituting the government of Canada which are inconsistent with justice and the common rights of British subjects."[1] Although the combined Upper Canadian vote easily defeated this amendment, Baldwin, Hincks and four other Upper Canadians voted in favour of it. Hincks spoke at some length in its support. He attacked the provision of the Union Act whereby the imperial parliament fixed a civil list for Canada. He declared that the basis of representation now established was unjust : in Upper Canada there were forty-two members, twenty-six of whom were returned by constituencies consisting of three hundred and fifty thousand souls, while the remaining sixteen only represented sixty-three thousand. The representation of Lower Canada was equally out of proportion. " It is," he said, "idle to concede responsible government unless there is a fair representation of the people." The suppression of the French language as an official medium, he denounced as an " unjust and cruel provision."

[1] *Journal of the Legislative Assembly,* Vol. I., p. 64.

Hincks's speech was, however, but a further "waste of powder." The amendment was voted down by fifty to twenty-five.

With the termination of this preliminary debate upon responsible government and the rejection of Neilson's amendment, the government had safely passed its initial difficulties, and was free to turn to the work of positive legislation. That the issue involved in the debate was not, however, one of merely abstract interest, amply appears from the correspondence of Lord Sydenham and the view which he took of his constitutional position in the government of Canada. In describing the attempt of the Reform party to "ensure a stormy opening" of the parliament, he wrote (June 27th, 1841): "My officers, (ministers!) though the best men, I believe, for their departments that can be found, were, unfortunately, many of them, unpopular from their previous conduct, and none of them sufficiently acquainted with the manner in which a government *through* parliament should be conducted to render us any assistance in this matter. *I had therefore to fight the whole battle myself.* . . . The result, however, has been complete success. *I have got the large majority of the House ready to support me upon any question that can arise.* . . . Except the rump of the old House of Assembly of Lower Canada and two or three ultra-Radicals who have gone over with *my solicitor-general, whom I have got rid of*, every member is cordially with me and with my government."

Thus established on a fair working basis, with the question of responsible government for the moment set aside, the administration was able to proceed with its programme. In the ensuing session, which lasted until September 17th, 1841, it managed to make good a large part of its promises. A vigorous programme of public works was instituted. Backed by the imperial guarantee of the interest on a £1,500,000 sterling loan, the province undertook an expenditure of £1,659,682 on works of public utility. The Welland Canal, hitherto in the hands of a private company, was bought up by the government, which spent £450,000 on its improvement. The navigation of the St. Lawrence, which, as has been seen, was still obstructed by intervening rapids, was aided by a vote of £696,182 for the construction of canals at Cornwall and Lachine; £58,500 was laid out upon deepening the channel in Lake St. Peter; and £25,000 on the construction of roads in the Eastern Townships and in the Baie des Chaleurs district. A sum of £45,000 was devoted to the Burlington Canal. The remainder of the money was appropriated largely to the construction of new roads in Upper Canada. This question of public works introduced serious divisions among the members of the Reform party. Hincks who was, to use his own phrase, a "warm supporter" of public works,[1] voted

---

[1] *Reminiscences*, p. 69.

with the government. The French-Canadians, on the other hand, opposed the policy of public expenditure wherever it seemed, in their opinion, to favour Upper Canada unduly. Baldwin, for the sake of party cohesion, was inclined to side with the French-Canadians, and so preserve a united opposition. Aylwin endeavoured to secure a vote of the House to the effect that no debt should be incurred on public works save with the consent of a majority from Lower Canada. Baldwin voted in favour of it, but found only one of his Upper Canadian followers prepared to go to this length. On the matter of road building in western Canada, Baldwin and Hincks again found themselves voting on opposite sides. Thanks to the divisions in the ranks of their opponents, the ministry were enabled to carry on the government with a fair show of support.

Certain other measures of the session were also of considerable importance. The criminal law was modified by measures reducing its severity. The pillory was abolished and the number of capital offences considerably reduced. The provincial tariff was revised, the duties on imported merchandise being advanced from two and one-half to five per cent. A resolution of the House of Assembly affirmed the necessity of abolishing seigniorial tenure in Lower Canada and a commission was appointed for its consideration. A bill in reference to the corrupt practices which had been prevalent in the recent election, excited great public attention and caused more difficulty to the government than any other measure of the session. Petitions had come up to the House from Terrebonne (where LaFontaine had been defeated) and elsewhere praying the assembly to cancel the elections. Technical flaws in the petitions prevented their reception. A bill brought into the House to overcome the difficulty and permit the reception of the petitions was passed by a large majority, receiving the support, not only of the entire Reform party, but of Sir Allan MacNab and the Upper Canadian Tories. The influence of the government caused the bill to be rejected in the legislative council. This was only one of eighteen measures rejected during the session by the Upper House, a circumstance which served to show that on its present nominated basis it might prove an obstructive influence.

But the measure of the greatest importance adopted during the session was the law in reference to municipal government. As this was a subject with which, in the sequel, the LaFontaine-Baldwin administration was intimately associated, a brief account of the legislation under Lord Sydenham is here necessary. The institution of democratic self-government is nowhere complete until it is accompanied by the establishment of self-governing bodies for local affairs. Parliamentary reform, therefore, naturally goes hand in hand with municipal reform. This had already been seen in England, where the great reform of parliament in 1832 had been followed in 1835 by the introduction of municipal self-government. It was now proposed to take an initial step in this same direction in regard to the local government of Upper Canada. Until this time there existed in the districts into which Upper Canada was divided, no elective municipal bodies. The justices of the peace, nominated by the Crown, had exercised in their quarter sessions a supervision over local affairs and had levied local taxation. In the Lower Province local taxation had not been raised previous to Lord Sydenham's administration. The latter had sought to insert into the Act of Union provisions for district government but, finding the imperial parliament averse to such detailed legislation, he had, by means of the special council, created in Lower Canada municipal bodies consisting of nominees of the Crown. It was not proposed to alter the system thus established in Lower Canada, where the government still felt apprehensive of giving full play to the principle of election. The bill presented to the united parliament referred, therefore, only to Upper Canada. This occasioned a peculiar difficulty. If the local bodies established were to be entirely elective, the French might with justice complain of the special privileges thus accorded to the British part of the province. If, on the other hand, the municipal institutions of Upper Canada were framed after the model of those already created by the special council in Lower Canada, the

British section of the province would cry out against the denial of representative government.

In this delicate situation the government attempted a middle course. The provisions of the bill permitted the inhabitants of the districts of Upper Canada to form themselves into municipal bodies. Councillors were to be elected in each district, but the warden, the treasurer and the clerk, were to be nominated by the Crown. The bill as thus drawn had the disadvantage which attends all measures of compromise ; it met with opponents on both sides. Mr. Viger, on behalf of the French-Canadians, entered an energetic protest[1] on the ground that Upper Canada was unduly favoured. " I will express myself," he said, " as sufficiently selfish to oppose such great advantages being accorded to the Upper Canadians alone." Robert Baldwin and the generality of his following objected, on the ground that the advantages conferred were not sufficiently great and that all the municipal offices ought to be made elective.

Here again Hincks found himself compelled to differ from his leader and, in a speech of considerable power, undertook to defend this course in regard to the bill, and to free himself from the charges of desertion now brought against him by his fellow Reformers. To him it seemed that half a loaf was better than no bread. He would have preferred that local elective government might also have been con-

[1] Turcotte, *Le Canada sous l'Union*, pp. 98, 99.

ceded to Lower Canada, but if this could not be obtained he saw no reason to deny it to Upper Canada on that account. He would have preferred that all the offices should have been elective, but he was willing, in default of this, to accept the modified self-government granted by the bill. " I acknowledge myself," he said, "to be a party man, and that I have ever been most anxious to act in concert with that political party to which I have been long and zealously attached. . . . I have been held up in public prints as having sold myself to the government. From political opponents I can expect nothing else but such attacks, but, sir, I confess I have been pained at the insinuations which have proceeded from other quarters. . . . I can assert that my vote in favour of this bill is as conscientious and independent as that of any honourable member on the floor of this House."

Baldwin, in rising to reply, denied that he had had any share in originating, repeating, or sanctioning any insinuations against Mr. Hincks's behaviour towards the party. The means of demonstrating the groundlessness of such insinuations rested with Mr. Hincks himself. He assured the honourable member for Oxford that if a time should come when the political tie which bound them to each other was to be severed forever, it would be to him by far the most painful event which had occurred in the course of his political life. Nevertheless, in spite of these words of conciliation, the temporary breach occasioned by the divergent policy of the leaders of the Upper Canadian Reformers tended to widen. Hincks, with the best of motives, was drawn towards the practical programme of the government. He not only voted with them on the question of public works and municipal institutions, but took issue with his leader also in the votes on the usury laws, the Upper Canadian roads and other matters. His services on the special committee in regard to currency and banking still further commended him to the government as a political expert, of whose services the country ought not to be deprived.

To meet the charges now freely brought against him in the liberal press, Hincks published in his *Examiner* a letter (September 15th, 1841) in which he fully explains the motives of his conduct. "The formation of a new ministry on the declared principle of acting in concert having failed, all parties were compelled to look to the measures of the administration, and we can now declare that, previous to the session of parliament, our opinion was given repeatedly and decidedly, that in the event of failure to obtain such an administration as would be entirely satisfactory, the policy of the Reform party was to give to the administration such a support as would enable it to carry out liberal measures which we had no doubt would be brought forward." In the face of so consistent an explanation the charges brought against Hincks of having "sold himself to the government" and of "having *ratted from his party* "[1] fell entirely to the ground. The support of Hincks, and of four French-Canadian members of like mind, enabled the government to carry the municipal bill by a narrow majority. The question of a more extended form of local self-government remained, however, in the foreground of the Reform programme, and received no final settlement until the passage of the statute known as the Baldwin Act in 1849.

The Act for the establishment of a system of common schools passed both Houses of parliament with but little opposition. The people of Upper Canada were firm believers in the advantages of public education. Especially was this the case with those who came of Loyalist stock, and among whom the traditions of New England still survived. Until this period, however, no successful attempt had been made to establish a general system of elementary schools. The government of the province had committed the mistake of beginning at the wrong end of the scale, and ambitious attempts to institute grammar schools and secondary colleges had preceded any efforts towards the education of the mass of the people.[2] Governor Simcoe, eager to extend to

[1] The expression is quoted by Major Richardson, *Eight Years in Canada* (1847), from a virulent Montreal article in which Hincks is called an "adder," and his career a "libel on colonial politics."

[2] N. Burwash, *Egerton Ryerson* (Makers of Canada Series), pp. 53 *et seq.*

his Loyalist settlers the advantages that their forefathers had enjoyed in Massachusetts or Connecticut, planned the institution of a university at York,
with grammar schools at Cornwall, Kingston, Newark and Sandwich, a proposal which failed of adoption. A little later, however, (1807) grammar
schools were instituted in each of the eight districts of the province. These were supplemented by
private schools, such as those of Dr. Strachan and
Dr. Baldwin mentioned above. But to the generality of the people these advanced schools were of
no utility, and the settlers were forced to rely on
their own efforts and on spontaneous coöperation
for the teaching of their children.

Not until 1816 was the attempt made to organize by an Act of the legislature a system of
elementary schools. Under this Act the people
of any locality might organize themselves for the
building and maintenance of a school, for whose
management they elected three of their number as trustees. A general grant of funds was made
by the legislature in aid of schools thus organized,
while in every district a board of education appointed by the lieutenant-governor exercised a general
supervision over the trustees of each school. This
statute had been supplemented by further legislation in the same direction,[1] providing for the institution of a provincial board and for district examination of teachers. The intention of these statutes had

---

[1] Acts of 1820, 1823, 1824.

been better than their operation. Neither attendance at schools nor local taxation in support of them had been made compulsory, and a large majority of the children of the province were still without adequate education. Day, the solicitor-general of Lower Canada, in introducing the measure, stated that not more than one child out of eighteen was in attendance at the existing elementary schools to whose support the government contributed. In Lower Canada the condition of things was still less advanced. There existed as yet "no legal establishment, no provision of the law by which the people could obtain access to education." Such schools as existed were private establishments founded and supported in great measure by the Church. The secondary colleges of this kind were sufficiently numerous and efficient, but of elementary schools, especially in the rural parts of the country, there was a sad lack.

The present law[1] provided an annual grant of two hundred thousand dollars for primary schools, —eighty thousand for Upper Canada, one hundred and twenty thousand for the Lower Province. It enacted that the district council in each district should act as a board of education, distributing the annual government grant, assessing on the inhabitants of the different school districts the sums necessary for the erection of new schools. Within each of these school areas a board of commissioners was

[1] 4 and 5 Vict., c. 18.

to be elected who should act as the trustees of the school, appointing the teacher and regulating the course of study. A fee of one shilling and three pence per month was to be exacted for each child in attendance, save in cases of extreme poverty. The principal objections raised to the bill as first drafted turned on the question of religious instruction. A great number of petitions were presented to the assembly praying that the Bible should be adopted as a book of instruction in the elementary school curriculum. To meet the views of the petitioners a separate school clause[1] was added to the Act, whereby inhabitants possessing a religious faith different from that of the majority, might establish and maintain a school of their own and receive a proportion of the government grant.

In spite of the success of their practical policy, the session was not destined to end in unqualified victory for the administration. On September 3rd, (1841) Baldwin presented to the assembly a series of resolutions affirming the principle of responsible government. The government succeeded in voting down the resolutions in the form in which they were presented, but only at the price of substituting for them a set of resolutions almost equivalent. These resolutions, hereafter associated with the name of Robert Baldwin, stand as the definite achievement of the United Reformers in their first

[1] 4 and 5 Vict., c. 18, sec. XI.

constitutional struggle under the union. They read as follows :[1]

1. "That the most important, as well as most undoubted, of the political rights of the people of this province is that of having a provincial parliament for the protection of their liberties, for the exercise of a constitutional influence over the executive departments of their government, and for legislation upon all matters of internal government."[2]

2. "That the head of the executive government of the province being, within the limits of his government, the representative of the sovereign, is responsible to the imperial authority alone ; but that, nevertheless, the management of our local affairs can only be conducted by him, by and with the assistance, counsel and information of subordinate officers in the province."[3]

3. "That in order to preserve between the different branches of the provincial parliament that harmony which is essential to the peace, welfare and good government of the province, the chief

[1] *Journal of the Legislative Assembly*, Vol. I., September 3rd, 1841, pp. 480, 481.

[2] Baldwin's resolution had ended. . . . "legislation upon all matters which do not, on the grounds of abolute necessity, constitutionally belong to the jurisdiction of the imperial parliament as the paramount authority of the legislature."

[3] Baldwin's resolution had read . . . . "is not constitutionally responsible to any other than the authorities of the empire." The meaning is that the governor is properly to be considered dissociated from the party government of the province.

advisers of the representative of the sovereign, constituting a provincial administration under him, ought to be men possessed of the confidence of the representatives of the people, thus affording a guarantee that the well-understood wishes and interests of the people, which our gracious sovereign has declared shall be the rule of the provincial government, will, on all occasions, be faithfully represented and advocated."[1]

4. "That the people of this province, have, moreover, a right to expect from such provincial administration the exertion of their best endeavours that the imperial authority, within its constitutional limits, shall be exercised in the manner most consistent with their wishes and interests.[2]

[1] Baldwin's resolution read : "That in order to preserve that harmony between the different branches of the provincial parliament which is essential to the happy conduct of public affairs, the principal of such subordinate officers, advisers of the representative of the sovereign, and constituting as such the provincial administration under him, as the head of the provincial government, ought always to be men possessed of the public confidence, whose opinions and policy harmonizing with those of the representatives of the people, would afford a guarantee that the well-understood wishes and interests of the people, which our gracious sovereign has declared shall be the rule of the provincial government, will at all times be faithfully represented to the head of that government and through him to the sovereign and imperial parliament."

[2] Baldwin's resolution was a much more direct affirmation of principle. It read : "That as it is practically always optional with such advisers to continue in or retire from office, at pleasure, this House has the constitutional right of holding such advisers politically responsible for every act of the provincial government of a local character, sanctioned by such government while such advisers continue in office."

DEATH OF SYDENHAM

It is said that the resolutions in their final form were drafted by Lord Sydenham himself. It would be difficult to say just what would have been the scope of their operation had that energetic and purposeful nobleman remained at the head of Canadian affairs. But his melancholy and untimely death, just as the session came to a close, gave a new turn to the current of history and rendered it possible for those who had opposed his administration to put into operation the principles of government whose validity he had conceded. A fall from his horse (September 4th, 1841) resulted in injuries which proved too much for his constitution, already enfeebled by the severity of his labours, to withstand. He lingered for a fortnight, his mind still busied with public cares, worn out with insomnia and racked with unceasing suffering. On the seventeenth of the month, while the governor-general was hovering between life and death, the parliament was prorogued in his name by the officer commanding the forces at Kingston. On Sunday, September 19th, Lord Sydenham breathed his last. His memory has been variously judged. A well-known French-Canadian historian[1] has denounced the "political tyranny which he exercised against the Liberals of the population," and has spoken of his "hand of iron" pressed heavily upon French Canada. A British-Canadian historian of prominence[2] has

[1] Turcotte, *Le Canada sous l'Union*, p. 106.

[2] John McMullen, *History of Canada*, (1868), p. 496.

111

called him the "merchant pacificator of Canada," and ranked his achievements with those of Wolfe and Brock. But all are united in testifying to his untiring zeal, his wide range of knowledge and the integrity of his personal character.

CHAPTER V

THE FIRST LAFONTAINE-BALDWIN MINISTRY

THE sudden death of Lord Sydenham occasioned an interregnum in the government of the province, during which time the administration was carried on under Sir Richard Jackson, commander of Her Majesty's forces in Canada. On October 7th, 1841, a new governor-general was appointed in the person of Sir Charles Bagot, who arrived at Kingston on Monday, January 10th, 1842. The news of his appointment had been the subject of a premature jubilation on the part of the thorough-going Tories of the MacNab faction. The nominee of the Tory government of Sir Robert Peel, and himself known for a Tory of the old school, Sir Charles was expected to restore to Canada an atmosphere of official conservatism which should recall the serener days of the Family Compact. The sequel showed that Sir Charles was prepared to do nothing of the kind. He was, indeed, a Tory, but his long parliamentary and diplomatic training had stood him in good stead. As an undersecretary of state for foreign affairs and on diplomatic missions at Paris, Washington and St. Petersburg, he had learned the value of the ways of peace. At the Hague, whither he had been sent in connection with the recent disruption of the

113

kingdom of the Netherlands, he had already had to face the problem of rival religions and hostile races. The natural affability and kindness of his temperament, combined with the enlightened wisdom of advancing years, led him to seek rather to conciliate existing differences than to inflame anew the smouldering embers of partisan animosity. Devoid of the personal egotism which had so often converted colonial governors into "domineering proconsuls," Sir Charles was willing to entrust the task of practical government to the hands most able to undertake it. For the role of pacificator, the new governor-general was well suited. His distinguished bearing and upright carriage, and the ease with which he mingled with all classes of colonial society rapidly assured him in the province a personal esteem destined greatly to facilitate that conciliation of rival parties which it was his hope to accomplish.

It only remained for Bagot to find, among the political groups which divided his parliament, a party, or a union of parties, strong enough to enable him to carry on the government on these lines. As the parliament was not summoned for eight months after his arrival, Sir Charles had ample time to look about him and to consider the political situation which he was called upon to face. Visits to Toronto, Montreal and Quebec brought him into contact with the political leaders of the hour, and enabled him to realize that, with the ministry

114

as it at the moment existed, it would not be possible long to carry on the government. Indeed the Draper ministry had owed its continued existence solely to the recognized value of certain of the measures which it had initiated. It had enjoyed a sort of political armistice, at the close of which a renewed and triumphant onslaught of its opponents might naturally be expected. In particular the new governor realized that it would be impossible to carry on the government of the country without an adequate support from the French-Canadians. He made it, therefore, his aim from the outset to adopt towards them an attitude of friendliness and confidence. Several important appointments to office were made from among their ranks. Judge Vallières, one of Sir John Colborne's former antagonists, was made chief-justice of Montreal; Dr. Meilleur, a French-Canadian scholar of distinction, became superintendent of public instruction. As a result of this policy Bagot was greeted in Lower Canada with signal enthusiasm and his memory has still an honoured place in the annals of the province.

Meantime it had become evident even to Mr. Draper that some reconstruction of the ministry and some decided modification of its policy were urgently demanded. French Canada was still loud in its complaints against its lack of proper representation in the cabinet, against the injustice of the present electoral divisions, and against local government by appointed officers. "The government," said *Le*

Canadien, a leading journal in the Reform interest, "may keep us in a state of political inferiority, it may rob us, it may oppress us. It has the support of an army and of the whole power of the empire to enable it to do so. But never will we ourselves give it our support in its attempt to enslave and degrade us." The tone of the province was clearly seen in the bye-elections which took place during the recess of parliament. D. B. Papineau, a brother of the exiled leader, was elected for Ottawa, James Leslie, who had been one of the victims of the election frauds of 1841, was elected for Verchères. Most significant of all was the return to parliament of Louis Hippolyte LaFontaine. Baldwin, it will be remembered, had been elected in 1841 for two constituencies, Hastings and the fourth riding of York. He had accepted the seat for Hastings, and the constituency of York was thereby without a representative. He proposed to his constituents that they should bear witness to the reality of the Anglo-French Reform alliance by electing LaFontaine as their representative. LaFontaine accepted with cordiality the proposal of his ally. " I cannot but regard such a generous and liberal offer," he wrote in answer to the formal invitation from the Reform committee of the riding, " as a positive and express condemnation, on the part of the freeholders, of the gross injustice done to several Lower Canadian constituencies, which, in reality, have been deprived of their elective franchise, and which, in consequence of vio-

Sir Louis H. LaFontaine

lence, riots and bloodshed, are now represented in the united parliament by men in whom they place no confidence."

To his new constituency LaFontaine issued an address in which he urged the need of coöperation between the French and English parties. "Apart from the considerations of social order, from the love of peace and political freedom, our common interests would alone establish sympathies which, sooner or later, must have rendered the mutual coöperation of the mass of the two populations necessary to the march of government. . . . The political contest commenced at the last session has resulted in a thorough union in parliament between the members who represent the majority of both peoples. That union secures to the provincial government solid support in carrying out those measures which are required to establish peace and contentment." LaFontaine's candidacy was successful and he was elected in September, 1841, by a majority of two hundred and ten votes.

It was the design of Bagot to meet the impending difficulties of the situation, before the meeting of parliament, by such a reconstruction of his ministry as should convert it into a coalition in which all parties might be represented. To men of moderate views, of the type of Sir Charles Bagot, there is an especial fascination in the idea of a political coalition. To subordinate the petty differences of party animosity to the broader considerations of national welfare, is a task so congenial to their own temperament that they do not realize how difficult it is for others. To gather into a single happy family the radical and the reactionary, the clerical and the secularist, is a hope as tempting as it is fatuous. The initial success which had attended Bagot's efforts, the enthusiasm of his reception in French Canada, concealed for the moment the difficulties of the peaceful reunion which he proposed. At Montreal the governor had been received by a " procession upwards of a mile in length, while the hundred banners and flags which fluttered in the gentle breeze, together with the animating strains of martial music, formed a *tout ensemble* which had never before been witnessed in Canada."[1]

"The millenium," wrote a British correspondent, a month or two later, "has certainly arrived. Lord Ashburton has settled all difficulties between John Bull and Brother Jonathan, and the lion and the lamb are seen lying down together in Sir Charles Bagot's cabinet." This last allusion referred to the elevation of Francis Hincks and Henry Sherwood to executive office. On June 9th, 1842, Hincks was given the post of inspector-general. Previous to the union this position (in each province) had been of a somewhat routine character, the chief duties of its incumbent being to vouch for the correctness of the warrants

[1] New York *Albion*, Saturday, June 4th, 1842.

issued on the receiver-general.[1] But even in Sydenham's time it was intended that the office should be
converted into what might be called a ministry of
finance, and that the inspector-general should hold a
seat in the legislature as the official exponent of the
financial policy of the government. The voluntary
retirement of the Hon. John Macauley of Kingston, inspector-general for Upper Canada, had made
an opening, and Hincks was accordingly given
the position of inspector-general of Canada, while
the former incumbent of the office in Lower Canada was made deputy-inspector for the united provinces.

It had been charged against Hincks that, even
during the preceding session of the parliament,
the prospect of this office had been held out as a bait
to allure him from his allegiance to the Reformers.
But according to his own statement[2] no approaches
of this kind were made to him at all during the year
1841. Nor did he intend, in accepting a seat in the
executive council, which was to accompany the
inspectorship, to forego any of his previous principles. In his address to his Oxford constituents on
the occasion of his reëlection on appointment to
office, he said : " I have accepted office without the
slightest compromise of my well-known political
principles, and I shall not continue to hold it unless
the administration with which I am connected shall

[1] Hincks, *Reminiscences,* p. 81.

[2] *Reminiscences,* p. 80.

be supported by the public opinion of the country."
Nevertheless the bitter comments of the rival factions on Hincks's appointment showed already the impossibilities of a general reconciliation. "The appointment of Mr. Hincks to the lucrative and important office of inspector-general," said a contemporary journalist,[1] "has been received with strong expressions of disapproval by the great bulk of the *loyal party* of the province. . . . Mr. Hincks has long conducted a journal which has been accused of ministering sedition to its readers, and at the breaking out of Mackenzie's rebellion he stood with his arms folded, rendering no assistance towards quelling the atrocious attempt of that mountebank. . . . It is for these reasons that the honours now bestowed on him are so objectionable to a great part of the people." It will be noted that both now and later it was an article of faith with the Tories that they were the only *loyal* part of the population, a fiction which rendered any political compromise with them all the more difficult to effect.

In order to offset the appointment of Hincks, Bagot at the same time offered the post of solicitor-general for Upper Canada to Cartwright, a leading member of the MacNab party. Cartwright declined the office, and forwarded to Sir Charles Bagot a letter in explanation of his refusal. The recent appointment, he said, had been viewed with disapproval by

---

[1] Correspondent of the New York *Albion,* July 2nd, 1841.

120

the Conservative party to which he belonged. **He**
construed it as an evidence that the government
was indifferent to the political principles of its
supporters, even when their principles were un-
friendly to British supremacy. The cry for responsible government was a danger to the country,
and was a request incompatible with the position
of Canada as a British colony. Of this dangerous
movement, Mr. Hincks had been the "apologist."
He had been the defender of Papineau and
Mackenzie up to the very moment of the rebellion. To go into a government with "this
individual" would ruin Mr. Cartwright's character as a public man.[1] As Mr. Cartwright's objections appeared invincible, the post was
offered to one of his fellow Conservatives,
Henry Sherwood, a lawyer of Toronto. Mr.
Sherwood, contrary to the expectation of his
party, accepted the office, entering upon his
duties in July, 1842. The ministry was therefore
(in the month of August, 1842) of a decidedly
multi-coloured complexion, containing as it did,
representatives of the Tories, the Reformers,
and of the old council. But it was the intention
of Bagot to carry his principle of combination
still further, and to enlist, if possible, the services of the two men most influential in the
country, Baldwin and LaFontaine. Of LaFontaine's support the governor felt a particular need.

[1] See N. F. Davin, *The Irishman in Canada*, p. 478.

The ministry contained no French-Canadians, and of the special offices which were concerned exclusively with the affairs of Lower Canada, one (the office of solicitor-general) had been rendered vacant by the elevation of Mr. Day to the bench, while the incumbent of another (Ogden, the attorney-general) was absent in England. It was becoming clear that, unless a reconstruction could be effected, the present ministry would be left almost unsupported in the House. Mr. Draper seems to have accepted the situation with philosophic resignation. He was quite ready, if need be, to resign his own place, and he harboured no delusions about his ability to carry on the government with inadequate support. The meeting of parliament at Kingston (September 8th, 1842) was made the occasion of an attempt on the part of the governor to complete his system of coalition. His speech from the throne, while referring to the prosperous financial position of the government and the rapid progress of the public works undertaken, expressed an ardent wish that " a spirit of moderation and harmony might animate the counsels of the parliament." The debate on the address in answer to the speech was fixed for Friday, September 13th. On that afternoon the governor, who had already been in personal consultation with LaFontaine, wrote to him in the following terms :—

LAFONTAINE APPROACHED

"Government House,

"Kingston, September 13th, 1842.

"Sir :

"Having taken into my most earnest and anxious consideration the conversation which passed between us, I find my desire to invite to the aid of, and cordial coöperation with my government the population of French origin in this province, unabated. . . . I have, therefore, come, not without difficulty, to the conclusion that, for such an object, I will consent to the retirement of the attorney-general, Mr. Ogden, from the office which he now holds, upon its being distinctly understood that a provision will be made for him commensurate with his long and faithful services. Upon his retirement I am prepared to offer to you the situation of attorney-general for Lower Canada with a seat in my executive council. . . .

"Mr. Baldwin's differences with the government have arisen chiefly from his desire to act in concert with the representatives of the French portion of the population, and, as I hope these differences are now happily removed, I shall be willing to avail myself of this service. Mr. Draper has tendered me the resignation of his office. I shall always regret the loss of such assistance as he has uniformly afforded me, and I shall feel the imperative obligation of considering his claims upon the government, whenever an opportunity may offer of adequately acknowledging them. . . .

"From my knowledge of the sentiments entertained by all the gentlemen who now compose my constitutional advisers, I see no reason to doubt that a strong and united council might be formed on the basis of this proposition. In this persuasion I have gone to the utmost length to meet and even to surpass your demands, and if, after such an overture, I shall find that my efforts to secure the political tranquillity of the country are unsuccessful, I shall at least have the satisfaction of feeling that I have exhausted all the means which the most anxious desire to accomplish the great object has enabled me to devise.

"I have the honour, etc,

"C. BAGOT."

The promise was given in the same letter that the position of solicitor-general for Lower Canada should be filled according to LaFontaine's nomination, provided only that the person nominated was British. The commissionership of Crown lands was likewise to be offered to M. Girouard, a former associate and friend of LaFontaine during the constitutional struggle preceding the rebellion. At the same time a pension was to be granted to Mr. Davidson, the previous commissioner, an old servant of the government. That the proposal thus made went a long way towards meeting the demands of the Reform party can be seen by reading the comments on it in the Tory press, when the letter was subsequently read out in the assembly by Mr. Draper as a proof of the intractable attitude of the Reformers. "Incredible and humiliating as it may appear," said the Toronto *Church*, "it was really written by Sir Charles Bagot to Mr. LaFontaine. . . . A Radical ministry cannot last long. Loyal men need not despair; *they have God on their side.* We must begin to agitate for a dissolution of the union between Upper and Lower Canada, or a federal union of all the British North American provinces." It will be seen from this that the exasperated Tories claimed a monopoly, not only of loyalty to the Crown, but even of the sheltering protection of Providence.

Flattering as was Sir Charles Bagot's proposal, LaFontaine, after hurried consultation with his future colleague, did not see fit to accept it. It had been the aim of the Reform leaders not merely to obtain office for themselves personally but to force a resignation of the whole ministry, to be followed by a cabinet reconstruction in due form. Even with Draper absent, there were several members of the existing administration, notably Sherwood, the Tory solicitor-general just appointed, with whom they would find it difficult to coöperate. To accept the responsibility of providing pensions for Ogden and Davidson seemed to LaFontaine, wrongly perhaps, a bad constitutional precedent. The suggestion of giving pensions was not indeed without defence, under the circumstances. Davidson was an old public servant who had taken no active part in politics, and who had no wish to continue to hold an office which was now to be made a subject of party appointment and dismissal.[1] The office held by Ogden had also been non-political at the time of his assuming it. But a further objection to the proposal lay in the fact that the united Reformers were in complete command of the situation, and could afford to insist on better terms of entry upon office than those offered by Sir Charles Bagot.

Foiled in the plan of friendly reconstruction, there was nothing for it for the government but to fight its way with the address as best it might. The resolutions for the adoption of a cordial response to the speech from the throne were the signal for a debate of unusual interest and excitement, during which the galleries of the legislative chambers were packed with eager listeners who felt that the fate not only of the government, but of the system of government, hung on the issue. The newspapers of the day testify to the intense interest occasioned by the prospect of the approaching trial of strength. " This afternoon," writes the Toronto *Herald* of September 13th, "the great battle commenced. The war is even now being carried into the enemy's camp—excitement increases—members rave—the people wax furious—and where it will end no one can guess." " The House was so crowded," complained a local journalist, "that we were unable to obtain any space for

---

[1] Hincks, *Political History of Canada*, (a lecture) 1877, p. 26.

writing in, and had to rely on our recollection for an abstract of the day's proceedings."[1]

Mr. Draper was too keen a fighter to surrender tamely and without a struggle. He addressed the House in what was called by the Kingston *Chronicle*, "one of the most splendid and eloquent speeches we have ever heard." He submitted to the consideration of the assembly an account of the unsuccessful attempt to obtain the services of LaFontaine in the government. It had been recognized, he said, that it was absolutely right that the gentlemen representing the population of French Canada should have a share in the administration of affairs. It had not escaped attention that an alliance had been formed between the representatives of French Canada and the honourable member for Hastings. When the government had opened negotiations with the honourable member for the fourth riding of York (Mr. LaFontaine), it had appeared that the inclusion of Mr. Baldwin in the government was made a *sine qua non*. He (Mr. Draper) had felt that he could not remain in the council if Mr. Baldwin were brought into it. It was for this reason that he had tendered his resignation. Mr. Draper then read aloud the governor's letter to LaFontaine. On what grounds His Excellency's proposal had been declined he would leave to the honourable members opposite to explain.

[1] Correspondence of Toronto *Herald*.

LaFontaine and Baldwin both spoke in answer. LaFontaine spoke in French. At the opening of his speech he was interrupted by a member asking him to speak in English. LaFontaine refused. " Even were I as familiar with the English as with the French language," he said, " I should none the less make my first speech in the language of my French-Canadian compatriots, were it only to enter my solemn protest against the cruel injustice of that part of the Act of Union which seeks to proscribe the mother tongue of half the population of Canada." In the course of his speech LaFontaine dwelt upon the unfair position in which French Canada was placed and its lack of representation in the cabinet. He had no wish for office unless his acceptance of it should mean the introduction of a new régime. In default of that, " in the state of enslavement in which the iron hand of Lord Sydenham sought to hold the people of French Canada, in the presence of actual facts which still bespeak that purpose, he had (in refusing), but one duty to fulfil,—that of maintaining that personal honour which has distinguished his compatriots and to which their most embittered enemies are compelled to do homage."

Baldwin, following LaFontaine with an amendment to the address embodying a declaration of want of confidence, was able to feel that his hour of triumph had come. The government at the close of the last session had acquiesced in the resolutions affirming the principle of responsible government; these they must now repudiate or inevitably find themselves out of office. Baldwin could scarcely be called an eloquent speaker. His language was often cumbrous and was devoid of imagery. But in moments such as the present he was able to present a clear case with overwhelming force.[1] He challenged the government to abide by the principle which they had avowed. In that principle lay the future safety of the imperial connection and the union of the Canadas. " I will never yield my desire," he said, " to preserve the connection between this and the mother country : and although it is said a period must arrive demanding a separation, I, for my part, with the principle that has now been avowed being acted on, cannot subscribe to that opinion. If a conciliatory policy is adopted towards all the people of this country, such an opinion could have no existence. I was, and still am, an advocate of the union of the provinces, but an advocate not of a union of parchment, but a union of hearts and of free born men."

If, the speaker continued, the ministry believed it but an act of justice to the Lower Canadians to call some of their representatives to the councils of their sovereign's representative, why had they kept this conviction pent up in their own minds without the manliness to give it effect ? They admitted the justice of the principle but had not the manliness to give it effect. Out of

[1] Kingston *Chronicle and Gazette*, September 17th, 1842.

their own mouths they stood convicted. Other members joined in the debate. Aylwin denounced the government in unstinted terms. The letter to LaFontaine, he said, was a trick. It was intended to increase discord. Mr. Draper had said that he was unwilling to remain in office as a colleague of Mr. Baldwin. He could not act with the master, but he had no objection to acting with the disciple. This sneering allusion to Hincks provoked from that member an embittered denial of the aptness of the phrase. He had never been, he said, a *disciple* of Robert Baldwin; the great question on which they had agreed, and for which they had acted together, had been responsible government; that was now settled and conceded. The policy of the administration had been worthy of support, and he had supported it.

The attack thus opened on the government waged hotly through the sitting of the afternoon and evening. Barthe of Yamaska, Viger and others joined in the onslaught. When the debate was at last adjourned, a little before midnight, it was plain to all that if a vote should be taken on Baldwin's amendment the government must inevitably succumb. It was in vain that Sullivan in the Upper House had undertaken the defence of the government with his usual brilliance and power; in vain that he had tried to show that the Reformers were merely a party of obstruction, bent on impeding the legitimate operation of government for their own selfish ends. "Are we," he cried, "to carry on the government fairly and upon liberal principles, or *by dint of miserable majorities?* by the latter or by the united acclamations of the people? We wish to know, in fact, whether there is sufficient patriotism to allow us to work for the good of the people."

The argument against miserable majorities, whatever it might mean to a philosopher, was powerless to meet the situation or to save the government from its imminent defeat. Great, therefore, was the expectation of the public for a renewal of the struggle on the following day. The halls and galleries of the legislature were packed with an expectant audience. All the greater was the surprise of the spectators to find that the storm which had raged so fiercely in the House had now suddenly and entirely subsided. Very obviously something had happened. The members of the assembly, who yesterday had appeared instinct with an eager intentness, now sat with quiet composure in their luxurious chairs of "green moreen," meditating in silence or even chatting and joking with their fellows. There was for a moment a thrill of expectation in the audience when Hincks arose; he, if any one, might be expected, with his incisive speech and telling directness, to precipitate an encounter.[1] But, to the disappointment of the listening crowd in the galleries, the inspector-general merely moved

[1] See N. F. Davin, *The Irishman in Canada*, p. 481.

that the debate on Mr. Baldwin's amendment should be postponed till Friday. The quiet acceptance of this proposal by the House showed that the majority of the members were aware of its meaning. The government, unable to face the rising storm of opposition, had capitulated. Mr. Draper's resignation was again to be handed in, and a general reconstruction of the ministry was to be effected. Some few of the members ventured an immediate protest. Dr. Dunlop, an " independent " member for Huron, known as " Tiger Dunlop,"[1] denounced the contemplated adjustment. The political transformation that seemed about to be accomplished would introduce, he said, within a space of twenty-four hours, changes as extraordinary as those witnessed by Rip Van Winkle after a lapse of twenty years. The new ministry that was in the making would be as composite as Nebuchadnezzar's dream ; he would not be invidious enough to say who would be the head of gold or who the feet of brass, but the greater part of it he feared would be of dirt.

In despite, however, of Dr. Dunlop's sallies and the loud outcry of the Tory press, the proposed arrangement was carried to its completion. Baldwin withdrew his amendment ; Mr. Draper resigned, and LaFontaine and his colleague entered upon

---

[1] The epithet did not refer to the Doctor's pugnacity, but to his record as a tiger slayer in India. See W. J. Rattray, *The Scot in British North America*, Vol. II., pp. 445 et seq.

office. The change effected was not a complete
change of cabinet, inasmuch as Hincks, Killaly,
Sullivan and three others still remained in office.
As Hincks has pointed out, the name, "LaFontaine-Baldwin ministry" commonly applied to the
new executive group is therefore inaccurate.[1]
Sullivan was in reality the senior member of
the council. But in the wider sense of the
term the designation, "LaFontaine-Baldwin ministry," indicates the essential principle of its
reconstruction, and, as a matter of historical
nomenclature, has long met with a general acceptance. The formation of the ministry involved a
certain element of compromise. The disputed question of the pensions was left as a matter of individual voting, and in the sequel was satisfactorily
arranged, Ogden being given an imperial appointment and Davidson a collectorship of customs. It
was not, according to Hincks,[2] definitely and formally stipulated that the ministers left over from
the old ministry should retain their seats on condition of conforming to the policy of their new
chiefs. But, with the exception of Sullivan, their
known opinions were such as to render this conformity more or less a matter of course. The ministry as finally constituted—the change occupied two
or three weeks—was as follows :—

L. H. LaFontaine, attorney-general for Lower

[1] *Political History of Canada,* p. 27.

[2] *Op.cit,* p. 25.

Canada; Robert Baldwin, attorney-general for Upper Canada; R. B. Sullivan, president of the council; J. H. Dunn, receiver-general; Dominick Daly, provincial secretary for Lower Canada; S. B. Harrison, provincial secretary for Upper Canada; H. H. Killaly, president of the department of public works; F. Hincks, inspector-general of public accounts; T. C. Aylwin, solicitor-general for Lower Canada; J. E. Small, solicitor-general for Upper Canada; A. N. Morin, commissioner of Crown lands. The last named office had been declined by Mr. Girouard, whose name had been mentioned in Sir Charles Bagot's letter, and was, at LaFontaine's suggestion, conferred upon Morin, his most intimate friend and political associate.

The incoming ministers, in accordance with parliamentary practice, now resigned their seats and submitted themselves to their constituents for reelection. The election of LaFontaine in what the Tories called his "rotten borough" of the fourth riding of York, was an easy matter. Baldwin, on the other hand, encountered a stubborn opposition. The following newspaper extracts (both taken, it need hardly be said, from journals opposed to the new ministry) may give some idea of the elections of the period and the virulence of the party politics of the day.

"The Hastings election commenced on Monday. At half past ten the speeches began and lasted till three. Although Mr. Baldwin came in with a large procession and Mr. Murney had none, yet the latter was listened to with extreme attention, and spoke admirably. Mr. Baldwin could not be heard half the time, there was incessant talking while he spoke. At five o'clock on Tuesday evening the poll stood thus:—Murney, 130; Baldwin, 124. The poll does not close till Saturday night. Let every loyal man consider that on his single vote the election may depend, and let him immediately hasten and record it for Murney.

"The fourth riding election commenced on Monday. William Roe, Esq., a popular and loyal man, resident at Newmarket, opposes Mr. LaFontaine. The poll is held at David-town (fit place!). By the last accounts the votes stood thus:—LaFontaine, 191; Roe, 71. Mr. Roe was recovering his lost ground and will fight manfully to the last. Every out-voter should repair to his aid. Saturday will not be too late."

.   .   .   .

"The Hastings election has terminated in favour of Mr. Murney. The numbers at the last were:— Murney, 482; Baldwin, 433. A number of shanty-men having no votes were hired by Mr. Baldwin's party to create a disturbance. They did so, and ill-treated Mr. Murney's supporters. The latter, however, *rallied and drove their dastardly assailants from the field.* Two companies of the 23rd Regiment were sent from Kingston to keep the peace, and polling was most unjustly discontinued for one day. The returning officer, Mr. Sheriff Moodie, is described to us, on good authority, as having entirely identified himself with the Baldwin party. He has made such a return as will prevent Mr. Murney from taking his seat, and no doubt the tyrannical and anti-British majority in the House will sustain him in any injustice, especially if it be exceedingly glaring."

A less prejudiced journal[1] gives the following more impartial account of the same proceedings:— "On Wednesday, (October 5th), it appears that bodies of voters, armed with bludgeons, swords, and firearms, generally consisting of men who had no votes but attached to opposite parties, alternately succeeded in driving the voters of Mr. Baldwin and Mr. Murney from the polls. . . . One man had his arm nearly cut off by a stroke of a sword, and two others are not expected to live from the blows they have received. All the persons injured whom we have mentioned were supporters of Mr. Baldwin, but we understand that the riotous proceedings were about as great on the one side as the other."

Baldwin was of course compelled to seek another constituency. The election in the second riding of York had been declared void and Baldwin was put up as a candidate by well-intentioned friends, in despite of the fact that he had already arranged

[1] The Prince Edward *Gazette*, quoted by J. C. Dent, *Canada Since the Union*, Vol. I., p. 248.

to offer himself to a Lower Canadian constituency. The upshot was that Baldwin, who made no canvass of the York electors, was again beaten. But his allies in French Canada were now only too anxious to make a fitting return for his action in this respect towards LaFontaine. For the debt of gratitude incurred, an obvious means of repayment suggested itself. Several French-Canadian members offered to make way for the associate of their leader. Baldwin accepted the offer of Mr. Borne, the member for Rimouski, for which constituency he was finally elected (January 30th, 1843), but not until after the session had closed.

The incoming of the first LaFontaine-Baldwin ministry as thus constituted, offers an epoch-making date in the constitutional history of Canada. It may with reason be considered the first Canadian cabinet,[1] in which the principle of colonial self-government was embodied. This is not to say that it marks the establishment of responsible government in Canada, for to assign a date to that might be a matter of some controversy. Durham had recommended responsible government; Russell in his celebrated despatch had indicated, somewhat vaguely, perhaps, the sanction of the home government to its adoption; Sydenham had evaded, if not denied, it. Even after this date, as will appear

[1] "Canadian" in this sense refers to the two provinces then known as Canada. A responsible ministry had already been seen in Nova Scotia. See in this connection, Hon. J. W. Longley, *Joseph Howe* (Makers of Canada Series), Chapters iii, iv.

in the sequel, Metcalfe refused to accept it as the fundamental principle of Canadian government. Not until the coming of Lord Elgin can it be said that responsible government was recognized on both sides of the Atlantic as a permanent and essential part of the administration of the province. But it remains true that in this LaFontaine-Baldwin ministry we find for the first time a cabinet deliberately constituted as the delegates of the representatives of the people, and taking office under a governor willing to accept their advice as his constitutional guide in the government of the country.

The distinct advance that was thus made in the political evolution of the British colonial system becomes more apparent upon a nearer view of the attendant circumstances of the hour. At the present day the people of Britain and the British colonies have become so accustomed to the peaceful operation of cabinet government that they are inclined to take it for granted as an altogether normal phenomenon, the possibility and the utility of which are self-evident. It is no longer realized that responsible government, like the wider principle of government by majority rule, rests after all upon convention. Unless and until the minority of a country are willing to acquiesce in the control of the majority, the whole system of vote counting and legislation based on it is impossible. In a community where the voters defeated at the polls resort to violence and rebellion, majority rule loses its political significance, for this significance lies in the fact that it has become a general political habit of the community to accept the decision of the majority of themselves. On this presumed consensus, this general agreement to submit if voted down, rests the fabric of modern democratic government. The same is true, also, of the particular form of democratic rule known as cabinet or responsible government: it presupposes that the beaten party recognize the political right of their conquerors to take office; that they will not consider that the whole system of government has broken down merely because they have been voted out of power; nor meditate a resort to violent measures, as if the political victory of their opponents had dissolved the general bonds of allegiance. So much has this party acquiescence become in our day the traditional political habit, that in British, self-governing countries His Majesty's ministers and His Majesty's Opposition circulate in and out of office with decorous alternation, each side recognizing in the other an institution necessary to its own existence. But at the period of which we speak the case was different. To the thorough-going Tories the admission to office of LaFontaine, Baldwin and their adherents seemed a political crime. Loyalty raised its hands in pious horror at the sight of a ministry whom it persisted in associating with the lost cause of rebellion and sedition, and one of whose two leaders was under the permanent stigma attaching to an alien name and descent. Even the traditional lip service due to colonial governors was forgotten, and the Tory press openly denounced Bagot as a feeble-minded man led astray by a clique of seditious and irresponsible advisers.

The journals of the autumn of 1842 are filled with denunciations of the new government. "If the events of the past few weeks," wrote the Montreal *Gazette*, " are to be taken as a presage of the future —and who doubts it?—Lower Canada is no longer a place of sojourn for British colonists. A change has come over the spirit of our dream in the last few weeks, so sudden, so passing strange, that we have been scarcely able to comprehend its nature and extent. By degrees, however, the appalling truth develops itself. *Every post from Kingston confirms the fact that the British party has been deliberately handed over to the vindictive disposition of a French mob*, whose first efforts are directed towards the abrogation of those laws which protect property and promote improvement. Every step in the way of legislation since the 8th ultimate, has been a step backward, and the heel falls each time, with insulting ingenuity, on the necks of the British. 'Coming events cast their shadows before.' They are cast broadly and ominously, almost assuming in our sad and most reluctant eyes, the mysterious characters of sacred writ—MENE, MENE, TEKEL, UPHARSIN."

The Montreal *Transcript* was even more outspoken in its denunciation. " To a governor without any opinion of his own and ready to veer about at every breath of opposition, no worse field could have been presented than Canada. Were His Excellency only resolute, the presence of three or four men in his cabinet could not avail to render him powerless and passive. But from the moment that the patronage of the Crown was surrendered, in such an unexampled manner, to such men—*from the moment a seat in the cabinet was offered and pressed upon a man*[1] *who had fought in open rebellion and faced the fire of British musketry in a mad attempt to carry out his hostility to the government that then was*—from that moment the governor placed himself with his hands tied in the power of his new advisers." Another leading Conservative paper did not scruple to say that the " composition of the present cabinet is the germ of colonial separation from the mother country."

One can understand how great must have been the difficulties of Bagot's situation. It was not possible for him merely to fold his hands and to announce himself, with general approval, as the long-desired constitutional governor. If he attempted to actually govern, the Reformers would be up in arms ; if he left the government to his ministers, he must face the outcry of the Tory faction. The

---

[1] The reference is to Mr. Girouard who is said to have fought at St. Eustache.

ideal of one party was the abomination of the other. The French press was of course loud in its praise of the new policy. " To-day," said *La Minerve*, in speaking of the formation of the ministry, " commences a new era, and one which will be signalized by the administration of equal justice towards all our fellow-citizens and the return of popular confidence in the government." " The great principle of responsibility," said the same journal, " is thus formally and solemnly recognized by the representative of the Crown, and sealed with the approbation of the assembly. From this epoch dates a revolution, effected without blood or slaughter, but none the less glorious." But the more the French press praised Bagot's action, the more did the " loyal " newspapers denounce it, subjecting the governor to personal criticism and abuse entirely out of keeping with the system he laboured to introduce. " To hear the stupid *Aurore* and the venomous *Minerve* lauding a British governor," declared the Toronto *Patriot*, " is surely proof plain that he is not what he might be ; that he is a changed man and not worthy of the cordial sympathy of the Conservative and loyal press of Canada." It is small wonder that Bagot's health began to suffer severely from the anxiety and distress of mind occasioned by these malignant attacks upon his character.

A proper appreciation of the state of public feeling evidenced by such extracts renders clear the great significance of the LaFontaine-Baldwin alli-

ance in the history of Canada. Its importance is of
a double character. It afforded, in the first place,
an object lesson in the principle of responsible government; for it showed in actual operation a group
of ministers united in policy, backed by an overwhelming majority in the popular branch of the
legislature, and receiving the constitutional approval
of the governor, of whom they were the advisers.
Henceforth responsible government, the "one idea"
of Robert Baldwin, was no longer merely an "idea";
it was a known and tried system whose actual
operation had proved its possibility. Its trial, indeed, in the present case was but brief, yet brief as
it was, it remained as an ensample for future effort.
But the new government had a further significance.
It indicated the only possible policy by which the
racial problem in the political life of Canada could
find an adequate solution. To the old-time Tory
the absorption, suppression, or at any rate the subordination of French Canada seemed the natural,
one might say the truly British and loyal, method
of governing the united country. From now on a
new path of national development is indicated in
the alliance and coöperation of the two races, each
contributing its distinctive share to the political life
of the country, and each finding in the other a
healthful stimulus and support. This is the principle, entirely contrary to the doctrines of the older
school, first introduced by the alliance of Baldwin
and LaFontaine, which has since governed the

destinies of Canada. On the validity of this principle the future of the country has been staked.

If we pass from the general consideration of the ministry before us to the legislative history of its first session, there is but little to record. The session was but of a month's duration (September 8th to October 12th, 1842), the new ministers during the first part of it were still seeking reëlection, and time was lacking for a wide programme of reform. Such measures as were carried, however, indicated clearly the policy which it proposed to follow: to conciliate the people of French Canada by removing some of the more burdensome restrictions imposed by the special council and to make at least a beginning of a programme of reform, was the cardinal aim of the government. The first law placed upon the statute-book for the session—the law in regard to elections—evinced this latter purpose. The elections of the day were notoriously corrupt. Fraud and violence had been the rule rather than the exception. Under the existing system there was but a single polling place for each constituency, an arrangement which favoured riotous proceedings and the assemblage of tumultuous crowds. The new election law[1] provided that there should be a separate polling place in each township or ward of every constituency, and that each elector should vote at the polling place of the district where his property

[1] *Statutes of Canada*, 6 Vict., c. 1.

was situated. Electors might be put on oath as to whether they had already voted. The polls were to stay open only two days. An oath in denial of bribery could be imposed on any voter, if it were demanded by two electors. Firearms and other weapons might be confiscated by the returning officer, under penalty, in case of resistance, of fine and imprisonment. Under similar penalties it was forbidden to make use of ensigns, standards or flags, " as party flags," to distinguish the supporters of a particular candidate, either on election day or for a fortnight before or after ; a similar prohibition was laid down against "ribbons," "labels" and "favours" used as party badges. These last clauses offered an easy mark for the raillery of the Conservative press, and offered a favourable opportunity for wilful misinterpretation by pressing into service the neverfailing Union Jack and British loyalty. The *Patriot* of Toronto speaks as follows of the tyranny of the election law :—

" This law also prohibits, under penalties of fines of fifty pounds, and imprisonment for six months, or both, the exhibiting of any ensign, standard, colour, flag, ribbon, label or favour, whatever, or for any reason whatsoever, at any election or on any election day, or within a fortnight before or after such a day ! ! ! So that any body of honest electors who for a fortnight before or after an election (being a period of one month), *shall dare to hoist the Union Jack of Old England*, or wear a

green or blue ribbon in the button-hole, shall be
fined fifty pounds or imprisoned six months, or
both, under Mr. Baldwin's election bill. We defy
the whole world to match this bill for grinding and
insupportable tyranny. Verily, Messrs. LaFontaine
and Baldwin, ye use your victory over the poor,
loyal serfs of Canada with most honourable moderation! How long this Algerine Act will be
allowed to pollute our statute-book remains yet
to be seen."[1]

Another statute[2] of the session undertook to remedy the injustice done by Lord Sydenham towards the city constituencies of Montreal and Quebec. He had used the power conferred upon him
under the Act of Union[3] to reconstruct these constituencies by separating the cities from the sub-
urbs[4]; under the present statute the "ancient
boundaries and limits" of the cities were restored.
A further reversal of Lord Sydenham's policy was
seen in the repeal[5] of a series of ordinances by
which the special council had undertaken to alter
the system of law courts in Lower Canada. Sydenham's Act in reference to winter roads in Lower
Canada, a needlessly officious piece of legislation,

[1] Toronto *Patriot,* October, 1842.

[2] 6 Vict. c. 16.

[3] Section 21.

[4] Letters patent March 4th, 1841.

[5] By a statute 6 Vict., c. 13, the ordinances were 3 and 4 Vict., c.
45 : 4 Vict. c. 15 and 4 Vict. 19.

was also partially repealed.[1] A special duty of three shillings a quarter was imposed upon wheat from the United States; a loan of one million, five hundred thousand pounds sterling was authorized, and the sum of eighty-three thousand, three hundred and six pounds was voted for the civil list. A resolution was, moreover, passed by a large majority of the assembly (forty against twenty) declaring that Kingston was not suitable to be the seat of government. The session came to an end on October 12th, 1842. A useful beginning had been made but no legislation of a sweeping character had been passed. The adversaries of the government did not hesitate to taunt the ministry with having promised much and done little. "After all the *rumpus* about responsible government," said the Woodstock *Herald*, "the session is over, and we are all just as we were— waiting for something, we scarcely know what. But we all know that the parliament has shown itself nothing but a debating club."

At the time of their first ministry both LaFontaine and Baldwin may be said to have been entering upon the prime of life. Baldwin was thirty-eight years old, LaFontaine only thirty-four. In personal appearance they presented in many ways a contrast. LaFontaine was a man of striking presence, of more than ordinary stature, and robust and powerful

[1] The clause repealed had enacted that horses when driven double must be driven abreast. This was intended to improve the sleighing.

frame. His massive brow and regular features, the thoughtful cast of his countenance and the firm lines of the mouth, offered an almost exact resemblance to the face of the Emperor Napoleon. On his visiting the Invalides in Paris, LaFontaine was surrounded by the veterans of Napoleon's guard, who are said to have thrilled with emotion at seeing among them the walking image of their dead emperor. When Lady Mary Bagot, who remembered the emperor, saw LaFontaine for the first time she could not repress an exclamation of astonishment. " If I was not certain that he is dead," she cried, " I should say it was Napoleon." The habitual gravity of LaFontaine's manner and the dignity of his address enhanced still further the impression of power conveyed by his firm features and steady eye. His colleague was a man of different type and less striking in general appearance. In stature Baldwin stood rather above the average, being about five feet ten inches in height, though his heavy frame and the slight stoop of his broad shoulders prevented him from appearing a tall man. His eyes were grey and his hair of a dark brown, as yet untinged with grey. The features were lacking in mobility and the habitual expression of his face was that of serious thought, but the extreme kindliness of his heart and the truthfulness of his whole being, coupled with a manner that was unassuming and free from conceit, lent to his address a suggestion of rugged honesty and force and extreme gentleness, that won him the unfailing affection of those about him.

As the autumn progressed, disquieting rumours began to prevail in regard to the state of the governor-general's health. It is a strange thing that thrice running the destinies of Canada should have been profoundly affected by the premature death of those sent out to administer its government. "Canada has been too much for him," John Stuart Mill had said of Lord Durham. With equal truth might it be said that Canada had proved too much for Sir Charles Bagot. The governor had come to the country in excellent health. The firm and vigorous tone in which he had read his first and only speech from the throne had been the subject of general remark, and had seemed to indicate that Bagot was destined for a vigorous old age. But the cares of office weighed heavily upon him. He had not anticipated that his policy of good-will and conciliation would have exposed him to the bitter attacks of the discomfited Tories; still less had he expected that his conduct, as appears to have been the case, would have been an object of censure at the hands of the home government. It is undoubted that the symptoms of heart trouble and general decline which now began to appear were aggravated by the governor's sense of the failure of his mission as peacemaker, and by the distress caused by the crude brutality of his critics.

149

BALDWIN LAFONTAINE HINCKS

The autumn months of 1842 must indeed have been full of bitterness to Bagot. The opposition to his administration had assumed a personal note, for which the rectitude of his intentions gave no warrant. Organizations called Constitutional Societies, in remembrance of Tory loyalty before the rebellion, had sprung into new life. The parent society at Toronto[1] was reproduced in organizations in the country districts. The "anti-British policy of Sir Charles Bagot" was denounced in the plainest terms. His ministry was openly branded as a ministry of traitors and rebels. The influence of Edward Gibbon Wakefield and other private advisers was made a salient point of attack, and the governor was represented as surrounded by a group of counsellors—"the Hinckses, the Wakefields and the Girouards, remarkable for nothing but bitter hatred to monarchical and loyal institutions." The press of the mother country joined in the outcry. The *Times* undertook to demonstrate the folly of admitting to the ministry a man like LaFontaine, "who," it asserted, "had had a price set upon his head." The *Morning Herald*[2] went still further; it declared the whole system of representative institutions in Lower Canada a mistake. That province, it said, needed "despotic government,—strong, just and good—administered by a

[1] Organized October 28th, 1842, or, as it was called, "reorganized," (from the Society of 1832).

[2] October 23rd, 1842.

150

governor-general responsible to parliament." " If Sir Charles Bagot be right," it argued, " then Lord Gosford and Sir Francis Head must have been wrong," which evidently was absurd.

In how far the British government itself joined in these censorious attacks cannot accurately be told, but Bagot had certainly received from Lord Stanley, the colonial secretary, letters condemning the policy he had seen fit to adopt. The Duke of Wellington had denounced the acceptance of the new Canadian ministry by the governor as surrendering to a party still affected with treason. "The Duke of Wellington," wrote Sir Robert Peel, " has been thunderstruck by the news from Canada. He considers what has happened as likely to be fatal to the connection with England. . . Yesterday he read to me all the despatches, and commented on them most unreservedly. He perpetually said, 'What a fool the man [Bagot] must have been, to act as he has done ! and what stuff and nonsense he has written ! and what a bother he makes about his policy and his measures, when there are no measures but rolling himself and his country in the mire !'" Even Peel himself felt by no means easy about the situation, nor did he accept the absolute validity of the constitutional principle as applied to Canadian government. "I would not," he wrote to Stanley, "voluntarily throw myself into the hands of the French party through fear of being in a minority. . . . I would not allow the French party to dictate the appointment of men tainted by charges, or vehement suspicion, of sedition or disaffection to British authority, to be ministers."[1]

As the winter drew on it was evident that Sir Charles could no longer adequately fulfil his duties. He was obliged to postpone the meeting of the parliament which was to have taken place in November. His physicians urgently recommended that he should relinquish his office, and the oncoming of a winter of unwonted severity still further taxed his failing strength. He forwarded to the home government a request for his recall. In view of his enfeebled condition, the government was able to grant his prayer without seeming to reflect upon the character of his administration. But Bagot was not destined to see England again. Though released from office on March 30th, 1843, the day on which he yielded place to Sir Charles Metcalfe, he was no longer in a condition to undertake the homeward voyage, and was compelled to remain at Alwington House, in Kingston. Six weeks later, (May 19th, 1843), his illness terminated in death. Before going out of office he had uttered a wish to his assembled ministers that they would be mindful to defend his memory. The prayer was not unnecessary, for the bitter invective of his foes was not hushed even in the presence of death.

[1] C. S. Parker, *Sir Robert Peel from his Private Papers* (London, 1899), Vol. I., pp 379 *et seq.*

DEATH OF BAGOT

" Even when Sir Charles Bagot breathed his last," says a chronicler of the time, himself a Tory and a disappointed place-hunter, " such was the exasperation of the public mind, that they (*sic*) scarcely accorded to him the common sentiments of regret which the departure of a human being from among his fellow-men occasions. . . . The Toronto *Patriot* in particular, the deadly and uncompromising enemy of the administration of the day, hesitated not to proclaim that the head of the government was an imbecile and a slave, while other journals, even less guarded in their language, boldly pronounced a wish that his death might free the country •from the state of thraldom into which it was reduced."[1] Every good cause has its martyrs. The governor-general had played his part honestly and without self-interest, and when the list of those is written who have up-built the fabric of British colonial government, the name of Bagot should find an honoured place among their number.

[1] Major Richardson, *Eight Years in Canada*, p. 213. Chapters xiv. and xv. of Richardson's work may be consulted for characteristic abuse of Sir Charles Bagot.

CHAPTER VI

THE COMING OF METCALFE

ON March 29th, 1843, the little town of King-ston was once more astir with expectancy and interest over the arrival of a new governor-general. Sir Charles Metcalfe had sailed from Liverpool to Boston, and thence had journeyed overland to Kingston, the country being in that inclement season "one mass of snow."[1] His journey terminated in a drive across the frozen lake and river, and a state entry, with no little pageantry, into his colonial capital. "He came," said a Kingston correspondent of the time, "from the American side, in a close-bodied sleigh drawn by four greys. He was received on arriving at the foot of Arthur Street by an immense concourse of people. The male population of the place turned out *en masse* to greet Sir Charles, which they did with great enthusiasm. The various branches of the fire department, the Mechanics' Institution and the national societies, turned out with their banners, which, with many sleighs decorated with flags, made quite a show. Sir Charles Metcalfe is a thorough-looking Englishman, with a jolly visage."

[1] The winter was exceptionally severe. "Governor Metcalfe," said a New York official at Albany, "you'll admit, I think, that this is a clever body of snow for a young country."

BALDWIN LAFONTAINE HINCKS

In the drama of responsible government in Canada, it was the unfortunate lot of this "thorough-looking Englishman with a jolly visage," to be cast for the part of villain. His attempt to strangle the infant Hercules in its cradle, to reassert the claim of the governor to the actual control of the administration, forms the most important and critical episode of the story before us and merits a treatment in some detail. Such a treatment may, perhaps, be best introduced by a discussion of the personality and personal opinions of the new governor, and in particular of his opinions on the vexed question of colonial administration. The word "villain" that has just been used, must be understood in a highly figurative sense. Metcalfe was a man of many admirers. Gibbon Wakefield has pronounced him a statesman "whom God made greater than the colonial office."[1] Macaulay indicates for him a perhaps even higher range of distinction in calling him, "the ablest civil servant I ever knew in India." His enthusiastic biographer[2] tells us that on his retiring from his administration of Jamaica, the "coloured population kneeled to bless him," while "all classes of society and all sects of Christians sorrowed for his departure, and the Jews set an example of Christian love by praying for him in their synagogues." In face of such a record it seems almost a pity that Sir Charles should have aban-

[1] Fisher's *Colonial Magazine*, July, 1844.
[2] J. W. Kaye, *Life of Lord Metcalfe*, 1859.

doned the coloured populations of Jamaica and Hyderabad to assume the care of the uncoloured people of Canada. That Metcalfe was an upright, honourable man, disinterested in his motives and conscientious in the performance of what he took to be his duty, is hardly open to doubt. But it may well be doubted whether the antecedent training that he had received had not unfitted, rather than fitted, him for the position he was now called upon to assume.

In the British system a great gulf is fixed between the administration of a dependency and the governorship of a self-governing colony. Of the greatness of this gulf Metcalfe appears to have had no proper appreciation, and he was, in consequence, unable to rid his mind of the supposed parallel between the different parts of the empire in which he had been called upon to act as governor. In a letter which he addressed to Colonel Stokes, one of his Indian correspondents, during his troubles in Canada, he undertakes to make his difficulties with the Canadian legislature apparent by the following interesting analogy : "Fancy such a state of things in India, with a Mohammedan council and a Mohammedan assembly, and you will have some notion of my position." In view of the very limited number of Mohammedans in the Canadian assembly, it is to be presumed that the notion thus communicated would be a somewhat artificial one.

Sir Charles Metcalfe, at the time of his coming to Canada, was fifty-eight years old.[1] For some time previous he had been suffering from a dangerous and painful malady—a cancerous growth in the left cheek—which had occasioned his retirement from his previous position. An operation performed in England had seemed to remove all danger of a fatal termination of the disorder, and Sir Charles, in coming to Canada, hoped that he had at last recovered from his long affliction.

What may seem strange in connection with Metcalfe's régime in Canada, and his attitude towards Canadian political parties, was that he was not, as far as British politics were concerned, a Tory or a friend of the royal prerogative. He was, on the contrary, to use the words of his biographer, "a Whig and something more than a Whig." The same authority[2] has further described him as "a statesman known to be saturated through and through with Liberal opinions." Metcalfe himself, in a letter written shortly before his appointment, spoke of his own opinions and his political position in the following terms: "In the present predominance of Toryism among the constituencies, there is no chance for a man who is for the abolition of the Corn Laws, vote by ballot, extension of the suffrage, amelioration of the Poor Laws for the benefit of the poor, equal rights to all sects of

[1] He was born on January 30th, 1785.

[2] J. W. Kaye, *Life of Lord Metcalfe*, Vol. II., p. 452.

Christians in matters of religion, and equal rights to all men in civil matters."[1]

On the strength of such a declaration it might have been supposed that Metcalfe would have gravitated naturally towards the Reform party of Canada, at the basis of whose programme civil and religious equality and the doctrine of equal rights lay as a corner-stone. But the lamp of Metcalfe's Liberalism burned dim in the colonial atmosphere. His inclinations were all on the side of the Tory party, whose fervid and ostentatious loyalty offered a cheering contrast to the stiff-necked independence of the Reformers. "It is," he said, "the only party with which I can sympathize. I have no sympathy with the anti-British rancour of the French party or the selfish indifference towards our country of the Republican party. Yet these are the parties with which I have to coöperate." The expression, "Republican party," shows that the incessant accusation of disloyalty brought by the Conservative journalists against their opponents, was not without its effect upon the governor's mind. By sheer force of iteration the Conservatives had convinced themselves that they were the one and only section of the people truly loyal to the Crown ; and since the governor was the immediate and visible representative of the Crown in Canada, there was a natural temptation to construe this attitude into a declaration of personal allegiance.

[1] Letter to Mr. Mangles, January 13th, 1843.

But although Metcalfe might plead guilty to a spontaneous sympathy with the Tory party, he had no intention of identifying or allying himself with any of the rival factions. On the contrary, he cherished, as had his predecessors, the belief that his proper attitude and vocation should be that of the peacemaker, the wise administrator enabled by the altitude of his office to compose the differences that severed his fractious subordinates. " I dislike extremely," he said, "the notion of governing as a supporter of any particular party. I wish to make the patronage of the government conducive to the conciliation of all parties by bringing into the public service the men of greatest merit and efficiency, without any party distinction."[1]

The governor seems, however, to have recognized that he could not disregard the fact that the party at present in power had the support of the assembly behind them. " Fettered as I am," he wrote, " by the necessity of acting with a council brought into place by a coalition of parties, and at present in possession of a decided majority in the representative assembly, I must in some degree forego my own inclinations in those respects." It was his intention, he told the colonial secretary, to treat the executive council with the confidence and cordiality due to the station which they occupied, but he was prepared to *be on his guard against any encroachments.* This last

---

[1] Metcalfe to Stanley, April 24th, 1843

phrase touches the root of the matter. Of what nature were the "encroachments" which Metcalfe was determined not to permit? How did he interpret his own position in reference to the executive officers that were his constitutional advisers? What, in other words, was his opinion on the application of responsible government? The answer to this question can best be found by an examination of Metcalfe's own statements as they appear in his confidential correspondence with the colonial office.

"Lord Durham's meaning," he wrote,[1] "seems to have been that the governor should conduct his administration in accordance with public feeling, represented by the popular branch of the legislature, and it is obvious that without such concordance the government could not be successfully administered. There is no evidence in what manner Lord Durham would have carried out the system which he advocated, as it was not brought into effect during his administration. Lord Sydenham arranged the details by which the principle was carried into execution. In forming the executive council he made it a rule that the individuals composing it should be members of the popular branch of the legislature, to which, I believe, there was only one exception: the gentleman appointed to be president being a member of the legislative council. Lord

---

[1] Metcalfe to Stanley, April 24th, 1843. Metcalfe's colonial despatches can be found in the *Selections from the Papers of Lord Metcalfe*, (London, 1885, Ed., J. W. Kaye).

Sydenham had apparently no intention of surrendering the government into the hands of the executive council. On the contrary, he ruled the council, and exercised great personal influence in the election of members to the representative assembly. . . . I am not aware that any great change took place during that period of the administration of Sir Charles Bagot which preceded the meeting of the legislature, but this event was instantly followed by a full development of the consequences of making the officers of the government virtually dependent for the possession of their places on the pleasure of the representative body. The two extreme parties in Upper Canada most violently opposed to one another, coalesced solely for the purpose of turning out the office-holders, or, as it is now termed, the ministry of that day, with no other bond of union, and with a mutual understanding that having accomplished that purpose, they would take the chance of the consequences, and should be at liberty to follow their respective courses. The French party also took part in this coalition, and from its compactness and internal union, formed its greatest strength. These parties together accomplished their joint purpose. They had expected to do so by a vote of the assembly, but in that were anticipated by the governor-general, who in apprehension of the threatened vote of want of confidence in members of his council, opened negotiations with the leaders of the French party, and that negotiation terminated in the resignation or removal from the council of those members who belonged to what is called by themselves the Conservative party, and in the introduction of five members of the united French and Reform parties. . . . *These events were regarded by all parties in the country as establishing in full force the system of responsible government* of which the practical execution had before been incomplete. From that time the tone of the members of the council and the tone of the public voice regarding responsible government has been greatly exalted. The council are now spoken of by themselves and others generally as the 'ministers,' the 'administration,' the 'cabinet,' the 'government,' and so forth. *Their pretensions are according to this new nomenclature.* They regard themselves as a responsible ministry, *and expect that the policy and conduct of the governor shall be subservient to their views and party policy.*"

Very similar in tone is a despatch of May 12th, 1843, in which the governor declared that none of his predecessors had really been face to face with the problem of granting or withholding self-government. "Lord Durham," he said, "had no difficulty in writing at leisure in praise of responsible government. . . Lord Sydenham put the *idea* in force without suffering himself to be much restrained by it. . . Sir Charles Bagot yielded to the coercive effect of Lord Sydenham's arrangements. *Now comes the tug of war*, and supposing absolute submission to be out of the question, I cannot say that I see the end of the struggle if the parties alluded to really mean to maintain it." The part that the new governor intended to play in this impending tug of war is clearly indicated in this communication to Lord Stanley. He had no intention of adapting himself to the position of a merely nominal head of the government, controlled by the advice of his ministers.

"I am required," he wrote, "to give myself up entirely to the council; to submit absolutely to their dictation; to have no judgment of my own; to bestow the patronage of the government exclusively on their partisans; to proscribe their opponents; and to make some public and unequivocal declaration of my adhesion to these conditions—including the complete nullification of Her Majesty's government—a course which he [Mr. LaFontaine], under self-deception, denominates Sir Charles Bagot's policy, although it is very certain that Sir Charles Bagot meant no such thing. Failing of submission to these stipulations, I am threatened with the resignation of Mr. LaFontaine for one, and both he and I are fully aware of the serious consequences likely to follow the execution of that menace, from the blindness ,with which the French-Canadian party follow their leader. . . . The sole question is, to describe it without disguise, whether the governor shall be wholly and completely a tool

in the hands of the council, or whether he shall have
any exercise of his own judgment in the administration of the government. Such a question has
not come forward as a matter of discussion, but
there is no doubt the leader of the French party
speaks the sentiments of others of his council
beside himself. . . . *As I cannot possibly adopt
them, I must be prepared for the consequences of
a rupture with the council*, or at least the most
influential portion of it. It would be very im-
prudent on my part to hasten such an event, or to
allow it to take place under present circumstances,
if it can be avoided—*but I must expect it, for I
cannot consent to be the tool of a party*. . . .
Government by a majority is the explanation of
responsible government given by the leader in
this movement, and government without a majority
must be admitted to be ultimately impracticable.
But the present question, the one which is coming
on for trial in my administration, is not whether the
governor shall so conduct his government as to
meet the wants and wishes of the people, and
obtain their suffrages by promoting their welfare
and happiness—nor whether he shall be responsible
for his measures to the people, through their representatives—but whether he shall, or shall not, have
a voice in his own council. . . . The tendency and
object of this movement is to throw off the government of the mother country in internal affairs
entirely—but to be maintained and supported at

her expense, and to have all the advantages of connection, as long as it may suit the majority of the people of Canada to endure it. This is a very intelligible and very convenient policy for a Canadian aiming at independence, but the part that the representative of the mother country is required to perform in it is by no means fascinating."

The tenor of Sir Charles Metcalfe's correspondence cited above, which belongs to the period between his assumption of the government and the meeting of the parliament, shows that the difficulties which were presently to culminate in the "Metcalfe Crisis" were already appearing on the horizon. Meantime the new governor was made the recipient of flattering addresses from all parts of the country and from citizens of all shades of opinion. The difficulties of Metcalfe's position can be better understood when one considers the varied nature of these addresses and the conflicting sentiments expressed. Some were sent up from Reform constituencies whose citizens expressed the wish that he might continue to tread in the path marked out by his predecessor. Others were from "loyal and constitutional societies" whose prayer it was that he might resist the designing encroachments of his anti-British advisers. The people of the township of Pelham, for example, declared that they "had learned with unfeigned sorrow that unusual efforts had been made to weaken His Excellency's opinion of Messrs. Baldwin and LaFontaine and the other members of his cabinet." The Constitutional Society of Orillia begged to "state their decided disapproval of the policy pursued by our late governor-general." "We have not the slightest wish," they said, "to dictate to your Excellency, but, conscientiously believing that it would tend to the real good, happiness, and prosperity of the country, we in all humility venture to recommend the dismissal of the following members from your councils: The Hon. Messrs. Harrison, LaFontaine, Baldwin, Hincks and Small." In some cases[1] rival addresses, breathing entirely opposed sentiments were sent up from the same place. It is small wonder that Metcalfe became deeply impressed by the bitterness of party faction existing in Canada.

"The violence of party spirit," he wrote to Lord Stanley,[2] "forces itself on one's notice immediately on arrival in the colony; and threatens to be the source of all the difficulties which are likely to impede the successful administration of the government for the welfare and happiness of the country." In this statement may be found the basis for such defense as can be made for Metcalfe's conduct in Canada. He was honestly convinced that the antipathy between the rival factions was assuming dangerous proportions, and that it threatened to culminate in a renewal of civil strife. In this position of affairs it seemed to

[1] For example the addresses from the Talbot district.

[2] April 25th, 1843.

167

him his evident duty to alleviate the situation by using such influence and power as he considered to be lawfully entrusted to him, to counteract the intensity of the party struggle. In particular it seemed to him that his right of making appointments to government offices ought to be exercised with a view to general harmony, and not at the dictates and in the interests of any special political group. "I wish," he wrote, "to make the patronage of the government conducive to the conciliation of all parties, by bringing into the public service the men of greatest merit and efficiency, without any party distinction."

This sentiment is no doubt, as a sentiment, very admirable. But what Metcalfe did not realize was that it was equivalent to saying that he intended to distribute the patronage of the government as *he* thought advisable, and not as the ministry, representing the voice of a majority of the people, might think advisable. Metcalfe seems to have been aware from the outset that his views on this matter would not be readily endorsed by his ministers. He spoke of the question of the patronage as "the point on which he most proximately expected to incur a difference with them." Indeed it may be asserted that Metcalfe was convinced that he must, sooner or later, come to open antagonism with his cabinet. As early as June, 1843, he wrote to Stanley: "Although I see no reason now to apprehend an immediate rupture, I am sensible that it may happen at any time. If all [of the ministers] were of the same mind with three or four it would be more certain. But there are moderate men among them, and they are not all united in the same unwarrantable expectations."

It is not difficult to infer from what has gone before that Metcalfe had but little personal sympathy with the two leaders of his cabinet. In his published correspondence we have no direct personal estimate of LaFontaine and Baldwin. But the account given by his "official" biographer of the two Canadian statesmen undoubtedly reflects opinion gathered from the governor-general's correspondence, and is of interest in the present connection. "The two foremost men in the council," writes Kaye,[1] "[were] Mr. LaFontaine and Mr. Baldwin, the attorneys-general for Lower and Upper Canada. The former was a French-Canadian and the leader of his party in the colonial legislature. . . . All his better qualities were natural to him; his worse were the growth of circumstances. Cradled, as he and his people had been, in wrong, smarting for long years under the oppressive exclusiveness of the dominant race, he had become mistrustful and suspicious; and the doubts which were continually floating in his mind had naturally engendered there indecision and infirmity of purpose." How little real justifica-

---

[1] Kaye's *Life of Lord Metcalfe* was written at the request of Metcalfe's trustee. Many thousand letters, written to and by Metcalfe, were put in the hands of his biographer.

tion there was for this last expression of opinion
may be gathered from the comments thereupon
published by Francis Hincks in later years. " I can
hardly believe that there is a single individual in
the ranks of either party," he says "who would
admit that Kaye was correct in attributing to [Sir]
Louis LaFontaine 'indecision and infirmity of
purpose.' I can declare for my own part that I
never met a man less open to such an imputation."[1]
Metcalfe's biographer saw fit, however, to qualify
his strictures of LaFontaine by stating that he
was a "just and honourable man" and that "his
motives were above suspicion."

A still less flattering portrait is drawn by the
same author when he goes on to speak of Robert
Baldwin. "Baldwin's father," says Kaye,[2] "had
quarrelled with his party,[3] and, with the characteristic
bitterness of a renegade, had brought up his son in
extremest hatred of his old associates, and had
instilled into him the most liberal *(sic)* opinions.
Robert Baldwin was an apt pupil; and there was
much in the circumstances by which he was surrounded,—in the atrocious misgovernment of his
country . . . —to rivet him in the extreme opinions
he had imbibed in his youth. So he grew up to be

[1] *Political History of Canada*, p. 16.

[2] J. W. Kaye, *Life of Lord Metcalfe*. Vol. II., pp. 490, 491. The
errors of fact made by Mr. Kaye in reference to Baldwin's parentage,
etc., need no correction.

[3] By this is meant the Family Compact of which Kaye supposes
Dr. Baldwin to have been a member.

an enthusiast, almost a fanatic. He was thoroughly
in earnest; thoroughly conscientious; but he was
to the last degree uncompromising and intolerant.
He seemed to delight in strife. The might of mild-
ness he laughed to scorn. It was said of him that
he was not satisfied with a victory unless it was
gained by violence—that concessions were valueless
to him unless he wrenched them with a strong hand
from his opponent. Of an unbounded arrogance and
self-conceit, he made no allowances for others, and
sought none for himself. There was a sort of sub-
lime egotism about him—a magnificent self-esteem,
which caused him to look upon himself as a patriot,
whilst he was serving his own ends by the promotion
of his ambition, the gratification of his vanity or
spite. His strong passions and his uncompromising
spirit made him a mischievous party leader and a
dangerous opponent. His influence was very great.
He was not a mean man : he was above corruption :
and there were many who accepted his estimate of
himself and believed him to be the only pure
patriot in the country. During the illness of Sir
Charles Bagot he had usurped the government. The
activity of Sir Charles Metcalfe, *who did everything
for himself, and exerted himself to keep every one in
his proper place*, was extremely distasteful to him."
It is an old saying that there is no witness whose
testimony is so valid as that of an unwilling witness :
and it is possible to read between the lines of this
biased estimate a truer picture of the man. " In

this dark photograph," says the author of *The Irishman in Canada*,[1] "the impartial eye recognizes the statesman, the patriot, the great party leader, who was not to be turned away by fear or favour from the work before him."

As early as May, 1843, an important episode took place in reference to the question of appointments, a question destined later to be the cause of the resignation of the ministry. The matter is of special historical significance in that LaFontaine saw fit to draw up a memorandum explaining what had occurred and putting definitely on record the attitude assumed by himself and his colleagues in their interpretation of their relation to the governor-general. The facts in question were as follows.[2] The office of provincial aide-de-camp for Lower Canada had fallen vacant. The post was a sinecure, the salary for which was voted yearly by the assembly. A certain Colonel De Salaberry, a son of the De Salaberry of Chateauguay, came to Kingston to solicit the office. He had an interview with Sir Charles Metcalfe, as a result of which it was reported that he had received the promise of the appointment. The private secretary of the governor-general, a certain Captain Higginson, met LaFontaine at a dinner given by His Excellency in Kingston. Higginson

---

[1] N. F. Davin, *The Irishman in Canada*, p. 490.

[2] See *The Pilot*, September 18th, 1844 ; also Hincks's *Reminiscences*, pp. 93 *et seq.*

discussed the vacant office with LaFontaine and was informed that, if the post were given to Colonel De Salaberry, the appointment would be viewed with disfavour by the people of Lower Canada. On this Higginson asked the attorney-general if he might, at his convenience, have an opportunity of discussing with him the present political situation. LaFontaine granted this request and Higginson called upon him at his office next day. A conversation of some three hours duration ensued in which the question of the nature and meaning of responsible government was discussed at full length. Captain Higginson declared that he was acting in the matter in a purely personal character and not as the accredited agent of the governor-general. This was probably true in the technical and formal sense, but it cannot be doubted that Higginson was expressing the known sentiments of Sir Charles Metcalfe, and that he duly reported the conversation to the governor, whose subsequent actions were evidently influenced thereby. The substance of the argument may best be given in the words of LaFontaine's published memorandum.[1]

"Being requested by Captain Higginson to explain to him what was understood by responsible government, the councillor[2] informed him of the

[1] Space will not permit the presentation of the entire document, which may be found (in translation) in Hincks's *Reminiscences*, pp. 98 *et seq.*

[2] LaFontaine writes in the third person, speaking of himself as a "member of the executive council," a "councillor," etc.

opinions which had been so often expressed on this subject as well in the House as elsewhere. He explained to him that the councillors were responsible for all the acts of the government with regard to local matters, that they were so held by members of the legislature, that they could only retain office so long as they possessed the confidence of the representatives of the people, and that whenever this confidence should be withdrawn from them they would retire from the administration; that these were the principles recognized by the resolutions of September 3rd, 1841, and that it was on the faith of these principles being carried out that he had accepted office. The question of consultation and non-consultation was brought on the tapis with reference to the exercise of patronage, that is to say, the distribution of places at the disposal of the government. The councillor informed Captain Higginson that the responsibility of the members of the administration, extending to all the acts of the government in local matters, comprehending therein the appointment to offices, consultation in all those cases became necessary, it being afterwards left to the governor to adopt or reject the advice of his councillors; His Excellency not being bound, and it not being possible to bind him, to follow that advice, but, on the contrary, having a right to reject it : but in this latter case, if the members of council did not choose to assume the responsibility of the act that the governor wished to perform, contrary to their advice, they had the means of relieving themselves from it by exercising their power of resigning." As Captain Higginson appears to have demurred to this interpretation of the meaning of the September resolutions, LaFontaine asked him to state the construction which he himself put upon them. Higginson replied,—and in replying may properly be considered to have expressed the sentiments of Sir Charles Metcalfe,—that although the governor ought to choose his councillors "from among those supposed to have the confidence of the people," nevertheless "each member of the administration ought to be responsible only for the acts of his own department, and consequently that he ought to have the liberty of voting with or against his colleagues whenever he judged fit; that by this means an administration composed of the principal members of each party might exist advantageously for all parties, and would furnish the governor the means of better understanding the views and opinions of each party, and would not fail, under the auspices of the governor, to lead to the reconciliation of all." From these views La-Fontaine expressed an emphatic and unqualified dissent. " If," he said, " the opinions [thus] expressed upon the sense of the resolutions of 1841 were those of the governor-general, and if His Excellency was determined to make them the rule for conducting his government, the sooner he made it known to the members of the council the better, in

order to avoid all misunderstanding between them."
LaFontaine added that in such a case he himself
would feel it his duty to tender his resignation.
Since there is undeniable evidence that Higginson
related this conversation in full to Sir Charles
Metcalfe, it is plain that henceforth the latter was
quite aware of the point of view taken by his
cabinet, and must have felt that a persistence in
the course he contemplated could not but lead to
an open rupture. Indeed it appears to have been
very shortly after this incident that he wrote to
Lord Stanley that his "attempts to conciliate all
parties are criminal in the eyes of the council, or at
least of the most formidable member of it."

As yet, however, the difficulties that were impending between the governor and his ministers
were unknown to the country at large. The "want
of cordiality and confidence" between Metcalfe and
his advisers had indeed become "a matter of public
rumour,"[1] but His Excellency had been careful in
his answers to the addresses praying for the removal
of the ministry to rebuke the spirit of partisan bitterness in which they were couched.[2] The governor
was consequently able to summon parliament in
the autumn of 1843 with a fair outward show of
harmony, and it was not until near the close of the
year that the smouldering quarrel broke into a

[1] The phrases are taken from LaFontaine's letter of November
27th, 1843, cited in the following chapter.

[2] Kaye, Vol. II., p. 510.

flame. Meantime the parliament had passed through a session of great activity and interest, and had undertaken a range of legislation which rapidly developed the extent and meaning of the Reform programme. In this, the third session of the first parliament, which lasted from September 28th until December 9th (1843), the ministry enjoyed in the assembly an overwhelming support. Of the eighty-four members of the House, some sixty figured as the supporters of the government; and even in the legislative council, the appointment of Dr. Baldwin, the father of the attorney-general, Æmilius Irving and others, lent support to the government. Mr. Draper, on the other hand, now elevated to a seat in the legislative council, embarked on a determined and persistent opposition to the measures of the administration. Six new members had been elected during the recess to fill vacancies in the assembly. Prominent among these was Edward Gibbon Wakefield, elected for Beauharnois, notable presently as one of the defenders of Sir Charles Metcalfe. Wakefield had already attained a certain notoriety in England for his views on the "art of colonization," and for the theories of land settlement which he had endeavoured to put into practice in Australia and New Zealand.[1] He had already spent some time in Canada with Lord

---

[1] See *Dictionary of National Biography*, Art. Wakefield, E.G. See also W. P. Reeves, *State Experiments in Australia and New Zealand*, (1902), Vol. I., Ch. vi.

Durham in an unofficial capacity, and had had some share in the preparation of the report. He had returned to Canada in 1841, and as has been already noted, had been on intimate terms with Bagot and his ministry. He was anxious, according to Hincks, to press a certain land scheme of his invention on the government, and it was their refusal to meet his views which led him presently to oppose their policy and to become the confidential adviser and the apologist of Sir Charles Metcalfe.

Hopelessly outvoted as they were in the Lower House, the Tories and other opponents of the government nevertheless maintained a spirited opposition. Sir Allan MacNab and his adherents persisted at every available opportunity in raising the racial question, in reviving uncomfortable recollections of 1837, and in assuming a tone of direct personal attack, the impotence of which against the solid majority of the government lent it an added venom.[1] The government in its turn was well represented in debate. Baldwin, LaFontaine and Hincks were all members of the assembly; being now united in policy, the combined power of their leadership and the ardour which they put into their legislative duties, easily held their followers together

[1] The following extract is illustrative of the amenities of the day :— "Then Mr. Johnston came into full play—right and left he dashed into the supporters of the bill with his peculiar sarcasm—he told one honourable gentleman from Montreal that he never yet had had the manliness to express an independent opinion—told others that they would make good feather breeches to hatch eggs, etc., etc."—Kingston *Whig,* October 1843.

and enabled them to enjoy a continued and un-wavering support. A sort of natural division of labour had been instituted among them. The larger measures of the Reform programme were intro-duced by Baldwin: LaFontaine was especially concerned with the alterations to be effected in the judicial system of Lower Canada and cognate matters, while Hincks assumed the care of fiscal and commercial legislation.

A contemporary account[1] of Francis Hincks during the session of 1843, gives a vivid idea of the legislature of the day and the prominent part played in its deliberations by the inspector-general. " He [Mr. Hincks] had a portable desk beside him and a heap of papers. He was as busy as a nailer, writing, reading, marking down pages, whispering to the men on the front seat, sending a slip of paper to this one and that one, a hint to the member speaking; there was no mistaking that man. Presently he stood up and started off full drive, —half a dozen voices cry out, ' Hear, hear !' ' No ! No !' He picks up a slip of paper and the whole House is silent. The figures come tumbling out like potatoes from a basket. He snatches up a journal or some other document, and having established his position he goes ahead again. The inspector-general, Mr. Hincks, is decidedly the man of that House. When one has observed with what attention

---

[1] *The Examiner*, October 25th, 1843. Hincks had severed his con-nection with this paper on assuming office.

he is listened to by every member, when we look up to the reporters, who are, during half the time when the other speakers are up, looking on wearily, now all hard at their tasks, catching every word they can lay hold of, it is not difficult to guess how it has happened that Francis Hincks has been one of the best abused men that ever lived in Canada. No wonder the old Compact hated him : they foresaw in him a sad enemy to vermin. He is a real terrier. He speaks much too rapidly ; and in consequence runs into a very disagreeable sort of stammering. His manner of reading off statistical quotations is peculiarly censurable. It is impossible for reporters to take down the figures correctly, and the honourable gentleman should reflect of what great importance it is to himself and the ministry that all such matter be correctly reported."

The measures of the session included altogether sixty-four statutes assented to by the governor, with nine other bills reserved for the royal assent, of which four subsequently became law. Of these, many were of an entirely subordinate character and need no mention, but the more important measures require some notice. Among the matters to which the attention of the House was early directed was the question of the seat of government. Lord Sydenham's selection of Kingston had given dissatisfaction in both sections of the province, and many representations had been forwarded to the home government requesting that some other

Notre Dame Street, Montreal, 1840

capital might be selected. Montreal, Quebec and Toronto all aspired to the coveted honour. Even Bytown, as the present city of Ottawa was then called, was favoured by some persons, owing to its inland situation and its immunity from frontier attack. But in point of wealth, importance and natural situation, Montreal seemed obviously destined to be the capital of Canada. It was at this time a city of over forty thousand inhabitants. Its position at the head of ocean navigation rendered it, as now, the commercial emporium of the country, and the narrow streets near the water front,—St. Paul and Notre Dame, then the principal mercantile streets of the town,—were crowded during the season of navigation with the rush of its seagoing commerce. The extreme beauty of the situation of the city, its historical associations and its manifest commercial greatness of the future, ought to have placed the superiority of its claims beyond a question. But the racial antagonism, which was the dominant feature of the politics of the hour, rendered the question one of British interest as opposed to French. Montreal was indeed by no means an entirely French city. It numbered several thousand British inhabitants, had two daily newspapers published in English and had in it (to quote the words of Dr. Taché in the assembly) more "real English, more out and out John Bulls, than either Kingston or Toronto."

But the Conservatives of Upper Canada persisted in identifying Montreal with the Lower Canadian province. " It is not," said the New York *Albion* in an editorial article,[1] " a mere matter of holding parliamentary sessions in this place or in that, that is involved ; it is a matter that carries with it the great question of English or French supremacy for the future." Legally speaking the matter lay with the imperial government[2] (acting through the governor-general) but a representation[3] was made to Sir Charles Metcalfe and communicated by him to the Canadian parliament to the effect that " Her Majesty's government decline to come to a determination in favour of any place as the future seat of government, without the advice of the provincial legislature." It was, however, made a proviso that the choice must be between Kingston and Montreal; Quebec and Toronto " being alike too remote from the centre of the province." In accordance with this message a resolution was introduced by Robert Baldwin, and seconded by LaFontaine (November 2nd, 1843), advising the Crown to remove the seat of government to Montreal. The members of the administration (with the exception of Mr. Harrison, the member for Kingston, who now resigned his post as provincial secretary) were entirely in favour of the measure. Sir Charles Metcalfe himself sup-

[1] November 11th, 1843.

[2] 3 and 4 Vict. c. 35, Sec. xxx.

[3] See *Journal of the Legislative Assembly*, October 6th, 1842.

182

ported it. But the Tories persisted in regarding it as a betrayal of Upper Canada. In the legislative council Mr. Draper had already succeeded in passing resolutions condemning the proposed change, on the ground that the retention of the capital in Upper Canada was a virtual condition of the union of the two provinces. Sir Allan MacNab took even higher ground: he regarded the journey to and from Kingston and the sojourn in the British atmosphere of Upper Canada as a necessary training for the French-Canadian deputies, whereby they might acquire, by infection as it were, something of the spirit of the British constitution.[1]

In despite of the Conservative opposition, the resolution favouring the transfer of the government was carried in the assembly by a vote of fifty-one to twenty-seven (November 3rd, 1843). In the legislative council the presence of the newly-appointed members enabled the same resolution to be adopted. An attempt was made by the Tories to refuse to consider the question, on the ground that Mr. Draper's recent resolution had already dealt with it. This contention was rejected by the Speaker, who insisted that the resolution must be duly voted on; whereupon an indignant councillor, Mr. Morris, said he "must protest in the most solemn manner against

---

[1] See speech of Robert Baldwin (*La Minerve*, November 16th, 1843) in which he describes the French-Canadian members "sitting at the feet of the honourable knight as a political Gamaliel."

this proceeding, took his hat, made his bow to
the Speaker and left the chamber followed by
twelve other members of the council for Upper
Canada."

A measure of the session, the work of LaFontaine,
for which the Reform party are entitled to great
credit, was the Act for securing the independence of
the legislative assembly.[1] The aim of this statute
was to consolidate the system of cabinet government by removing placemen from the assembly.
It enacted that after the end of the present parliament a large number of office-holders should be
disqualified for election. The list included judges,
officers of the courts, registrars, customs officers,
public accountants and many other minor officials.
The holders of the ministerial offices were of course
outside of the scope of the statute, which thus aimed
to place the relation of the legislature to the holding of office on the same footing as in the mother
country. The reasonableness of this measure was
admitted even by opponents of the government,
but the question of its constitutionality having
been raised in the legislative council, it was reserved
by the governor for the assent of the Crown. This
assent was duly granted.

The reorganization of the judicial system of
Lower Canada with a view to render the administration of justice more easy and less expensive was
carried forward by LaFontaine in a series of five

[1] 7 Vict. c. 65.

statutes.[1] The district and division courts that had
been established under Mr. Draper's government
(September 18th, 1841)[2] were abolished in favour of
a simpler system of circuit courts : a new court of
appeal was organized and provision made for the
summary trial of small causes.

Among the bills laid before parliament, in whose
preparation Baldwin was chiefly concerned, a prominent place should be given to the bill for the
discouragement of secret societies. During the
summer and autumn of 1843 the province of Upper
Canada had been the scene of deplorable and riotous strife between the rival factions into which the
Irish settlers of the colony were divided. With the
large immigration from the British Isles during the
preceding years, a great number of Irish had come
into the country. Unfortunately these had seen fit
to carry with them into Canada the unhappy
quarrels of their native country, and nowhere was
the strife of Orangemen and Repealers, Protestants and Catholics, more ardent than in the little
Canadian capital. The events of the year 1843,
during which all Ireland was in a frenzy of excitement over O'Connell's agitation for repeal, naturally precipitated a similar agitation in Canada.
Here the situation was further aggravated by the
fact that the two parties of Irishmen were in a sort

[1] 7 Vict. cc. 16, 17, 18, 19, 20. The statutes are very elaborate : it
is quite impossible in the present limited space to give any proper idea
of their purport.

[2] 4 and 5 Vict. c. 20.

of natural alliance with the rival political factions of Canada. The Orangemen, with their ostentatious attachment to the British Crown, found allies in the Tories, while their Catholic opponents had much in common with their co-religionists of French Canada. Orange lodges had sprung into being throughout Upper Canada: "Hibernian societies" of Irish Catholics flaunted in defiance the colours and insignia of their associations.[1]

In such a state of affairs, collisions between the rival parties were inevitable. At Kingston, on the anniversary of the battle of the Boyne, serious troubles occurred; several persons were wounded, and one killed; the troops had to be called out to maintain order. On a later occasion the streets were placarded with bills announcing rival assemblages, one in aid of the cause of repeal, the other for preventing the repeal meeting, "peaceably if we can, forcibly if we must." The unofficial action of the governor and the cabinet prevented the holding of the meetings.

Sir Charles Metcalfe was obviously alarmed at the prospect of a general conflagration. Rumours had reached him that the Irish of New York were busily engaged at drill under French officers, and that an invasion of Canada was to be attempted. "It is supposed," he wrote to Stanley,[2] "that if any collision were to occur in Ireland between the

[1] See Kaye, Vol. II., pp. 502 *et seq.*
[2] July 8th, 1843.

ORANGE DISTURBANCES

government and the disaffected, it would be followed by the pouring of myriads of Roman Catholic Irish into Canada from the United States." It is just possible that this apprehension caused the governor to look more than ever towards the Tories as an ultimate support. In the course of the month of July he had an interview with a Mr. Gowan (then grand-master of the Grand Orange Lodge of Canada and a man of the greatest influence), after which the grand-master wrote a mysterious confidential letter to a friend, in which he told his correspondent "not to be surprised if Baldwin, Hincks and Harrison should *walk*." Mr. Gowan said, furthermore, that he had given his views to the governor *maturely and in writing*.[1] It is quite possible that the grand-master had recommended a reconstruction of the government as the price of obtaining the support of the Orange order. Meantime, however, the tumults of the rival Irish factions continued unabated. At Toronto, for example, during the time when legislation in regard to secret societies was being discussed, an Orange mob gathered in the streets one November night, having amongst them a cart with a gibbet and effigies of Baldwin and Hincks placarded with the word "Traitors," which effigies were burnt during a scene of great confusion before the residence of Dr. Baldwin.[2]

[1] Gowan's letter is quoted by N. F. Davin, *The Irishman in Canada*, p. 492.

[2] *The Examiner*, November 8th, 1843.

BALDWIN LAFONTAINE HINCKS

It was in order to discourage, as far as possible, the manifestations of the Irish societies that Baldwin introduced (October 9th, 1843) his bill in regard to secret societies. The provisions of the bill declared all societies (with the exception of the Freemasons) to be illegal if their members were bound together by secret oaths and signs: members of such societies were to be incapable of holding office or of serving on juries : all persons holding public office were to be called upon to declare that they belonged to no such societies: innkeepers who permitted society meetings on their premises were to lose their licenses. Drastic as this measure appears, it must be borne in mind that the secret societies bill was introduced as a government measure with the knowledge and consent of Sir Charles Metcalfe. It passed the House by a large majority, fifty-five votes being cast in favour of it and only thirteen against it.[1] Nevertheless, Sir Charles saw fit to reserve it for the royal sanction, which in the sequel was refused. It is true that the legislature had already adopted a law of a more general nature in regard to demonstrations tending to disturb the public peace, and that this additional legislation was viewed by many as special legislation against a particular class. But the ministry, as will be seen later, considered that, under the circumstances, Metcalfe had gone beyond his constitutional functions in withholding his assent.

[1] *Journal of the Legislative Assembly*, November 4th, 1843.

TARIFFS AND SCHOOLS

Two Acts of the session[1] which elicited a general approval were Hincks's measures for the protection of agriculture against the competition of the United States. The latter country had recently adopted a high tariff system whereby the Canadians found themselves excluded from the American market. The present statute did not profess to institute a definite and permanent policy of protection, but claimed to remedy the unequal conditions imposed on the farming population under the existing customs system, which put duties on merchandise but allowed foreign agricultural produce and live stock to come in free. Under these Acts a duty of £1 10s. was to be paid on imported horses, £1 on cattle; and on all grains other than wheat, duties of from two to three shillings per quarter.

In order to remedy the defective operation of the existing school law two new statutes were adopted.[2] Fifty thousand pounds a year were now to be given by the government to elementary schools. The difficulties which had arisen under Mr. Draper's Act in regard to the apportionment of the government grant were to be obviated by a division of the money between Upper and Lower Canada in the ratio of twenty to thirty thousand pounds until a census should be taken, after which the division was to be according to population. In the second of

[1] 7 Vict. cc. 1 and 2.

[2] 7 Vict. c. 9 and 7 Vict. c. 29.

the school Acts (which dealt only with Upper Canada) it was provided that the government grant should be distributed among the localities according to population; that the townships (or towns or cities as the case might be) should levy on their inhabitants a sum at least equal to, but not more than double, the government grant. Fees were still to be charged for instruction in the common schools, but a clause of the Act (section 49) enabled the council of any town or city to establish free schools by by-law. The Act continued to recognize the system of separate schools, which might be established either by Protestants or Roman Catholics on the application of ten or more freeholders or householders.

The school law was mainly in amplification and in extension of the existing system. A measure in regard to education of a much more distinctive character, and which evoked a furious opposition both within and without the House, was Robert Baldwin's University of Toronto bill. Although this measure was not finally adopted, the university question remained for years in the forefront of the political issues of the day, until the matter was finally set at rest by the statute enacted under the second LaFontaine-Baldwin administration.[1]

[1] The administration of 1848 should more properly be called the Baldwin-LaFontaine administration, since Robert Baldwin was its senior member. But it has been customary to use the designation in the text.

THE UNIVERSITY QUESTION

As the name Robert Baldwin will always be associated with the successful removal of all denominational character from the University of Toronto, some explanation of the question at issue is here in place. The present University of Toronto originated in an antecedent institution called King's College.[1] The first impetus towards the creation of this college had been given by Governor Simcoe, who called the attention of the imperial government to the wisdom of making provision for a provincial university and to the possibility of effecting this by an appropriation of Crown lands. In 1797 the two Houses of the legislature of Upper Canada petitioned the Crown to make an appropriation of a certain portion of the waste lands of the colony as a fund for the establishment and support of a respectable grammar school in each district of the province, and also of a college or university. In 1799 the land grant was made. It consisted of five hundred and fifty thousand, two hundred and seventy-four acres of land. Beyond this nothing was done for many years. Meantime a certain part of the land was set aside for special educational objects ; one hundred and ninety thousand, five hundred and seventy-three acres were appropriated in 1823 for district grammar schools, and in 1831, sixty-two thousand, nine hundred and ninety-six acres were given to Upper

[1] See J. Loudon, *History of the University of Toronto*, printed in *Canada, an Encyclopædia*, 1898.

Canada College.[1] At length in 1827 a royal charter was issued for a university to be known as the University of King's College. Under this document the conduct of the university and of its teaching was vested in a corporation consisting of the chancellor, the president and the professors. Certain clauses of the charter gave to King's College a denominational character: the bishop of the diocese was to be, *ex officio*, its visitor, and the archdeacon of York (at that time Dr. John Strachan) its *ex officio* president: the university was to have a faculty of divinity, all students in which must subscribe to the Thirty-nine Articles of the Church of England: the same test was prescribed for all members of the university council.

The issue of this charter had occasioned a violent agitation. Vigorous protest was raised against the peculiar privileges thus extended to the Church of England. The opposition to the charter prevented any further action being taken towards the actual establishment of the college. Finally, in 1837, a statute[2] was passed by the legislature of Upper Canada which revised the terms of the royal charter. It provided that the judges of the court of king's bench should be the visitors of the college, that the president need not be the incumbent of any particular ecclesiastical office, that no religious

---

[1] In 1828 part of the original grant of land was exchanged for an equal portion of land belonging to the Clergy Reserves.

[2] *Statutes of Upper Canada,* 7 Will. IV. c. 16.

tests should be required of students, and that no professor, nor member of the council, need be a member of the Church of England. The statute still left the faculty of divinity as a part of the university, and left it necessary for every professor and member of the council to subscribe to a belief in the Trinity and in the divine inspiration of the Scripture. Even after the charter had been thus modified, a further delay was occasioned by the rebellion of 1837, and it was not until 1842 that the building of King's College actually commenced, the corner-stone being laid by Sir Charles Bagot in his capacity of chancellor of the university. In April of 1843 actual teaching had begun, the old parliament buildings on Front Street, Toronto, being used as temporary premises. Meantime the long delay which had been encountered in the creation of the provincial university, and the somewhat arrogant claims that had been put forward by Dr. Strachan and the extreme Anglicans, had led the members of the other sects to make efforts towards the establishment of denominational colleges of their own. The Methodists incorporated in 1836 an institution which opened its doors at Cobourg in the following year under the name of the Upper Canada Academy.[1] In 1841 an Act of the parliament of Canada[2] conferred on the academy the power to grant degrees, and gave it the name

[1] See Egerton Ryerson, *Story of My Life*, Chap. xiv.

[2] 4 and 5 Vict. c. 37.

of Victoria College. The Presbyterians, acting under a royal charter, established Queen's College at Kingston, which entered on the work of teaching in 1842. The Roman Catholics had founded in the same town a seminary known as the College of Regiopolis.

To Robert Baldwin and those who were able to take a broad-minded view of the question of higher education in Canada and to consider the future as well as the present, the separate foundation of these denominational universities appeared a decided error. It meant that, in the future, Canadian education would run upon sectarian lines and that a narrow scholasticism would usurp the place of a wider culture. The theologian would be substituted for the man of learning. More than this, the present system was in violation of that doctrine of equal rights which was the foundation of Robert Baldwin's political creed ; for the opulent land grant enjoyed by King's College gave to it a form of state support which was denied to its sister institutions. The measure which Baldwin presented to the parliament in remedy of the situation was sweeping in character. It proposed to create an institution to be known as the University of Toronto, of which the existing sectarian establishments should be the colleges. The executive academic body of the university was to consist of the governor-general as chancellor, together with a vice-chancellor and council chosen from the different colleges. With this was to be a

Queen's College, Kingston, 1840

board of control made up of dignitaries of the respective churches together with various public officials. The essential principle of Baldwin's bill lay in the fact that all the denominational colleges involved were put on an equal footing. Each retained its own faculty of divinity, the university granting a doctor's degree in divinity to graduates of all the divinity faculties alike. The property that had been granted by the state to King's College was to become the property of the University of Toronto. It proposed, in a word, a general federation of the existing sectarian institutions into a single provincial establishment looking to the state for its support, including denominational colleges as its affiliated members but itself of an entirely unsectarian character. To those acquainted with the recent history of educational development in Ontario, the wisdom of the idea of federation needs no commentary.

At the present day the general principle of the bill—the secularization of state education—meets with a ready support; but the proposal of the measure aroused in Upper Canada a storm of opposition. First and foremost the opposition came from the Anglicans, to whom the measure seemed a piece of godless iconoclasm directed at their dearest privileges. Dr. John Strachan, whose intense convictions and untiring energy made him the most formidable champion of the Church of England, led the attack on the bill. Strachan was by instinct

a fighting man who did not spare the weight of his
blows in a good cause. He forwarded to the parliament a thunderous petition, presented by "John,
by Divine Permission First Bishop of Toronto,"
the intemperate language of which bespeaks the
character of the man. "The leading object of the
bill," so began the prayer, "is to place all forms of
error on an equality with truth, by patronizing
equally within the same institution an unlimited
number of sects, whose doctrines are absolutely
irreconcilable : a principle in its nature atheistical,
and so monstrous in its consequences that, if successfully carried out, it would utterly destroy all
that is pure and holy in morals and religion, and
lead to greater corruption than anything adopted
during the madness of the French Revolution. . . .
Such a fatal departure from all that is good is without a parallel in the history of the world."[1]

A whirlwind of discussion followed the legislative
progress of the bill. It was argued that parliament
had no legal right to abrogate the royal charter of
King's College; that the proposed measure was
equivalent to a confiscation of the property of the
college ; more than that it was argued that the
provincial parliament was not empowered to create
a university at all. These were the arguments of the
lawyer, to which the churchmen added their cry of
horror at the desecration of the privileges of the
Church. The violence of "John, by Divine Per-

[1] *Journal of the Legislative Assembly*, November 6th, 1843.

mission," etc., was imitated by lesser luminaries. " Here we have," screamed "Testis," in a hysterical contribution to a leading Anglican paper,[1] "the true atheistical character of the popular dogma of responsible government. This is its fruit, its bitter, poisonous fruit; this is the broad road to destruction into which its many votaries are rushing headlong." Draper in the legislative council (November 24th, 1843) opposed the bill in a speech excellent in its masterly analysis, in which the really weak points of the bill—its interference with charter rights and its peculiar degrees in assorted divinity—were exposed with an unsparing hand. But in spite of opposition from outside, the bill was making its way through the legislature and had reached its second reading when its further progress was stopped by an event which threw the whole country into a turmoil of excitement.

[1] *The Church,* November 17th, 1843.

CHAPTER VII

THE METCALFE CRISIS

THE newspapers of the early forties, adhering to the decorous traditions of the older school, knew nothing of the modern system of sensational headings and exaggerated type. But the news which, at the close of November, 1843, spread rapidly through the country, startled many of them into large capitals and abundant notes of exclamation. The LaFontaine-Baldwin ministry, with an unbroken majority behind it, had gone suddenly out of office! "Dismissed!" triumphantly shouted the Tories, and forthwith, without waiting for further details of what had happened, an exultant song of praise flowed from the pens of Conservative editors in laudation of the stout-hearted governor who had vindicated British loyalty against the treacheries of aliens and Radicals. "The news from Canada," sang back in echo the New York *Albion*, "is of a right cheering character: the Franco-Radical cabinet has gone to the tomb of the Capulets amid the shouts of every loyal man in the province. The governor-general, Sir Charles Metcalfe, (and thrice honoured be his name!) has thrown off the incubus of a disloyal faction and the queen's representative stands redeemed and disenthralled."

199

But the ministry had not, as presently appeared, been dismissed; they had, with one exception only, handed in a collective resignation in protest against what they regarded as the unconstitutional conduct of the governor-general. This was at last the rupture which Metcalfe five months before had told Lord Stanley might "happen any day." The vexed question of the patronage and the governor's reservation of the Secret Societies Bill had led the cabinet to force the matter to an issue. It has been seen above that Metcalfe had resolved that the exercise of the right of appointment to office should not be removed from his hands. To this policy he had adhered. Several cases had already occurred in which the governor-general had offered, and even conferred, official positions without any consultation with his ministry. Among these was the important post of speaker of the legislative council,[1] which was offered successively, though without finding acceptance, to two members of the Conservative party. Finally toward the end of November, 1843, it reached the ears of the cabinet that a certain Mr. Powell, the son of Colonel Powell (also of the Conservative party) had been appointed by Sir Charles Metcalfe to be clerk of the peace for the Dalhousie district. The position, in and of itself, was no great affair. But the ministry, considering a principle of prime importance to be involved, decided to bring the matter to a final test.

[1] The holder of this office under the Act of Union was nominated and removed by the governor-general (3 and 4 Vict. c. Section xxxv).

RESIGNATION OF THE CABINET

On November 24th Baldwin and LaFontaine called upon the governor-general and held with him a long colloquy which was renewed at a meeting of the executive council the next day. The two ministers, to use the words of Metcalfe's biographer, "pressed their demands with energy and resolution: but Metcalfe, in his own placid way, was equally energetic and resolute." On the day following (November 26th, 1843) the ministry resigned. As the course of action thus adopted and the crisis which followed constitute a turning point in the political history of Canada, and form the most important episode in the public career of the united leaders, it is well to follow in some detail the threads of the vexed controversy to which their resignation gave rise. At the instance of Sir Charles Metcalfe, LaFontaine drew up an official statement of the reasons of the resignation, which, together with a rejoinder by the governor-general, was duly laid before the Houses of parliament.[1] The ministerial statement runs as follows:—

"Mr. LaFontaine, in compliance with the request of the governor-general, and in behalf of himself and his late colleagues, who have felt it to be their duty to tender a resignation of office, states, for His

[1] These are to be found in the *Journals of the Assembly* and in all the newspapers of the day : they also appear in the pamphlet printed by H. W. Rowsell (Toronto, 1844) under the title *Addresses presented to His Excellency the Rt. Hon. Sir Chas. T. Metcalfe, Bart. G.C.B.* This document and other publications on the controversy appear in the Baldwin Pamphlets, 1844, now in the Toronto Public Library.

Excellency's information, the substance of the explanation which they purpose to offer in their places in parliament. They avowedly took office upon the principle of responsibility to the representatives of the people in parliament, and with a full recognition on their parts of the following resolutions introduced into the legislative assembly with the knowledge and sanction of Her Majesty's representative in this province, on September 3rd, 1841." (Here follows a citation of the resolutions given in Chapter IV. above.)

"They have lately understood that His Excellency took a widely different view of the position, duties, and responsibilities of the executive council, from that under which they accepted office, and through which they have been enabled to conduct the parliamentary business of the government, sustained by a large majority of the popular branch of the legislature.

"Had the difference of opinion between His Excellency and themselves, and, as they have reason to believe, between His Excellency and the parliament and people of Canada generally, been merely theoretical, the members of the late executive council might, and would, have felt it to be their duty to avoid any possibility of collision which might have a tendency to disturb the tranquil and amicable relations which apparently subsisted between the executive government and the provincial parliament. But the difference of opinion has led not merely to appointments to office against their advice, but to appointments, and proposals to make appointments, of which they were not informed in any manner, until all opportunity of offering advice respecting them had passed by, and to a determination on the part of His Excellency to reserve for the expression of Her Majesty's pleasure thereon a bill introduced into the provincial parliament with His Excellency's knowledge and consent as a government measure, without an opportunity being given to the members of the executive council to state the probability of such a reservation. They, therefore, felt themselves in the anomalous position of being, according to their own avowals and solemn public pledges, responsible for all the acts of the executive government and parliament, and at the same time not only without the opportunity of offering advice respecting these acts, but without the knowledge of their existence, until informed of them from private and unofficial sources.

"When the members of the late executive council offered their humble remonstrances to His Excellency on this condition of public affairs, His Excellency not only frankly explained the difference of opinion existing between him and the council, but stated that, from the time of his arrival in the country, he had observed an antagonism between him and them on the subject, and notwithstanding that the members of the council repeatedly and distinctly explained to His

Excellency that they considered him free to act contrary to their advice, and only claimed an opportunity of giving such advice and of knowing, before others, His Excellency's intentions, His Excellency did not in any manner remove the impression left upon their minds, by his avowal, that there was an antagonism between him and them, and a want of that cordiality and confidence which would enable them, in their respective stations, to carry on public business to the satisfaction of His Excellency or of the country.

"The want of this cordiality and confidence had already become a matter of public rumour: and public opinion not only extended it to acts, upon which there were apparent grounds for difference of opinion, but to all measures of government involving political principles. His Excellency, on the one hand, was supposed to be coerced by his council into a course of policy which he did not approve of, and the council were made liable to the accusation of assuming the tone and position of responsible advisers of the government, without, in fact, asserting the right of being consulted thereupon.

"While His Excellency disavowed any intention of altering the course of administration of public affairs which he found on his arrival in Canada, he did not disguise the opinion that these affairs would be more satisfactorily managed by and through the governor himself, without any necessity of concord

204

amongst the members of the executive council or obligation on their part to defend or support in parliament the acts of the governor. To this opinion of His Excellency, as one of theory, the members of the executive council might not have objected; but when, on Saturday last, they discovered that it was the real ground of all their differences with His Excellency, and of the want of confidence and cordiality between His Excellency and the council since his arrival, they felt it impossible to continue to serve Her Majesty, as executive councillors for the affairs of this province, consistently with their duty to Her Majesty, or to His Excellency, or with their public and often repeated pledges in the provincial parliaments, if His Excellency would see fit to act upon his opinion of their functions and responsibilities."

The document written by Sir Charles Metcalfe in answer to this on the following day (November 28th, 1843) runs as follows :—

"The governor-general observes with regret in the explanation which the gentlemen who have resigned their seats in the executive council propose to offer in their places in parliament, a total omission of the circumstances which he regards as forming the real grounds of their resignation ; and as this omission may have proceeded from their not considering themselves at liberty to disclose the circumstances, it becomes necessary that he should state them.

"On Friday, Mr. LaFontaine and Mr. Baldwin came to the government house, and after some other matters of business, and some preliminary remarks as to the cause of their proceeding, demanded of the governor-general that he should agree to make no appointment, and no offer of an appointment, without previously taking the advice of the council; that the lists of candidates should, in every instance, be laid before the council; that they should recommend any others at discretion, and that the governor-general, in deciding after taking their advice, should not make any appointment prejudicial to their influence. In other words, that the patronage of the Crown should be surrendered to the council for the purchase of parliamentary support; for, if the demand did not mean that, it meant nothing, as it cannot be imagined that the mere form of taking advice without regarding it, was the process contemplated.

"The governor-general replied that he would not make any such stipulation, and could not degrade the character of his office, nor violate his duty, by such a surrender of the prerogative of the Crown.

"He appealed to the number of appointments made by him on the recommendation of the council, or the members of it in their departmental capacity, and to instances in which he had abstained from conferring appointments on their opponents, as furnishing proofs of the great consideration which he had evinced towards the council in the distribution of the patronage of the Crown.

"He at the same time objected, as he had always done, to the exclusive distribution of patronage with party views, and maintained the principle that office ought in every instance to be given to the man best qualified to render efficient service to the state; and where there was no such preëminence, he asserted the right to exercise his discretion.

"He understood from Messrs. LaFontaine and Baldwin, that their continuance in office depended upon his final decision with regard to their demand; and it was agreed that at the council to be assembled the next day, that subject should be fully discussed.

"He accordingly met the council on Saturday, convinced that they would resign, as he would not recede from the resolution which he had formed, and the same subject became the principal topic of discussion. Three or more distinct propositions were made to him, over and over again, sometimes in different terms, but always aiming at the same purpose, which, in his opinion, if accomplished, would have been a virtual surrender into the hands of the council of the prerogative of the Crown: and on his uniformly replying to these propositions in the negative, his refusal was each time followed by 'Then we must resign,' or words to that purport, from one or more of his council. In the course of the conversations which, both on Friday and Saturday, followed the explicit demand made by the council regarding the patronage of the Crown, that demand being based on the construction put by some of the gentlemen on the meaning of 'Responsible Government,' different opinions were elicited on the abstract theory of that still undefined question as applicable to a colony—a subject on which considerable difference of opinion is known everywhere to prevail; but the governor-general, during those conversations, protested against its being supposed that he is practically adverse to the system of responsible government, which has been here established : which he has hitherto pursued without deviation, and to which it is fully his intention to adhere. . . . If, indeed, by responsible government the gentlemen of the late council mean that the council is to be supreme, and the authority of the governor-general a nullity, then he cannot agree with them, and must declare his dissent from that perversion of the acknowledged principle. . . . Allusion is made in the proposed explanation of the gentlemen of the late council, to the governor-general's having determined to reserve for the consideration of Her Majesty's government, one of the bills passed by the two legislative Houses. That is the Secret Societies Bill. If there is any part of the functions of the governor in which he is more than any other bound to exercise an independent judgment, it must be in giving the royal assent to Acts of parliament. With regard to this duty he has special instructions from Her Majesty to reserve every Act of an unusual or extraordinary character. Undoubtedly the Secret Societies Bill answers that description, being unexampled in British legislation. The gentlemen of the late council heard his sentiments on it expressed to them. He told them that it was an arbitrary and unwise measure, and not even calculated to effect the end it had in view. He had given his consent to its being introduced into parliament, because he had promised, soon after his assumption of the government, that he would sanction legislation on the subject as a substitute for executive measures which he refused to adopt on account of their proscriptive character : although he deprecates the existence of societies which tend to foment religious and civil discord. The gentlemen of the late council cannot fail to remember with what pertinacity those measures were pressed on him, and can hardly be unaware of what would have followed at that time, if, in addition to rejecting the proscriptive measures urged, he had refused to permit any legislation on the subject."[1]

[1] About a fortnight afterwards (December 11th, 1843) Metcalfe wrote to Lord Stanley as follows : "Late on the following day, Mr. LaFontaine sent me a written statement of the explanation, which he and his colleagues proposed to give in their places in parliament, of the grounds of their resignation. A copy is enclosed. It is a most disingenuous production, suppressing entirely the immediate matter upon which their resignation took place, and trumping up a vague assertion of differences on the theory of responsible government as applicable to a colony, which had been expressed in the freedom of conversation as matters of opinion but not as grounds of procedure, and were, therefore, very unfairly used for the purpose to which this misrepresentation was

The two above documents, which were soon
scattered broadcast throughout Canada, represent
the official version of the opposing sides of the
political controversy which raged throughout the
next twelve months. The resignation of the La-
Fontaine-Baldwin ministry was no ordinary event.
The whole principle of British colonial government
was staked upon the issue; and upon both sides of
the Atlantic events in Canada were followed with
an exceptional interest. Only during periods of
actual rebellion or war, has there ever been in this
country an era of more intense political excitement. The question of responsible government and
of its proper meaning and application in Canada,
became the supreme issue of the day, and both in
and out of parliament, in the press, on the hustings,
and from the housetops, it was made the subject of

applied. Had the gentlemen openly avowed that their object was to
make the council supreme and to prostrate the British government and
to reduce the authority of the governor to a nullity, there would have
been truth in their statements of a difference between us, as I never
can admit that construction of responsible government in a colony."
"Correspondence of Lord Metcalfe," *Canadian Archives.* A little later
(December 26th, 1843) Metcalfe wrote to Lord Stanley: "It is said
that they [the late council] were beginning to totter in parliament.
Some clauses in the judicature bills for Lower Canada, brought in by
Mr. LaFontaine, had been thrown out owing to Mr. Viger's opposition
on principle to the arrangement therein proposed of judges sitting as a
part of the Court of Appeal on the hearing of appeals from their own
judgments. Mr. Baldwin's King's College University Bill was threatened with certain failure and would probably have been lost on the
day after their resignation, if the latter had not furnished a pretext for
withdrawing it without assigning the prospect of defeat as the cause.

violent and virulent argumentation. The Reformers had had no intention, in offering their resignation to the governor, of surrendering their claim to the political control of the country : the resignation was not an act of submissive meekness but an act of defiance. It was intended as the prelude of an organized campaign of resistance to Sir Charles Metcalfe, which should either drive him from his office or compel him to admit the ministerial principle in its entirety. Metcalfe, on his part, bent not before the storm, but with British resolution braced himself squarely on his feet to face the rising gale of opposition. Not an inch would he retreat : not a syllable would he retract. Till the British government might summon him home, he was there to govern Canada, with a ministry if he could, but without a ministry if he must.

Their Assessment Bill likewise gave general dissatisfaction in Upper Canada, and they had been compelled to modify it considerably. These and some other occasional symptoms of defection, although not affecting their general majority in the House, were regarded as omens of approaching weakness, and it is supposed that, in order to recover waning popularity and power, they sought a rupture with the governor, determined to make use of it for the purpose of raising a popular cry in their favour. . . . This explanation has obtained some currency; but I cannot say that I give full credence to it. . . . A more obvious motive may be found in other circumstances. There were several bills before the parliament which, if passed into laws, would have created several new appointments with considerable salaries. . . . To secure the distribution of this patronage was, I conceive, the immediate object of their demand, or one for the surrender of the patronage into their hands." *Selections from the Papers of Lord Metcalfe*, London, 1855. [Ed., J. W. Kaye.]

Mistaken as the views of the governor-general undoubtedly were, there is much to admire in the spirit of indomitable firmness with which he was prepared to confront single-handed, if need be, the whole population of the colony. As the controversy waxed hot, the amenities of political discussion were thrown aside and the divinity that hedges a governor-general was dissipated in a storm of personal attack : the cry of despot, tyrant and autocrat, was heard on all sides, while the satirists of the time dubbed His Excellency "Charles the Simple," and added the still more crushing epithet of "Old Square Toes." But Metcalfe was not left to fight single-handed : Mr. Draper's adherents were with him from the start. To the Tories the aspect of a governor proposing to actually govern was as welcome as sunshine after storm, while needy politicians, office-seekers and personal opponents of the late ministry rallied eagerly to the cause. The people of Canada were soon divided into two great factions, the supporters and the enemies of Metcalfe. Meetings, banquets, speeches, addresses, pamphlets and fierce editorial articles became the order of the day, and the strife of the political combatants waxed more and more furious with the realization that it must culminate in a general election which might mean to either party a general and irretrievable disaster.

The first trial of strength in the momentous conflict was on the floor of the parliament itself. Great was the excitement in and around the legislature, when the news of the ministerial resignation became public. "The library of the assembly," wrote a private correspondent from Kingston, "was crowded with letter writers eager to circulate the news from Sandwich to Gaspé, and no sound met the ear but the harsh scratching of the pens as they rushed over the paper. In the lobbies and on the landing-places small groups were congregated discussing the news. The politician as he walked the street was button-held (sic) by many a curious and excited enquirer. The stagnation which usually characterizes the metropolis has been converted into a bustling and earnest animation."

On November 27th, LaFontaine briefly announced to the House the fact that the ministry, with the exception of Mr. Daly, had resigned office. Two days later Baldwin presented to the assembly the reasons for the resignation, and an exciting debate followed, culminating in a triumphant vote of confidence in the ministry. It is unnecessary to repeat at length the arguments presented for and against the ministry, which were practically identical with those contained in the official letters just quoted. Baldwin in his opening speech declared that the ministry had accepted office on principles they had publicly and privately avowed. These principles, he said, had received the sanction of a large majority of the representatives of the people. The ministry stood pledged to maintain them. The head of the government entertained views widely differing from his ministers on the duties and responsibilities of their office: this had left nothing for them but to resign. Baldwin read to the House the resolutions of 1841, in which he and his colleagues found the justification of their present conduct. Hincks, Price, Christie and others supported Baldwin in the assembly, while Sullivan defended the conduct of the late ministry before the legislative council in a speech of exceptional brilliancy and power. Beside the overwhelming arguments thus presented, the defence of the governor-general, in the hands of Mr. Daly, seemed tame and insignificant, and the attempt of the latter to show that Metcalfe was prepared to live up to the September resolutions carried no conviction.

Nor was the fierce onslaught of Sir Allan Mac-Nab on the outgoing cabinet of any greater efficacy. He made no attempt to reconcile the conduct of the governor with the principles of responsible government. He attacked the principles themselves. To him the September resolutions were as chaff to be driven before the wind. Responsible government, he said, should never have been conceded: if persisted in, it could lead to nothing but the ultimate separation of the colony from the mother country. MacNab's defence of Metcalfe was of a character little likely to defend, and the governor, despite his instinctive sympathy with the Tories, might have wished to be saved from his friends; for Metcalfe found himself in the painful position of being defended by one set of adherents on the ground that he had maintained responsible government, and by the other on the ground that responsible government was not worth maintaining.

Of far more consequence to the cause of the outgoing cabinet was the defection of Mr. Viger. Denis Benjamin Viger had long been one of the prominent leaders of the popular party in Lower Canada and had suffered imprisonment for the cause. The principle of responsible government and the claims of the French-Canadians had had no more ardent supporter than Mr. Viger, and at this time, with the dignity of seventy winters upon him, he was still viewed as one of the leaders of his people. It was not without deep emotion[1] that Viger now announced to the House that he could not endorse the conduct of the leaders of his party. The principle of responsible government he was willing to admit, but the present occasion, he said, offered no adequate grounds for a step so momentous as that which they had seen fit to take.[2] The debate was finally closed by the passage of a resolution, presented by Mr. Price, to the effect that " an humble address be presented to His Excellency, humbly representing to His Excellency the deep regret felt

[1] *La Minerve,* December 11th, 1843.

[2] Mr. Viger afterwards published his views on the situation in full in a pamphlet entitled, *La Crise Ministerielle,* (1844).

by this House at the retirement of certain members of the provincial administration on the question of their right to be consulted on what this House unhesitatingly avows to be the prerogative of the Crown,—appointments to office : and further, to assure His Excellency that the advocacy of this principle entitles them to the confidence of the House, being in strict accordance with the principles embraced in the resolutions adopted in the House on September 3rd, 1841." The motion was carried by forty-six votes against twenty-three. On December 9th, 1843, the parliament was prorogued.

Meantime the governor-general was without a ministry. At the moment of prorogation, Mr. Dominick Daly enjoyed the unique honour of being sole adviser to the Crown. On the twelfth of the month (Dec. 1843) Mr. Draper was sworn in as executive councillor, and Mr. Viger, with whom negotiations had at once been opened by Sir Charles Metcalfe, entered also into the service of the government. It was announced in the administration newspapers that these gentlemen constituted a provisional government, and that the governor-general would organize a regular cabinet at the earliest possible moment. Meantime the Reform journals loudly denounced this new form of personal rule.

The prorogation of parliament was the signal for the organization of a vigorous campaign of opposition on the part of the Reform party, whose leaders threw themselves with great ardour into the work of rousing the country in anticipation of a coming election. Baldwin and LaFontaine, returning to the practice of the law in their respective cities, headed the agitation. Hincks, who had severed his connection with the *Examiner* on assuming office in 1842, now determined to return to newspaper work. As Montreal was to be the future capital of the province, he came to that city shortly after the rising of the House and looked about him for the purchase of a suitable journal. A paper called the *Times*,—moderately liberal in its complexion,— being at that time without an editor, Hincks acted gratuitously in that capacity for some little while, hoping ultimately to purchase the paper; but finding difficulty in arranging matters with the proprietors, he established (March 5th, 1844) a journal of his own under the name of the *Pilot*. Adopting the same device as he had already used with success in the case of the *Examiner*, Hincks printed at the head of his first issue a quotation from Lord Durham's report in favour of responsible government and backed it up with an opening editorial in which he plunged at once into the present controversy. "If the representative of the sovereign," said the *Pilot*, "is in practice to make appointments according to his own personal opinion, and to reject the bills relating to our local affairs because he thinks them unnecessary or inexpedient, it would be infinitely better that the mockery of representative institutions was abolished." The journalistic career in those days was not without its dangers and difficulties. Hincks and his newspaper were denounced on all sides by the Tory press: he was likened to Marat, to Robespierre and to the iconoclasts of the French revolution. An embittered Orangeman,[1] incensed at certain expressions used by a correspondent of the *Pilot*, endeavoured to force a duel upon the editor. But in spite of all difficulties Hincks persevered, and remained at his editorial work in Montreal throughout the next four years.

In addition to his editorial work on the *Pilot*, Hincks endeavoured to influence opinion in the mother country by contributing a series of letters to the London *Morning Chronicle*. These were intended to offset the arguments that were being laid before the British public by Gibbon Wakefield. The latter, whom the Reformers now regarded as

[1] The gentleman in question was Colonel Ogle R. Gowan. A correspondent of the *Pilot*, in discussing the well-known episode of the queen's refusal to dismiss the ladies of the bedchamber and its relation to the royal prerogative, had said: "His [Sir Robert Peel's] demand was complied with, though Colonel Gowan *falsely* asserted the contrary at Kingston." Gowan wrote to Hincks (March 12th, 1844) asking the name and address of the correspondent. "Should you decline to accede to my demand," he said, "I beg you will refer me to a friend on your behalf to meet Captain Weatherly of this city, who will arrange a meeting between us." Hincks managed to appease the irate colonel by explaining that the *falseness* of the argument and not the *veracity* of the speaker was the matter in question.

a snake that they had unwittingly warmed in the
bosom of the party, had become the bitter enemy
of the late ministry. He had endeavoured to persuade the assembly to adopt an amendment nullify-
ing the vote of confidence. Failing in this, he had
published a pamphlet[1] in defence of the conduct
of Metcalfe, and was at this time busily contributing articles to the London press on the
Canadian question. Wakefield in these writings
undertook to make a double misrepresentation ; to
misrepresent Canadian affairs to the people of Great
Britain, and to misrepresent British opinion thereupon to the people of Canada. "The quantity of
sympathy with Messrs. Baldwin and LaFontaine
existing in the United Kingdom," he wrote, "is
very minute." The resignation of the ministry he
interpreted, not as arising out of the question of
responsible government, but simply as a political
trick : the difficulty encountered with the university
bill and other Upper Canadian legislation had made
the Reform party anxious to divert public attention
from its ill success by the familiar device of drag-
ging a herring across the scent. Responsible government was merely the herring in question. Hincks
easily exposes the fallacies of Wakefield's argu-

---

[1] *A View of Sir Charles Metcalfe's Government in Canada* (London,
1844). See also an article, *Sir Charles Metcalfe in Canada (Fisher's
Colonial Magazine*, 1844) and letters in the *Colonial Gazette* ; see also
Edward Gibbon Wakefield by R. Garnett, London, 1898. Dr. Garnett
speaks of Wakefield as "exercising *irresponsible* government in Canada
as the secret counsellor of Sir Charles Metcalfe."

ment; for Wakefield's letters to the press before and after the ministerial rupture were essentially inconsistent. On October 27th, 1843, Wakefield had written that he would have no objection to a quarrel between Metcalfe and the ministers if he "could be sure that the governor would pick well his ground of quarrel." Again on November 25th he wrote to a correspondent: "The governor-general has had, I think, the opportunity of breaking with his ministers on tenable ground and has let it slip. . . . I am unwilling to do him the bad turn of shooting the bird which I suppose him to be aiming at behind the hedge of reserve which conceals him from vulgar eyes." In his letter to the *Colonial Gazette*, after the rupture, and in his pamphlet, Wakefield tries to put the quarrel in the quite different light described above. In his letters to the *Chronicle* Hincks not only shows the inconsistency of his adversary's position, but makes a pitiless exposure of the reasons underlying Wakefield's self-interested desertion of the Reform party.[1]

While Hincks was thus busily occupied at Montreal, Baldwin, who had returned to Toronto after the prorogation of the House, was heading the agitation against Metcalfe in Upper Canada. A public banquet was held in honour of the ex-ministers (December 28th, 1843) at the North American Hotel, Robert Baldwin being the guest

[1] See Hincks's letters to the *Morning Chronicle*, July 24th, 1844, etc.

of the evening. Mr. Ridout, of the Upper Canada Bank, proposed the health of Messrs. LaFontaine, Baldwin and the other members of the cabinet, the "steadfast champions of responsible government," to which Baldwin replied in a long speech, subsequently printed in full in the Reform journals of both Upper and Lower Canada. A Reform Association was founded in Toronto whose branches rapidly spread over the whole of the province. Under the auspices of the new association there was held in Toronto towards the end of March of the new year,[1] the first of a series of great meetings organized throughout the country. So great was the enthusiasm attendant upon this gathering that the hall of the association, situated in a building on the corner of Front and Scott Streets, was quite inadequate to accommodate the crowd that clamoured for admission, and hundreds were turned from the doors. Robert Baldwin, who occupied the chair, was the central figure of the occasion, and the address with which he opened the proceedings of this first general meeting of the Reform Association, ranks among his most striking speeches.[2] Loud and continued cheering greeted him as he rose to speak, and was renewed at intervals in the pauses of his discourse.

"Our objects," said the speaker, in announcing the formation of the association, "are open and

[1] March 25th, 1844.

[2] *Baldwin Pamphlets* (1844), Toronto Public Library.

avowed. We seek no concealment for we have nothing to conceal. We demand the practical application of the principles of the constitution of our beloved mother country to the administration of all our local affairs. Not one hair's breadth farther do we go, or desire to go: but not with one hair's breadth short of that will we ever be satisfied. . . . Earnestly I recommend to all who value the principles of the British constitution, and to whom the preservation of the connection with the mother country is dear, to lend their aid by joining this organization. Depend upon it, the day will come when one of the proudest boasts of our posterity will be, that they can trace their descent to one who has his name inscribed on this great roll of the contenders for colonial rights."

After fully developing the nature of colonial self-government and quoting from Lord Durham's report and the September resolutions in support of his contention, Baldwin went on to show the utter insufficiency of responsible government as conceived by Sir Charles Metcalfe. His Excellency's system meant nothing more or less than the old disastrous methods of personal government brought back again. "If we are to have the old system," said Baldwin, "then let us have it under its own name, the 'Irresponsible System,' the 'Compact System,' or any other name adapted to its hideous deformities; but let us not be imposed

222

upon by a mere name. We have been adjured," he continued, alluding to an answer recently given by Metcalfe to a group of petitioners, "with reference to this new-fangled responsible government, in a style and manner borrowed with no small degree of care from that of the eccentric baronet [1] who once represented the sovereign in this part of Her Majesty's dominions, to 'keep it,' to 'cling to it,' not to 'throw it away'!! You all, no doubt, remember the story of little Red Ridinghood, and the poor child's astonishment and alarm, as she began to trace the features of the wolf instead of those of her venerable grandmother: and let the people of Canada beware lest, when they begin to trace the real outlines of this new-fangled responsible government, and are calling out in the simplicity of their hearts, 'Oh, grandmother, what great big eyes you have!' it may not, as in the case of little Red Ridinghood, be too late, and the reply to the exclamation, 'Oh, grandmother, what a great big mouth you have!' be 'That's to gobble you up the better, my child.'"

Baldwin was ably followed by his cousin, Robert Sullivan, by William Hume Blake, and a long list of other speakers. Notable among these was one whose name was subsequently to become famous in the annals of Canadian Liberalism. George Brown, a young Scottish emigrant, had just established at Toronto (March 5th, 1844) a weekly

[1] Sir F. B. Head.

newspaper called the *Globe*, founded in the interest of the Reform party. The *Globe* was a fighting paper from the start, and the power of its opening editorials with their unsparing onslaughts on the governor-general was already spreading its name from one end of the province to the other. In reality there were strong points of disagreement between the editor of the *Globe* and the leading Reformers, who at this time aided and encouraged his enterprise, and Brown was destined ultimately to substitute for the moderate doctrines of the Reformers of the union, the programme of the thorough-going Radical. But agreement in opposition is relatively easy. The day of the Radicals and the Clear Grits[1] was not yet, and for the time Brown was heart and soul with the cause of the ex-ministers. In his speech on this occasion he drew a satirical picture of the operation of responsible government *à la* Metcalfe. " Imagine yourself, sir," he said to the chairman, " seated at the top of the council table, and Mr. Draper at the bottom,— on your right hand we will place the Episcopal Bishop of Toronto (Dr. John Strachan) and on your left the Reverend Egerton Ryerson,—on the right of Mr. Draper sits Sir Allan MacNab, and on his left Mr. Hincks. We will fill up the other chairs with gentlemen admirably adapted for their situations

[1] The relation of George Brown to the Clear Grits to whom he was at first opposed is traced by J. Lewis in his *George Brown* (Makers of Canada Series).

by the most extreme imaginable differences of opinion—we will seat His Excellency at the middle of the table, on a chair raised above the warring elements below, *prepared to receive the advice of his constitutional conscience-keepers.* We will suppose you, sir, to rise and propose the opening of King's College to all Her Majesty's subjects,—and then, sir, we will have the happiness of seeing the discordant-producing-harmony-principle in the full vigour of peaceful operation."

Resolutions were adopted at the meeting endorsing the principles and conduct of the late administration and condemning in strong terms the interim government of Sir Charles Metcalfe. "We have commenced the campaign," said the *Globe*, in commenting on the proceedings, "the ball has received its first impulse in this city,—let it be taken up in every village, and in every hamlet of the country." At these meetings Baldwin was a frequent speaker and addresses from all parts of the country were forwarded to him. Not the least interesting among them was an address from his constituents of Rimouski setting forth that "a public meeting of the citizens of the different parishes of the county had been held immediately after mass on Sunday, February 4th," and that resolutions had been adopted fully approving the "conduct in parliament of the Hon. Robert Baldwin." In the course of the summer Baldwin not only spoke in various towns of Upper Canada but found time also, in July, to visit the Lower Provinces. In his own constituency, the county of Rimouski, Baldwin's tour became a triumphal procession. The inhabitants flocked to meet him and his visit was made the occasion of universal gaiety and merry-making. The village street of Kamouraska was decorated with flags and a long *cortège* of vehicles accompanied the Reform leader on his entry : the river at Rimouski was crossed in a boat gaily adorned with bunting for the occasion, while repeated salvos of musketry attended the transit of Baldwin and his party. At Rimouski village itself, an assembly of some four hundred parishioners with their *curé* at their head was marshalled before the village church to present an address of welcome. Everywhere the cordial hospitality of the people was conjoined with the warmest expressions of political approval.

A shower of addresses fell also upon Sir Charles Metcalfe, addresses of advice, of hearty approval, and of angry expostulation. The "inhabitants of the town of London" begged to "approach His Excellency with feelings of gratitude and admiration which they could not sufficiently express." The townspeople of Orillia had been "particularly disgusted with the studied insult so continually offered to all the faithful and loyal of the land, and by the advancement to situations of honour and employment of suspected and disloyal persons."

A SHOWER OF ADDRESSES

The Tories of Toronto, Belleville, and a host of other places, sent up similar addresses. On the other hand, "the magistracy, freeholders, and inhabitants generally of the district of Talbot, observed with painful regret the unhappy rupture between His Excellency and a council which possessed so largely the confidence of the people. The principle of responsible government, which has occasioned this rupture, they had fondly hoped had been so clearly defined and so fully recognized and established as to obviate all difficulty and altercation for the future."[1] The district council of Gore took upon itself to go even further. They assured His Excellency that "public opinion in this district and, we believe, throughout the length and breadth of Canada, will fully sustain the late executive council in the stand they have taken, and in the views they have expressed." Altogether some hundred addresses were forwarded to the governor-general. The greater part of them, as might be expected, emanated from Conservative sources and chorused a jubilant approbation of Metcalfe's conduct. British loyalty, the old flag and the imperial connection were put to their customary illogical use, and did duty for better arguments against responsible government. Even the "Mohawk Indians of the Bay of Quinté" were pressed into political service. On the subject of responsible

[1] As against this address a rival faction of the people of Talbot sent up expressions of hearty approval of Metcalfe's conduct.

government the ideas of the chiefs were doubtless a little hazy and they discreetly avoided it, but their prayer that the "Great Spirit would long spare their gracious Mother to govern them" may be taken as a rude paraphrase of the Tory argument against the ministry. They regretted "the removal of the great council fire from Cataraqui to some hundred miles nearer the sun's rising," but lapsed into language much less convincingly Indian by saying that "the question is simply this, whether this country is to remain under the protection and government of the queen, or to become one of the United States."

The Mohawk Indians were not the only ones who insisted on saying that this latter was the main question at issue. There was at Kingston a rising young barrister and politician of the Tory party, John A. Macdonald by name, who at this juncture coöperated in founding a United Empire Association.

Meantime the condition of affairs in Canada, and the fact that Metcalfe was conducting the government of the country with an executive council which consisted of only three persons, were exciting attention in the mother country and had become the subject of debate in the imperial parliament. Ever since the agitation and rebellion of 1837, there had been in the House of Commons a group of Radical members who were ready at any time to espouse the cause of the colonists against the governors. This was done, it must in fairness be admitted, largely in ignorance of actual Canadian affairs. The sympathy of the British Radicals proceeded partly from the general philanthropy that marked their thought, partly from their abstract and doctrinaire conception of individual rights, and partly also from their desire to use the colonial agitation as a weapon of attack against the Tory government. Hume and Roebuck, it will be remembered, had been in correspondence with Mackenzie and Papineau. They had been the London agents of the Canadian Alliance Association founded by Mackenzie in 1834. Since that period the cause of self-government in Canada had found consistent supporters among the British Radicals. But the bearing of this sympathetic connection must not be misinterpreted. Trained in the narrow school of " little Englandism " the Radicals regarded every colony as necessarily moving towards the manifest destiny of ultimate independence, and the historic value of their sympathetic connection with the Baldwin-LaFontaine party in the present crisis cannot be very highly estimated. Indeed a little examination shows that between the ideas of the British Radicals and those of Robert Baldwin and his party, a great gulf was fixed. To the former, colonial self-government was justified as a necessary prelude to colonial independence: to the latter, it appeared as a bond—as the only stable and permanent bond—which would maintain intact the connection with the mother country. This latter point cannot be too strongly emphasized. There is hardly a speech made by Robert Baldwin at this period in which he does not assert his devotion to the unity of the empire and his firm belief that responsible government in the colonies was the true means of its maintenance. With the lapse of sixty years the narrow view of the British Radicals has been discredited and lost from sight in the larger prospect of an imperial future. But no portion of that discredit should fall upon the Reformers of Canada, to whom at this moment they offered their support.

In answer to a question in the House of Commons, Lord Stanley, the colonial secretary, had (February 2nd, 1844) declared that the imperial government fully approved of the conduct of Sir Charles Metcalfe.[1] Although Sir Charles

[1] There appears to be little doubt that Stanley's confidential letters to Metcalfe supported the latter in his quarrel with the Reformers. Hincks in his *Reminiscences* gives it as his opinion that Metcalfe, at the time of his leaving England, had received instructions from the colonial secretary to the effect that he was to make it his business to prevent the establishment of responsible government in Canada. "Sir Charles Metcalfe," he writes (p. 89), "was selected with the object of overthrowing the new system of government." The formal instructions to Metcalfe under date of February 24th, 1843, were identical with those sent to Lord Sydenham under date of August 30th, 1840. (See *Canadian Archives Report, 1905,* pp. 115-21.) But it is known that Metcalfe had a confidential interview with Lord Stanley before leaving England and that he received private communications from him in regard to the ministerial crisis. The following passage occurs in a MS. letter of LaFontaine to Baldwin under date of January 28th,

Metcalfe, he said, went out to carry out the views of the government at home, yet he was equally determined to *resist any demands inconsistent with the dignity of the Crown; in pursuing this course he would have the entire support of the home government.* A still more emphatic approval of Metcalfe's conduct, together with a declaration of the principles of colonial government, was given by Lord Stanley some four months later (May 30th, 1844) in a debate which was presently known in Canada as the "great debate." The statements made by Lord Stanley on that occasion, and the concurrence expressed by Lord John Russell, leave no doubt that neither the British statesmen of the Conservative party nor their Liberal opponents had as yet accepted the principle of colonial autonomy as we now know it. They were still haunted by the lingering idea that a colony must of necessity be subservient to its governor, and that complete self-government meant independence of Great Britain.

Mr. Roebuck had called the attention of the House of Commons to the condition of affairs in Canada, and the colonial secretary made a lengthy speech in reply. "The honourable member," he said, "drew *an analogy between the position of the ministers in the colony and the position of the*

1844 : "Holmes received this morning a letter from Dunn who states that a person, upon whose word he can rely, had just informed him that the governor had received despatches from Lord Stanley approving his conduct. *That is a matter of course.*" (*Baldwin Correspondence*, Toronto Public Library.)

ministers of the Crown in the mother country. He [Lord Stanley] *denied the analogy.* The constitution of Canada was so framed as to render it impossible that it could possess all the ingredients of the British constitution." In Great Britain, he said, the Crown "exercised great influence because of the love, veneration, and attachment of the people. The governor was entirely destitute of the influence thus attached to royalty. . . . The House of Lords exercised the power derived from rank, station, wealth, territorial possession and hereditary title. The council [legislative] in Canada had none of these adventitious advantages." The reasoning thus presented by the colonial secretary seems to bear in the wrong direction.[1] But his remarks which follow essentially reveal the attitude of his mind on the question. " Place the governor of Canada," he said, " in a state of absolute dependence on his council and they at once would make Canada an independent and republican colony. . . . *It was inconsistent with a monarchical government that the governor should be nominally responsible, and yet was to be stripped of all power and authority, and to be reduced to that degree of power which was vested in the sovereign of this country: it was inconsistent with colonial dependence altogether and was overlooking altogether the distinction which must subsist between an independ-*

[1] *La Minerve* (July 1st, 1844) contains an interesting discussion of this debate.

ent country and a colony subject to the domination of the mother country. . . . The power for which a minister is responsible in England is not his own power but the power of the Crown, of which he is for the time the organ. *It is obvious that the executive councillor of a colony is in a situation totally different.* The governor, under whom he serves, receives his orders from the Crown of England. But can the colonial council be the advisers of the Crown of England? Evidently not, for the Crown has other advisers for the same functions and with superior authority."

In the latter part of his speech Lord Stanley dealt more directly with the question of colonial appointments: his remarks show all too plainly that he too persisted in dividing the Canadians into two groups of "rebels" and "honest men," and in viewing the present controversy as a strife between the two. "Did not the honourable and learned gentleman," he asked, referring to Mr. Roebuck, "think that the minority in a colonial society, be it Tory, Radical, Whig, French, or English, had more chance of fair play if the honours and rewards in the gift of the government were distributed by the Crown than if they were dispensed exclusively by political partisans." The magnificent stupidity of this remark can be realized if one imagines Lord Stanley being asked whether it might not be advisable to allow the queen to make personal appointments to all offices in order to shelter the British minority from the rapacity of the Conservative party. But what Stanley had in his mind becomes clear when he goes on to say :— " Would it be consistent with the dignity, the honour, the metropolitan interests of the Crown that its patronage should be used by the administration [of Canada] to reward the very men who had held back in the hour of danger ? and would it be just or becoming to proscribe and drive from the service of the country those who, in the hour of peril, had come forward to manifest their loyalty and to maintain the union of Canada with the Crown of England ?" The union of Canada and England had as little to do with the present argument as the union of Sweden and Norway, but the reference to it passed current in both countries for nobility of sentiment. Lord Stanley concluded his remarks by referring to the LaFontaine-Baldwin ministry as " unprincipled demagogues " and " mischievous advisers."

Stanley's defense of Metcalfe and his views on colonial self-government read somewhat strangely at the present day. What is still more strange is that the Liberal leader, Lord John Russell, who spoke on the same occasion, was prepared to put the same interpretation on the Canadian situation. He would, he said, have condemned Sir Charles Metcalfe if he had said that he would *in no case* take the opinion of his executive council respecting appointments ; but it would be impossible for the governor to say that he would in all cases follow the will of the executive council. Sir Robert Peel and Mr. Charles Buller, one of the principal collaborators of Lord Durham in the composition of his report, spoke also to the same effect.

During all this time Sir Charles Metcalfe remained without a ministry. Even the two new councillors in office, Draper and Viger, had merely been sworn in as executive councillors without being assigned to offices of emolument. As the spring passed and the summer wore on, the chances of being able to obtain a ministry on anything like a representative basis still appeared remote. The Tories of the assembly had given to Sir Charles Metcalfe from the outset a cordial support, but in view of the overwhelming numbers of the Reformers and French-Canadians, the attempt to construct a ministry from the ranks of the Tories would have been foredoomed to failure. On the other hand, the governor-general was well aware that continued government without a ministry meant ruin to his cause and tended of itself to prove the contention of his opponents. No effort was spared, therefore, to obtain support from the Reform party itself and to encourage secession from the ranks of the French-Canadians by tempting offers of office. It was hoped that the example of Mr. Viger might induce others of his nationality to desert the cause of the late administration. Barthe, a fellow-prisoner of Viger in the days of the rebellion, and since then editor of *L'Avenir du Canada* and member for Yamaska, had been offered a seat in the cabinet shortly after the ministerial resignation and had refused. Four French-Canadians in turn had rejected the offer of the position of attorney-general for Lower Canada, and the same position had been offered in vain to two British residents. Viger found himself with but small support among his fellow-countrymen. It was in vain that he appealed to them in a pamphlet[1] in which he sought to prove that LaFontaine and Baldwin had acted without constitutional warrant. The subtleties of Mr. Viger's arguments availed nothing against the instinctive sympathy of the French-Canadians with their chosen leader. At the end of the month of June, Mr. Draper, anxious to realize the situation at first hand, visited the Lower Province and spent some weeks in a vain attempt at obtaining organized support for the government. As a result of his investigations he wrote to Sir Charles Metcalfe that " after diligently prosecuting his inquiries and extending his observations in all possible quarters, he could come to no other conclusion than that the aid of the French-Canadian party was not to be obtained on any other than the impossible terms of the restoration of Baldwin and LaFontaine."[2]

[1] See *La Crise Ministerielle et M. Denis Benjamin Viger*, (Kingston, 1844,) published also in English (*Baldwin Pamphlets*, 1844, Toronto Public Library).

[2] Kaye, *Life of Metcalfe*, 1854, Vol. II, pp. 552, 553.

"The difficulty, indeed," says Metcalfe's biographer, "seemed to thicken. According to Mr. Draper, it was one from which there was no escape. After the lapse of seven months, during which the country had been without an executive government, Metcalfe was told by one of the ablest, the most clear-headed and one of the most experienced men in the country, that it was impossible to form a ministry, according to the recognized principle of responsible government, without the aid of the French-Canadian party, and that aid it was impossible to obtain. What was to be done?" Well might the governor-general and his private advisers ask themselves this question. As Mr. Draper himself informed His Excellency, the want of an executive government was beginning to have a disastrous effect upon the commerce and credit of the country. The revenue must inevitably be soon affected, the administration of justice was already hampered for want of a proper officer to represent the Crown in the courts of law, while the public mind was filled with disquieting apprehensions for the future which were beginning to paralyze the industrial life of the province.[1]

The whole summer of 1844 was one of intense political excitement. Agitation meetings, and political speeches became the order of the day, and political demonstrations on a large scale were organized by the rival parties. On May 12th a

[1] See Kaye, *op. cit.* Vol. II, p. 553.

general meeting of the Reform Association had been held at Toronto. At this Robert Baldwin played a principal part, and in his speech on the occasion reiterated his attachment to the British connection and his belief that the policy of his party was the only one that could lead to permanent imperial stability. He presented to the meeting an address which he had drafted for presentation to the people of Canada, and which was adopted with enthusiasm. Its concluding sentences sounded a note of warning and appeal:— "This is not a mere party struggle. It is Canada against her oppressors. The people of Canada claiming the British constitution against those who withhold it : the might of public opinion against faction and corruption."

The newspapers during these months contained little else than fiery disputation on the all-absorbing topic of the hour. Pamphlets poured from the colonial press in an abundant shower, and editors, lawyers, assemblymen and divines hastened to add each his contribution to the political controversy engendered by the situation. The Reform Alliance started a series of "tracts for the people" designed to elucidate the leading principles and disputed points of the whole controversy. Hincks, Buchanan, Ryerson, Sullivan and a swarm of others hastened into the fray, iterating and reiterating the well-worn arguments for and against the late ministry and soundly belabouring one another with political invective and personal abuse. The great bulk of the literature of the Metcalfe controversy is of but little interest or novelty. It is somewhat difficult to read through the forty pages of print in which "Zeno" (of Quebec) undertakes to show that the resistance of Metcalfe and his satellites to responsible government was but the "expiring howl of that mercenary class who, by servility, venality and corruption, have marred the prosperity of the colony." Equally difficult is it to follow the tortuous argumentation of Isaac Buchanan in his *Five Letters Against the Baldwin Faction.* Buchanan, who was a moderate Reformer now turned against his late leaders, writes with the bitterness of a renegade, and his letters are of some interest as illustrating the wilful distortion of Robert Baldwin's opinions and objects at the hands of his opponents. "How many are there," he asks, "who are out and out supporters of Mr. Baldwin who do not conscientiously wish that Canada was a state of the union to-morrow?" "Mr. Baldwin," he says, "was weakening the very foundations of colonial society," and supports the statement by an afflicting ancedote of a recent experience in England.

"On the subject of Baldwin's past character," says Buchanan, "the question was again and again put to me in England. Did he not prefer his party to his country, at the late rebellion, declining to fight against the former or to turn out in defence of the latter? I remember well the feeling remark of one gentleman of the most liberal British politics, and whose bosom beats as high as any man's for the cause of freedom, —'*Well, poor Mr. Baldwin may be a patriot, but he is not a Briton.*'"

There is, however, one episode of the Metcalfe controversy—namely, the literary duel between the Rev. Egerton Ryerson and the Hon. R. B. Sullivan, late president of the council—which deserves more than a passing notice. In both Upper and Lower Canada, Metcalfe had spared no pains to win men of prominence of all parties to his cause by flattering offers of public office. Egerton Ryerson, already famous in the colony as a leader of the Methodist Church, as president of Victoria College and as an opponent of the exclusive claim of the Church of England to the Clergy Reserves, was one of those who were said by the Reformers to have felt the "draw of vice-regal blandishments."[1] The announcement early in 1844 that Ryerson had been interviewed by the governor-general, and that his appointment as superintendent of education with a seat in the cabinet was under consideration, was declared by the *Globe* (March 8th, 1844) to be an "alarming feeler." Subsequently, when Ryerson, in the ensuing May, published his famous defence of Sir Charles

[1] N. F. Davin, *The Irishman in Canada*, p. 504.

240

RYERSON DEFENDS METCALFE

Metcalfe[1] and was later in the year duly appointed to be superintendent of education, his enemies did not scruple to say that Mr. Ryerson had sold himself to the Metcalfe government for a price, and had become a traitor to the cause of public liberty. But whatever may be thought of the correctness or incorrectness of Ryerson's views on the ministerial controversy, the contention that his literary services had been bought, cannot stand. His appointment to office rests on a solid basis of merit and had long been under consideration. No one in the province had given more earnest thought to the problem of public education than had Egerton Ryerson, and the question of his appointment as superintendent of common schools had already been discussed by Lord Sydenham. It appears also, on good authority, that Sir Charles Metcalfe had determined to appoint Ryerson to some such position before the rupture with the LaFontaine-Baldwin cabinet occurred.[2] It must, therefore, in fairness be admitted that the defence of Sir Charles Metcalfe was inspired by no self-seeking motives, but proceeded from a genuine conviction that the course adopted by the late cabinet was unconstitutional and dangerous to the public welfare.

[1] *Sir Charles Metcalfe Defended Against the Attacks of his late Councillors*, Toronto, 1844.

[2] See Egerton Ryerson, *Story of My Life* (Edited by J. G. Hodgins) Chap. xliii : see also N. Burwash, *Egerton Ryerson* (Makers of Canada Series) Chap. v.

From the literary point of view, Ryerson's defence is an extremely able document and is written, not with the ponderous periods of the theologian, but with a vigour of style and a freedom of phrase which drew down upon the head of its author the taunt of being a "political swashbuckler." The central point of the argument of the pamphlet is the attempt to prove that the conduct of the late ministry was contrary to British precedent. " If the ministry," argued Ryerson, " objected to the governor's appointments, the proper course for them consisted in immediate resignation, not in attempting to bind the governor with a pledge in regard to appointments of the future. It was," he said, " contrary to British usage for them to remain in office twenty-four hours, much less weeks or months, after the head of the executive had performed acts or made appointments which they did not choose to justify before parliament and before the country. It was contrary to British usage for them to complain of and condemn a policy or acts to which they had become voluntary parties by their continuing in office. It was contrary to British usage for them to go to the sovereign to discuss principles and debate policy, instead of tendering their resignations for his past acts." This line of reasoning, though rendered plausible by an imposing show of precedent and argument, need not be taken very seriously. The ministry had, in fact, resigned on account of the past acts of the governor, not on the strength of any single one, but rather by reason of the accumulation of many. For the entire ministry to have resigned the first time the governor undertook to make a minor appointment on his own account would have been plainly impossible: equally impossible was it to allow the governor to continue indefinitely making such appointments. The essence of the situation lay, therefore, in the future rather than the past.

Ryerson's pamphlet called forth an answer from an opponent of as good fighting mettle as himself. The *Thirteen Letters on Responsible Government*, published by Robert Sullivan, are certainly equal to Ryerson's defence in point of logic and in the presentation of the law, and easily surpass it in facility of style, while the caustic wit, for which the writer was distinguished, adds to the brilliance of his work. Sullivan signed himself "Legion" to indicate that his name was not one but many. He prefaces his work with a mock-heroic "Argument," or table of contents, in which he endeavours at the outset to put his theological opponent in a ludicrous light. Thus he announces as the subject of Letter IV, the "doctor's [Ryerson's] discovery that Cincinnatus was one of the Knights of the Round Table, from which he infers that Mr. Baldwin stole his ideas on responsible government from the days of chivalry." Later we read that " 'Legion' repudiates his relatives and absolves his godfathers on the ground of the doctor's monopoly of the calendar of saints," while the letters conclude with a "panoramic view of the doctor's iniquitous career—his death struggle with 'Legion' and his hideous writhings graphically described," after which "'Legion' carries off the doctor amidst yells and imprecations." Apart from witticisms, personalities, and stinging satire, Sullivan's letters are of great importance in the Metcalfe controversy from the fact that the writer takes issue with Lord Stanley, whose views on colonial government he considers entirely erroneous. As a rule the writers on behalf of the Reform party endeavoured to so interpret Stanley's expressions as to make them appear favourable to the attitude taken by the LaFontaine-Baldwin cabinet. In the light of what has been quoted above, this will be seen to be a hopeless task. Sullivan takes a bolder, and at the same time a surer, stand. "Lord Stanley's argument," he says, "if it proves anything, proves that we should not have representative institutions at all: that public opinion should not prevail in anything, because it wants the ingredient of aristocratic influence. . . . There is not the slightest doubt, in the mind of any one, but that the governor of this province is bound to obey the orders of Her Majesty's secretary of state for the colonies, however opposed these orders may be to the advice of the council, for the time being. But there is as little doubt but that when a secretary of state gives such orders with respect to the administration of our local affairs, he violates the principle of responsible government as explained in the resolutions of 1841, to which Sir Charles Metcalfe subscribed."

That a good many of "Legion's" shafts had struck home is seen in the furious rejoinder published by Egerton Ryerson. In this the distinguished divine almost forgets the dignity of his divinity. He compares his opponent to Barère and likens the Reform Association to the Committee of Public Safety of the French Revolution :—" Whether 'Legion' drank, fiddled and danced," he writes, " when Sir F. Head was firing the country, or when Lount and Mathews were hanging on the gallows, I have not the means of knowing : but a man who can charge the humane and benevolent Sir Charles Metcalfe with being an inhuman and bloodthirsty Nero, can easily be conceived to sing and shout at scenes over which patriotism and humanity weep." To Baldwin himself, the writer is almost as unsparing. Baldwin had just delivered an address to the electors of Middlesex in which he exhorted the Tories " to forget all minor differences and to act as if they remembered only that they were Canadians, since as Canadians we have a country and are a people." This patriotic utterance Ryerson sees fit to misinterpret. " In reading this passage of Mr. Baldwin's address," he says, " I could not keep from my thoughts two passages in very different books, the one a parable in the Book of Judges, in which 'the bramble said unto the trees, if in truth ye annoint me king over you, then come and put your trust in my shadow : and if not, let fire come out of the bramble, and devour the cedars of Lebanon.' The other passage which Mr. Baldwin's address brought to my recollection, is one of Æsop's Fables, where the fox that had lost its tail exhorted his brethren of all shades and sizes to imitate his example as the best fashion of promoting their comfort and elevation."

The party war of pamphlets, speeches and addresses continued unabated throughout the summer. As the autumn drew on the efforts of Metcalfe and Draper to obtain at least the semblance of a representative cabinet met with better success. Towards the end of August a Mr. James Smith, a Montreal lawyer of no particular prominence, and never as yet a member of any legislative body,[1] accepted the position of attorney-general for Lower Canada. A recruit of more imposing name was found in Denis B. Papineau, brother of the French-Canadian leader of 1837, to whom was given the office of commissioner of Crown lands.

Papineau, who had hitherto been an adherent of the Lower Canadian Reform party, shared with Viger the odium of being a renegade from his party, and was subsequently accused by Robert Baldwin on the floor of the House with having

[1] H. J. Morgan, *Sketches of Celebrated Canadians*, 1862.

approved the resignation of the previous ministry and then usurped the position they had seen fit to abandon.[1] Papineau, whose character had stood high with his compatriots, claimed in reply that his acceptance of office did not rest on personal grounds, but that he had seen fit, on mature reflection, to modify his opinion of the present controversy. William Morris of Brockville[2] accepted at the same time the post of receiver-general. Mr. Draper being now definitely appointed to be attorney-general for Upper Canada, Mr. Viger, president of the council, and Mr. Daly being still provincial secretary, Metcalfe found himself, at the opening of September (1844), with something approaching a complete ministry. It was thought wiser for the present to place no Tories in the cabinet. Mr. Henry Sherwood was, however, given the post of solicitor-general for Upper Canada without a seat in the executive council, and towards the close of the year W. B. Robinson, a brother of Chief-justice Robinson and a Tory of the old school, became inspector-general. Metcalfe was now ready to try conclusions with his adversaries. He dissolved the parliament on September 23rd, and writs, returnable on November 12th, were issued for a new election.

[1] Speech in answer to Address from the Throne, 1844.

[2] See above, p. 83.

CHAPTER VIII

IN OPPOSITION

THE elections of the autumn of 1844 were carried on amid an unsurpassed political excitement, and both sides threw themselves into the struggle with an animosity that seriously endangered the peace of the country. Whatever may be thought of the constitutionality of Metcalfe's conduct during the recent session of parliament, there can be no doubt that he went outside of his proper sphere in the part he took in the parliamentary election. His personal influence and his personal efforts were used to the full in the interests of the Draper government. Indeed, there now existed, between the governor-general and the leaders of the Reform party, a feeling of personal antagonism that gave an added bitterness to the contest. The governor-general had not scrupled to denounce the Reformers publicly as enemies of British sovereignty: in answer to an address sent up to him from the county of Drummond in which reference was made to the "measures and proceedings of a party tending directly in our opinion to the terrible result of separation from British connection and rule," Metcalfe stated that he had "abundant reason to know that you have accurately described the designs of the late executive council."

This intemperate language brought about the resignation of LaFontaine from his position as queen's counsel, a step immediately followed by a similar resignation on the part of Baldwin. The resignations were accompanied by letters to the provincial secretary in which the accusation of hostility to British sovereignty was indignantly denied. The same denial was repeated by the Reform leaders in the public addresses to their constituents, inserted in full length, according to the custom of the day, in the party newspapers, in spite of which Metcalfe and the Tories persisted in viewing the contest as one between loyalty and treason. "He felt," said Metcalfe's biographer, "that he was fighting for his sovereign against a rebellious people." For the rank and file of the Tory following, excuse may be found in the exigencies of party warfare; but for Metcalfe, as governor of the country, no apology can be offered, save perhaps the honesty of his conviction. "I regard the approaching election," he wrote (September 26th, 1844), "as a very important crisis, the result of which will demonstrate whether the majority of Her Majesty's Canadian subjects are disposed to have responsible government in union with British connection and supremacy, or will struggle for a sort of government that is impracticable consistently with either."

The result of the election gave a narrow majority to Mr. Draper's administration, but the contest

was accompanied by such violence and disorder at
the polls that the issue cannot be regarded as
indicating the real tenor of public opinion. In this
violence, it must be confessed, both parties participated. The Irish, mindful of their late contest
with the Orangemen and the fate of the Secret
Societies Bill, were solid for the Reform party, and
their solidity assumed at many polling places its
customary national form. It was charged by the
enemies of Baldwin that gangs of Irishmen were
hired in Upper Canada to control the voters by the
power of the club.[1] Nor were the Tories behind
hand in the use of physical force, and on both
sides inflammatory handbills and placards incited
the voters to actual violence. " The British party,"
said Metcalfe himself, "were resolved to oppose
force by force and organized themselves for
resistance."

As the issue of the elections became known, it
appeared that the Reformers had carried Lower
Canada by a sweeping majority, but that the adherents of the government had scored a still more
complete victory in the Upper Province. LaFontaine, who had decided to present himself again to
the electors of Terrebonne rather than to continue
to represent an Upper Canadian constituency, was
elected almost unanimously. Out of fifteen hundred
voters who assembled in despite of bad roads and
bad weather, only about a score were prepared to

[1] N. F. Davin, *The Irishman in Canada*, p. 513.

support a local attorney—a Mr. Papineau—who had been nominated to oppose LaFontaine. A mere show of hands was sufficient to settle the election without further formalities. Morin was elected for two constituencies. Aylwin was returned for Quebec, and of the forty-two members for Lower Canada, only sixteen could be counted as supporters of the government. D. B. Papineau was elected for Ottawa county, but his colleague, Viger, whose prestige among the French-Canadians was permanently impaired,[1] was defeated by Wolfred Nelson, the former leader of the rebellion. The city of Montreal, henceforth to be the capital of Canada, signalized itself by returning two supporters of the administration. But their success was due solely to the arrangement of voting districts made by the government; for the city contained an overwhelming majority of French-Canadian and Irish adherents of the Reform party.[2] In Upper Canada, of the forty-two members elected, the government could count thirty as its adherents. MacNab, Sherwood, W. B. Robinson, John A. Macdonald of Kingston, and many other Tories were elected. Baldwin, who had bidden farewell to the constituency of Rimouski, was elected for the fourth riding of York, but Hincks was

[1] See Turcotte, *Le Canada sous l' Union*, pp. 157 *et seq.*

[2] These facts are admitted by Metcalfe. See Kaye, Vol. II. See also Hincks's *Political History of Canada*, pp. 35, 36.

beaten in Oxford[1] and remained out of parliament until 1848. John Henry Dunn, also a member of the late cabinet, was beaten in Toronto. The Tories stuck at nothing to carry the elections in Upper Canada. To their affrighted loyalty the end justified the means. Returns were in some cases wilfully falsified. Elsewhere the voters were driven from the polls and violence carried to such an extent that the troops were called out to quell the disorder, while throughout the province the militia were warned to be in readiness for possible emergencies. Only seven decided Reformers, among them Baldwin, Small and Price, were returned to parliament from Upper Canada. Taking the two sections of the province together and making due allowance for doubtful members, it appeared that the government might claim at the very outside, forty-six supporters in a House of eighty-four members. Even this narrow margin of support could not be relied upon. On the vote for the speakership, for example, Sir Allan MacNab was elected by only a majority of three.

On these terms, for want of any better, Mr. Draper had now to undertake the government of

[1] Hincks presented a petition to the assembly protesting against the election of his opponent, Mr. Robert Riddell. He claimed that the deputy returning officers had refused to admit the votes of persons who had come to the province previous to 1820, although, under an Act of the parliament of Upper Canada, such persons, if willing to take the oath of allegiance, were entitled to vote. The petition was not granted.

the country. It was a difficult task, and for one less skilled in the arts of political management it would have been impossible. The administration could hardly rest upon a satisfactory footing unless an adequate support could be obtained from the French of Lower Canada: on the other hand, any attempt to gain this support was apt to alienate the Upper Canadian Tories, now definitely in alliance with Mr. Draper and represented in his cabinet by Robinson, the new inspector-general. The leader of the government was therefore compelled to preserve, as best he might, a balance of power in a chronic condition of unstable equilibrium. That Mr. Draper did continue to carry on his government for nearly three years speaks volumes for his political dexterity.

It is no part of the present narrative to follow in detail the legislative history of Mr. Draper's administration. The seat of government had now been transferred to Montreal, where the parliament was given as its quarters a building that had formerly been St. Anne's market. It was a capacious edifice some three hundred and fifty feet in length by fifty in breadth, with two large halls on the ground floor which served for the House of Assembly and the legislative council, the hall of the assembly containing ample galleries with seats for five hundred spectators.[1] The parliament came together on

[1] A. Leblond de Brumath, *Histoire Populaire de Montréal* (1890) pp. 379, 380

November 28th, 1844, and remained in session until the end of March of the ensuing year. During Mr. Draper's administration under Lord Sydenham, he had maintained himself in office, as has been seen, by adopting the measures desired by the Opposition as his own policy. This method of stealing his opponent's thunder was a favourite artifice of the leader of the government, and during the present session he made a liberal use of it. Acts in reference to the schools and municipalities of Lower Canada were passed, which carried forward the educational reforms already commenced. In order to conciliate, if possible, the Reformers of Lower Canada, steps were taken towards restoring the French language to its official position. It was known to the government that LaFontaine had it under consideration to put before the assembly a resolution urging upon the imperial government the claims of the people of Lower Canada to have their language placed upon an equal footing with English in the proceedings of the legislature. LaFontaine's intention was accordingly forestalled, and Denis Papineau, the commissioner of Crown lands, proposed to the assembly to vote an address to the imperial government asking for a repeal of the clause of the Act of Union[1] which made English the sole

---

[1] Act of Union, Section xli. "All journals, entries, and all written or printed proceedings of what nature soever of the said legislative council and legislative assembly . . . shall be in the English language only." Speaking in French was not, of course, contrary to the law.

official language. The motion was voted by acclamation amid general enthusiasm and the home
government, after some delay, saw fit to act upon
it.[1] The adminstration was less happy in its attempt
to deal with the still outstanding university question. Mr. Draper presented a University Bill,
closely analogous to that of Robert Baldwin; but
finding the opposition of the Tories was at once
aroused against such a proposed spoliation of
the Church, the bill was dropped without coming
to a vote. With these and other minor measures,
and with much wrangling over the crop of contested elections that remained as a legacy from the
late conflict, the time of the assembly was occupied
until the end of the month of March.

Before the session had yet come to an end, the
news was received that the home government
intended raising Sir Charles Metcalfe to the peerage. In view of Metcalfe's long and useful career
in other parts of the empire, such a step was not
necessarily to be regarded as a special official
approval of his conduct in Canada; but among
the Reformers the announcement occasioned great
indignation. The violence of party antagonism had
by no means subsided : at the very opening of the
session Baldwin had endeavoured to carry through
the assembly a vote of censure against the governor-general for having violated the principles of
the constitution by governing without a ministry.

[1] See below, page 287.

METCALFE MADE A PEER

The news that Metcalfe, instead of censure, was now to obtain an elevation to the peerage, drew forth from the members of the Opposition expressions of protest in language which the passions of the hour rendered unduly intemperate. Aylwin declared to the assembly that it would be more fitting that Metcalfe should be recalled and put on trial, rather than that he should receive the dignity of a peer. Even Robert Baldwin made use of somewhat immoderate expressions of disapproval. Utterances of this kind might perhaps have been spared, for the untoward fate that had fallen upon the two preceding governors of Canada now cast its shadow plainly on the governor-general, and it was becoming evident that Baron Metcalfe of Fern Hill was not long destined to enjoy earthly honours. Before coming to Canada he had suffered severely, as has been said above, from a cancerous growth upon the cheek: an operation had for the time arrested the progress of the disease, but all efforts towards a radical cure had proved unavailing. The sufferings of the distinguished patient had now become constant and his sight seriously affected. The rapid decline of his health made it apparent that he was no longer fit for the arduous duties of his position, and his friends began to urge him to ask for his recall. But Lord Metcalfe, with the indomitable courage that was his leading virtue, still held heroically to what he considered to be the post of duty.

Meantime, having got through one parliamentary session, Mr. Draper was anxious to avoid, if possible, encountering another upon the same terms. Draper appears to have realized that the great error of his past policy had been his failure to reckon with the strength of the united French-Canadian vote. This had upset his former ministry under Lord Sydenham, and the experience of the Metcalfe crisis had shown him that, even with the full support of a governor-general, the government could not be satisfactorily carried on without French-Canadian support. Mr. Draper now determined to obtain this support, and to retrieve his past errors by the formation of a new variety of political coalition. Of the Reform party of Upper Canada he had but little fear. Their representation in parliament was now seriously depleted, and even among their remaining members of the assembly, divisions had existed during the past session; on the other hand, the star of the Tories was in the ascendant and that party might always be counted upon to offset in Upper Canada the political influence of the Reformers. If then, Mr. Draper argued, the French-Canadian party under LaFontaine could be induced to break loose from Baldwin and his adherents and to join forces with the Ministerialists of Upper Canada, a combination could be formed that would hold a strong majority in both of the ancient provinces. We have here the beginnings of that system of a "double majority,"—a majority, that is, in both Upper and Lower Canada,—which became the will o' the wisp of the rival politicians, and which many persons were presently inclined to invest with a constitutional sanctity, as forming part of the necessary machinery of Canadian government.[1] It was characteristic of the ways and means of Mr. Draper, to whom the term "artful dodger" has often been applied, that he was prepared to throw overboard his French-Canadian men of straw (Viger and Papineau) to make way for LaFontaine, Morin, and their friends.

In order to attain his purpose, Mr. Draper in the autumn of 1845 entered into indirect negotiations with LaFontaine, Mr. Caron, the speaker of the legislative council, acting as a go-between. In the three-cornered correspondence that ensued the question of a ministerial reconstruction along the lines of the new alliance was fully discussed. Draper at first had interviews with Caron in which he suggested that the ministry might be strengthened by the addition of leading French-Canadian Reformers. Caron conveyed this suggestion to LaFontaine in a letter of September 7th, 1845.

[1] On the principle of the "double majority" see Dent, *The Past Forty Years*, Vol. II. pp. 20 *et seq.* Hincks's *Political History* (p. 28) contains interesting matter in this connection. "Up to the time of my leaving Canada in 1855," writes Hincks, "no political alliance was formed on the principle of securing majorities from the two provinces." The Draper-Caron-LaFontaine correspondence here referred to is given in Hincks's *Reminiscences*.

Mr. Draper's ideas, gathered thus at one remove and intentionally expressed with vagueness, may be seen in the following passage from Mr. Caron's letter. "He [Mr. Draper] told me that Mr. Viger could be easily *prevailed upon to retire*, and that Mr. Papineau desired nothing better: that both these situations should be filled up by French-Canadians: he seemed desirous that Morin should be president of the council . . . he spoke of the office of solicitor-general, which, he said, ought to be filled by one of our origin . . . he also spoke of an assistant secretaryship, the incumbent of which ought to receive handsome emoluments . . . This was about all he could for the present offer to our friends, who, when in power, might themselves strive afterwards to make their share more considerable. As regarded *you* [LaFontaine], he said that nothing would afford him greater pleasure than to have you as his colleague, but that, as the governor and yourself could not meet, the idea of having you form part of the administration must be given up so long as Lord Metcalfe remained in power: that it would be unjust to sacrifice a man of your influence and merit . . . but that this difficulty could easily be made to disappear by giving you an appointment with which you would be satisfied. . . . *As to Mr. Baldwin, he said little about;* but I understood, as I did in my first conversation, that *he thought he would retire of himself.*"

FAILURE OF DRAPER'S PLAN

Such was Mr. Draper's plan. LaFontaine's attitude in the dealings which followed is entirely above reproach. Mr. Draper's method of approach he considered to be irregular and unconstitutional; nor did the glittering bribe of "handsome emoluments" and "an appointment with which he would be satisfied," conceal from him the real meagreness of Mr. Draper's offer. The artful attorney-general was indeed merely offering to buy off a number of leading French-Canadians with offers of office and salary. It appears, however, that if Mr. Draper had been willing to go further and entirely reconstruct the Lower Canadian part of his cabinet so as to place it in the hands of the Reformers, LaFontaine would have been willing to make terms with him. This statement must not, however, be misunderstood. The arrangement contemplated was viewed by LaFontaine, not as the purchase of the Lower Canadian party by Mr. Draper, but as the purchase of Mr. Draper by the Lower Canadian party. The plan was fully discussed between LaFontaine and Hincks in Montreal. Nor did LaFontaine conceal anything of the negotiations in question from Robert Baldwin. The plan contemplated by LaFontaine and Hincks would merely have amounted to a further consolidation of the united French and English Reform party by adding to its ranks Mr. Draper and his immediate adherents. The danger of further secession, in pursuance of the example of Denis, Papineau and Viger, would thus be minimized. The undoubted parliamentary talents of Mr. Draper would lend a valuable support to the cause, and the Tories of Upper Canada would remain in hopeless isolation. In a letter of September 23rd, 1845,[1] LaFontaine wrote very freely to Baldwin of the whole matter, and enclosed a translation of his letter to Caron. "Mr. Hincks," he said, "whom I saw this morning, seemed to be favourable to the plan, if it was effected, admitting that it would immediately crush the reaction in Quebec, and would strengthen you in Upper Canada. For my part I think Mr. Draper would be very glad to have an opportunity to act with the Liberal party : he knows he is not liked by the Tory party and that they wish to get rid of him. However, that is his own business."

If so powerful a combination of parties, and one so obviously advantageous to the interests of his race could have been formed, LaFontaine was perfectly willing, if need be, to retire from his leadership of the party in order to facilitate the new arrangement. "What French-Canadians should do above everything," he wrote, "is to remain united and to make themselves respected. I will not serve as a means of dividing my compatriots. If an administration is formed which merits my confidence, I will support it with all my heart. If it has not my confidence but possesses that of the

[1] *MS. Letters of LaFontaine to Baldwin.* Baldwin Correspondence, (Toronto Public Library.)

majority of my compatriots, not being able to support it, I will willingly resign my seat, rather than cast division in our ranks." But to meet LaFontaine's views, Mr. Draper would have been called upon to go further than he had intended. To break entirely with the Canadian Tories and to throw overboard Mr. Dominick Daly,—the "permanent secretary," as he was now facetiously entitled,—was more than Mr. Draper had bargained for. These difficulties caused the negotiations to hang fire until the recall of Lord Metcalfe changed the position of affairs. "The whole affair," says a Canadian historian, "suddenly collapsed, and the only result was to intensify the political atmosphere, and aggravate the quarrel between a weak government and a powerful opposition."[1]

Among the correspondence of Robert Baldwin in reference to the proposed reconstruction of parties, appears a letter of considerable interest addressed to LaFontaine which bears no date, but which was probably written in the autumn of 1845, after the failure of Mr. Caron's negotiations. Baldwin expresses an emphatic disapproval of any attempt to set up the principle of a "double majority." Such a system of government would be calculated, in his opinion, rather to intensify than to obliterate the racial animosity and end in precipitating a desperate struggle for supremacy. "You already know," he wrote, "my opinion of the 'double

[1] Fennings Taylor, *Portraits of British Americans*, Vol. I. p. 322.

majority' as respects the interests of the province at large. When I gave you that opinion I hesitated to dwell on what appears to me to be its extreme danger to our Lower Canadian friends of French origin themselves. . . . I speak not of the present public men of the province, or of the course which they or any of them may take. Some may be swept away from the arena altogether; others may retire; but in the event of such an arrangement being carried out, all who remain upon the political sea will, I am satisfied, have to go with the stream. The arrangement will be viewed as one based essentially upon a natural, original distinction and equally uninfluenced by the political principles. *British and French will then become in reality, what our opponents have so long wished to make them, the essential distinctions of party, and the final result will scarcely admit of doubt.* The schemes of those who looked forward to the union as a means of crushing the French-Canadians, and who advocated it with no other views, will then be crowned with success, and the latter will themselves have become the instruments to accomplish it. That this will be the final result of any successful attempt to reorganize the ministry upon such a foundation, I have no doubt whatever. It will not, however, be injurious to the French-Canadian portion of our population alone. It appears to me equally clear that it will be most calamitous to the country in general. It will perpetuate distinctions, initiate animosities, sever the bonds of political sympathy and sap the foundation of political morality."[1]

In the autumn of 1845 the progress of Lord Metcalfe's malady was such as rapidly to render him unfit for further exertions. His disease had almost destroyed his sight and his constant sufferings rendered the transaction of official business a matter of extreme difficulty. At the end of October he asked for his recall. But the imperial government, aware of his distressing condition, had anticipated his request, and Stanley had already forwarded to him the official acceptance of a resignation which he might use at any time that seemed proper to him. " You will retire, whenever you retire," wrote the colonial secretary, " with the entire approval and admiration of Her Majesty's government." Lord Metcalfe left Montreal at the end of November, 1845, and returned to England. All attempts to stay the ravages of his dreadful malady proved unavailing and after months of suffering, borne with admirable constancy, he died on September 5th, 1846. Not even the melancholy circumstances of Lord Metcalfe's departure from Canada could still the animosity of his opponents, and a section of the Reform press greeted the news of his retirement with untimely exultation.

On Metcalfe's departure the government was entrusted to Lord Cathcart, commander of the

[1] *Baldwin Correspondence*, (Toronto Public Library.)

forces, at first as administrator and afterwards as governor-general. Cathcart was a soldier, a veteran of the Peninsula and Waterloo, whose main interest in the Canadian situation lay in the question whether the dispute then pending in regard to the Oregon territory would end in war with the United States. Indeed it was on account of the threatening aspect of the boundary question that the imperial government had elevated Cathcart to the governorship. The matter of responsible government concerned him not, and during his administration he left the civil government of the country to his ministers to conduct as best they might. Their best was indeed but poor. In the session of parliament that ran from March 20th until June 9th, 1846, the government was quite unable to maintain itself. Mr. Draper tried in vain to repeat his thunder-stealing policy and although he carried through parliament an Act to provide for a civil list, which was intended (with imperial consent) to take the place of the existing imperial arrangement,[1] his government on other measures was repeatedly defeated. In the summer and autumn of the year, difficulties crowded upon Mr. Draper. The Draper-Caron correspondence was made public,[2] whereat many Tories took offence and Sherwood, the solicitor-general, dropped out of Mr. Draper's cabinet.

[1] See above, p. 68.

[2] See *La Minerve*, April 9th, 1846, and following issues.

A NEW BRITISH CABINET

The leader of the government had failed in his attempted alliance with the Liberals of Lower Canada, and had excited resentment and distrust in the minds of his Tory following. It was indeed becoming very evident that the only method of salvation for the Draper government was to make it a government without Mr. Draper.

Meantime events had happened in England calculated to exercise an immediate effect upon the course of Canadian policy. With the disruption of the Tories over the passage of the Corn Law Repeal (in the summer of 1846), Sir Robert Peel's government had come to an end, and the Liberals under Lord John Russell had come into power. With Lord John was associated as colonial secretary, Earl Grey, the son of the great Whig prime minister of the Reform Bill. The name of the second Earl Grey will always be associated with the establishment of actual democratic government in the mother country by means of parliamentary reform: that of the third will be forever connected with the final and definite adoption of the principle of colonial self-government. The moment was a critical one. The abandonment of the older system of commercial restrictions had destroyed the doctrine that the value of the colonies lay in the monopoly of their trade by the mother country.[1] To the Radical wing of the British party

[1] See in this connection Earl Grey's *Colonial Policy* (1853) Vol. I, p. 13.

this seemed to mean that the time had come to permit the colonies to depart in peace. But to Lord Grey, himself a former under-secretary of state for the colonies, and enlightened by the study of recent events in Canada, and by the similar struggle that had been in progress in Nova Scotia,[1] it appeared that the time was opportune for establishing the colonial system upon another and more durable basis, and for the creation of such a system of government as might combine colonial liberty with imperial stability. He repudiated the idea of abandoning the dependencies of the empire to a separate destiny. "The nation," he said, "has incurred a responsibility of the highest kind which it is not at liberty to throw off."

The advent to power of the British Liberal ministry was viewed by the Reform party in Canada as most auspicious for their cause. "I cannot help regarding it as a circumstance full of promise," said Robert Baldwin at a public dinner (November 11th, 1846) given to him by the Reform electors of the east riding of Halton, "that the imperial councils should at the present time be presided over by the statesman who, as colonial secretary, has given the imperial imprimatur to the doctrines of Lord Durham's Report, and the colonial department directed by one so nearly connected with the great statesman to whom England and the colonies were both so

[1] See Longley's *Joseph Howe* (Makers of Canada Series), Chap. iii.

much indebted for that invaluable state document."[1]
The new British cabinet could not, of course,
put forth an official repudiation of the conduct
of its predecessors towards the colonies. This
would have been contrary to the most obvious
considerations of imperial policy, and would also
have been unadvisable owing to the attitude taken
in earlier years by Lord John Russell himself.
But the cabinet were fully aware, none the less,
that the situation in British North America
could only be met by a frank recognition of
the right of the colonists of Nova Scotia and
Canada to manage their own affairs. The sphere
of action which Lord Grey considered proper
for a governor to assume may be best understood by a despatch addressed by him to Sir
John Harvey, lieutenant-governor of Nova Scotia,
(November 3rd, 1846). "This," says Lord Grey
himself, "contains the best explanation I can give
of the . . . means to be adopted for the purpose
of bringing into full and successful operation *the
system of constitutional government which it seemed
to be the desire of the inhabitants of British North
America to have established among them.*" Harvey,

[1] The speech to the electors of Halton was one of a series of
addresses delivered by Baldwin on a tour of Western Canada
in the autumn of 1846. The Tory journals affected to sneer
at the "quacksalving tour of agitation" (Toronto *Patriot*, November, 1846) undertaken by the Reform leader ; but the enthusiasm
excited by Baldwin's speeches made it manifest that the Tories
could not again look for a repetition of their victory of two years
past.

whose executive council was incomplete and unable to carry on the government, had found himself in a situation analogous to that in Canada. "I am of opinion," runs Lord Grey's despatch,[1] "that, under all the circumstances of the case, the best course for you to adopt is to call upon the members of your present executive council to propose to you the names of the gentlemen whom they would recommend to supply the vacancies which I understand to exist in the present board. If they should be successful in submitting to you an arrangement to which no valid objection arises, you will of course continue to carry on the government through them, so long as it may be possible to do so satisfactorily, and as they possess the necessary support from the legislature. Should the present council fail in proposing to you an arrangement which it would be proper for you to accept, it would then be your natural course, in conformity with the practice in analogous cases in this country, to apply to the opposite party: and should you be able through their assistance to form a satisfactory council, there will be no impropriety in dissolving the assembly upon their advice: such a measure, under those circumstances, being the only mode of escaping from the difficulty which would otherwise exist of carrying on the government of the province upon the principles of the constitution. The object with which I recommend to you this course, is

[1] See *House of Commons Sessional Papers*, No. 621 of 1848, p. 8.

that of making it apparent that any transfer which may take place of political power from the hands of one party in the province to those of another, is the result, not of an act of yours, but of the wishes of the people themselves. . . . In giving, therefore, all fair and proper support to your council for the time being, you will carefully avoid any acts which can possibly be supposed to imply the slightest personal objection to their opponents, and also refuse to assent to any measures which may be proposed to you by your council which may appear to you to involve an improper exercise of the authority of the Crown for party rather than for public objects. In exercising, however, this power of refusing to sanction measures which may be submitted to you by your council, you must recollect that this power of opposing a check upon extreme measures proposed by the party for the time in the government, depends entirely for its efficacy upon its being used sparingly and with the greatest possible discretion. *A refusal to accept advice tendered to you by your council is a legitimate ground for its members to tender to you their resignation,*—a course which they would doubtless adopt, should they feel that the subject on which a difference had arisen between you and themselves was one upon which public opinion would be in their favour. *Should it prove to be so, concession to their views must sooner or later become inevitable,* since it cannot be too distinctly acknowledged

271

that it is neither possible nor desirable to carry on the government of any of the British provinces in North America in opposition to the opinion of the inhabitants."

In order to carry into effect in the province of Canada the views thus indicated, the new British government determined to send out to the colony a governor-general whose especial task it should be to set right the unfortunate situation created by the mistaken policy of Lord Metcalfe. The conclusion of the Oregon treaty had by this time removed any immediate prospect of rupture with the United States, and it was no longer necessary to retain a military man at the head of Canadian affairs. The choice of the Liberal government fell upon Lord Elgin. Elgin presented, in many respects, a marked contrast to the governors who had preceded him. He was still a young man, and his vigorous health and ardent spirits gave reason to hope that he was destined to break the spell that seemed to hang over the Canadian governors, and that there was little likelihood of his dying in office. His proficiency in the French language, his geniality and the charm of his address, prepared for him, from the moment of his landing, a social and personal success. But these advantages were the least of Lord Elgin's qualifications for his new position. His chief claim to distinction, and the fact which gives his name a high and enduring place in the record of Canadian history, was his masterly grasp of the colonial situation, and the course he was prepared to take in instituting a real system of colonial self-government.

Lord Durham recommended responsible government: Baldwin and LaFontaine contended for it: Lord Grey sanctioned it, and Lord Elgin, as governor-general, first successfully applied it. For this full credit should be given to him. There seems to have been in the minds of Lord Grey and Lord John Russell some lingering of the old leaven,—a certain reservation in the grant of colonial autonomy they were prepared to make. The fact appears in certain passages of the despatch quoted above, and it is not difficult to find in Lord Grey's other writings expressions of opinion which imply a hesitancy to accept the doctrine of colonial self-government in its entire sense.[1] Lord John Russell in earlier years (1836) had told the House of Commons that the demands of the Canadian Reformers were incompatible with British sovereignty.[2] Prior to his departure for the colony Lord Elgin had, indeed, been given by the colonial

[1] See in this connection B. Holland, *Imperium et Libertas* (1901), Part II., Chap. iv. and Lord Grey's *Colonial Policy*, Vol. II., Letter v.

[2] "The House of Assembly of Lower Canada have asked for an elective legislative council and an executive council, which shall be responsible to them and not to the government and Crown of Great Britain. We consider that these demands are inconsistent with the relations between a colony and the mother country, and that it would be better to say at once, 'Let the two countries separate,' than for us to pretend to govern the colony afterwards."—Speech of May 16th, 1836.

secretary the most liberal instructions in regard to the conduct of the Canadian government. Had he been of the temper of Lord Metcalfe or Lord Sydenham, he could easily have assumed a certain latitude in his application of the constitutional system. But Lord Elgin was not so minded. He was inclined, if anything, to improve on his instructions, and having grasped the fundamental idea of colonial self-government, was determined to bring it fully into play.

Lord Elgin was a thorough believer in the doctrines enunciated in Lord Durham's Report. Moreover, his marriage with Durham's daughter gave him an especial and sympathetic interest in proving the truth of Lord Durham's views. "I still adhere," he wrote to his wife, "to my opinion that the real and effectual vindication of Lord Durham's memory and proceedings will be the success of a governor-general of Canada who works out his views of government fairly." Where Lord Elgin showed a political sagacity far in advance of the governors who had preceded him was in his perception of the fact that a governor, in frankly accepting his purely constitutional position, did not thereby abandon his prestige and influence in the province, nor cease to be truly representative of the British Crown. Sydenham's pride had revolted at the prospect of nonentity: Metcalfe's loyalty had taken fright at the spectre of colonial independence; but Elgin had the insight to perceive and to demonstrate the real nature of the governor's position. He was once asked, later on, "whether the theory of the responsibility of provincial ministers to the provincial parliament, and of the consequent duty of the governor to remain absolutely neutral in the strife of political parties, had not a necessary tendency to degrade his office into that of a mere *roi fainéant*." This Elgin emphatically denied. "I have tried," he said, "both systems. In Jamaica, there was no responsible government; but I had not half the power I have here, with my constitutional and changing cabinet."[1]

Lord Elgin left England at the beginning of January, 1847, and entered Montreal on the twentyninth of the month. The people of the city, irrespective of political leanings, united in an address of welcome, and, in the perplexed state of Canadian politics, all parties were inclined to look to the new governor to give a definite lead to the current of affairs. It was strongly in Elgin's favour that neither party associated his past career with the cause of their opponents. In British politics a Tory, he came to Canada as the appointee of a British Liberal government. "Lord Elgin," said Hincks in the *Pilot*, "is said to be a Tory and

---

[1] Elgin had been governor of Jamaica. See Walrond's *Letters of Lord Elgin*, and citations by A. Todd, *Parliamentary Government in the British Colonies* (1880), p. 59.

there is no doubt that he is of a Tory family. We look upon his bias as an English politician with the most perfect indifference. We do not think it matters one straw to us Canadians whether our governor is a Tory or a Whig, more especially a Tory of the Peel school. We have to rely on ourselves not the governor; and if we are true to ourselves, the private opinions of the governor will be of very little importance."

At the time of Lord Elgin's arrival, the Draper government was reaching its last stage of decrepitude. "The ministry," in the words of a Canadian writer, "were as weak as a lot of shelled pease." In the spring of the year (April and May, 1847) a partial reconstruction of the ministry was made with a view of rallying the support of the malcontent Tories. Mr. Draper himself abandoned his place, his fall being broken by his appointment as puisne judge of the court of queen's bench. John A. Macdonald, destined from now on to figure in the forefront of Canadian politics, entered the ministry as receiver-general; Sherwood became attorney-general of Upper Canada, and other changes were made. But inasmuch as the reconstructed cabinet—the Sherwood-Daly ministry, as it is called—contained no other French-Canadian than Mr. Papineau, it was plainly but a makeshift and could not hope to conduct with success the administration of the country. As soon as parliament was summoned (June 2nd, 1847) the

Reformers commenced a vigorous and united onslaught. Baldwin, seconded by LaFontaine, moved an amendment to the address in which, while congratulating Lord Elgin upon his recent marriage with Lord Durham's daughter, he declared that it was to Lord Durham that the country owed the recognition of the principle of responsible government, and to Lord Elgin that the parliament looked for the application of it. LaFontaine followed with an eloquent denunciation of those of his compatriots who had lent their support in parliament to a ministry whose cardinal principle was hostility to their race. "You have," he said, "sacrificed honour to love of office: you have let yourselves become passive instruments in the hands of your colleagues: you have sacrificed your country and ere long you will reap your reward."

After a heated debate of three days the government was able to carry the address by a majority of only two votes. Nor had it any better fortune during the session of two months which ensued. The ministry was not in a position to introduce any measures of prime importance, and even upon minor matters sustained repeated defeats. The only legislation possible under the circumstances were measures of evident and urgent public utility into which party considerations did not enter. The incorporation of companies to operate the new "magnetic telegraph," as the newspapers of the day called it, are noticeable among these. Still more necessary was the legislation for the relief of the vast crowds of indigent Irish immigrants, driven from their own country by the terrible famine of 1846-7, and to whose other sufferings were added the ravages of ship-fever and other contagious diseases. In the public consideration of this question Robert Baldwin took a prominent place and aided in the foundation of the Emigration Association of Toronto.

The ill-success of the reconstructed government, and the universal desire for a strong and stable administration which could adequately cope with the many difficulties of the hour, clearly necessitated a dissolution of parliament. Lord Elgin, though without personal bias against the existing cabinet, felt that it was no longer representative of the feelings of the people, among whom the current of public opinion had now set strongly in favour of the Reform party. Elgin dissolved the parliament on December 6th, 1847, the writs for the new election being returnable on the twenty-fourth of the following January. The general election which ensued was an unbroken triumph for the Reformers. In Upper Canada twenty-six of the forty-two members returned belonged to the Liberal party, while in the lower part of the province only half a dozen of those elected were partisans of the expiring government. Baldwin was again elected in the fourth riding of York, the same county returning also, in Blake and Price, two of his strongest supporters. Francis Hincks, who was absent from Canada, being at this time on a five months' tour to his native land, was elected for Oxford in his absence. Sir Allan MacNab and John A. Macdonald were among the Conservatives reëlected; Sherwood narrowly escaped defeat, while John Cameron, the solicitor-general, Ogle R. Gowan, the Orange leader, and many others of the party lost their seats. In Lower Canada the Reformers were irresistible: even the city of Montreal repented of its sins by returning LaFontaine and a fellow-Reformer as its members. LaFontaine was also returned for Terrebonne, but elected to sit for Montreal. The result of the election left nothing for the Conservatives but to retire as gracefully as might be to the shades of Opposition and wait for happier times.

CHAPTER IX

THE SECOND LAFONTAINE-BALDWIN MINISTRY

THE second LaFontaine-Baldwin administration,[1] which extended from the beginning of 1848 until the retirement of the two Reform leaders in the summer of 1851, has earned in Canadian history the honourable appellation of the "great ministry." Its history marks the culmination of the lifework of Robert Baldwin and Louis LaFontaine and the justification of their political system. It is a commonplace of history that every great advance in the structure of political institutions brings with it an acceleration of national progress. This is undoubtedly true of the LaFontaine-Baldwin ministry, whose inception signalizes the final acceptance of the principle of responsible government. This fact lent to it a vigour and activity which enabled it to achieve a legislative record with which the work of no other ministry during the period of the union can compare. The settlement of the school system, the definite foundation of the University of Toronto on the basis to which it owes its present eminence, the organization of municipal government, the opening of the railroad system of Canada,—these are among the political achievements of the "great

[1] See note on page 190.

ministry." More than all this is the fact that the
LaFontaine-Baldwin ministry indicates the first
real pacification of French Canada, the passing
of the "strife of two nations warring within the
bosom of a single state" and the beginning of that
joint and harmonious citizenship of the two races
which has become the corner-stone of the structure
of Canadian government. The ministry stands thus
at the turning-point of an era. The forces of racial
antipathy, separation and rebellion, scarce checked
by the union of 1840, here pass into that broader
movement which slowly makes towards Canadian
confederation and the creation of a continental
Dominion.

Towards the change of national life thus indicated other and more material forces were also
tending. The era of the "great ministry" belongs
to the time when the advent of the railroad and
the telegraph was unifying and consolidating the
industrial and social life of the country. Sandwich
and Gaspé no longer appeared the opposite ends
of the earth. The toilsome journey that separated
the chief cities of Upper from those of Lower Canada was soon to become a thing of the past, and a
more active intercourse and more real sympathy
between the eastern and western sections of the
country to take the place of their former political
and social isolation. Lord Elgin once said that the
true solution of the Canadian question would be
found when both the French and the English in-

habitants should be divided into Conservative and Liberal parties whose formation should rest upon grounds of kindred sentiments and kindred interests. For this the changes now operative in the country were preparing the way: the old era was passing away and a new phase of national life was destined to take its place. Looking back upon the period we can see that the LaFontaine-Baldwin administration marks the time of transition, the essential point of change from the Canada of the rebellion epoch to the Canada of the confederation.

The result of the election of 1847-8 had made it a foregone conclusion that the Conservative government must retire from office. Lord Elgin called the parliament together at Montreal on February 25th, 1848, and the vote on the election of the speaker showed at once the relative strength of the parties in the assembly. It having been proposed that Sir Allan MacNab, the late speaker of the House, be again elected, Baldwin proposed the name of Morin in his stead: while paying tribute to the qualifications of Sir Allan in other respects, he held it fitting that the speaker should be able to command both the French and English languages. A vote of fifty-four to nineteen proved the overwhelming strength of the Reformers. The answer to the speech from the throne, as was of course to be expected, was met by an amendment, proposed by Robert Baldwin, to the effect that

the present ministry did not enjoy the confidence
of the country. The amendment being carried by
a vote of fifty-four to twenty (March 3rd, 1848),
the Conservative ministers tendered their resignation. Lord Elgin at once sent for LaFontaine and
the latter, in consultation with Baldwin, proceeded
to form the ministry which bears their names. The
ministry as thus constituted (March 11th, 1848)
was as follows :—

For Lower Canada: L. H. LaFontaine, attorney-
general; James Leslie, president of the executive
council; R. E. Caron, president of the legislative
council; E. P. Taché, chief commissioner of public works ; T. C. Aylwin, solicitor-general ; L. M.
Viger, receiver-general.

For Upper Canada: Robert Baldwin, attorney-
general ; R. B. Sullivan, provincial secretary ; F.
Hincks, inspector-general; J. H. Price, commissioner of Crown lands ; Malcolm Cameron, assistant commissioner of public works ; W. H. Blake,[1]
solicitor-general.

Frequent mention has already been made of
most of the above. Leslie, who had for many years
represented the county of Verchères, and Malcolm
Cameron, who had been a bitter opponent of Sir
F. B. Head and had held a minor office under
Bagot, represented the more Radical wing of the
Reform party. The name of (Sir) Etienne Taché,

[1] Mr. Blake, who was absent in Europe, did not enter on office until
April, 1849.

twice subsequently prime minister, is of course well known. Taché had formerly been in the assembly for six years (1841-6), had since held the office of deputy adjutant-general, and was now, along with James Leslie, given a seat in the legislative council. Various other additions were presently made to the Upper House in order to redress the balance of parties therein and more adequately to represent the French-Canadian population.

Lord Elgin, although determined not to identify himself in sympathy with either of the Canadian parties, seems, none the less, to have entertained a high idea of the ability and integrity of his new ministers. " My present council," he wrote to Lord Grey, " unquestionably contains more talent, and has a firmer holder on the confidence of parliament and of the people than the last. There is, I think, moreover, on their part, a desire to prove, by proper deference for the authority of the governor-general (which they all admit has in my case never been abused), that they were libelled when they were accused of impracticability and anti-monarchical tendencies." The governor was determined to let the leaders of the ministry feel that they need fear no repetition of their difficulties with Sir Charles Metcalfe. In an initial interview with Baldwin and LaFontaine he took pains to assure them of the course he intended to pursue. " I spoke to them," he wrote after-

wards,[1] "in a candid and friendly tone; told them
I thought there was a fair prospect, if they were
moderate and firm, of forming an administration
deserving and enjoying the confidence of parliament: that they might count on all proper support
and assistance from me."

It was not possible for the ministry to undertake
a serious programme of legislation during the
session of 1848. Those of the ministers who belonged to the assembly—including LaFontaine
and Baldwin—had of course to present themselves to their constituents for reëlection. This
proved an easy matter, the elections being either
carried by acclamation or by large majorities. But
Lord Elgin and his ministers both preferred to
bring the session to a close, in order to leave time
for the mature consideration of the measures to
be adopted on the re-assembling of parliament. The
legislature was accordingly postponed from March
23rd, 1848, until the opening of the following
year. The parliamentary session which then ensued
(dating from January 18th until May 30th, 1849)
was unprecedented in the importance of its legislation and the excitement occasioned by its measures. The speech from the throne announced a
vigorous programme of reform. Electoral reform,
the revision of the judicature system of both
provinces, the constitution of the university of
King's College, the completion of the St. Lawrence

[1] Walrond, *Letters of Lord Elgin*, p. 52.

canals, and the regulation of the municipal system were among the subjects on which the parliament would be asked to legislate. The question of an interprovincial railroad from Quebec to Halifax and the transfer of the postal department from the imperial to the Canadian authorities, were also to be brought under consideration.

Two important announcements were also made by Lord Elgin on behalf of the imperial government. The legislature was informed that the imperial parliament had passed an Act in repeal of the clause of the Act of Union which had declared English to be the sole official language of the legislature. With instinctive tact and courtesy the governor-general demonstrated the reality of the change thus effected, by himself reading his speech in French as well as English, a proceeding which drew forth enthusiastic praise from the press of Lower Canada. The other announcement was no less calculated to enlist the sympathies of French Canada. "I am authorized to inform you," said Lord Elgin, "that it is Her Majesty's purpose to exercise the prerogative of mercy in favour of all persons who are still liable to penal consequences for political offences arising out of the unfortunate occurrences of 1837 and 1838, and I have the queen's commands to invite you to confer with me in passing an Act to give full effect to Her Majesty's most gracious intentions."[1]

[1] *Journals of the Legislative Assembly*, January 18th, 1849.

The debate which followed on the address is notable for the trial of strength that occurred between LaFontaine and Louis-Joseph Papineau, the former leader of the popular party in the days of the rebellion. When the agitation in Lower Canada had broken into actual insurrection, Papineau had fled the country with a price upon his head. For two years he had lived in the United States; thence he passed to France where he spent some eight years, his time being chiefly passed in the cultured society of the capital. As yet no general law of amnesty had been passed to permit the return of the "rebels" of 1837. But in many individual instances the government had seen fit to grant a pardon. LaFontaine, during his first ministry, had urged upon Sir Charles Metcalfe the wisdom of a general amnesty. Unable to obtain this he had secured from the governor-general the authorization of a *nolle prosequi* in the case of Papineau. This was in 1843. The ex-leader did not, however, see fit to avail himself of his liberty to return to Canada until the year 1847. On his return in that year he had presented himself in the ensuing general election to the constituency of St. Maurice, and the prestige of his bygone career sufficed for his election. He once again found himself a member of a Canadian assembly.

For Papineau's historic reputation among his compatriots, it would have been better had he never returned to Canada. True, he had been absent from the country but ten years, yet he came back to a Canada that knew him not. The charm of his personal address, the magniloquence of his oratory were still there, but the leadership of Louis-Joseph Papineau was gone forever. There were some in the province who could not forget that Papineau had fled from his misguided followers at the darkest hour of their fortunes. There were others—and these the bulk of his compatriots—who felt that the lapse of time and the march of events had rendered Papineau and his bygone agitation an issue of the past, an issue that could not serve as a rallying-point for French Canada in the altered circumstances of the hour. Of this great change Papineau himself realized nothing. He was still preaching the old doctrine of 1837, the uncompromising hostility to British rule and the veiled republicanism of his former days. In the brief session of 1848 he had angrily inveighed against the prorogation of parliament and had urged, to prevent it, a stoppage of supplies! Now, at the opening of the session of 1849, he rose to utter an impassioned but meaningless attack against the policy of LaFontaine. The great upheaval of European democracy of 1848, of which he had witnessed the approaching signals, had appealed to Papineau's imagination. It ill sufficed him to live in a country in which there was no ruthless despotism to denounce, no grinding tyranny to oppose, no political martyrdom to attain. In default of a real tyranny he must invent one. He denounced the union of the Canadas, he denounced the legislative council, he denounced responsible government. "The constitution of the country," he cried, "is false, tyrannical and calculated to demoralize its people. Conceived by statesmen of a narrow and malevolent genius, it has had up till the present, and can only have in the future, effects that are dangerous, results that are ruinous and disastrous." Most bitterly of all did he denounce those of his race who had accepted and aided to establish the present system and who, for the sake of office and power, had bartered the proud independence of an unconquered race.

The reply of LaFontaine to Papineau ranks among his finest speeches. Inferior perhaps to his former leader in the arts of eloquence, he far excelled him in the balance and vigour of his intellect. The utter futility of Papineau's adherence to the old uncompromising doctrines of the past, he easily exposed. " What," he asked, "would have been the consequences of the adoption of this conflict to the bitter end, that we are reproached with not having adopted? If, instead of accepting the offers made to them . . . the representatives of Lower Canada had persistently held aloof, the French-Canadians would have never shared in the government of the country. They would have been crushed. Would you with your system of

unending conflict have ever obtained the repeal
of the clause of the Act of Union that proscribes
our language? . . . If, in 1842, we had adopted
that system should we now be in a position to
solicit, to urge, as we have been doing, the return
of our exiled compatriots?"

It might, perhaps, have been more magnanimous
on the part of LaFontaine had he omitted to give
his arguments a personal allusion. But the ingrati-
tude of Papineau, who owed it to LaFontaine's
efforts and to the system of conciliation which he
denounced, that he was able again to tread the soil
of his native country, stung LaFontaine to the
quick. He continued: "If we had not accepted
office in the ministry of 1842, should we have been
in a position to obtain for the honourable member
himself, permission to return to his country, to
obtain which I did not hesitate, in order to overcome the repeated refusals of Sir Charles Metcalfe,
to offer my resignation of lucrative offices I then
enjoyed? Yet, behold now this man obeying his
old-time instinct of pouring forth insult and out-
rage, and daring in the presence of these facts to
accuse me, and with me my colleagues, of venality,
of a sordid love of office and of servility to those in
power! To hear him, he alone is virtuous, he alone
loves our country, he alone is devoted to the
fatherland. . . . But since he bespeaks such virtue,
I ask him at least to be just. Where would the
honourable member be to-day, if I had adopted

this system of a conflict to the bitter end? He would be at Paris, fraternizing, I suppose, with the red republicans, the white republicans, or the black republicans, and approving, one after the other, the fluctuating constitutions of France!"[1]

But though routed in debate by LaFontaine and unable any longer to lead the assembly, Papineau was not without a certain following. Some of the more ardent of the younger spirits among the French-Canadians were still attracted by the prestige of his name and by the violence of his democratic principles, and espoused his cause. There began to appear a Radical wing of the French-Canadian Reformers, pressing upon the government a still greater acceleration of democratic progress and a still more complete recognition of the claims of their nationality. The Radical movement was as yet, however, but a more rapid eddy in the broad stream of reform that in the meantime was moving fast enough.

One hundred and ninety acts of parliament were passed during the session of 1849 and received the governor's assent. Many of these—the Tariff Act,[2] the Amnesty Act,[3] the Railroad Acts,[4] the Judicature Acts,[5] the Rebellion Losses Act,[6] the Municipal Corporations Act,[7] and the Act to amend the charter of the university established at Toronto[8]—

---

[1] Speech of January 23rd, 1849. (Translated from *La Minerve*.)
[2] 12 Vict. c. 1.   [3] 12 Vict. c. 13.   [4] 12 Vict. cc. 28, 29.
[5] 12 Vict. cc. 38, 41, 63, 64.   [6] 12 Vict. c. 58.
[7] 12 Vict. c. 81.   [8] 12 Vict. c. 82.

are measures of first-rate importance. With the two last mentioned the name of Robert Baldwin will always be associated. It will be remembered that during his previous ministry Baldwin had brought in a bill for the revision of the charter of King's College and for the consolidation of the denominational colleges of the country into a single provincial institution. Against this measure a loud outcry had been raised by the Tories, on the ground that it effected a spoliation of the Anglican Church which had hitherto exercised a dominant influence over King's College, and whose doctrines were taught in the faculty of divinity of that institution. The rupture with Sir Charles Metcalfe had prevented the passage of the bill. Mr. Draper had introduced a measure of similar character, but had seen fit to abandon it on account of the opposition excited among his own adherents. The measure, which Baldwin carried through parliament in 1849, creating the University of Toronto in place of King's College, has been said by Sir John Bourinot to have "placed the university upon that broad basis on which it still rests." A former president of the University of Toronto, in a recent history of the institution,[1] has seen fit to disparage Robert Baldwin's Act, drawing attention to the needless complexity of its clauses, the failure of its attempt to affiliate

[1] See J. Loudon, *History of the University of Toronto. Canada: an Encyclopædia*, Vol. IV.

the sectarian colleges, and to the fact that a revision of its provisions became necessary a few years later (1853). But the great merit of Baldwin's University Act lay, not in its treatment of the details of organization but in the cardinal point of establishing a system of higher education, non-sectarian in its character, in whose benefits the adherents of all creeds might equally participate.

The faculty of divinity and the degree in divinity were now abolished, and the control of the university entirely withdrawn from the Church, except for the fact that the different denominational colleges were each entitled to a representative on the senate of the university. The system of government instituted was, indeed, cumbrous. Academic powers and the nominations to the professoriate were placed in the hands of a senate, consisting of a chancellor, vice-chancellor, the professors and twelve nominated members,—six chosen by the government, six by the denominational colleges. A further body called the caput, or council, made up of the president and deans of faculties, and certain others, exercised disciplinary powers. An endowment board, appointed jointly by the government, the senate, the caput, etc., managed the property of the university. Various other powers were vested in the faculties, the deans of faculties and in subordinate authorities. The elaborate regulation of the whole structure and the lack of elasticity in its organization were in marked contrast to the more simple provisions of the charter of King's College. No religious tests for professoriate and students were to be imposed. It was further enacted that neither the chancellor nor any government representative on the senate should be a "minister, ecclesiastic or teacher, under or according to any form or profession of religious faith or worship."

Provision was made under the Act for the incorporation in the University of Toronto of the denominational colleges. To obtain incorporation they were to forego their existing power of conferring degrees. As the colleges were unwilling to do this unless they were granted a share of the provincial endowment for their own teaching purposes, the scheme of consolidation failed. Victoria and Queen's Universities remained upon their separate and sectarian bases, and thus one of the purposes of Baldwin's Act was defeated. Moreover, a section of the adherents of the Anglican Church refused to countenance the new establishment. Bishop Strachan, who had denounced the godless iconoclasm of Baldwin's previous University Bill, again headed the agitation against a secular university. Furious at the passage of the measure, he called upon the members of his Church to raise funds for a university of their own, headed the subscription himself with a contribution of five thousand dollars, and, undeterred by his advancing years, betook himself to England to obtain sympathy and help towards the founda-

BALDWIN LAFONTAINE HINCKS

tion of an Anglican College. The result of his endeavours was the foundation of Trinity College in 1851.

The Municipal Corporations Act of 1849, commonly known as the Baldwin Act, constitutes another of the permanent political achievements of Robert Baldwin. Many years ago the Upper Canada *Law Journal* remarked of this Act and of the revision of the judicial system, "Had Mr. Baldwin never done more than enact our municipal and jury laws, he would have done enough to entitle his memory to the lasting respect of the inhabitants of this province. Neighbouring provinces are adopting the one and the other almost intact, as an embodiment of wisdom united with practical usefulness, equally noted for simplicity and for completeness of detail not to be found elsewhere." Quite recently Professor Shortt has said,[1] "Looking at the Baldwin Act in its historic significance, we must admit it to have been a most comprehensive and important measure, whose beneficial influence has been felt, not merely in Ontario, but more or less throughout the Dominion. . . . In all essential principles its spirit and purpose are embodied in our present municipal system."

[1] *University of Toronto Studies : History and Economics*, Vol. II. No. 2. *Municipal Government in Ontario*. The following account of the steps leading to the Baldwin Act is largely based on Professor Shortt's admirable monograph.

LOCAL GOVERNMENT

The Baldwin Act represents the culmination and final triumph of the agitation for local self-government that had, for over fifty years, run a parallel course with the movement for responsible government. In the earlier years of Upper Canadian settlement, the government had been very chary of investing the settlers with rights of local management. Townships indeed existed, but these were merely areas plotted out by the surveyor for convenience in the allotment of land, and were not incorporated units of government. Nor was incorporation given to the districts or larger areas into which the province was subdivided. Even the villages and towns had at first no rights of self-government. The management of local affairs and the assessment of local taxes were left to the justices of the peace, sitting in quarter sessions, these being officers appointed by the governor and representing, of course, the solid cohesion of the governing class. The settlers, many of whom had been used to better things in their New England homes, constantly protested. At times they organized themselves in their townships on a voluntary basis. Various bills for giving power to the people of the townships, as such, were brought before the legislature, but met with a distrustful rejection at the hands of the governing oligarchy. Only a few unimportant matters—the election of petty officers, such as fence-viewers and pound-keepers—were handed over to the people.

The system thus established proved increasingly unjust and inconvenient: unjust, since it contributed to the privileges of the colonial aristocracy: inconvenient, especially in the growing towns where matters such as markets, fire protection, street-paving, etc., urgently demanded an organized municipal control. The pressure of the situation presently forced the government to grant some rights of self-government to the towns. A severe fire at Kingston in 1812 proved an object-lesson to a population that dwelt in wooden houses. An Act of parliament[1] gave special powers to the magistrates in regard to Kingston, and an Act of a year later put York, Sandwich and Amhertsburg upon the same footing. Belleville was presently granted the right to *elect* a police board, the first actual use of the democratic principle in town government. Brockville, after a long fight against the government, obtained an Act of parliament which set up the Brockville town board as a body corporate.[2] The powers granted were limited, but the Act was a step in advance. A similar limited incorporation was extended to Hamilton, York and other towns (1832-4). Meantime the Reform party had vigorously taken up the cry for local self-government. Durham recommended in his Report "the establishment of a good system of municipal institutions

[1] 56 Geo. III. c. 33.
[2] 2 Will. IV. c. 17.

throughout this province." The Draper government, under Lord Sydenham, as has been seen, had endeavoured to enlist popular support by passing a Local Government Act (1841). But the fear of Tory opposition prevented Mr. Draper from doing more than incorporating the districts of Upper Canada with a partially elective government.[1] It remained for Baldwin, in one comprehensive statute, to establish the entire system of local government in Upper Canada upon the democratic basis of popular election.

The text of the Baldwin Act fills some fifty pages of the statute-book; but its ground plan is excellent in its logic and simplicity, and can be explained in a few words. The districts are abolished as areas of government in favour of counties with townships as their subdivisions. The township now became an incorporated body with power to construct highways, school buildings, etc. Its inhabitants elected five councillors, who appointed one of their number to be "reeve" of the township, and, in townships having a population of more than five hundred, another to be deputy-reeve. The reeves and deputy-reeves of the townships constituted the county council and elected from among themselves the "warden" of the county. The county council thus incorporated had authority over county roads, bridges and grammar schools, with other usual municipal powers. Within

[1] See pp. 100, 101, above.

the area of the county the Act recognized also police villages, incorporated villages, towns and cities, representing an ascending series of corporate powers and a correspondingly increasing independence from the control of the county council. The police village was merely a hamlet to whose inhabitants the county committed the election of police trustees who should take steps to prevent fires, etc. An incorporate village was a body corporate with an elected council and a reeve, and practically on the same footing as a township. Still further powers were given to the town, with an elected council and a mayor and reeve chosen thereby. At the apex of urban government were placed the cities, Toronto, Hamilton and Kingston, and any others whose population should reach fifteen thousand. The city, with a mayor, aldermen and common councillors, constituted a county in itself, special powers being also delegated to it. Taken as a whole the Act is uniform in plan, excellent both in its fundamental principle and in the consistency of its detail; though frequently amended, it remains as the basis of local self-government in Ontario at the present day.

In addition to the University and Municipal Acts, Baldwin was also largely responsible for the Acts revising the judicial system of Upper Canada, creating a court of common pleas and a court of error and appeal, and freeing the court of chancery from the delays which had hitherto impaired its

300

utility, by altering its procedure and increasing the number of its judges from one to three.

The allotment of legislative business among the leaders of the Reform party proceeded on the same lines as during the former ministry. While the political legislation was entrusted to Baldwin and LaFontaine, Hincks undertook the preparation of commercial and economic measures. These at the moment were of especial importance. The adoption of free trade by England had involved the loss of the preference enjoyed under earlier statutes by Canadian agricultural exports to the mother country. This had precipitated in Canada a severe commercial depression: the winter of 1848-9 had been a winter of discontent, and Lord Elgin had written home of the "downward progress of events." A vigorous policy was needed in order to revive the industries of the country, and to this Hincks addressed himself with characteristic energy. Already various charters had been granted for the construction of railways in Canada: the road from LaPrairie to St. Johns[1] (Quebec) had been built as early as 1837, and by the year 1848 a part of what afterwards became the Grand Trunk line from Montreal to Portland was already constructed, while work had been begun upon the Great Western and Northern Railways. Hincks,

[1] The importance of this line lay in the fact that it connected the St. Lawrence navigation (through the Richelieu River) with that of Lake Champlain and the Hudson.

realizing the importance of the development of the Canadian transportation system, now inaugurated a policy of active governmental aid to railway construction. An Act of parliament guaranteed, for any railway of more than seventy-five miles in length, the payment of six per cent. interest on half the cost of its construction. Anxious at the same time to stimulate trade with the United States in order to compensate the country for the loss of its commercial privileges with Great Britain, Hincks endeavoured to bring about a system of reciprocal free trade in natural products between Canada and the republic. An Act of the legislature accordingly declared all duties on this class of imports to be removed as soon as the congress of the United States should take similar action. Unfortunately the opposition of the American senate interposed a long delay, and it was not until five years later that an international treaty at last brought the system of reciprocity into effect. Meantime the Customs Act of 1849 revised existing duties, altering many of them to an *ad valorem* basis and placing the average duty at about thirteen and one-quarter per cent.

The legislative measures that fell to the share of LaFontaine were the political bills relating to Lower Canada. Here also the judicial system was amended, a court of queen's bench being established with four judges of its own, and the superior court also undergoing a revision. A general law of amnesty gave effect to the intention of the Crown. An attempt to carry a bill for redistributing the seats in the legislature failed of its purpose. It was LaFontaine's object to give to each province seventy-five instead of forty-two members, in order to permit a subdivision of the larger constituencies: the equality of representation between the two provinces was to be retained, although it was now evident that Upper Canada would soon surpass in population the lower section of the province. For a measure of this kind a majority of two-thirds was necessitated by the Act of Union. The opposition to the bill came from the Upper Canadian Tories and from Papineau and certain other French-Canadian Radicals, who insisted on carrying the democratic principle of equal representation to its full extent, even against the interests of their own nationality. LaFontaine's measure fell short of the required two-thirds by one vote. Of far more importance was a measure now before parliament for whose introduction LaFontaine was responsible, and whose passage almost threatened to bring the country to a civil war. The Rebellion Losses Bill is, however, of such importance as to require a chapter to itself.

CHAPTER X

THE REBELLION LOSSES BILL

THE Act of Indemnification of 1849, or—to give it the name by which it was known during its passage through parliament and by which it is still remembered—the Rebellion Losses Bill, is of unparalleled importance in the history of Canada. The bill was a measure for the compensation of persons in Lower Canada whose property had suffered in the suppression of the rebellion of 1837 and 1838. It excited throughout Canada a furious opposition. It was denounced both in Canada and in England as a scheme for rewarding rebels. Its passage led to open riots in Montreal, to the invasion of the legislature by a crowd of malcontents, to the burning of the houses of parliament and to the mobbing of Lord Elgin in the streets of the city. These facts alone would have made it an episode of great prominence in the narrative of our history; but the bill is of still greater importance in the development of the constitution of Canada. The fact that in despite of the opposition of the Loyalists, in despite of the flood of counter-petitions and addresses, in despite of the imminent prospect of civil strife, Lord Elgin fulfilled his constitutional duty, refused to dissolve the parliament or to reserve the bill for the royal sanction, and that the home government accepted the situation and refused to interfere, shows that we have here arrived at the complete realization of colonial self-government. The passage of the Rebellion Losses Bill gives to the doctrine of the right of the people of the colony to manage their own affairs, the final seal of a general acceptance.

The circumstances leading to the introduction of the measure were as follows. The outbreak of 1837-8 had occasioned throughout the two provinces a very considerable destruction of private property. Some of this had been caused by the overt acts of the rebels; but there had also been a good deal of property destroyed, injured or confiscated by the troops and the Loyalists in the suppression of the rebellion.

It was, from the beginning, the intention of the government to make reparation to persons who had suffered damage from the acts of rebels. The parliament of Upper Canada had passed an Act (1 Vict. c. 13) appointing commissioners to estimate the damages, and had presently voted (2 Vict. c. 48) the issue of some four thousand pounds in debentures in payment of the claims. The special council of Lower Canada had taken similar action. But the question of damage done in suppressing the outbreak was of a somewhat different complexion. A part of the property destroyed was the property of persons actually in arms against the government. To these, plainly enough, no compensation was owing. In other cases the owners of injured property were adherents of the government, whose losses were occasioned either fortuitously or by the necessities of war. To these, equally clearly, a compensation ought to be paid. But between these two classes was a large number of persons whose property had suffered, who were not openly and provably rebels but who had belonged to the disaffected class, or who at any rate were identified in race and sympathy with the disaffected part of the population. This element gave to the equities of the question a very perplexed appearance.

In the last session of its existence the parliament of Upper Canada had adopted an Act (October 22nd, 1840)[1] voting compensation on a large scale for damage done by the troops *and otherwise*. The sum of forty thousand pounds was to be applied to claims preferred under the Act. As no means were laid down for raising the necessary funds, this Act remained inoperative. Then followed the union of the Canadas and the election of a joint parliament. In despite of repeated petitions and individual representations to the government nothing more was done in regard to Rebellion Losses Claims until the year 1845 when the Draper government passed an Act to render operative the Upper Canadian statute of 1840.

[1] 3 Vict. c. 76.

The funds for the measure were to be supplied out of the receipts from tavern licenses for Upper Canada, which were set aside for that purpose. The sums collected under this Act of parliament between April 5th, 1845 and January 24th, 1849, amounted to £38,658.

At the time when Mr. Draper's Act of 1845 was before parliament, the Reformers of Lower Canada protested against the inequity of extending to one section of the country a privilege not enjoyed by the other, and demanded similar legislation for Lower Canada. The government, presumably in order to obtain their support for its own measure, indicated its readiness to act upon this demand, and a unanimous address was presented to Lord Metcalfe (February 28th, 1845) asking him to institute an enquiry into the losses sustained in Lower Canada during the period of the insurrection. A commission consisting of five persons was accordingly appointed (November 24th, 1845). The commissioners were asked to distinguish between participants in the rebellion and persons innocent of complicity, but they were also informed that " the object of the executive government was merely to obtain a general estimate of the rebellion losses, the particulars of which should form the subject of more minute investigation thereafter under legislative authority." The result was that the commission found themselves compelled to report that "the want of power to proceed to a strict and regular investigation of the losses in question left the commissioners no other resource than to trust to the allegation of the claimants as to the amount and nature of their losses." Needless to say that, under the circumstances, many of the allegations in question were very wide of the truth : the total sum claimed amounted to over two hundred and forty thousand pounds, and of this it is said that about twenty-five thousand pounds represented claims of persons who had been convicted by court-martial of complicity in the rebellion. It will easily be understood that under these circumstances the cry arose from the Canadian Tories and their British sympathizers that the whole scheme amounted to nothing more than plundering the public treasury in favour of the disloyal. It was impossible for the government to take action upon a report of so unreliable a character. Indeed it is likely that the government was anxious merely to tide the matter over as best it might. It voted some ten thousand pounds in payment of claims that had been certified in Lower Canada before the union, and with that it let the matter rest.

As the question stood at the opening of the LaFontaine-Baldwin administration, it is plain that a grave injustice rested upon many injured persons in Lower Canada as compared with their fellow-citizens of Upper Canada who had received compensation for their losses : granted that there were black sheep among the claimants, this did not affect the validity of the other claims. It was this injustice that LaFontaine, whose constant policy it was to safeguard the rights of his nationality, now determined to rectify. Early in the session he moved, seconded by Robert Baldwin, a series of seven resolutions, reciting the failure of the previous commission and demanding the appointment of a new body with proper powers, and the payment of claims. The resolutions, carried by large majorities (the vote on the first one, for example, was fifty-two to twenty) were followed (February 27th) by the introduction of a bill to bring them into effect. The measure was entitled, "An Act to provide for the indemnification of parties in Lower Canada whose property was destroyed during the rebellion of the years 1837 and 1838."[1] There was no difficulty, as far as voting power went in carrying the bill through parliament. It was passed by the House of Assembly (March 9th, 1849) by a vote of forty-seven to eighteen, and accepted without amendment by the legislative council by twenty against fourteen votes. The fact that the measure received overwhelming support in a legislature only recently elected, must be carefully noted in considering the constitutional aspect of the question involved.

Under the provisions of the Act the governor-general was empowered to appoint five com-

[1] The Act is 12 Vict. c. 58.

missioners whose duty it should be "faithfully and without partiality to enquire into and to ascertain the amount of the losses sustained during the rebellion." The commissioners were given authority to summon witnesses and examine them under oath. For the payment of the claims the governor was empowered to issue debentures, payable out of the consolidated revenue of the province at or within twenty years after the date of issue and bearing interest at six per cent. The maximum amount to be expended on the claims (including the expenses incurred under the Act and the sum of £9,986 issued in debentures under the Act of June 9th, 1846[1]) was not to exceed £100,000; if the claims allowed amounted to a higher total, a proportionate distribution was to be effected. The Act also provided that no claim should be recognized on the part of any persons "who had been convicted of treason during the rebellion, or who, having been taken into custody, had submitted to Her Majesty's will and been transported to Bermuda."

The introduction and explanation of the bill before parliament naturally fell to the task of LaFontaine, who made a number of speeches in its support, traversing the whole question of indemnity from 1837 onwards and affording an admirable history of the measure. Baldwin took but little part in the debates on the Rebellion

[1] 9 Vict. c. 65.

Losses Bill. It has often been said that this was from lack of sympathy with the measure, and insinuations of this kind were made in the House of Assembly. But a speech made by Baldwin during the debate on the introduction of the preliminary resolutions (February 27th, 1849) emphatically affirms his concurrence in LaFontaine's proposed measure. He had been accused, he said, of wilfully abstaining from speaking on the measure, but this was an error, for he had merely refrained from speaking because there was no necessity to do so. The whole matter had been set in such a clear light by his friends that it would be impossible to elucidate it still further. In the brief speech which followed, Baldwin went on to show that the measure contemplated by the resolutions would merely do for Lower Canada what had already been done for the upper part of the province. If the resolutions failed to indicate how to avoid indemnifying any who had taken up arms, so too had the Act of 1841.[1]

The passage of the bill was, of course, an easy matter as far as obtaining a majority went. But nothing could exceed the furious opposition excited both within and without the parliament by the introduction of the bill. The old battle of the rebellion was fought over again. With Papineau back in the assembly, Mackenzie now revisiting the country under the Amnesty Act, the legis-

[1] 3 Vict. c. 76.

lature in session at Montreal and a French-Canadian at the head of the administration, it seemed to the excited Tories as if the days of 1837 had come back, and that they must rally again to fight the cause of British loyalty against the encroachments of an alien race. The bill for payment of the losses seemed like the crowning triumph of their foes, and the cry, "No pay for rebels," resounded throughout the province. Many Canadian writers, as for example, the late Sir John Bourinot in his *Lord Elgin*, have seen in the opposition of the Tories nothing more than a party contest, the familiar game in which a likely issue is seized upon in the hope of a sudden overthrow of the government. "The issue," he says, "was not one of public principle or of devotion to the Crown, it was simply a question of obtaining a party victory *per fas aut nefas*."[1]

The issue was not, indeed, in the real truth of the matter, a question of devotion to the Crown and the retention of the British connection. But the Tories, many of them, in all honesty saw it so. One has but to read the newspapers of the day to realize that something more than a mere party question was at issue. It was a contest in which right and justice were fighting hand to hand against a blind but honest fanaticism to whose distorted vision the Rebellion Losses Bill undid the work of the Loyalists of 1837. The rabble of the Montreal streets

[1] *Lord Elgin* (Makers of Canada Series), p. 68.

that burned the houses of parliament were doubtless inspired by no higher motive than the fierce lust
of destruction that animates an inflamed and unprincipled mob. But the opposition of Sir Allan
MacNab and the reputable leaders of Conservatism
was based on a genuine conviction that the safety
of the country was at stake. In the blindness of
their rage the Tories lost from sight entirely that
they themselves had sanctioned the payment of
compensation for losses in Upper Canada, that the
Draper government had itself originated the present movement, and that the bill expressly stipulated that nothing should be paid to "rebels" in
the true sense of the term. The reasoned logic of
LaFontaine's presentation of the bill fell upon ears
which the passion of the hour made deaf to
argument: the fiery invective of Solicitor-general
Blake, who answered the Tory accusation of disloyalty with a counter-accusation of the same
character, only maddened them to fury. In the
debate on the second reading of the bill the parliament became a scene of wild confusion. MacNab
had called the French-Canadians "aliens and
rebels." Blake in return taunted him with the
disloyalty that prompts a meaningless and des-
tructive opposition.

"I am not come here," said Blake,[1] "to learn
lessons of loyalty from honourable gentlemen

[1] An excellent account of the debate is given by Dent, *Canada Since
the Union*, Vol. II. pp. 151 *et seq.*

opposite. . . . I have no sympathy with the would-be loyalty of honourable gentlemen opposite, which, while it at all times affects peculiar zeal for the prerogative of the Crown, is ever ready to sacrifice the liberty of the subject. This is not British loyalty: it is the spurious loyalty which at all periods of the world's history has lashed humanity into rebellion. . . . The expression 'rebel' has been applied by the gallant knight opposite to some gentlemen on this side of the House, but I tell gentlemen on the other side that their public conduct has proved that *they* are the rebels to their constitution and country." For a man of MacNab's fighting temper, this was too much. "If the honourable member means to apply the word 'rebel' to me," he shouted, "I must tell him that it is nothing else than a lie." In a moment the House was in an uproar: Blake and MacNab were only prevented from coming to blows by the intervention of the sergeant-at-arms, while a storm of shouts and hisses from the crowded galleries added to the confusion of the House. Blake and MacNab were taken into custody by the sergeant-at-arms, several of the wilder spirits of the galleries were arrested, and the debate ended for the day.

Of the various arguments advanced against the bill in the Canadian parliament and elsewhere, two only are worth considering. It was said in the first place that under the terms of the bill a certain number of persons who, in heart if not in act, had been rebels would receive compensation. This was undoubtedly true, but was also unavoidable. Unless one were to have given to the commissioners inquisitorial and discretionary powers, unless, that is to say, they had been allowed to declare any one in retrospect a rebel simply on their general opinion of his conduct,—a remedy that would have been worse than the evil it strove to cure,—it is undoubtedly true that many of the disaffected inhabitants of the Lower Canada of 1837 could claim compensation. But it must be borne in mind that they could not claim compensation *for being disaffected*, but simply for having lost their property. The Act did the best that could be done. It accepted the only legal definition of "rebel" that was possible; namely, persons previously convicted as such. These it excluded. To all others who could prove damages compensation was to be given.

The other objection was perhaps more serious. It was urged against the bill that the Upper Canadian losses had been paid out of a special fund raised in Upper Canada; namely, the proceeds of the tavern licenses paid in that part of the province. The bill of 1849 proposed to pay the Lower Canadian losses out of the general fund of (united) Canada. By this method, it was argued, the people of Upper Canada were called upon to pay all of their own damages and a share of those of their neighbours. The answer made by the administration to this argument may be found in the speeches delivered by LaFontaine in March, 1849, and in a circular drawn up in Montreal, presumably by Hincks, in defence of the government, and subsequently printed in the London *Times*.[1] It ran as follows:—

The proceeds of tavern licenses, in both provinces, had previously formed part of the general fund. When Mr. Draper's Act of 1845 was passed, these proceeds were removed from the general fund and alienated to special uses in each section of the province. In Lower Canada they were given to the municipalities: in Upper Canada they were applied to the payment of the rebellion losses. Now in Upper Canada the sums in question were considerably greater than in Lower Canada: the license taxes in the one case amounted (taking an average of the last four years) to £9,664; in the other case to only £5,557. Hence, argued LaFontaine, the effect of the proceeding was to give to Upper Canada an overplus of £4,107 a year, which was equivalent to a capital sum of £68,454. The same kind of segregation had also (in 1846) been made of the marriage license proceeds, in which case the surplus accruing amounted to £1,785 and represented a capital of £29,764. Putting the two together it appears, according to LaFontaine's view of it, that Upper Canada thus received the equivalent of a capital sum of £98,000. Since the present bill only asked for £90,000 (the other

[1] March 23rd, 1849.

£10,000 of the £100,000 representing claims already certified), Lower Canada was only asking what was well within its rights. This argument of LaFontaine may, or may not, appear convincing. Since the Upper Canadian license tax was paid by the people of Upper Canada, it is hard to see that the surplus of its proceeds over the tax in Lower Canada had anything to do with the case. It must be remembered also that the Lower Canadian tax was used in Lower Canada. But the argument is part of the history of the time and is here given for what it is worth.

Intense excitement prevailed throughout Canada during the parliamentary discussion of the bill. Public meetings of protest were held by the Tories throughout the country. Petitions poured in against the measure, many of them directed to Lord Elgin himself, in order, if possible, to force him from his ground of constitutional neutrality. Resolutions were drawn up at a meeting in Toronto praying the queen to disallow the bill if it should pass. In many places the excitement thus occasioned led to violent demonstrations, in some cases, as at Belleville, to open riots. The inflamed state of public feeling at this period and the exasperation of the Tories are evidenced by the disturbances which occurred at Toronto on the reappearance of William Lyon Mackenzie. On this occasion Baldwin, Blake and the ex-leader of the rebels were burned in effigy in the streets of the town. The following is the exultant account given of the burning by the Toronto *Patriot*, the most thorough-going organ of Toryism.

"On Thursday evening [March 22nd, 1849], the inhabitants of Toronto witnessed a very uncommon spectacle—more uncommon than surprising at this time. The attorney-general, the proud solicitor-general and the hero of Gallows Hill were associated in one common fate, amid the cheers and exultations of the largest concourse of people beheld in Toronto since the election of Dunn and Buchanan. The three dolls,—would that their originals had been as harmless !—were elevated on long poles and paraded round the town, visiting the residences of the three noble individuals, and subsequently two of them were burned near Mr. Baldwin's residence and the third opposite Mr. McIntosh's, in Yonge Street, the house in which the humane and gallant Mackenzie had taken up his abode. It would be impossible to describe the expressions of indignation and disgust on the part of the people towards the triumvirate."

The scene was concluded by smashing in the front windows of the McIntosh house with a volley of stones. The partisan press spared no efforts to arouse a desperate opposition to the bill. "Men of Canada of British origin," pleaded the *Church*,[1] a forceful publication devoted to

[1] March 29th, 1849.

319

Anglican Toryism and the doctrines of Dr. Strachan, "no sleep to the eyes, no slumber to the eyelids, until you have avenged this most atrocious, this most unparalleled insult!" In the same month the New York *Herald* declared that the "fate of Canada was near at hand." "This may be the commencement," it said, "of a struggle which will end in the consummation so devoutly wished by the majority of the people,— a complete and perfect separation of those provinces from the rule of England."

In the mother country, both in and out of parliament, loud protests were raised against the measure. The London *Times* interpreted it as the selfish machination of a rebel faction. "As things have been turned upside down since 1838," said a *Times* editorial on the Canadian situation, "and what was then the rebel camp is now the government of Canada, it is obvious that no measure of compensation is likely to pass which does not include some of the offending gentlemen themselves in the bill of damages made out. The alternative is either no compensation to anybody, or to all alike. This must be very annoying to the Royalists *(sic)*, who marched to and fro, and who incurred expense, wounds, and loss of health by their prompt succour of the state. . . . If we would judge of the feelings excited in the breast of such ardent Royalists as Sir Allan MacNab, we must suppose a parliament of Chartists and Repealers, not only dividing among themselves all the offices of the State, but also compensating one another for their past sufferings with magnificent grants from the treasury." It is to be noted that the usual Tory designation of their party as Loyalists is not strong enough for the *Times* in this issue, which implies a still more chivalrous degree of devotion to the throne by using the term Royalists. The same article speaks of the "*loyal* population of Canada being considerably excited," talks of their settled "impression that rebellion has been rewarded and loyalty insulted by the British Crown," and describes Canada as a "colony that hangs by a thread."[1]

The crowning event in the agitation against the Act of Indemnification was the riot at Montreal, which broke out on the news that Lord Elgin had given his assent to the bill. This was on April 25th, 1849. Lord Elgin's consent to the measure was, of course, the result of due deliberation, but the immediate circumstances of giving assent were of a somewhat hurried character. Among other bills awaiting his sanction was the new tariff bill. Navigation was just opening at Montreal and the sudden news that an incoming vessel was sighted in the river induced Lord Elgin, at the request of the ministry,[2] to proceed in haste to the houses

[1] London *Times*, March 21st, 1849.

[2] Hincks went out to "Monklands" to request the governor-general to assent at once to the tariff bill. *Reminiscences*, p. 194.

of parliament. It seemed to Lord Elgin that he might as well take advantage of the occasion to assent to the other bills that were also waiting his approval. The news that the bill had become law spread rapidly through the town, and the haste of Lord Elgin's proceedings gave an entirely false colour to what had happened. As the governor-general left the houses of parliament "after the consummation of his nefarious act," (to use the words of a Tory journalist),[1] he was greeted with the "groans and curses" of a crowd that had assembled about the building. As he drove through the city on his way to his official residence of "Monklands," the groans and curses were accompanied with a shower of random missiles. Stones crashed against the sides of the governor's carriage and rotten eggs bespattered it with filth, but no serious harm was done to its occupants. As the evening drew on the excitement throughout the city increased apace. The fire bells of the town were rung to call the people into the streets, and a printed announcement was passed through the crowd that a mass meeting would be held at eight o'clock in the Champ de Mars.

All this time the House was in session. MacNab warned the ministry that a riot was brewing, but the government were reluctant to make a precipitate call for military help. At eight o'clock the wide expanse of the Champ de Mars was filled

[1] Montreal *Courier*.

with a surging and excited mob, howling with applause as it listened to speeches in denunciation of the tyranny that had been perpetrated. Presently from among the crowd the cry arose, " To the parliament house," and the rioters, ready for any violence, hurried through the narrow streets of the lower town to the legislative building. On their way they wrecked the offices of the *Pilot* with a shower of stones. A few minutes later a similar volley burst in the windows of the house of parliament. The members fled from the hall in confusion, while the rioters invaded the building and filled the hall of the assembly itself. The furniture, chandeliers and fittings of the hall were smashed to pieces in the wild rage of destruction. A member of the crowd took his seat in the speaker's chair and shouted, " I dissolve this House."

While the tumult and destruction were still in progress, the cry was raised, " The parliament house is on fire." The west end of the building, doubtless deliberately fired by the rioters, was soon a sheet of flames. The fire spread fiercely from room to room and from wing to wing of the building. " The fury and rapidity with which the flames spread," said an eye-witness, "can hardly be imagined : in less than fifteen minutes the whole of the wing occupied by the House of Assembly was in flames, and, owing to the close connection between the two halls of the legislature, the

chamber of the legislative council was involved
in the same destruction." The fierce light of the
flames illuminated the city from the mountain to
the river, and spread fear in the hearts of its inhabitants. The firemen who arrived on the scene
were forcibly held back from staying the progress
of the fire, and the houses of the parliament of
Canada burned fiercely to ruin. The assembly
library of twenty thousand volumes perished in the
flames. MacNab, with characteristic loyalty, rescued
from the burning building the portrait of his beloved queen. The military, at length arrived on
the ground, stayed the progress of further violence,
but the wild excitement that pervaded the popu-
lace of the city boded further trouble. Next evening the riots broke out again. Attacks were made
on the houses of Hincks and Wolfred Nelson.
The boarding house on St. Antoine Street, occupied by Baldwin and Price, was assaulted with a
shower of stones: LaFontaine's residence—a new
house which he had just purchased, but where he
was fortunately not at that moment in residence
—was attacked, the furniture demolished, and the
stables given to the flames. Not until the evening
of the twenty-seventh did the troops, aided by
a thousand special constables armed with cutlasses
and pistols, succeed in restoring order to the
streets.

Three days later the governor-general, attempting to drive into the city from his residence,

where he had remained since the twenty-fifth, was again attacked. As he passed through the streets on his way to the government offices in the Château de Ramezay on Notre Dame Street, volleys of stones and other missiles greeted the progress of his carriage. Before reaching his destination Lord Elgin found his way blocked with a howling, furious crowd, while shouts of "Down with the governor-general" urged the mob to violence. The governor's escort of troops succeeded in forcing back the crowd and effecting his entrance into the building, but his return journey was converted into a precipitate flight, the crowd pursuing the vice-regal carriage in "cabs, *calèches* and everything that would run." Fortunately Lord Elgin escaped unhurt, but his brother was severely injured by a stone hurled after the carriage and several of his escort were hurt. Such were the disgraceful scenes which lost for Montreal the dignity of being the seat of government.

It was but natural that the progress of events in Canada should excite great attention in the mother country. In the British parliament, the government of Lord John Russell was prepared to defend the right of the Canadians to legislate as they pleased in regard to the matter at issue. Mr. Roebuck and the Radicals went even further and defended the equity of the bill itself. The Peelites, or at any rate the greater part of them, voted with the government against interference. But the thorough-going Tories insisted on viewing the issue as one between loyalty and treason, and demanded that the imperial government should either disallow the Act or contravene its operation by an Act of the British parliament. In the middle of the month of June the Canadian question was debated both in the House of Commons and in the House of Lords. Not the least important of those who appeared as the champions of the Canadian Tories was Mr. Gladstone. His rising reputation, the especial attention he had devoted to colonial questions, and the fact that he had been Lord Stanley's successor as colonial secretary in the cabinet of Sir Robert Peel, combined to render him a formidable adversary to the Canadian ministry. His speech on the Rebellion Losses Act shows his usual marvellous command of detail and powers of presentation. Mr. Gladstone's great objection to the Canadian statute was that, in his opinion, a large number of virtual rebels would receive compensation under its operation: he begged that Lord John Russell's government would either disallow the Act or obtain from the Canadian parliament an amendment of its provisions which should place the compensation on a basis more strictly defined. But what is still more noticeable in Mr. Gladstone's speech is his opinion that the government had allowed Lord Elgin too great latitude in the matter, and that the scope of the Act exceeded the proper limits of colonial power. "It might not be politic for the colonial secretary," he said, "to interpose his advice in respect to merely local matters, but it was his first duty to tender his advice regarding measures which involved not only imperial rights but the honour of the Crown. That advice ought not to be delayed until a measure assumed the form of a statute, but should be given at the first possible moment, and before public opinion was appealed to in the country."

Roebuck, Disraeli and others participated in the debate and a certain Mr. Cochrane, representing the outraged patriotism of the extreme Tories, referred in scathing terms to Baldwin and LaFontaine, speaking of them as fugitives from justice in the days of the rebellion.

The speech of Mr. Gladstone on the Canadian question is of especial importance in the present narrative in that it called forth an answer from the pen of Francis Hincks, in the form of a letter to the London *Times*.[1] Shortly after the passage of the indemnification bill Hincks had left Montreal (May 14th, 1849) for England. The object of his visit was, in the first place, of a financial character, the Canadian government being anxious to negotiate its securities in the London market. But the inspector-general acted also as a special envoy to the imperial cabinet in regard to the great question of the day and discussed the Rebellion Losses question with Lord John Russell and Earl Grey.

[1] London *Times*, June 20th, 1849.

Hincks also conversed on the subject in detail with Mr. Gladstone who found himself unable to adopt the views of the Canadian minister.

In his letter to the *Times*, Hincks deals at some length with Mr. Gladstone's arguments in regard to the "payment of rebels." In the debates in the recent session of the Canadian parliament, Hincks had said that certain persons convicted of high treason in Upper Canada had received compensation under the Upper Canada Rebellion Losses Act, which was carried into effect by Tory commissioners under instructions from a Tory government. Both Disraeli and Gladstone had dissented from this. Disraeli had broadly asserted that there had been no rebels in Upper Canada, and that consequently no restrictive clauses were necessary in the Act for that section of the province. Gladstone had said that "there was no ground to suppose that any rebel had received any sum by way of compensation." Hincks, by a very accurate citation of individual cases, shows that there *were* rebels in Upper Canada and that *some* of them, at any rate, had received compensation under the Act. Hincks does not mean to imply that, as a consequence of this, the government should expressly seek to reward the rebels of the Lower Province. "I do not of course mean to contend that, if it be wrong rebels should be compensated for their losses, the fact that they were so compensated in Upper Canada is any excuse for the Lower Canada Act. But I do contend that it is highly discreditable to a party which, when in power, admitted claims of this description without the slightest complaint, to agitate the entire province, to get up an excitement which they themselves are unable to control, because their opponents have introduced a measure much more stringent in its details, but under which it is possible that some parties suspected or accused of treason, but never convicted, may be paid."

The letter concludes with some interesting paragraphs in which the writer discusses the strictures that had been passed in the course of the debate in the House of Commons[1] upon the leaders of the Canadian ministry. "Nothing can be more untrue," writes Hincks, "than the allegation that any member of the present administration was implicated in the rebellion. No reward was ever offered for the apprehension of any one of them. Mr. Baldwin never was a fugitive from justice. Such absurd statements as I have heard regarding occurrences in Canada, only prove that it is very unsafe for parties at a distance of three thousand miles to interfere in our affairs. I confess, however, that I was not very sorry that the members of the House of Commons had an opportunity afforded them of hearing at least

[1] See especially the speech of Mr. B. Cochrane (London *Times*, June 15th, 1849) and his reference to Baldwin, LaFontaine, Papineau, and the "arch-traitor Mackenzie."

one speech in the true Canadian Tory spirit, as they are enabled to judge of the manner in which the passions of the mob of Montreal were inflamed.

"Let me, in conclusion," wrote Hincks, "say a word or two regarding 'French domination.' I should imagine that the author of *Coningsby* [Mr. Disraeli] understands the meaning of getting up a 'good cry' to serve party purposes. The cry of the Canadian Tory party is 'French domination,' and it is especially intended to excite the sympathy of people in England who understand little about our politics, but who are naturally inclined to sympathize with a British party governed by French influence. A little reflection would convince them that 'French domination' cannot exist in the united province. I need scarcely say that it is wholly untrue that it does exist. The administration consists of five members from Upper Canada and five from Lower Canada. The former represent some of the most important constituencies in Upper Canada. If the administration of the government or of the legislature were made subservient to French influence, is it probable, I would ask, that the government would be supported by the British people of Upper Canada? All I shall say in conclusion is, that I claim for myself and my colleagues from Upper Canada— and in truth and justice I should say for my Lower Canadian colleagues also—that we have as much true British feeling as any member of that party which seems to wish to monopolize it."

The financial purpose of Hincks's visit to England—the strengthening of the credit of the colony in the London market—was accomplished with marked success. The inspector-general realized that the agitation occasioned by recent events, and the pervading ignorance in reference to the economic position and prospects of Canada, seriously prejudiced the securities of the province in the eyes of the British investors. To meet this situation, Hincks prepared and published in London a pamphlet entitled, *Canada and its Financial Resources*. In this publication he shows that the money hitherto borrowed by the Canadian government had been employed in public works of a sound and reproductive character. The imperial guarantee loan of £1,500,000 and the issue of provincial debentures of a somewhat larger sum make a gross total of £3,223,839, and represent the larger part of the cost of the public works of the province, the total cost being estimated by Hincks at £3,703,781 sterling. In order to show the utility and profitableness of the expenditure thus made, Hincks composed a series of tables showing the growth and progress of the colony for the last twenty-five years. The population of Upper Canada had risen, between 1824 and 1848, from 151,097 to 723,000 inhabitants: Lower Canada, whose population in 1825 had stood at 423,630, now contained 766,000 souls. The land under cultivation in Upper Canada had increased during the same period from 535,212 to 2,673,820 acres : the yield of local taxation in Upper Canada had increased from £10,235 to £86,058 ; while the estimated revenue for the united province in the current year stood at £574,640, a sum whose proportion to the public debt showed the stable condition of the provincial finances. Although financial and fiscal discussion forms the major part of Hincks's pamphlet, he deals also with the political situation, reasserts the essential loyalty of the Reform party, urges the necessity for the further development of the province and calls for imperial aid in the building of an intercolonial railway. The effect of this pamphlet and of the series of letters of a similar character which Hincks contributed to the *Daily Mail* in the following August, was most happy. An increasing confidence on the part of the British public in the financial soundness of the Canadian government, tended to offset the unfortunate effect produced by the agitation over the Act of Indemnification.

The attitude of Lord Elgin in regard to the Rebellion Losses Bill has been much discussed. At the time of the adoption of the measure his conduct was made the subject of mistaken censure from various quarters. He was blamed for not having refused his assent to the bill: he was blamed for not having dissolved the parliament: he was blamed for having afterwards remained for weeks at "Monklands" without having insisted on forcing his way into the city under military protection. But time has justified his conduct in every respect. One must read the journals of the time to appreciate how much the governor-general was called upon to bear, and with what grave responsibility the office of constitutional head of the country becomes invested in moments of danger. The Tory press was filled with bitter personal attacks. "This man's father," said the Montreal *Courier*, "was denounced by the noblest bard, but one, that England ever produced, as the Robber of the Greek Temples;[1] his son will be heard of in future times as the man who lost for England the noble colony won by the blood of Wolfe." Compare with this the utterance of Lord Elgin made at the same time. "I am prepared to bear any amount of obloquy that may be cast upon me, but, if I can possibly prevent it, no stain of blood shall rest upon my name."

In his treatment of the Rebellion Losses Bill and his firm conviction that it was his duty to give his assent, Lord Elgin achieved for Canada one of the greatest victories of its constitutional progress. "By reserving the bill," wrote Lord Elgin afterwards, "I should only throw on Her Majesty's

[1] The reference is, of course, to the collection of the Elgin marbles.

government a responsibility which rests, and I
think, ought to rest, on me. . . . If I had dissolved parliament, I might have produced a rebellion, but assuredly I should not have procured
a change of ministry." As the sight of flame and
the sound of riot drifts into the past, a momentous
achievement appears written large on the surface
of our history by Lord Elgin's acceptance of the
Act of Indemnification. It signified that, from now
on, the government of Canada, whether conducted
ill or well, was at least to be conducted by the
people—the majority of the people—of Canada
itself. The history of responsible government in
our country reaches here its culmination.

CHAPTER XI

THE END OF THE MINISTRY

THE story of responsible government, with which the present volume is mainly concerned, practically ends, as has just been said, with the passage of the Rebellion Losses Bill. The history of the concluding sessions of the LaFontaine-Baldwin administration, of the disintegration of the ministry and of the reconstruction of the Reform government under Hincks and Morin, belongs elsewhere. It has, moreover, already received ample treatment in other volumes of the present series.[1] We are here approaching the days of the Clear Grits, of Radicals breaking from Reformers, of a *Parti Rouge*, of recrudescent Toryism and the political match-making of the coalition era. But some brief account of the decline and end of the LaFontaine-Baldwin administration may here be appended.

Union in opposition is notoriously easier than union in office. Opposition is a negative function, the work of government is positive. It was but natural, therefore, that with the accession of the Reform party to power and the definite acceptance of the great principle which had held them to-

---

[1] See Sir J. Bourinot, *Lord Elgin*, and John Lewis, *George Brown*.

gether, differences of opinion which had been held in abeyance during the struggle for power, now began to make themselves felt. The Reformers were by profession a party of progress, and it was natural that some among them should aim at a more rapid rate of advance than others. "It cannot be expected," wrote Hincks, reviewing in later days the period before us, "that there will be the same unanimity among the members of a party of progress as in one formed to resist organic changes: in the former there will always be a section dissatisfied with what they think the inertness of their leaders."[1]

Moreover, the great upheaval of the Rebellion Losses agitation tended to throw into a strong light all existing differences of opinion and to intensify political feeling. The movement towards annexation with the United States in the summer of 1849, which led a number of the British residents of Montreal to sign a manifesto in its favour, was doubtless dictated as much by political spite as by serious conviction.[2] But it is characteristic, none the less, of the precipitating influence exercised upon the formation of parties by the great agitation. In addition to this, the recent events in Europe—chartism and the repeal move-

[1] *Political History*, p. 39.

[2] Sir John Abbott speaking in the senate in 1889 said that the "annexation manifesto was the outburst of a movement of petulance." See also J. Pope, *Life of Sir John A. Macdonald*, Vol. I., p. 70.

ment in the British Isles, and the democratic revolutions on the continent—gave a strong impulse to the doctrines of Radicalism, and at the same time repelled many people from the party of progress and directed them towards the party of order and stability. The years of the mid-century were consequently an era in which the formation and movements of parties were modified under new and powerful impulses.

In despite of this, the LaFontaine-Baldwin administration throughout the years 1849 and 1850 remained in a position of exceptional power. It suffered indeed to some extent from the desertion of Malcolm Cameron who resigned his place in a ministry that moved too slowly for his liking (December, 1849), and from the elevation of so strong a combatant as Mr. Blake to the calmer atmosphere of the bench. But it gained something also from the propitious circumstances of the time. The cloud of commercial depression that had hung over Canada was passing away. The removal of the last of the British Navigation Acts in 1849—for which Baldwin, a convinced free trader, and his fellow-Reformers had long since petitioned the imperial government—brought to the ports of the St. Lawrence in the ensuing year an entry of nearly one hundred foreign vessels: the completion of the works on the Welland Canal, on which in all some $6,269,000 had been expended, seemed to inaugurate a new era for the shipping trade of the

Great Lakes, while the prospect of an early reciprocity with the United States and the Maritime Provinces, and the extension of the railroad system, were rapidly reviving the agriculture and commerce of the united provinces. The bountiful harvest of 1850 came presently to add the climax to the national prosperity.

The ministry, therefore, in despite of the progress of Radicalism, which was soon to threaten its existence, was able in the session of 1850 to carry out several reform measures of great importance. The seat of government had meantime, in accordance with an address from the legislature, been transferred to the city of Toronto, which was henceforth to alternate with Quebec, in four year periods, in the honour of being the provincial capital. The appearance of Lord Elgin at the old parliament buildings on Front Street was greeted with loud acclamations from a loyal population, and the Tory party, after one or two unsuccessful attempts to undo the Act of Indemnification by further legislation, found themselves compelled to accept the inevitable. The reorganization of the postal system, now transferred to the control of Canada, with the lowering of postal rates, was one of the leading reforms effected in the session. A new school law for Upper Canada carried out more completely the system inaugurated under Mr. Draper's Act,[1] and confirmed the principle of granting separate schools

---

[1] See above p. 255.

to Roman Catholics. An improved jury system, a reorganization of the division courts and certain amendments in the election law, were also among the results of the session's work. It was noted with congratulation by the friends of the ministry that not a single bill adopted by the legislature was reserved by the governor-general. The *Globe* in calling attention to the fact, "unprecedented in Canadian history," declared that it proved "the practical existence of responsible government."

The legislative success of the session of 1850 was perhaps more apparent than real. Some great questions of practical reform—notably those of the Clergy Reserves and of Seigniorial Tenure—were still pressing for solution. In these two vexed problems, which had stood before the politicians of the two Canadas for a generation past like twin riddles of the sphinx, were contained the eternal problem of the Church and the State, and the like problem of landed aristocracy against unlanded democracy. On these the party of the Reformers could find no common ground of agreement. These two issues and the natural drift of political thought of the time were bringing out more clearly each day the difference between Radicals and Reformers. Neither Baldwin nor LaFontaine had anything of the complexion of a Radical. The former, indeed, showed in his private walk of life much of that reverence for the things and ideas of the past, which is often a part of the inconsistent equipment of the Liberal politician. In his Municipal Act his resuscitation of the Saxon term "reeve" had excited the kindly ridicule of his contemporaries. LaFontaine too had much that was conservative in his temperament, and though in his younger years no over zealous practitioner of religion, he set his face strongly against anything that savoured of spoliation of the rightful claims of the Church. As against the moderation and tempered zeal of the chiefs, the intemperate haste and unqualified doctrines of some of their followers now began to stand in rude contrast. The latter urged the full measure of the Democratic programme. "Take from the churches," they said, "their reserved lands that are merely a relic of old time ecclesiastical privilege, change this mediæval seignior of Lower Canada and his tenants into ordinary property-holders, and give us in our constitutions a full and untrammelled application of the principles of popular election,—an elected assembly, an elected Upper House and an elected governor at the head."

Many of the leaders of the new Radicalism were men not without influence in the community. There was, in Upper Canada, William Lyon Mackenzie, now returned from his ungrateful exile to fish in the troubled waters as an Independent, and aspiring again to popular leadership; Dr. John Rolph, the agitator of the pre-rebellion days, who had ridden out with Baldwin to interview the rebels at Montgomery's tavern, and who, like Mackenzie, had known the bitterness of exile; Macdougall, a lawyer by title but by predilection a politician and journalist, once a contributor to the *Examiner* but now the editor of a Radical publication called the *North American*. With these was Malcolm Cameron, the recently resigned commissioner of public works. Out of this material was being formed the new party of the Radicals, a party that boasted that it wanted only men of " clear grit," and whose members presently became known as the Clear Grits.[1] Their platform, which shows the infection of European democratic movements, consisted of the following demands: The application of the elective principle to all the officials and institutions of the country, from the head of the government downwards; universal suffrage; vote by ballot; biennial parliaments; abolition of the property qualification for members of parliament; a fixed term for the holding of general elections and for the meeting of the legislature; retrenchment; abolition of pensions to judges; abolition of the courts of common pleas and chancery and the enlargement of the jurisdiction of the court of queen's bench; reduction of lawyers' fees; free trade; direct taxation; an amended jury law; abolition or modification of the usury laws; abolition of primogeniture; secular-

[1] Mackenzie called himself Independent, but naturally fell into alliance with the Grits.

ization of the Clergy Reserves and the abolition of the rectories that had been created out of that endowment.[1]

Such was the original group of the Clear Grits. In later times their designation—or at least the term "Grit"—was applied to the Reformers generally and especially to the adherents of George Brown.[2] But in the beginning Brown had little sympathy with the new party and remained, in spite of certain Radical leanings, an adherent of LaFontaine and Baldwin till the last. His paper, the *Globe*, at first denounced the Grits as "a miserable clique of office-seeking, bunkum-talking cormorants, that met in a certain lawyer's office on King Street [Macdougall's] and announced their intention to form a new party on Clear Grit principles."

At the same time in Lower Canada a Radical party, following the lead of Papineau, was being formed in opposition to the policy of LaFontaine. The career of Papineau has been the subject of so many conflicting opinions, has met with such extremes of approbation and censure, that it is difficult to hazard an opinion on the merit of his political conduct at this time. With LaFontaine and the ministry he was entirely out of sympathy. Lord Elgin, who spoke of him as "Guy Fawkes,

[1] Platform adopted at a meeting of the party at Markham, March 23rd, 1850.

[2] John Lewis, *George Brown* (Makers of Canada Series), pp. 40, 41.

viewed him with dislike. But among his compatriots a group of the younger men, now called the *Parti Rouge* and including A. A. Dorion, Doutre, Dessaules and others, followed the lead of Papineau and advocated a programme of an equally Radical character to that of the Clear Grits. In their party organ, *L'Avenir*, they demanded universal suffrage, the repeal of the union with Upper Canada, the abolition of the church tithes and election of the Upper House, while many of them openly advocated republicanism and annexation to the United States. In the legislature of 1850 Papineau maintained against the measures of LaFontaine an unremitting opposition, and made common cause with MacNab and his party in voting against the government. To add to the difficulties that were gathering about the administration, Brown, of the *Globe* (hitherto their firm supporter), incited by the agitation in England over the Ecclesiastical Titles controversy, commenced an outcry against Roman Catholicism and all its works.

By far the worst difficulties of the ministry lay, however, in the Clergy Reserves question.[1] The history of this long-standing controversy may be epitomized thus: the Constitutional Act of 1791[2] empowered the Crown to set apart in each prov-

---

[1] See Charles Lindsey, *The Clergy Reserves.*

[2] 31 Geo. III. c. 31. See W. Houston, *Documents Illustrative of the Canadian Constitution,* for text of the Act with comments.

ince for the maintenance and support of a Protestant clergy one-eighth of the public lands as yet unallotted: the Crown also had power to erect and endow rectories out of the reserve, whose incumbents should be "presented" by the governor, after the practice of presentation in England. In other words, the aim of the Act was to create in the two provinces an endowed State Church. The same statute gave to the parliament of each province power to alter or repeal these arrangements as it might see fit, provided always that such action was sanctioned by the imperial parliament. The Reserves had been at first exclusively claimed and enjoyed by the Church of England. Grave dissatisfaction arose. The other Protestant Churches claimed that the terms of the Act permitted of their participation in the reserve. The settlers also complained that the arrangement impeded settlement, hindered the making of roads and tended to interpose waste spaces among the farms of the colonies.

In 1819 an opinion, delivered by the law officers of the Crown, declared that the ministers of the Church of Scotland were entitled to a share in the Reserves. The old Reform party in Upper Canada of the days before the rebellion, protested against this form of State aid to the two Churches. Some Reformers wanted all sects to participate, others wished the whole system abolished. In 1831 the imperial government had invited the legislature of Upper Canada to adopt a measure for the settlement of the question. Nothing, however, was agreed upon. No special endowments of rectories were made until 1836, when Sir John Colborne signed patents creating forty-four of them. This occasioned still louder protest. In Lower Canada, already settled and less subject to the allotment of new lands, the matter of the Clergy Reserves never became an acute question. It was the policy of the Roman Catholic Church not to oppose ecclesiastical endowment by the State.[1]

In 1840 the parliament of Upper Canada passed an Act distributing the lands among the various Protestant sects. This Act was disallowed, but an imperial Act[2] of 1840 made a new disposition of the Reserves. Certain parts of the Church land had already[3] been sold. The funds arising from these sales were to be distributed, in the proportion of two to one, between the Churches of England and Scotland. The rest of the Reserves were now to be sold. Of the proceeds arising, one-third was to go to the Church of England, one-sixth to the Church of Scotland, and the remainder, at the discretion of the governor in council, was to be applied to "purposes of public worship and religious instruction in Canada."

[1] In Upper Canada 2,395,687 acres were reserved ; in Lower Canada 934,050 acres.

[2] 3 and 4 Vict. c. 78.

[3] In virtue of 7 and 8 Geo. IV. c. 62.

In accordance with this, distribution was made of
these funds among the Dissenting denominations.

Such was the position of the Reserves question
in the year 1850 : the Church lands, while no
longer blocking settlement,[1] since they were offered
for sale when allotted, constituted a fund of which
the Anglican Church received the lion's share, but
in which all Protestant denominations participated.
Many of the Reform party were anxious to leave
the matter where it was, but the Radicals were
determined to have done with all connection between Church and State and to force the question
to an issue. Price, the commissioner of Crown
lands, in the session of 1850, brought in a series
of resolutions declaring the reservation of the
public domain for religious purposes to have long
been a source of intense discontent, and asking the
imperial parliament to grant to the Canadian legislature plenary powers to deal with the lands as it
should see fit. One of these resolutions (June 21st,
1850) read : "No religious denomination can be
held to have such vested interest in the revenue
derived from the proceeds of the said Clergy Reserves as should prevent further legislation with
respect to the disposal of them." On Price's resolutions, which were finally carried, the ministry was
divided. Hincks, who had seconded the resolutions,

[1] Previous to 1827 the lands reserved could not be sold for the
benefit of the Church. They could only be leased. In 1827 power was
given to sell one-quarter of the land. The amount which could be sold
in any one year was limited to one hundred thousand acres.

346

was in favour of the secularization of the Reserves. Of this policy he had been a consistent advocate for many years past.[1]

Secularization, however, could only be accomplished by first inducing the imperial parliament to repeal the Act of 1840 and to refer the whole question to the Canadian legislature. Hincks's practical political experience told him that this end could be best accomplished by avoiding any action which might antagonize the British parliament, and in especial the House of Lords, by seeming to make Canadian jurisdiction a menace to the privileges of the Church. "It was clearly our policy," he wrote subsequently, "to ask for a repeal of the imperial Act on the ground of our constitutional right to settle the question according to Canadian opinion, and not to declare to a body sufficiently prejudiced and containing a bench of bishops, that our object was secularization." Hincks was, therefore, of opinion that the existing ministry should content itself with asking for the repeal. The policy to be afterwards adopted could be agreed upon in its own time. Though aware of the difference of opinion between himself and certain of his colleagues, he saw nothing in that difference to demand a reconstruction of the administration. Whatever the individual opinions of the ministers

---

[1] *Reminiscences,* pp. 278 *et seq.* Hincks published a series of letters on the Clergy Reserves question in the Montreal *Herald*, December, 1882.

might be on the subject, there were no immediate measures, he argued, which the Canadian government could take towards secularization. " To have broken up the LaFontaine government," he wrote, " because its leader would not pledge himself to support secularization, when it was uncertain whether we could obtain the repeal of the imperial Act of 1840, would have been an act of consummate folly, indeed hardly short of madness."

Nevertheless, the divergence of opinion in the cabinet was a palpable fact. LaFontaine believed in Canadian control: he desired the repeal of the Act of 1840: but he did not believe in the policy of secularization. Rightly conceiving that the alienation of the Reserves to other than religious purposes was the intent of Price's resolution quoted above, he gave his vote against it. Baldwin, to his deep regret, found himself compelled to vote against LaFontaine on this resolution. His attitude, as expressed in his speech on this occasion, honest though it was, was hardly calculated to hold political support. He admitted that previous to the imperial Act of 1840, he had, along with his fellow-Reformers, believed in the secularization of the Reserves and their application to provincial education: the passage of the Act had altered his opinion and he believed they ought to adhere as far as possible to the purpose it indicated. He did not regard the reserved lands as being entirely the property of the people, but recognized the vested interest created

348

by imperial legislation. At the same time he expressed himself as opposed to any union between Church and State, and declared that he did not regard the Act of 1840 as necessarily a final settlement. With this rather vague statement of his position, Baldwin voted in favour of the resolution condemned by LaFontaine. The opportunity offered by the evident lack of union on the part of the ministry was not lost on the Opposition. Even before the vote referred to, Boulton of the Conservative party tried to amend one of the resolutions by substituting a motion, "that, in the language of the Hon. Robert Baldwin in his address to the electors of the fourth riding of the county of York on December 8th, 1847, preparatory to the last election, when an adviser of the Crown on a great public question avows a scheme which his colleagues dare not approve, public safety and public morals require that they should separate."

The difference of opinion thus evinced among the members of the ministry was not calculated to strengthen their hold on their majority. At the same time the parallel question of seigniorial tenure[1] was weakening their support in Lower Canada. This was a legacy of the old French régime under which about eight million *arpents* of land had been granted to the seigniors on a feudal

---

[1] An admirable account of the system is to be found in the recent work of Professor W. H. Munro of Harvard University, *The Seigniorial System in Canada*. (Longmans, Green, & Co., N. Y., 1907.)

basis. The holders of land *(censitaires)* under the seigniors had a permanent right of occupancy but were
compelled to pay fixed yearly dues in money and
in kind, and in the event of their selling out their
tenancy must pay one-twelfth of the purchase price
to their lord. The latter had also various vexatious
privileges, such as the *droit de banalité*, or sole
right of grinding corn. Whatever may have been
the merits of the system in aiding the first establishment of the colony, it had long since become an
anachronism. Agitation against the tenure had gone
on for years, but with the exception of a law of
1825 which permitted the seignior and *censitaire* by
joint consent to terminate the tenure, nothing had
been done. Granted that the system was to be
abolished, the difficult question remained, how to
abolish it. Was the land to be handed over to the
censitaire as his property in fee simple, or was it to
be given to the seignior as his absolute property, or
was some adjustment, involving proper compensation, possible? The Reformers of Lower Canada
were much divided; some of them wished to see
the seigniors expropriated without compensation;
others to expropriate them with compensation;
others to leave the matter to voluntary arrangement aided by legislation, but not compulsory; and
others, finally, such as Papineau (himself a seignior)
wished to leave the matter where it was. LaFontaine, while believing in the historic value of
the system, considered it injurious at the present

time to the interests of agriculture; he wished to
see it abolished, but wished to find means to respect
the interests of the seigniors by a proper compensation. The reference of the matter to a committee,
and the presentation of various tentative bills,
afforded no solution, and the matter dragged forward from the session of 1850 to that of 1851, while
the prolonged delay led several of the Reformers to
accuse LaFontaine of deliberately temporizing for
fear of losing parliamentary support.

The end of the great ministry came in the succeeding session, that of 1851. The opposition of the
Clear Grits to the government was growing more
and more pronounced and the two unsolved questions proved a standing hindrance to the reunion of
the Reform party. A Canadian writer[1] has said
that the Reform party had become too ponderous
to be held together and that it broke of its own
weight. Indeed the united strength of the Reformers, Radicals, Clear Grits, Independents and the
Parti Rouge, so completely outnumbered the Conservatives, that it was vain to expect to find
all sections of the party disregarding their own
special views for the sake of continuing to outvote
so small a minority. The temptation was rather for
the leaders of the separate groups to court new alli-
ances, which might convert their subordinate position in the Reform party into a dominant position in a new combination. In this way we can

---

[1] F. Taylor, *Portraits of British Americans,* Vol. III, p. 84.

understand the vote which, midway in the session of 1851, led to the resignation of Robert Baldwin.

Mackenzie, who was aiding the Clear Grits in their persistent opposition to the cabinet, brought in a motion (June 26th, 1851) in favour of abolishing the court of chancery—one of the reforms recommended in the platforms of the Clear Grits. This court, formerly a valid subject of grievance, had been reorganized by Baldwin in his Act of 1849, and he had seen no reason to regard its present operation as unsatisfactory. Mackenzie's motion was rejected, but its rejection was only effected by the votes of LaFontaine and his French-Canadian supporters: twenty-seven of the Upper Canadian votes were given against Baldwin, many of them representing the opinion of Upper Canadian lawyers. Under happier auspices Baldwin might not have regarded this vote as a matter of vital importance, for he had never professed himself a believer in the doctrine of the "double majority,"[1] the need, that is to say, of a majority support in each section of the province at the same time. But the mortification arising in this instance was coupled with a realization of the difficulties that were thickening about the government, and with a knowledge that the

[1] Turcotte *(Canada sous l'Union*, p. 173*)* says that Baldwin by his resignation sanctioned the principle of the "double majority." But compare Hincks, *Political History*, p. 28. See also letter of Baldwin to LaFontaine, cited above, pp. 263-5.

Reform party was passing under other guidance than that of its early leaders. The vote on the chancery question was merely made the occasion for a resignation which could henceforth only be a question of time.

Baldwin's resignation was tendered on June 30th, 1851. All parties united in courteous expressions of appreciation of his great services to the country, and the chivalrous MacNab expressed his regret at the determination of his old-time adversary. Almost immediately after the resignation of Baldwin, LaFontaine expressed his intention of retiring from public life after the close of the session. He, too, had wearied of the struggle to maintain union where none was. The committee on seigniorial tenure, moreover, reported a proposal for a bill which LaFontaine found himself compelled to consider a measure of confiscation. The consciousness that his views on this all-important subject could no longer command a united support confirmed him in his intention to abandon political life. Indeed, for some years, LaFontaine had suffered keenly from the disillusionment that attends political life. As far back as September 23rd, 1845, he had expressed his weariness of office in a confidential letter to Baldwin. "As to myself," he wrote, "I sincerely hope I will never be placed in a situation to be obliged to take office again. The more I see, the more I feel disgusted. It seems as if duplicity, deceit, want of sincerity, selfishness, were virtues. It gives me a poor idea of human nature."[1]

The parliamentary session terminated on August 30th, 1851. It was generally known throughout the country that LaFontaine would carry into effect, in the ensuing autumn, the intention of resignation which he had expressed. His approaching retirement from public life was made the occasion of a great banquet in his honour held at the St. Lawrence Hotel, Montreal, (October 1st, 1851.) Morin, the life-long associate in the political career of the leader of French Canada, occupied the chair, while Leslie, Holmes, Nelson and other prominent Reformers were among those present. The speech of LaFontaine on this occasion, on which he bid farewell to public life, is of great interest. In it he passes in review the political evolution of French Canada during his public career.

"Twenty-one years ago," said LaFontaine,[2] "when first I entered upon political life, we were under a very different government. I refer to the method of its administration. We had a government in which the parliament had no influence,—the government of all British colonies. Under this government the people had no power, save only the power of refusing subsidies. This was the sole resource of the House of Assembly, and we can

[1] *MS. Letters of LaFontaine and Baldwin.* Toronto Public Library.

[2] The speech is translated from *La Minerve*, October 4th, 1851.

readily conceive with what danger such a resource was fraught. It was but natural that this system should give occasion to many abuses.

"We commenced, therefore, our struggle to extirpate these abuses, to establish that form of government that it was our right to have and which we have to-day,—true representative English government. Let it be borne in mind that under our former system of government all our struggles were vain and produced only that racial hate and animosity which is happily passing from us to-day, and which, I venture to hope, this banquet may tend still further to dissipate.

"I hope that I give offence to none if, in speaking of the union of the provinces, I say that history will record the fact that the union was a project, which, in the mind of its author, aimed at the annihilation *(anéantissement)* of the French-Canadians. It was in this light that I regarded it. But after having subsequently examined with care this rod of chastisement that had been prepared against my compatriots, I besought some of the most influential among them to let me make use of this very instrument to save those whom it was designed to ruin, to place my fellow-countrymen in a better position than any they had ever occupied. I saw that this measure contained in itself the means of giving to the people the control which they ought to have over the government, of establishing a real government in Canada. It was under these circumstances that I entered parliament. The rest you know. From this moment we began to understand *responsible government*, the favourite watchword of to-day; it was then that it was understood that the governor must have as his executive advisers men who possessed the confidence of the public, and it was thus that I came to take part in the administration.

"For fifteen months things went fairly well. Then came the struggle between the ministry, of which I formed part, and Governor Metcalfe. The result of this struggle has been that you have in force in this country, the true principles of the English constitution. Power to-day is in the hands of the people. . . .

"I have said that the union was intended to annihilate the French-Canadians. But the matter has resulted very differently. The author of the union was mistaken. He wished to degrade one race among our citizens, but the facts have shown that both races among us stand upon the same footing. The very race that had been trodden under foot *(dans l'abaissement)* now finds itself, in some sort by this union, in a position of command to-day. Such is the position in which I leave the people of my race. I can only deprecate the efforts now made to divide the population of French Canada, but I have had a long enough experience to assure you that such efforts cannot succeed: my compatriots have too much common sense to forget that, if divided, they would be powerless and we be, to use the expression of a Tory of some years ago, 'destined to be dominated and led by the people of another race.' For myself, I spurn the efforts that are made to sunder the people of French Canada. Never will they succeed."

LaFontaine resigned in October, 1851. The break-up of the ministry was, of course, followed by a general election in which he played no part. Baldwin presented himself to the electors of the fourth riding of York and was defeated by Hartman, a Clear Grit. In his speech to the electors, after the announcement of his defeat, he declared that he had felt it his duty once more to place himself before them and "not to take upon himself the responsibility of originating the disruption of a bond which had been formed and repeatedly renewed between him and the electors of the north riding." With the election of 1851, Robert Baldwin's public career entirely terminates. From that time until his death, seven years later, he lived in complete retirement at "Spadina." Though but forty-seven years of age at the time of his resignation, his health had suffered much from the assiduity of his parliamentary labours. In 1854 he was created a Companion of the Bath, and in the following year the government of John A. Macdonald offered him the position of chief-justice of the common pleas. This offer, and the later invitation (1858) to accept a nomination for the legislative council (then become elective), Baldwin's failing health compelled him to decline. He died on December 9th, 1858, and was buried in the family sepulchre, called St. Martin's Rood, on the Spadina estate, whence his remains were subsequently removed to St. James Cemetery, Toronto.

LaFontaine, in retiring from political life at the age of forty-four, had yet a distinguished career before him on the bench. Returning, after his resignation, to legal occupations, he was appointed in 1853 chief-justice of Lower Canada, and in the year following was created a baronet in recognition of his distinguished career. As chief-justice, Sir Louis LaFontaine presided over the sittings of the seigniorial tenure court established for the adjustment of claims under the Act of 1854, and attained a distinction as a jurist which rivalled his eminence as a political leader. In 1860 LaFontaine, whose first wife, as has been seen,[1] had died many years before, married a Madame Kinton, widow of an English officer.[2] Of this marriage were born two sons, both of whom died young. Sir Louis LaFontaine died at Montreal, February 26th, 1864.

It is beyond the scope of the present volume to follow the subsequent political career of Francis

[1] See page 47.

[2] See L. O. David, *Biographies Canadiennes* (Montreal, 1870): Sir Louis H. LaFontaine.

Hincks. His reconstruction of the Reform party, his joint premiership with Morin, and the "sleepless vigilance" of his policy of railroad development and public improvement, form an important chapter in the history of Canada to which Sir John Bourinot and other authors of the present series have done ample justice. Hincks's career as a colonial governor in Barbadoes and Guiana, his subsequent return to Canada as Sir Francis Hincks, and the story of his services as minister of finance (1869-73) under Sir John A. Macdonald, lie altogether apart from the subject-matter of this book. Sir Francis Hincks died August 18th, 1885, after a long, active and useful life. His *Reminiscences of his Public Life*, published in 1884, is precisely one of those books which it is greatly to be desired that men who have taken a large part in public affairs would more frequently give to the world. For Canadian political history from 1840 to 1854, it will always remain an authority of the first importance.

It may, at first sight, appear strange that the two great Reformers, whose joint career has been chronicled in the foregoing pages, should have abandoned political life at an age when most statesmen are but on the threshold of their achievements. But the resignation of Baldwin and LaFontaine meant that their work was done. To find a real basis of political union between French and British Canada, to substitute for the strife of unreconciled races the fellow-citizenship of two great peoples, and set up in the foremost of British colonies an ensample of self-government that should prove the lasting basis of empire,—this was the completed work by which they had amply earned the rest of eventide after the day of toil.

INDEX

INDEX

A

INDEX

INDEX

L

LAMBTON, JOHN, see *Durham, Lord*

LaFontaine-Baldwin ministry (first), 113 *et seq.*; the first Canadian cabinet in which the principle of colonial self-government was embodied, 137, 138; goes out of office, 199 *et seq.*; second administration, 281 *et seq.*, 309; holds a position of exceptional power throughout 1849-50, 337; carries out reform measures of importance, 338, 339; its difficulty with the Clergy Reserve question, 343-9; in relation to seigniorial tenure, 349-51; end of the great ministry, 351, 354

LaFontaine, Louis H., early life, 47; sails to England, 48; arrested in 1838, 49; views on relation of responsible government to the union, 57; receives advances from Sydenham, 61; meets Hincks, 63; defeated at Terrebonne, 70, 79, 82; LaFontaine-Baldwin ministry (first), 113 *et seq.*, 137, 138, 199, 210, 234; elected for fourth riding of York, 116, 117; overtures from Bagot, 121-6; addresses the assembly in French, 128; enters cabinet, 133; reëlected in fourth riding of York, 134; contests fourth riding, 135; denounced by the *Patriot*, 146; criticized by Metcalfe, 164; his relation to Metcalfe, 166; dismissal recommended, 167; opinions of Kaye, 169; conversation with Captain Higginson, 173; speech in assembly, 178; seconds resolution for moving the seat of government, 182; prepares bill to remove office-holders from parliament, 184; reorganizes judicial system of Lower Canada, 184; LaFontaine-Baldwin administration, propriety of the name, 190 (note); resigns office (1843), 199 *et seq.*; interview with Metcalfe, 201; official statement on resignation, 201; announces resignation, 213; denounced by Lord Stanley, 234; opposed by Viger, 236; resigns position of queen's counsel, 250; elected in Terrebonne (1844), 251; correspondence with Caron, 259 *et seq.*; writes to Baldwin regarding Caron affair, 262; attacks adherents of Denis Papineau, 277; elected in Montreal, 279; LaFontaine-Baldwin administration (second), 281 *et seq.*, 309; attorney-general, 284; interview with Lord Elgin, 285; urges an amnesty, 288; attacked by Louis-Joseph Papineau, 289; speech against Louis-Joseph Papineau, 290-2; reorganizes judicial system of Lower Canada, 303; moves resolution on Rebellion Losses, 310; speeches on Rebellion Losses, 311, 312; argument on Rebellion Losses question, 317; his residence mobbed, 324; not in favour of the secularization of the Clergy Reserves, 348; determines to retire from political life, 353; tendered a banquet on his approaching retirement, 354;

367

INDEX

INDEX

LORD ELGIN

Elgin a Kincardine

LORD ELGIN

BY

SIR JOHN GEORGE BOURINOT

TORONTO

MORANG & CO., LIMITED

1910

EDITORS' NOTE

THE late Sir John Bourinot had completed and revised the following pages some months before his lamented death. The book represents more satisfactorily, perhaps, than anything else that he has written the author's breadth of political vision and his concrete mastery of historical fact. The life of Lord Elgin required to be written by one possessed of more than ordinary insight into the interesting aspects of constitutional law. That it has been singularly well presented must be the conclusion of all who may read this present narrative.

CONTENTS

CONTENTS

CHAPTER I

EARLY CAREER

THE Canadian people have had a varied experience in governors appointed by the imperial state. At the very commencement of British rule they were so fortunate as to find at the head of affairs Sir Guy Carleton—afterwards Lord Dorchester—who saved the country during the American revolution by his military genius, and also proved himself an able civil governor in his relations with the French Canadians, then called "the new subjects," whom he treated in a fair and generous spirit that did much to make them friendly to British institutions. On the other hand they have had military men like Sir James Craig, hospitable, generous, and kind, but at the same time incapable of understanding colonial conditions and aspirations, ignorant of the principles and working of representative institutions, and too ready to apply arbitrary methods to the administration of civil affairs. Then they have had men who were suddenly drawn from some inconspicuous position in the parent state, like Sir Francis Bond Head, and allowed by an apathetic or ignorant colonial office to prove their want of discretion, tact, and even common sense at a very critical stage of Canadian

1

affairs. Again there have been governors of the highest rank in the peerage of England, like the Duke of Richmond, whose administration was chiefly remarkable for his success in aggravating national animosities in French Canada, and whose name would now be quite forgotten were it not for the unhappy circumstances of his death.[1] Then Canadians have had the good fortune of the presence of Lord Durham at a time when a most serious state of affairs imperatively demanded that ripe political knowledge, that cool judgment, and that capacity to comprehend political grievances which were confessedly the characteristics of this eminent British statesman. Happily for Canada he was followed by a keen politician and an astute economist who, despite his overweening vanity and his tendency to underrate the ability of "those fellows in the colonies"—his own words in a letter to England— was well able to gauge public sentiment accurately and to govern himself accordingly during his short term of office. Since the confederation of the provinces there has been a succession of distinguished governors, some bearing names famous in the history of Great Britain and Ireland, some bringing to the discharge of their duties a large knowledge of public business gained in the government of the parent state and her wide empire, some gifted with a happy faculty of expressing

[1] He was bitten by a tame fox and died of hydrophobia at Richmond, in the present county of Carleton, Ontario.

2

themselves with ease and elegance, and all equally influenced by an earnest desire to fill their important position with dignity, impartiality, and affability.

But eminent as have been the services of many of the governors whose memories are still cherished by the people of Canada, no one among them stands on a higher plane than James, eighth earl of Elgin and twelfth earl of Kincardine, whose public career in Canada I propose to recall in the following narrative. He possessed to a remarkable degree those qualities of mind and heart which enabled him to cope most successfully with the racial and political difficulties which met him at the outset of his administration, during a very critical period of Canadian history. Animated by the loftiest motives, imbued with a deep sense of the responsibilities of his office, gifted with a rare power of eloquent expression, possessed of sound judgment and infinite discretion, never yielding to dictates of passion but always determined to be patient and calm at moments of violent public excitement, conscious of the advantages of compromise and conciliation in a country peopled like Canada, entering fully into the aspirations of a young people for self-government, ready to concede to French Canadians their full share in the public councils, anxious to build up a Canadian nation without reference to creed or race—this distinguished nobleman must be always placed by a

Canadian historian in the very front rank of the great administrators happily chosen from time to time by the imperial state for the government of her dominions beyond the sea. No governor-general, it is safe to say, has come nearer to that ideal, described by Sir Edward Bulwer Lytton, when secretary of state for the colonies, in a letter to Sir George Bowen, himself distinguished for the ability with which he presided over the affairs of several colonial dependencies. "Remember," said Lord Lytton, to give that eminent author and statesman his later title, "that the first care of a governor in a free colony is to shun the reproach of being a party man. Give all parties, and all the ministries formed, the fairest play. . . . . After all, men are governed as much by the heart as by the head. Evident sympathy in the progress of the colony; traits of kindness, generosity, devoted energy, where required for the public weal; a pure exercise of patronage; an utter absence of vindictiveness or spite; the fairness that belongs to magnanimity: these are the qualities that make governors powerful, while men merely sharp and clever may be weak and detested."

In the following chapters it will be seen that Lord Elgin fulfilled this ideal, and was able to leave the country in the full confidence that he had won the respect, admiration, and even affection of all classes of the Canadian people. He came to the country when there existed on all sides doubts as to the satisfactory working of the union of 1840, suspicions as to the sincerity of the imperial authorities with respect to the concession of responsible government, a growing antagonism between the two nationalities which then, as always, divided the province. A very serious economic disturbance was crippling the whole trade of the country, and made some persons—happily very few in number—believe for a short time that independence, or annexation to the neighbouring republic, was preferable to continued connection with a country which so grudgingly conceded political rights to the colony, and so ruthlessly overturned the commercial system on which the province had been so long dependent. When he left Canada, Lord Elgin knew beyond a shadow of a doubt that the two nationalities were working harmoniously for the common advantage of the province, that the principles of responsible government were firmly established, and that the commercial and industrial progress of the country was fully on an equality with its political development.

The man who achieved these magnificent results could claim an ancestry to which a Scotsman would point with national pride. He could trace his lineage to the ancient Norman house of which "Robert the Bruce"—a name ever dear to the Scottish nation—was the most distinguished member. He was born in London on July 20th, 1811. His father was a general in the British army, a representative peer in the British parliament from 1790-1840, and an ambassador to several European courts; but he is best known to history by the fact that he seriously crippled his private fortunes by his purchase, while in the East, of that magnificent collection of Athenian art which was afterwards bought at half its value by the British government and placed in the British Museum, where it is still known as the "Elgin Marbles." From his father, we are told by his biographer,[1] he inherited "the genial and playful spirit which gave such a charm to his social and parental relations, and which helped him to elicit from others the knowledge of which he made so much use in the many diverse situations of his after life." The deep piety and the varied culture of his mother "made her admirably qualified to be the depository of the ardent thoughts and aspirations of his boyhood." At Oxford, where he completed his education after leaving Eton, he showed that unselfish spirit and consideration for the feelings of others which were the recognized traits of his character in after life. Conscious of the unsatisfactory state of the family's fortunes, he laboured strenuously even in college to relieve his father as much as possible of the expenses of his education. While living very much to himself, he never failed to

[1] "Letters and Journals of James, eighth Earl of Elgin, etc." Edited by Theodore Walrond, C.B. For fuller references to works consulted in the writing of this short history, see *Bibliographical Note* at the end of this book.

win the confidence and respect even at this youthful age of all those who had an opportunity of knowing his independence of thought and judgment. Among his contemporaries were Mr. Gladstone, afterwards prime minister; the Duke of Newcastle, who became secretary of state for the colonies and was chief adviser of the Prince of Wales—now Edward VII—during his visit to Canada in 1860; and Lord Dalhousie and Lord Canning, both of whom preceded him in the governor-generalship of India. In the college debating club he won at once a very distinguished place. "I well remember," wrote Mr. Gladstone, many years later, "placing him as to the natural gift of eloquence at the head of all those I knew either at Eton or at the University." He took a deep interest in the study of philosophy. In him —to quote the opinion of his own brother, Sir Frederick Bruce, "the Reason and Understanding, to use the distinctions of Coleridge, were both largely developed, and both admirably balanced. . . . . He set himself to work to form in his own mind a clear idea of each of the constituent parts of the problem with which he had to deal. This he effected partly by reading, but still more by conversation with special men, and by that extraordinary logical power of mind and penetration which not only enabled him to get out of every man all he had in him, but which revealed to these men themselves a knowledge of their own imperfect and crude conceptions, and made them constantly

7

unwilling witnesses or reluctant adherents to views which originally they were prepared to oppose. . . ." The result was that, "in an incredibly short time he attained an accurate and clear conception of the essential facts before him, and was thus enabled to strike out a course which he could consistently pursue amid all difficulties, because it was in harmony with the actual facts and the permanent conditions of the problem he had to solve." Here we have the secret of his success in grappling with the serious and complicated questions which constantly engaged his attention in the administration of Canadian affairs.

After leaving the university with honour, he passed several years on the family estate, which he endeavoured to relieve as far as possible from the financial embarrassment into which it had fallen ever since his father's extravagant purchase in Greece. In 1840, by the death of his eldest brother, George, who died unmarried, James became heir to the earldom, and soon afterwards entered parliament as member for the borough of Southampton. He claimed then, as always, to be a Liberal-Conservative, because he believed that "the institutions of our country, religious as well as civil, are wisely adapted, when duly and faithfully administered, to promote, not the interest of any class or classes exclusively, but the happiness and welfare of the great body of the people"; and because he felt that, "on the maintenance of these institutions, not

8

only the economical prosperity of England, but, what is yet more important, the virtues that distinguish and adorn the English character, under God, mainly depend."

During the two years Lord Elgin remained in the House of Commons he gave evidence to satisfy his friends that he possessed to an eminent degree the qualities which promised him a brilliant career in British politics. Happily for the administration of the affairs of Britain's colonial empire, he was induced by Lord Stanley, then secretary of state for the colonies, to surrender his prospects in parliament and accept the governorship of Jamaica. No doubt he was largely influenced to take this position by the conviction that he would be able to relieve his father's property from the pressure necessarily entailed upon it while he remained in the expensive field of national politics. On his way to Jamaica he was shipwrecked, and his wife, a daughter of Mr. Charles Cumming Bruce, M.P., of Dunphail, Stirling, suffered a shock which so seriously impaired her health that she died a few months after her arrival in the island when she had given birth to a daughter.[1] His administration of the government of Jamaica was distinguished by a strong desire to act discreetly and justly at a time

[1] Lady Elma, who married, in 1864, Thomas John Howell-Thurlow-Cumming Bruce, who was attached to the staff of Lord Elgin in his later career in China and India, etc., and became Baron Thurlow on the death of his brother in 1874. See "Debrett's Peerage."

when the economic conditions of the island were still seriously disturbed by the emancipation of the negroes. Planter and black alike found in him a true friend and sympathizer. He recognized the necessity of improving the methods of agriculture, and did much by the establishment of agricultural societies to spread knowledge among the ignorant blacks, as well as to create a spirit of emulation among the landlords, who were still sullen and apathetic, requiring much persuasion to adapt themselves to the new order of things, and make efforts to stimulate skilled labour among the coloured population whom they still despised. Then, as always in his career, he was animated by the noble impulse to administer public affairs with a sole regard to the public interests, irrespective of class or creed, to elevate men to a higher conception of their public duties. "To reconcile the planter"—I quote from one of his letters to Lord Stanley—"to the heavy burdens which he was called to bear for the improvement of our establishments and the benefit of the mass of the population, it was necessary to persuade him that he had an interest in raising the standard of education and morals among the peasantry; and this belief could be imparted only by inspiring a taste for a more artificial system of husbandry." "By the silent operation of such salutary convictions," he added, "prejudices of old standing are removed; the friends of the negro and of the proprietary classes find themselves almost

10

unconsciously acting in concert, and conspiring to complete that great and holy work of which the emancipation of the slave was but the commencement."

At this time the relations between the island and the home governments were always in a very strained condition on account of the difficulty of making the colonial office fully sensible of the financial embarrassment caused by the upheaval of the labour and social systems, and of the wisest methods of assisting the colony in its straits. As it too often happened in those old times of colonial rule, the home government could with difficulty be brought to understand that the economic principles which might satisfy the state of affairs in Great Britain could not be hastily and arbitrarily applied to a country suffering under peculiar difficulties. The same unintelligent spirit which forced taxation on the thirteen colonies, which complicated difficulties in the Canadas before the rebellion of 1837, seemed for the moment likely to prevail, as soon as the legislature of Jamaica passed a tariff framed naturally with regard to conditions existing when the receipts and expenditures could not be equalized, and the financial situation could not be relieved from its extreme tension in any other way than by the imposition of duties which happened to be in antagonism with the principles then favoured by the imperial government. At this critical juncture Lord Elgin successfully interposed

11

between the colonial office and the island legislature, and obtained permission for the latter to manage this affair in its own way. He recognized the fact, obvious enough to any one conversant with the affairs of the island, that the tariff in question was absolutely necessary to relieve it from financial ruin, and that any strenuous interference with the right of the assembly to control its own taxes and expenses would only tend to create complications in the government and the relations with the parent state. He was convinced, as he wrote to the colonial office, that an indispensable condition of his usefulness as a governor was "a just appreciation of the difficulties with which the legislature of the island had yet to contend, and of the sacrifices and exertions already made under the pressure of no ordinary embarrassments."

Here we see Lord Elgin, at the very commencement of his career as a colonial governor, fully alive to the economic, social, and political conditions of the country, and anxious to give its people every legitimate opportunity to carry out those measures which they believed, with a full knowledge and experience of their own affairs, were best calculated to promote their own interests. We shall see later that it was in exactly the same spirit that he administered Canadian questions of much more serious import.

Though his government in Jamaica was in every sense a success, he decided not to remain any longer than three years, and so wrote in 1845 to Lord Stanley. Despite his earnest efforts to identify himself with the island's interests, he had led on the whole a retired and sad life after the death of his wife. He naturally felt a desire to seek the congenial and sympathetic society of friends across the sea, and perhaps return to the active public life for which he was in so many respects well qualified. In offering his resignation to the colonial secretary he was able to say that the period of his administration had been "one of considerable social progress"; that "uninterrupted harmony" had "prevailed between the colonists and the local government"; that "the spirit of enterprise" which had proceeded from Jamaica for two years had "enabled the British West Indian colonies to endure with comparative fortitude, apprehensions and difficulties which otherwise might have depressed them beyond measure."

It was not, however, until the spring of 1846 that Lord Elgin was able to return on leave of absence to England, where the seals of office were now held by a Liberal administration, in which Lord Grey was colonial secretary. Although his political opinions differed from those of the party in power, he was offered the governor-generalship of Canada when he declined to go back to Jamaica. No doubt at this juncture the British ministry recognized the absolute necessity that existed for removing all political grievances that arose from the tardy concession of responsible

13

government since the death of Lord Sydenham, and for allaying as far as possible the discontent that generally prevailed against the new fiscal policy of the parent state, which had so seriously paralyzed Canadian industries. It was a happy day for Canada when Lord Elgin accepted this gracious offer of his political opponents, who undoubtedly recognized in him the possession of qualities which would enable him successfully, in all probability, to grapple with the perplexing problems which embarrassed public affairs in the province. He felt (to quote his own language at a public dinner given to him just before his departure for Canada) that he undertook no slight responsibilities when he promised "to watch over the interests of those great offshoots of the British race which plant themselves in distant lands, to aid them in their efforts to extend the domain of civilization, and to fulfil the first behest of a benevolent Creator to His intelligent creatures—'subdue the earth'; to abet the generous endeavour to impart to these rising communities the full advantages of British laws, British institutions, and British freedom; to assist them in maintaining unimpaired—it may be in strengthening and confirming—those bonds of mutual affection which unite the parent and dependent states."

Before his departure for the scene of his labours in America, he married Lady Mary Louisa Lambton, daughter of the Earl of Durham, whose short career in Canada as governor-general and high

14

commissioner after the rebellion of 1837 had such a remarkable influence on the political conditions of the country. Whilst we cannot attach too much importance to the sage advice embodied in that great state paper on Canadian affairs which was the result of his mission to Canada, we cannot fail at the same time to see that the full vindication of the sound principles laid down in that admirable report is to be found in the complete success of their application by Lord Elgin. The minds of both these statesmen ran in the same direction. They desired to give adequate play to the legitimate aspirations of the Canadian people for that measure of self-government which must stimulate an independence of thought and action among colonial public men, and at the same time strengthen the ties between the parent state and the dependency by creating that harmony and confidence which otherwise could not exist in the relations between them. But while there is little doubt that Lord Elgin would under any circumstances have been animated by a deep desire to establish the principles of responsible government in Canada, this desire must have been more or less stimulated by the tender ties which bound him to the daughter of a statesman whose opinions where so entirely in harmony with his own. In Lord Elgin's temperament there was always a mingling of sentiment and reason, as may be seen by reference to his finest exhibitions of eloquence. We can well believe that a deep reverence for the memory of a great man, too soon removed from the public life of Great Britain, combined with the natural desire to please his daughter when he wrote these words to her:—"I still adhere to my opinion that the real and effectual vindication of Lord Durham's memory and proceedings will be the success of a governor-general of Canada who works out his views of government fairly. Depend upon it, if this country is governed for a few years satisfactorily, Lord Durham's reputation as a statesman will be raised beyond the reach of cavil." Now, more than half a century after he penned these words and expressed this hope, we all perceive that Lord Elgin was the instrument to carry out this work.

Here it is necessary to close this very brief sketch of Lord Elgin's early career, that I may give an account of the political and economic conditions of the dependency at the end of January, 1847, when he arrived in the city of Montreal to assume the responsibilities of his office. This review will show the difficulties of the political situation with which he was called upon to cope, and will enable us to obtain an insight into the high qualifications which he brought to the conduct of public affairs in the Canadas.

CHAPTER II

POLITICAL CONDITION IN CANADA

TO understand clearly the political state of Canada at the time Lord Elgin was appointed governor-general, it is necessary to go back for a number of years. The unfortunate rebellions which were precipitated by Louis-Joseph Papineau and William Lyon Mackenzie during 1837 in the two Canadas were the results of racial and political difficulties which had gradually arisen since the organization of the two provinces of Upper and Lower Canada under the Constitutional Act of 1791. In the French section, the French and English Canadians—the latter always an insignificant minority as respects number—had in the course of time formed distinct parties. As in the courts of law and in the legislature, so it was in social and everyday life, the French Canadian was in direct antagonism to the English Canadian. Many members of the official and governing class, composed almost exclusively of English, were still too ready to consider French Canadians as inferior beings, and not entitled to the same rights and privileges in the government of the country. It was a time of passion and declamation, when men of fervent eloquence, like Papineau, might have

17

aroused the French as one man, and brought about a general rebellion had they not been ultimately thwarted by the efforts of the moderate leaders of public opinion, especially of the priests who, in all national crises in Canada, have happily intervened on the side of reason and moderation, and in the interests of British connection, which they have always felt to be favourable to the continuance and security of their religious institutions. Lord Durham, in his memorable report on the condition of Canada, has summed up very expressively the nature of the conflict in the French province. "I expected," he said, "to find a contest between a government and a people; I found two nations warring in the bosom of a single state; I found a struggle, not of principles, but of races."

While racial antagonisms intensified the difficulties in French Canada, there existed in all the provinces political conditions which arose from the imperfect nature of the constitutional system conceded by England in 1791, and which kept the country in a constant ferment. It was a mockery to tell British subjects conversant with British institutions, as Lieutenant-Governor Simcoe told the Upper Canadians in 1792, that their new system of government was "an image and transcript of the British constitution." While it gave to the people representative institutions, it left out the very principle which was necessary to make them work harmoniously—a government responsible to the

18

legislature, and to the people in the last resort, for the conduct of legislation and the administration of affairs. In consequence of the absence of this vital principle, the machinery of government became clogged, and political strife convulsed the country from one end to the other. An "irrepressible conflict" arose between the government and the governed classes, especially in Lower Canada. The people who in the days of the French régime were without influence and power, had gained under their new system, defective as it was in essential respects, an insight into the operation of representative government, as understood in England. They found they were governed, not by men responsible to the legislature and the people, but by governors and officials who controlled both the executive and legislative councils. If there had always been wise and patient governors at the head of affairs, or if the imperial authorities could always have been made aware of the importance of the grievances laid before them, or had understood their exact character, the differences between the government and the majority of the people's representatives might have been arranged satisfactorily. But, unhappily, military governors like Sir James Craig only aggravated the dangers of the situation, and gave demagogues new opportunities for exciting the people. The imperial authorities, as a rule, were sincerely desirous of meeting the wishes of the people in a reasonable and fair spirit, but unfortunately for the country, they were too often ill-advised and ill-informed in those days of slow communication, and the fire of public discontent was allowed to smoulder until it burst forth in a dangerous form.

In all the provinces, but especially in Lower Canada, the people saw their representatives practically ignored by the governing body, their money expended without the authority of the legislature, and the country governed by irresponsible officials. A system which gave little or no weight to public opinion as represented in the House of Assembly, was necessarily imperfect and unstable, and the natural result was a deadlock between the legislative council, controlled by the official and governing class, and the House elected by the people. The governors necessarily took the side of the men whom they had themselves appointed, and with whom they were acting. In the maritime provinces in the course of time, the governors made an attempt now and then to conciliate the popular element by bringing in men who had influence in the assembly, but this was a matter entirely within their own discretion. The system of government as a whole was worked in direct contravention of the principle of responsibility to the majority in the popular House. Political agitators had abundant opportunities for exciting popular passion. In Lower Canada, Papineau, an eloquent but impulsive man, having rather the qualities of an agitator than those of a statesman, led the majority of his compatriots.

For years he contended for a legislative council elected by the people: and it is curious to note that none of the men who were at the head of the popular party in Lower Canada ever recognized the fact, as did their contemporaries in Upper Canada, that the difficulty would be best solved, not by electing an Upper House, but by obtaining an executive which would only hold office while supported by a majority of the representatives in the people's House. In Upper Canada the radical section of the Liberal party was led by Mr. William Lyon Mackenzie, who fought vigorously against what was generally known as the "Family Compact," which occupied all the public offices and controlled the government.

In the two provinces these two men at last precipitated a rebellion in which blood was shed and much property destroyed, but which never reached any very extensive proportions. In the maritime provinces, however, where the public grievances were of less magnitude, the people showed no sympathy whatever with the rebellious elements of the upper provinces.

Amid the gloom that overhung Canada in those times there was one gleam of sunshine for England. Although discontent and dissatisfaction prevailed among the people on account of the manner in which the government was administered, and of the attempts of the minority to engross all power and influence, there was still a sentiment in favour of British connection, and the annexationists were relatively few in number. Even Sir Francis Bond Head—in no respect a man of sagacity—understood this well when he depended on the militia to crush the outbreak in the upper province; and Joseph Howe, the eminent leader of the popular party, uniformly asserted that the people of Nova Scotia were determined to preserve the integrity of the empire at all hazards. As a matter of fact, the majority of leading men, outside of the minority led by Papineau, Nelson and Mackenzie, had a conviction that England was animated by a desire to act considerately with the provinces and that little good would come from precipitating a conflict which could only add to the public misfortunes, and that the true remedy was to be found in constitutional methods of redress for the political grievances which undoubtedly existed throughout British North America.

The most important clauses of the Union Act, which was passed by the imperial parliament in 1840 but did not come into effect until February of the following year, made provision for a legislative assembly in which each section of the united provinces was represented by an equal number of members—forty-two for each and eighty-four for both; for the use of the English language alone in the written or printed proceedings of the legislature; for the placing of the public indebtedness of the two provinces at the union as a first charge on the revenues of the united provinces; for a two-thirds vote of the members of each House before any change could be made in the representation. These enactments, excepting the last which proved eventually to be in their interest, were resented by the French Canadians as clearly intended to place them in a position of inferiority to the English Canadians. Indeed it was with natural indignation they read that portion of Lord Durham's report which expressed the opinion that it was necessary to unite the two races on terms which would give the domination to the English. "Without effecting the change so rapidly or so roughly," he wrote, "as to shock the feelings or to trample on the welfare of the existing generation, it must henceforth be the first and steady purpose of the British government to establish an English population, with English laws and language, in this province, and to trust its government to none but a decidedly English legislature."

French Canadians dwelt with emphasis on the fact that their province had a population of 630,000 souls, or 160,000 more than Upper Canada, and nevertheless received only the same number of representatives. French Canada had been quite free from the financial embarrassment which had brought Upper Canada to the verge of bankruptcy before the union; in fact the former had actually a considerable surplus when its old constitution was revoked on the outbreak of the rebellion. It was,

23

consequently, with some reason, considered an act of injustice to make the people of French Canada pay the debts of a province whose revenue had not for years met its liabilities. Then, to add to these decided grievances, there was a proscription of the French language, which was naturally resented as a flagrant insult to the race which first settled the valley of the St. Lawrence, and as the first blow levelled against the special institutions so dear to French Canadians and guaranteed by the Treaty of Paris and the Quebec Act. Mr. LaFontaine, whose name will frequently occur in the following chapters of this book, declared, when he presented himself at the first election under the Union Act, that "it was an act of injustice and despotism"; but, as we shall soon see, he became a prime minister under the very act he first condemned. Like the majority of his compatriots, he eventually found in its provisions protection for the rights of the people, and became perfectly satisfied with a system of government which enabled them to obtain their proper position in the public councils and restore their language to its legitimate place in the legislature.

But without the complete grant of responsible government it would never have been possible to give to French Canadians their legitimate influence in the administration and legislation of the country, or to reconcile the differences which had grown up between the two nationalities before the union and

24

seemed likely to be perpetuated by the conditions of the Union Act just stated. Lord Durham touched the weakest spot in the old constitutional system of the Canadian provinces when he said that it was not " possible to secure harmony in any other way than by administering the government on those principles which have been found perfectly efficacious in Great Britain." He would not "impair a single prerogative of the crown"; on the contrary he believed " that the interests of the people of these provinces require the protection of prerogatives which have not hitherto been exercised." But he recognized the fact as a constitutional statesman that "the crown must, on the other hand, submit to the necessary consequences of representative institutions; and if it has to carry on the government in unison with a representative body, it must consent to carry it on by means of those in whom that representative body has confidence." He found it impossible "to understand how any English statesman could have ever imagined that representative and irresponsible government could be successfully combined." To suppose that such a system would work well there "implied a belief that French Canadians have enjoyed representative institutions for half a century without acquiring any of the characteristics of a free people; that Englishmen renounce every political opinion and feeling when they enter a colony, or that the spirit of Anglo-Saxon freedom is utterly changed and weakened among those who are transplanted across the Atlantic."

No one who studies carefully the history of responsible government from the appearance of Lord Durham's report and Lord John Russell's despatches of 1839 until the coming of Lord Elgin to Canada in 1847, can fail to see that there was always a doubt in the minds of the imperial authorities—a doubt more than once actually expressed in the instructions to the governors— whether it was possible to work the new system on the basis of a governor directly responsible to the parent state and at the same time acting under the advice of ministers directly responsible to the colonial parliament. Lord John Russell had been compelled to recognize the fact that it was not possible to govern Canada by the old methods of administration—that it was necessary to adopt a new colonial policy which would give a larger measure of political freedom to the people and ensure greater harmony between the executive government and the popular assemblies. Mr. Poulett Thomson, afterwards Lord Sydenham, was appointed governor-general with the definite objects of completing the union of the Canadas and inaugurating a more liberal system of colonial administration. As he informed the legislature of Upper Canada immediately after his arrival, in his anxiety to obtain its consent to the union, he had received "Her Majesty's commands to administer the government of

these provinces in accordance with the well understood wishes and interests of the people." When
the legislature of the united provinces met for the
first time, he communicated two despatches in
which the colonial secretary stated emphatically
that, "Her Majesty had no desire to maintain any
system or policy among her North American subjects which opinion condemns," and that there was
"no surer way of gaining the approbation of the
Queen than by maintaining the harmony of the
executive with the legislative authorities." The
governor-general was instructed, in order "to maintain the utmost possible harmony," to call to his
councils and to employ in the public service "those
persons who, by their position and character, have
obtained the general confidence and esteem of the
inhabitants of the province." He wished it to be
generally made known by the governor-general
that thereafter certain heads of departments would
be called upon "to retire from the public service as
often as any sufficient motives of public policy
might suggest the expediency of that measure." It
appears, however, that there was always a reservation in the minds of the colonial secretary and of
governors who preceded Lord Elgin as to the meaning of responsible government and the methods of
carrying it out in a colony dependent on the Crown.
Lord Sydenham himself believed that the council
should be one "for the governor to consult and no
more"; that the governor could "not be responsible

to the government at home and also to the legislature of the province," for if it were so "then all colonial government becomes impossible." The governor, in his opinion, "must therefore be the minister [*i.e.*, the colonial secretary], in which case he cannot be under control of men in the colony." But it was soon made clear to so astute a politician as Lord Sydenham that, whatever were his own views as to the meaning that should be attached to responsible government, he must yield as far as possible to the strong sentiment which prevailed in the country in favour of making the ministry dependent on the legislature for its continuance in office. The resolutions passed by the legislature in support of responsible government were understood to have his approval. They differed very little in words—in essential principle not at all—from those first introduced by Mr. Baldwin. The inference to be drawn from the political situation of that time is that the governor's friends in the council thought it advisable to gain all possible credit with the public in connection with the all-absorbing question of the day, and accordingly brought in the following resolutions in amendment to those presented by the Liberal chief:—

"1. That the head of the executive government of the province, being within the limits of his government the representative of the sovereign, is responsible to the imperial authority alone, but that nevertheless the management of our local affairs can only be conducted by him with the assistance, counsel, and information of subordinate officers in the province.

"2. That in order to preserve between the different branches of the provincial parliament that harmony which is essential to the peace, welfare, and good government of the province, the chief advisers of the representative of the sovereign, constituting a provincial administration under him, ought to be men possessed of the confidence of the representatives of the people; thus affording a guarantee that the well-understood wishes and interests of the people—which our gracious sovereign has declared shall be the rule of the provincial government—will on all occasions be faithfully represented and advocated.

"3. That the people of this province have, moreover, the right to expect from such provincial administration the exercise of their best endeavours that the imperial authority, within its constitutional limits, shall be exercised in the manner most consistent with their well-understood wishes and interests."

It is quite possible that had Lord Sydenham lived to complete his term of office, the serious difficulties that afterwards arose in the practice of responsible government would not have occurred. Gifted with a clear insight into political conditions and a thorough knowledge of the working of representative institutions, he would have understood that if parliamentary government was ever to

29

be introduced into the colony it must be not in a half-hearted way, or with such reservations as he had had in his mind when he first came to the province. Amid the regret of all parties he died from the effects of a fall from his horse a few months after the inauguration of the union, and was succeeded by Sir Charles Bagot, who distinguished himself in a short administration of two years by the conciliatory spirit which he showed to the French Canadians, even at the risk of offending the ultra loyalists who seemed to think, for some years after the union, that they alone were entitled to govern the dependency.

The first ministry after that change was composed of Conservatives and moderate Liberals, but it was soon entirely controlled by the former, and never had the confidence of Mr. Baldwin. That eminent statesman had been a member of this administration at the time of the union, but he resigned on the ground that it ought to be reconstructed if it was to represent the true sentiment of the country at large. When Sir Charles Bagot became governor the Conservatives were very sanguine that they would soon obtain exclusive control of the government, as he was known to be a supporter of the Conservative party in England. It was not long, however, before it was evident that his administration would be conducted, not in the interests of any set of politicians, but on principles of compromise and justice to all political parties, and, above all, with the hope of conciliating the French Canadians and bringing them into harmony with the new conditions. One of his first acts was the appointment of an eminent French Canadian, M. Vallières de Saint-Réal, to the chief-justiceship of Montreal. Other appointments of able French Canadians to prominent public positions evoked the ire of the Tories, then led by the Sherwoods and Sir Allan MacNab, who had taken a conspicuous part in putting down the rebellion of 1837-8. Sir Charles Bagot, however, persevered in his policy of attempting to stifle racial prejudices and to work out the principles of responsible government on broad national lines. He appointed an able Liberal and master of finance, Mr. Francis Hincks, to the position of inspector-general with a seat in the cabinet. The influence of the French Canadians in parliament was now steadily increasing, and even strong Conservatives like Mr. Draper were forced to acknowledge that it was not possible to govern the province on the principle that they were an inferior and subject people, whose representatives could not be safely entrusted with any responsibilities as ministers of the Crown. Negotiations for the entrance of prominent French Canadians in opposition to the government went on without result for some time, but they were at last successful, and the first LaFontaine-Baldwin cabinet came into existence in 1842, largely through the instrumentality of Sir Charles Bagot. Mr. Baldwin was a statesman whose greatest desire was the success of responsible government without a single reservation. Mr. LaFontaine was a French Canadian who had wisely recognized the necessity of accepting the union he had at first opposed, and of making responsible government an instrument for the advancement of the interests of his compatriots and of bringing them into unison with all nationalities for the promotion of the common good. The other prominent French Canadian in the ministry was Mr. A. N. Morin, who possessed the confidence and respect of his people, but was wanting in the energy and ability to initiate and press public measures which his leader possessed.

The new administration had not been long in office when the governor-general fell a victim to an attack of dropsy, complicated by heart disease, and was succeeded by Sir Charles Metcalfe, who had held prominent official positions in India, and was governor of Jamaica previous to Lord Elgin's appointment. No one who has studied his character can doubt the honesty of his motives or his amiable qualities, but his political education in India and Jamaica rendered him in many ways incapable of understanding the political conditions of a country like Canada, where the people were determined to work out the system of parliamentary government on strictly British principles. He could have obtained little assistance from British statesmen had he been desirous of mastering and applying the principles of responsible government to the dependency. Their opinions and instructions were still distinguished by a perplexing vagueness. They would not believe that a governor of a dependency could occupy exactly the same relation with respect to his responsible advisers and to political parties as is occupied with such admirable results by the sovereign of England. It was considered necessary that a governor should make himself as powerful a factor as possible in the administration of public affairs—that he should be practically the prime minister, responsible, not directly to the colonial legislature, but to the imperial government, whose servant he was and to whom he should constantly refer for advice and assistance whenever in his opinion the occasion arose. In other words it was almost impossible to remove from the mind of any British statesman, certainly not from the colonial office of those days, the idea that parliamentary government meant one thing in England and the reverse in the colonies, that Englishmen at home could be entrusted with a responsibility which it was inexpedient to allow to Englishmen or Frenchmen across the sea. The colonial office was still reluctant to give up complete control of the local administration of the province, and wished to retain a veto by means of the governor, who considered official favour more desirable than the approval of any colonial legislature. More or less imbued with such views, Sir Charles Metcalfe was bound to come into conflict

33

with LaFontaine and Baldwin, who had studied deeply the principles and practice of parliamentary government, and knew perfectly well that they could be carried out only by following the precedents established in the parent state.

It was not long before the rupture came between men holding views so diametrically opposed to each other with respect to the conduct of government. The governor-general decided not to distribute the patronage of the Crown under the advice of his responsible ministry, as was, of necessity, the constitutional practice in England, but to ignore the latter, as he boldly declared, whenever he deemed it expedient. "I wish," he wrote to the colonial secretary, "to make the patronage of the government conducive to the conciliation of all parties by bringing into the public service men of the greatest merit and efficiency without any party distinction." These were noble sentiments, sound in theory, but entirely incompatible with the operation of responsible government. If patronage is to be properly exercised in the interests of the people at large, it must be done by men who are directly responsible to the representatives of the people. If a governor-general is to make appointments without reference to his advisers, he must be more or less subject to party criticism, without having the advantage of defending himself in the legislature, or of having men duly authorized by constitutional usage to do so. The revival of that personal government which had

34

evoked so much political rancour, and brought governors into the arena of party strife before the rebellion, was the natural result of the obstinate and unconstitutional attitude assumed by Lord Metcalfe with respect to appointments to office and other matters of administration.

All the members of the LaFontaine-Baldwin government, with the exception of Mr. Dominick Daly, resigned in consequence of the governor's action. Mr. Daly had no special party proclivities, and found it to his personal interests to remain his Excellency's sole adviser. Practically the province was without an administration for many months, and when, at last, the governor-general was forced by public opinion to show a measure of respect for constitutional methods of government, he succeeded after most strenuous efforts in forming a Conservative cabinet, in which Mr. Draper was the only man of conspicuous ability. The French Canadians were represented by Mr. Viger and Mr. Denis B. Papineau, a brother of the famous rebel, neither of whom had any real influence or strength in Lower Canada, where the people recognized LaFontaine as their true leader and ablest public man. In the general election which soon followed the reconstruction of the government, it was sustained by a small majority, won only by the most unblushing bribery, by bitter appeals to national passion, and by the personal influence of the governor-general, as was the election which immediately preceded the rising in Upper Canada. In later years, Lord Grey[1] remarked that this success was "dearly purchased, by the circumstance that the parliamentary opposition was no longer directed against the advisers of the governor but against the governor himself, and the British government, of which he was the organ." The majority of the government was obtained from Upper Canada, where a large body of people were misled by appeals made to their loyalty and attachment to the Crown, and where a large number of Methodists were influenced by the extraordinary action of the Rev. Egerton Ryerson, a son of a United Empire Loyalist, who defended the position of the governor-general, and showed how imperfectly he understood the principles and practice of responsible government. In a life of Sir Charles Metcalfe,[2] which appeared shortly after his death, it is stated that the governor-general "could not disguise from himself that the government was not strong, that it was continually on the brink of defeat, and that it was only enabled to hold its position by resorting to shifts and expedients, or what are called tactics, which in his inmost soul Lord Metcalfe abhorred."

The action of the British ministry during this crisis in Canadian affairs proved quite conclusively

[1] "The Colonial Policy of Lord John Russell's Administration," by Earl Grey, London, 1857. See Vol. I, p. 205.

[2] The "Life and Correspondence of Charles, Lord Metcalfe," by John W. Kaye, London, 1858.

that it was not yet prepared to concede responsible government in its fullest sense. Both Lord Stanley, then secretary of state for the colonies, and Lord John Russell, who had held the same office in a Whig administration, endorsed the action of the governor-general, who was raised to the peerage under the title of Baron Metcalfe of Fernhill, in the county of Berks. Earthly honours were now of little avail to the new peer. He had been a martyr for years to a cancer in the face, and when it assumed a most dangerous form he went back to England and died soon after his return. So strong was the feeling against him among a large body of the people, especially in French Canada, that he was bitterly assailed until the hour when he left, a dying man. Personally he was generous and charitable to a fault, but he should never have been sent to a colony at a crisis when the call was for a man versed in the practice of parliamentary government, and able to sympathize with the aspirations of a people determined to enjoy political freedom in accordance with the principles of the parliamentary institutions of England. With a remarkable ignorance of the political conditions of the province—too often shown by British statesmen in those days—so great a historian and parliamentarian as Lord Macaulay actually wrote on a tablet to Lord Metcalfe's memory:—"In Canada, not yet recovered from the calamities of civil war, he reconciled contending factions to each other and to the mother country." The truth is, as written by Sir Francis Hincks[1] fifty years later, "he embittered the party feeling that had been considerably assuaged by Sir Charles Bagot."

Lord Metcalfe was succeeded by Lord Cathcart, a military man, who was chosen because of the threatening aspect of the relations between England and the United States on the question of the Oregon boundary. During his short term of office he did not directly interfere in politics, but carefully studied the defence of the country and quietly made preparations for a rupture with the neighbouring republic. The result of his judicious action was the disappearance of much of the political bitterness which had existed during Lord Metcalfe's administration. The country, indeed, had to face issues of vital importance to its material progress. Industry and commerce were seriously affected by the adoption of free trade in England, and the consequent removal of duties which had given a preference in the British markets to Canadian wheat, flour, and other commodities. The effect upon the trade of the province would not have been so serious had England at this time repealed the old navigation laws which closed the St. Lawrence to foreign shipping and prevented the extension of commerce to other markets. Such a course might have immediately compensated

[1] "Reminiscences of his public life," by Sir Francis Hincks, K.C.M.G., C.B., Montreal, 1884.

Canadians for the loss of those of the motherland. The anxiety that was generally felt by Canadians on the reversal of the British commercial policy under which they had been able to build up a very profitable trade, was shown in the language of a very largely signed address from the assembly to the Queen. "We cannot but fear," it was stated in this document, "that the abandonment of the protective principle, the very basis of the colonial commercial system, is not only calculated to retard the agricultural improvement of the country and check its hitherto rising prosperity, but seriously to impair our ability to purchase the manufactured goods of Great Britain—a result alike prejudicial to this country and the parent state." But this appeal to the selfishness of British manufacturers had no influence on British statesmen so far as their fiscal policy was concerned. But while they were not prepared to depart in any measure from the principles of free trade and give the colonies a preference in British markets over foreign countries, they became conscious that the time had come for removing, as far as possible, all causes of public discontent in the provinces, at this critical period of commercial depression. British statesmen had suddenly awakened to the mistakes of Lord Metcalfe's administration of Canadian affairs, and decided to pursue a policy towards Canada which would restore confidence in the good faith and justice of the imperial government. "The Queen's representative"—this is a citation from a London paper[1] supporting the Whig government— "should not assume that he degrades the Crown by following in a colony with a constitutional government the example of the Crown at home. Responsible government has been conceded to Canada, and should be attended in its workings with all the consequences of responsible government in the mother country. What the Queen cannot do in England the governor-general should not be permitted to do in Canada. In making imperial appointments she is bound to consult her cabinet; in making provincial appointments the governor-general should be bound to do the same."

The Oregon dispute had been settled, like the question of the Maine boundary, without any regard to British interests in America, and it was now deemed expedient to replace Lord Cathcart by a civil governor, who would be able to carry out, in the valley of the St. Lawrence, the new policy of the colonial office, and strengthen the ties between the province and the parent state.

As I have previously stated, Lord John Russell's ministry made a wise choice in the person of Lord Elgin. In the following pages I shall endeavour to show how fully were realized the high expectations of those British statesmen who sent him across the Atlantic at this critical epoch in the political and industrial conditions of the Canadian dependency.

[1] See "McMullen's History of Canada," Vol. II (2nd Ed.), p. 201.

CHAPTER III

POLITICAL DIFFICULTIES

LORD ELGIN made a most favourable impression on the public opinion of Canada from the first hour he arrived in Montreal, and had opportunities of meeting and addressing the people. His genial manner, his ready speech, his knowledge of the two languages, his obvious desire to understand thoroughly the condition of the country and to pursue British methods of constitutional government, were all calculated to attract the confidence of all nationalities, classes, and creeds. The supporters of responsible government heard with infinite pleasure the enunciation of the principles which would guide him in the discharge of his public duties. "I am sensible," he said in answer to a Montreal address, "that I shall but maintain the prerogative of the Crown, and most effectually carry out the instructions with which Her Majesty has honoured me, by manifesting a due regard for the wishes and feelings of the people and by seeking the advice and assistance of those who enjoy their confidence."

At this time the Draper Conservative ministry, formed under such peculiar circumstances by Lord Metcalfe, was still in office, and Lord Elgin, as in

duty bound, gave it his support, although it was
clear to him and to all other persons at all conversant with public opinion that it did not enjoy
the confidence of the country at large, and must
soon give place to an administration more worthy
of popular favour. He recognized the fact that the
crucial weakness in the political situation was "that
a Conservative government meant a government
of Upper Canadians, which is intolerable to the
French, and a Radical government meant a government of French, which is no less hateful to the
British." He believed that the political problem of
"how to govern united Canada"—and the changes
which took place later showed he was right—would
be best solved "if the French would split into a
Liberal and Conservative party, and join the Upper
Canada parties which bear corresponding names."
Holding these views, he decided at the outset to
give the French Canadians full recognition in the
reconstruction or formation of ministries during his
term of office. And under all circumstances he was
resolved to give "to his ministers all constitutional
support, frankly and without reserve, and the benefit of the best advice" that he could afford them in
their difficulties. In return for this he expected that
they would, "in so far as it is possible for them to
do so, carry out his views for the maintenance of
the connection with Great Britain and the advancement of the interests of the province." On this tacit
understanding, they—the governor-general and the

Draper-Viger cabinet—had "acted together harmoniously," although he had "never concealed from them that he intended to do nothing" which would "prevent him from working cordially with their opponents." It was indispensable that "the head of the government should show that he has confidence in the loyalty of all the influential parties with which he has to deal, and that he should have no personal antipathies to prevent him from acting with leading men."

Despite the wishes of Lord Elgin, it was impossible to reconstruct the government with a due regard to French Canadian interests. Mr. Caron and Mr. Morin, both strong men, could not be induced to become ministers. The government continued to show signs of disintegration. Several members resigned and took judgeships in Lower Canada. Even Mr. Draper retired with the understanding that he should also go on the bench at the earliest opportunity in Upper Canada. Another effort was made to keep the ministry together, and Mr. Henry Sherwood became its head; but the most notable acquisition was Mr. John Alexander Macdonald as receiver-general. From that time this able man took a conspicuous place in the councils of the country, and eventually became prime minister of the old province of Canada, as well as of the federal dominion which was formed many years later in British North America, largely through his instrumentality. From his first entrance into politics he showed that versatility of intellect, that readiness to adapt himself to dominant political conditions and make them subservient to the interests of his party, that happy faculty of making and keeping personal friends, which were the most striking traits of his character. His mind enlarged as he had greater experience and opportunities of studying public life, and the man who entered parliament as a Tory became one of the most Liberal-Conservatives who ever administered the affairs of a colonial dependency, and, at the same time, a statesman of a comprehensive intellect who recognized the strength of British institutions and the advantage of British connection.

The obvious weakness of the reconstructed ministry was the absence of any strong men from French Canada. Mr. Denis B. Papineau was in no sense a recognized representative of the French Canadians, and did not even possess those powers of eloquence—that ability to give forth "rhetorical flashes"—which were characteristic of his reckless but highly gifted brother. In fact the ministry as then organized was a mere makeshift until the time came for obtaining an expression of opinion from the people at the polls. When parliament met in June, 1847, it was quite clear that the ministry was on the eve of its downfall. It was sustained only by a feeble majority of two votes on the motion for the adoption of the address to the governor-general. The opposition, in which LaFontaine, Baldwin, Aylwin, and Chauveau were the most prominent figures, had clearly the best of the argument in the political controversies with the tottering ministry. Even in the legislative council resolutions, condemning it chiefly on the ground that the French province was inadequately represented in the cabinet, were only negatived by the vote of the president, Mr. McGill, a wealthy merchant of Montreal, who was also a member of the administration.

Despite the weakness of the government, the legislature was called upon to deal with several questions which pressed for immediate action. Among the important measures which were passed was one providing for the amendment of the law relating to forgery, which was no longer punishable by death. Another amended the law with respect to municipalities in Lower Canada, which, however, failed to satisfy the local requirements of the people, though it remained in force for eight years, when it was replaced by one better adapted to the conditions of the French province. The legislature also discussed the serious effects of free trade upon Canadian industry, and passed an address to the Crown praying for the repeal of the laws which prevented the free use of the St. Lawrence by ships of all nations. But the most important subject with which the government was called upon to deal was one which stifled all political rivalry and national prejudices, and demanded the earnest consideration of

45

all parties. Canada, like the rest of the world, had heard of an unhappy land smitten with a hideous plague, of its crops lying in pestilential heaps and of its peasantry dying above them, of fathers, mothers, and children ghastly in their rags or nakedness, of dead unburied, and the living flying in terror, as it were, from a stricken battlefield. This dreadful Irish famine forced to Canada upwards of 100,000 persons, the greater number of whom were totally destitute and must have starved to death had they not received public or private charity. The miseries of these unhappy immigrants were aggravated to an inconceivable degree by the outbreak of disease of a most malignant character, stimulated by the wretched physical condition and by the disgraceful state of the pest ships in which they were brought across the ocean. In those days there was no effective inspection or other means taken to protect from infection the unhappy families who were driven from their old homes by poverty and misery. From Grosse Isle, the quarantine station on the Lower St. Lawrence, to the most distant towns in the western province, many thousands died in awful suffering, and left helpless orphans to evoke the aid and sympathy of pitying Canadians everywhere. Canada was in no sense responsible for this unfortunate state of things. The imperial government had allowed this Irish immigration to go on without making any effort whatever to prevent the evils that followed it from Ireland to the banks of the St. Lawrence and the Great Lakes. It was a heavy burden which Canada should never have been called upon to bear at a time when money was scarce and trade was paralyzed by the action of the imperial parliament itself. Lord Elgin was fully alive to the weighty responsibility which the situation entailed upon the British government, and at the same time did full justice to the exertions of the Canadian people to cope with this sad crisis. The legislature voted a sum of money to relieve the distress among the immigrants, but it was soon found entirely inadequate to meet the emergency.

Lord Elgin did not fail to point out to the colonial secretary "the severe strain" that this sad state of things made, not only upon charity, but upon the very loyalty of the people to a government which had shown such culpable negligence since the outbreak of the famine and the exodus from the plague-stricken island. He expressed the emphatic opinion that "all things considered, a great deal of forbearance and good feeling had been shown by the colonists under this trial." He gave full expression to the general feeling of the country that "Great Britain must make good to the province the expenses entailed on it by this visitation." He did full justice to the men and women who showed an extraordinary spirit of self-sacrifice, a positive heroism, during this national crisis. "Nothing," he wrote, "can exceed the devotion of the nuns and Roman Catholic priests, and the conduct of the clergy and of many of the laity of other denominations has been most exemplary. Many lives have been sacrificed in attendance on the sick, and administering to their temporal and spiritual need. . . This day the Mayor of Montreal, Mr. Mills, died, a very estimable man, who did much for the immigrants, and to whose firmness and philanthropy we chiefly owe it, that the immigrant sheds here were not tossed into the river by the people of the town during the summer. He has fallen a victim to his zeal on behalf of the poor plague-stricken strangers, having died of ship fever caught at the sheds." Among other prominent victims were Dr. Power, Roman Catholic Bishop of Toronto, Vicar-General Hudon of the same church, Mr. Roy, curé of Charlesbourg, and Mr. Chaderton, a Protestant clergyman. Thirteen Roman Catholic priests, if not more, died from their devotion to the unhappy people thus suddenly thrown upon their Christian charity. When the season of navigation was nearly closed, a ship arrived with a large number of people from the Irish estates of one of Her Majesty's ministers, Lord Palmerston. The natural result of this incident was to increase the feeling of indignation already aroused by the apathy of the British government during this national calamity. Happily Lord Elgin's appeals to the colonial secretary had effect, and the province was reimbursed eventually for the heavy expenses incurred by it in its efforts to fight disease, misery and death. English statesmen, after these painful experiences, recognized the necessity of enforcing strict regulations for the protection of emigrants crossing the ocean, against the greed of ship-owners. The sad story of 1847-8 cannot now be repeated in times when nations have awakened to their responsibilities towards the poor and distressed who are forced to leave their old homes for that new world which offers them well-paid work, political freedom, plenty of food and countless comforts.

In the autumn of 1847, Lord Elgin was able to seek some relief from his many cares and perplexities of government in a tour of the western province, where, to quote his own words, he met " a most gratifying and encouraging reception." He was much impressed with the many signs of prosperity which he saw on all sides. "It is indeed a glorious country," he wrote enthusiastically to Lord Grey, "and after passing, as I have done within the last fortnight, from the citadel of Quebec to the falls of Niagara, rubbing shoulders the while with its free and perfectly independent inhabitants, one begins to doubt whether it be possible to acquire a sufficient knowledge of man or nature, or to obtain an insight into the future of nations, without visiting America." During this interesting visit to Upper Canada, he seized the opportunity of giving his views on a subject which may be considered one of his hobbies, one to which he devoted much attention while in Jamaica, and this was the formation of agricultural associations for the purpose of stimulating scientific methods of husbandry.

Before the close of the first year of his administration Lord Elgin felt that the time had come for making an effort to obtain a stronger ministry by an appeal to the people. Accordingly he dissolved parliament in December, and the elections, which were hotly contested, resulted in the unequivocal condemnation of the Sherwood cabinet, and the complete success of the Liberal party led by LaFontaine and Baldwin. Among the prominent Liberals returned by the people of Upper Canada were Baldwin, Hincks, Blake, Price, Malcolm Cameron, Richards, Merritt and John Sandfield Macdonald. Among the leaders of the same party in Lower Canada were LaFontaine, Morin, Aylwin, Chauveau and Holmes. Several able Conservatives lost their seats, but Sir Allan MacNab, John A. Macdonald, Mr. Sherwood and John Hillyard Cameron succeeded in obtaining seats in the new parliament, which was, in fact, more notable than any other since the union for the ability of its members. Not the least noteworthy feature of the elections was the return of Mr. Louis J. Papineau, and Mr. Wolfred Nelson, rebels of 1837-8, both of whom had been allowed to return some time previously to the country. Mr. Papineau's career in parliament was not calculated to strengthen his position in impartial history. He proved beyond a doubt that he was only a demagogue, incapable of learning lessons of wise statesmanship during the years of reflection that were given him in exile. He continued to show his ignorance of the principles and workings of responsible government. Before the rebellion which he so rashly and vehemently forced on his credulous, impulsive countrymen, so apt to be deceived by flashy rhetoric and glittering generalities, he never made a speech or proposed a measure in support of the system of parliamentary government as explained by Baldwin and Howe, and even W. Lyon Mackenzie. His energy and eloquence were directed towards the establishment of an elective legislative council in which his compatriots would have necessarily the great majority, a supremacy that would enable him and his following to control the whole legislation and government, and promote his dominant idea of a *Nation Canadienne* in the valley of the St. Lawrence. After the union he made it the object of his political life to thwart in every way possible the sagacious, patriotic plans of LaFontaine, Morin, and other broad-minded statesmen of his own nationality, and to destroy that system of responsible government under which French Canada had become a progressive and influential section of the province.

As soon as parliament assembled at the end of February, the government was defeated on the vote for the speakership. Its nominee, Sir Allan MacNab, received only nineteen votes out of fifty-four, and Morin, the Liberal candidate, was then unanimously chosen. When the address in reply to the governor-general's speech came up for consideration, Baldwin moved an amendment, expressing a want of confidence in the ministry, which was carried by a majority of thirty votes in a house of seventy-four members, exclusive of the speaker, who votes only in case of a tie. Lord Elgin received and answered the address as soon as it was ready for presentation, and then sent for LaFontaine and Baldwin.

He spoke to them, as he tells us himself, "in a candid and friendly tone," and expressed the opinion that "there was a fair prospect, if they were moderate and firm, of forming an administration deserving and enjoying the confidence of parliament." He added that "they might count on all proper support and assistance from him." When they "dwelt on difficulties arising out of pretensions advanced in various quarters," he advised them "not to attach too much importance to such considerations, but to bring together a council strong in administrative talent, and to take their stand on the wisdom of their measures and policy." The result was the construction of a powerful government by LaFontaine with the aid of Baldwin. "My present council," Lord Elgin wrote to the colonial secretary, "unquestionably contains more talent, and has a firmer hold on the confidence of parliament and of the people than the last. There is, I think, moreover, on their part, a desire to prove, by proper deference for the authority of the governor-general (which they all admit has in my case never been abused), that they were libelled when they were accused of impracticability and anti-monarchical tendencies." These closing words go to show that the governor-general felt it was necessary to disabuse the minds of the colonial secretary and his colleagues of the false impression which the British government and people seemed to entertain, that the Tories and Conservatives were alone to be trusted in the conduct of public affairs. He saw at once that the best way of strengthening the connection with Great Britain was to give to the strongest political party in the country its true constitutional position in the administration of public affairs, and identify it thoroughly with the public interests.

The new government was constituted as follows:

Lower Canada.—Hon. L. H. LaFontaine, attorney-general of Lower Canada; Hon. James Leslie, president of the executive council; Hon. R. E. Caron, president of the legislative council; Hon. E. P. Taché, chief commissioner of public works; Hon. I. C. Aylwin, solicitor-general for Lower Canada; Hon. L. M. Viger, receiver-general.

Upper Canada.—Hon. Robert Baldwin, attorney-general of Upper Canada; Hon. R. B. Sullivan, provincial secretary; Hon. F. Hincks, inspector-general; Hon. J. H. Price, commissioner of crown lands; Hon. Malcolm Cameron, assistant commissioner of public works; Hon. W. H. Blake, solicitor-general.

The LaFontaine-Baldwin ministry must always occupy a distinguished place in the political history of the Canadian people. It was the first to be formed strictly in accordance with the principles of responsible government, and from its entrance into public life must be dated a new era in which the relations between the governor and his advisers were at last placed on a sound constitutional basis, in which the constant appeals to the imperial government on matters of purely provincial significance came to an end, in which local self-government was established in the fullest sense compatible with the continuance of the connection with the empire. It was a ministry notable not only for the ability of its members, but for the many great measures which it was able to pass during its term of office—measures calculated to promote the material advancement of the province, and above all to dispel racial prejudices and allay sectional antagonisms by the adoption of wise methods of compromise, conciliation and justice to all classes and creeds.

In Lord Elgin's letters of 1848 to Earl Grey, we can clearly see how many difficulties surrounded the discharge of his administrative functions at this time, and how fortunate it was for Canada, as well as for Great Britain, that he should have been able to form a government which possessed so fully the confidence of both sections of the province, irrespective of nationality. The revolution of February in Paris, and the efforts of a large body of Irish in the United States to evoke sympathy in Canada on behalf of republicanism were matters of deep anxiety to the governor-general and other friends of the imperial state. "It is just as well," he wrote at this time to Lord Grey, "that I should have arranged my ministry, and committed the flag of Great Britain to the custody of those who are supported by the large majority of the representatives and constituencies of the province, before the arrival of the astounding news from Europe which reached us by the last mail. There are not wanting here persons who might, under different circumstances, have attempted by seditious harangues, if not by overt acts, to turn the example of France, and the sympathies of the United States to account."

Under the circumstances he pressed upon the imperial authorities the wisdom of repealing that clause of the Union Act which restricted the use of the French language. "I am for one deeply convinced," and here he showed he differed from Lord Durham, "of the impolicy of all such attempts to denationalize the French. Generally speaking, they produce the opposite effect from that intended, causing the flame of national prejudice and animosity to burn more fiercely." But he went on to say, even were such attempts successful, what would be the inevitable result: "You may perhaps Americanize, but, depend upon it, by methods of this description you will never Anglicize the French inhabitants of the province. Let them feel, on the other hand, that their religion, their habits, their prepossessions, their prejudices, if you will, are more considered and respected here than in other portions of this vast continent, who will venture to say that the last hand which waves the British flag on American ground may not be that of a French Canadian?"[1]

Lord Elgin had a strong antipathy to Papineau—"Guy Fawkes Papineau," as he called him in one of his letters—who was, he considered, "actuated by the most malignant passions, irritated vanity, disappointed ambition and national hatred," always ready to wave "a lighted torch among combustibles." Holding such opinions, he seized every practical opportunity of thwarting Papineau's persistent efforts to create a dangerous agitation among his impulsive countrymen. He shared fully the great desire of the bishops and clergy to stem the immigration of large numbers of French Canadians into the United States by the establishment of an association for colonization purposes. Papineau endeavoured to attribute this exodus to the effects of the policy of the imperial government, and to gain control of this association with the object of using it as a means of stimulating a feeling against England, and strengthening himself

[1] These concluding words of Lord Elgin recall a similar expression of feeling by Sir Etienne Pascal Taché, " That the last gun that would be fired for British supremacy in America would be fired by a French Canadian."

56

in French Canada by such insidious methods. Lord
Elgin, with that intuitive sagacity which he applied
to practical politics, recognized the importance of
identifying himself with the movement initiated by
the bishops and their friends, of putting himself
"in so far as he could at its head," of imparting
to it "as salutary a direction as possible, and
thus wresting from Papineau's hands a potent instrument of agitation." This policy of conciliating
the French population, and anticipating the great
agitator in his design, was quite successful. To use
Lord Elgin's own language, " Papineau retired to
solitude and reflection at his seigniory, ' La Petite
Nation,'" and the governor-general was able at the
same time to call the attention of the colonial
secretary to a presentment of the grand jury of
Montreal, "in which that body adverts to the
singularly tranquil, contented state of the province."

It was at this time that Lord Elgin commenced
to give utterance to the views that he had formed
with respect to the best method of giving a stimulus to the commercial and industrial interests that
were so seriously crippled by the free trade policy
of the British government. So serious had been its
effects upon the economic conditions of the province
that mill-owners, forwarders and merchants had
been ruined " at one fell swoop," that the revenue
had been reduced by the loss of the canal dues paid
previously by the shipping engaged in the trade

promoted by the old colonial policy of England, that private property had become unsaleable, that not a shilling could be raised on the credit of the province, that public officers of all grades, including the governor-general, had to be paid in debentures which were not exchangeable at par. Under such circumstances it was not strange, said the governor-general, that Canadians were too ready to make unfavourable comparisons between themselves and their republican neighbours. "What makes it more serious," he said, "is that all the prosperity of which Canada is thus robbed is transplanted to the other side of the line, as if to make Canadians feel more bitterly how much kinder England is to the children who desert her, than to those who remain faithful. It is the inconsistency of imperial legislation, and not the adoption of one policy rather than another, which is the bane of the colonies."

He believed that "the conviction that they would be better off if they were annexed," was almost universal among the commercial classes at that time, and the peaceful condition of the province under all the circumstances was often a matter of great astonishment even to himself. In his letters urging the imperial government to find an immediate remedy for this unfortunate condition of things, he acknowledged that there was "something captivating in the project of forming this vast British Empire into one huge *Zollverein*, with free interchange of commodities, and uniform duties against the world without; though perhaps without some federal legislation it might have been impossible to carry it out."[1] Undoubtedly, under such a system "the component parts of the empire would have been united by bonds which cannot be supplied under that on which we are now entering," but he felt that, whatever were his own views on the subject, it was then impossible to disturb the policy fixed by the imperial government, and that the only course open to them, if they hoped "to keep the colonies," was to repeal the navigation laws, and to allow them "to turn to the best possible account their contiguity to the States, that they might not have cause for dissatisfaction when they contrasted their own condition with that of their neighbours."

Some years, however, passed before the governor-general saw his views fully carried out. The imperial authorities, with that extraordinary indifference to colonial conditions which too often distinguished them in those times, hesitated until well into 1849 to follow his advice with respect to the navigation

---

[1] Fifty years after these words were written, debates have taken place in the House of Commons of the Canadian federation in favour of an imperial Zollverein, which would give preferential treatment to Canada's products in British markets. The Conservative party, when led by Sir Charles Tupper, emphatically declared that "no measure of preference, which falls short of the complete realization of such a policy, should be considered final or satisfactory." England, however, still clings to free trade.

laws, and the Reciprocity Treaty was not successfully negotiated until a much later time. He had the gratification, however, before he left Canada of seeing the beneficial effects of the measures which he so earnestly laboured to promote in the interests of the country.

CHAPTER IV

THE INDEMNIFICATION ACT

THE legislature opened on January 18th, 1849, when Lord Elgin had the gratification of informing French Canadians that the restrictions imposed by the Union Act on the use of their language in the public records had been removed by a statute of the imperial parliament. For the first time in Canadian history the governor-general read the speech in the two languages; for in the past it had been the practice of the president of the legislative council to give it in French after it had been read in English from the throne. The session was memorable in political annals for the number of useful measures that were adopted. In later pages of this book I shall give a short review of these and other measures which show the importance of the legislation passed by the LaFontaine-Baldwin ministry. For the present I shall confine myself to the consideration of a question which created an extraordinary amount of public excitement, culminated in the destruction of valuable public property, and even threatened the life of the governor-general, who during one of the most trying crises in Canadian history, displayed a coolness and patience, an indifference to all personal considerations, a political sagacity and a strict adherence to sound methods of constitutional government, which entitle him to the gratitude of Canadians, who might have seen their country torn asunder by internecine strife, had there been then a weak and passionate man at the head of the executive. As it will be seen later, he, like the younger Pitt in England, was " the pilot who weathered the storm." In Canada, the storm, in which the elements of racial antagonism, of political rivalry and disappointment, of spoiled fortunes and commercial ruin raged tumultuously for a while, threatened not only to drive Canada back for years in its political and material development, but even to disturb the relations between the dependency and the imperial state.

The legislation which gave rise to this serious convulsion in the country was, in a measure, an aftermath of the rebellious risings of 1837 and 1838 in Upper and Lower Canada. Many political grievances had been redressed since the union, and the French Canadians had begun to feel that their interests were completely safe under a system of government which gave them an influential position in the public councils. The restoration of their language to its proper place in a country composed of two nationalities standing on a sure footing of equal political and civil rights, was a great consolation to the French people of the east. The pardon extended to the rash men who were directly concerned in

the events of 1837 and 1838, was also well calculated to heal the wounds inflicted on the province
during that troublous period. It needed only the
passage of another measure to conceal the scars
of those unhappy days, and to bury the past in
that oblivion in which all Canadians, anxious for
the unity and harmony of the two races and the
satisfactory operation of political institutions, were
sincerely desirous of hiding it forever. This measure
was pecuniary compensation from the state for
certain losses incurred by people in French Canada
in consequence of the wanton destruction of property during the revolt. The obligation of the
state to give such compensation had been fully
recognized before and after the union.

The special council of Lower Canada and the
legislature of Upper Canada had authorized the
payment of an indemnity to those loyal inhabitants
in their respective provinces who had sustained losses
during the insurrections. It was not possible, however, before the union, to make payments out of the
public treasury in accordance with the ordinance of
the special council of Lower Canada and the statute
of the legislature of Upper Canada. In the case of
both provinces these measures were enacted to
satisfy the demands that were made for compensation by a large number of people who claimed to
have suffered losses at the outbreak of the rebellions,
or during the raids from the United States which
followed these risings and which kept the country

in a state of ferment for months. The legislature of the united provinces passed an act during its first session to extend compensation to losses occasioned in Upper Canada by violence on the part of persons " acting or assuming to act " on Her Majesty's behalf "for the suppression of the said rebellion or for the prevention of further disturbances." Funds were also voted out of the public revenues for the payment of indemnities to those who had met with the losses set forth in this legislation affecting Upper Canada. It was, on the whole, a fair settlement of just claims in the western province.

The French Canadians in the legislature supported the measure, and urged with obvious reason that the same consideration should be shown to the same class of persons in Lower Canada. It was not, however, until the session of 1845, when the Draper-Viger ministry was in office, that an address was passed to the governor-general, Lord Metcalfe, praying him to take such steps as were necessary "to insure to the inhabitants of that portion of this province, formerly Lower Canada, an indemnity for just losses suffered during the rebellions of 1837 and 1838." The immediate result was the appointment of commissioners to make inquiry into the losses sustained by " Her Majesty's loyal subjects" in Lower Canada "during the late unfortunate rebellion." The commissioners found some difficulty in acting upon their instructions, which called upon them to distinguish the cases of those " who had joined, aided or abetted the said rebellion, from the cases of those who had not done so," and they accordingly applied for definite advice from Lord Cathcart, whose advisers were still the Draper-Viger ministry. The commissioners were officially informed that " it was his Excellency's intention that they should be guided by no other description of evidence than that furnished by the sentences of the courts of law." They were further informed that it was only intended that they should form a general estimate of the rebellion losses, " the particulars of which must form the subject of more minute inquiry hereafter, under legislative authority."

During the session of 1846 the commissioners made a report which gave a list of 2,176 persons who made claims amounting in the aggregate to £241,965. At the same time the commissioners expressed the opinion that £100,000 would be adequate to satisfy all just demands, and directed attention to the fact that upwards of £25,503 were actually claimed by persons who had been condemned by a court-martial for their participation in the rebellion. The report also set forth that the inquiry conducted by the commissioners had been necessarily imperfect in the absence of legal power to make a minute investigation, and that they had been compelled largely to trust to the allegations of the claimants who had laid their cases before them, and that it was only from data collected in

this way that they had been able to come to conclusions as to the amount of losses.

When the Draper-Viger ministry first showed a
readiness to take up the claims of Lower Canada
for the same compensation that had been granted
to Upper Canada, they had been doubtless influenced, not solely by the conviction that they
were called upon to perform an act of justice, but
mainly by a desire to strengthen themselves in the
French province. We have already read that their
efforts in this direction entirely failed, and that they
never obtained in that section any support from the
recognized leaders of public opinion, but were
obliged to depend upon Denis B. Papineau and
Viger to keep up a pretence of French Canadian
representation in the cabinet. It is, then, easy to
believe that, when the report of the commissioners
came before them, they were not very enthusiastic
on the subject, or prepared to adopt vigorous
measures to settle the question on some equitable
basis, and remove it entirely from the field of
political and national conflict.

They did nothing more than make provision for
the payment of £9,986, which represented claims
fully investigated and recognized as justifiable before
the union, and left the general question of indemnity
for future consideration. Indeed, it is doubtful if the
Conservative ministry of that day, the mere creation
of Lord Metcalfe, kept in power by a combination of
Tories and other factions in Upper Canada, could

have satisfactorily dealt with a question which required the interposition of a government having the confidence of both sections of the province. One thing is quite certain. This ministry, weak as it was, Tory and ultra-loyalist as it claimed to be, had recognized by the appointment of a commission, the justice of giving compensation to French Canada on the principles which had governed the settlement of claims from Upper Canada. Had the party which supported that ministry been influenced by any regard for consistency or principle, it was bound in 1849 to give full consideration to the question, and treat it entirely on its merits with the view of preventing its being made a political issue and a means of arousing racial and sectional animosities. As we shall now see, however, party passion, political demagogism, and racial hatred prevailed above all high considerations of the public peace and welfare, when parliament was asked by the LaFontaine-Baldwin ministry to deal seriously and practically with the question of indemnity to Lower Canada.

The session was not far advanced when La-Fontaine brought forward a series of resolutions, on which were subsequently based a bill, which set forth in the preamble that " in order to redeem the pledge given to the sufferers of such losses . . . it is necessary and just that the particulars of such losses, not yet paid and satisfied, should form the subject of more minute inquiry under legislative authority (see p. 65 *ante*) and that the same, so far only as they may have arisen from the total or partial, unjust, unnecessary or wanton destruction of dwellings, buildings, property and effects . . . should be paid and satisfied." The act provided that no indemnity should be paid to persons "who had been convicted of treason during the rebellion, or who, having been taken into custody, had submitted to Her Majesty's will, and been transported to Bermuda." Five commissioners were to be appointed to carry out the provisions of the act, which also provided £400,000 for the payment of legal claims.

Then all the forces hostile to the government gathered their full strength for an onslaught on a measure which such Tories as Sir Allan Mac-Nab and Henry Sherwood believed gave them an excellent opportunity of arousing a strong public sentiment which might awe the governor-general and bring about a ministeral crisis. The issue was not one of public principle or of devotion to the Crown, it was simply a question of obtaining a party victory *per fas aut nefas*. The debate on the second reading of the bill was full of bitterness, intensified even to virulence. Mr. Sherwood declared that the proposal of the government meant nothing else than the giving of a reward to the very persons who had been the cause of the shedding of blood and the destruction of property throughout the country. Sir Allan MacNab went so far in a moment of passion as to insult the French Canadian people by calling them "aliens and rebels." The solicitor-general, Mr. Hume Blake,[1] who was Irish by birth, and possessed a great power of invective, inveighed in severe terms against "the family compact" as responsible for the rebellion, and declared that the stigma of "rebels" applied with complete force to the men who were then endeavouring to prevent the passage of a bill which was a simple act of justice to a large body of loyal people. Sir Allan MacNab instantly became furious and said that if Mr. Blake called him a rebel it was simply a lie.

Then followed a scene of tumult, in which the authority of the chair was disregarded, members indulged in the most disorderly cries, and the people in the galleries added to the excitement on the floor by their hisses and shouts. The galleries were cleared with the greatest difficulty, and a hostile encounter between Sir Allan and Mr. Blake was only prevented by the intervention of the sergeant-at-arms, who took them into custody by order of the House until they gave assurances that they would proceed no further in the unseemly dispute. When the debate was resumed on the following day, LaFontaine brought it again to the proper level of argument and reason, and

[1] The father of the Hon. Edward Blake, the eminent constitutional lawyer, who occupied for many years a notable place in Canadian politics, and is now (1902) a member of the British House of Commons.

showed that both parties were equally pledged to a measure based on considerations of justice, and declared positively that the government would take every possible care in its instructions to the commissioners that no rebel should receive any portion of the indemnity, which was intended only as a compensation to those who had just claims upon the country for the losses that they actually sustained in the course of the unfortunate rebellion.

At this time the Conservative and ultra-loyal press was making frantic appeals to party passions and racial prejudices, and calling upon the governor-general to intervene and prevent the passage of a measure which, in the opinion of loyal Canadians, was an insult to the Crown and its adherents. Public meetings were also held and efforts made to arouse a violent feeling against the bill. The governor-general understood his duty too well as the head of the executive to interfere with the bill while passing through the two Houses, and paid no heed to these passionate appeals dictated by partisan rancour, while the ministry pressed the question to the test of a division as soon as possible. The resolutions and the several readings of the bill passed both Houses by large majorities. The bill was carried in the assembly on March 9th by forty-seven votes against eighteen, and in the legislative council on the 15th, by fifteen against fourteen. By an analysis of the division in the popular chamber, it will be seen that out of thirty-one members from Upper Canada seventeen supported and fourteen opposed the bill, while out of ten Lower Canadian members of British descent there were six who voted yea and four nay. The representatives of French Canada as a matter of course were arrayed as one in favour of an act of justice to their compatriots. During the passage of the bill its opponents deluged the governor-general with petitions asking him either to dissolve the legislature or to reserve the bill for the consideration of the imperial government. Such appeals had no effect whatever upon Lord Elgin, who was determined to adhere to the well understood rules of parliamentary government in all cases of political controversy.

When the bill had passed all its stages in the two Houses by large majorities of both French and English Canadians, the govenor-general came to the legislative council and gave the royal assent to the measure, which was entitled "An Act to provide for the indemnification of parties in Lower Canada whose property was destroyed during the rebellion in the years 1837 and 1838." No other constitutional course could have been followed by him under all the circumstances. In his letters to the colonial secretary he did not hesitate to express his regret "that this agitation should have been stirred, and that any portion of the funds of the province should be diverted now from much more useful purposes to make good losses sustained by individuals in the rebellion," but he believed that "a great deal of property was cruelly and wantonly destroyed" in Lower Canada, and that "this government, after what their predecessors had done, and with Papineau in the rear, could not have helped taking up this question." He saw clearly that it was impossible to dissolve a parliament just elected by the people, and in which the government had a large majority. "If I had dissolved parliament," to quote his own words, "I might have produced a rebellion, but assuredly I should not have procured a change of ministry. The leaders of the party know that as well as I do, and were it possible to play tricks in such grave concerns, it would have been easy to throw them into utter confusion by merely calling upon them to form a government. They were aware, however, that I could not for the sake of discomfiting them hazard so desperate a policy; so they have played out their game of faction and violence without fear of consequences."

His reasons for not reserving the bill for the consideration of the British government must be regarded as equally cogent by every student of our system of government, especially by those persons who believe in home rule in all matters involving purely Canadian interests. In the first place, the bill for the relief of a corresponding class of persons in Upper Canada, "which was couched in terms very nearly similar, was not reserved," and it was "difficult to discover a sufficient reason, so far as the representative of the Crown was concerned, for dealing with the one measure differently from the other." And in the second place, "by reserving the bill he should only throw upon Her Majesty's government or (as it would appear to the popular eye in Canada) on Her Majesty herself, a responsibility which rests and ought to rest" upon the governor-general of Canada. If he passed the bill, "whatever mischief ensues may probably be repaired," if the worst came to the worst, "by the sacrifice" of himself. If the case were referred to England, on the other hand, it was not impossible that Her Majesty might "only have before her the alternative of provoking a rebellion in Lower Canada, by refusing her assent to a measure chiefly affecting the interests of the *habitants* and thus throwing the whole population into Papineau's hands, or of wounding the susceptibilities of some of the best subjects she has in the province."

A Canadian writer at the present time can refer only with a feeling of indignation and humiliation to the scenes of tumult, rioting and incendiarism, which followed the royal assent to the bill of indemnity. When Lord Elgin left Parliament House —formerly the Ste. Anne market—a large crowd insulted him with opprobrious epithets. In his own words he was "received with ironical cheers and hootings, and a small knot of individuals, consisting, it has since been ascertained, of persons

of a respectable class in society, pelted the carriage
with missiles which must have been brought for
that purpose." A meeting was held in the open air,
and after several speeches of a very inflammatory
character had been made, the mob rushed to the
parliament building, which was soon in flames. By
this disgraceful act of incendiarism most valuable
collections of books and documents were destroyed,
which, in some cases, could not be replaced. Supporters of the bill were everywhere insulted and
maltreated while the excitement was at its height.
LaFontaine's residence was attacked and injured.
His valuable library of books and manuscripts,
some of them very rare, was destroyed by fire
—a deplorable incident which recalls the burning
and mutilation of the rich historical collections of
Hutchinson, the last loyalist governor of Massachusetts, at the commencement of the American
revolution in Boston.

A few days later Lord Elgin's life was in actual
danger at the hands of the unruly mob, as he was
proceeding to Government House—then the old
Château de Ramezay on Notre Dame Street—to
receive an address from the assembly. On his
return to Monklands he was obliged to take a
circuitous route to evade the same mob who were
waiting with the object of further insulting him
and otherwise giving vent to their feelings.

The government appears to have been quite unconscious that the public excitement was likely to

Burning of the Parliament Buildings, Montreal, 1849

assume so dangerous a phase, and had accordingly taken none of those precautions which might have prevented the destruction of the Parliament House and its valuable contents. Indeed it would seem that the leaders of the movement against the bill had themselves no idea that the political storm which they had raised by their inflammatory harangues would become a whirlwind so entirely beyond their control. Their main object was to bring about a ministerial crisis. Sir Allan MacNab, the leader of the opposition, himself declared that he was amazed at the dangerous form which the public indignation had at last assumed. He had always been a devoted subject of the sovereign, and it is only just to say that he could under no circumstances become a rebel, but he had been carried away by his feelings and had made rash observations more than once under the belief that the bill would reward the same class of men whom he and other loyalists had fought against in Upper Canada. Whatever he felt in his heart, he and his followers must always be held as much responsible for the disturbances of 1849 as were Mackenzie and Papineau for those of 1837. Indeed there was this difference between them: the former were reckless, but at least they had, in the opinion of many persons, certain political grievances to redress, while the latter were simply opposing the settlement of a question which they were bound to consider fairly and impartially, if they had any respect for former

pledges. Papineau, Mackenzie and Nelson may well
have found a measure of justification for their past
madness when they found the friends of the old
"family compact" and the extreme loyalists of
1837 and 1838 incited to insult the sovereign in
the person of her representative, to create racial
passion and to excite an agitation which might
at any moment develop into a movement most
fatal to Canada and her connection with England.

Happily for the peace of the country, Lord
Elgin and his councillors showed a forbearance and
a patience which could hardly have been expected
from them during the very serious crisis in which
they lived for some weeks. "I am prepared," said
Lord Elgin at the very moment his life was in
danger, "to bear any amount of obloquy that may
be cast upon me, but, if I can possibly prevent it,
no stain of blood shall rest upon my name." When
he remained quiet at Monklands and decided not
to give his enemies further opportunities for out-
bursts of passion by paying visits to the city, even
if protected by a military force, he was taunted by
the papers of the opposition with cowardice for
pursuing a course which, we can all now clearly
see, was in the interests of peace and order. When
at a later time LaFontaine's house was again
attacked after the arrest of certain persons implicated in the destruction of the Parliament House,
and one of the assailants was killed by a shot fired
from inside, he positively refused to consent to

martial law or any measures of increased rigour until a further appeal had been made to the mayor and corporation of the city. The issue proved that he was clearly right in his opinion of the measures that should be taken to restore order at this time. The law-abiding citizens of Montreal at once responded to a proclamation of the mayor to assist him in the maintenance of peace, and the coroner's jury—one member being an Orangeman who had taken part in the funeral of the deceased—brought in a unanimous verdict, acquitting LaFontaine of all blame for the unfortunate incident that had occurred during the unlawful attack on his residence.

The Montreal disturbances soon evoked the indignation of the truly loyal inhabitants of the province. Addresses came to the governor-general from all parts to show him that the riots were largely due to local causes, "especially to commercial distress acting on religious bigotry and national hatred." He had also the gratification of learning that his constitutional action was fully justified by the imperial government, as well as supported in parliament where it was fully discussed. When he offered to resign his office, he was assured by Lord Grey that "his relinquishment of that office, which, under any circumstances, would be a most serious blow to Her Majesty's service and to the province, could not fail, in the present state of affairs, to be most injurious to the public welfare, from the encouragement which it would give to those who have been concerned in the violent and illegal opposition which has been offered to your government." In parliament, Mr. Gladstone, who seems never to have been well-informed on the subject, went so far as to characterize the Rebellion Losses Bill as a measure for rewarding rebels, but both Lord John Russell, then leader of the government, and his great opponent, Sir Robert Peel, gave their unqualified support to the measure. The result was that an amendment proposed by Mr. Herries in favour of the disallowance of the act was defeated by a majority of 141.

This action of the imperial authorities had the effect of strengthening the public sentiment in Canada in support of Lord Elgin and his advisers. The government set to work vigorously to carry out the provisions of the law, appointing the same commissioners as had acted under the previous ministry, and was able in a very short time to settle definitely this very disturbing question. It was deemed inexpedient, however, to keep the seat of government at Montreal. After a very full and anxious consideration of the question, it was decided to act on the recommendation of the legislature that it should thereafter meet alternately at Toronto and Quebec, and that the next session should be held at Toronto in accordance with this arrangement. This "perambulating system" was tried for several years, but it proved so inconvenient and expensive that the legislature in 1858 passed an address to Her

Majesty praying her to choose a permanent capital. The place selected was the city of Ottawa, on account of its situation on the frontier of the two provinces, the almost equal division of its population into French and English, its remoteness from the American borders, and consequently its comparative security in time of war. Some years later it became the capital of the Dominion of Canada— the confederation of provinces and territories extending across the continent.

In the autumn of 1849 Lord Elgin made a tour of the western part of the province of Upper Canada for the purpose of obtaining some expression of opinion from the people in the very section where the British feeling was the strongest. On this occasion he was attended only by an aide-de-camp and a servant, as an answer to those who were constantly assailing him for want of courage. Here and there, as he proceeded west, after leaving French Canada, he was insulted by a few Orangemen, notably by Mr. Ogle R. Gowan, who appeared on the wharf at Brockville with a black flag, but apart from such feeble exhibitions of political spite he met with a reception, especially west of Toronto, which proved beyond cavil that the heart and reason of the country, as a whole, were undoubtedly in his favour, and that nowhere was there any actual sympathy with the unhappy disturbances in Montreal. He had also the gratification soon after his return from this pleasant tour to receive from the British government an official notification that he had been raised to the British peerage under the title of Baron Elgin of Elgin in recognition of his distinguished services to the Crown and empire in America.

But it was a long time before Lord Elgin was forgiven by a small clique of politicians for the part he had taken in troubles which ended in their signal discomfiture. The political situation continued for a while to be aggravated by the serious commercial embarrassment which existed throughout the country, and led to the circulation of a manifesto, signed by leading merchants and citizens of Montreal, urging as remedies for the prevalent depression a revival of colonial protection by England, reciprocal free trade with the United States, a federal union or republic of British North America, and even annexation to the neighbouring states as a last resort. This document did not suggest rebellion or a forceable separation from England. It even professed affection for the home land; but it encouraged the idea that the British government would doubtless yield to any colonial pressure in this direction when it was convinced that the step was beyond peradventure in the interest of the dependency. The manifesto represented only a temporary phase of sentiment and is explained by the fact that some men were dissatisfied with the existing condition of things and ready for any change whatever. The movement found no active or general response among the great mass of thinking people; and it was impossible for the Radicals of Lower Canada to persuade their compatriots that their special institutions, so dear to their hearts, could be safely entrusted to their American republican neighbours. All the men who, in the thoughtlessness of youth or in a moment of great excitement, signed the manifesto—notably the Molsons, the Redpaths, Luther H. Holton, John Rose, David Lewis Mac-Pherson, A. A. Dorion, E. Goff Penny—became prominent in the later public and commercial life of British North America, as ministers of the Crown, judges, senators, millionaires, and all devoted subjects of the British sovereign.

When Lord Elgin found that the manifesto contained the signatures of several persons holding office by commission from the Queen, he made an immediate inquiry into the matter, and gave expression to the displeasure of the Crown by removing from office those who confessed that they had signed the objectionable document, or declined to give any answer to the queries he had addressed to them. His action on this occasion was fully justified by the imperial government, which instructed him "to resist to the utmost any attempt that might be made to bring about a separation of Canada from the British dominions." But while Lord Elgin, as the representative of the Queen, was compelled by a stern sense of duty to condemn such acts of infidelity to the empire, he did not conceal from himself that there was a great deal in the economic conditions of the provinces which demanded an immediate remedy before all reason for discontent could disappear. He did not fail to point out to Lord Grey that it was necessary to remove the causes of the public irritation and uneasiness by the adoption of measures calculated to give a stimulus to Canadian industry and commerce. "Let me then assure your Lordship," he wrote in November 1849, "and I speak advisedly in offering this assurance, that the dissatisfaction now existing in Canada, whatever may be the forms with which it may clothe itself, is due mainly to commercial causes. I do not say that there is no discontent on political grounds. Powerful individuals and even classes of men are, I am well aware, dissatisfied with the conduct of affairs. But I make bold to affirm that so general is the belief that, under the present circumstances of our commercial condition, the colonists pay a heavy pecuniary fine for their fidelity to Great Britain, that nothing but the existence of an unwonted degree of political contentment among the masses has prevented the cry for annexation from spreading like wildfire through the province." He then proceeded again to press upon the consideration of the government the necessity of following the removal of the imperial restrictions upon navigation and shipping in the colony, by the establishment of a reciprocity of trade between the United States and the British North American

Provinces. The change in the navigation laws took place in 1849, but it was not possible to obtain larger trade with the United States until several years later, as we shall see in a future chapter when we come to review the relations between that country and Canada.

Posterity has fully justified the humane, patient and discreet constitutional course pursued by Lord Elgin during one of the most trying ordeals through which a colonial governor ever passed. He had the supreme gratification, however, before he left the province, of finding that his policy had met with that success which is its best eulogy and justification. Two years after the events of 1849, he was able to write to England that he did not believe that "the function of the governor-general under constitutional government as the moderator between parties, the representative of interests which are common to all the inhabitants of the country, as distinct from those that divide them into parties, was ever so fully and so frankly recognized." He was sure that he could not have achieved such results if he had had blood upon his hands. His business was "to humanize, not to harden." One of Canada's ablest men—not then in politics—had said to him: "Yes, I see it all now, you were right, a thousand times right, though I thought otherwise then. I own that I would have reduced Montreal to ashes before I would have endured half of what you did," and he added, "I should have been justified, too."

"Yes," answered Lord Elgin, "you would have been justified because your course would have been perfectly defensible; but it would not have been the best course. Mine was a better one." And the result was this, in his own words: "700,000 French reconciled to England, not because they are getting rebel money; I believe, indeed that no rebels will get a farthing; but because they believe that the British governor is just. 'Yes,' but you may say, 'this is purchased by the alienation of the British.' Far from it, I took the whole blame upon myself; and I will venture to affirm that the Canadian British were never so loyal as they are at this hour; [this was, remember, two years after the burning of Parliament House] and, what is more remarkable still, and more directly traceable to this policy of forbearance, never, since Canada existed, has party spirit been more moderate, and the British and French races on better terms than they are now; and this in spite of the withdrawal of protection, and of the proposal to throw on the colony many charges which the imperial government has hitherto borne."

Canadians at the beginning of the twentieth century may also say as Lord Elgin said at the close of this letter, *Magna est Veritas.*

CHAPTER V

THE END OF THE LAFONTAINE-BALDWIN
MINISTRY, 1851

THE LaFontaine-Baldwin government remained in office until October, 1851, when it was constitutionally dissolved by the retirement of the prime minister soon after the resignation of his colleague from Upper Canada, whose ability as a statesman and integrity as a man had given such popularity to the cabinet throughout the country. It has been well described by historians as "The Great Ministry." During its existence Canada obtained a full measure of self-government in all provincial affairs. Trade was left perfectly untrammeled by the repeal in June, 1849, of the navigation laws, in accordance with the urgent appeals of the governor-general to the colonial secretary. The immediate results were a stimulus to the whole commerce of the province, and an influx of shipping to the ports of the St. Lawrence. The full control of the post-office was handed over to the Canadian government. This was one of the most popular concessions made to the Canadian people, since it gave them opportunities for cheaper circulation of letters and newspapers, so necessary in a new and sparsely settled country, where the people were

85

separated from each other in many districts by long distances. One of the grievances of the Canadians before the union had been the high postage imposed on letters throughout British North America. The poor settlers were not able to pay the three or four shillings, and even more, demanded for letters mailed from their old homes across the sea, and it was not unusual to find in country post-offices a large accumulation of dead letters, refused on account of the expense. The management of the postal service by imperial officers was in every way most unsatisfactory; it was chiefly carried on for the benefit of a few persons, and not for the convenience or consolation of the many who were always anxious for news of their kin in the "old country." After the union there was a little improvement in the system, but it was not really administered in the interests of the Canadian people until it was finally transferred to the colonial authorities. When this desirable change took place, an impulse was soon given to the dissemination of letters and newspapers. The government organized a post-office department, of which the head was a postmaster-general with a seat in the cabinet.

Other important measures made provision for the introduction of the decimal system into the provincial currency, the taking of a census every ten years, the more satisfactory conduct of parliamentary elections and the prevention of corruption, better facilities for the administration of justice in the two provinces, the abolition of primogeniture with respect to real estate in Upper Canada, and the more equitable division of property among the children of an intestate, based on the civil law of French Canada and old France.

Education also continued to show marked improvement in accordance with the wise policy adopted since 1841. Previous to the union popular education had been at a very low ebb, although there were a number of efficient private schools in all the provinces where the children of the well-to-do classes could be taught classics and many branches of knowledge. In Lower Canada not one-tenth of the children of the *habitants* could write, and only one-fifth could read. In Upper Canada the schoolmasters as a rule, according to Mrs. Anna Jameson,[1] were "ill-fed, ill-clothed, ill-paid, or not paid at all." In the generality of cases they were either Scotsmen or Americans, totally unfit for the positions they filled. As late as 1833 Americans or anti-British adventurers taught in the greater proportion of the schools, where the pupils used United States text-books replete with sentiments hostile to England—a wretched state of things stopped by legislation only in 1846. Year by year after the union improvements were made in the school system, with the object of giving every possible educational facility to rich and poor alike.

[1] See her "Winter Studies and Summer Rambles in Canada." London, 1838.

In the course of time elementary education became practically free. The success of the system in the progressive province of Upper Canada largely rested on the public spirit of the municipalities. It was engrafted on the municipal institutions of each county, to which provincial aid was given in proportion to the amount raised by local assessment. The establishment of normal schools and public libraries was one of the useful features of school legislation in those days. The merits of the system naturally evoked the sympathy and praise of the governor-general, who was deeply interested in the intellectual progress of the country. The development of "individual self-reliance and local exertion under the superintendence of a central authority exercising an influence almost exclusively moral is the ruling principle of the system."

Provision was also made for the imparting of religious instruction by clergymen of the several religious denominations recognized by law, and for the establishment of separate schools for Protestants or Roman Catholics whenever there was a necessity for them in any local division. On the question of religious instruction Lord Elgin always entertained strong opinions. After expressing on one occasion his deep gratification at the adoption of legislation which had "enabled Upper Canada to place itself in the van among the nations in the important work of providing an efficient system of education for the whole community," he proceeded to commend the fact that "its foundation was laid deep in the framework of our common Christianity." He showed then how strong was the influence of the moral sense in his character: "While the varying opinions of a mixed religious society are scrupulously respected . . . . it is confidently expected that every child who attends our common schools shall learn there that he is a being who has an interest in eternity as well as in time; that he has a Father towards whom he stands in a closer and more affecting and more endearing relationship than to any earthly father, and that that Father is in heaven." But since the expression of these emphatic opinions the tendency of legislation in the majority of the provinces—but not in French Canada, where the Roman Catholic clergy still largely control their own schools—has been to encourage secular and not religious education. It would be instructive to learn whether either morality or Christianity has been the gainer.

It is only justice to the memory of a man who died many years after he saw the full fruition of his labours to say that Upper Canada owes a debt of gratitude to the Rev. Egerton Ryerson for his services in connection with its public school system. He was far from being a man of deep knowledge or having a capacity for expressing his views with terseness or clearness. He had also a large fund of personal vanity which made him sometimes a busybody when

89

inaction or silence would have been wiser for himself. We can only explain his conduct in relation to the constitutional controversy between Lord Metcalfe and the Liberal party by the supposition that he could not resist the blandishments of that eminent nobleman, when consulted by him, but allowed his reason to be captured and then gave expression to opinions and arguments which showed that he had entirely misunderstood the seriousness of the political crisis or the sound practice of the parliamentary system which Baldwin, LaFontaine and Howe had so long laboured to establish in British North America. The books he wrote can never be read with profit or interest. His "History of the United Empire Loyalists" is probably the dullest book ever compiled by a Canadian, and makes us thankful that he was never able to carry out the intention he expressed in a letter to Sir Francis Hincks of writing a constitutional history of Canada. But though he made no figure in Canadian letters, and was not always correct in his estimate of political issues, he succeeded in making for himself a reputation for public usefulness in connection with the educational system of Upper Canada far beyond that of the majority of his Canadian contemporaries.

The desire of the imperial and Canadian governments to bury in oblivion the unhappy events of 1837 and 1838 was very emphatically impressed by the concession of an amnesty in 1849 to all the persons who had been engaged in the rebellions. In the time of Lord Metcalfe, Papineau, Nelson, and other rebels long in exile, had been allowed to return to Canada either by virtue of special pardons granted by the Crown under the great seal, or by the issue of writs of *nolle prosequi*. The signal result of the Amnesty Act passed in 1849 by the Canadian legislature, in accordance with the recommendation in the speech from the throne, was the return of William Lyon Mackenzie, who had led an obscure and wretched life in the United States ever since his flight from Upper Canada in 1837, and had gained an experience which enabled him to value British institutions more highly than those of the republic.

An impartial historian must always acknowledge the fact that Mackenzie was ill-used by the family compact and English governors during his political career before the rebellion, and that he had sound views of constitutional government which were well worthy of the serious consideration of English statesmen. In this respect he showed more intelligence than Papineau, who never understood the true principles of parliamentary government, and whose superiority, compared with the little, pugnacious Upper Canadian, was the possession of a stately presence and a gift of fervid eloquence which was well adapted to impress and carry away his impulsive and too easily deceived countrymen. If Mackenzie had shown more control of his temper and confined himself to such legitimate constitutional agitation as was stirred up by a far abler man, Joseph Howe, the father of responsible government in the maritime provinces, he would have won a far higher place in Canadian history. He was never a statesman; only an agitator who failed entirely throughout his passionate career to understand the temper of the great body of Liberals—that they were in favour not of rebellion but of such a continuous and earnest enunciation of their constitutional principles as would win the whole province to their opinions and force the imperial government itself to make the reforms imperatively demanded in the public interests.[1] But, while we cannot recognize in him the qualities of a safe political leader, we should do justice to that honesty of purpose and that spirit of unselfishness which placed him on a far higher plane than many of those men who belonged to the combination derisively called the "family compact," and who never showed a willingness to consider other interests than their own. Like Papineau, Mackenzie became a member of the provincial legislature, but only to give additional evidence that he

[1] "I am inclined," wrote Lord Durham, "to view the insurrectionary movements which did take place as indicative of no deep-rooted disaffection, and to believe that almost the entire body of the reformers of this province sought only by constitutional means to attain those objects for which they had so long peaceably struggled before the unhappy troubles occasioned by the violence of a few unprincipled adventurers and heated enthusiasts."

did not possess the capacity for discreet, practical statesmanship possessed by Hincks and Baldwin and other able Upper Canadians who could in those days devote themselves to the public interests with such satisfactory results to the province at large.

It was Baldwin who, while a member of the ministry, succeeded in carrying the measure which created the University of Toronto, and placed it on the broad basis on which it has rested ever since. His measure was the result of an agitation which had commenced before the union. Largely through the influence of Dr. Strachan, the first Anglican bishop of Upper Canada, Sir Peregrine Maitland, when lieutenant-governor, had been induced to grant a charter establishing King's College "at or near York" (Toronto), with university privileges. Like old King's in Nova Scotia, established before the beginning of the century, it was directly under the control of the Church of England, since its governing body and its professors had to subscribe to its thirty-nine articles. It received an endowment of the public lands available for educational purposes in the province, and every effort was made to give it a provincial character though conducted entirely on sectarian principles. The agitation which eventually followed its establishment led to some modifications in its character, but, for all that, it remained practically under the direction of the Anglican bishop and clergy, and did not obtain the support or approval of any dissenters. After the union a large edifice was commenced in the city of Toronto, on the site where the legislative and government buildings now stand, and an energetic movement was made to equip it fully as a university.

When the Draper-Viger ministry was in office, it was proposed to meet the growing opposition to the institution by establishing a university which should embrace three denominational colleges— King's College, Toronto, for the Church of England, Queen's College, Kingston, for the Presbyterians, and Victoria College, Cobourg, for the Methodists— but the bishop and adherents of the Anglican body strenuously opposed the measure, which failed to pass in a House where the Tories were in the ascendant. Baldwin had himself previously introduced a bill of a similar character as a compromise, but it had failed to meet with any support, and when he came into office he saw that he must go much further and establish a non-sectarian university if he expected to carry any measure on the subject in the legislature. The result was the establishment of the University of Toronto, on a strictly un-denominational foundation. Bishop Strachan was deeply incensed at what he regarded as a violation of vested rights of the Church of England in the University of King's College, and never failed for years to style the provincial institution "the God-less university." In this as in other matters he failed to see that the dominant sentiment of the country would not sustain any attempt on the part of a single denomination to control a college which obtained its chief support from public aid. Whilst every tribute must be paid to the zeal, energy, and courage of the bishop, we must at the same time recognize the fact that his former connection with the family compact and his inability to understand the necessity of compromise in educational and other matters did much injury to a great church.

He succeeded unfortunately in identifying it with the unpopular and aristocratic party, opposed to the extension of popular government and the diffusion of cheap education among all classes of people. With that indomitable courage which never failed him at a crisis he set to work to advance the denomination whose interests he had always at heart, and succeeded by appeals to English aid in establishing Trinity College, which has always occupied a high position among Canadian universities, although for a while it failed to arouse sympathy in the public mind, until the feelings which had been evoked in connection with the establishment of King's had passed away. An effort is now (1901) being made to affiliate it with the same university which the bishop had so obstinately and bitterly opposed, in the hope of giving it larger opportunities for usefulness. Its complete success of late has been impeded by the want of adequate funds to maintain those departments of scientific instruction now imperatively demanded in modern education. When this affiliation takes place, the friends of Trinity, conversant with its history from its beginning, believe that the portrait of the old bishop, now hanging on the walls of Convocation Hall, should be covered with a dark veil, emblematic of the sorrow which he would feel were he to return to earth and see what to him would be the desecration of an institution which he built as a great remonstrance against the spoliation of the church in 1849.

The La Fontaine-Baldwin ministry also proved itself fully equal to the demands of public opinion by its vigorous policy with respect to the colonization of the wild lands of the province, the improvement of the navigation of the St. Lawrence, and the construction of railways. Measures were passed which had the effect of opening up and settling large districts by the offer of grants of public land at a nominal price and very easy terms of payment. In this way the government succeeded in keeping in the country a large number of French Canadians who otherwise would have gone to the United States, where the varied industries of a very enterprising people have always attracted a large number of Canadians of all classes and races.

The canals were at last completed in accordance with the wise policy inaugurated after the union by Lord Sydenham, whose commercial instincts at once recognized the necessity of giving western trade easy access to the ocean by the improvement of the great waterways of Canada. It had always been the ambition of the people of Upper Canada before the union to obtain a continuous and secure system of navigation from the lakes to Montreal. The Welland Canal between Lakes Erie and Ontario was commenced as early as 1824 through the enterprise of Mr. William Hamilton Merritt— afterwards a member of the LaFontaine-Baldwin ministry—and the first vessel passed its locks in 1829; but it was very badly managed, and the legislature, after having aided it from time to time, was eventually obliged to take control of it as a provincial work. The Cornwall Canal was also undertaken at an early day, but work had to be stopped when it became certain that the legislature of Lower Canada, then controlled by Papineau, would not respond to the aspirations of the west and improve that portion of the St. Lawrence within its provincial jurisdiction.

Governor Haldimand had, from 1779-1782, constructed a very simple temporary system of canals to overcome the rapids called the Cascades, Cedars and Côteau, and some slight improvements were made in these primitive works from year to year until the completion of the Beauharnois Canal in 1845. The Lachine Canal was completed, after a fashion, in 1828, but nothing was done to give a continuous river navigation between Montreal and the west until 1845, when the Beauharnois Canal was first opened. The Rideau Canal originated in the experiences of the war of 1812-14, which showed the necessity of a secure inland communication between Montreal and the country on Lake Ontario; but though first constructed for defensive purposes, it had for years decided commercial advantages for the people of Upper Canada, especially of the Kingston district. The Grenville Canal on the Ottawa was the natural continuation of this canal, as it ensured uninterrupted water communication between Bytown—now the city of Ottawa—and Montreal.

The heavy public debt contracted by Upper Canada prior to 1840 had been largely accumulated by the efforts of its people to obtain the active sympathy and coöperation of the legislature of French Canada, where Papineau and his followers seemed averse to the development of British interests in the valley of the St. Lawrence. After the union, happily for Canada, public men of all parties and races awoke to the necessity of a vigorous canal policy, and large sums of money were annually expended to give the shipping of the lakes safe and continuous navigation to Montreal. At the same time the channel of Lake St. Peter between Montreal and Quebec was improved by the harbour commissioners of the former city, aided by the government. Before the LaFontaine-Baldwin cabinet left office, it was able to see the complete success of this thoroughly Canadian

98

or national policy. The improvement of this canal system—now the most magnificent in the world—has kept pace with the development of the country down to the present time.

It was mainly, if not entirely, through the influence of Hincks, finance minister in the government, that a vigorous impulse was given to railway construction in the province. The first railroad in British North America was built in 1837 by the enterprise of Montreal capitalists, from La Prairie on the south side of the St. Lawrence as far as St. Johns on the Richelieu, a distance of only sixteen miles. The only railroad in Upper Canada for many years was a horse tramway, opened in 1839 between Queenston and Chippewa by the old portage road round the falls of Niagara. In 1845 the St. Lawrence and Atlantic Railway Company—afterwards a portion of the Grand Trunk Railway—obtained a charter for a line to connect with the Atlantic and St. Lawrence Railway Company of Portland, in the State of Maine. The year 1846 saw the commencement of the Lachine Railway. In 1849 the Great Western, the Northern, and the St. Lawrence and Atlantic Railways were stimulated by legislation which gave a provincial guarantee for the construction of lines not less than seventy-five miles in length. In 1851 Hincks succeeded in passing a measure which provided for the building of a great trunk line connecting Quebec with the western limits of

Upper Canada. It was hoped at first that this road would join the great military railway contemplated between Quebec and Halifax, and then earnestly advocated by Howe and other public men of the maritime provinces with the prospect of receiving aid from the imperial government. If these railway interests could be combined, an intercolonial rail-road would be constructed from the Atlantic seaboard to the lakes, and a great stimulus given not merely to the commerce but to the national unity of British North America. In case, however, this great idea could not be realized, it was the intention of the Canadian government to make every possible exertion to induce British capitalists to invest their money in the great trunk line by a liberal offer of assistance from the provincial exchequer, and the municipalities directly interested in its construction.

The practical result of Hincks's policy was the construction of the Grand Trunk Railway of Canada, not by public aid as originally proposed, but by British capitalists. The greater intercolonial scheme failed in consequence of the conflict of rival routes in the maritime provinces, and the determination of the British government to give its assistance only to a road that would be constructed at a long distance from the United States frontier, and consequently available for military and defensive purposes—in fact such a road as was actually built after the confederation of the provinces with the aid of an imperial guarantee. The history of the negotiations between the Canadian government and the maritime provinces with respect to the intercolonial scheme is exceedingly complicated. An angry controversy arose between Hincks and Howe; the latter always accused the former of a breach of faith, and of having been influenced by a desire to promote the interests of the capitalists concerned in the Grand Trunk without reference to those of the maritime provinces. Be that as it may, we know that Hincks left the wordy politicians of Nova Scotia and New Brunswick to quarrel over rival routes, and, as we shall see later, went ahead with the Grand Trunk, and had it successfully completed many years before the first sod on the Intercolonial route was turned.

In addition to these claims of the LaFontaine-Baldwin government to be considered "a great ministry," there is the fact that, through the financial ability of Hincks, the credit of the province steadily advanced, and it was at last possible to borrow money in the London market on very favourable terms. The government entered heartily into the policy of Lord Elgin with respect to reciprocity with the United States, and the encouragement of trade between the different provinces of British North America. It was, however, unable to dispose of two great questions which had long agitated the province—the abolition of the seigniorial tenure, which was antagonistic to settlement and colonization, and the secularization of the clergy reserves, granted to the Protestant clergy by the Constitutional Act of 1791. These questions will be reviewed at some length in later chapters, and all that it is necessary to say here is that, while the LaFontaine-Baldwin cabinet supported preliminary steps that were taken in the legislature for the purpose of bringing about a settlement of these vexatious subjects, it never showed any earnest desire to take them up as parts of its ministerial policy, and remove them from political controversy.

Indeed it is clear that LaFontaine's conservative instincts, which became stronger with age and experience of political conditions, forced him to proceed very slowly and cautiously with respect to a movement that would interfere with a tenure so deeply engrafted in the social and economic structure of his own province, while as a Roman Catholic he was at heart always doubtful of the justice of diverting to secular purposes those lands which had been granted by Great Britain for the support of a Protestant clergy. Baldwin was also slow to make up his mind as to the proper disposition of the reserves, and certainly weakened himself in his own province by his reluctance to express himself distinctly with respect to a land question which had been so long a grievance and a subject of earnest agitation among the men who supported him in and out of the legislature. Indeed when he presented himself for the last time before his constituents in 1857, he was emphatically attacked on the hustings as an opponent of the secularization of the reserves for refusing to give a distinct pledge as to the course he would take on the question. This fact, taken in connection with his previous utterances in the legislature, certainly gives force to the opinion which has been more than once expressed by Canadian historians that he was not prepared, any more than LaFontaine himself, to divert funds given for an express purpose to one of an entirely different character. Under these circumstances it is easy to come to the conclusion that the LaFontaine-Baldwin ministry was not willing at any time to make these two questions parts of its policy—questions on which it was ready to stand or fall as a government.

The first step towards the breaking up of the ministry was the resignation of Baldwin following upon the support given by a majority of the Reformers in Upper Canada to a motion presented by William Lyon Mackenzie for the abolition of the court of chancery and the transfer of its functions to the courts of common law. The motion was voted down in the House, but Baldwin was a believer in the doctrine that a minister from a particular province should receive the confidence and support of the majority of its representatives in cases where a measure affected its interests exclusively. He had taken some pride in the passage of the act which reorganized the court, reformed old abuses in its practice, and made it, as he was convinced, useful in litigation ; but when he found that his efforts in this direction were condemned by the votes of the very men who should have supported him in the province affected by the measure, he promptly offered his resignation, which was accepted with great reluctance not only by LaFontaine but by Lord Elgin, who had learned to admire and respect this upright, unselfish Canadian statesman. A few months later he was defeated at an election in one of the ridings of York by an unknown man, largely on account of his attitude on the question of the clergy reserves. He never again offered himself for parliament, but lived in complete retirement in Toronto, where he died in 1858. Then the people whom he had so long faithfully served, after years of neglect, became conscious that a true patriot had passed away.

LaFontaine placed his resignation in the hands of the governor-general, who accepted it with regret. No doubt the former had deeply felt the loss of his able colleague, and was alive to the growing belief among the Liberal politicians of Upper Canada that the government was not proceeding fast enough in carrying out the reforms which they considered necessary. LaFontaine had become a Conservative as is usual with men after some experience of the responsibilities of public administration, and probably felt that he had better retire before he lost his influence with his party, and before the elements of disintegration that were forming within it had fully developed. After his retirement he returned to the practice of law, and in 1853 he became chief justice of the court of appeal of Lower Canada on the death of Sir James Stuart. At the same time he received from the Crown the honour of a baronetcy, which was also conferred on the chief justice of Upper Canada, Sir John Beverley Robinson.

Political historians justly place LaFontaine in the first rank of Canadian statesmen on account of his extensive knowledge, his sound judgment, his breadth of view, his firmness in political crises, and above all his desire to promote the best interests of his countrymen on those principles of compromise and conciliation which alone can bind together the distinct nationalities and creeds of a country peopled like Canada. As a judge he was dignified, learned and impartial. His judicial decisions were distinguished by the same lucidity which was conspicuous in his parliamentary addresses. He died ten years later than the great Upper Canadian, whose honoured name must be always associated with his own in the annals of a memorable epoch, when the principles of responsible government were at last, after years of perplexity and trouble, carried out in their entirety, and when the French Canadians had come to recognize as a truth that under no other system would it have been possible for them to obtain that influence in the public councils to which they were fully entitled, or to reconcile and unite the diverse interests of a great province, divided by the Ottawa river into two sections, the one French and Roman Catholic, and the other English and Protestant.

CHAPTER VI

THE HINCKS-MORIN MINISTRY

WHEN LaFontaine resigned the premiership the ministry was dissolved and it was necessary for the governor-general to choose his successor. After the retirement of Baldwin, Hincks and his colleagues from Upper Canada were induced to remain in the cabinet and the latter became the leader in that province. He was endowed with great natural shrewdness, was deeply versed in financial and commercial matters, had a complete comprehension of the material conditions of the province, and recognized the necessity of rapid railway construction if the people were to hold their own against the competition of their very energetic neighbours to the south. His ideas of trade, we can well believe, recommended themselves to Lord Elgin, who saw in him the very man he needed to help him in his favourite scheme of bringing about reciprocity with the United States. At the same time he was now the most prominent man in the Liberal party so long led by Baldwin and LaFontaine, and the governor-general very properly called upon him to reconstruct the ministry. He assumed the responsibility and formed the government known in the political history of

107

Canada as the Hincks-Morin ministry; but before we consider its *personnel* and review its measures, it is necessary to recall the condition of political parties at the time it came into power.

During the years Baldwin and LaFontaine were in office, the politics of the province were in the process of changes which eventually led to important results in the state of parties. The *Parti Rouge* was formed in Lower Canada out of the extreme democratic element of the people by Papineau, who, throughout his parliamentary career since his return from exile, showed the most determined opposition to LaFontaine, whose measures were always distinguished by a spirit of conservatism, decidedly congenial to the dominant classes in French Canada where the civil and religious institutions of the country had much to fear from the promulgation of republican principles.

The new party was composed chiefly of young Frenchmen, then in the first stage of their political growth—notably A. A. Dorion, J. B. E. Dorion *(l'enfant terrible)*, R. Doutre, Dessaules, Labrèche, Viger, and Laflamme; L. H. Holton, and a very few men of British descent were also associated with the party from its commencement. Its organ was *L'Avenir* of Montreal, in which were constantly appearing violent diatribes and fervid appeals to national prejudice, always peculiar to French Canadian journalism. It commenced with a programme in which it advocated universal suffrage, the abolition of property qualification for members of the legislature, the repeal of the union, the abolition of tithes, a republican form of government, and even, in a moment of extreme political aberration, annexation to the United States. It was a feeble imitation of the red republicanism of the French revolution, and gave positive evidences of the inspiration of the hero of the fight at St. Denis in 1837. Its platform was pervaded not only by hatred of British institutions, but with contempt for the clergy and religion generally. Its revolutionary principles were at once repudiated by the great mass of French Canadians and for years it had but a feeble existence. It was only when its leading spirits reconstructed their platform and struck out its most objectionable planks, that it became something of a factor in practical Canadian politics. In 1851 it was still insignificant numerically in the legislature, and could not affect the fortunes of the Liberal party in Lower Canada then distinguished by the ability of A. N. Morin, P. J. O. Chauveau, R. E. Caron, E. P. Taché, and L. P. Drummond. The recognized leader of this dominant party was Morin, whose versatile knowledge, lucidity of style, and charm of manner gave him much strength in parliament. His influence, however, as I have already said, was too often weakened by an absence of energy and of the power to lead at national or political crises.

Parties in Upper Canada also showed the signs

of change. The old Tory party had been gradually modifying its opinions under the influence of responsible government, which showed its wisest members that ideas that prevailed before the union had no place under the new, progressive order of things. This party, nominally led by Sir Allan MacNab, that staunch old loyalist, now called itself Conservative, and was quite ready, in fact anxious, to forget the part it took in connection with the rebellion losses legislation, and to win that support in French Canada without which it could not expect to obtain office. The ablest man in its councils was already John Alexander Macdonald, whose political sagacity and keenness to seize political advantages for the advancement of his party, were giving him the lead among the Conservatives. The Liberals had shown signs of disintegration ever since the formation of the "Clear Grits," whose most conspicuous members were Peter Perry, the founder of the Liberal party in Upper Canada before the union; William McDougall, an eloquent young lawyer and journalist; Malcolm Cameron, who had been assistant commissioner of public works in the LaFontaine-Baldwin government; Dr. John Rolph, one of the leaders of the movement that ended in the rebellion of 1837; Caleb Hopkins, a western farmer of considerable energy and natural ability; David Christie, a well-known agriculturist; and John Leslie, the proprietor of the Toronto *Examiner*,

110

the chief organ of the new party. It was organized as a remonstrance against what many men in the old Liberal party regarded as the inertness of their leaders to carry out changes considered necessary in the political interests of the country. Its very name was a proof that its leaders believed there should be no reservation in the opinion held by their party—that there must be no alloy or foreign metal in their political coinage, but it must be clear Grit. Its platform embraced many of the cardinal principles of the original Reform or Liberal party, but it also advocated such radical changes as the application of the elective principle to all classes of officials (including the governor-general), universal suffrage, vote by ballot, biennial parliaments, the abolition of the courts of chancery and common pleas, free trade and direct taxation.

The Toronto *Globe*, which was for a short time the principal exponent of ministerial views, declared that many of the doctrines enunciated by the Clear Grits "embody the whole difference between a republican form of government and the limited monarchy of Great Britain." *The Globe* was edited by George Brown, a Scotsman by birth, who came with his father in his youth to the western province and entered into journalism, in which he attained eventually signal success by his great intellectual force and tenacity of purpose. His support of the LaFontaine-Baldwin ministry gradually dropped from a moderate enthusiasm to a positive coolness, from its failure to carry out the principles urged by *The Globe*—especially the secularization of the clergy reserves. Then he commenced to raise the cry of French domination and to attack the religion and special institutions of French Canada with such virulence that at last he became "a governmental impossibility," so far as the influence of that province was concerned. He supported the Clear Grits in the end, and became their recognized leader when they gathered to themselves all the discontented and radical elements of the Liberal party which had for some years been gradually splitting into fragments. The power of the Clear Grits was first shown in 1851, when William Lyon Mackenzie succeeded in obtaining a majority of Reformers in support of his motion for the abolition of the court of chancery, and forced the retirement of Baldwin, whose conservatism had gradually brought him into antagonism with the extremists of his old party.

Although relatively small in numbers in 1851, the Clear Grits had the ability to do much mischief, and Hincks at once recognized the expediency of making concessions to their leaders before they demoralized or ruined the Liberal party in the west. Accordingly, he invited Dr. Rolph and Malcolm Cameron to take positions in the new ministry. They consented on condition that the secularization of the clergy reserves would be a part of the ministerial policy. Hincks then

112

presented the following names to the governor-general:

Upper Canada.—Hon. F. Hincks, inspector-general; Hon. W. B. Richards, attorney-general of Upper Canada; Hon. Malcolm Cameron, president of the executive council; Hon. John Rolph, commissioner of crown lands; Hon. James Morris, postmaster-general.

Lower Canada.—Hon. A. N. Morin, provincial secretary; Hon. L. P. Drummond, attorney-general of Lower Canada; Hon. John Young, commissioner of public works; Hon. R. E. Caron, president of legislative council; Hon. E. P. Taché, receiver-general.

Later, Mr. Chauveau and Mr. John Ross were appointed solicitors-general for Lower and Upper Canada, without seats in the cabinet.

Parliament was dissolved in November, when it had completed its constitutional term of four years, and the result of the elections was the triumph of the new ministry. It obtained a large majority in Lower Canada, and only a feeble support in Upper Canada. The most notable acquisition to parliament was George Brown, who had been defeated previously in a bye-election of the same year by William Lyon Mackenzie, chiefly on account of his being most obnoxious to the Roman Catholic voters. He was assuming to be the Protestant champion in journalism, and had made a violent attack on the Roman Catholic faith on the occasion of the appointment of Cardinal Wiseman as Archbishop of Westminster, an act denounced by extreme Protestants throughout the British empire as an unconstitutional and dangerous interference by the Pope with the dearest rights of Protestant England. As soon as Brown entered the legislature he defined his political position by declaring that, while he saw much to condemn in the formation of the ministry and was dissatisfied with Hincks's explanations, he preferred giving it for the time being his support rather than seeing the government handed over to the Conservatives. As a matter of fact, he soon became the most dangerous adversary that the government had to meet. His style of speaking —full of facts and bitterness—and his control of an ably conducted and widely circulated newspaper made him a force in and out of parliament. His aim was obviously to break up the new ministry, and possibly to ensure the formation of some new combination in which his own ambition might be satisfied. As we shall shortly see, his schemes failed chiefly through the more skilful strategy of the man who was always his rival—his successful rival —John A. Macdonald.

During its existence the Hincks-Morin ministry was distinguished by its energetic policy for the promotion of railway, maritime and commercial enterprises. It took the first steps to stimulate the establishment of a line of Atlantic steamers by the offer of a considerable subsidy for the carriage of mails between Canada and Great Britain. The first contract was made with a Liverpool firm, McKean, McLarty & Co., but the service was not satisfactorily performed, owing, probably — according to Hincks — to the war with Russia, and it was necessary to make a new arrangement with the Messrs. Allan, which has continued, with some modification, until the present time.

The negotiations for the construction of an intercolonial railway having failed for the reasons previously stated, (p. 100), Hincks made successful applications to English capitalists for the construction of the great road always known as the Grand Trunk Railway of Canada. It obtained a charter authorizing it to consolidate the lines from Quebec to Richmond, from Quebec to Rivière du Loup, and from Toronto to Montreal, which had received a guarantee of $3,000 a mile in accordance with the law passed in 1851. It also had power to build the Victoria bridge across the St. Lawrence at Montreal, and lease the American line to Portland. By 1860, this great national highway was completed from Rivière du Loup on the lower St. Lawrence as far as Sarnia and Windsor on the western lakes. Its early history was notorious for much jobbery, and the English shareholders lost the greater part of the money which they invested in this Canadian undertaking.[1] It cost the province

[1] For a succinct history of this road see "Eighty Years' Progress of British North America," Toronto, 1863.

from first to last upwards of $16,000,000 but it was, on the whole, money expended in the interests of the country, whose internal development would have been very greatly retarded in the absence of rapid means of transit between east and west. The government also gave liberal aid to the Great Western Railway, which extended from the Niagara river to Hamilton, London and Windsor, and to the Northern road, which extended north from Toronto, both of which, many years later, became parts of the Grand Trunk system.

In accordance with its general progressive policy, the Hincks-Morin ministry passed through the legislature an act empowering municipalities in Upper Canada, after the observance of certain formalities, to borrow money for the building of railways by the issue of municipal debentures guaranteed by the provincial government. Under this law a number of municipalities borrowed large sums to assist railways and involved themselves so heavily in debt that the province was ultimately obliged to come to their assistance and assume their obligations. For years after the passage of this measure, Lower Canada received the same privileges, but the people of that province were never carried away by the enthusiasm of the west and never burdened themselves with debts which they were unable to pay. The law, however, gave a decided impulse at the outset to railway enterprise in Upper Canada, and would have been a positive public

advantage had it been carried out with some degree of caution.

The government established a department of agriculture to which were given control of the taking of a decennial census, the encouragement of immigration, the collection of agricultural and other statistics, the establishment of model farms and agricultural schools, the holding of annual exhibitions and fairs, and other matters calculated to encourage the cultivation of the soil in both sections of the province. Malcolm Cameron became its first minister in connection with his nominal duties as president of the executive council —a position which he had accepted only on condition that it was accompanied by some more active connection with the administration of public affairs.

For three sessions the LaFontaine-Baldwin ministry had made vain efforts to pass a law increasing the representation of the two provinces to one hundred and thirty or sixty-five members for each section. As already stated the Union Act required that such a measure should receive a majority of two-thirds in each branch of the legislature. It would have become law on two occasions had it not been for the factious opposition of Papineau, whose one vote would have given the majority constitutionally necessary. When it was again presented in 1853 by Mr. Morin, it received the bitter opposition of Mr. Brown, who was now formulating the doctrine of representation by population which after-

wards became so important a factor in provincial politics that it divided west from east, and made government practically impossible until a federal union of the British North American provinces was brought about as the only feasible solution of the serious political and sectional difficulties under which Canada was suffering. A number of prominent Conservatives, including Mr. John A. Macdonald, were also unfavourable to the measure on the ground that the population of Upper Canada, which was steadily increasing over that of Lower Canada, should be equitably considered in any readjustment of the provincial representation. The French Canadians, who had been forced to come into the union in 1841 with the same representation as Upper Canada with its much smaller population, were now unwilling to disturb the equality originally fixed while agreeing to an increase in the number of representatives from each section. The bill, which became law in 1853, was entirely in harmony with the views entertained by Lord Elgin when he first took office as governor-general of Canada. In 1847 he gave his opinion to the colonial secretary that "the comparatively small number of members of which the popular bodies who determine the fate of provincial administrations" consisted was "unfavourable to the existence of a high order of principle and feeling among official personages." When a defection of two or three individuals from a majority of ten or so put

an administration in peril, " the perpetual patch-work and trafficking to secure this vote and that (not to mention other evils) so engrosses the time and thoughts of ministers that they have not leisure for matters of greater moment." He clearly saw into the methods by which his first unstable ministry, which had its origin in Lord Metcalfe's time, was alone able to keep its feeble majority. " It must be remembered," he wrote in 1847, "that it is only of late that the popular assemblies in this part of the world have acquired the right of deter-mining who shall govern them—of insisting, as we phrase it, that the administration of affairs shall be conducted by persons enjoying their confidence. It is not wonderful that a privilege of this kind should be exercised at first with some degree of recklessness, and that while no great principles of policy are at stake, methods of a more questionable character for winning and retaining the confidence of these arbiters of destiny should be resorted to."

While the Hincks government was in office, the Canadian legislature received power from the imperial authorities—as I shall show later—to settle the question of the clergy reserves on condition that protection should be given to those members of the clergy who had been beneficiaries under the Consti-tutional Act of 1791. A measure was passed for the settlement of the seigniorial tenure question on an equitable basis, but it was defeated in the legislative council by a large majority amongst which we see the names of several seigneurs directly interested in the measure. It was not fully discussed in that chamber on the ground that members from Upper Canada had not had a sufficient opportunity of studying the details of the proposed settlement and of coming to a just conclusion as to its merits. The action of the council under these circumstances was severely criticized, and gave a stimulus to the movement that had been steadily going on for years among radical reformers of both provinces in favour of an elective body.

The result was that in 1854 the British parliament repealed the clauses of the Union Act of 1840 with respect to the upper House, and gave full power to the Canadian legislature to make such changes as it might deem expedient—another concession to the principle of local self-government. It was not, however, until 1856, that the legislature passed a bill giving effect to the intentions of the imperial law, and the first elections were held for the council. Lord Elgin was always favourable to this constitutional change. "The position of the second chamber of our body politic"—I quote from a despatch of March, 1853—"is at present wholly unsatisfactory. The principle of election must be introduced in order to give to it the influence which it ought to possess, and that principle must be so applied as to admit of the working of parliamentary government (which I for one am certainly not prepared to abandon for the American system) with two

elective chambers. . . . . When our two legislative
bodies shall have been placed on this improved
footing, a greater stability will have been imparted
to our constitution, and a greater strength." Lord
Elgin's view was adopted and the change was made.

It is interesting to note that so distinguished
a statesman as Lord Derby, who had been colonial secretary in a previous administration, had
only gloomy forebodings of the effects of this
elective system applied to the Upper House. He
believed that the dream that he had of seeing the
colonies form eventually "a monarchical government, presided over by one nearly and closely allied
to the present royal family," would be proved
quite illusory by the legislation in question. "Nothing," he added, "like a free and regulated monarchy
could exist for a single moment under such a
constitution as that which is now proposed for
Canada. From the moment that you pass this
constitution, the progress must be rapidly towards
republicanism, if anything could be more really republican than this bill." As a matter of fact a very
few years later than the utterance of these gloomy
words, Canada and the other provinces of British
North America entered into a confederation "with
a constitution similar in principle to that of the
United Kingdom"—to quote words in the preamble
of the Act of Union—and with a parliament of
which the House of Commons is alone elective.
More than that, Lord Derby's dream has been in a

measure realized and Canada has seen at the head of her executive a governor-general—the present Duke of Argyle—"nearly and closely allied to the present royal family" of England, by his marriage to the Princess Louise, the fourth daughter of Queen Victoria, who accompanied her husband to Ottawa.

One remarkable feature of the Imperial Act dealing with this question of the council, was the introduction of a clause which gave authority to a mere majority of the members of the two Houses of the legislature to increase the representation, and consequently removed that safeguard to French Canada which required a two-thirds vote in each branch. As the legislature had never passed an address or otherwise expressed itself in favour of such an amendment of the Union Act, there was always a mystery as to the way it was brought about. Georges Étienne Cartier always declared that Papineau was indirectly responsible for this imperial legislation. As already stated, the leader of the Rouges had voted against the bill increasing the representation, and had declaimed like others against the injustice which the clause in the Union Act had originally done to French Canada. "This fact," said Cartier, "was known in England, and when leave was given to elect legislative councillors, the amendment complained of was made at the same time. It may be said then, that if Papineau had not systematically opposed the increase of representation, the change in

122

question would have never been thought of in England." Hincks, however, was attacked by the French Canadian historian, Garneau, for having suggested the amendment while in England in 1854. This, however, he denied most emphatically in a pamphlet which he wrote at a later time when he was no longer in public life. He placed the responsibility on John Boulton, who called himself an independent Liberal and who was in England at the same time as Hincks, and probably got the ear of the colonial secretary or one of his subordinates in the colonial office, and induced him to introduce the amendment which passed without notice in a House where very little attention was given, as a rule, to purely colonial questions.

In 1853 Lord Elgin visited England, where he received unqualified praise for his able administration of Canadian affairs. It was on this occasion that Mr. Buchanan, then minister of the United States in London, and afterwards a president of the Republic, paid this tribute to the governor-general at a public dinner given in his honour.

"Lord Elgin," he said, "has solved one of the most difficult problems of statesmanship. He has been able, successfully and satisfactorily, to administer, amidst many difficulties, a colonial government over a free people. This is an easy task where the commands of a despot are law to his obedient servants, but not so in a colony where the people feel that they possess the rights and privileges of native-born Britons. Under his enlightened government, Her Majesty's North American provinces have realized the blessings of a wise, prudent and prosperous administration, and we of the neighbouring nation, though jealous of our rights, have reason to be abundantly satisfied with his just and friendly conduct towards ourselves. He has known how to reconcile his devotion to Her Majesty's service with a proper regard to the rights and interests of a kindred and neighbouring people. Would to heaven we had such governors-general in all the European colonies in the vicinity of the United States!"

On his return from England Lord Elgin made a visit to Washington and succeeded in negotiating the reciprocity treaty which he had always at heart. It was not, however, until a change of government occurred in Canada, that the legislature was able to give its ratification to this important measure. This subject is of such importance that it will be fully considered in a separate chapter on the relations between Canada and the United States during Lord Elgin's term of office.

In 1854 the Roman Catholic inhabitants of Quebec and Montreal were deeply excited by the lectures of a former monk, Father Gavazzi, who had become a Protestant and professed to expose the errors of the faith to which he once belonged. Much rioting took place in both cities, and blood was shed in Montreal, where the troops, which had been called out, suddenly fired on the mob. Mr. Wilson, the mayor, who was a Roman Catholic, was accused of having given the order to fire, but he always denied the charge, and Hincks, in his "Reminiscences," expresses his conviction that he was not responsible. He was persuaded that " the firing was quite accidental, one man having discharged his piece from misapprehension, and others having followed his example until the officers threw themselves in front, and struck up the firelocks." Be this as it may, the Clear Grits in the West promptly made use of this incident to attack the government on the ground that it had failed to make a full investigation into the circumstances of the riot. As a matter of fact, according to Hincks, the government did take immediate steps to call the attention of the military commandant to the matter, and the result was a court of inquiry which ended in the removal of the regiment—then only a few days in Canada—to Bermuda for having shown "a want of discipline." Brown inveighed very bitterly against Hincks and his colleagues, as subject to Roman Catholic domination in French Canada, and found this unfortunate affair extremely useful in his systematic efforts to destroy the government, to which at no time had he been at all favourable.

Several changes took place during 1853 in the *personnel* of the ministry, which met parliament on June 13th, with the following members holding portfolios: Hon. Messrs. Hincks, premier and inspector-general; John Ross, formerly solicitor-general west in place of Richards, elevated to the bench, attorney-general for Upper Canada; James Morris, president of the legislative council, in place of Mr. Caron, now a judge; John Rolph, president of the executive council; Malcolm Cameron, postmaster-general; A. N. Morin, commissioner of crown lands; L. P. Drummond, attorney-general for Lower Canada; Mr. Chauveau, formerly solicitor east, provincial secretary; J. Chabot, commissioner of public works in place of John Young, resigned on account of differences on commercial questions; and E. P. Taché, receiver-general. Dunbar Ross became solicitor-general east, and Joseph C. Morrison, solicitor-general west.

The government had decided to have a short session, pass a few necessary measures and then appeal to the country. The secularization of the reserves, and the question of the seigniorial tenure were not to be taken up until the people had given an expression of opinion as to the ministerial policy generally. As soon as the legislature met, Cauchon, already prominent in public life, proposed an amendment to the address, expressing regret that the government had no intention "to submit immediately a measure to settle the question of the seigniorial tenure." Then Sicotte, who had not long before declined to enter the ministry, moved to

add the words "and one for the secularization of
the clergy reserves." These two amendments were
carried by a majority of thirteen in a total division
of seventy-one votes. While the French Liberals
continued to support Morin, all the Upper Canadian opponents of the government, Conservatives and Clear Grits, united with a number of
Hincks's former supporters and Rouges in Lower
Canada to bring about this ministerial defeat. The
government accordingly was obliged either to
resign or ask the governor-general for a dissolution.
It concluded to adhere to its original determination, and go at once to the country. The
governor-general consented to prorogue the legislature with a view to an immediate appeal to
the electors. When the Usher of the Black Rod
appeared at the door of the assembly chamber,
to ask the attendance of the Commons in the
legislative council, a scene of great excitement
occurred. William Lyon Mackenzie made one
of his vituperative attacks on the government,
and was followed by John A. Macdonald, who
declared its course to be most unconstitutional.
When at last the messenger from the governor-
general was admitted by order of the speaker, the
House proceeded to the council chamber, where
members were electrified by another extraordinary incident. The speaker of the assembly was
John Sandfield Macdonald, an able Scotch Canadian, in whose character there was a spirit of

vindictiveness, which always asserted itself when he received a positive or fancied injury. He had been a solicitor-general of Upper Canada in the LaFontaine-Baldwin government, and had never forgiven Hincks for not having promoted him to the attorney-generalship, instead of W. B. Richards, afterwards an eminent judge of the old province of Canada, and first chief justice of the Supreme Court of the Dominion. Hincks had offered him the commissionership of crown lands in the ministry, but he refused to accept any office except the one on which his ambition was fixed. Subsequently, however, he was induced by his friends to take the speakership of the legislative assembly, but he had never forgiven what he considered a slight at the hands of the prime minister in 1851. Accordingly, when he appeared at the Bar of the Council in 1853, he made an attempt to pay off this old score. As soon as he had made his bow to the governor-general seated on the throne, Macdonald proceeded to read the following speech, which had been carefully prepared for the occasion in the two languages:

"May it please your Excellency: It has been the immemorial custom of the speaker of the Commons' House of Parliament to communicate to the throne the general result of the deliberations of the assembly upon the principal objects which have employed the attention of parliament during the period of their labours. It is not now part of my duty thus to address your Excellency, inasmuch as there has been no act passed or judgment of parliament obtained since we were honoured by your Excellency's announcement of the cause of summoning of parliament by your gracious speech from the throne. The passing of an act through its several stages, according to the law and custom of parliament (solemnly declared applicable to the parliamentary proceedings of this province, by a decision of the legislative assembly of 1841), is held to be necessary to constitute a session of parliament. This we have been unable to accomplish, owing to the command which your Excellency has laid upon us to meet you this day for the purpose of prorogation. At the same time I feel called upon to assure your Excellency, on the part of Her Majesty's faithful Commons, that it is not from any want of respect to yourself, or to the august personage whom you represent in these provinces, that no answer has been returned by the legislative assembly to your gracious speech from the throne."

It is said by those who were present on this interesting occasion that His Excellency was the most astonished person in the council chamber. Mr. Fennings Taylor, the deputy clerk with a seat at the table, tells us in a sketch of Macdonald that Lord Elgin's face clearly marked " deep displeasure and annoyance when listening to the speaker's address," and that he gave " a motion of angry impatience when he found himself obliged to listen to the repetition in French of the reproof which had evidently galled him in English." This incident was in some respects without parallel in Canadian parliamentary history. There was a practice, now obsolete in Canada as in England, for the speaker, on presenting the supply or appropriation bill to the governor-general for the royal assent, to deliver a short address directing attention to the principal measures passed during the session about to be closed.[1] This practice grew up in days when there were no responsible ministers who would be the only constitutional channel of communication between the Crown and the assembly. The speaker was privileged, and could be instructed as "the mouth-piece" of the House, to lay before the representative of the Sovereign an expression of opinion on urgent questions of the day. On this occasion Mr. Macdonald was influenced entirely by personal spite, and made an unwarrantable use of an old custom which was never intended, and could not be constitutionally used, to insult the representative of the Crown, even by inference. Mr. Macdonald was not even correct in his interpretation of the constitution, when he positively declared that an act was necessary to constitute a session. The Crown makes a session by summoning

[1] "Portraits of British Americans," Montreal, 1865, vol. I., pp. 99-100. See Bourinot's "Parliamentary Procedure," p. 573n. The last occasion on which a Canadian speaker exercised this old privilege was in 1869, and then Mr. Cockburn made only a very brief reference to the measures of the session.

and opening parliament, and it is always a royal prerogative to prorogue or dissolve it at its pleasure even before a single act has passed the two Houses. Such a scene could never have occurred with the better understanding of the duties of the speaker and of the responsibilities of ministers advising the Crown that has grown up under a more thorough study of the practice and usages of parliament, and of the principles of responsible government. This little political episode is now chiefly interesting as giving an insight into one phase of the character of a public man, who afterwards won a high position in the parliamentary and political life of Canada before and after the confederation of 1867, not by the display of a high order of statesmanship, but by the exercise of his tenacity of purpose, and by reason of his reputation for a spiteful disposition which made him feared by friend and foe.

Immediately after the prorogation, parliament was dissolved and the Hincks-Morin ministry presented itself to the people, who were now called upon to elect a larger number of representatives under the act passed in 1853. Of the constitutionality of the course pursued by the government in this political crisis, there can now be no doubt. In the first place it was fully entitled to demand a public judgment on its general policy, especially in view of the fact, within the knowledge of all persons, that the opposition in the assembly was composed of discordant elements, only temporarily brought together by the hope of breaking up the government. In the next place it felt that it could not be justified by sound constitutional usage in asking a parliament in which the people were now imperfectly represented, to settle definitely such important questions as the clergy reserves and the seigniorial tenure. Lord Elgin had himself no doubt of the necessity for obtaining a clear verdict from the people by means of "the more perfect system of representation" provided by law. In the debate on the Representation Bill in 1853, John A. Macdonald did not hesitate to state emphatically that the House should be governed by English precedents in the position in which it would soon be placed by the passage of this measure. "Look," he said, "at the Reform Bill in England. That was passed by a parliament that had been elected only one year before, and the moment it was passed, Lord John Russell affirmed that the House could not continue after it had declared that the country was not properly represented. How can we legislate on the clergy reserves until another House is elected, if this bill passes? A great question like this cannot be left to be decided by a mere accidental majority. We can legislate upon no great question after we have ourselves declared that we do not represent the country. Do these gentlemen opposite mean to say that they will legislate on a question affecting the rights of people yet unborn, with the fag-end of a parliament dishonoured by its own confessions of incapacity?" Hincks in his "Reminiscences," printed more than three decades later than this ministerial crisis, still adhered to the opinion that the government was fully justified by established precedent in appealing to the country before disposing summarily of the important questions then agitating the people. Both Lord Elgin and Sir John A. Macdonald—to give the latter the title he afterwards received from the Crown—assuredly set forth the correct constitutional practice under the peculiar circumstances in which both government and legislature were placed by the legislation increasing the representation of the people.

The elections took place in July and August of 1854, for in those times there was no system of simultaneous polling on one day, but elections were held on such days and as long as the necessities of party demanded.[1] The result was, on the whole, adverse to the government. While it still retained a majority in French Canada, its opponents returned in greater strength, and Morin himself was defeated in Terrebonne, though happily for the interests of his party he was elected by acclamation at the same time in Chicoutimi. In Upper Canada the ministry did not obtain half the vote of the sixty-five representatives now elected to the

[1] It was not until 1874 when Mr. Alexander Mackenzie was first minister of a Liberal government that simultaneous polling at a general election was required by law, but it had existed some years previously in Nova Scotia.

legislature by that province. This vote was distributed as follows : Ministerial, 30 ; Conservatives, 22 ; Clear Grits, 7 ; and Independents, 6. Malcolm Cameron was beaten in Lambton, but Hincks was elected by two constituencies. One auspicious result of this election was the disappearance of Papineau from public life. He retired to his pretty château on the banks of the Ottawa, and the world soon forgot the man who had once been so prominent a figure in Canadian politics. His graces of manner and conversation continued for years to charm his friends in that placid evening of his life so very different from those stormy days when his eloquence was a menace to British institutions and British connection. Before his death, he saw Lower Canada elevated to an independent and influential position in the confederation of British North America which it could never have reached as that *Nation Canadienne* which he had once vainly hoped to see established in the valley of the St. Lawrence.

The Rouges, of whom Papineau had been leader, came back in good form and numbered nineteen members. Antoine A. Dorion, Holton, and other able men in the ranks of this once republican party, had become wise and adopted opinions which no longer offended the national and religious susceptibilities of their race, although they continued to show for years their radical tendencies which prevented them from ever obtain-

134

ing a firm hold of public opinion in a practically Conservative province, and becoming dominant in the public councils for any length of time.

The fifth parliament of the province of Canada was opened by Lord Elgin on February 5th, 1854, and the ministry was defeated immediately on the vote for the speakership, to which Mr. Sicotte—a dignified cultured man, at a later time a judge— was elected. On this occasion Hincks resorted to a piece of strategy which enabled him to punish John Sandfield Macdonald for the insult he had levelled at the governor-general and his advisers at the close of the previous parliament. The government's candidate was Georges Étienne Cartier, who was first elected in 1849 and who had already become conspicuous in the politics of his province. Sicotte was the choice of the Opposition in Lower Canada, and while there was no belief among the politicians that he could be elected, there was an understanding among the Conservatives and Clear Grits that an effort should be made in his behalf, and in case of its failure, then the whole strength of the opponents of the ministry should be so directed as to ensure the election of Mr. Macdonald, who was sure to get a good Reform vote from the Upper Canadian representatives. These names were duly proposed in order, and Cartier was defeated by a large majority. When the clerk at the table had called for a vote for Sicotte, the number who stood up in his favour was quite insignificant, but before the Nays were taken, Hincks arose quickly and asked that his name be recorded with the Yeas. All the ministerialists followed the prime minister and voted for Sicotte, who was consequently chosen speaker by a majority of thirty-five. But all that Hincks gained by such clever tactics was the humiliation for the moment of an irascible Scotch Canadian politician. The vote itself had no political significance whatever, and the government was forced to resign on September 8th. The vote in favour of Cartier had shown that the ministry was in a minority of twelve in Upper Canada, and if Hincks had any doubt of his political weakness it was at once dispelled on September 7th when the House refused to grant to the government a short delay of twenty-four hours for the purpose of considering a question of privilege which had been raised by the Opposition. On this occasion, Dr. Rolph, who had been quite restless in the government for some time, voted against his colleagues and gave conclusive evidence that Hincks was deserted by the majority of the Reform party in his own province, and could no longer bring that support to the French Canadian ministerialists which would enable them to administer public affairs.

The resignation of the Hincks-Morin ministry begins a new epoch in the political annals of Canada. From that time dates the disruption of the old Liberal party which had governed the country so successfully since 1848, and the formation of a powerful combination which was made up of the moderate elements of that party and of the Conservatives, which afterwards became known as the Liberal-Conservative party. This new party practically controlled public affairs for over three decades until the death of Sir John A. Macdonald, to whose inspiration it largely owed its birth. With that remarkable capacity for adapting himself to political conditions, which was one of the secrets of his strength as a party leader, he saw in 1854 that the time had come for forming an alliance with those moderate Liberals in the two provinces who, it was quite clear, had no possible affinity with the Clear Grits, who were not only small in numbers, but especially obnoxious to the French Canadians as a people on account of the intemperate attacks made by Mr. Brown in the Toronto *Globe* on their revered institutions.

The representatives who supported the late ministry were still in larger numbers than any other party or faction in the House, and it was obvious that no government could exist without their support. Sir Allan MacNab, who was the oldest parliamentarian, and the leader of the Conservatives—a small but compact party—was then invited by the governor-general to assist him by his advice, during a crisis when it was evident to the veriest political tyro that the state of parties in the assembly rendered it very difficult to form a

137

stable government unless a man could be found
ready to lay aside all old feelings of personal and
political rivalry and prejudice and unite all factions
on a common platform for the public advantage.
All the political conditions, happily, were favourable for a combination on a basis of conciliation
and compromise. The old Liberals in French Canada under the influence of LaFontaine and Morin
had been steadily inclining to Conservatism with
the secure establishment of responsible government
and the growth of the conviction that the integrity
of the cherished institutions of their ancient province could be best assured by moving slowly
(festina lente), and not by constant efforts to
make radical changes in the body politic. The
Liberals, of whom Hincks was leader, were
also very distrustful of Brown, and clearly saw
that he could have no strength whatever in a
province where French Canada must have a guarantee that its language, religion, and civil law,
were safe in the hands of any government that
might at any time be formed. The wisest men
among the Conservatives also felt that the time
had arrived for adopting a new policy since the old
questions which had once evoked their opposition
had been at last settled by the voice of the people,
and could no longer constitutionally or wisely be
made matters of continued agitation in or out of
parliament. "The question that arose in the minds
of the old Liberals," as it was said many years

138

later by Thomas White, an able journalist and politician,[1] "was this: shall we hand over the government of this country to the men who, calling themselves Liberals, have broken up the Liberal party by the declaration of extravagant views, by the enunciation of principles far more radical and reckless than any we are prepared to accept, and by a restless ambition which we cannot approve? Or shall we not rather unite with the Conservatives who have gone to the country declaring, in reference to the great questions which then agitated it, that if the decision at the polls was against them, they would no longer offer resistance to their settlement, but would, on the contrary, assist in such solution of them as would forever remove them from the sphere of public or political agitation." With both Liberals and Conservatives holding such views, it was easy enough for John A. Macdonald to convince even Sir Allan MacNab that the time had come for forgetting the past as much as possible, and constituting a strong government from the moderate elements of the old parties which had served their turn and now required to be remodelled on a wider basis of common interests. Sir Allan MacNab recognized the necessity of bringing his own views

[1] See "The Last Forty Years, or Canada Since the Union of 1841," by John Charles Dent, Toronto, 1881, vol. II., p. 309. Mr. White became Minister of the Interior in Sir John Macdonald's government (1885-88) but died suddenly in the midst of a most active and useful administrative career.

into harmony with those of the younger men of his party who were determined not to allow such an opportunity for forming a powerful ministry to pass by. The political situation, indeed, was one calculated to appeal to both the vanity and self-interest of the veteran statesman, and he accordingly assumed the responsibility of forming an administration. He communicated immediately with Morin and his colleagues in Lower Canada, and when he received a favourable reply from them, his next step was to make arrangements, if possible, with the Liberals of Upper Canada. Hincks was only too happy to have an opportunity of resenting the opposition he had met with from Brown and the extreme Reformers of the western province, and opened negotiations with his old supporters on the conditions that the new ministry would take immediate steps for the secularization of the clergy reserves, and the settlement of the seigniorial tenure, and that two members of the administration would be taken from his own followers. The negotiations were successfully closed on this basis of agreement, and on September 11th the following ministers were duly sworn into office:

Upper Canada.—Hon. Sir Allan MacNab, president of the executive council and minister of agriculture; Hon. John A. Macdonald, attorney-general of Upper Canada; Hon. W. Cayley, inspector-general; Hon. R. Spence, postmaster-general; Hon. John Ross, president of the legislative council.

Lower Canada.—Hon. A. N. Morin, commissioner of crown lands; Hon. L. P. Drummond, attorney-general for Lower Canada; Hon. P. J. O. Chauveau, provincial secretary; Hon. E. P. Taché, receiver-general; Hon. J. Chabot, commissioner of public works.

The new cabinet contained four Conservatives, and six members of the old ministry. Henry Smith, a Conservative, became solicitor-general for Upper Canada, and Dunbar Ross continued in the same office for Lower Canada, but neither of them had seats in the cabinet. The Liberal-Conservative party, organized under such circumstances, was attacked with great bitterness by the leaders of the discordant factions, who were greatly disappointed at the success of the combination formed through the skilful management of Messrs. J. A. Macdonald, Hincks and Morin.

The coalition was described as "an unholy alliance" of men who had entirely abandoned their principles. But an impartial historian must record the opinion that the coalition was perfectly justified by existing political conditions, that had it not taken place, a stable government would in all probability have been for some time impossible, and that the time had come for the reconstruction of parties with a broad generous policy which would ignore issues at last dead, and be more in

harmony with modern requirements. It might with
some reason be called a coalition when the reconstruction of parties was going on, but it was really
a successful movement for the annihilation of old
parties and issues, and for the formation on their
ruins of a new party which could gather to itself
the best materials available for the effective conduct of public affairs on the patriotic platform of
the union of the two races, of equal rights to all
classes and creeds, and of the avoidance of purely
sectional questions calculated to disturb the union
of 1841.

The new government at once obtained the support of a large majority of the representatives from
each section of the province, and was sustained by
the public opinion of the country at large. During
the session of 1854 measures were passed for the
secularization of the reserves, the removal of the
seigniorial tenure, and for the ratification of the
reciprocity treaty with the United States. As I
have only been able so far in this historical narrative to refer in a very cursory manner to these very
important questions, I propose now to give in the
following chapter a succinct review of their history
from the time they first came into prominence
down to their settlement at the close of Lord
Elgin's administration in Canada.

CHAPTER VII

THE HISTORY OF THE CLERGY RESERVES, (1791-1854)

FOR a long period in the history of Canada the development of several provinces was more or less seriously retarded, and the politics of the country constantly complicated by the existence of troublesome questions arising out of the lavish grants of public lands by the French and English governments. The territorial domain of French Canada was distributed by the king of France, under the inspiration of Richelieu, with great generosity, on a system of a modified feudal tenure, which, it was hoped, would strengthen the connection between the Crown and the dependency by the creation of a colonial aristocracy, and at the same time stimulate the colonization and settlement of the valley of the St. Lawrence ; but, as we shall see in the course of the following chapter, despite the wise intentions of its promoters, the seigniorial tenure gradually became, after the conquest, more or less burdensome to the *habitants*, and an impediment rather than an incentive to the agricultural development and peopling of the province. Even little Prince Edward Island was troubled with a land question as early as 1767, when it was still

143

known by the name St. John, given it in the days of French rule. Sixty-seven townships, containing in the aggregate 1,360,600 English acres, were conveyed in one day by ballot, with a few reservations to the Crown, to a number of military men, officials and others, who had real or supposed claims on the British government. In this wholesale fashion the island was burdened with a land monopoly which was not wholly removed until after the union with the Canadian Dominion in 1873. Though some disputes arose in Nova Scotia and New Brunswick between the old and new settlers with respect to the ownership of lands after the coming of the Loyalists, who received, as elsewhere, liberal grants of land, they were soon settled, and consequently these maritime provinces were not for any length of time embarrassed by the existence of such questions as became important issues in the politics of Canada. Extravagant grants were also given to the United Empire Loyalists who settled on the banks of the St. Lawrence and Niagara rivers in Upper Canada, as some compensation for the great sacrifices they had made for the Crown during the American revolution. Large tracts of this property were sold either by the Loyalists or their heirs, and passed into the hands of speculators at very insignificant prices. Lord Durham in his report cites authority to show that not " one-tenth of the lands granted to United Empire Loyalists had been occupied by the persons to whom they were granted, and in a great proportion of cases not occupied at all." The companies which were also in the course of time organized in Great Britain for the purchase and sale of lands in Canada, also received extraordinary favours from the government. Although the Canada Company, which is still in existence, was an important agency in the settlement of the province of Upper Canada, its possession of immense tracts—some of them, the Huron Block, for instance, locked up for years— was for a time a great public grievance.

But all these land questions sank into utter insignificance compared with the dispute which arose out of the thirty-sixth clause of the Constitutional Act of 1791, which provided that there should be reserved for the maintenance and support of a "Protestant clergy," in the provinces of Upper and Lower Canada, "a quantity of land equal in value to a seventh part of grants that had been made in the past, or might be made in the future." Subsequent clauses of the same act made provision for the erection and endowment of one or more rectories in every township or parish, "according to the establishment of the Church of England," and at the same time gave power to the legislature of the two provinces "to vary or repeal" these enactments of the law with the important reservation that all bills of such a character could not receive the royal assent until thirty days after they had been laid before both Houses of the imperial

145

parliament. Whenever it was practicable, the lands were reserved under the act among those already granted to settlers with the intention of creating parishes as soon as possible in every settled township throughout the province. However, it was not always possible to carry out this plan, in consequence of whole townships having been granted *en bloc* to the Loyalists in certain districts, especially in those of the Bay of Quinté, Kingston and Niagara, and it was therefore necessary to carry out the intention of the law in adjoining townships where no lands of any extent had been granted to settlers.

The Church of England, at a very early period, claimed, as the only " Protestant clergy " recognized by English law, the exclusive use of the lands in question, and Bishop Mountain, who became in 1793 Anglican bishop of Quebec, with a jurisdiction extending over all Canada, took the first steps to sustain this assertion of exclusive right. Leases were given to applicants by a clerical corporation established by the Anglican Church for the express purpose of administering the reserves. For some years the Anglican claim passed without special notice, and it is not until 1817 that we see the germ of the dispute which afterwards so seriously agitated Upper Canada. It was proposed in the assembly to sell half the lands and devote the proceeds to secular purposes, but the sudden prorogation of the legislature by Lieutenant-Governor Gore, prevented any definite action on the resolutions, although the debate that arose on the subject had the effect of showing the existence of a marked public grievance. The feeling at this time in the country was shown in answers given to circulars sent out by Robert Gourlay, an energetic Scottish busy-body, to a number of townships, asking an expression of opinion as to the causes which retarded improvement and the best means of developing the resources of the province. The answer from Sandwich emphatically set forth that the reasons of the existing depression were the reserves of land for the Crown and clergy, "which must for long keep the country a wilderness, a harbour for wolves, and a hindrance to compact and good neighbourhood; defects in the system of colonization; too great a quantity of land in the hands of individuals who do not reside in the province, and are not assessed for their property."

The select committee of the House of Commons on the civil government of Canada reported in 1828 that "these reserved lands, as they are at present distributed over the country, retard more than any other circumstance the improvement of the colony, lying as they do in detached portions of each township and intervening between the occupations of actual settlers, who have no means of cutting roads through the woods and morasses which thus separate them from their neighbours." It appears, too, that the quantity of land actually reserved was in excess of that which appears to have been contemplated by the

Constitutional Act. "A quantity equal to one-seventh of all grants," wrote Lord Durham in his report of 1839, "would be one-eighth of each township, or of all the public land. Instead of this proportion, the practice has been ever since the act passed, and in the clearest violation of its provisions, to set apart for the clergy in Upper Canada, a seventh of all the land, which is a quantity equal to a sixth of the land granted. . . . In Lower Canada the same violation of the law has taken place, with this difference—that upon every sale of Crown and clergy reserves, a fresh reserve for the clergy has been made, equal to a fifth of such reserves." In that way the public in both provinces was systematically robbed of a large quantity of land, which, Lord Durham estimated, was worth about £280,000 at the time he wrote. He acknowledges, however, that the clergy had no part in "this great misappropriation of the public property," but that it had arisen "entirely from heedless misconception, or some other error of the civil government of the province." All this, however, goes to show the maladministration of the public lands, and is one of the many reasons the people of the Canadas had for considering these reserves a public grievance.

When political parties were organized in Upper Canada some years after the war of 1812-14, which had for a while united all classes and creeds for the common defence, we see on one side a Tory compact for the maintenance of the old condition of things, the control of patronage, and the protection of the interests of the Church of England; on the other, a combination of Reformers, chiefly composed of Methodists, Presbyterians, and Baptists, who clamoured for reforms in government and above all for relief from the dominance of the Anglican Church, which, with respect to the clergy reserves and other matters, was seeking a *quasi* recognition as a state church. As the Puritans of New England at the commencement of the American Revolution inveighed against any attempt to establish an Anglican episcopate in the country as an insidious attack by the monarchy on their civil and religious liberty—most unjustly, as any impartial historian must now admit[1]—so in Upper Canada the dissenters made it one of their strongest grievances that favouritism was shown to the Anglican Church in the distribution of the public lands and the public patronage, to the detriment of all other religious bodies in the province. The bitterness that was evoked on this question had much to do with bringing about the rebellion of 1837. If the whole question could have been removed from the arena of political discussion, the Reformers would have been deprived of one of their most potent agencies to create a feeling against the

[1] See remarks of Dr. Kingsford in his "History of Canada" (vol. VII., pp. 266-273), showing how unjust was the clamour raised by the enemies of the church in New England when a movement was in progress for the establishment of a colonial episcopate simply for purposes of ordination and church government.

"family compact" and the government at Toronto.
But Bishop Strachan, who was a member of both the
executive and legislative councils—in other words,
the most influential member of the "family compact"—could not agree to any compromise which
would conciliate the aggrieved dissenters and at
the same time preserve a large part of the claim
made by the Church of England. Such a compromise in the opinion of this sturdy, obstinate ecclesiastic, would be nothing else than a sop to his
Satanic majesty. It was always with him a battle
à l'outrance, and as we shall soon see, in the end he
suffered the bitterness of defeat.

In these later days when we can review the
whole question without any of the prejudice and
passion which embittered the controversy while it
was a burning issue, we can see that the Church of
England had strong historical and legal arguments
to justify its claim to the exclusive use of the clergy
reserves. When the Constitutional Act of 1791 was
passed, the only Protestant clergy recognized in
British statutes were those of the Church of England, and, as we shall see later, those of the established
Church of Scotland. The dissenting denominations
had no more a legal status in the constitutional
system of England than the Roman Catholics, and
indeed it was very much the same thing in some
respects in the provinces of Canada. So late as 1824
the legislative council, largely composed of Anglicans, rejected a bill allowing Methodist ministers

to solemnize marriages, and it was not until 1831 that recognized ministers of all denominations were placed on an equality with the Anglican clergy in such matters. The employment of the words "Protestant clergy" in the act, it was urged with force, was simply to distinguish the Church of England clergy from those of the Church of Rome, who, otherwise, would be legally entitled to participate in the grant.

The loyalists, who founded the province of Upper Canada, established formally by the Constitutional Act of 1791, were largely composed of adherents of the Church of England, and it was one of the dearest objects of Lieutenant-Governor Simcoe to place that body on a stable basis and give it all the influence possible in the state. A considerable number had also settled in Lower Canada, and received, as in other parts of British North America, the sympathy and aid of the parent state. It was the object of the British government to make the constitution of the Canadas "an image and transcript" as far as possible of the British system of government. In no better way could this be done, in the opinion of the framers of the Constitutional Act, than by creating a titled legislative council;[1] and though this effort came to naught, it is noteworthy as showing the

[1]A clause of the act of 1791 provided that the sovereign might, if he thought fit, annex hereditary titles of honour to the right of being summoned to the legislative council in either province, but no titles were ever conferred under the authority of this imperial statute.

151

tendency at that time of imperial legislation. If such a council could be established, then it was all important that there should be a religious body, supported by the state, to surround the political institutions of the country with the safeguards which a conservative and aristocratic church like that of England would give. The erection and endowment of rectories "according to the establishment of the Church of England"—words of the act to be construed in connection with the previous clauses —was obviously a part of the original scheme of 1791 to anglicize Upper Canada and make it as far as possible a reflex of Anglican England.

It does not appear that at any time there was any such feeling of dissatisfaction with respect to the reserves in French Canada as existed throughout Upper Canada. The Protestant clergy in the former province were relatively few in number, and the Roman Catholic Church, which dominated the whole country, was quite content with its own large endowments received from the bounty of the king or private individuals during the days of French occupation, and did not care to meddle in a question which in no sense affected it. On the other hand, in Upper Canada, the arguments used by the Anglican clergy in support of their claims to the exclusive administration of the reserves were constantly answered not only in the legislative bodies, but in the Liberal papers, and by appeals to the imperial government. It was contended that the phrase "Protestant clergy" used in the Constitutional Act, was simply intended to distinguish all Protestant denominations from the Roman Catholic Church, and that, had there been any intention to give exclusive rights to the Anglican Church, it would have been expressly so stated in the section reserving the lands, just as had been done in the sections specially providing for the erection and endowment of Anglican rectories.

The first successful blow against the claims of the English Church in Canada was struck by that branch of the Presbyterian Church known in law as the Established Church of Scotland. It obtained an opinion from the British law officers in 1819, entirely favourable to its own participation in the reserves on the ground that it had been fully recognized as a state church, not only in the act uniting the two kingdoms of England and Scotland, but in several British statutes passed later than the Constitutional Act whose doubtful phraseology had originated the whole controversy. While the law officers admitted that the provisions of this act might be "extended also to the Church of Scotland, if there are any such settled in Canada (as appears to have been admitted in the debate upon the passing of the act)," yet they expressed the opinion that the clauses in question did not apply to dissenting ministers, since they thought that "the term 'Protestant clergy' could apply only to Protestant clergy recognized and established by law." We shall see a little further on the truth of the old adage that "lawyers will differ" and that in 1840, twenty-one years later than the expression of the opinion just cited, eminent British jurists appeared to be more favourable to the claims of denominations other than the Church of Scotland.

Until 1836—the year preceding the rebellion—the excitement with respect to the reserves had been intensified by the action of Sir John Colborne, lieutenant-governor of Upper Canada, who, on the eve of his departure for England, was induced by Bishop Strachan to sign patents creating and endowing forty-four rectories[1] in Upper Canada, representing more than 17,000 acres of land in the aggregate or about 486 for each of them. One can say advisedly that this action was most indiscreet at a time when a wise administrator would have attempted to allay rather than stimulate public irritation on so serious a question. Until this time, says Lord Durham, the Anglican clergy had no exclusive privileges, save such as might spring from their efficient discharge of their sacred duties, or from the energy, ability or influence of members of their body—notably Bishop Strachan, who practically controlled the government in religious and even secular matters. But, continued Lord Durham, the last public act of Sir John Colborne made it quite understood that every rector pos-

---

[1] Thirteen other patents were left unsigned by the lieutenant-governor and consequently had no legal force.

sessed "all the spiritual and other privileges enjoyed by an English rector," and that though he might "have no right to levy tithes" (for even this had been made a question), he was "in all other respects precisely in the same position as a clergyman of the established church in England." "This is regarded," added Lord Durham, "by all other teachers of religion in this country as having at once degraded them to a position of legal inferiority to the clergy of the Church of England; and it has been most warmly resented. In the opinion of many persons, this was the chief predisposing cause of the recent insurrection, and it is an abiding and unabated cause for discontent."

As soon as Sir John Colborne's action was known throughout the province, public indignation among the opponents of the clergy reserves and the Church of England took the forms of public meetings to denounce the issue of the patents, and of memorials to the imperial government calling into question their legality and praying for their immediate annulment. An opinion was obtained from the law officers of the Crown that the action taken by Sir John Colborne was "not valid and lawful," but it was given on a mere *ex parte* statement of the case prepared by the opponents of the rectories; and the same eminent lawyers subsequently expressed themselves favourably as to the legality of the patents when they were asked to reconsider the whole question, which was set forth in a very elaborate report prepared under the direction of Bishop Strachan. It is convenient to mention here that this phase of the clergy reserve question again came before able English counsel at the Equity Bar, when Hincks visited London in 1852. After they had given an opinion unfavourable to the Colborne patents on the case as submitted to them by the Canadian prime minister, it was deemed expedient to submit the whole legal question to the Court of Chancery in Upper Canada, which decided unanimously, after a full hearing of the case, that the patents were valid. But this decision was not given until 1856, when the whole matter of the reserves had been finally adjusted, and the validity of the creation of the rectories was no longer a burning question in Upper Canada.

When Poulett Thomson came to Canada in the autumn of 1839 as governor-general, he recognized the necessity of bringing about an immediate settlement of this very vexatious question, and of preventing its being made a matter of agitation after the union of the two provinces. The imperial authorities had already disallowed an act passed by the legislature of Upper Canada of 1838 to reinvest the clergy reserves in the Crown, and it became necessary for Lord Sydenham—to give the governor-general's later title—to propose a settlement in the shape of a compromise between the various Protestant bodies interested in the reserves. Lord Sydenham was opposed to the application of these lands to general education as proposed in several bills which had passed the assembly, but had been rejected by the legislative council owing to the dominant influence of Bishop Strachan. "To such a measure," says Lord Sydenham's biographer,[1] "he was opposed; first because it would have taken away the only fund exclusively devoted to purposes of religion, and secondly, because, even if carried in the provincial legislature, it would evidently not have obtained the sanction of the imperial parliament. He therefore entered into personal communication with the leading individuals among the principal religious communities, and after many interviews, succeeded in obtaining their support to a measure for the distribution of the reserves among the religious communities recognized by law, in proportion to their respective numbers."

Lord Sydenham's efforts to obtain the consent "of leading individuals among the principal religious communities" did not succeed in preventing a strong opposition to the measure after it had passed through the legislature. Dr. Ryerson, a power among the Methodists, denounced it, after he had at the outset shown an inclination to support it, and the Bishop of Toronto was also among its most determined opponents. Lord Sydenham's well-meaning attempt to settle the question was

[1] "Memoirs of the Life of the Right Honourable Charles Lord Sydenham, G.C.B.," edited by his brother G. Poulett Scrope, M.P.; London, 1843.

thwarted at the very outset by the reference of the
bill to English judges, who reported adversely on
the ground that the power "to vary or repeal"
given in the Constitutional Act of 1791 was only
prospective, and did not authorize the provincial legislature to divert the proceeds of the lands already
sold from the purpose originally contemplated in
the imperial statute. The judges also expressed the
opinion on this occasion that the words "Protestant
clergy" were large enough to include and did
include "other clergy than those of the Church of
Scotland." In their opinion these words appeared,
"both in their natural force and meaning, and still
more from the context of the clauses in which they
are found, to be there used to designate and intend
a clergy opposed in doctrine and discipline to the
clergy of the Church of Rome, and rather to aim at
the encouragement of the Protestant religion in
opposition to the Romish Church, than to point
exclusively to the clergy of the Church of England." But as they did not find on the statute
book the acknowledgment by the legislature of any
other clergy answering the description of the law,
they could not specify any other except the Church
of Scotland as falling within the imperial statute.

Under these circumstances the imperial government at once passed through parliament a bill
(3 and 4 Vict., c. 78) which re-enacted the Canadian measure with the modifications rendered necessary by the judicial opinion just cited. This act put

an end to future reservations, and at the same time recognized the claims of all the Protestant bodies to a share in the funds derived from the sales of the lands. It provided for the division of the reserves into two portions—those sold before the passing of the act and those sold at a later time. Of the previous sales, the Church of England was to receive two-thirds and the Church of Scotland one-third. Of future sales, the Church of England would receive one-third and the Church of Scotland one-sixth, while the residue could be applied by the governor-in-council "for purposes of public worship and religious instruction in Canada," in other words, that it should be divided among those other religious denominations that might make application at any time for a share in these particular funds.

This act, however, did not prove to be a settlement of this disturbing question. If Bishop Strachan had been content with the compromise made in this act, and had endeavoured to carry out its provisions as soon as it was passed, the Anglican Church would have obtained positive advantages which it failed to receive when the question was again brought into the arena of angry discussion. In 1844 when Henry Sherwood was solicitor-general in the Draper-Viger Conservative government he proposed an address to the Crown for the passing of a new imperial act, authorizing the division of the land itself instead of the income arising from its

159

sales. His object was to place the lands, allotted to the Church of England, under the control of the church societies, which could lease them, or hold them for any length of time at such prices as they might deem expedient. In the course of the debate on this proposition, which failed to receive the assent of the House, Baldwin, Price, and other prominent men expressed regret that any attempt should be made to disturb the settlement made by the imperial statute of 1840, which, in their opinion, should be regarded as final.

A strong feeling now developed in Upper Canada in favour of a repeal of the imperial act, and the secularization of the reserves. The Presbyterians— apart from the Church of Scotland—were now influenced by the Scottish Free Church movement of 1843 and opposed to public provision for the support of religious denominations. The spirit which animated them spread to other bodies, and was stimulated by the uncompromising attitude still assumed by the Anglican bishop, who was anxious, as Sherwood's effort proved, to obtain advantages for his church beyond those given it by the act of 1840. When the LaFontaine-Baldwin ministry was formed, the movement for the secularization of the reserves among the Upper Canadian Liberals, or Reformers as many preferred to call their party, became so pronounced as to demand the serious consideration of the government; but there was no inclination shown by the French

Canadians in the cabinet to disturb the settlement of 1840, and the serious phases of the Rebellion Losses Bill kept the whole question for some time in the background. After the appearance of the Clear Grits in Upper Canadian politics, with the secularization of the reserves as the principal plank in their platform, the LaFontaine-Baldwin cabinet felt the necessity of making a concession to the strong feeling which prevailed among Upper Canadian Reformers. As they were divided in opinion on the question and could not make it a part of the ministerial policy, Price, commissioner of Crown lands, was induced in the session of 1850 to introduce on his sole responsibility an address to the Crown, praying for the repeal of the imperial act of 1840, and the passage of another which would authorize the Canadian legislature to dispose of the reserves as it should deem most expedient, but with the distinct understanding that, while no particular sect should be considered as having a vested right in the property, the emoluments derived by existing incumbents should be guaranteed during their lives. Mr. Price—the same gentleman who had objected some years previously to the reopening of the question—showed in the course of his speech the importance which the reserves had now attained. The number of acres reserved to this time was 2,395,687, and of sales, under two statutes, 1,072,453. These sales had realized £720,756, of which £373,899 4s. 4d. had been paid, and £346,856 15s. 8d. remained still due. Counting the interest on the sum paid, a million of pounds represented the value of the lands already sold, and when they were all disposed of there would be realized more than two millions of pounds. Price also pointed out the fact that only a small number of persons had derived advantages from these reserves. Out of the total population of 723,000 souls in Upper Canada, the Church of England claimed 171,000 and the Church of Scotland 68,000, or a total of 239,000 persons who received the lion's share, and left comparatively little to the remaining population of 484,000 souls. Among the latter the Roman Catholics counted 123,707 communicants and received only £700 a year; the Wesleyans, with 90,363 adherents, received even a still more wretched pittance. Furthermore 269,000 persons were entirely excluded from any share whatever in the reserves. In the debate on the resolutions for the address LaFontaine did not consider the imperial act a finality, and was in favour of having the reserves brought under the control of the Canadian legislature, but he expressed the opinion most emphatically that all private rights and endowments conferred under the authority of imperial legislation should be held inviolate, and so far as possible, carried into effect. Baldwin's observations were remarkable for their vagueness. He did not object to endowment for religious purposes, although he was opposed to any union between church and

162

state. While he did not consider the act of 1840 as a final settlement, inasmuch as it did not express the opinion of the Canadian people, he was not then prepared to commit himself as to the mode in which the property should be disposed of. Hincks affirmed that there was no desire on the part of members of the government to evade their responsibilities on the question, but they were not ready to adopt the absurd and unconstitutional course that was pressed on them by the Clear Grits, of attempting to repeal an imperial act by a Canadian statute.

Malcolm Cameron and other radical Reformers advocated the complete secularization of the reserves, while Cayley, Macdonald, and other Conservatives, urged that the provisions of the imperial act of 1840 should be carried out to the fullest extent, and that the funds, then or at a future time at the disposal of the government "for the purposes of public worship and religious instruction" under the act, should be apportioned among the various denominations that had not previously had a share in the reserves. When it came to a division, it was clear that there was no unanimity on the question among the ministers and other supporters. Indeed, the summary given above of the remarks made by LaFontaine, Baldwin, and Hincks, affords conclusive evidence of the differences of opinion that existed between them and of their reluctance to express themselves definitely on the subject. The majority of the French members, Messrs. LaFontaine, Cauchon, Chabot, Chauveau, LaTerrière and others, voted against the resolution which affirmed that "no religious denomination can be held to have such vested interest in the revenue derived from the proceeds of the said clergy reserves as should prevent further legislation with reference to the disposal of them, but this House is nevertheless of opinion that the claims of existing incumbents should be treated in the most liberal manner." Baldwin and other Reformers supported this clause, which passed by a majority of two. The address was finally adopted on a division of forty-six Yeas and twenty-three Nays—"the minority containing the names of a few Reformers who would not consent to pledge themselves to grant, for the lives of the existing incumbents, the stipends on which they had accepted their charges—some perhaps having come from other countries to fill them and having possibly thrown up other preferments."[1] The address was duly forwarded to England by Lord Elgin, with a despatch in which he explained at some length the position of the whole question. In accordance with the principle which guided him throughout his administration of Canadian affairs— to give full scope to the right of the province to manage its own local concerns—he advised Lord Grey to repeal the imperial act of 1840 if he

[1] Sir Francis Hincks's "Reminiscences of his Public Life," p. 283.

wished "to preserve the colony." Lord Grey admitted that the question was one exclusively affecting the people of Canada and should be decided by the provincial legislature. It was the intention of the government, he informed Lord Elgin, to introduce a bill into parliament for this purpose; but action had to be deferred until another year when, as it happened unfortunately for the province, Lord John Russell's ministry was forced to resign, and was succeeded by a Conservative administration led by the Earl of Derby.

The Canadian government soon ascertained from Sir John Pakington, the new colonial secretary, that the new advisers of Her Majesty were not "inclined to give their consent and support to any arrangement the result of which would too probably be the diversion to other purposes of the only public fund . . . . which now exists for the support of divine worship and religious instruction in the colony." It was also intimated by the secretary of state that the new government was quite ready to entertain a proposal for reconsidering the mode of distributing the proceeds of the sales of the reserves, while not ready to agree to any proposal that might "divert forever from its sacred object the fund arising from that portion of the public lands of Canada which, almost from the period of the British conquest of that province, has been set apart for the religious instruction of the people." Hincks, who was at that time in England, at once wrote to Sir John Pakington, in very emphatic terms, that he viewed "with grave apprehension the prospect of collision between Her Majesty's government and the parliament of Canada, on a question regarding which such strong feelings prevailed among the great mass of the population." The people of Canada were convinced that they were "better judges than any parties in England of what measures would best conduce to the peace and welfare of the province." As respects the proposal "for reconsidering the mode of distributing the income of the clergy reserves," Hincks had no hesitation in saying that "it would be received as one for the violation of the most sacred constitutional rights of the people."

As soon as the Canadian legislature met in 1852, Hincks carried an address to the Crown, in which it was urged that the question of the reserves was "one so exclusively affecting the people of Canada that its decision ought not to be withdrawn from the provincial legislature, to which it properly belongs to regulate all matters concerning the domestic interests of the province." The hope was expressed that Her Majesty's government would lose no time in giving effect to the promise made by the previous administration and introduce the legislation necessary "to satisfy the wishes of the Canadian people." In the debate on this address, Morin, the leader of the French section of the cabinet, clearly expressed himself in favour of the secularization of the reserves in accordance with the views entertained by his Upper Canadian colleagues. It was consequently clear that the successors of the LaFontaine-Baldwin ministry were fully pledged to a vigorous policy for the disposal of this vexatious dispute.

A few months after Lord Elgin had forwarded this address to the Crown, the Earl of Derby's administration was defeated in the House of Commons, and the Aberdeen government was formed towards the close of 1852, with the Duke of Newcastle as secretary of state for the colonies. One of Sir John Pakington's last official acts was to prepare a despatch unfavourable to the prayer of the assembly's last address, but it was never sent to Canada, though brought down to parliament. At the same time the Canadian people heard of this despatch they were gratified by the announcement that the new ministers had decided to reverse the policy of their predecessors and to meet the wishes of the Canadian legislature. Accordingly, in the session of 1853, a measure was passed by the imperial parliament to give full power to the provincial legislature to vary or repeal all or any part of the act of 1840, and to make all necessary provisions respecting the clergy reserves or the proceeds derived from the same, on the express condition that there should be no interference with the annual stipends or allowances of existing incumbents as long as they lived. The Hincks-Morin ministry was then urged to bring in at once a measure disposing finally of the question, in accordance with the latest imperial act; but, as we have read in a previous chapter, it came to the opinion after anxious deliberation that the existing parliament was not competent to deal with so important a question. It also held that it was a duty to obtain an immediate expression of opinion from the people, and the election of a House in which the country would be fully represented in accordance with the legislation increasing the number of representatives in the assembly.

The various political influences arrayed against Hincks in Upper Canada led to his defeat, and the formation of the MacNab-Morin Liberal-Conservative government, which at once took steps to settle the question forever. John A. Macdonald commenced this new epoch in his political career by taking charge of the bill for the secularization of the reserves. It provided for the payment of all moneys arising from the sales of the reserves into the hands of the receiver-general, who would apportion them amongst the several municipalities of the province according to population. All annual stipends or allowances, charged upon the reserves before the passage of the imperial act of 1853, were continued during the lives of existing incumbents, though the latter could commute their stipends or allowances for their value in money, and in this way create a small permanent endowment for the advantage of the church to which they belonged.

168

THE CONTROVERSY CLOSED

After nearly forty years of continuous agitation, during which the province of Upper Canada had been convulsed from the Ottawa to Lake Huron, and political parties had been seriously embarrassed, the question was at last removed from the sphere of party and religious controversy. The very politicians who had contended for the rights of the Anglican clergy were now forced by public opinion and their political interests to take the final steps for its settlement. Bishop Strachan's fight during the best years of his life had ended in thorough discomfiture. As the historian recalls the story of that fight, he cannot fail to come to the conclusion that the settlement of 1854 relieved the Anglican Church itself of a controversy which, as long as it existed, created a feeling of deep hostility that seriously affected its usefulness and progress. Even Lord Elgin was compelled to write in 1851 "that the tone adopted by the Church of England here has almost always had the effect of driving from her even those who would be most disposed to co-operate with her if she would allow them." At last freed from the political and the religious bitterness which was so long evoked by the absence of a conciliatory policy on the part of her leaders, this great church is able peacefully to teach the noble lessons of her faith and win that respect among all classes which was not possible under the conditions that brought her into direct conflict with the great mass of the Canadian people.

CHAPTER VIII

SEIGNIORIAL TENURE

THE government of Canada in the days of the
French régime bore a close resemblance to
that of a province of France. The governor was
generally a noble and a soldier, but while he was
invested with large military and civil authority by
the royal instructions, he had ever by his side a
vigilant guardian in the person of the intendant,
who possessed for all practical purposes still more
substantial powers, and was always encouraged to
report to the king every matter that might appear
to conflict with the principles of absolute government laid down by the sovereign. The superior
council of Canada possessed judicial, administrative
and legislative powers, but its action was limited
by the decrees and ordinances of the king, and its
decisions were subject to the veto of the royal
council of the parent state. The intendant, generally a man of legal attainments, had the special
right to issue ordinances which had the full effect
of law—in the words of his commission "to order
everything as he shall see just and proper." These
ordinances regulated inns and markets, the building
and repairs of churches and presbyteries, the construction of bridges, the maintenance of roads, and

all those matters which could affect the comfort, the convenience, and the security of the community at large. While the governmental machinery was thus modelled in a large measure on that of the provincial administration of France, the territory of the province was subject to a modified form of the old feudal system which was so long a dominant condition of the nations of Europe, and has, down to the present time left its impress on their legal and civil institutions, not even excepting Great Britain itself. Long before Jacques Cartier sailed up the River St. Lawrence this system had gradually been weakened in France under the persistent efforts of the Capets, who had eventually, out of the ruin of the feudatories, built up a monarchy which at last centralized all power in the king. The policy of the Capets had borne its full, legitimate fruit by the time Louis XIV ascended the throne. The power of the great nobles, once at the head of practically independent feudatories, had been effectually broken down, and now, for the most part withdrawn from the provinces, they ministered only to the ambition of the king, and contributed to the dissipation and extravagance of a voluptuous court.

But while those features of the ancient feudal system, which were calculated to give power to the nobles, had been eliminated by the centralizing influence of the king, the system still continued in the provinces to govern the relations between the *noblesse* and the peasantry who possessed their lands on old feudal conditions regulated by the customary or civil law. These conditions were, on the whole, still burdensome. The noble who spent all his time in attendance on the court at Versailles or other royal palaces could keep his purse equal to his pleasures only by constant demands on his feudal tenants, who dared no more refuse to obey his behests than he himself ventured to flout the royal will.

Deeply engrafted as it still was on the social system of the parent state, the feudal tenure was naturally transferred to the colony of New France, but only with such modifications as were suited to the conditions of a new country. Indeed all the abuses that might hinder settlement or prevent agricultural development were carefully lopped off. Canada was given its *seigneurs*, or lords of the manor, who would pay fealty and homage to the sovereign himself, or to the feudal superior from whom they directly received their territorial estate, and they in their turn leased lands to peasants, or tillers of the soil, who held them on the modified conditions of the tenure of old France. It was not expedient, and indeed not possible, to transfer a whole body of nobles to the wilderness of the new world—they were as a class too wedded to the gay life of France—and all that could be done was to establish a feudal tenure to promote colonization, and at the same time possibly create a landed gentry who might be a shadowy reflection of the French *noblesse*, and could, in particular cases, receive titles directly from the king himself.

This seigniorial tenure of New France was the most remarkable instance which the history of North America affords of the successful effort of European nations to reproduce on this continent the ancient aristocratic institutions of the old world. In the days when the Dutch owned the Netherlands, vast estates were partitioned out to certain "patroons," who held their property on *quasi* feudal conditions, and bore a resemblance to the *seigneurs* of French Canada. This manorial system was perpetuated under English forms when the territory was conquered by the English and transformed into the colony of New York, where it had a chequered existence, and was eventually abolished as inconsistent with the free conditions of American settlement. In the proprietary colony of Maryland the Calverts also attempted to establish a landed aristocracy, and give to the manorial lords certain rights of jurisdiction over their tenants drawn from the feudal system of Europe. For Carolina, Shaftesbury and Locke devised a constitution which provided a territorial nobility, called *landgraves* and *caciques*, but it soon became a mere historical curiosity. Even in the early days of Prince Edward Island, when it was necessary to mature a plan of colonization, it was gravely proposed to the British government that the whole island should be divided into "hundreds," as in England, or into "baronies," as in Ireland, with courts-baron, lords of manors, courts-leet, all under the direction of a lord paramount; but while this ambitious aristocratic scheme was not favourably entertained, the imperial authorities chose one which was most injurious in its effects on the settlement of this fertile island.

It was Richelieu who introduced this modified form of the feudal system into Canada, when he constituted, in 1627, the whole of the colony as a fief of the great fur-trading company of the Hundred Associates on the sole condition of its paying fealty and homage to the Crown. It had the right of establishing seigniories as a part of its undertaking to bring four thousand colonists to the province and furnish them with subsistence for three years. Both this company and its successor, the Company of the West Indies, created a number of seigniories, but for the most part they were never occupied, and the king revoked the grants on the ground of non-settlement, when he resumed possession of the country and made it a royal province. From that time the system was regulated by the *Coutume de Paris*, by royal edicts, or by ordinances of the intendant.

The greater part of the soil of Canada was accordingly held *en fief* or *en seigneurie*. Each grant varied from sixteen *arpents*—an *arpent* being about five-sixths of an English acre—by fifty, to ten leagues by twelve. We meet with other forms of tenure in the partition of land in the days of the French régime—for instance, *franc aleu noble* and *franc aumone* or *mortmain*, but these were exceptional grants to charitable, educational, or religious institutions, and were subject to none of the ordinary obligations of the feudal tenure, but required, as in the latter case, only the performance of certain devotional or other duties which fell within their special sphere. Some grants were also given in *franc aleu roturier*, equivalent to the English tenure of free and common socage, and were generally made for special objects.[1]

The *seigneur*, on his accession to the estate, was required to pay homage to the king, or to his feudal superior from whom he derived his lands. In case he wished to tranfer by sale or otherwise his seigniory, except in the event of direct natural succession, he had to pay under the *Coutume de Paris* —which, generally speaking, regulated such seigniorial grants—a *quint* or fifth part of the whole purchase money to his feudal superior, but he was allowed a reduction *(rabat)* of two-thirds if the money was promptly paid down. In special cases, land transfers, whether by direct succession or otherwise, were subject to the rule of *Vixen le*

[1] See on these points an excellent article on the feudal system of Canada in the *Queen's Quarterly* (Kingston, January, 1899) by Dr. W. Bennett Munro. Also *Droit de banalité*, by the same, in the report of the Am. Hist. Ass., Washington, for 1899, Vol. I.

français, which required the payment of *relief,* or one year's revenue, on all changes of ownership, or a payment of gold *(une maille d'or).* It was obligatory on all seigniors to register their grants at Quebec, to concede or sub-infeudate them under the rule of *jeu de fief,* and settle them with as little delay as practicable. The Crown also reserved in most cases its *jura regalia* or *regalitates,* such as mines and minerals, lands for military or defensive purposes, oak timber and masts for the building of the royal ships. It does not, however, appear that military service was a condition on which the seigniors of Canada held their grants, as was the case in France under the old feudal tenure. The king and his representative in his royal province held such powers in their own hands. The seignior had as little influence in the government of the country as he had in military affairs. He might be chosen to the superior council at the royal pleasure, and was bound to obey the orders of the governor whenever the militia were called out. The whole province was formed into a militia district, so that in time of war the inhabitants might be obliged to perform military service under the royal governor or commander-in-chief of the regular forces. A captain was appointed for each parish—generally conterminous with a seigniory—and in some cases there were two or three. These captains were frequently chosen from the seigniors, many of whom —in the Richelieu district entirely—were officers

177

of royal regiments, notably of the Carignan-Salières. The seigniors had, as in France, the right of dispensing justice, but with the exception of the Seminary of St. Sulpice of Montreal, it was only in very rare instances they exercised their judicial powers, and then simply in cases of inferior jurisdiction *(basse justice)*. The superior council and intendant adjudicated in all matters of civil and criminal importance.

The whole success of the seigniorial system, as a means of settling the country, depended on the extent to which the seigniors were able to grant their lands *en censive* or *en roture*. The *censitaire* who held his lands in this way could not himself sub-infeudate. The grantee *en roture* was governed by the same rules as the one *en censive* except with respect to the descent of lands in cases of intestacy. All land grants to the *censitaires*—or as they preferred to call themselves in Canada, *habitants*—were invariably shaped like a parallelogram, with a narrow frontage on the river varying from two to three *arpents*, and with a depth from four to eight *arpents*. These farms, in the course of time assumed the appearance of a continuous settlement on the river and became known in local phraseology as *Côtes*—for example, Côte des Neiges, Côte St. Louis, Côte St. Paul, and many other picturesque villages on the banks of the St. Lawrence. In the first century of settlement the government induced the officers and soldiers of the Carignan-Salières regi-

178

ment to settle lands along the Richelieu river and to build palisaded villages for the purposes of defence against the war-like Iroquois; but, in the rural parts of the province generally, the people appear to have followed their own convenience with respect to the location of their farms and dwellings, and chose the banks of the river as affording the easiest means of intercommunication. The narrow oblong grants, made in the original settlement of the province, became narrower still as the original occupants died and their property was divided among the heirs under the civil law. Consequently at the present day the traveller who visits French Canada sees the whole country divided into extremely long and narrow parallelograms each with fences and piles of stones as boundaries in innumerable cases.

The conditions on which the *censitaire* held his land from the seignior were exceedingly easy during the greater part of the French régime. The *cens et rentes* which he was expected to pay annually, on St. Martin's day, as a rule, varied from one to two *sols* for each superficial *arpent*, with the addition of a small quantity of corn, poultry, and some other article produced on the farm, which might be commuted for cash, at current prices. The *censitaire* was also obliged to grind his corn at the seignior's mill *(moulin banal)*, and though the royal authorities at Quebec were very particular in pressing the fulfilment of this obligation, it does not appear to

179

have been successfully carried out in the early days of the colony on account of the inability of the seigniors to purchase the machinery, or erect buildings suitable for the satisfactory performance of a service clearly most useful to the people of the rural districts. The obligation of baking bread in the seigniorial oven was not generally exacted, and soon became obsolete as the country was settled and each *habitant* naturally built his own oven in connection with his home. The seigniors also claimed the right to a certain amount of statute labour *(corvée)* from the *habitants* on their estates, to one fish out of every dozen caught in seigniorial waters, and to a reservation of wood and stone for the construction and repairs of the manor house, mill, and church in the parish or seigniory. In case the *censitaire* wished to dispose of his holding during his lifetime, it was subject to the *lods et ventes*, or to a tax of one-twelfth of the purchase money, which had to be paid to the seignior, who usually as a favour remitted one-fourth on punctual payment. The most serious restriction on such sales was the *droit de retraite*, or right of the seignior to pre-empt the same property himself within forty days from the date of the sale.

There was, no doubt, at the establishment of the seigniorial tenure, a disposition to create in Canada, as far as possible, an aristocratic class akin to the *noblesse* of old France, who were a social order quite distinct from the industrial and commercial classes, though they did not necessarily bear titles. Under the old feudal system the possession of land brought nobility and a title, but in the modified seigniorial system of Canada the king could alone confer titular distinctions. The intention of the system was to induce men of good social position—like the *gentils-hommes* or officers of the Carignan regiment—to settle in the country and become seigniors. However, the latter were not confined to this class, for the title was rapidly extended to shopkeepers, farmers, sailors, and even mechanics who had a little money and were ready to pay for the cheap privilege of becoming nobles in a small way. Titled seigniors were very rare at any time in French Canada. In 1671, Des Islets, Talon's seigniory, was erected into a barony, and subsequently into an earldom (Count d'Orsainville). François Berthelot's seigniory of St. Laurent on the Island of Orleans was made in 1676 an earldom, and that of Portneuf, Réné Robineau's, into a barony. The only title which has come down to the present time is that of the Baron de Longueuil, which was first conferred on the distinguished Charles LeMoyne in 1700, and has been officially recognized by the British government since December, 1880.

The established seigniorial system bore conclusive evidence of the same paternal spirit which sent shiploads of virtuous young women (sometimes *marchandises mêlées*) to the St. Lawrence to become wives of the forlorn Canadian bachelors, gave trousseaux of cattle and kitchen utensils to the newly wed, and encouraged by bounties the production of children. The seigniories were the ground on which these paternal methods of creating a farming community were to be developed, but despite the wise intentions of the government the whole machinery was far from realizing the results which might reasonably have been expected from its operation. The land was easily acquired and cheaply held, facilities were given for the grinding of grain and the making of flour; fish and game were quickly taken by the skilful fisherman and enterprising hunter, and the royal officials generally favoured the *habitants* in disputes with the seigniors.

Unlike the large grants made by the British government after the conquest to loyalists, Protestant clergy, and speculators—grants calculated to keep large sections of the country in a state of wildness — the seigniorial estates had to be cultivated and settled within a reasonable time if they were to be retained by the occupants. During the French dominion the Crown sequestrated a number of seigniories for the failure to observe the obligation of cultivation. As late as 1741 we find an ordinance restoring seventeen estates to the royal domain, although the Crown was ready to reinstate the former occupants the moment they showed that they intended to perform their duty of settlement. But all the care that was taken to encourage settlement was for a long time

without large results, chiefly in consequence of the
nomadic habits of the young men on the seigniories.
The fur trade, from the beginning to the end of
French dominion, was a serious bar to steady industry on the farm. The young *gentilhomme* as well
as the young *habitant* loved the free life of the forest
and river better than the monotonous work of the
farm. He preferred too often making love to the im-
pressionable dusky maiden of the wigwam rather
than to the stolid, devout damsel imported for his
kind by priest or nun. A raid on some English post
or village had far more attraction than following the
plough or threshing the grain. This adventurous
spirit led the young Frenchman to the western
prairies where the Red and Assiniboine waters
mingle, to the foot-hills of the Rocky Mountains,
to the Ohio and Mississippi, and to the Gulf of
Mexico. But while Frenchmen in this way won
eternal fame, the seigniories were too often left in
a state of savagery, and even those *seigneurs* and
habitants who devoted themselves successfully to
pastoral pursuits found themselves in the end har-
assed by the constant calls made upon their military services during the years the French fought to
retain the imperial domain they had been the first
to discover and occupy in the great valleys of
North America. Still, despite the difficulties which
impeded the practical working of the seigniorial
system, it had on the whole an excellent effect on
the social conditions of the country. It created a

friendly and even parental relation between *seigneur*, *curé*, and *habitant*, who on each estate constituted as it were a seigniorial family, united to each other by common ties of self-interest and personal affection. If the system did not create an energetic self-reliant people in the rural communities, it arose from the fact that it was not associated with a system of local self-government like that which existed in the colonies of England. The French king had no desire to see such a system develop in the colonial dependencies of France. His governmental system in Canada was a mild despotism intended to create a people ever ready to obey the decrees and ordinances of royal officials, over whom the commonalty could exercise no control whatever in such popular elective assemblies as were enjoyed by every colony of England in North America.

During the French régime the officials of the French government frequently repressed undue or questionable exactions imposed, or attempted to be imposed, on the *censitaires* by greedy or extravagant seigniors. It was not until the country had been for some time in the possession of England that abuses became fastened on the tenure, and retarded the agricultural and industrial development of the province. The *cens et rentes* were unduly raised, the *droit de banalité* was pressed to the extent that if a *habitant* went to a better or more convenient mill than the seignior's, he had to

184

pay tolls to both, the transfer of property was hampered by the *lods et ventes* and the *droit de retraite,* and the claim always made by the seigniors to the exclusive use of the streams running by or through the seigniories was a bar to the establishment of industrial enterprise. Questions of law which arose between the *seigneur* and *habitant* and were referred to the courts were decided in nearly all cases in favour of the former. In such instances the judges were governed by precedent or by a strict interpretation of the law, while in the days of French dominion the intendants were generally influenced by principles of equity in the disputes that came before them, and by a desire to help the weaker litigant, the *censitaire.*

It took nearly a century after the conquest before it was possible to abolish a system which had naturally become so deeply rooted in the social and economic conditions of the people of French Canada. As the abuses of the tenure became more obvious, discontent became widespread, and the politicians after the union were forced at last to recognize the necessity of a change more in harmony with modern principles. Measures were first passed better to facilitate the optional commutation of the tenure of lands *en roture* into that of *franc aleu roturier,* but they never achieved any satisfactory results. LaFontaine did not deny the necessity for a radical change in the system, but he was too much wedded to the old institutions of his native province to take the initiative for its entire removal. Mr. Louis Thomas Drummond, who was attorney-general in both the Hincks-Morin and MacNab-Morin ministries, is deserving of honourable mention in Canadian history for the leading part he took in settling this very perplexing question. I have already shown that his first attempt in 1853 failed in consequence of the adverse action of the legislative council, and that no further steps were taken in the matter until the coming into office of the MacNab or Liberal-Conservative government in 1854, when he brought a bill into parliament to a large extent a copy of the first. This bill became law after it had received some important amendments in the upper House, where there were a number of representatives of seigniorial interests, now quite reconciled to the proposed change and prepared to make the best of it. It abolished all feudal rights and duties in Lower Canada, "whether bearing upon the *censitaire* or *seigneur*," and provided for the appointment of commissioners to enquire into the respective rights of the parties interested. In order to enable them to come to correct conclusions with respect to these rights, all questions of law were first submitted to a seigniorial court composed of the judges of the Queen's Bench and Superior Court in Lower Canada. The commissioners under this law were as follows:—Messrs. Chabot, H. Judah, S. Lelièvre, L. Archambault, N. Dumas, J. G. Turcotte, C.

Delagrave, P. Winter, J. G. Lebel, and J. B.
Varin. The judges of the seigniorial court were:—
Chief Justice Sir Louis H. LaFontaine, president;
Judges Bowen, Aylwin, Duval, Caron, Day, Smith,
Vanfelson, Mondelet, Meredith, Short, Morin, and
Badgley. Provision was also made by parliament
for securing compensation to the seigniors for the
giving up of all legal rights of which they were
deprived by the decision of the commissioners. It
took five years of enquiry and deliberation before
the commissioners were able to complete their
labours, and then it was found necessary to vote
other funds to meet all the expenses entailed by a
full settlement of the question.

The result was that all lands previously held *en
fief, en arrière fief, en censive,* or *en roture,* under
the old French system, were henceforth placed on
the footing of lands in the other provinces, that is
to say, free and common socage. The seigniors received liberal remuneration for the abolition of the
lods et ventes, droit de banalité, and other rights
declared legal by the court. The *cens et ventes* had
alone to be met as an established rent *(rente con-
stituée)* by the *habitant,* but even this change was
so modified and arranged as to meet the exigencies
of the *censitaires,* the protection of whose interests
was at the basis of the whole law abolishing this
ancient tenure. This radical change cost the country from first to last over ten million dollars,
including a large indemnity paid to Upper Canada

for its proportion of the fund taken from public revenues of the united provinces to meet the claims of the seigniors and the expenses of the commission. The money was well spent in bringing about so thorough a revolution in so peaceable and conclusive a manner. The *habitants* of the east were now as free as the farmers of the west. The seigniors themselves largely benefited by the capitalization in money of their old rights, and by the untrammelled possession of land held *en franc aleu roturier*. Although the seigniorial tenure disappeared from the social system of French Canada nearly half a century ago, we find enduring memorials of its existence in such famous names as these:—Nicolet, Verchères, Lotbinière, Berthier, Rouville, Joliette, Terrebonne, Sillery, Beaupré, Bellechasse, Portneuf, Chambly, Sorel, Longueuil, Boucherville, Chateauguay, and many others which recall the seigniors of the old régime.

CHAPTER IX

CANADA AND THE UNITED STATES

IN a long letter which he wrote to Earl Grey
in August, 1850, Lord Elgin used these significant words : "To render annexation by violence
impossible, or by any other means improbable as
may be, is, as I have often ventured to repeat, the
polar star of my policy." To understand the full
significance of this language it is only necessary to
refer to the history of the difficulties with which
the governor-general had to contend from the first
hour he came to the province and began his efforts
to allay the feeling of disaffection then too prevalent throughout the country—especially among the
commercial classes—and to give encouragement to
that loyal sentiment which had been severely
shaken by the indifference or ignorance shown by
British statesmen and people with respect to the
conditions and interests of the Canadas. He was
quite conscious that, if the province was to remain
a contented portion of the British empire, it could
be best done by giving full play to the principles
of self-government among both nationalities who
had been so long struggling to obtain the application of the parliamentary system of England in
the fullest sense to the operation of their own

internal affairs, and by giving to the industrial and commercial classes adequate compensation for the great losses which they had sustained by the sudden abolition of the privileges which England had so long extended to Canadian products—notably, flour, wheat and lumber—in the British market.

Lord Elgin knew perfectly well that, while this discontent existed, the party which favoured annexation would not fail to find sympathy and encouragement in the neighbouring republic. He recalled the fact that both Papineau and Mackenzie, after the outbreak of their abortive rebellion, had many abettors across the border, as the infamous raids into Canada clearly proved. Many people in the United States, no doubt, saw some analogy between the grievances of Canadians and those which had led to the American revolution. "The mass of the American people," said Lord Durham, "had judged of the quarrel from a distance; they had been obliged to form their judgment on the apparent grounds of the controversy; and were thus deceived, as all those are apt to be who judge under such circumstances, and on such grounds. The contest bore some resemblance to that great struggle of their own forefathers, which they regard with the highest pride. Like that, they believed it to be the contest of a colony against the empire, whose misconduct alienated their own country; they considered it to be a contest undertaken by a people professing to seek independence of distant control, and extension of popular privileges." More than that, the striking contrast which was presented between Canada and the United States "in respect to every sign of productive industry, increasing wealth, and progressive civilization" was considered by the people of the latter country to be among the results of the absence of a political system which would give expansion to the energies of the colonists and make them self-reliant in every sense.

Lord Durham's picture of the condition of things in 1838-9 was very painful to Canadians, although it was truthful in every particular. "On the British side of the line," he wrote, "with the exception of a few favoured spots, where some approach to American prosperity is apparent, all seems waste and desolate." But it was not only "in the difference between the larger towns on the two sides" that we could see "the best evidence of our own inferiority." That "painful and undeniable truth was most manifest in the country districts through which the line of national separation passes for one thousand miles." Mrs. Jameson in her "Winter Studies and Summer Rambles," written only a year or two before Lord Durham's report, gives an equally unfavourable comparison between the Canadian and United States sides of the western country. As she floated on the Detroit river in a little canoe made of a hollow tree, and saw on one side "a city with its towers, and spires, and animated population," and on the other "a little straggling hamlet with all the symptoms of apathy, indolence, mistrust, hopelessness," she could not help wondering at this "incredible difference between the two shores," and hoping that some of the colonial officials across the Atlantic would be soon sent "to behold and solve the difficulty."

But while Lord Durham was bound to emphasize this unsatisfactory state of things he had not lost his confidence in the loyalty of the mass of the Canadian people, notwithstanding the severe strain to which they had been subject on account of the supineness of the British government to deal vigorously and promptly with grievances of which they had so long complained as seriously affecting their connection with the parent state and the development of their material resources. It was only necessary, he felt, to remove the causes of discontent to bring out to the fullest extent the latent affection which the mass of French and English Canadians had been feeling for British connection ever since the days when the former obtained guarantees for the protection of their dearest institutions and the Loyalists of the American Revolution crossed the frontier for the sake of Crown and empire. "We must not take every rash expression of disappointment," wrote Lord Durham, "as an indication of a settled aversion to the existing constitution; and my own observation convinces me that the predominant feeling of all the British population of the North

192

American colonies is that of devoted attachment to the mother country. I believe that neither the interests nor the feelings of the people are incompatible with a colonial government, wisely and popularly administered." His strong conviction then was that if connection with Great Britain was to be continuous, if every cause of discontent was to be removed, if every excuse for interference "by violence on the part of the United States" was to be taken away, if Canadian annexationists were no longer to look for sympathy and aid among their republican neighbours, the Canadian people must be given the full control of their own internal affairs, while the British government on their part should cease that constant interference which only irritated and offended the colony. "It is not by weakening," he said, "but strengthening the influence of the people on the government; by confining within much narrower bounds than those hitherto allotted to it, and not by extending the interference of the imperial authorities in the details of colonial affairs, that I believe that harmony is to be restored, where dissension has so long prevailed; and a regularity and vigour hitherto unknown, introduced into the administration of these provinces." And he added that if the internal struggle for complete self-government were renewed "the sympathy from without would at some time or other re-assume its former strength."

Lord Elgin appeared on the scene at the very

time when there was some reason for a repetition of that very struggle, and a renewal of that very "sympathy from without" which Lord Durham imagined. The political irritation, which had been smouldering among the great mass of Reformers since the days of Lord Metcalfe, was seriously aggravated by the discontent created by commercial ruin and industrial paralysis throughout Canada as a natural result of Great Britain's ruthless fiscal policy. The annexation party once more came to the surface, and contrasts were again made between Canada and the United States seriously to the discredit of the imperial state. "The plea of self-interest," wrote Lord Elgin in 1849, "the most powerful weapon, perhaps, which the friends of British connection have wielded in times past, has not only been wrested from my hands but transferred since 1846 to those of the adversary." He then proceeded to contrast the condition of things on the two sides of the Niagara, only "spanned by a narrow bridge, which it takes a foot passenger about three minutes to cross." The inhabitants on the Canadian side were "for the most part United Empire Loyalists" and differed little in habits or modes of thought and expression from their neighbours. Wheat, their staple product, grown on the Canadian side of the line, "fetched at that time in the market from 9d. to 1s. less than the same article grown on the other." These people had protested against the Montreal annexation movement, but Lord Elgin was nevertheless confident that the large majority firmly believed "that their annexation to the United States would add one-fourth to the value of the produce of their farms."

In dealing with the causes of discontent Lord Elgin came to exactly the same conclusion which, as I have just shown, was accepted by Lord Durham after a close study of the political and material conditions of the country. He completed the work of which his eminent predecessor had been able only to formulate the plan. By giving adequate scope to the practice of responsible government, he was able to remove all causes for irritation against the British government, and prevent annexationists from obtaining any sympathy from that body of American people who were always looking for an excuse for a movement—such a violent movement as suggested by Lord Elgin in the paragraph given above—which would force Canada into the states of the union. Having laid this foundation for a firm and popular government, he proceeded to remove the commercial embarrassment by giving a stimulus to Canadian trade by the repeal of the navigation laws, and the adoption of reciprocity with the United States. The results of his efforts were soon seen in the confidence which all nationalities and classes of the Canadian people felt in the working of their system of government, in the strengthening of the ties between the imperial state and the dependency,

195

and in the decided stimulus given to the shipping and trade throughout the provinces of British North America.

I have already in the previous chapters of this book dwelt on the methods which Lord Elgin so successfully adopted to establish responsible government in accordance with the wishes of the Canadian people, and it is now only necessary to refer to his strenuous efforts during six years to obtain reciprocal trade between Canada and the United States. It was impossible at the outset of his negotiations to arouse any active interest among the politicians of the republic as long as they were unable to see that the proposed treaty would be to the advantage of their particular party or of the nation at large. No party in congress was ready to take it up as a political question and give it that impulse which could be best given by a strong partisan organization. The Canadian and British governments could not get up a "lobby" to press the matter in the ways peculiar to professional politicians, party managers, and great commercial or financial corporations. Mr. Hincks brought the powers of his persuasive tongue and ingenious intellect to bear on the politicians at Washington, but even he with all his commercial acuteness and financial knowledge was unable to accomplish anything. It was not until Lord Elgin himself went to the national capital and made use of his diplomatic tact and amenity of demeanour that a successful result was reached. No governor-general who ever visited the United States made so deep an impression on its statesmen and people as was made by Lord Elgin during this mission to Washington, and also in the course of the visits he paid to Boston and Portland where he spoke with great effect on several occasions. He won the confidence and esteem of statesmen and politicians by his urbanity, dignity, and capacity for business. He carried away his audiences by his exhibition of a high order of eloquence, which evoked the admiration of those who had been accustomed to hear Webster, Everett, Wendell Phillips, Choate, and other noted masters of oratory in America.

He spoke at Portland after his success in negotiating the treaty, and was able to congratulate both Canada and the United States on the settlement of many questions which had too long alienated peoples who ought to be on the most friendly terms with each other. He was now near the close of his Canadian administration and was able to sum up the results of his labours. The discontent with which the people of the United States so often sympathized had been brought to an end "by granting to Canadians what they desired—the great principle of self-government." "The inhabitants of Canada at this moment," he went on to say, "exercise as much influence over their own destinies and government as do the people of the United States. This is the only cause of misunderstanding that ever existed; and this cannot arise when the circumstances which made them at variance have ceased to exist."

The treaty was signed on June 5th, 1854, by Lord Elgin on the part of Great Britain, and by the Honourable W. L. Marcy, secretary of state, on behalf of the United States, but it did not legally come into force until it had been formally ratified by the parliament of Great Britain, the congress of the United States, and the several legislatures of the British provinces. It exempted from customs duties on both sides of the line certain articles which were the growth and produce of the British colonies and of the United States— the principal being grain, flour, breadstuffs, animals, fresh, smoked, and salted meats, fish, lumber of all kinds, poultry, cotton, wool, hides, ores of metal, pitch, tar, ashes, flax, hemp, rice, and unmanufactured tobacco. The people of the United States and of the British provinces were given an equal right to navigate the St. Lawrence river, the Canadian canals and Lake Michigan. No export duty could be levied on lumber cut in Maine and passing down the St. John or other streams in New Brunswick. The most important question temporarily settled by the treaty was the fishery dispute which had been assuming a troublesome aspect for some years previously. The government at Washington then began to raise the issue that the three mile limit to which their fishermen could be confined should follow the sinuosities of the coasts, including bays; the object being to obtain access to the valuable mackerel fisheries of the Bay of Chaleurs and other waters claimed to be exclusively within the territorial jurisdiction of the maritime provinces. The imperial government generally sustained the contention of the provinces—a contention practically supported by the American authorities in the case of Delaware, Chesapeake, and other bays on the coasts of the United States—that the three mile limit should be measured from a line drawn from headland to headland of all bays, harbours, and creeks. In the case of the Bay of Fundy, however, the imperial government allowed a departure from this general principle when it was urged by the Washington government that one of its headlands was in the territory of the United States, and that it was an arm of the sea rather than a bay. The result was that foreign fishing vessels were shut out only from the bays on the coasts of Nova Scotia and New Brunswick within the Bay of Fundy. All these questions were, however, placed in abeyance for twelve years, by the Reciprocity Treaty of 1854, which provided that the inhabitants of the United States could take fish of any kind, except shell fish, on the sea coasts, and shores, in the bays, harbours, and creeks of any British province, without any restriction as to distance, and had also permission to land on these coasts and shores for the purpose of drying their nets and curing their fish. The same privileges were extended to British citizens on the eastern sea coasts and shores of the United States, north of the 36th parallel of north latitude—privileges of no practical value to the people of British North America compared with those they gave up in their own prolific waters. The farmers of the agricultural west accepted with great satisfaction a treaty which gave their products free access to their natural market, but the fishermen and seamen of the maritime provinces, especially of Nova Scotia, were for some time dissatisfied with provisions which gave away their most valuable fisheries without adequate compensation, and at the same time refused them the privilege—a great advantage to a ship-building, ship-owning province—of the coasting trade of the United States on the same terms which were allowed to American and British vessels on the coasts of British North America. On the whole, however, the treaty eventually proved of benefit to all the provinces at a time when trade required just such a stimulus as it gave in the markets of the United States. The aggregate interchange of commodities between the two countries rose from an annual average of $14,230,763 in the years previous to 1854 to $33,492,754 gold currency, in the first year of its existence; to $42,944,754 gold currency, in the second year; to $50,339,770 gold currency in the third year; and to no less a sum than $84,070,955 at war prices, in the thirteenth year when it was terminated by the United States in accordance with the provision, which allowed either party to bring it to an end after a due notice of twelve months at the expiration of ten years or of any longer time it might remain in force. Not only was a large and remunerative trade secured between the United States and the provinces, but the social and friendly intercourse of the two countries necessarily increased with the expansion of commercial relations and the creation of common interests between them. Old antipathies and misunderstandings disappeared under the influence of conditions which brought these communities together and made each of them place a higher estimate on the other's good qualities. In short, the treaty in all respects fully realized the expectations of Lord Elgin in working so earnestly to bring it to a successful conclusion.

However, it pleased the politicians of the United States, in a moment of temper, to repeal a treaty which, during its existence, gave a balance in favour of the commercial and industrial interests of the republic, to the value of over $95,000,000 without taking into account the value of the provincial fisheries from which the fishermen of New England annually derived so large a profit. Temper, no doubt, had much to do with the action of the United States government at a time when it was irritated by the sympathy extended to the Confederate States by many persons in the provinces as well as in Great Britain—notably by Mr. Gladstone himself. No doubt it was thought that the repeal of the treaty would be a sort of punishment to the people of British North America. It was even felt— as much was actually said in congress—that the result of the sudden repeal of the treaty would be the growth of discontent among those classes in Canada who had begun to depend upon its continuance, and that sooner or later there would arise a cry for annexation with a country from which they could derive such large commercial advantages. Canadians now know that the results have been very different from those anticipated by statesmen and journalists on the other side of the border. Instead of starving Canada and forcing her into annexation, they have, by the repeal of the Reciprocity Treaty, and by their commercial policy ever since, materially helped to stimulate her self-reliance, increase her commerce with other countries, and make her largely a self-sustaining, independent country. Canadians depend on themselves—on a self-reliant, enterprising policy of trade—not on the favour or caprice of any particular nation. They are always quite prepared to have the most liberal commercial relations with the United States, but at the same time feel that a reciprocity treaty is no longer absolutely essential to their prosperity, and cannot under any circumstances have any particular effect on the political destiny of the Canadian confederation whose strength and unity are at length so well assured.

CHAPTER X

FAREWELL TO CANADA

LORD ELGIN assumed the governor-generalship of Canada on January 30th, 1847, and
gave place to Sir Edmund Head on December
19th, 1854. The address which he received from
the Canadian legislature on the eve of his departure
gave full expression to the golden opinions which
he had succeeded in winning from the Canadian
people during his able administration of nearly
eight years. The passionate feeling which had been
evoked during the crisis caused by the Rebellion
Losses Bill had gradually given way to a true
appreciation of the wisdom of the course that he
had followed under such exceptionally trying circumstances, and to the general conviction that his
strict observance of the true forms and methods of
constitutional government had added strength and
dignity to the political institutions of the country
and placed Canada at last in the position of a semi-
independent nation. The charm of his manner could
never fail to captivate those who met him often in
social life, while public men of all parties recognized
his capacity for business, the sincerity of his convictions, and the absence of a spirit of intrigue in
connection with the administration of public affairs

and his relations with political parties. He received evidences on every side that he had won the confidence and respect and even affection of all nationalities, classes, and creeds in Canada. In the very city where he had been maltreated and his life itself endangered, he received manifestations of approval which were full compensation for the mental sufferings to which he was subject in that unhappy period of his life, when he proved so firm, courageous and far-sighted. In well chosen language—always characteristic of his public addresses—he spoke of the cordial reception he had met with, when he arrived a stranger in Montreal, of the beauty of its surroundings, of the kind attention with which its citizens had on more than one occasion listened to the advice he gave to their various associations, of the undaunted courage with which the merchants had promoted the construction of that great road which was so necessary to the industrial development of the province, of the patriotic energy which first gathered together such noble specimens of Canadian industry from all parts of the country, and had been the means of making the great World's Fair so serviceable to Canada; and then as he recalled the pleasing incidents of the past, there came to his mind a thought of the scenes of 1849, but the sole reference he allowed himself was this: "And I shall forget—but no, what I might have to forget is forgotten already, and therefore I cannot tell you what I shall forget."

The last speech which he delivered in the picturesque city of Quebec gave such eloquent expression to the feelings with which he left Canada, is such an admirable example of the oratory with which he so often charmed large assemblages, that I give it below in full for the perusal of Canadians of the present day who had not the advantage of hearing him in the prime of his life.

"I wish I could address you in such strains as I have sometimes employed on similar occasions—strains suited to a festive meeting; but I confess I have a weight on my heart and it is not in me to be merry. For the last time I stand before you in the official character which I have borne for nearly eight years. For the last time I am surrounded by a circle of friends with whom I have spent some of the most pleasant days of my life. For the last time I welcome you as my guests to this charming residence which I have been in the habit of calling my home.[1] I did not, I will frankly confess it, know what it would cost me to break this habit, until the period of my departure approached, and I began to feel that the great interests which have so long engrossed my attention and thoughts were passing out of my hands. I had a hint of what my feelings really were upon this point—a pretty broad hint too—one lovely morning in June last, when I returned to Quebec after my temporary absence in England, and landed in the coves below Spencer-

[1] "Spencerwood," the governor's private residence.

wood (because it was Sunday and I did not want to make a disturbance in the town), and when with the greetings of the old people in the coves who put their heads out of the windows as I passed along, and cried 'Welcome home again,' still ringing in my ears, I mounted the hill and drove through the avenue to the house door, I saw the drooping trees on the lawn, with every one of which I was so familiar, clothed in the tenderest green of spring, and the river beyond, calm and transparent as a mirror, and the ships fixed and motionless as statues on its surface, and the whole landscape bathed in that bright Canadian sun which so seldom pierces our murky atmosphere on the other side of the Atlantic. I began to think that persons were to be envied who were not forced by the necessities of their position to quit these engrossing interests and lovely scenes, for the purpose of proceeding to distant lands, but who are able to remain among them until they pass to that quiet corner of the garden of Mount Hermon, which juts into the river and commands a view of the city, the shipping, Point Levi, the Island of Orleans, and the range of the Laurentine; so that through the dim watches of that tranquil night which precedes the dawning of the eternal day, the majestic citadel of Quebec, with its noble train of satellite hills, may seem to rest forever on the sight, and the low murmur of the waters of St. Lawrence, with the hum of busy life on their surface, to fall ceaselessly on the ear. I cannot bring myself to believe that the future has in store for me any interests which will fill the place of those I am now abandoning. But although I must henceforward be to you as a stranger, although my official connection with you and your interests will have become in a few days matter of history, yet I trust that through some one channel or other, the tidings of your prosperity and progress may occasionally reach me; that I may hear from time to time of the steady growth and development of those principles of liberty and order, of manly independence in combination with respect for authority and law, of national life in harmony with British connection, which it has been my earnest endeavour, to the extent of my humble means of influence, to implant and to establish. I trust, too, that I shall hear that this House continues to be what I have ever sought to render it, a neutral territory, on which persons of opposite opinions, political and religious, may meet together in harmony and forget their differences for a season. And I have good hope that this will be the case for several reasons, and, among others, for one which I can barely allude to, for it might be an impertinence in me to dwell upon it. But I think that without any breach of delicacy or decorum I may venture to say that many years ago, when I was much younger than I am now, and when we stood towards each other in a relation somewhat different from that which has recently subsisted between us, I learned to look up to Sir Edmund Head with respect, as a gentleman of the highest character, the greatest ability, and the most varied accomplishments and attainments. And now, ladies and gentlemen, I have only to add the sad word— Farewell. I drink this bumper to the health of you all, collectively and individually. I trust that I may hope to leave behind me some who will look back with feelings of kindly recollection to the period of our intercourse; some with whom I have been on terms of immediate official connection, whose worth and talents I have had the best means of appreciating, and who could bear witness at least, if they please to do so, to the spirit, intentions, and motives with which I have administered your affairs; some with whom I have been bound by the ties of personal regard. And if reciprocity be essential to enmity, then most assuredly I can leave behind me no enemies. I am aware that there must be persons in so large a society as this, who think that they have grievances to complain of, that due consideration has not in all cases been shown to them. Let them believe me, and they ought to believe me, for the testimony of a dying man is evidence, even in a court of justice, let them believe me, then, when I assure them, in this the last hour of my agony, that no such errors of omission or commission have been intentional on my part. Farewell, and God bless you."

Before I proceed to review some features of his administration in Canada, to which it has not been possible to do adequate justice in previous chapters of this book, I must very briefly refer to the eminent services which he was able to perform for the empire before he closed his useful life amid the shadows of the Himalayas. On his return to England he took his seat in the House of Lords, but he gave very little attention to politics or legislation. On one occasion, however, he expressed a serious doubt as to the wisdom of sending to Canada large bodies of troops, which had come back from the Crimea, on the ground that such a proceeding might complicate the relations of the colony with the United States, and at the same time arrest its progress towards self-independence in all matters affecting its internal order and security.

This opinion was in unison with the sentiments which he had often expressed to the secretary of state during his term of office in America. While he always deprecated any hasty withdrawal of imperial troops from the dependency as likely at that time to imperil its connection with the mother country, he believed most thoroughly in educating Canadians gradually to understand the large measure of responsibility which attached to self-government. He was of opinion "that the system of relieving colonists altogether from the duty of self-defence must be attended with injurious effects upon themselves." "It checks," he continued, "the growth of national and manly morals. Men seldom think anything worth preserving for which they are never asked to make a sacrifice." His view was that, while it was desirable to remove imperial troops gradually and throw the responsibility of self-defence largely upon Canada, "the movement in that direction should be made with due caution." "The present"—he was writing to the secretary of state in 1848 when Canadian affairs were still in an unsatisfactory state—"is not a favourable moment for experiments. British statesmen, even secretaries of state, have got into the habit lately of talking of the maintenance of the connection between Great Britain and Canada with so much indifference, that a change of system in respect to military defence incautiously carried out might be presumed by many to argue, on the part of the mother country, a disposition to prepare the way for separation." And he added three years later: "If these communities are only truly attached to the connection and satisfied of its permanence (and as respects the latter point, opinions here will be much influenced by the tone of statesmen at home), elements of self-defence, not moral elements only, but material elements likewise, will spring up within them spontaneously as the product of movements from within, not of pressure from without. Two millions of people in a northern latitude can do a good deal in the way of helping themselves, when their hearts are in the right place." Before two decades of years had passed away, the foresight of these suggestions was clearly shown. Canada had become a part of a

THE QUESTION OF SELF-DEFENCE

British North American confederation, and with the development of its material resources, the growth of a national spirit of self-reliance, the new Dominion, thus formed, was able to relieve the parent state of the expenses of self-defence, and come to her aid many years later when her interests were threatened in South Africa. If Canada has been able to do all this, it has been owing to the growth of that spirit of self-reliance—of that principle of self-government—which Lord Elgin did his utmost to encourage. We can then well understand that Lord Elgin, in 1855, should have contemplated with some apprehension the prospect of largely increasing the Canadian garrisons at a time when Canadians were learning steadily and surely to cultivate the national habit of depending upon their own internal resources in their working out of the political institutions given them by England after years of agitation, and even suffering, as the history of the country until 1840 so clearly shows. It is also easy to understand that Lord Elgin should have regarded the scheme in contemplation as likely to create a feeling of doubt and suspicion as to the motives of the imperial government in the minds of the people of the United States. He recalled naturally his important visit to that country, where he had given eloquent expression, as the representative of the British Crown, to his sanguine hopes for the continuous amity of peoples allied to each other by so many ties of kindred and interest, and had also succeeded after infinite labour in negotiating a treaty so well calculated to create a common sympathy between Canada and the republic, and stimulate that friendly intercourse which would dispel many national prejudices and antagonisms which had unhappily arisen between these communities in the past. The people of the United States might well, he felt, see some inconsistency between such friendly sentiments and the sending of large military reinforcements to Canada.

In the spring of 1857 Lord Elgin accepted from Lord Palmerston a delicate mission to China at a very critical time when the affair of the lorcha "Arrow" had led to a serious rupture between that country and Great Britain. According to the British statement of the case, in October, 1856, the Chinese authorities at Canton seized the lorcha although it was registered as a British vessel, tore down the British flag from its masthead, and carried away the crew as prisoners. On the other hand the Chinese claimed that they had arrested the crew, who were subjects of the emperor, as pirates, that the British ownership had lapsed some time previously, and that there was no flag flying on the vessel at the time of its seizure. The British representatives in China gave no credence to these explanations but demanded not only a prompt apology but also the fulfilment of "long evaded treaty obligations." When these peremptory demands were not at once complied with, the British

212

proceeded in a very summary manner to blow up Chinese forts, and commit other acts of war, although the Chinese only offered a passive resistance to these efforts to bring them to terms of abject submission. Lord Palmerston's government was condemned in the House of Commons for the violent measures which had been taken in China, but he refused to submit to a vote made up, as he satirically described it, "of a fortuitous concourse of atoms," and appealed to the country, which sustained him. While Lord Elgin was on his way to China, he heard the news of the great mutiny in India, and received a letter from Lord Canning, then governor-general, imploring him to send some assistance from the troops under his direction. He at once sent "instructions far and wide to turn the transports back and give Canning the benefit of the troops for the moment." It is impossible, say his contemporaries, to exaggerate the importance of the aid which he so promptly gave at the most critical time in the Indian situation. "Tell Lord Elgin," wrote Sir William Peel, the commander of the famous Naval Brigade at a later time, "that it was the Chinese expedition which relieved Lucknow, relieved Cawnpore, and fought the battle of December 6th." But this patriotic decision delayed somewhat the execution of Lord Elgin's mission to China. It was nearly four months after he had despatched the first Chinese contingent to the relief of the Indian authorities, that another body of troops arrived in China and he was able to proceed vigorously to execute the objects of his visit to the East. After a good deal of fighting and bullying, Chinese commissioners were induced in the summer of 1859 to consent to sign the Treaty of Tientsin, which gave permission to the Queen of Great Britain to appoint, if she should see fit, an ambassador who might reside permanently at Pekin, or visit it occasionally according to the pleasure of the British government, guaranteed protection to Protestants and Roman Catholics alike, allowed British subjects to travel to all parts of the empire, under passports signed by British consuls, established favourable conditions for the protection of trade by foreigners, and indemnified the British government for the losses that had been sustained at Canton and for the expenses of the war.

Lord Elgin then paid an official visit to Japan, where he was well received and succeeded in negotiating the Treaty of Yeddo, which was a decided advance on all previous arrangements with that country, and prepared the way for larger relations between it and England. On his return to bring the new treaty to a conclusion, he found that the commissioners who had gone to obtain their emperor's full consent to its provisions, seemed disposed to call into question some of the privileges which had been already conceded, and he was consequently forced to assume that peremptory tone which experience of the Chinese has shown can alone bring them to understand the full measure of their responsibilities in negotiations with a European power. However, he believed he had brought his mission to a successful close, and returned to England in the spring of 1859.

How little interest was taken in those days in Canadian affairs by British public men and people, is shown by some comments of Mr. Walrond on the incidents which signalized Lord Elgin's return from China. "When he returned in 1854 from the government of Canada," this writer naively admits, " there were comparatively few persons in England who knew anything of the great work he had done in the colony. But his brilliant successes in the East attracted public interest and gave currency to his reputation." He accepted the position of postmaster-general in the administration just formed by Lord Palmerston, and was elected Lord Rector of Glasgow; but he had hardly commenced to study the details of his office, and enjoy the amenities of the social life of Great Britain, when he was again called upon by the government to proceed to the East, where the situation was once more very critical. The duplicity of the Chinese in their dealings with foreigners had soon shown itself after his departure from China, and he was instructed to go back as Ambassador Extraordinary to that country, where a serious rupture had occurred between the English and Chinese while an expedition of the former was on its way to Pekin to obtain the formal ratification of the Treaty of Tientsin. The French government, which had been a party to that treaty, sent forces to coöperate with those of Great Britain in obtaining prompt satisfaction for an attack made by the Chinese troops on the British at the Peiho, the due ratification of the Treaty of Tientsin, and payment of an indemnity to the allies for the expenses of their military operations.

The punishment which the Chinese received for their bad faith and treachery was very complete. Yuen-ming-yuen, the emperor's summer palace, one of the glories of the empire, was levelled to the ground as a just retribution for treacherous and criminal acts committed by the creatures of the emperor at the very moment it was believed that the negotiations were peacefully terminated. Five days after the burning of the palace, the treaty was fully ratified between the emperor's brother and Lord Elgin, and full satisfaction obtained from the imperial authorities at Pekin for their shameless disregard of their solemn engagements. The manner in which the British ambassador discharged the onerous duties of his mission, met with the warm approval of Her Majesty's government and when he was once more in England he was offered by the prime minister the governor-generalship of India.

He accepted this great office with a full sense of the arduous responsibilities which it entailed upon him, and said good-bye to his friends with words which showed that he had a foreboding that he might never see them again—words which proved unhappily to be too true. He went to the discharge of his duties in India in that spirit of modesty which was always characteristic of him. "I succeeded," he said, "to a great man (Lord Canning) and a great war, with a humble task to be humbly discharged." His task was indeed humble compared with that which had to be performed by his eminent predecessors, notably by Earl Canning, who had established important reforms in the land tenure, won the confidence of the feudatories of the Crown, and reorganized the whole administration of India after the tremendous upheaval caused by the mutiny. Lord Elgin, on the other hand, was the first governor-general appointed directly by the Queen, and was now subject to the authority of the secretary of state for India. He could consequently exercise relatively little of the powers and responsibilities which made previous imperial representatives so potent in the conduct of Indian affairs. Indeed he had not been long in India before he was forced by the Indian secretary to reverse Lord Canning's wise measure for the sale of a fee-simple tenure with all its political as well as economic advantages. He was able, however, to carry out loyally the wise and equitable policy of his predecessor towards the feudatories of England with firmness and dignity and with good effect for the British government.[1]

[1] See article on Lord Elgin in "Encyclopædia Britannica" (9th ed.), Vol. VIII., p. 132.

In 1863 he decided on making a tour of the northern parts of India with the object of making himself personally acquainted with the people and affairs of the empire under his government. It was during this tour that he held a Durbar or Royal Court at Agra, which was remarkable even in India for the display of barbaric wealth and the assemblage of princes of royal descent. After reaching Simla his peaceful administration of Indian affairs was at last disturbed by the necessity—one quite clear to him—of repressing an outburst of certain Nahabee fanatics who dwelt in the upper valley of the Indus. He came to the conclusion that "the interests both of prudence and humanity would be best consulted by levelling a speedy and decisive blow at this embryo conspiracy." Having accordingly made the requisite arrangements for putting down promptly the trouble on the frontier and preventing the combination of the Mahommedan inhabitants in those regions against the government, he left Simla and traversed the upper valleys of the Beas, the Ravee, and the Chenali with the object of inspecting the tea plantations of that district and making inquiries as to the possibility of trade with Ladâk and China. Eventually, after a wearisome journey through a most picturesque region, he reached Dhurmsala—"the place of piety"—in the Kangra valley, where appeared the unmistakable symptoms of the fatal malady which soon caused his death.

LAST DAYS

The closing scenes in the life of the statesman have been described in pathetic terms by his brother-in-law, Dean Stanley.[1] The intelligence that the illness was mortal "was received with a calmness and fortitude which never deserted him" through all the scenes which followed. He displayed "in equal degrees, and with the most unvarying constancy, two of the grandest elements of human character—unselfish resignation of himself to the will of God, and thoughtful consideration down to the smallest particulars, for the interests and feelings of others, both public and private." When at his own request, Lady Elgin chose a spot for his grave in the little cemetery which stands on the bluff above the house where he died, "he gently expressed pleasure when told of the quiet and beautiful aspect of the place chosen, with the glorious view of the snowy range towering above, and the wide prospect of hill and plain below." During this fatal illness he had the consolation of the constant presence of his loving wife, whose courageous spirit enabled her to overcome the weakness of a delicate constitution. He died on November 20th, 1863, and was buried on the following day beneath the snow-clad Himalayas.[2]

[1] In the "North British Review," quoted by Walrond, pp. 458-461.

[2] Lord Elgin's eldest son (9th Earl) Victor Alexander Bruce, who was born in 1849, at Monklands, near Montreal, was Viceroy of India 1894-9. See Debrett's Peerage, arts. Elgin and Thurton for particulars of Lord Elgin's family.

If at any time a Canadian should venture to this quiet station in the Kangra valley, let his first thought be, not of the sublimity of the mountains which rise far away, but of the grave where rest the remains of a statesman whose pure unselfishness, whose fidelity to duty, whose tender and sympathetic nature, whose love of truth and justice, whose compassion for the weak, whose trust in God and the teachings of Christ, are human qualities more worthy of the admiration of us all than the grandest attributes of nature.

None of the distinguished Canadian statesmen who were members of Lord Elgin's several administrations from 1847 until 1854, or were then conspicuous in parliamentary life, now remain to tell us the story of those eventful years. Mr. Baldwin died five years before, and Sir Louis Hypolite LaFontaine three months after the decease of the governor-general of India, and in the roll of their Canadian contemporaries there are none who have left a fairer record. Mr. Hincks retired from the legislature of Canada in 1855, when he accepted the office of governor-in-chief of Barbadoes and the Windward Islands from Sir William Molesworth, colonial secretary in Lord Palmerston's government, and for years an eminent advocate of a liberal colonial policy. This appointment was well received throughout British North America by Mr. Hincks's friends as well as political opponents, who recognized the many merits of this able politician and administrator. It was considered, according to the London *Times*, as "the inauguration of a totally different system of policy from that which has been hitherto pursued with regard to our colonies." "It gave some evidence," continued the same paper, "that the more distinguished among our fellow-subjects in the colonies may feel that the path of imperial ambition is henceforth open to them." It was a direct answer to the appeal which had been so eloquently made on more than one occasion by the Honourable Joseph Howe[1] of Nova Scotia, to extend imperial honours and offices to distinguished colonists, and not reserve them, as was too often the case, for Englishmen of inferior merit. "This elevation of Mr. Hincks to a governorship," said the Montreal *Pilot* at the time, "is the most practicable comment which can possibly be offered upon the solemn and sorrowful complaints of Mr. Howe, anent the neglect with which the colonists are treated by the imperial government. So sudden, complete and noble a disclaimer on the part of Her Majesty's minister for the colonies must have startled the delegate from Nova Scotia, and we trust that his turn may not be far distant." Fifteen years later, Mr. Howe himself became a lieutenant-governor of Nova Scotia, and an inmate of the very

[1] See Mr. Howe's eloquent speeches on the organization of the empire, in his "Speeches and Public Letters," (Boston, 1859), vol. II., pp. 175-207.

government house to which he was not admitted in the stormy days when he was fighting the battle of responsible government against Lord Falkland.

Mr. Hincks was subsequently appointed governor of British Guiana, and at the same time received a Commandership of the Bath as a mark of "Her Majesty's approval honourably won by very valuable and continued service in several colonies of the empire." He retired from the imperial service with a pension in 1869, when his name was included in the first list of knights which was submitted to the Queen on the extension of the Order of St. Michael and St. George for the express purpose of giving adequate recognition to those persons in the colonies who had rendered distinguished service to the Crown and empire. During his Canadian administration Lord Elgin had impressed upon the colonial secretary that it was "very desirable that the prerogative of the Crown, as the fountain of honour, should be employed, in so far as this can properly be done, as a means of attaching the outlying parts of the empire to the throne." Two principles ought, he thought, "as a general rule to be attended to in the distribution of imperial honours among colonists." Firstly they should appear "to emanate directly from the Crown, on the advice, if you will, of the governors and imperial ministers, but not on the recommendation of the local executive." Secondly, they "should be conferred, as much as possible, on the eminent persons who are no longer engaged actively in political life." The first principle has, generally speaking, guided the action of the Crown in the distribution of honours to colonists, though the governors may receive suggestions from and also consult their prime ministers when the necessity arises. These honours, too, are no longer conferred only on men actively engaged in public life, but on others eminent in science, education, literature, and other vocations of life.[1]

In 1870 Sir Francis Hincks returned to Canadian public life as finance minister in Sir John Macdonald's government, and held the office until 1873, when he retired altogether from politics. Until the last hours of his life he continued to show that acuteness of intellect, that aptitude for public business, that knowledge of finance and commerce, which made him so influential in public affairs. During his public career in Canada previous to 1855, he was the subject of bitter attacks for his political acts, but nowadays impartial history can admit that, despite his tendency to commit the province to heavy expenditures, his energy, enterprise and financial ability did good service to the country at large. He was also attacked as having used his public position to promote his own pecuniary interests, but he courted and obtained inquiry into the most serious of such accusations, and

[1] See on this subject Todd's "Parliamentary Government in the British Colonies," pp. 313-329.

although there appears to have been some careless-
ness in his connection with various speculations,
and at times an absence of an adequate sense of his
responsibility as a public man, there is no evidence
that he was ever personally corrupt or dishonest.
He devoted the close of his life to the writing of his
"Reminiscences," and of several essays on questions
which were great public issues when he was so
prominent in Canadian politics, and although none
of his most ardent admirers can praise them as
literary efforts of a high order, yet they have an
interest so far as they give us some insight into
disputed points of Canada's political history. He
died in 1885 of the dreadful disease small-pox in
the city of Montreal, and the veteran statesman
was carried to the grave without those funeral
honours which were due to one who had filled with
distinction so many important positions in the
service of Canada and the Crown. All his contemporaries when he was prime minister also lie in
the grave and have found at last that rest which
was not theirs in the busy, passionate years of their
public life. Sir Allan MacNab, who was a spend-
thrift to the very last, lies in a quiet spot beneath
the shades of the oaks and elms which adorn the
lovely park of Dundurn in Hamilton, whose people
have long since forgotten his weaknesses as a man,
and now only recall his love for the beautiful city
with whose interests he was so long identified, and
his eminent services to Crown and state. George

Brown, Hincks's inveterate opponent, continued for years after the formation of the first Liberal-Conservative administration, to keep the old province of Canada in a state of political ferment by his attacks on French Canada and her institutions until at last he succeeded in making government practically unworkable, and then suddenly he rose superior to the spirit of passionate partisanship and racial bitterness which had so long dominated him, and decided to aid his former opponents in consummating that federal union which relieved old Canada of her political embarrassment and sectional strife. His action at that time is his chief claim to the monument which has been raised in his honour in the great western city where he was for so many years a political force, and where the newspaper he established still remains at the head of Canadian journalism.

The greatest and ablest man among all who were notable in Lord Elgin's days in Canada, Sir John Alexander Macdonald—the greatest not simply as a Canadian politician but as one of the builders of the British empire—lived to become one of Her Majesty's Privy Councillors of Great Britain, a Grand Cross of the Bath, and prime minister for twenty-one years of a Canadian confederation which stretches for 3,500 miles from the Atlantic to the Pacific ocean. When death at last forced him from the great position he had so long occupied with distinction to himself and advantage

225

to Canada, the esteem and affection in which he was held by the people, whom he had so long served during a continuous public career of half a century, were shown by the erection of stately monuments in five of the principal cities of the Dominion—an honour never before paid to a colonial statesman. The statues of Sir John Macdonald and Sir Georges Cartier—statues conceived and executed by the genius of a French Canadian artist—stand on either side of the noble parliament building where these statesmen were for years the most conspicuous figures; and as Canadians of the present generation survey their bronze effigies, let them not fail to recall those admirable qualities of statesmanship which distinguished them both— above all their assertion of those principles of compromise, conciliation and equal rights which have served to unite the two races in critical times when the tide of racial and sectional passion and political demagogism has rushed in a mad torrent against the walls of the national structure which Canadians have been so steadily and successfully building for so many years on the continent of North America.

CHAPTER XI

POLITICAL PROGRESS

IN the foregoing pages I have endeavoured to review—very imperfectly, I am afraid—all those important events in the political history of Canada from 1847 to 1854, which have had the most potent influence on its material, social, and political development. Any one who carefully studies the conditions of the country during that critical period of Canadian affairs cannot fail to come to the conclusion that the gradual elevation of Canada from the depression which was so prevalent for years in political as well as commercial matters, to a position of political strength and industrial prosperity, was largely owing to the success of the principles of self-government which Lord Elgin initiated and carried out while at the head of the Canadian executive. These principles have been clearly set forth in his speeches and in his despatches to the secretary of state for the colonies as well as in instructive volumes on the colonial policy of Lord John Russell's administration by Lord Grey, the imperial minister who so wisely recommended Lord Elgin's appointment as governor-general. Briefly stated these principles are as follows :—

That it is neither desirable nor possible to carry on the government of a province in opposition to the opinion of its people.

That a governor-general can have no ministers who do not enjoy the full confidence of the popular House, or, in the last resort, of the people.

That the governor-general should not refuse his consent to any measure proposed by the ministry unless it is clear that it is of such an extreme party character that the assembly or people could not approve of it.

That the governor-general should not identify himself with any party but make himself "a mediator and moderator between all parties."

That colonial communities should be encouraged to cultivate "a national and manly tone of political morals," and should look to their own parliaments for the solution of all problems of provincial government instead of making constant appeals to the colonial office or to opinion in the mother country, "always ill-informed, and therefore credulous, in matters of colonial politics."

That the governor-general should endeavour to impart to these rising communities the full advantages of British laws, British institutions, and British freedom, and maintain in this way the connection between them and the parent state.

We have seen in previous chapters how industriously, patiently, and discreetly Lord Elgin laboured to carry out these principles in the adminis-

228

tration of his government. In 1849 he risked his
own life that he might give full scope to the
principles of responsible government with respect
to the adjustment of a question which should be
settled by the Canadian people themselves without
the interference of the parent state, and on the
same ground he impressed on the imperial government the necessity of giving to the Canadian
legislature full control of the settlement of the
clergy reserves. He had no patience with those
who believed that, in allowing the colonists to
exercise their right to self-government in matters
exclusively affecting themselves, there was any
risk whatever so far as imperial interests were
concerned. One of his ablest letters was that which
he wrote to Earl Grey as an answer to the unwise
utterances of the prime minister, Lord John Russell, in the course of a speech on the colonies in
which, "amid the plaudits of a full senate, he
declared that he looked forward to the day when
the ties which he was endeavouring to render so
easy and mutually advantageous would be severed."
Lord Elgin held it to be "a perfectly unsound and
most dangerous theory, that British colonies could
not attain maturity without separation," and in this
connection he quoted the language of Mr. Baldwin
to whom he had read that part of Lord John Russell's speech to which he took such strong exception.
"For myself," said the eminent Canadian, "if the
anticipations therein expressed prove to be well

founded, my interest in public affairs is gone forever. But is it not hard upon us while we are labouring, through good and evil report, to thwart the designs of those who would dismember the empire, that our adversaries should be informed that the difference between them and the prime minister of England is only one of time? If the British government has really come to the conclusion that we are a burden to be cast off, whenever a favourable opportunity offers, surely we ought to be warned." In Lord Elgin's opinion, based on a thorough study of colonial conditions, if the Canadian or any other system of government was to be successful, British statesmen must "renounce the habit of telling the colonies that the colonial is a provisional existence." They should be taught to believe that "without severing the bonds which unite them to England, they may attain the degree of perfection, and of social and political development to which organized communities of free men have a right to aspire." The true policy in his judgment was "to throw the whole weight of responsibility on those who exercise the real power, for after all, the sense of responsibility is the best security against the abuse of power; and as respects the connection, to act and speak on this hypothesis—that there is nothing in it to check the development of healthy national life in these young communities." He was "possessed," he used the word advisedly, "with the idea that it was possible to maintain on the soil of North

America, and in the face of Republican America, British connection and British institutions, if you give the latter freely and trustingly." The history of Canada from the day those words were penned down to the beginning of the twentieth century proves their political wisdom. Under the inspiring influence of responsible government Canada has developed in 1902, not into an independent nation, as predicted by Lord John Russell and other British statesmen after him, but into a confederation of five millions and a half of people, in which a French Canadian prime minister gives expression to the dominant idea not only of his own race but of all nationalities within the Dominion, that the true interest lies not in the severance but in the continuance of the ties that have so long bound them to the imperial state.

Lord Elgin in his valuable letters to the imperial authorities, always impressed on them the fact that the office of a Canadian governor-general has not by any means been lowered to that of a mere subscriber of orders-in-council—of a mere official automaton, speaking and acting by the orders of the prime minister and the cabinet. On the contrary, he gave it as his experience that in Jamaica, where there was no responsible government, he had "not half the power" he had in Canada "with a constitutional and changing cabinet." With respect to the maintenance of the position and due influence of the governor, he used language which gives a true solution of the problem involved in the adaptation of parliamentary government to the colonial system. "As the imperial government and parliament gradually withdraw from legislative interference, and from the exercise of patronage in colonial affairs, the office of governor tends to become, in the most emphatic sense of the term, the link which connects the mother country and the colony, and his influence the means by which harmony of action between the local and imperial authorities is to be preserved. It is not, however, in my humble judgment, by evincing an anxious desire to stretch to the utmost constitutional principles in his favour, but, on the contrary, by the frank acceptance of the conditions of the parliamentary system, that this influence can be most surely extended and confirmed. Placed by his position above the strife of parties—holding office by a tenure less precarious than the ministers who surround him—having no political interests to serve but those of the community whose affairs he is appointed to administer—his opinion cannot fail, when all cause for suspicion and jealousy is removed, to have great weight in colonial councils, while he is set at liberty to constitute himself in an especial manner the patron of those larger and higher interests—such interests, for example, as those of education, and of moral and material progress in all its branches—which, unlike the contests of party, unite instead of dividing the members of the body politic."

232

As we study the political history of Canada for the fifty years which have elapsed since Lord Elgin enunciated in his admirable letters to the imperial government the principles which guided him in his Canadian administration, we cannot fail to see clearly that responsible government has brought about the following results, which are at once a guarantee of efficient home government and of a harmonious coöperation between the dependency and the central authority of the empire.

The misunderstandings that so constantly occurred between the legislative bodies and the imperial authorities, on account of the latter failing so often to appreciate fully the nature of the political grievances that agitated the public mind, and on account of their constant interference in matters which should have been left exclusively to the control of the people directly interested, have been entirely removed in conformity with the wise policy of making Canada a self-governing country in the full sense of the phrase. These provinces are as a consequence no longer a source of irritation and danger to the parent state, but, possessing full independence in all matters of local concern, are now among the chief sources of England's pride and greatness.

The governor-general instead of being constantly brought into conflict with the political parties of the country, and made immediately responsible for the continuance of public grievances, has gained in dignity and influence since he has been removed

from the arena of public controversy. He now
occupies a position in harmony with the principles
that have given additional strength and prestige to
the throne itself. As the legally accredited representative of the sovereign, as the recognized head
of society, he represents what Bagehot has aptly
styled "the dignified part of our constitution,"
which has much value in a country like ours where
we fortunately retain the permanent form of monarchy in harmony with the democratic machinery
of our government. If the governor-general is a
man of parliamentary experience and constitutional
knowledge, possessing tact and judgment, and
imbued with the true spirit of his high vocation—
and these high functionaries have been notably so
since the commencement of confederation—he can
sensibly influence, in the way Lord Elgin points
out, the course of administration and benefit the
country at critical periods of its history. Standing
above all party, having the unity of the empire at
heart, a governor-general can at times soothe the
public mind, and give additional confidence to the
country, when it is threatened with some national
calamity, or there is distrust abroad as to the
future. As an imperial officer he has large responsibilities of which the general public has naturally
no very clear idea, and if it were possible to obtain
access to the confidential and secret despatches
which seldom see the light in the colonial office—
certainly not in the lifetime of the men who wrote

them—it would be found how much, for a quarter of a century past, the colonial department has gained by having had in the Dominion, men, no longer acting under the influence of personal feeling through being made personally responsible for the conduct of public affairs, but actuated simply by a desire to benefit the country over which they preside, and to bring Canadian interests into union with those of the empire itself.

The effects on the character of public men and on the body politic have been for the public advantage. It has brought out the best qualities of colonial statesmanship, lessened the influence of mere agitators and demagogues, and taught our public men to rely on themselves in all crises affecting the welfare and integrity of the country. Responsible government means self-reliance, the capacity to govern ourselves, the ability to build up a great nation.

When we review the trials and struggles of the past that we may gain from them lessons of confidence for the future, let us not forget to pay a tribute to the men who have laid the foundations of these communities, still on the threshold of their development, and on whom the great burden fell; to the French Canadians who, despite the neglect and indifference of their kings, amid toil and privation, amid war and famine, built up a province which they have made their own by their patience and industry, and who should, differ as we may

from them, evoke our respect for their fidelity to
the institutions of their origin, for their appreciation
of the advantages of English self-government, and
for their coöperation in all great measures essential
to the unity of the federation; to the Loyalists of
last century who left their homes for the sake of
"king and country," and laid the foundations of
prosperous and loyal English communities by the
sea and by the great lakes, and whose descendants
have ever stood true to the principles of the institutions which have made Britain free and great; to
the unknown body of pioneers some of whose
names perhaps still linger on a headland or river or
on a neglected gravestone, who let in the sunlight
year by year to the dense forests of these countries,
and built up by their industry the large and thriv-
ing provinces of this Dominion; above all, to the
statesmen—Elgin, Baldwin, LaFontaine, Morin,
Howe, and many others—who laid deep and firm,
beneath the political structure of this confederation,
those principles of self-government which give
harmony to our constitutional system and bring
out the best qualities of an intelligent people. In
the early times in which they struggled they had
to bear much obloquy, and their errors of judgment
have been often severely arraigned at the bar of
public opinion; many of them lived long enough to
see how soon men may pass into oblivion; but we
who enjoy the benefit of their earnest endeavours,
now that the voice of the party passion of their

times is hushed, should never forget that, though they are not here to reap the fruit of their labours, their work survives in the energetic and hopeful communities which stretch from Cape Breton to Victoria.

CHAPTER XII

A COMPARISON OF SYSTEMS

IN one of Lord Elgin's letters we are told that, when he had as visitors to government house in 1850, Sir Henry Bulwer, the elder brother of Lord Lytton, and British minister to the United States, as well as Sir Edmund Head, his successor in the governorship of Canada, he availed himself of so favourable an opportunity of reassuring them on many points of the internal policy of the province on which they were previously doubtful, and gave them some insight into the position of men and things on which Englishmen in those days were too ignorant as a rule. One important point which he impressed upon them—as he hoped successfully—was this: "That the faithful carrying out of the principles of constitutional government is a departure from the American model, not an approximation to it, and, therefore, a departure from republicanism in its only workable shape." The fact was: "The American system is our old colonial system, with, in certain cases, the principle of popular election substituted for that of nomination by the Crown." He was convinced "that the concession of constitutional government has a tendency to draw the colonists" towards England and not towards republicanism; "firstly, because it slakes that thirst for self-government which seizes on all British communities when they approach maturity; and secondly because it habituates the colonists to the working of a political mechanism which is both intrinsically superior to that of the Americans, and more unlike it than our old colonial system." In short, he felt very strongly that " when a people have been once thoroughly accustomed to the working of such a parliamentary system as ours they never will consent to resort to this irresponsible mechanism."

Since these significant words were written half a century ago, Canadians have been steadily working out the principles of parliamentary government as understood and explained by Lord Elgin, and have had abundant opportunities of contrasting their experiences with those of their neighbours under a system in many respects the very reverse of that which has enabled Canada to attain so large a measure of political freedom and build up such prosperous communities to the north of the republic, while still remaining in the closest possible touch with the imperial state. I propose now to close this book with some comparisons between the respective systems of the two countries, and to show that in this respect as in others Lord Elgin proved how deep was his insight into the working of political institutions, and how thoroughly he had mastered the problem of the best methods of administering

240

the government of a great colonial dependency, not solely with a regard to its own domestic interests but with a view of maintaining the connection with the British Crown, of which he was so discreet and able a servant.

It is especially important to Canadians to study the development of the institutions of the United States, with the view of deriving benefit from their useful experiences, and avoiding the defects that have grown up under their system. All institutions are more or less on trial in a country like Canada, which is working out great problems of political science under decided advantages, since the ground is relatively new, and the people have before them all the experiences of the world, especially of England and the United States, in whose systems Canadians have naturally the deepest interest. The history of responsible government affords another illustration of a truth which stands out clear in the history of nations, that those constitutions which are of a flexible character, the natural growth of the experiences of centuries, and which have been created by the necessities and conditions of the times, possess the elements of real stability, and best ensure the prosperity of a people. The great source of the strength of the institutions of the United States lies in the fact that they have worked out their government in accordance with certain principles, which are essentially English in their origin, and have been naturally developed

241

since their foundation as colonial settlements, and whatever weaknesses their system shows have chiefly arisen from new methods, and from the rigidity of their constitutional rules of law, which separate too sharply the executive and the legislative branches of government. Like their neighbours the Canadian people have based their system on English principles, but they have at the same time been able to keep pace with the progress of the unwritten constitution of England, to adapt it to their own political conditions, and to bring the executive and legislative authorities to assist and harmonize with one another.

Each country has its "cabinet council," but the one is essentially different from the other in its character and functions. This term, the historical student will remember, was first used in the days of the Stuarts as one of derision and obloquy. It was frequently called "junto" or "cabal," and during the days of conflict between the commons and the king it was regarded with great disfavour by the parliament of England. Its unpopularity arose from the fact that it did not consist of men in whom parliament had confidence, and its proceedings were conducted with so much secrecy that it was impossible to decide upon whom to fix responsibility for any obnoxious measure. When the constitution of England was brought back to its original principles, and harmony was restored between the Crown and the parliament, the cabinet became no longer a term of reproach, but a position therein was regarded as the highest honour in the country, and was associated with the efficient administration of public affairs, since it meant a body of men responsible to parliament for every act of government.[1] The old executive councils of Canada were obnoxious to the people for the same reason that the councils of the Stuarts, and even of George III, with the exception of the régime of the two Pitts, became unpopular. Not only do we in Canada, in accordance with our desire to perpetuate the names of English institutions use the name "cabinet" which was applied to an institution that gradually grew out of the old privy council of England, but we have even incorporated in our fundamental law the older name of "privy council," which itself sprang from the original "permanent" or "continual" council of the Norman kings. Following English precedent, the Canadian cabinet or ministry is formed out of the privy councillors, chosen under the law by the governor-general, and when they retire from office they still retain the purely honorary distinction. In the United States the use of the term "cabinet" has none of the significance it has with us, and if it can be compared at all to any English institutions it might be to the old cabinets who acknowledged responsibility to the king, and were only so many heads of departments in the

[1] See Todd's "Parliamentary Government in England," vol. II., p. 101.

king's government. As a matter of fact the comparison would be closer if we said that the administration resembles the cabinets of the old French kings, or to quote Professor Bryce, "the group of ministers who surround the Czar or the Sultan, or who executed the bidding of a Roman emperor like Constantine or Justinian." Such ministers like the old executive councils of Canada, "are severally responsible to their master, and are severally called in to counsel him, but they have not necessarily any relations with one another, nor any duty or collective action." Not only is the administration conducted on the principle of responsibility to the president alone, in this respect the English king in old irresponsible days, but the legislative department is itself constructed after the English model as it existed a century ago, and a general system of government is established, lacking in that unity and elasticity which are essential to its effective working. On the other hand the Canadian cabinet is the cabinet of the English system of modern times and is formed so as to work in harmony with the legislative department, which is a copy, so far as possible, of the English legislature.

The special advantages of the Canadian or English system of parliamentary government, compared with congressional government, may be briefly summed up as follows :—

(1) The governor-general, his cabinet, and the popular branch of the legislature are governed in

244

Canada, as in England, by a system of rules, conventions and understandings which enable them to work in harmony with one another. The Crown, the cabinet, the legislature, and the people, have respectively certain rights and powers which, when properly and constitutionally brought into operation, give strength and elasticity to our system of government. Dismissal of a ministry by the Crown under conditions of gravity, or resignation of a ministry defeated in the popular House, bring into play the prerogatives of the Crown. In all cases there must be a ministry to advise the Crown, assume responsibility for its acts, and obtain the support of the people and their representatives in parliament. As a last resort to bring into harmony the people, the legislature, and the Crown, there is the exercise of the supreme prerogative of dissolution. A governor, acting always under the advice of responsible ministers, may, at any time, generally speaking, grant an appeal to the people to test their opinion on vital public questions and bring the legislature into accord with the public mind. In short, the fundamental principle of popular sovereignty lies at the very basis of the Canadian system.

On the other hand, in the United States, the president and his cabinet may be in constant conflict with the two Houses of Congress during the four years of his term of office. His cabinet has no direct influence with the legislative bodies, inasmuch as they have no seats therein. The political complexion of congress does not affect their tenure of office, since they depend only on the favour and approval of the executive; dissolution, which is the safety valve of the English or Canadian system—"in its essence an appeal from the legal to the political sovereign"—is not practicable under the United States constitution. In a political crisis the constitution provides no adequate solution of the difficulty during the presidential term. In this respect the people of the United States are not sovereign as they are in Canada under the conditions just briefly stated.

(2) The governor-general is not personally brought into collision with the legislature by the direct exercise of a veto of its legislative acts, since the ministry is responsible for all legislation and must stand or fall by its important measures. The passage of a measure of which it disapproved as a ministry would mean in the majority of cases a resignation, and it is not possible to suppose that the governor would be asked to exercise a prerogative of the Crown which has been in disuse since the establishment of responsible government and would now be a revolutionary measure even in Canada.

In the United States there is danger of frequent collision between the president and the two legislative branches, should a very critical exercise of the veto, as in President Johnson's time, occur at a time when the public mind was deeply agitated. The chief magistrate loses in dignity and influence whenever the legislature overrides the veto, and congress becomes a despotic master for the time being.

(3) The Canadian minister, having control of the finances and taxes and of all matters of administration, is directly responsible to parliament and sooner or later to the people for the manner in which public functions have been discharged. All important measures are initiated by the cabinet, and on every question of public interest the ministers are bound to have a definite policy if they wish to retain the confidence of the legislature. Even in the case of private legislation they are also the guardians of the public interests and are responsible to the parliament and the people for any neglect in particular.

On the other hand in the United States the financial and general legislation of congress is left to the control of committees, over which the president and his cabinet have no direct influence, and the chairman of which may have ambitious objects in direct antagonism to the men in office.

(4) In the Canadian system the speaker is a functionary who certainly has his party proclivities, but it is felt that as long as he occupies the chair all political parties can depend on his justice and impartiality. Responsible government makes the premier and his ministers responsible for the constitution of the committees and for the opinions

and decisions that may emanate from them. A government that would constantly endeavour to shift its responsibilities on committees, even of its own selection, would soon disappear from the treasury benches. Responsibility in legislation is accordingly ensured, financial measures prevented from being made the footballs of ambitious and irresponsible politicians, and the impartiality and dignity of the speakership guaranteed by the presence in parliament of a cabinet having the direction and supervision of business.

On the other hand, in the United States, the speaker of the House of Representatives becomes, from the very force of circumstances, a political leader, and the spectacle is presented—in fact from the time of Henry Clay—so strange to us familiar with English methods, of decisions given by him with clearly party objects, and of committees formed by him with purely political aims, as likely as not with a view to thwart the ambition either of a president who is looking to a second term or of some prominent member of the cabinet who has presidential aspirations. And all this lowering of the dignity of the chair is due to the absence of a responsible minister to lead the House. The very position which the speaker is forced to take from time to time—notably in the case of Mr. Reed[1]—is clearly the result of the defects in the constitutional

[1] He was speaker of the House of Representatives from 1895 to 1899.

system of the United States, and is so much evidence that a responsible party leader is an absolute necessity in congress. A legislature must be led, and congress has been attempting to get out of a crucial difficulty by all sorts of questionable shifts which only show the inherent weakness of the existing system.

In the absence of any provision for the unity of policy between the executive and legislative authorities of the United States, it is impossible for any nation to have a positive guarantee that a treaty it may negotiate with the former can be ratified. The sovereign of Great Britain enters into treaties with foreign powers with the advice and assistance of his constitutional advisers, who are immediately responsible to parliament for their counsel in such matters. In theory it is the prerogative of the Crown to make a treaty; in practice it is that of the ministry. It is not constitutionally imperative to refer such treaties to parliament for its approval—the consent of the Crown is sufficient; but it is sometimes done under exceptional circumstances, as in the case of the cession of Heligoland. In any event the action of the ministry in the matter is invariably open to the review of parliament, and the ministry may be censured by an adverse vote for the advice given to the sovereign, and forced to retire from office. In the United States the senate must ratify all treaties by a two-thirds vote, but unless there is a majority in that House of the same political complexion as the president the treaty may be refused. No cabinet minister is present to lead the House, as in England, and assume all the responsibility of the president's action. It is almost impossible to suppose that an English ministry would consent to a treaty that would be unpopular in parliament and the country. The existence of the government would depend on its action. In the United States both president and senate have divided responsibilities. The constitution makes no provision for unity in such important matters of national obligation.

The great advantages of the English, or Canadian, system lie in the interest created among all classes of the people by the discussions of the different legislative bodies. Parliamentary debate involves the fate of cabinets, and the public mind is consequently led to study all issues of importance. The people know and feel that they must be called upon sooner or later to decide between the parties contending on the floor of the legislature, and consequently are obliged to give an intelligent consideration to public affairs. Let us see what Bagehot, ablest of critics, says on this point:—

"At present there is business in their attention (that is to say, of the English or Canadian people). They assist at the determining crisis; they assist or help it. Whether the government will go out or remain is determined by the debate and by the division in parliament. And the opinion out of doors, the secret pervading disposition of society, has a great influence on that division. The nation feels that its judgment is important, and it strives to judge. It succeeds in deciding because the debates and the discussions give it the facts and arguments. But under the presidential government the nation has, except at the electing moment, no influence; it has not the ballot-box before it; its virtue is gone and it must wait till its instant of despotism again returns. There are doubtless debates in the legislature, but they are prologues without a play. The prize of power is not in the gift of the legislature. No presidential country needs to form daily delicate opinions, or is helped in forming them."

Then when the people do go to the ballot-box, they cannot intelligently influence the policy of the government. If they vote for a president, then congress may have a policy quite different from his; if they vote for members of congress, they cannot change the opinions of the president. If the president changes his cabinet at any time, they have nothing to say about it, for its members are not important as wheels in the legislative machinery. Congress may pass a bill of which the people express their disapproval at the first opportunity when they choose a new congress, but still it may remain on the statute-book because the senate holds views different from the newly elected House, and cannot be politically changed until after a long series of legislative elections. As Professor Woodrow Wilson well puts it in an able essay:—[1]

"Public opinion has no easy vehicle for its judgments, no quick channels for its action. Nothing about the system is direct and simple. Authority is perplexingly subdivided and distributed, and responsibility has to be hunted down in out-of-the-way corners. So that the sum of the whole matter is that the means of working for the fruits of good government are not readily to be found. The average citizen may be excused for esteeming government at best but a haphazard affair upon which his vote and all his influence can have but little effect. How is his choice of representative in congress to affect the policy of the country as regards the questions in which he is most interested if the man for whom he votes has no chance of getting on the standing committee which has virtual charge of those questions? How is it to make any difference who is chosen president? Has the president any great authority in matters of vital policy? It seems a thing of despair to get any assurance that any vote he may cast will even in an infinitesimal degree affect the essential courses of administration. There are so many cooks mixing their ingredients in the national broth that it seems hopeless, this thing of changing one cook at a time."

Under such a system it cannot be expected that the people will take the same deep interest in elec-

[1] "Congressional Government," pp. 301, 332.

tions and feel as directly responsible for the character of the government as when they can at one election and by one verdict decide the fate of a government, whose policy on great issues must be thoroughly explained to them at the polls. This method of popular government is more real and substantial than a system which does not allow the people to influence congressional legislation and administrative action through a set of men sitting in congress and having a common policy.

I think it does not require any very elaborate argument to show that when men feel and know that the ability they show in parliament may be sooner or later rewarded by a seat on the treasury benches, and that they will then have a determining voice in the government of the country, be it dominion or province, they must be stimulated by a keener interest in public life, a closer watchfulness over legislation and administration, a greater readiness for discussing all public questions, and a more studied appreciation of public opinion outside the legislative halls. Every man in parliament is a premier *in posse*. While asking my readers to recall what I have already said as to the effect of responsible government on the public men and people of Canada, I shall also here refer them to some authorities worthy of all respect.

Mr. Bagehot says with his usual clearness :—[1]

"To belong to a debating society adhering to an

[1] "The English Constitution," pp. 95, 96.

executive (and this is no inapt description of a congress under a presidential constitution) is not an object to stir a noble ambition, and is a position to encourage idleness. The members of a parliament excluded from office can never be comparable, much less equal, to those of a parliament not excluded from office. The presidential government by its nature divides political life into two halves, an executive half and a legislative half, and by so dividing it, makes neither half worth a man's having—worth his making it a continuous career— worthy to absorb, as cabinet government absorbs, his whole soul. The statesmen from whom a nation chooses under a presidential system are much inferior to those from whom it chooses under a cabinet system, while the selecting apparatus is also far less discerning."

An American writer, Prof. Denslow,[1] does not hesitate to express the opinion very emphatically that "as it is, in no country do the people feel such an overwhelming sense of the littleness of the men in charge of public affairs" as in the United States. And in another place he dwells on the fact that "responsible government educates office-holders into a high and honourable sense of their accountability to the people," and makes "statesmanship a permanent pursuit followed by a skilled class of men."

Prof. Woodrow Wilson says that,[2] so far from men

[1] In the *International Review*, March, 1877.

[2] "Congressional Government," p. 94.

being trained to legislation by congressional government, "independence and ability are repressed under the tyranny of the rules, and practically the favour of the popular branch of congress is concentrated in the speaker and a few—very few—expert parliamentarians." Elsewhere he shows that "responsibility is spread thin, and no vote or debate can gather it." As a matter of fact and experience, he comes to the conclusion "the more power is divided the more irresponsible it becomes and the petty character of the leadership of each committee contributes towards making its despotism sure by making its duties interesting."

Professor James Bryce, it will be admitted, is one of the fairest of critics in his review of the institutions of the United States; but he, too, comes to the conclusion[1] that the system of congressional government destroys the unity of the House (of representatives) as a legislative body; prevents the capacity of the best members from being brought to bear upon any one piece of legislation, however important; cramps debate; lessens the cohesion and harmony of legislation; gives facilities for the exercise of underhand and even corrupt influence; reduces responsibility; lowers the interest of the nation in the proceedings of congress.

In another place,[2] after considering the relations between the executive and the legislature, he ex-

[1] "The American Commonwealth," I., 210 *et seq.*

[2] *Ibid.*, pp. 304, 305.

presses his opinion that the framers of the constitution have "so narrowed the sphere of the executive as to prevent it from leading the country, or even its own party in the country." They endeavoured "to make members of congress independent, but in doing so they deprived them of some of the means which European legislators enjoy of learning how to administer, of learning even how to legislate in administrative topics. They condemned them to be architects without science, critics without experience, censors without responsibility."

And further on, when discussing the faults of democratic government in the United States—and Professor Bryce, we must remember, is on the whole most hopeful of its future—he detects as amongst its characteristics "a certain commonness of mind and tone, a want of dignity and elevation in and about the conduct of public affairs, and insensibility to the nobler aspects and finer responsibilities of national life." Then he goes on to say[1] that representative and parliamentary system "provides the means of mitigating the evils to be feared from ignorance or haste, for it vests the actual conduct of affairs in a body of specially chosen and presumably qualified men, who may themselves intrust such of their functions as need peculiar knowledge or skill to a smaller governing body or bodies selected in respect of their more

[1] *Ibid.*, Chap. 95, vol. III.

eminent fitness. By this method the defects of democracy are remedied while its strength is retained." The members of American legislatures, being disjoined from the administrative offices, "are not chosen for their ability or experience; they are not much respected or trusted, and finding nothing exceptional expected from them, they behave as ordinary men."

"If corruption," wrote Judge Story, that astute political student, "ever silently eats its way into the vitals of this Republic, it will be because the people are unable to bring responsibility home to the executive through his chosen ministers."[1]

As I have already stated in the first pages of this chapter, long before the inherent weaknesses of the American system were pointed out by the eminent authorities just quoted, Lord Elgin was able, with that intuitive sagacity which he applied to the study of political institutions, to see the unsatisfactory working of the clumsy, irresponsible mechanism of our republican neighbours.

"Mr. Fillmore," he is writing in November, 1850, "stands to his congress very much in the same relation in which I stood to my assembly in Jamaica. There is the same absence of effective responsibility in the conduct of legislation, the same want of concurrent action between the parts of the political machine. The whole business of legislation in the American congress, as well as in the state legisla-

[1] "Commentaries," sec. 869.

tures, is conducted in the manner in which railway business was conducted in the House of Commons at a time when it is to be feared that, notwithstanding the high standard of honour in the British parliament, there was a good deal of jobbing. For instance, our reciprocity measure was pressed by us at Washington last session just as a railway bill in 1845 or 1846 would have been pressed in parliament. There was no government to deal with. The interests of the union as a whole, distinct from local and sectional interests, had no organ in the representative bodies; it was all a question of canvassing this member of congress or the other. It is easy to perceive that, under such a system, jobbing must become not the exception but the rule,"—remarks as true in 1901 as in 1850.

It is important also to dwell on the fact that in Canada the permanency of the tenure of public officials and the introduction of the secret ballot have been among the results of responsible government. Through the influence and agency of the same system, valuable reforms have been made in Canada in the election laws, and the trial of controverted elections has been taken away from partisan election committees and given to a judiciary independent of political influences. In these matters the irresponsible system of the United States has not been able to effect any needful reforms. Such measures can be best carried by ministers having the initiation and direction of legislation and must necessarily be retarded when power is divided among several authorities having no unity of policy on any question.

Party government undoubtedly has its dangers arising from personal ambition and unscrupulous partisanship, but as long as men must range themselves in opposing camps on every subject, there is no other system practicable by which great questions can be carried and the working of representative government efficiently conducted. The framers of the constitution of the United States no doubt thought they had succeeded in placing the president and his officers above party when they instituted the method of electing the former by a body of select electors chosen for that purpose in each state, who were expected to act irrespective of all political considerations. A president so selected would probably choose his officers also on the same basis. The practical results, however, have been to prove that in every country of popular and representative institutions party government must prevail. Party elects men to the presidency and to the floor of the Senate and House of Representatives, and the election to those important positions is directed and controlled by a political machinery far exceeding in its completeness any party organization in England or in Canada. The party convention is now the all important portion of the machinery for the election of the president, and the safeguard provided by the constitution for the choice of the best man is a mere nullity. One thing is quite certain, that party government under the direction of a responsible ministry, responsible to parliament and the people for every act of administration and legislation, can have far less dangerous tendencies than a party system which elects an executive not amenable to public opinion for four years, divides the responsibilities of government among several authorities, prevents harmony among party leaders, does not give the executive that control over legislation necessary to efficient administration of public affairs, and in short offers a direct premium to conflict among all the authorities of the state—a conflict, not so much avoided by the checks and balances of the constitution as by the patience, common sense, prudence, and respect for law which presidents and their cabinets have as a rule shown at national crises. But we can clearly see that, while the executive has lost in influence, congress has gained steadily to an extent never contemplated by the founders of the constitution, and there are thoughtful men who say that the true interests of the country have not always been promoted by the change. Party government in Canada ensures unity of policy, since the premier of the cabinet becomes the controlling part of the political machinery of the state; no such thing as unity of policy is possible under a system which gives the president neither the dignity of a governor-general, nor the strength of a premier, and splits up political power among any number of would-be party leaders, who adopt or defeat measures by private intrigues, make irresponsible recommendations, and form political combinations for purely selfish ends.[1]

It seems quite clear then that the system of responsible ministers makes the people more immediately responsible for the efficient administration of public affairs than is possible in the United States. The fact of having the president and the members of congress elected for different terms, and of dividing the responsibilities of government among these authorities does not allow the people to exercise that direct influence which is ensured, as the experience of Canada and of England proves, by making one body of men immediately responsible to the electors for the conduct of public affairs at frequently recurring periods, arranged by well understood rules, so as to ensure a correct expression of public opinion on all important issues. The committees which assist in governing this country are the choice of the people's representatives assembled in parliament, and every four or five years and sometimes even sooner in case of a crisis, the people have to decide on the wisdom of the choice.

The system has assuredly its drawbacks like all systems of government that have been devised and worked out by the brain of man. In all frankness I confess that this review would be incomplete were

[1] See Story's "Commentaries," sec. 869.

I not to refer to certain features of the Canadian system of government which seem to me on the surface fraught with inherent danger at some time or other to independent legislative judgment. Any one who has closely watched the evolution of this system for years past must admit that there is a dangerous tendency in the Dominion to give the executive—I mean the ministry as a body—too superior a control over the legislative authority. When a ministry has in its gift the appointment not only of the heads of the executive government in the provinces, that is to say, of the lieutenant-governors, who can be dismissed by the same power at any moment, but also of the members of the Upper House of Parliament itself, besides the judiciary and numerous collectorships and other valuable offices, it is quite obvious that the element of human ambition and selfishness has abundant room for operation on the floor of the legislature, and a bold and skilful cabinet is also able to wield a machinery very potent under a system of party government. In this respect the House of Representatives may be less liable to insidious influences than a House of Commons at critical junctures when individual conscience or independent judgment appears on the point of asserting itself. The House of Commons may be made by skilful party management a mere recording or registering body of an able and determined cabinet. I see less liability to such silent though potent influences in a system which makes the president and a House of Representatives to a large degree independent of each other, and leaves his important nominations to office under the control of the senate, a body which has no analogy whatever with the relatively weak branch of the Canadian parliament, essentially weak while its membership depends on the government itself. I admit at once that in the financial dependence of the provinces on the central federal authority, in the tenure of the office of the chief magistrates of the provinces, in the control exercised by the ministry over the highest legislative body of Canada, that is, highest in point of dignity and precedence, there are elements of weakness; but at the same time it must be remembered that, while the influence and power of the Canadian government may be largely increased by the exercise of its great patronage in the hypothetical cases I have suggested, its action is always open to the approval or disapproval of parliament and it has to meet an opposition face to face. Its acts are open to legislative criticism, and it may at any moment be forced to retire by public opinion operating upon the House of Commons.

On the other hand the executive in the United States for four years may be dominant over congress by skilful management. A strong executive by means of party wields a power which may be used for purposes of mere personal ambition, and may by clever management of the party machine

263

and with the aid of an unscrupulous majority retain power for a time even when it is not in accord with the true sentiment of the country; but under a system like that of Canada, where every defect in the body politic is probed to the bottom in the debates of parliament, which are given by the public press more fully than is the practice in the neighbouring republic, the people have a better opportunity of forming a correct judgment on every matter and giving an immediate verdict when the proper time comes for an appeal to them, the sovereign power. Sometimes this judgment is too often influenced by party prejudices and the real issue is too often obscured by skilful party management, but this is inevitable under every system of popular government; and happily, should it come to the worst, there is always in the country that saving remnant of intelligent, independent men of whom Matthew Arnold has written, who can come forward and by their fearless and bold criticism help the people in any crisis when truth, honour and justice are at stake and the great mass of electors fail to appreciate the true situation of affairs. But we may have confidence in the good sense and judgment of the people as a whole when time is given them to consider the situation of affairs. Should men in power be unfaithful to their public obligations, they will eventually be forced by the conditions of public life to yield their positions to those who merit public confidence. If it should ever happen in Canada that public opinion has become so low that public men feel that they can, whenever they choose, divert it to their own selfish ends by the unscrupulous use of partisan agencies and corrupt methods, and that the highest motives of public life are forgotten in a mere scramble for office and power, then thoughtful Canadians might well despair of the future of their country; but, whatever may be the blots at times on the surface of the body politic, there is yet no reason to believe that the public conscience of Canada is weak or indifferent to character and integrity in active politics. The instincts of an English people are always in the direction of the pure administration of justice and the efficient and honest government of the country, and though it may sometimes happen that unscrupulous politicians and demagogues will for a while dominate in the party arena, the time of retribution and purification must come sooner or later. English methods must prevail in countries governed by an English people and English institutions.

It is sometimes said that it is vain to expect a high ideal in public life, that the same principles that apply to social and private life cannot always be applied to the political arena if party government is to succeed; but this is the doctrine of the mere party manager, who is already too influential in Canada as in the United States, and not of a true patriotic statesman. It is wiser to believe that the

265

nobler the object the greater the inspiration, and at all events, it is better to aim high than to sink low. It is all important that the body politic should be kept pure and that public life should be considered a public trust. Canada is still young in her political development, and the fact that her population has been as a rule a steady, fixed population, free from those dangerous elements which have come into the United States with such rapidity of late years, has kept her relatively free from any serious social and political dangers which have afflicted her neighbours, and to which I believe they themselves, having inherited English institutions and being imbued with the spirit of English law, will always in the end rise superior. Great responsibility, therefore, rests in the first instance upon the people of Canada, who must select the best and purest among them to serve the country, and, secondly, upon the men whom the legislature chooses to discharge the trust of carrying on the government. No system of government or of laws can of itself make a people virtuous and happy unless their rulers recognize in the fullest sense their obligations to the state and exercise their powers with prudence and unselfishness, and endeavour to elevate and not degrade public opinion by the insidious acts and methods of the lowest political ethics. A constitution may be as perfect as human agencies can make it, and yet be relatively worthless while the large responsibilities and powers entrusted to the governing body—

responsibilities and powers not embodied in acts of parliament—are forgotten in view of party triumph, personal ambition, or pecuniary gain. "The laws," says Burke, "reach but a very little way. Constitute government how you please, infinitely the greater part of it must depend upon the exercise of the powers which are left at large to the prudence and uprightness of ministers of state. Even all the use and potency of the laws depend upon them. Without them your commonwealth is no better than a scheme upon paper, and not a living, active, effective organization."

BIBLIOGRAPHICAL NOTE

For accounts of the whole career of Lord Elgin see *Letters and Journals of James, Eighth Earl of Elgin*, etc., edited by Theodore Walrond, C.B., with a preface by his brother-in-law, Dean Stanley (London 2nd. ed., 1873); for China mission, *Narrative of the Earl of Elgin's Mission to China and Japan*, by Lawrence Oliphant, his private secretary (Edinburgh, 1869); for the brief Indian administration, *The Friend of India* for 1862-63. Consult also article in vol. 8 of *Encyclopædia Britannica*, 9th ed. ; John Charles Dent's *Canadian Portrait Gallery* (Toronto, 1880), vol. 2, which also contains a portrait; W. J. Rattray's *The Scot in British North America* (Toronto, 1880) vol. 2, pp. 608-641.

For an historical review of Lord Elgin's administration in Canada, see J. C. Dent's *The Last Forty Years, or Canada since the Union of 1841* (Toronto, 1881), chapters XXIII-XXXIV inclusive, with a portrait; Louis P. Turcotte's *Le Canada Sous l'Union* (Quebec, 1871), chapters I-IV, inclusive ; Sir Francis Hincks's *Reminiscences of His Public Life* (Montreal, 1884) with a portrait of the author ; Joseph Pope's *Memoirs of the Rt. Hon. Sir John A. Macdonald, G.C.B.* (Ottawa and London, 1894), with portraits of the great statesman, vol. 1, chapters IV-VI inclusive ; Lord Grey's *Colonial Policy of Lord John Russell's Administration* (London, 2nd ed., 1853), vol. 1 ; Sir C. B. Adderley's *Review of the Colonial Policy of Lord John Russell's Administration, by Earl Grey, and Subsequent Colonial History* (London, 1869).

For accounts of the evolution of responsible government in Canada consult the works by Dent, Turcotte, Rattray, Hincks, Grey and Adderley, just mentioned ; Lord Durham's *Report on the Affairs of British North America*, submitted to parliament, 1839 ; Dr. Alpheus Todd's *Parliamentary Government in The British Colonies* (2nd ed. London, 1894) ; Bourinot's *Manual of the Constitutional History of Canada* (Toronto, 1901); his *Canada under British Rule* (London and Toronto, 1901), chapters VI-VIII inclusive ; *Memoir of the Life of the Rt. Hon. Lord Sydenham, etc.*, by his brother G. Poulett Scrope, M.P., (London, 1843), with a portrait of that nobleman ; *Life and Correspondence of Charles, Lord Metcalfe*, by J. W. Kaye (London, new ed., 1858).

For comparisons between the parliamentary government of Great

Britain or Canada, and the congressional system of the United States, see Walter Bagehot's *English Constitution* and other political essays (New York, 1889); Woodrow Wilson's *Congressional Government* (Boston, 1885); Dr. James Bryce's *American Commonwealth* (London, 1888); Bourinot's *Canadian Studies in Comparative Politics*, in *Trans. Roy. Soc. Can.*, vol. VIII, sec. 2 (old ser.), and in separate form (Montreal, 1891). Other books and essays on the same subject are noted in a bibliography given in *Trans. Roy. Soc. Can.*, vol. XI, old ser., sec. 2, as an appendix to an article by Sir J. G. Bourinot on Parliamentary Government in Canada.

The reader may also profitably consult the interesting series of sketches (with excellent portraits) of the lives of Sir Francis Hincks, Sir A. MacNab, Sir L. H. LaFontaine, R. Baldwin, Bishop Strachan, L. J. Papineau, John Sandfield Macdonald, Antoine A. Dorion, Sir John A. Macdonald, George Brown, Sir E. P. Taché, P. J. O. Chauveau, and of other men notable from 1847-1854, in the *Portraits of British Americans* (Montreal 1865-67), by J. Fennings Taylor, who was deputy clerk of the old legislative council, and later of the senate of Canada, and a contemporary of the eminent men whose careers he briefly and graphically describes. Consult also Dent's *Canadian Portrait Gallery*, which has numerous portraits.

INDEX